Fundamentals of
HUMAN RESOURCE MANAGEMENT Canadian Edition

D0478083

Raymond A. Noe
Ohio State University

John R. Hollenbeck
Michigan State University

Barry Gerhart
University of Wisconsin–Madison

Patrick M. Wright
Cornell University

Sandra Steen
University of Regina

**McGraw-Hill
Ryerson**

Toronto   Montréal   Boston   Burr Ridge, IL   Dubuque, IA   Madison, WI   New York
San Francisco   St. Louis   Bangkok   Bogotá   Caracas   Kuala Lumpur   Lisbon   London
Madrid   Mexico City   Milan   New Delhi   Santiago   Seoul   Singapore   Sydney   Taipei

The McGraw·Hill Companies

McGraw-Hill
Ryerson

FUNDAMENTALS OF HUMAN RESOURCE MANAGEMENT
Canadian Edition

ISBN-13: 978-0-07-090799-7

ISBN-10: 0-07-090799-4

2 3 4 5 6 7 8 9 10 TCP 0 9 8 7 6

Printed and bound in Canada

Publisher: Lynn Fisher

Sponsoring Editor: Kim Brewster

Developmental Editor: Tracey Haggert

Senior Marketing Manager: Kelly Smyth

Senior Supervising Editor: Margaret Henderson

Copy Editor: Erin Moore

Production Coordinator: Janie Deneau

Permissions Editor: Christine Lomas

Typeface: 10.5/12 Goudy

Composition: Dianna Little

Cover Design: Dianna Little

Cover Image: © Digital Vision/Getty Images

Printer: Transcontinental Printing Group

Library and Archives Canada Cataloguing in Publication

Fundamentals of human resource management/Raymond A.
Noe ... [et al.].—Canadian ed.

Includes bibliographical references and index.
ISBN 0-07-090799-4

1. Personnel management—Textbooks. I. Noe, Raymond A.

HF5549.F848 2005   658.3   C2005-904011-4

In memory of my Mom
—R. A. N.

To my parents, Harold and Elizabeth, my wife, Patty,
and my children, Jennifer, Marie, Timothy, and Jeffrey
—J. R. H.

To my parents, Robert and Shirley, my wife, Heather,
and my children, Chris and Annie
—B. G.

To my parents, Patricia and Paul, my wife, Mary, and
my sons, Michael and Matthew
—P. M. W.

To my grandfather, Walter, my husband, Aaron, and my
children, Matt and Jessica
—S. L. S.

About the Authors

Raymond A. Noe is the Robert and Anne Hoyt Professor of Management at The Ohio State University. He was previously a professor in the Department of Management at Michigan State University and the Industrial Relations Center of the Carlson School of Management, University of Minnesota. He received his BS in psychology from The Ohio State University and his MA and PhD in psychology from Michigan State University. Professor Noe conducts research and teaches undergraduate as well as MBA and PhD students in human resource management, managerial skills, quantitative methods, human resource information systems, training, employee development, and organizational behaviour. He has published articles in the *Academy of Management Journal, Academy of Management Review, Journal of Applied Psychology, Journal of Vocational Behavior,* and *Personnel Psychology.* Professor Noe is currently on the editorial boards of several journals including *Personnel Psychology, Journal of Business and Psychology, Journal of Training Research,* and *Journal of Organizational Behavior.* Professor Noe has received awards for his teaching and research excellence, including the Herbert G. Heneman Distinguished Teaching Award in 1991 and the Ernest J. McCormick Award for Distinguished Early Career Contribution from the Society for Industrial and Organizational Psychology in 1993. He is also a fellow of the Society for Industrial and Organizational Psychology.

John R. Hollenbeck is Professor of Management at the Eli Broad Graduate School of Business Administration at Michigan State University. He received his PhD in management and organizational behaviour from New York University in 1984. Professor Hollenbeck is the editor of *Personnel Psychology* and has served on the editorial boards of *Academy of Management Journal, Organizational Behavior and Human Decision Processes,* the *Journal of Management,* and the *Journal of Applied Psychology.* Professor Hollenbeck has been recognized for both his research and teaching. He was the first recipient of the Ernest J. McCormick Award for Distinguished Early Career Contribution to the field of Industrial and Organizational Psychology in 1992 and was the 1987 Teacher–Scholar Award winner at Michigan State University. Dr. Hollenbeck's research focuses on self-regulation theories of work motivation, employee separation and acquisition processes, and team decision making and performance.

Barry Gerhart is the John and Barbara Keller Distinguished Chair in Business at University of Wisconsin–Madison. He was previously the Frances Hampton Currey Professor and Area Coordinator, Organization Studies in the Owen School of Management at Vanderbilt University and Associate Professor and Chairman of the Department of Human Resource Studies, School of Industrial and Labor Relations at Cornell University. He received his BS in psychology form Bowling Green University in 1979 and his PhD in industrial relations from the University of Wisconsin–Madison in 1985. His research is in the areas of compensation/rewards, human resource strategy staffing, and employee attitudes. Professor Gerhart has worked with a variety of organizations including TRW, Corning, and Hewitt Associates. His work has appeared in the *Academy of Management Journal, Industrial and Labor Relations Review, Administrative Science Quarterly, International Journal of Human Resource Management,* and the *Journal of Applied Psychology.* He was co-recipient of the 1991 Scholarly Achievement Award, Human Resources Division, Academy of Management.

Patrick M. Wright is Professor of Human Resource Studies and Research Director of the Center for Advanced Human Resource Studies in the School of Industrial and Labor Relations at Cornell University. He was formerly Associate Professor of Management and Coordinator of the Master of Science in Human Resource Management program in the College of Business Administration and Graduate School of Business at Texas A & M University. He holds a BA in psychology from Wheaton College, and an MBA and PhD in organizational behaviour/ human resource management from Michigan State University. He teaches, conducts research, and consults in the areas of personnel selection, employee motivation, and strategic human resource management. His research articles have appeared in journals such as the *Academy of Management Journal, Journal of Applied Psychology, Organizational Behavior and Human Decision Processes, Journal of Management,* and *Human Resource Management Review.* He has served on the editorial boards of *Journal of Applied Psychology* and *Journal of Management* and also serves as an ad hoc reviewer for *Organizational Behavior and Human Decision Making Processes, Academy of Management Journal,* and *Academy of Management Review.* In addition, he has consulted for a number of organizations, including Whirlpool Corporation, Amoco Oil Company, and the North Carolina state government.

Sandra Steen is a Lecturer of Human Resource Management in the Faculty of Business Administration at the University of Regina's Business School. Sandra has an integrated education and background in both Human Resource Management and Organization Development Consulting. She has 25 years of leading, managing, training, teaching, and consulting across a wide range of organizations in the private, public, and not-for-profit sectors. Her knowledge base combines both theory gained from an MBA focusing on human resource management/organizational behaviour from the University of Regina as well as from practitioner and consultant perspectives. Her professional affiliations include the Saskatchewan Training and Development Association and the Saskatchewan Council of Human Resource Associations. Sandra also holds the designation of Certified Human Resource Professional.

Brief Contents

Contents

Preface

Welcome to the first Canadian edition of *Fundamentals of Human Resource Management*. This is a fully Canadianized text, created to give students, supervisors, managers, entrepreneurs, and leaders a brief, focused introduction to HRM in Canada that is rich in content and relevant in its strategic application. We have developed a new text that is geared toward envisioning, developing, and implementing the people practices that will not only help to make organizations great, but will also help make organizations great places to work.

This text is comprised of 12 concise chapters that feature the right balance between theory and practice, and present the material in a manner that is relevant to the Canadian student. This text is built on the foundations of the highly successful U.S. first edition, rewritten and reworked into a Canadian edition designed for the Canadian marketplace. Here is how we have created this first Canadian edition of *Fundamentals of Human Resource Management*:

- written fewer chapters to accommodate the 12-week semester

- placed the entire text in a Canadian context. This includes providing a comprehensive overview of the Canadian legal framework for human resource management, a thorough discussion of Canadian labour relations and compensatory practices, and assessing human resource trends and management in Canada

- added the most relevant and up-to-date statistics, figures, and tables to support and clarify the chapter content

- featured Canadian examples in the pedagogical elements throughout the text and showcased a mix of Canadian and relevant international companies in the end-of-chapter cases

Emphasis on the Whole Picture

Human resource management affects every aspect of the workforce. Labour or management, employer or employee, student or professional, we all have a vested interest in effective human resource management. This book provides coverage of all the expected HRM topics such as analyzing jobs, planning, recruiting, selecting, training, developing, and compensating employees, managing performance, and handling labour relations. In addition, we have strived to give you more of what you may need to understand, facilitate, and contribute to achieving extraordinary results in organizations of all types and sizes. We have rounded out our discussion of HRM in Canada by including those topics that we feel represent the additional expectations of the progressive human resource professional and leader, such as managing human resources globally, adopting a total rewards approach to compensating and rewarding employees, and creating a high-performance work environment where employees' hearts and minds are engaged.

Balanced and Relevant Examples

You will find a broad range of Canadian examples featuring organizations from coast to coast that are leading the way in proactive human resource management. As a globally conscious Canadian human resource professional and instructor, I understand the world is getting smaller and smaller every day. Technological capabilities and greater personal and professional movement across international borders means more and more people will contribute to the effective management of human resources in countries in addition to Canada. Whether as part of a multinational or working for a foreign-owned company, Canadian students of human resource management need to be prepared to consider global opportunities. Consequently, we included a chapter on developments in global HRM to help broaden the perspective of students who may choose a career working for organizations that operate globally.

Pedagogical Features

Each of these features has been designed to take human resource management out of the classroom and into the real world—either with a practical exercise, a trip to the Internet, a headline news feature, or through an example of a best practice or innovation in the workplace.

Integrated Learning System

Great care was used in the creation of the supplemental materials to accompany *Fundamentals of Human Resource Management*. Whether you are a seasoned faculty member or a newly minted instructor, you will find the support materials to be comprehensive and practical.

i-Learning Sales Specialist

Your Integrated Learning Sales Specialist is a McGraw-Hill Ryerson representative who has the experience, product knowledge, training, and support to help you assess and integrate any of the below-noted products, technology, and services into your course for optimum teaching and learning performance. Whether it's how to use our test bank software, helping your students improve their grades, or how to put your entire course online, your *i*-Learning Sales Specialist is there to help. Contact your local *i*-Learning Sales Specialist today to learn how to maximize all McGraw-Hill Ryerson resources!

i-Learning Services Program

McGraw-Hill Ryerson offers a unique *i*Services package designed for Canadian faculty. Our mission is to equip providers of higher education with superior tools and resources required for excellence in teaching. For additional information visit www.mcgrawhill.ca/highereducation/eservices/.

Instructors' Supplements

Instructor's CD-ROM

The CD-ROM includes an electronic version of the Instructor's Manual, the EZ Test Computerized Test Bank, and Microsoft® PowerPoint® Presentations.

Instructors can use this resource to access many of the supplements associated with the text and create custom presentations, exam questions, and Microsoft® PowerPoint® lecture slides. All of these instructor's supplements are also available for download in the Instructor's Resource Centre of the Online Learning Centre at www.mcgrawhill.ca/college/noe.

Instructor's Manual

The Instructor's Manual includes a wealth of information to assist instructors in presenting this text and their course to its best advantage. It includes lecture notes, answers to end-of-chapter questions, and other valuable aids.

EZ Test Computerized Test Bank

McGraw-Hill's EZ Test is a flexible and easy-to-use electronic testing program. The program allows instructor's to create tests from book-specific items. It accommodates a wide range of question types and instructors may add their own questions. Multiple versions of the test can be created and any test can be exported to use with course management systems such as WebCT, BlackBoard, or PageOut. The program is available for Windows and Macintosh environments.

Microsoft® PowerPoint® Presentations

A complete set of PowerPoint slides for each chapter are provided.

Fundamentals of Human Resource Management Video Package

The video package contains carefully selected segments from current CBC programming as well as segments from the McGraw-Hill Management Video Library. It is an excellent supplement to lectures and useful for generating in-class discussions.

PageOut

McGraw-Hill's unique point-and-click course Web site tool enables users to create a full-featured, professional quality course Web site without knowing HTML coding. PageOut is free for instructors, and lets you post your syllabus online, assign McGraw-Hill OLC content, add Web links, and maintain an online grade book. (And if you're short on time, we even have a team ready to help you create your site.)

Primis Online

You can customize this text and save your students money off bookstore prices by using McGraw-Hill's Primis Online digital database, the largest online collection of texts, readings, and cases. Contact your McGraw-Hill *i*-Learning Sales Specialist for more information.

WebCT/BlackBoard

This text is available in two of the most popular course-delivery platforms—WebCT and BlackBoard—for more user-friendly and enhanced features. Contact your McGraw-Hill *i*-Learning Sales Specialist for more information.

Instructor Online Learning Centre— www.mcgrawhill.ca/college/noe

Along with the Student OLC (see below), *Fundamentals of Human Resource Management* includes a password-protected Web site for instructors. The site offers downloadable supplements including those found on the Instructor's CD ROM, and a series of other resources.

Group-Video Resource Manual

This new manual contains everything an instructor needs to successfully integrate McGraw-Hill technology and additional group activities into the classroom. It includes a menu of items you can use as teaching tools in class. All of the Build Your Management Skills (self-assessments and Test Your Knowledge) exercises have teaching notes included here, with additional PowerPoint slides (in printed form) to use in class. All of the HotSeat DVD segments have teaching notes with additional PowerPoints (in printed form) included here as well. In addition, group exercises are included with anything a professor would need to use this exercise in class—handouts, figures, etc.

The manual is organized into 25 topics such as ethics, decision-making, change, and leadership. Each of the teaching resources is then organized by topic for easy inclusion in the professor's lecture. A matrix is included at the front of the manual that references each resource by topic.

Student Supplements

Student Online Learning Centre— www.mcgrawhill.ca/college/noe

Fundamentals of Human Resource Management Online Learning Centre (OLC) is a Web site that follows the text chapter-by-chapter, with additional experiential materials, such as "What's Your HR IQ?" and quizzes to enhance the text and the classroom experience. Students can review concepts or prepare for exams by taking the self-grading quizzes that accompany each chapter or work through interactive exercises. The site also contains Web links to relevant human resource management sites and resources and other supplemental information that complements the text material.

CCH Canada BusinessWorks© CD-ROM

Use the tools the professionals use! Available as a bundled option, CCH Canada BusinessWorks CD-ROM provides a snapshot of the BusinessWorks information database. This CD-ROM gives students and instructors access to laws, regulations, and developments in all major areas of human resource management including Health and Safety, Employment Standards, and Industrial Relations.

Acknowledgments

The first Canadian edition of *Fundamentals of Human Resource Management* represents the collaborative efforts of an extraordinary publishing team at McGraw-Hill Ryerson: Kim Brewster, Sponsoring Editor; Tracey Haggert, Developmental Editor; Christine Lomas, Permissions Editor; Margaret Henderson, Senior Supervising Editor; and Erin Moore, Copy Editor.

I want to acknowledge the many reviewers of this Canadian edition for their detailed, helpful and timely comments. Their suggestions helped improve this textbook and ensured that the text meets the needs of the Canadian marketplace:

Alex Kondra, *Acadia University*
Carol Ann Samhaber, *Algonquin College*
Alec Lee, *Camosun College*
Gary Robinson, *Centennial College*
Maureen Nummelin, *Conestoga College*
David Morrison, *Durham College*
Ruthanne Krant, *Georgian College*
Suzanne Kavanagh, *George Brown College*
Donald Schepens, *Grant MacEwan College*
Anne Harper, *Humber College Institute of Technology and Advanced Learning*
Kate Muller, *Humber College Institute of Technology and Advanced Learning*
Frank Vuo, *Lethbridge Community College*
Nelson Lacroix, *Niagara College*
David Inkster, *Red Deer College*
Jim Hebert, *Red River College of Applied Arts, Science and Technology*
Barbara Lipton, *Seneca College of Applied Arts and Technology*
Michael Barrett, *University of Alberta*
Maria Rotundo, *University of Toronto*

Finally, I would like to express my appreciation to my husband, Aaron, and to our children, Matt and Jessica, for their enthusiasm and flexibility.

FEATURES

Chapter 8

Developing Employees for Future Success

What Do I Need to Know? After reading this chapter, you should be able to:

1. Discuss how development is related to training and careers.
2. Identify the methods organizations use for employee development.
3. Describe how organizations use assessment of personality type, work behaviors, and job performance to plan employee development.
4. Explain how job experiences can be used for developing skills.
5. Summarize principles for setting up successful mentoring programs.
6. Tell how managers and peers develop employees through coaching.
7. Identify the steps in the process of career management.
8. Discuss how organizations are meeting the challenges of the "glass ceiling," succession planning, and dysfunctional managers.

Introduction

The managers at Irving Oil, Ltd. a family-owned company known for its tankers, truck stops, and refinery towers, are telling stories and painting with watercolours as they learn to lead. The St. John-based company has teamed up with the workplace learning provider, Forum Corporation to teach leadership skills to managers.

For many years, managers at Irving Oil have traditionally focused on corporate values that include a business strategy based on a rewarding working environment that ...hat." "We ...e way that

Although it is hard to measure the full impact of this leadership development initiative, Saint John refinery employees have been giving the company a higher rating for leadership in recent surveys. Irving Oil recently received a Human Resources Innovation Award from Atlantic Canada Human Resources Awards (ACHRA) for its Mutual Value Promise (MVP) program that includes a wide range of learning and development opportunities for employees and managers.[1] In addition, Irving was recently named North American refiner of the year by Hart Publications, a major energy sector publisher based in the United States. Irving is the first Canadian company to receive this annual reward, which examines a refiner's environmental performance, ability to produce clean fuel, and investment in facilities and employees.[2]

employee development The combination of formal education, job experiences, relationships, and assessment of personality and competencies to help employees prepare for the future of their careers.

As we noted in Chapter 1, employees' commitment to their organization depends on how their managers treat them. To "win the war for talent" managers must be able to identify high-potential employees, make sure the organization uses the talents of these people, and reassure them of their value, so that they do not become dissatisfied and leave the organization. Managers also must be able to listen. Although new employees need strong direction, they expect to be able to think independently and be treated with respect. In all these ways, managers provide for **employee development**—the combination of formal education, job experiences, relationships, and assessment of personality and competencies to help employees

---

Chapter 2

The Legal Context for Human Resource Management and Providing a Healthy and Safe Workplace

What Do I Need to Know? After reading this chapter, you should be able to:

1. Describe the legal framework for Human Resource Management in Canada.
2. Summarize the major federal and provincial laws impacting Human Resource Management.
3. Identify the agencies that enforce employment equality and privacy legislation and describe their roles.
4. Describe ways employers can avoid illegal discrimination and meet the duty to accommodate.
5. Define harassment and discuss how employers can eliminate or minimize it.
6. Explain the context for Occupational Health and Safety regulations.
7. Describe how Occupational Health and Safety regulations are enforced including employee rights and responsibilities.
8. Discuss ways employers promote worker safety and health.

BEST PRACTICES

The "Best Practices" boxes give specific examples of what is working well in HRM. Illustrating real world best practices helps to apply the content. Examples include: "Building a New Model for Labour Relations" and "OMNI's Success in Managing Diversity."

E-HRM

The "E-HRM" boxes appear in each chapter and emphasize the increasing use of technology in human resource management today and how it is changing the way things are getting done. Examples include: "Simulation Turns Recruitment into a Two-Way Street" and "Creating Job Descriptions Online."

HR HOW TO

The "HR How To" boxes discuss steps to creating HRM initiatives. This feature clarifies roles and functions of human resource professionals. Examples include: "Testing 101" and "Setting Up a Mentoring Program."

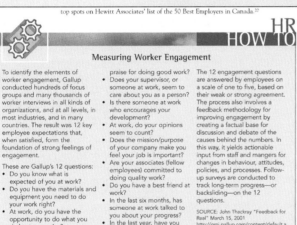

top spots on Hewitt Associates' list of the 50 Best Employers in Canada.[20]

HR HOW TO

Measuring Worker Engagement

To identify the elements of worker engagement, Gallup conducted hundreds of focus groups and many thousands of worker interviews in all kinds of organizations, and at all levels, in most industries, and in many countries. The result was 12 key employee expectations that, when satisfied, form the foundation of strong feelings of engagement.

These are Gallup's 12 questions:
- Do you know what is expected of you at work?
- Do you have the materials and equipment you need to do your work right?
- At work, do you have the opportunity to do what you do best every day?
- In the last seven days, have you received recognition or praise for doing good work?
- Does your supervisor, or someone at work, seem to care about you as a person?
- Is there someone at work who encourages your development?
- At work, do your opinions seem to count?
- Does the mission/purpose of your company make you feel your job is important?
- Are your associates (fellow employees) committed to doing quality work?
- Do you have a best friend at work?
- In the last six months, has someone at work talked to you about your progress?
- In the last year, have you had opportunities at work to learn and grow?

The 12 engagement questions are answered by employees on a scale of one to five, based on their weak or strong agreement. The process also involves a feedback methodology for improving engagement by creating a factual base for discussion and debate of the causes behind the numbers. In this way, it yields actionable input from staff and mangers for changes in behaviour, attitudes, policies, and processes. Follow-up surveys are conducted to track long-term progress—or backsliding—on the 12 questions.

SOURCE: John Thackray "Feedback for Real" March 15, 2001 http://gmj.gallup.com/content/default.asp?ci=811. Retrieved: November 28, 2004.

E-HRM

From Filling in Forms to Brainstorming the Firm's Next Big Innovation

Vacation. Illness. Promotions. Many roads lead to the human resources department. But with the evolution of technology, more and more of these roads are leading employees to an HR portal. Every organization needs to manage employee information effectively to make the most of its diverse talents, services, and information. Originally designed to disseminate information quickly, the employee intranet has become a common feature of many workplaces.

Over time, this type of intranet has evolved from a static repository of company information to a collaborative meeting place where which can be helpful to employees searching for sensitive information. Through a portal, employees can quickly and easily share their ideas and contribute to projects, accessing the sites through the office intranet or outside work through a Web browser.

Labatt Breweries of Canada set up an intranet called "The Pub." Its goals were to improve overall communication with employees located in eight breweries from coast-to-coast, and eliminate silos of information between business units. Using the portal, Labatt was able to improve employee communications significantly and now 70 percent of its at Labatt. "Through our intranet, we've been able to deliver immense value to our employees by providing tools that enable them to make better informed decisions and increase their productivity. The business value of bringing employees closer together is apparent when you look at the individual contributions and recommendations for greater innovation that come in through The Pub."

Team building through virtual communities of interest created through the HR portal can also translate directly into improvements in the day-to-day functioning of a company. Work teams that may have members too busy to meet

FEATURES

CHAPTER SUMMARIES recap the "What Do I Need to Know?" objectives from the beginning of each chapter with brief summary discussions.

CASES in each chapter look at organizations and how their practices illustrate or apply concepts from the chapter. They provide external examples to bring into a lecture, along with questions for assignments or classroom discussion.

VIDEO CASES at the end of each Part include summaries and challenging questions about current HRM issues. Teaching notes to the video cases are included in the Instructor's Manual.

Summary

1. Define human resource management, identify the responsibilities of human resource departments, and explain how human resource management contributes to an organization's performance.

   Human resource management consists of an organization's "people practices"—the policies, practices, and systems that influence employees' behaviour, attitudes, and performance. HR departments have responsibility for a variety of functions. The HRM process begins with analyzing and designing jobs, then recruiting and selecting employees to fill those jobs. Training and development equip employees to carry out their present jobs and follow a career path in the organization. Performance management ensures employees' activities and outputs match the organization's goals. Human resource departments also plan and administer the organization's pay and benefits. They carry out activities in support of employee relations, such as communication programs and collective bargaining. Conducting all these activities involves the establishment and administration of human resource policies. Management also depends on human resource professionals for help in ensuring compliance with legislation, as well as for support for the organization's strategy—for example, human resource planning and change management. HRM contributes to organizational performance by influencing who works for the organization and how these people work. These human resources, if well managed, have the potential to be a source of sustainable competitive advantage, contributing to basic objectives such as productivity, profits, and customer satisfaction.

2. Summarize areas in which human resource management can support organizational strategies.

   HR professionals should be familiar with the organization's strategy and may even play a role in developing the strategy. Specific HR practices vary according to the type of strategy. Productivity improvements require HR leadership including effective feedback and rewards. When organizations with international operations hire employees in foreign countries where they operate, they need to be cognizant of the differences in culture and business practices. Even small businesses serving local markets discover that qualified candidates include skilled immigrants who account for a significant and growing share of the Canadian labour market.

3. Identify the skills, certification, and ethical requirements of human resource professionals.

   Human resource management requires substantial skills in the area of strategic contributions to organizational success, including HR technical skills as well as planning, implementing, and measuring organizational results of strategic HR initiatives. Human resource professionals also require business acumen, and the ability to manage client relationships including managers, and employees as well as to maintain an effective work environment when required to manage a group or area within the human resources department. Many human resource professionals have achieved the nationally standardized designation, Certified Human Resource Professional (CHRP). Human resource professionals are required to uphold high ethical standards. Some areas in which ethical issues arise include adherence to legislation, protecting confidentiality, and maintaining professional competence.

4. Explain the role of supervisors in human resource management.

   Although many organizations have human resource departments, non-HR managers must be familiar with the basics of HRM and their own role with regard to managing human resources. Supervisors typically have responsibilities related to all the HR functions. Supervisors help analyze work, interview job candidates, participate in selection decisions, provide training, conduct performance appraisals, and recommend pay increases. On a day-to-day basis, supervisors represent the company to their employees, so they also play an important role in employee relations.

5. Describe typical careers in human resource management.

   Careers in human resource management may involve specialized work in fields such as recruiting, training, or labour relations. HR professionals may also be generalists, performing the full range of HR activities described in this chapter. People in these positions usually have a university degree or college diploma in business or the social sciences.

6. Describe trends in the labour force composition and how they affect human resource management.

Case: Suncor Strives for a Representative Workforce

Suncor Energy Inc. is a world leader in mining and extracting crude oil from Alberta's oil sands. Suncor also explores for, develops, and markets natural gas, operates major refineries in Sarnia, Ontario and Denver, Colorado and is actively involved in renewable energy initiatives such as wind power projects. Suncor also operates a chain of Sunoco service stations across Ontario and Phillips 66 service stations in Colorado and Wyoming. Suncor employs approximately 4,000 employees.

Nineteen percent of Suncor's employees are women, 7 percent are visible minorities and in the last eight years, the Aboriginal workforce in its oil sands division has grown to more than 10 percent from 3 percent. Heather Kennedy, vice-president of human resources and community affairs, says 10 percent is good, but not good enough. To attract more Aboriginal employees to better reflect the local population, Suncor sponsors scholarships, literacy and mentorship programs, and each summer hires 130 students, up to a third of them Aboriginal.

One beneficiary is Florida Proulx, from the Athabasca Chipewyan First Nation. A summer accounting assistant in 2002, she has since been hired by Suncor and plans to become a certified general accountant. Before that, she worked for an employment centre in Wood Buffalo, where she helped find jobs for Aboriginal peoples, many of them at Suncor. "The company is proactive," Proulx says.

"They go out and meet people in smaller communities and let them know they're there. Consultation is part of operating in the oilpatch—companies must show regula-

tors they have consulted with stakeholders. But it's also good business," says Heather Kennedy. "We're equals in this region. It's not a matter of meeting our obligations, but working with Aboriginals to determine what their needs and our needs are, and pulling them together."

Suncor recently sponsored an event held in conjunction with the National Aboriginal Achievement Foundation Awards to provide opportunities for high-school students from across Canada to meet Aboriginal role models and leaders such as Tina Keeper, television star of *North of 60* and the Honorable Pearl Calahasen, minister of Aboriginal Affairs and Northern Development. The National Aboriginal Achievement Foundation Awards were developed to encourage and celebrate excellence in the Aboriginal community.

Questions

1. How may Suncor benefit from employing a diverse workforce and supporting Aboriginal initiatives?

2. What does Suncor's human resource department need to do to ensure these potential benefits are achieved? *Refer to the Human Resource Management functions and responsibilities identified in Table 1.1 in developing your answer.*

SOURCES: www.suncor.com; Richard W. Yerema, *Canada's Top 100 Employers 2004* (Toronto: Mediacorp Canada Inc.), p. 325; "Aboriginal Voices," *Canadian Business*, March 29–April 11, 2004 p. 50; www.naof.ca/svmw.right.html. Retrieved: April 3, 2004.

Excalibur Case: Le Cirque du Soleil: How to Manage Growth

You are a team of consultants specializing in human resources and labour relations management. Your firm of consultants enjoys a good reputation for the quality of the services offered, especially to large-scale international companies. Having heard tell of the excellence of your services, Cirque du Soleil has approached you. After several meetings with representatives from their Human Resources Department, you have noted the following facts:

Cirque du Soleil

Founded in 1984 by a group of young street performers, Cirque du Soleil has been in constant evolution since its creation. The company enjoys excellent international recognition and is reputed to have reinvented circus arts. While Cirque du Soleil had sales of $1.7 million, 50 employees, and 23 performers in 1984, in 2000, reached $407 million and it employed 1,370 employees and 445 performers. It presented seven shows in 2000 on three continents: North America, Europe, and Asia.

Also, to manage adequately all its personnel, it has four separate headquarters. As well as International Headquarters in Montreal, it has four other head offices: Headquarters–America, also in Montreal, Headquarters–Europe in Amsterdam, Headquarters–Las Vegas in Las Vegas, and lastly, Headquarters–Asia-Pacific in Singapore.

While Cirque du Soleil would like to find and exploit new niches related to presenting shows, most of its revenues come from ticket sales. Thus, the nucleus of the Cirque remains presenting shows. The Cirque has four fixed shows, two touring shows in Asia, one in North America, and another in Europe. A touring show comprises 150 to 200 people, including 50 to 70 performers, and it has to relocate, on average, every six weeks, which demands very skilled logistics and effective planning of the entry authorizations for the different countries on the tour. Relocating means moving personnel, their baggage,

---

CBC VIDEO CASE: High Anxiety

Many North American employees are concerned about job loss due to offshoring and outsourcing. As thousands of jobs flood out of the U.S., fear and loathing of offshoring and outsourcing and the companies that send jobs to China and India is evident. Anxiety runs deep not only among employees who work in the manufacturing sector but among employees in other sectors as well. This anxiety has accelerated among the middle-class as better and better jobs are exported out of the country.

Canadians have tended to be less vocal so far because the outsourcing and offshoring trend has been slower to impact Canada. However, Canadian organizational examples show that more work will be outsourced to lower labour cost countries such as China in the future. For example, although an early production run of Mitel's latest telephone will likely be handled in Canada, ongoing production will take place in China where workers are paid one-tenth of Canadian salaries.

One Canadian manufacturer interviewed suggests that as lower-level jobs leave, ultimately "higher-skilled labour jobs will remain in Canada" and that jobs in North America will continue to "move upscale." However, fears and concerns are raised that the U.S. may plunge into "full scale protectionism" that could harm not only Canada's economy, but potentially even trigger a global recession.

SOURCE: Based on "High Anxiety," CBC Venture 918, March 14, 2004.

Questions

1. Would you be willing to pay more for a product to protect jobs in Canada? Why or why not?

2. The video suggests that although offshoring will result in the export of lower-skilled jobs, higher-skilled jobs will remain in Canada. Do you agree or disagree with this assessment? Why or why not?

REVIEW AND DISCUSSION QUESTIONS at the end of each chapter help link the contents in the chapter to potential applications requiring critical thinking.

WHAT'S YOUR HR IQ? sections at the end of each chapter reference the assessment activities included on the Online Learning Centre, which are hands-on activities to reinforce the specific chapter content.

---

petencies. They establish competency-based pay systems, or structures that set pay according to the employees' level of knowledge and what they are capable of doing. This encourages employees to be more flexible and adapt to changing technology. However, if the organization does not also provide systems in which employees can apply new skills, it may be paying them for skills they do not actually use.

4. Describe how organizations recognize individual, team, and organizational performance through the use of incentives.
Incentive pay is tied to individual performance, profits, or other measures of success. Organizations select forms of incentive pay to energize, direct, or influence employees' behaviour. Employees must value the rewards, have the resources they need to meet the standards, and believe the pay plan is fair. Organizations may recognize individual performance through such incentives as piecework rates, merit pay, sales commissions, and bonuses for meeting individual performance objectives. Common group incentives include gainsharing, bonuses, and team awards. Incentives for meeting organizational objectives include profit sharing and stock ownership.

5. Discuss the role of benefits and services as a part of employee total rewards.
Like pay, benefits and services help employers attract, retain, and provide a source of motivation for employees. The variety of possible benefits and services also helps employers tailor their offerings to attract the right types of employees. Employees expect at least a minimum level of benefits, and providing more than the minimum helps an organization compete in the labour market. Benefits and services are also a significant expense, but employers provide benefits and services because employees value them and many are required by law.

6. Summarize the types of employee benefits and services offered by employers.
Employers must contribute to the Canada Pension Plan/Quebec Pension Plan, Employment Insurance, and Workers' Compensation. In addition, employers offer various kinds of insurance, retirement plans, and

paid leave. Due to the increasing costs of providing employee benefits, many Canadian organizations are seeking ways to hold back the costs. Many employers have responded to work–life role conflicts by offering family-friendly benefits. Organizations need to establish objectives and select benefits that support those objectives. Flexible benefits are a means to give employees control over the benefits they receive.

7. Discuss the importance of effectively communicating the organization's approach to total rewards.
A comprehensive communications strategy is needed to help employees understand and value all the components in an organization's approach to total rewards. Managers and the human resource department share responsibility for this important requirement. Technology can provide employees access to information and other tools associated with administration of compensation and rewards. Employers have many options for communicating information about total rewards including online or printed rewards statements, presentations, videos, meetings, brochures, intranets, memos, and email. Using a combination of media increases employees' understanding.

8. Discuss issues related to compensating and rewarding executives.
Executive compensation has drawn public scrutiny because top executive compensation is much higher than average workers' pay. Chief executive officers have an extremely large impact on the organization's performance, but critics complain that when performance falters, executive pay does not decline as fast as the organization's profits or stock price. In addition, executive pay usually combines long-term and short-term incentives as well as additional benefits and services not provided to all employees. Incentives and additional benefits and services should be motivating but also meet standards for equity. Performance measures should encourage behaviour that is in the organization's best interests, including ethical behaviour. Executives need to follow ethical standards that prevent them from engaging in insider trading or deceptive practices designed to manipulate the organization's stock price.

Review and Discussion Questions

1. Some individuals evaluate prospective employers' job offers based only on direct pay considerations. What additional factors should be considered when evaluating job offers from employers?

2. Why might an organization choose to pay employees more than the market rate? Why might it choose to pay less? What are the consequences of paying more or less than the market rate?

---

3. What are the advantages of establishing pay ranges, rather than specific pay levels, for each job? What are the drawbacks of this approach?

4. Suppose a small start-up business wants to establish a competency-based pay structure? What would be some advantages of this approach? List the issues the company should be prepared to address in setting up this system. Consider the kinds of information you will need and the ways employees may react to the new pay structure.

5. With some organizations and jobs, pay is primarily wages or salaries, and with others, incentive pay is more important. For each of the following jobs, state whether you think the pay should emphasize base pay (wages and salaries) or incentive pay (bonuses, profit sharing, and so on). Give a reason for each.
   a. An accountant at a manufacturing company
   b. A salesperson for a software company
   c. A mechanic for a major airline

6. Why do some organizations link incentive pay to the organization's overall performance? Is it appropriate

to use stock performance as an incentive for employees at all levels? Why or why not?

7. Why do employers provide employee benefits, rather than providing all compensation in the form of pay and letting employees buy the services they want?

8. Of the benefits discussed in this chapter, list the ones you consider essential, i.e., the benefits you would require in any job offer. Why are these benefits important to you?

9. Why is it important to communicate information about total rewards? Suppose you work in the HR department of a company that has decided to add new elements to its total rewards—dental and vision care plus an increased budget to support learning and development opportunities for all employees. How would you recommend communicating this change? What information should your messages include?

10. Do you think executive compensation is too high? Why or why not?

What's Your HR IQ?   www.mcgrawhill.ca/college/noe

The Online Learning Centre offers more ways to check what you've learned so far. Find experiential exercises as well as Test Your Knowledge Quizzes, Videos, and many other resources at www.mcgrawhill.ca/college/noe

Excalibur Case: Smith Rubber   EXCALIBUR

Located in the Eastern Townships region of Quebec, Smith Rubber grew from a small family-owned business into a medium-sized company. The organization is now facing a great deal of competition within Quebec and across North America. Its success has always been tied to its ability to compete with Japanese and Mexican companies that also supply the automobile industry.

Steve Smith Jr. is now president of Smith Rubber. At the time of his promotion some years ago, the company was not unionized. During this period he wondered how to best recognize employees and reward their performance while encouraging them to increase productivity. He hesitated about increasing wages because he feared losing his competitive edge if his fixed costs rose.

Three years ago, Smith Rubber had a particularly good year in terms of sales and profits. As a result, Steve thought that a Christmas bonus would be the best way to reward employees. In fact, he told David Sanders, his human resource manager, "There is nothing like cold hard

cash to make employees work harder." He set out his bonus system as follows:

Compensation	Bonus
$30,000 and under	$2,500
$30,001–$35,000	$3,000
$35,001–$40,000	$3,500
$40,001–$45,000	$4,000
$45,001–$50,000	$4,500
$50,001 or higher	10% of salary

The bonuses were a hit. Many employees thanked the president personally. Moreover, in February, David Sanders received many positive comments from supervisors, saying that employees were working harder.

The following year there was a slump in the automobile industry, and competitors abroad made dramatic cuts in their costs by using robots in their assembly lines. It was difficult for Smith Rubber to compete and sales dropped by 5 percent, while profits plunged by 15 percent. Steve de-

Part 1

The Human Resource Environment

Strategies, Trends, and Challenges in Human Resource Management

1. Define human resource management, identify the responsibilities of human resource departments, and explain how human resource management contributes to an organization's performance.

2. Summarize areas in which human resource management can support organizational strategies.

3. Identify the skills, certification, and ethical requirements of human resource professionals.

4. Explain the role of supervisors in human resource management.

5. Describe typical careers in human resource management.

6. Describe trends in the labour force composition and how they affect human resource management.

7. Discuss how high-performance work systems and technological developments are affecting human resource management.

8. Explain how the nature of the employment relationship is changing and how the need for flexibility affects human resource management.

Introduction

"One award. 69,873 reasons." For the second year in a row, RBC Financial Group ranked first in the KPMG-sponsored Ipsos-Reid Canada's Most Respected Corporations survey. In full page national newspaper ads, RBC credited this success to its

Canada's Most Respected Corporation

RBC attributes success to its employees and thanks them for their commitment to serving the needs of clients and communities.

LO1

human resource management (HRM)
The policies, practices, and systems that influence employees' behaviour, attitudes, and performance.

69,873 employees in Canada and around the world. "People who put their values and commitment to work serving the needs of clients and communities everyday. To all of them, we say: 'Thanks.' "[1]

A consensus of 255 of the leading CEOs in Canada gave RBC Financial Group the first mention in six of the eight performance categories of the annual Most Admired and Respected Corporation survey. The CEOs indicated that they selected RBC Financial as the most admired and respected organization because of its "vision, focus, discipline or good strategy." RBC Financial received this top ranking in the areas of Human Resource Management, Corporate Social Responsibility, Corporate Governance, Best Long Term Investment Value, Financial Performance, and Top of Mind Most Admired or Respected. In making their selection in the Human Resource Management category, CEOs were to consider factors including workplace training, senior level succession planning, harmonious labour relations, and productivity enhancements.[2]

With 12 million customers and $413 billion of assets, RBC Financial is a successful organization that invests in its employees. In 2003, RBC spent $133 million on employee learning—an average of more than $1,900 per employee. RBC has approximately 19,000 employees in management-level positions; 50 percent are women. It is estimated that 30 percent of all RBC employees work in some form of flexible work arrangement. Perhaps, it is no coincidence that RBC receives as many as 13,000 résumés each month![3]

Organizations of all sizes and in all industries are increasingly recognizing the importance of people. "This is a time of rapid change in the market—a time when Canadian organizations are constantly trying to keep pace and remain competitive. In today's knowledge-based economy, we rely on people to generate, develop, and implement ideas."[4]

Human resource management (HRM), centres on the policies, practices, and systems that influence employees' behaviour, attitudes, and performance. Many companies refer to HRM as "people practices." Figure 1.1 emphasizes that there are several important HRM practices: analyzing work and designing jobs, attracting potential employees (recruiting), choosing employees (selection), teaching employees how to perform their jobs and preparing them for the future (training and development), evaluating their performance (performance management), rewarding employees (compensation), creating a positive work environment (employee relations), and

FIGURE 1.1

Human Resource Management Practices

supporting the organization's strategy (HR planning and change management). An organization performs best when all of these practices are managed well. At companies with effective HRM, employees and customers tend to be more satisfied, and the companies tend to be more innovative, have greater productivity, and develop a more favourable reputation in the community.[5]

In this chapter, we introduce the scope of human resource management including the ways in which HRM supports organizational strategy. We begin by discussing why human resource management is an essential element of an organization's succcess. We then turn to the elements of managing human resources: the roles and skills needed for effective human resource management. Next, the chapter describes how all managers, not just human resource professionals, participate in the activities related to human resource management. We then provide an overview of careers in human resource management and the highlights of practices covered in the remainder of the book. The chapter concludes by discussing a variety of trends and developments that impact HRM.

Human Resources and Company Performance

Managers and economists traditionally have seen human resource management as a necessary expense, rather than as a source of value to their organizations. Economic value is usually associated with *capital*—equipment, technology, and facilities. However, research has demonstrated that HRM practices can be valuable.[6] Decisions such as whom to hire, what to pay, what training to offer, and how to evaluate employee performance directly affect employees' motivation and ability to provide goods and services that customers value. Companies that attempt to increase their competitiveness by investing in new technology and promoting quality throughout the organization also invest in state-of-the-art staffing, training, and compensation practices.[7]

The concept of "human resource management" implies that employees are *resources* of the employer. As a type of resource, **human capital** means the organization's employees, described in terms of their training, experience, judgment, intelligence, relationships, and insight—the employee characteristics that can add economic value to the organization. In other words, whether it manufactures automobiles or forecasts the weather, for an organization to succeed at what it does, it needs employees with

human capital
An organization's employees, described in terms of their training, experience, judgment, intelligence, relationships, and insight.

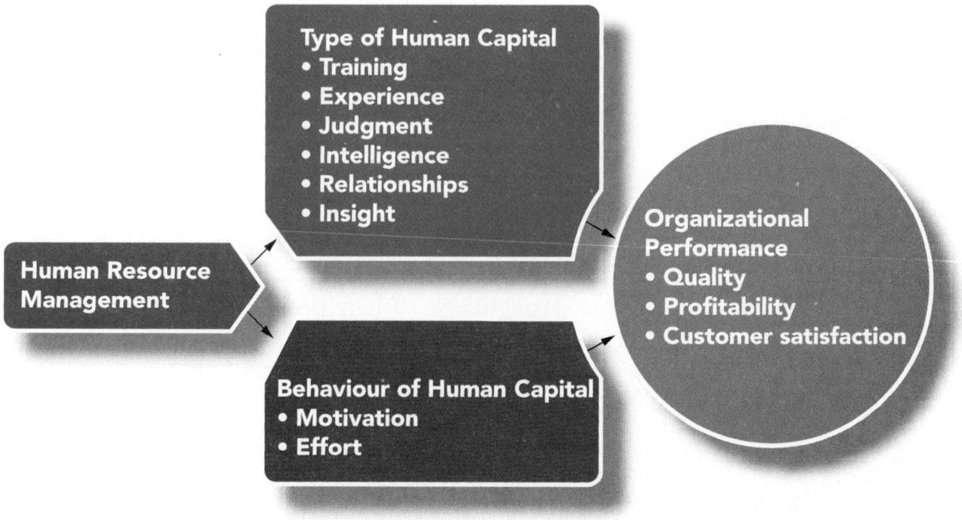

FIGURE 1.2

Impact of Human Resource Management

At WestJet, a key focus is on keeping employees motivated, trained, and compensated effectively. In turn, there is a low turnover rate and a high rate of customer satisfaction.

certain qualities, such as particular kinds of training and experience. This view means employees in today's organizations are not interchangeable, easily replaced parts of a system but the source of the company's success or failure. By influencing *who* works for the organization and *how* those people work, human resource management therefore contributes to such basic measures of an organization's success as quality, profitability, and customer satisfaction. Figure 1.2 shows this relationship.

Human resource management is critical to the success of organizations because human capital has certain qualities that make it valuable. In terms of business strategy, an organization can succeed if it has a *sustainable competitive advantage* (is better than competitors at something, and can hold that advantage over a sustained period of time). Therefore, we can conclude that organizations need the kind of resources that will give them such an advantage. Human resources have these necessary qualities:

- Human resources are *valuable*. High-quality employees provide a needed service as they perform many critical functions.
- Human resources are *rare* in the sense that a person with high levels of the needed skills and knowledge is not common. An organization may spend months looking for a talented and experienced manager or technician.
- Human resources *cannot be imitated*. To imitate human resources at a high-performing competitor, you would have to figure out which employees are providing the advantage and how. Then you would have to recruit people who can do precisely the same thing and set up the systems that enable those people to imitate your competitor.
- Human resources have *no good substitutes*. When people are well trained and highly motivated, they learn, develop their abilities, and care about customers. It is difficult to imagine another resource that can match committed and talented employees.

These qualities imply that human resources have enormous potential. An organization realizes this potential through the ways it practises human resource management.

Effective management of human resources can form the foundation of a **high-performance work system**—an organization in which technology, organizational structure, people, and processes all work together to give an organization an advantage in the competitive environment. As technology changes the ways organizations manufacture, transport, communicate, and keep track of information, human resource management must ensure that the organization has the right kinds of people to meet the new challenges. Maintaining a high-performance work system may include development of training programs, recruitment of people with new skill sets, and establishment of rewards for such behaviours as teamwork, flexibility, and learning. In the next chapter, we will see some of the changes that human resource managers are planning for, and Chapter 12 examines high-performance work systems in greater detail.

high-performance work system
An organization in which technology, organizational structure, people, and processes all work together to give an organization an advantage in the competitive environment.

Responsibilities of Human Resource Departments

In all but the smallest organizations, a human resource department is responsible for the functions of human resource management. On average, an organization has one HR staff person for every 100 employees served by the department. Table 1.1 details the responsibilities of human resource departments. These responsibilities include the practices introduced in Figure 1.1 plus two areas of responsibility that support those practices: (1) establishing and administering human resource policies and (2) ensuring compliance with labour laws.

Although the human resource department has responsibility for these areas, many of the tasks may be performed by supervisors or others inside or outside the organization.

FUNCTION	RESPONSIBILITIES
Analysis and design of work	Work analysis; job design; job descriptions
Recruitment and selection	Identifies needs; recruiting; interviewing and screening; deployment of staff; and outplacement
Training and development	Orientation; learning strategies; design, deliver, and evaluate programs; career development
Performance management	Integrates performance measures; performance appraisal systems; assists and coaches supervisors
Total compensation	Develop and administer compensation and incentive programs; benefit program design and implementation; pension plans; payroll
Employee and labour relations	Terms and conditions of employment, communication; employee involvement; labour relations
Human resource policies	Policy guidance and implementation; create and manage systems to collect and safeguard HR information
Compliance with legislation	Policies to ensure compliance with all legal requirements; reporting requirements
Support for strategy	Strategic partner in organizational change and development; human resource planning

TABLE 1.1

Responsibilities of HR Departments

SOURCE: Based on Canadian Council of Human Resources Associations National Standards for Human Resources Professionals, www.cchra-caarh.ca/en/phaseIreport/. Retrieved: March 22, 2004.

No two human resource departments have precisely the same roles because of differences in organization sizes and characteristics of the workforce, the industry, and management's values. In some companies, the HR department handles all the activities listed in Table 1.1. In others, it may share the roles and duties with managers and supervisors of other departments such as finance, operations, or information technology. When managers and supervisors actively perform a variety of HR activities, the HR department usually retains responsibility for consistency and compliance with all legal requirements. In some companies, the HR department actively advises top management. In others, the department responds to top-level management decisions and implements staffing, training, and compensation activities in light of company strategy and policies.

Let's take an overview of the HR functions and some of the options available for carrying them out. Human resource management involves both the selection of which options to use and the activities of using those options. Later chapters of the book will explore each function in greater detail.

Analyzing and Designing Jobs

job analysis
The process of getting detailed information about jobs.

job design
The process of defining the way work will be performed and the tasks that a given job requires.

To produce their given product or service (or set of products or services) companies require that a number of tasks be performed. The tasks are grouped together in various combinations to form jobs. Ideally, the tasks should be grouped in ways that help the organization to operate efficiently and to obtain people with the right qualifications to do the jobs well. This function involves the activities of job analysis and job design. **Job analysis** is the process of getting detailed information about jobs. **Job design** is the process of defining the way work will be performed and the tasks that a given job requires.

Recruiting and Hiring Employees

recruitment
The process through which the organization seeks applicants for potential employment.

selection
The process by which the organization attempts to identify applicants with the necessary knowledge, skills, abilities, and other characteristics that will help the organization achieve its goals.

Based on job analysis and design, an organization can determine the kinds of employees it needs. With this knowledge, it carries out the function of recruiting and hiring employees. **Recruitment** is the process through which the organization seeks applicants for potential employment. **Selection** refers to the process by which the organization attempts to identify applicants with the necessary knowledge, skills, abilities, and other characteristics that will help the organization achieve its goals. An organization makes selection decisions in order to add employees to its workforce, as well as to transfer existing employees to new positions.

At some organizations the selection process may focus on specific skills, such as experience with a particular programming language or type of equipment. At other organizations, selection may focus on general abilities, such as the ability to work as part of a team or find creative solutions. The focus an organization favours will affect many choices, from the way the organization measures ability, to the questions it asks in interviews, to the places it recruits. Table 1.2 lists employability skills, attitudes, and behaviours needed to participate and progress in today's dynamic world of work. HR professionals also provide guidance related to redeploying employees, termination, and outplacement.

Training and Developing Employees

Although organizations base hiring decisions on candidates' existing qualifications, most organizations provide ways for their employees to broaden or deepen their

FUNDAMENTAL SKILLS	PERSONAL MANAGEMENT SKILLS	TEAMWORK SKILLS
• Communicate • Manage information • Use numbers • Think and solve problems	• Demonstrate positive attitudes and behaviours • Be responsible • Be adaptive • Learn continuously • Work safely	• Work with others • Participate in projects and tasks

TABLE 1.2

Employability Skills 2000+

SOURCE: "Employability Skills 2000+"Brochure 2000 E/F (Ottawa: The Conference Board of Canada, 2000) www.conferenceboard.ca/education/learning-tools/employability-skills.htm. Retrieved: February 28, 2004.

knowledge, skills, and abilities. To do this, organizations provide for employee training and development. **Training** is a planned effort to enable employees to learn job-related knowledge, skills, and behaviour. For example, many organizations offer safety training to teach employees safe work habits. **Development** involves acquiring knowledge, skills, and behaviour that improve employees' ability to meet the challenges of a variety of new or existing jobs, including the client and customer demands of those jobs. Development programs often focus on preparing employees for management responsibility.

Managing Performance

Managing human resources includes keeping track of how well employees are performing relative to objectives such as job descriptions and goals for a particular position. The process of ensuring that employees' activities and outputs match the organization's goals is called **performance management.** The activities of performance management include specifying the tasks and outcomes of a job that contribute to the organization's success. Then various measures are used to compare the employee's performance over some time period with the desired performance. Often, rewards—the topic of the next section—are developed to encourage good performance.

Total Compensation and Rewards

Planning pay and benefits involves many decisions, often complex and based on knowledge of a multitude of legal requirements. An important decision is how much to offer in salary or wages, as opposed to bonuses, commissions, and other performance-related pay. Other decisions involve which benefits to offer, from retirement plans to various kinds of insurance to time off with pay. All such decisions have implications for the organization's bottom line, as well as for employee motivation.

Administering pay and benefits is another big responsibility. Organizations need systems for keeping track of each employee's earnings and benefits. Employees need information about their health plan, retirement plan, and other benefits. Keeping track of this involves extensive record keeping and reporting to management, employees, and others, while ensuring compliance with all applicable legislation.

training
A planned effort to enable employees to learn job-related competencies (i.e., knowledge, skills, and behaviour).

development
The acquisition of knowledge, skills, and behaviours that improve an employee's ability to meet changes in job requirements and in

performance management
The process of ensuring that employees' activities and outputs match the organization's goals.

Maintaining Positive Employee and Labour Relations

Organizations often depend on human resource professionals to help them identify and perform many of the tasks related to maintaining positive relations with employees. This function often includes providing for communications to employees.

In organizations where employees belong to a union, employee relations entails additional responsibilities. The organization periodically conducts collective bargaining to negotiate an employment contract with union members. The HR department also maintains communication with union representatives to ensure that issues are resolved as they arise.

Establishing and Administering Human Resource Policies

All the human resource activities described so far require fair and consistent decisions, and most require substantial record keeping. Organizations depend on their HR department to help establish policies related to hiring, discipline, promotions, benefits, and the other activities of human resource management.

All aspects of human resource management require HR professionals to collect and safeguard information. From the preparation of employee handbooks, to processing job applications, performance appraisals, benefits enrolment, and government-mandated reports, handling records about employees requires accuracy as well as sensitivity to employee privacy.

Ensuring Compliance with Federal and Provincial Legislation

As we will discuss in later chapters, especially Chapter 2, the government has many laws and regulations concerning the treatment of employees. These laws govern such matters as human rights, employment equity, employee safety and health, employee compensation and benefits, and employee privacy. Most managers depend on human resource professionals to help them keep up to date and on track with these requirements. Ensuring compliance with laws requires that human resource professionals keep watch over a rapidly changing legal landscape.

LO2

Supporting the Organization's Strategy

Traditional management thinking treated human resource management primarily as an administrative function, but managers today are beginning to see a more central role for HRM. They are beginning to look at HRM as a means to support a company's *strategy*—its plan for meeting broad goals such as profitability, quality, and market share.[8] This strategic role for HRM has evolved gradually. At many organizations, managers still treat HR professionals primarily as experts in designing and delivering HR systems. But at a growing number of organizations, HR professionals are strategic partners with other managers.[9] This means they use their knowledge of the business and of human resources to help the organization develop strategies and to align HRM policies and practices with those strategies.

In a recent study of almost 200 Canadian organizations surveyed by Deloitte Consulting and the University of Toronto's Centre of Industrial Relations, 41 percent of human resource leaders describe their departments as strategic partners while 31 percent still view themselves as administrative champions. Part of the problem for HR

Real GDP Per Capita Gap Between Canada and the United States and Real GDP Per Capita as a Proportion of U.S. Real GDP Per Capita (dollars, percent)

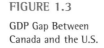

FIGURE 1.3

GDP Gap Between Canada and the U.S.

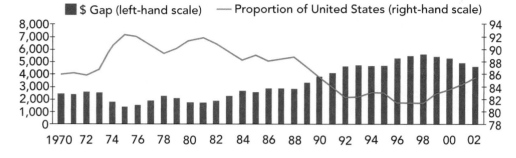

SOURCE: "Performance and Potential, 2003–2004: Defining the Canadian Advantage," A Special Report by the Conference Board of Canada, October 2003, p. 5.

professionals is that employees are concerned about getting help with traditional human resource administrative responsibilities such as completing benefit forms while executives want senior HR leaders to be partners in strategic planning.[10]

The specific ways in which human resource professionals support the organization's strategy vary according to their level of involvement and the nature of the strategy. Strategic issues include emphasis on productivity improvement, international expansion, and outsourcing decisions.

Productivity Improvement

To compete in today's global economy, companies need to enhance productivity. Canada's labour force productivity growth is forecast to average 1.5 percent per year between 2003 and 2015 compared with 1.7 percent per year in the United States. This productivity gap between Canada and the United States threatens Canada's ability to compete globally. As illustrated in Figure 1.3 the income gap has steadily increased between Canada and the United States. By 2002, the income gap stood at U.S. $4,779 and Canadian income per capita was 86 percent of the U.S. level. To eliminate the income gap by 2015, Canada's productivity would have to grow by 2.8 percent per year—a full 1.1 percentage points above the U.S. rate each year.[11]

Expanding into Global Markets

Companies are finding that to survive and prosper they must compete in international markets as well as fend off foreign competitors' attempts to gain ground in Canada. To meet these challenges, Canadian businesses must develop global markets, keep up with competition from overseas, hire from an international labour pool, and prepare employees for global assignments.

Study of companies that are successful and widely admired suggests that these companies not only operate on a multinational scale, but also have workforces and corporate cultures that reflect their global markets.[12] These companies, which include General Electric, Coca-Cola, Microsoft, RBC, and Intel, focus on customer satisfaction and innovation. In addition, they operate on the belief that people are the company's most important asset. Placing this value on employees requires the companies to emphasize human resource practices, including rewards for superior performance, measures of employee satisfaction, careful selection of employees, promotion from within, and investment in employee development.

The Global Workforce

For today's and tomorrow's employers, talent comes from a global workforce. Organizations with international operations hire at least some of their employees in the foreign countries where they operate. And even small businesses that stick close to home hire qualified candidates who are immigrants to Canada.

Technology is reducing barriers to overseas operations. Mark Braxton, chief technology officer for GM Onstar-Europe, believes that new technologies will open up opportunities for underdeveloped villages and communities in Africa, Asia, Europe, the United States, Central America, and South America by making it practical for employers to locate telephone service centres in places companies once would not have considered.[13] Economically deprived communities in Ireland, Brazil, and Mexico are being equipped with satellite links that give them access to universities, local government offices, and businesses. Hiring in such areas gives employers access to people with potential to be eager to work yet who will accept lower wages than elsewhere in the world. Challenges, however, may include employees' lack of familiarity with technology and corporate practices, as well as political and economic instability in the areas.

Despite the risks, many organizations that have hired globally are realizing high returns. For example, ABB Asea Brown Boveri (Europe's largest engineering company and a competitor to General Electric) was one of the first Western companies to seize a business opportunity when Asia was experiencing economic difficulties in the late 1990s.[14] With over 219,000 employees worldwide, ABB was considered a global company well before then. But when economic crisis lowered the cost of operating in Asia, the company laid off employees in Europe and North America, shifting production to low-cost countries in Asia. The changes required massive HR efforts for the layoffs and hiring, as well as training for the new Asian workers. For example, ABB sent employees to its electric motor facility in Shanghai, China, to train plant managers in ABB quality standards.

For an organization to operate in other countries, its HR practices must take into consideration differences in culture and business practices. Consider how Starbucks Coffee handled its expansion into Beijing, China.[15] Demand for qualified managers in Beijing exceeds the local supply. Employers therefore have to take steps to attract and retain managers. Starbucks researched the motivation and needs of potential managers. The company learned that in traditional Chinese-owned companies, rules and regulations allowed little creativity and self-direction. Starbucks distinguished itself as an employer by emphasizing its casual culture and opportunities for career development. The company also spends considerable time training employees.

Even hiring at home may involve selection of employees from other countries. The 1990s and beginning of the 21st century, like the beginning of the last century, have been years of significant immigration. Canada receives 250,000 immigrants each year, about 80 percent of whom are members of visible minorities.[16] The proportion of foreign-born was the highest in 70 years, at 18 percent of the total population in

Starbucks Coffee chairman Howard Schultz, left, poses with Yuji Tsunoda, president of Starbucks Japan, during the opening of the coffee-chain giant's 208th shop in Japan. Starbucks, which opens three stores a day worldwide, is a prime example of how companies can successfully compete in international markets.

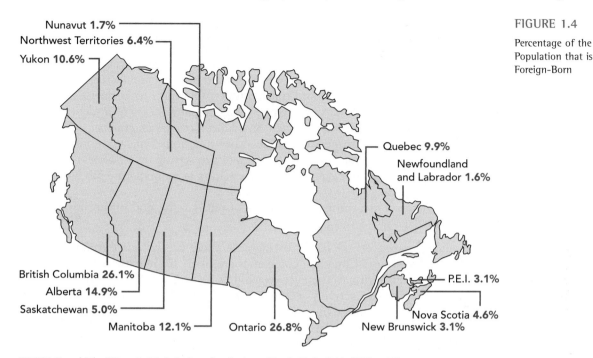

FIGURE 1.4

Percentage of the Population that is Foreign-Born

Nunavut **1.7%**
Northwest Territories **6.4%**
Yukon **10.6%**
Quebec **9.9%**
Newfoundland and Labrador **1.6%**
British Columbia **26.1%**
Alberta **14.9%**
Saskatchewan **5.0%**
P.E.I. **3.1%**
Nova Scotia **4.6%**
New Brunswick **3.1%**
Manitoba **12.1%**
Ontario **26.8%**

SOURCE: Kamal Dib, "Diversity Works", *Canadian Business*, March 29–April 11, 2004, p. 54.

2001.[17] The impact of immigration is especially significant in some regions of Canada. In 2001, more than one-fourth of the population of British Columbia and Ontario are foreign-born.[18]

Figure 1.4 illustrates the percentage of the population that is foreign-born for each province and territory. Canada's largest cities attract the largest number of immigrants. For example, 43.7 percent of Toronto's population and 37.5 percent of Vancouver's population are foreign-born.[19]

Because of declining population and labour shortages predicted for the future, employers will increasingly turn to immigrants to fill available job openings. In fact, Canada's current levels of immigration will need to increase by a multiple of 0.8 just to maintain replacement population levels.[20] Employers in tight labour markets—such as those seeking experts in computer science, engineering, and information systems—are especially likely to recruit international students.[21]

International Assignments

Besides hiring an international workforce, organizations must be prepared to send employees to other countries. This requires HR expertise in selecting employees for international assignments and preparing them for those assignments. Employees who take assignments in other countries are called **expatriates.**

Canadian companies must prepare employees to work in other countries. Canadian companies must carefully select employees to work abroad based on their ability to understand and respect the cultural and business norms of the host country. Qualified candidates also need language skills and technical ability. In Chapter 11, we discuss practices for training employees to understand other cultures.

expatriates
Employees who take assignments in other countries.

Outsourcing

outsourcing
The practice of having another company (a vendor, third-party provider, or consultant) provide services.

offshoring
Setting up a business enterprise in another country (e.g., building a factory in China).

Many organizations are increasingly outsourcing and offshoring business activities. **Outsourcing** refers to the practice of having another company (a vendor, third-party provider, or consultant) provide services. For instance, a manufacturing company might outsource its accounting and transportation functions to businesses that specialize in these activities. Outsourcing gives the company access to in-depth expertise and is often more economical as well. In addition to manufacturing, software development and call centre operations are other functions typically considered for outsourcing. **Offshoring**, on the other hand, refers to setting up a business enterprise in another country, e.g., setting up a factory in China to manufacture products at less cost than in Canada.

Overall there are two primary categories of outsourcing and offshoring implications to Canada:

- **Canadian companies are likely to increase their use of outsourcing and offshoring**. To cut costs Canadian companies are likely to increase their use of outsourcing and offshoring to the ever-growing list of countries such as India, China, and Mexico that are actively seeking economic diversification and investment. For example, Bombardier Inc.'s train unit now outsources low-level engineering work such as transferring two-dimensional drawings to 3D from peak capacity plants to a variety of outside firms around the world.[22] Montreal-based CGI Group Inc., Canada's largest computer services firm, has expanded its development operations in Bangalore and Mumbai India to 650 from 500 in the past year.[23] And as discussed in the Video Case at the end of Part 1, a growing number of North American companies are offshoring manufacturing operations to China to reduce costs.

- **Canada is losing its attractiveness as an outsourcing destination.** In 2004 Canada slipped from second to eighth place as an attractive outsourcing destination behind India, China, Malaysia, Czech Republic, Singapore, Philippines, and Brazil in a study conducted by A.T. Kearney.[24] For example, Canadian industries such as the auto industry could be threatened if the U.S. turned to other countries to put together automobiles.

Not only do HR departments help with a transition to outsourcing, but many HR functions are being outsourced. A survey by the Society for Human Resource Management found that almost three-quarters of companies outsource at least one HR function.[25] HR functions that are commonly outsourced include payroll administration, training, and recruitment and selection of employees. For example, BMO signed a ten-year contract with Exult Inc. to manage much of the bank's HR function. BMO's HR department was cut by half as Exult took over payroll and benefits administration, HR call centre management, employee records, and other administrative functions.[26] This arrangement frees HR managers at BMO to work on strategy and vision, focusing them on HRM responsibilities that add value to the business.

LO3

Skills and Certification of HR Professionals

With such varied responsibilities, human resource professionals need several important sets of skills. These areas of importance to professional practice in human resources are shown in Figure 1.5 —strategic contribution to organizational success, business acumen, managing client relationships, and professionalism.

The Certified Human Resource Professional (CHRP) designation has been nationally standardized at a specific threshold of professional practice for the HR professional.[27] Currently over 11,500 HR practitioners from across Canada have earned their designation from provincially administered CHRP programs.[28] To obtain the CHRP designation, new applicants are required to write two multiple-choice examinations:

- The first is the Knowledge Assessment based on general knowledge of all aspects of HRM.
- The second is the Professional Practice Assessment using case studies representing issues facing HR professionals.[29]

To help CHRP candidates prepare for their exams, an independent organization governed by the Canadian Council of Human Resources Associations—PARC (Professional Assessment and Resource Centre) provides guidelines, sample questions, and other resources to support CHRP candidates and HR professionals. The "E-HRM" feature provides sample interactive questions from the Knowledge and Professional Practice examinations.

Strategic Contributions to Organization Success

This portion of the profile includes HR technical skills as well as capabilities that address the areas of adding human capital value, planning and implementing strategic HR programs, and measuring organizational results.

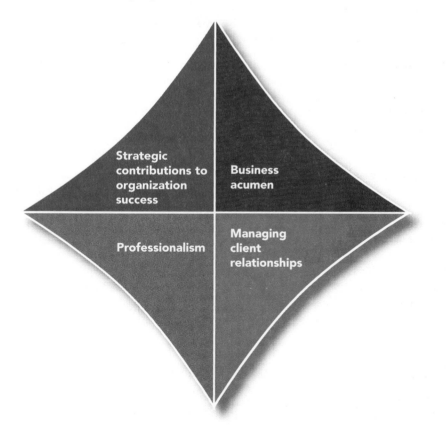

FIGURE 1.5

HR Professional Capabilities Profile

SOURCE: www.cchra_ccarh.ca/en/phaseIreport/part_I. Retrieved: March 23, 2004.

E-HRM

Certified Human Resource Professional (CHRP) National Examination Preparation

Certified Human Resource Professionals apply their knowledge to contribute to organizational effectiveness. The following questions are part of an interactive online tool to assist CHRP candidates prepare for the National Examinations. These questions and answers are a valuable resource to not only new CHRP candidates preparing for the examinations but also to current HR professionals who can access these questions and scenarios as a resource in implementing both strategic and day-to-day responsibilities.

Sample Knowledge Assessment Questions:

1. Which of the following are considered popular practices that help implement diversity management?
   a. Alternate work arrangements
   b. Mentoring and apprenticeship programs
   c. Support groups
   d. All of the above

2. Trend analysis has been a popular, systematic approach to forecasting labour demand for many years. Which of the following is not a step usually associated with this analysis?
   a. Select an appropriate business factor
   b. Plot historical trends
   c. Develop management forecasts
   d. Compute a productivity ratio

Sample Professional Practice Assessment Question:

3. The company that you work for as an HR consultant has just undergone a merger. The business that employs you is family owned and that the firm that the company is merging with is a U.S. firm. A number of employees have come to you and are extremely anxious about their future with the firm. Several employees have resigned and morale is very low. What would you do in this situation?
   a. Hire a consulting firm to conduct an attitude survey to find out how many employees are thinking of leaving in the next several months.
   b. Explain that the merger is a "done deal." There will be no impact on the way things have always been done. The employees are overreacting and should focus on their work.
   c. Identify the issues of most concern for all employees. Speak to senior managers, and develop a communications strategy that addresses the issues/concerns.
   d. Document the concerns and send an email to the manager of the employees explaining that morale is low and employees are thinking of leaving, and ask that senior managers speak to their employees.

SOURCE: Canadian Council of Human Resources Associations, Professional Standards Organization, www.cchra-ccarh.ca/parc/en/section_6/ss63e.asp. Retrieved: March 23, 2004.

Answers: 1: d; 2: d;
3: a = 2 points, b = 0 points,
c = 2 points, d = 5 points

Business Acumen

A sound foundation related to business fundamentals as well as the ability to manage outside HR contractors and other specialists, to project manage, and to identify, analyze, and advise on legal matters and legislative requirements are important capabilities of HR professionals today.

Managing Client Relationships

HR professionals interact with other managers in addressing organizational requirements. The ability to develop and maintain effective relationships with both managers and employees as clients is particularly important. In addition, the HR professional may manage a group or department within the human resources department requiring the ability to effectively establish and maintain an effective work environment.

Professionalism

Through personal and professional conduct, HR professionals play a critical role in advancing and promoting the profession.[30]

HR HOW TO

HRPAO's Code of Ethics

Each of the Human Resources Associations in Canada has a set of guidelines that provide standards of professional and ethical conduct for their members. The following ethical principles form the HRPAO's (Human Resources Professionals Association of Ontario) Code of Ethics.

1. Competence HR practitioners must maintain competence in carrying out professional responsibilities and provide services in an honest and diligent manner. They must ensure that activities engaged in are within the limits of their knowledge, experience, and skill. When providing services outside one's level of competence, or the profession, the necessary assistance must be sought so as not to compromise professional responsibility.

2. Legal Requirements HR practitioners must adhere to any statutory acts, regulations, or by-laws which relate to the field of Human Resources Management, as well as all civil and criminal laws, regulations, and statutes that apply in their jurisdiction.

They must not knowingly or otherwise engage in or condone any activity or attempt to circumvent the clear intention of the law.

3. Dignity in the Workplace HR practitioners support, promote, and apply the principles of human rights, equity, dignity, and respect in the workplace, within the profession, and in society as a whole.

4. Balancing Interests HR practitioners must strive to balance organizational and employee needs and interests in the practice of their profession.

5. Confidentiality HR practitioners must hold in strict confidence all confidential information acquired in the course of the performance of their duties and not divulge confidential information unless required by law and/or where serious harm is imminent.

6. Conflict of Interest HR practitioners must either avoid or disclose a potential conflict of interest that might influence or might be perceived to influence personal actions or judgments.

7. Professional Growth and Support of Other Professionals HR practitioners must maintain personal and professional growth in Human Resources Management by engaging in activities that enhance the credibility and value of the profession.

8. Enforcement The Canadian Council of Human Resources Associations works collaboratively with its Member Associations to develop and enforce high standards of ethical practice.

Ethics in Human Resource Management

ethics
The fundamental principles of right and wrong.

Whenever people's actions affect one another, ethical issues arise, and business decisions are no exception. **Ethics** refers to the fundamental principles of right and wrong; ethical behaviour is behaviour that is consistent with those principles. Business decisions, including HRM decisions, should be ethical, but the evidence suggests that is not always what happens. Recent surveys indicate that the general public and managers do not have positive perceptions of the ethical conduct of businesses. For example, in a survey conducted by the *Wall Street Journal*, 4 out of 10 executives reported they had been asked to behave unethically.[31]

Each of the HR Associations has a set of guidelines that identify standards for professional and ethical conduct of their members. The "HR How To" feature provides the Code of Ethics for the Human Resources Professionals Association of Ontario (HRPAO).

LO4

HR Responsibilities of Supervisors

Although many organizations have human resource departments, HR activities are by no means limited to the specialists who staff those departments. In large organizations, HR departments advise and support the activities of the other departments. In small organizations, there may be an HR specialist, but many HR activities are carried out by line supervisors. Either way, non-HR managers need to be familiar with the basics of HRM and their role with regard to managing human resources.

As we will see in later chapters, supervisors typically have responsibilities related to all the HR functions. Figure 1.6 shows some HR responsibilities that supervisors are likely to be involved in. Organizations depend on supervisors to help them determine what kinds of work need to be done (job analysis and design) and in what quantities (HR planning). Supervisors typically interview job candidates and participate in the decisions about which candidates to hire. Many organizations expect supervisors to train employees in some or all aspects of the employees' jobs. Supervisors conduct performance appraisals and may recommend pay increases. And, of course, supervisors play a key role in employee relations, because they are most often the voice of management for their employees, representing the company on a day-to-day basis. Throughout all these activities, supervisors can participate in HRM by taking into consideration the ways that decisions and policies will affect their employees. Understanding the princi-

FIGURE 1.6

Supervisors' Involvement in HRM: Typical Areas of Involvement

Help define jobs

Provide motivational environment, with support from pay, benefits, and other rewards

Forecast HR needs

Communicate policies and comply with legal requirements

Train, coach, and develop employees

Interview (and select) candidates

Recommend pay increases and promotions

Appraise performance

ples of communication, motivation, and other elements of human behaviour can help supervisors inspire the best from the organization's human resources.

Careers in Human Resource Management

LO5

The Government of Canada's National Occupational Classification (NOC) identifies two broad classifications of human resource occupations: Human Resource Specialists and Human Resource Managers, however, there are many different types of jobs in the HRM professions included in these classifications. Collectively, these two occupational classifications account for more than 73,000 members of Canada's labour force.[32]

Figures 1.7 and 1.8 provide summaries of average hourly earnings, employment outlook, and average levels of unemployment for Human Resource Specialists (NOC 1121) and Human Resource Managers (NOC 0112).

Specialists in Human Resources (NOC 1121)—At a Glance

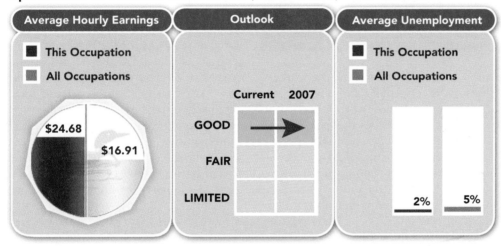

FIGURE 1.7

Average Hourly Earnings, Outlook, and Average Unemployment for Specialists in Human Resources

Human Resource Managers (NOC 0112)—At a Glance

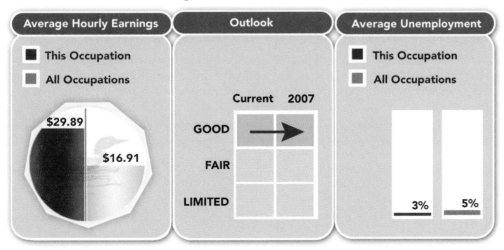

FIGURE 1.8

Average Hourly Earnings, Outlook, and Average Unemployment for Human Resource Managers

SOURCE: National Occupation Classification, 2003, Human Resources and Skills Development Canada, www.jobfutures.ca/jobfutures/noc/1121.shtml and www.jobfutures.ca/jobfutures/noc/0112.shtml. Retrieved: March 31, 2004. Reproduced with the permission of the Minister of Public Works and Government Services Canada, 2005.

HRPAO (Human Resources Professionals Association of Ontario) provides education, information services, seminars, government and media representation, online services, and publications such as *HR Professional.*

Some positions in HRM involve work in specialized areas such as recruiting, training, or labour and industrial relations. Other positions are generalists who usually perform the full range of HRM activities, including recruiting, training, compensation, and employee relations. Many recent entrants have a university degree or college diploma. HRPAO (Human Resource Professionals Association of Ontario) recently announced a transition to a degree requirement intended to advance the status of the CHRP among employers. In 2011, students enrolling for their CHRP will be required to have a degree.[33]

A well-rounded educational background will likely serve a person well in an HRM position. As one HR professional noted, "One of the biggest misconceptions is that [HRM] is all warm and fuzzy communications with the workers. Or that it is creative and involved in making a more congenial atmosphere for people at work. Actually it is both of those some of the time, but most of the time it is a big mountain of paperwork which calls on a myriad of skills besides the 'people' type. It is law, accounting, philosophy, and logic as well as psychology, spirituality, tolerance, and humility."[34]

In addition to the HRM professionals who hold the CHRP designation, many more are members of professional associations. The national professional organization for HRM in Canada is the Canadian Council of Human Resources Associations (CCHRA), which represents the collaborative efforts of ten provincial and specialist Human Resource Associations and includes more than 25,000 professionals across Canada. Visit the CCHRA's website at www.cchra-ccarh.ca to see their services and link to the associated provincial and specialist association websites.

Environmental Trends Impacting HRM

Major environmental trends that are impacting human resource management include changes related to composition of the workforce and how HRM can support a number of organizational strategies, from efforts to maintain high-performance work systems to changes in the organization's size and structure. Major changes in technology, especially the role of the Internet are changing organizations themselves, as well as providing new ways to carry out human resource management. Finally, we explore the changing nature of the employment relationship, in which careers and jobs are becoming more flexible.

internal labour force

An organization's workers (its employees and the people who work at the organization).

LO6

Change in the Labour Force

The *labour force* is a general way to refer to all the people willing and able to work. For an organization, the **internal labour force** consists of the organization's workers—its employees and the people who work at the organization. This internal labour force

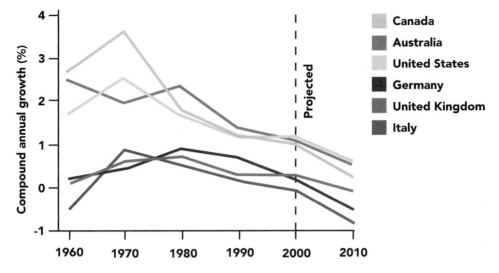

FIGURE 1.9

Decline of Labour Forces in Many Developed Countries by 2010

SOURCE: Andrew Wahl, "Leaders Wanted," *Canadian Business*, March 1–14, 2004, p. 32.

is drawn from the organization's **external labour market,** that is, individuals who are actively seeking employment. The number and kinds of people in the external labour market determine the kinds of human resources available to an organization (and their cost). Human resource professionals need to be aware of trends in the composition of the external labour market, because these trends affect the organization's options for creating a well-skilled, motivated internal labour force. One significant trend relates to the impending shortage of workers as the labour force actually shrinks in some developed countries. See Figure 1.9.

external labour market
Individuals who are actively seeking employment.

An Aging Workforce

"John Murphy has done the math, and it doesn't look good: over the next five years, his company will likely need to replace more than a quarter of its 11,000 employees. Murphy, executive vice-president of human resources at Ontario Power Generation, the Crown corporation that manages provincial electricity supply, says there isn't much he can do to avoid it. Average age of OPG's workforce is 45, its ranks filled with baby boomers who have their sights set on retirement. Many of those leaving the corporation in the next few years will be senior engineers and managers, who, after decades on the job, will give up their desk for good—taking valuable skills and experience with them."[35]

Canada's population and its labour force are aging. The fastest-growing age segment of the labour force will be workers aged 45 to 64, as the baby-boom generation (born 1946–1964) continues to age. There will be sustained growth in the working-age population until 2010 as the "echo-boom" generation (the children of the baby boomers) reaches working age.[36] However, as illustrated in Figure 1.10 growth of the labour force in Canada and other developed countries will decline dramatically after 2010 because of decreased numbers of the population aged 15 years and younger. By 2010, the labour forces in many developed countries will be shrinking.[37]

Human resource professionals will therefore spend much of their time on concerns related to retirement planning, retraining older workers, and motivating workers whose careers have plateaued. Organizations will struggle with ways to control the rising costs of health-related and other benefits. At the same time, organizations will have to find ways to attract, retain, and prepare the newest entrants to the labour force.

FIGURE 1.10

Age Distribution
Projection of the
Canadian Population
2006 and 2016

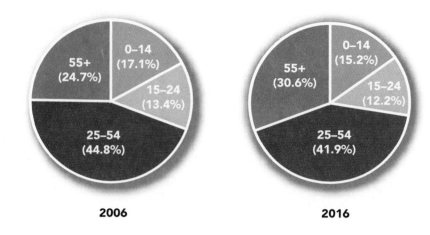

2006   **2016**

Note: Due to rounding, the totals do not always add up to the sum of the figure.

SOURCE: Adapted from Statistics Canada website, www.statcan.ca/english/Pgdb/demo23b.htm. Retrieved: April 2, 2004.

Generation X (born 1965–1980) grew up in the wake of the baby boomers. Dual-income families produced a generation of children with greater responsibility for taking care of themselves. Generation X employees are inclined to be cynical about the future because of their experience with recessions and downsizing and tend to be independent, technology-savvy, and results-driven. Generation Y (born 1981–2000) have been born and raised in a multicultural society resulting in tolerance to differences in race, religion, and culture.[38]

Employees view work as a means to self-fulfillment—that is, a means to more fully use their skills and abilities, meet their interests, and live a desirable lifestyle.[39] One report indicates that if employees receive opportunities to fully use and develop their skills, have greater job responsibilities, believe the promotion system is fair, and have a trustworthy manager who represents the employee's best interests, they are more committed to their companies.[40] Fostering these values requires organizations to develop HRM practices that provide more opportunity for individual contribution and entrepreneurship (in this context, taking responsibility for starting up something new).[41] Because many employees place more value on the quality of nonwork activities and family life than on pay and production, employees will demand more flexible work policies that allow them to choose work hours and the places where they work.

Employers will likely find that many talented older workers want to continue contributing through their work, though not necessarily in a traditional eight-to-five job. For organizations to attract and keep talented older workers, many will have to re-think the ways they design jobs. Phyllis Ostrowsky, in her mid-fifties, enjoyed her position as a store manager for 13 years, and she went out of her way to provide good customer service. But her job responsibilities and hours expanded to the point they became excessive. She eventually was working 12-hour days and was too busy to give customers the personal touch she liked to deliver. Ostrowsky therefore left her store job for a position as an office manager with another company.[42]

A Diverse Workforce

Another change affecting the Canadian labour force is that it is growing more diverse. Over 200 ethnic groups were reported in Canada's 2001 Census. Employment equity is now recognized as an effective Canadian tool for efficient use of skilled

FIGURE 1.11

HRM Practices That Support Diversity Management

SOURCE: Based on M. Loden and J. B. Rosener, *Workforce America!* (Homewood, IL: Business One Irwin, 1991).

human resources—and is increasingly borrowed by many industrialized countries. The four designated groups under the federal Employment Equity Act (women, Aboriginal peoples, persons with disabilities, and members of visible minorities) represent a strategic resource that numbers approximately 10 million out of 16.5 million individuals in Canada's labour force.[43] Employment equity considerations will be discussed in more detail in Chapter 2. Figure 1.11 summarizes ways in which HRM can support the management of diversity for organizational success.

"A diversified workforce has paid off at Lea International Ltd., a Markham, Ontario, company that creates transport and urban planning systems. It recently won a contract to redesign seven railway stations in Mumbai, India, for a commuter network that carries 6.1 million people a day. 'The fact that we have a workforce from around the world gives me competitive knowledge,' says president John Farrow, who points out that 34 percent of his employees are visible minorities and 12 percent are immigrants whose first language was not English."[44]

The banks also have good business cases for diversity: they need to reflect the communities and clients to which they sell services. "There is a natural tendency to hire people who look like the people on the other side of the counter," says Amy Hanen, vice-president of human resources policy and governance at CIBC.[45] The "Best Practices" feature discusses how one Canadian organization provides for effective integration of diverse cultures.

Participation rates of women in the labour force are increasing. In 2001, women represented 46 percent of Canada's paid workforce.[46] Even as recently as 1990, women made up only 9 percent of executive positions at the Bank of Montreal; now, they make up almost 33 percent.[47] The population of Aboriginal peoples reached nearly 1 million in 2001. One third of the Aboriginal population is under age 15, compared with 19 percent of the non-Aboriginal population thus providing opportunities for a significant source of skilled workers in the future.[48] Persons with disabilities comprise a productive but historically overlooked sector of the workforce. Some persons with disabilities require accommodation on the job to be effective, however,

OMNI's Success in Managing Diversity

OMNI, a multilingual TV station owned by Rogers Communications, Inc., is a leading provider of ethnocultural television programming. The station, which can be seen as a microcosm of the larger workplace community, is described as a virtual United Nations of nearly 400 employees who produce broadcasts in 44 languages, representing Cantonese, Portuguese, Italian, Hindi, Polish, and Ukrainian communities to name a few. Where there is such a great mix of employees, "people are acculturated and more accepting of differences," vice-president and general manager Madeline Ziniak says. However, this success in managing diversity does not happen without the planful effort of OMNI.

To help integrate employees from different cultures and create a harmonious workplace, OMNI conducts orientation sessions with a twofold aim:

- For employees new to Canada, they help to clarify expectations and accepted practices.
- For employees born and raised in Canada, they help to promote greater understanding and tolerance.

"We really do become citizens of the world here," Ms. Ziniak says. "So [employees become] very well-versed in the kind of interaction that is acceptable and respectful between different ethno-cultural communities." In addition, Ms. Ziniak says many training sessions focus on issues of communication, since "culturally, there's different ways of communicating. In some cultures, looking someone right in the eye is not respectful. In our courses, we say you have to look at the person directly." Specialized sessions like these run four or five times a year, and senior managers attend two annual conferences on diversity.

In addition, interoffice multicultural events help build understanding and tolerance while making minorities feel welcome. OMNI also hosts many international delegations, sent by the foreign affairs and international trade ministries, to learn about working in a diverse environment.

SOURCES: Sherry Noik-Bent, "By Being Visible: How to Manage Multiculti Maze," *The Globe and Mail*, November 24, 2004, pp. C1, C2; www.rogers.com.

more often than not, this accommodation can be provided at little or no cost, e.g., providing large print software or arranging office furniture to promote ease of access.[49]

Throughout this book, we will show how diversity affects HRM practices. For example, from a staffing perspective, it is important to ensure that tests used to select employees are not unfairly biased. From the perspective of work design, employees need flexible schedules that allow them to meet nonwork needs. In terms of training, it is clear that employees must be made aware of the damage that stereotypes can do. With regard to compensation and rewards, organizations are providing benefits such as child and elder care as a way to accommodate the needs of a diverse workforce.

Skill Deficiencies of the Workforce

The increasing use of computers to do routine tasks has shifted the kinds of skills needed for employees. Such qualities as physical strength and mastery of a particular piece of machinery are no longer important for many jobs. More employers are looking for mathematical, verbal, and interpersonal skills, such as the ability to solve math problems or reach decisions as part of a team. Often, when organizations are looking for technical skills, they are looking for skills related to computers and using the Internet. Today's employees must be able to handle a variety of responsibilities, interact with customers, and think creatively.

To find such employees, most organizations are looking for educational achievements. A college diploma or university degree is a basic requirement for many jobs today. Competition for qualified college and university graduates in many fields is intense. At the other extreme, workers with less education often have to settle for low-paying jobs. Some companies are unable to find qualified employees and instead rely on training to correct skill deficiencies.[50] Other companies team up with universities, colleges, and high schools to design and teach courses ranging from basic reading to design blueprint reading.

High-Performance Work Systems

LO7

Human resource management is playing an important role in helping organizations gain and keep an advantage over competitors by becoming high-performance work systems. These are organizations that have the best possible fit between their social system (people and how they interact) and technical system (equipment and processes).[51] As the nature of the workforce and the technology available to organizations have changed, so have the requirements for creating a high-performance work system. Customers are demanding high quality and customized products, employees are seeking flexible work arrangements, and employers are looking for ways to tap people's creativity and interpersonal skills. Such demands require that organizations make full use of their people's knowledge and skill, and skilled human resource management can help organizations do this.

Among the trends that are occurring in today's high-performance work systems are reliance on knowledge workers, employee engagement, the use of teamwork, and the increasing levels of education of the workforce. The following sections describe these three trends, and Chapter 12 will explore the ways HRM can support the creation and maintenance of a high-performance work system. HR professionals who keep up with change are well positioned to help create high-performance work systems.

Knowledge Workers

To meet their human capital needs, companies are increasingly trying to attract, develop, and retain knowledge workers. **Knowledge workers** are employees whose main contribution to the organization is specialized knowledge, such as knowledge of customers, a process, or a profession. Knowledge workers are especially needed for jobs in health services, business services, social services, engineering, and management.

Knowledge workers are in a position of power, because they own the knowledge that the company needs in order to produce its products and services, and they must share their knowledge and collaborate with others in order for their employer to succeed. An employer cannot simply order these employees to perform tasks. Managers depend on the employees' willingness to share information. Furthermore, skilled knowledge workers have many job opportunities, even in a slow economy. If they choose, they can leave a company and take their knowledge to another

knowledge workers
Employees whose main contribution to the organization is specialized knowledge, such as knowledge of customers, a process, or a profession.

Knowledge workers are employees whose value to their employers stems primarily from what they know. Engineers such as the ones pictured here have in-depth knowledge of their field and are hard to replace because of their special knowledge.

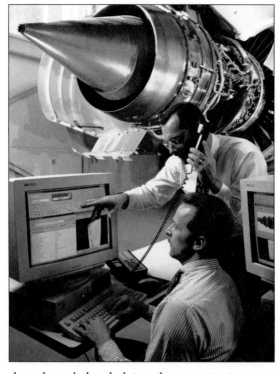

employer. Replacing them may be difficult and time-consuming.

As more organizations become knowledge-based, they must promote and capture learning at the level of employees, teams, and the overall organization.

The reliance on knowledge workers also affects organizations' decisions about the kinds of people they are recruiting and selecting.[52] They are shifting away from focusing on specific skills, such as how to operate a particular kind of machinery, and toward a greater emphasis on general cognitive skills (thinking and problem solving) and interpersonal skills. Employers are more interested in evidence that job candidates will excel at working in teams or interacting with customers. These skills also support an employee's ability to gather and share knowledge, helping the organization to innovate and meet customer needs. To the extent that technical skills are important, employers often are most interested in the ability to use information technology, including the Internet and statistical software.

The editors at *Canadian Business* recently spoke to academics, consultants, and industry representatives across Canada to find what the high demand jobs for skilled labour will be in the coming years. Table 1.3 summarizes their picks.

Employee Engagement

To completely benefit from employees' knowledge, organizations need a management style that focuses on developing and engaging employees. **Employee engagement** refers to the extent that employees are satisfied, committed to, and prepared to support what is important to the organization.

employee engagement
The extent that employees are satisfied, committed to, and prepared to support what is important to the organization.

TABLE 1.3

Some of Tomorrow's Hot Jobs

SECTOR	WANTED	CURRENT SALARY
Any	Managers of all types	Varies
Utilities	Engineers, load managers, line technicians	$44,000–$70,000
Oil and gas	Engineers, geologist, geophysicists, mechanics, equipment operators	$50,000–$150,000
Technology	Computer systems and software engineers	$47,000–$90,000
Health care	Surgeons, nurses, pharmacists	$32,000–$280,000
Financial services	Financial planners	$75,000–$500,000
Any	Accounting, insurance and finance professionals	$55,000–$235,000

SOURCE: Raizel Robin, "Tomorrow's Hot Jobs," *Canadian Business*, March 1–14, 2004, pp. 39, 40.

HRM practices such as performance management, training, career management, work design, and employee relations are important for creating employee engagement. Jobs must be designed to give employees the necessary latitude for making a variety of decisions. Employees must be properly trained to exert their wider authority and use information resources such as the Internet, as well as tools for communicating information. Employees also need feedback to help them evaluate their success. Pay and other rewards should reflect employees' authority and be related to successful handling of their responsibility. In addition, for engagement to occur, managers must be trained to link employees to resources within and outside the organization, such as customers, coworkers in other departments, and websites with needed information. Managers must also encourage employees to interact with staff throughout the organization, must ensure that employees receive the information they need, and must reward cooperation.

As with the need for knowledge workers, employee engagement shifts the recruiting focus away from technical skills and toward general cognitive and interpersonal skills. Employees who have responsibility for a final product or service must be able to listen to customers, adapt to changing needs, and creatively solve a variety of problems.

Teamwork

Modern technology places the information that employees need for improving quality and providing customer service right at the point of sale or production. As a result, the employees engaging in selling and producing must also be able to make decisions about how to do their work. Organizations need to set up work in a way that gives employees the authority and ability to make those decisions. One of the most popular ways to increase employee responsibility and control is to assign work to teams. **Teamwork** is the assignment of work to groups of employees with various skills who interact to assemble a product or provide a service.

teamwork
The assignment of work to groups of employees with various skills who interact to assemble a product or provide a service.

Increasing Levels of Education

The educational attainment of Canada's population is increasing. In 2001, 12.2 percent of Canada's population 15 years and older had a college certificate or diploma; 15.4 percent a university degree. These figures are up from 8.3 percent and 9.6 percent respectively, in 1986.[53]

In a recent survey conducted for a TD Bank Financial Group paper, economists Craig Alexander and Eric Lascalles examined the work of a dozen researchers to discover the rate of return of post-secondary education. The rate of return was calculated using the present value difference between the lifetime earnings of a post-secondary graduate and those of a high-school graduate, factoring in the cost of tuition, academic fees, and lost earnings while students were in school. Annual rates of return for a university degree ranged from 12 percent to 17 percent for men and 16 percent to 20 percent for women; for a college diploma, rates of return were between 15 percent and 28 percent for men, and 18 percent and 28 percent for women.[54]

Technological Change in HRM

Advances in computer-related technology have had a major impact on the use of information for managing human resources. Large quantities of employee data (including training records, skills, compensation rates, and benefits usage and cost) can eas-

human resource information system (HRIS)

A computer system used to acquire, store, manipulate, analyze, retrieve, and distribute information related to an organization's human resources.

ily be stored on personal computers and manipulated with user-friendly spreadsheets or statistical software. Often these features are combined in a **human resource information system (HRIS),** a computer system used to acquire, store, manipulate, analyze, retrieve, and distribute information related to an organization's human resources.[55] An HRIS can support strategic decision making, help the organization avoid lawsuits, provide data for evaluating programs or policies, and support day-to-day HR decisions.

The support of an HRIS can help HR professionals navigate the challenges of today's complex business environment. For example, rapidly changing technology can cause employees' skills to become obsolete. Organizations must therefore carefully monitor their employees' skills and the organization's needed skills. Often the employees and needs are distributed among several locations, perhaps among several countries, requiring a global HRIS. Northern Telecom has facilities in 90 countries, including the United Kingdom, China, and the United States, and needed access to information about employees located worldwide. The company has created a central database built on a common set of core elements. Anyone with authorization can view employee records from around the globe. Data on the number of employees, salaries, and recruiting efforts are continually updated as changes are made around the world. The system is customized to specific country needs, but several common data fields and elements are used globally. Northern Telecom's system has enabled managers around the world to obtain up-to-date employee data to meet customer needs and address internal staffing issues.[56]

Connectedness: A Changing Economy

The way business is conducted has changed rapidly during the past few years and will continue to do so. Many companies are connecting to the Internet to gain an advantage over (or keep up with) competitors. Greater use of the Internet has prompted the spread of **electronic business (e-business)**—any process that a business conducts electronically, especially business involving use of the Internet. E-business includes several forms of buying and selling goods and business services:

electronic business (e-business)

Any process that a business conducts electronically, especially business involving use of the Internet.

- Business-to-consumer transactions, such as purchasing books and tickets and conducting services, including banking, online.

TABLE 1.4

Summary of Connectedness Results for 2003

COUNTRY	RANK	OVERALL SCORE
United States	1	108
Canada	2	105
Sweden	2	105
Finland	4	101
United Kingdom	5	100
Australia	5	100
Germany	5	100
Japan	8	97
France	9	93
Italy	10	92

SOURCE: "Cashing in on Canadian Connectedness: The Move to Demonstrating Value," The Conference Board of Canada Briefing, April 2004, p. 2, www.conferenceboard.ca/boardwise. Retrieved: April 1, 2004.

- Business-to-business transactions, including sales among manufacturers, retailers, wholesalers, and construction firms.
- Consumer-to-consumer transactions—in particular, individuals buying and selling through auctions.

E-business relies on the Internet to enable buyers to obtain information online, directly order products and services, receive after-sale technical support, and view the status of orders and deliveries. Internet sites may also allow the customer and seller to communicate with each other through email, chat, and voice connections. Companies may set up customer service centres offering email and live telephone connections to provide help, advice, or product information not found on their websites.

Profitable e-businesses provide services that are information-intensive, rely on old-economy roots, and require little or no physical transportation of products. For example, eBay takes a cut of each sale on its auction site but is not directly involved in transporting items from sellers to buyers. Monster.ca charges companies to post job openings and see résumés but does not set up interviews between job candidates and employees. Travel websites such as Expedia earn a commission if the customer purchases a ticket, rents a car, or books a hotel room. Other old-economy businesses with strong brand recognition, such as FTD, the floral delivery service, have successfully used the Internet to complement telephone and flower store business. FTD can rely on local retailers to receive and ship orders using their own delivery vehicles. The Internet has given customers a new way to place orders.

At least 54 percent of Canadian businesses had a website in 2003, up from 28 percent in 1999. A recent study also found that although Canadians are less likely to order online, we rank third in the number of businesses that allow payments online. Overall, Canada lags the United States on several key indicators of e-business, including the number of leased lines connected to the Internet, the percentage of Internet users who buy online, the amount spent online, and total volumes of e-commerce per capita. Table 1.4 provides results from this benchmarking study against nine other Organisation for Economic Co-operation and Development (OECD) economies. Canada outperforms most of the comparator countries, trailing the United States but finishing in second place tied with Sweden. Other countries included in the study, such as the United Kingdom and Australia, are closing the gaps, however, Canada still retains high scores including excellence in e-learning and e-government applications. For example, the federal government recently committed $1.1 billion for the development of electronic health records.[57]

E–HRM Applications in Other Organizations

The development of e-business has included ways to move HRM activities onto the Internet. Electronic HRM applications let employees enrol in and participate in training programs online. Employees can go online to select from items in a benefits package and enrol in the benefits they choose. They can look up answers to HR-related questions and read company news. This processing and transmission of digitized HR information is called **electronic human resource management (e-HRM).**

E-HRM has the potential to change all traditional HRM functions. Table 1.5 shows some major implications of e-HRM. For example, employees in different geographic areas can work together. Use of the Internet lets companies search for talent without geographic limitations. Recruiting can include online job postings, applications, and candidate screening from the company's website or the websites of compa-

electronic human resource management (e-HRM)
The processing and transmission of digitized HR information, especially using computer networking and the Internet.

TABLE 1.5

Implications of
e-HRM for HRM
Practices

HRM PRACTICES	IMPLICATIONS OF E-HRM
Analysis and design of work	Employees in geographically dispersed locations can work together in virtual teams using video, email, and the Internet.
Recruiting	Post job openings online; candidates can apply for jobs online.
Selection	Online simulations, including tests, videos, and email, can measure job candidates' ability to deal with real-life business challenges.
Training	Online learning can bring training to employees anywhere, anytime.
Total Compensation	Employees can review salary and incentives information and seek information about and enrol in benefit plans.

nies that specialize in online recruiting, such as Monster.ca. Employees from different geographic locations can all receive the same training over the company's computer network.

Privacy is an important issue in e-HRM. A great deal of HR information is confidential and not suitable for posting on a website for everyone to see. Therefore, e-HRM typically is set up on an *intranet*, which is a network that uses Internet tools but limits access to authorized users in the organization.

Sharing of Human Resource Information

Information technology is changing the way HR departments handle record keeping and information sharing. Today, HR employees use technology to automate much of their work in managing employee records and giving employees access to information and enrolment forms for training, benefits, and other programs. As a result, HR employees play a smaller role in maintaining records, and employees now get information through **self-service.** This means employees have online access to information about HR issues such as training, benefits, compensation, and contracts; go online to enrol themselves in programs and services; and provide feedback through online surveys.

self-service
System in which employees have online access to information about HR issues and go online to enrol themselves in programs and provide feedback through surveys.

LO8

psychological contract
A description of what an employee expects to contribute in an employment relationship and what the employer will provide the employee in exchange for those contributions.

Change in the Employment Relationship

Economic downturns resulting in layoffs and bankruptcies have played a major role in changing the basic relationship between employers and employees.

A New Psychological Contract

We can think of the relationship between employers and employees in terms of a **psychological contract,** a description of what an employee expects to contribute in an employment relationship and what the employer will provide the employee in exchange for those contributions.[58] Unlike a written sales contract, the psychological contract is not formally put into words. Instead, it describes unspoken expectations that are widely held by employers and employees. In the traditional version of this psychological contract, organizations expected their employees to contribute time, effort, skills, abilities, and loyalty. In return, the organizations would provide job security and opportunities for promotion.

However, this arrangement is being replaced with a new type of psychological contract.[59] To stay competitive, modern organizations must frequently change the quality, innovation, creativeness, and timeliness of employee contributions and the skills needed to make those contributions. This need has led to organizational restructuring, mergers and acquisitions, layoffs, and longer hours for many employees. Companies demand excellent customer service and high productivity levels. They expect employees to take more responsibility for their own careers, from seeking training to balancing work and family. These expectations result in less job security for employees, who can count on working for several companies over the course of a career. Today, the average length of time a person holds a job is seven years (compared with eight years in 2000 and nine years in 1999).[60]

SPEED BUMP   **Dave Coverly**

FIGURE 1.12

A Family-Friendly Work Arrangement

In exchange for top performance and working longer hours without job security, employees want companies to provide flexible work schedules, effective work environments, more control over how they accomplish work, training and development opportunities, and financial incentives based on how the organization performs. (Figure 1.12 provides a humourous look at an employee who seems to have benefited from this modern psychological contract by obtaining a family-friendly work arrangement.) Employees realize that companies cannot provide employment security, so they want *employability*. This means they want their company to provide training and job experiences to help ensure that they can find other employment opportunities.

Flexibility

The new psychological contract largely results from the HRM challenge of building a committed, productive workforce in turbulent economic conditions that offer opportunity for financial success but can also quickly turn sour, making every employee expendable. From the organization's perspective, the key to survival in a fast-changing environment is flexibility. Organizations want to be able to change as fast as customer needs and economic conditions change. Flexibility in human resource management includes flexible staffing levels and flexible work schedules.

Flexible Staffing Levels

A flexible workforce is one the organization can quickly reshape and resize to meet its changing needs. To be able to do this without massive hiring and firing campaigns, organizations are using more **flexible staffing arrangements**. Flexible staffing arrange-

flexible staffing arrangements
Methods of staffing other than the traditional hiring of full-time employees (for example, use of independent contractors, on-call workers, temporary workers, and contract company workers).

ments are methods of staffing other than the traditional hiring of full-time employees. There are a variety of methods, with the following being most common:

- *Independent contractors* are self-employed individuals with multiple clients.
- *On-call workers* are persons who work for an organization only when they are needed.
- *Temporary workers* are employed by a temporary agency; client organizations pay the agency for the services of these workers.
- *Contract company workers* are employed directly by a company for a specific time specified in a written contract.

CBC News Online recently reported that an estimated one-third or greater of working Canadians are working in a non-standard work arrangement including part-time or casual status jobs, temporary or contract work, self-employment, holding multiple jobs, and those working from home.[61] More workers are choosing these arrangements, but preferences vary. Most independent contractors and contract workers have this type of arrangement by choice. In contrast, temporary agency workers and on-call workers are likely to prefer traditional full-time employment. With flexible staffing, organizations can more easily modify the number of their employees. Continually adjusting staffing levels is especially cost-effective for an organization that has fluctuating demand for its products and services. And when an organization downsizes by laying off temporary and part-time employees, the damage to morale among permanent full-time workers is likely to be less severe. From the employee's perspective, alternative work arrangements provide some flexibility for balancing work and nonwork activities.

Organization of this Book

This chapter has provided an overview of human resource management as well as a summary of challenges and trends impacting Canadian organizations, employees, and HR professionals. In this book, the topics are organized according to the broad areas of human resource management shown in Table 1.6. The numbers in the table refer to the part and chapter numbers.

Part 1 discusses several aspects of the human resource environment. To be effective, human resource management must begin with an awareness of the trends and challenges shaping this field, including changes in the workforce, technology, and society as well as the profession of HR itself. Such trends and issues are the topic of Chapter 1. On a more detailed level, human resource management must also ensure that the organization's actions comply with legal requirements, the topic of Chapter 2.

Part 2 explores the responsibilities involved in acquiring and selecting human resources. Chapter 3 covers the topics of analyzing work and designing jobs. Chapter 4 explains how to plan for human resource needs and recruit candidates to meet those needs. Chapter 5 discusses the selection of employees and their placement into jobs or teams.

In Part 3, the discussion turns to the development of human resources. Chapter 6 addresses various ways organizations train their employees to perform their jobs. Chapter 7 describes the various activities involved in managing performance, in-

TABLE 1.6

Topics Covered in This Book

cluding regular performance appraisals. Chapter 8 describes practices related to employee development—preparing employees for future jobs and helping to establish career paths that take into account employees' work interests, goals, values, and other career issues.

An important element of employee satisfaction is the employee's belief that he or she is being fairly compensated for the work performed. Part 4 addresses several topics related to compensation and rewards. Chapter 9 explores decisions related to the organization's overall pay structure, discusses ways organizations can use pay to recognize individual and group contributions to the organization's performance, considers benefits—forms of total compensation other than pay, and looks at how to create a total rewards culture.

Part 5 addresses a number of special topics that human resource managers face today. Chapter 10 discusses responsibilities of human resource management in organizations where employees have or are seeking union representation. Chapter 11 explores issues that arise when the organization has human resources working in more than one country. And Chapter 12, the last chapter, returns to the topic of high-performance organizations, taking a closer look at how human resource management can foster high performance.

Each chapter includes principles and examples showing how the human resource management practice covered in that chapter helps a company maintain high performance. "Best Practices" boxes highlight success stories related to these topics. "HR How To" boxes provide a more detailed look at how to carry out a practice in each of these areas. "E-HRM" boxes identify the ways that human resource professionals are applying information technology and the Internet to help their organizations excel in the fast-changing dynamic world.

Summary

1. Define human resource management, identify the responsibilities of human resource departments, and explain how human resource management contributes to an organization's performance.

   Human resource management consists of an organization's "people practices"—the policies, practices, and systems that influence employees' behaviour, attitudes, and performance. HR departments have responsibility for a variety of functions. The HRM process begins with analyzing and designing jobs, then recruiting and selecting employees to fill those jobs. Training and development equip employees to carry out their present jobs and follow a career path in the organization. Performance management ensures employees' activities and outputs match the organization's goals. Human resource departments also plan and administer the organization's pay and benefits. They carry out activities in support of employee relations, such as communication programs and collective bargaining. Conducting all these activities involves the establishment and administration of human resource policies. Management also depends on human resource professionals for help in ensuring compliance with legislation, as well as for support for the organization's strategy—for example, human resource planning and change management. HRM contributes to organizational performance by influencing who works for the organization and how these people work. These human resources, if well managed, have the potential to be a source of sustainable competitive advantage, contributing to basic objectives such as productivity, profits, and customer satisfaction.

2. Summarize areas in which human resource management can support organizational strategies.

   HR professionals should be familiar with the organization's strategy and may even play a role in developing the strategy. Specific HR practices vary according to the type of strategy. Productivity improvements require HR leadership including effective feedback and rewards. When organizations with international operations hire employees in foreign countries where they operate, they need to be cognizant of the differences in culture and business practices. Even small businesses serving local markets discover that qualified candidates include skilled immigrants who account for a significant and growing share of the Canadian labour market. Therefore, HRM requires knowledge of different cultures. Organizations also must be able to select and prepare employees for global assignments. Outsourcing requires effective job design, planning, recruitment and selection, and compensation practices to realize the potential benefits.

3. Identify the skills, certification, and ethical requirements of human resource professionals.

   Human resource management requires substantial skills in the area of strategic contributions to organizational success, including HR technical skills as well as planning, implementing, and measuring organizational results of strategic HR initiatives. Human resource professionals also require business acumen, and the ability to manage client relationships including managers, and employees as well as to maintain an effective work environment when required to manage a group or area within the human resources department. Many human resource professionals have achieved the nationally standardized designation, Certified Human Resource Professional (CHRP). Human resource professionals are required to uphold high ethical standards. Some areas in which ethical issues arise include adherence to legislation, protecting confidentiality, and maintaining professional competence.

4. Explain the role of supervisors in human resource management.

   Although many organizations have human resource departments, non-HR managers must be familiar with the basics of HRM and their own role with regard to managing human resources. Supervisors typically have responsibilities related to all the HR functions. Supervisors help analyze work, interview job candidates, participate in selection decisions, provide training, conduct performance appraisals, and recommend pay increases. On a day-to-day basis, supervisors represent the company to their employees, so they also play an important role in employee relations.

5. Describe typical careers in human resource management.

   Careers in human resource management may involve specialized work in fields such as recruiting, training, or labour relations. HR professionals may also be generalists, performing the full range of HR activities described in this chapter. People in these positions usually have a university degree or college diploma in business or the social sciences.

6. Describe trends in the labour force composition and how they affect human resource management.

   An organization's internal labour force comes from its external labour market—individuals who are actively seeking employment. In Canada, this labour market is aging and becoming more diverse. The share of women in the Canadian workforce has grown to nearly half of the total. To compete for talent, organizations must be flexible enough to meet the needs of older workers, possibly redesigning jobs. Organizations must recruit from a diverse population, establish bias-free HR systems, and help employees understand and appreciate cultural differences. Organizations also need employees with skills in decision making, customer service, and teamwork, as well as technical skills. The competition for such talent is intense. Organizations facing a skills shortage often hire employees who lack certain skills, then train them for their jobs.

7. Discuss how high-performance work systems and technological developments are affecting human resource management.

HRM can help organizations find and keep the best possible fit between their social system and technical system. Recruiting and selection decisions are especially important for organizations that rely on knowledge workers. Job design and appropriate systems for assessment and rewards have a central role in supporting employee engagement and teamwork.

The widespread use of the Internet includes HRM applications. Organizations search for talent globally using online job postings and screening candidates online. Organizations' websites feature information directed toward potential employees. Employees may receive training online. At many companies, online information sharing enables employee self-service for many HR needs, from application forms to training modules to information about the details of company policies and benefits.

8. Explain how the nature of the employment relationship is changing and how the need for flexibility affects human resource management.

The employment relationship takes the form of a "psychological contract" that describes what employees and employers expect from the employment relationship. Traditionally, organizations expected employees to contribute their skills and loyalty in exchange for job security and opportunities for promotion. Today, organizations are requiring top performance and longer work hours but often cannot provide job security. Organizations seek flexibility in staffing through non-standard work arrangements. They may use outsourcing as well as temporary and contract workers. The use of such workers can affect job design, as well as the motivation of the organization's permanent employees.

Review and Discussion Questions

1. How can human resource management contribute to a company's success?
2. Why do organizations outsource HRM functions? How does outsourcing affect the role of human resource professionals? As an HR professional, would you rather work for the HR department of a large organization or for an HR outsourcing firm such as Exult Inc.? Explain your answer.
3. What skills are important for success in human resource management? Which of these skills are already strengths of yours? Which would you like to develop further?
4. Traditionally, human resource management practices were developed and administered by the company's human resource department. Increasingly, line managers are playing an active HRM role. What are the potential benefits of line managers taking a more active role in HRM? Potential problems?
5. Does a career in human resource management appeal to you? Why or why not?
6. How does each of the following labour force trends affect HRM?
   a. Aging?
   b. Diversity?
   c. Skill deficiencies?
   d. Higher level of education?
7. What HRM functions could an organization provide through self-service? What are some advantages and disadvantages of using self-service for these functions?
8. How does the employment relationship typical of today's organizations differ from that of a generation ago?

What's Your HR IQ?   www.mcgrawhill.ca/college/noe

The Online Learning Centre offers more ways to check what you've learned so far. Find experiential exercises as well as Test Your Knowledge Quizzes, Videos, and many other resources at www.mcgrawhill.ca/college/noe.

Case: Suncor Strives for a Representative Workforce

Suncor Energy Inc. is a world leader in mining and extracting crude oil from Alberta's oil sands. Suncor also explores for, develops, and markets natural gas, operates major refineries in Sarnia, Ontario and Denver, Colorado and is actively involved in renewable energy initiatives such as wind power projects. Suncor also operates a chain of Sunoco service stations across Ontario and Phillips 66 service stations in Colorado and Wyoming. Suncor employs approximately 4,000 employees.

Nineteen percent of Suncor's employees are women, 7 percent are visible minorities and in the last eight years, the Aboriginal workforce in its oil sands division has grown to more than 10 percent from 3 percent. Heather Kennedy, vice-president of human resources and community affairs, says 10 percent is good, but not good enough. To attract more Aboriginal employees to better reflect the local population, Suncor sponsors scholarships, literacy and mentorship programs, and each summer hires 130 students, up to a third of them Aboriginal.

One beneficiary is Florida Prouix, from the Athabasca Chipwyan First Nation. A summer accounting assistant in 2002, she has since been hired by Suncor and plans to become a certified general accountant. Before that, she worked for an employment centre in Wood Buffalo, where she helped find jobs for Aboriginal peoples, many of them at Suncor. "The company is proactive," Proulx says.

"They go out and meet people in smaller communities and let them know they're there. Consultation is part of operating in the oilpatch—companies must show regula-

tors they have consulted with stakeholders. But it's also good business," says Heather Kennedy. "We're equals in this region. It's not a matter of meeting our obligations, but working with Aboriginals to determine what their needs and our needs are, and pulling them together."

Suncor recently sponsored an event held in conjunction with the National Aboriginal Achievement Foundation Awards to provide opportunities for high-school students from across Canada to meet Aboriginal role models and leaders such as Tina Keeper, television star of *North of 60* and the Honorable Pearl Calahasen, minister of Aboriginal Affairs and Northern Development. The National Aboriginal Achievement Foundation Awards were developed to encourage and celebrate excellence in the Aboriginal community.

Questions

1. How may Suncor benefit from employing a diverse workforce and supporting Aboriginal initiatives?

2. What does Suncor's human resource department need to do to ensure these potential benefits are achieved? *Refer to the Human Resource Management functions and responsibilities identified in Table 1.1 in developing your answer.*

SOURCES: www.suncor.com; Richard W. Yerema, *Canada's Top 100 Employers 2004* (Toronto: Mediacorp Canada Inc.), p. 325; "Aboriginal Voices," *Canadian Business*, March 29–April 11, 2004 p. 50; www.naaf.ca/naaaright.html. Retrieved: April 3, 2004.

Excalibur Case: Le Cirque du Soleil: How to Manage Growth

You are a team of consultants specializing in human resources and labour relations management. Your firm of consultants enjoys a good reputation for the quality of the services offered, especially to large-scale international companies. Having heard tell of the excellence of your services, Cirque du Soleil has approached you. After several meetings with representatives from their Human Resources Department, you have noted the following facts:

Cirque du Soleil

Founded in 1984 by a group of young street performers, Cirque du Soleil has been in constant evolution since its creation. The company enjoys excellent international recognition and is reputed to have reinvented circus arts. While Cirque du Soleil had sales of $1.7 million, 50 employees, and 23 performers in 1984, in 2000, sales reached $407 million and it employed 1,370 employees and 445 performers. It presented seven shows in 2000 on three conti-

nents: North America, Europe, and Asia.

Also, to manage adequately all its personnel, it has four separate headquarters. As well as International Headquarters in Montreal, it has four other head offices: Headquarters–America, also in Montreal, Headquarters–Europe in Amsterdam, Headquarters–Las Vegas in Las Vegas, and lastly, Headquarters–Asia-Pacific in Singapore.

While Cirque du Soleil would like to find and exploit new niches related to presenting shows, most of its revenues come from ticket sales. Thus, the nucleus of the Cirque remains presenting shows. The Cirque has four fixed shows, two touring shows in Asia, one in North America, and another in Europe. A touring show comprises 150 to 200 people, including 50 to 70 performers, and it has to relocate, on average, every six weeks, which demands very skilled logistics and effective planning of the entry authorizations for the different countries on the tour. Relocating means moving personnel, their baggage, and the Cirque's equipment from town to town. It also means lodging all these people and ensuring they get the required visas and work permits to be able to practice their art in the countries the tour is visiting. To reach the level of excellence set by Cirque du Soleil, talent scouts and recruiters travel the globe in search of artists, creators, coaches, musicians, etc. Consequently, the Cirque's performers and personnel come from more than 30 countries and speak various languages. Also, while the average age of employees is relatively young at 32, the age of the performers and employees varies from 3 to 62.

Development Project

As well as continuing to create and produce new shows, Cirque du Soleil wants to diversify its commercial activities. Indeed, it would like to see itself develop the production of audio-visual works such as the soundtracks of the different shows, explore the field of publishing and continue to promote some strategic agreements with partners in the hotel business. Cirque du Soleil has also set itself the objective of adding two or three tours within five years, which will bring the number of employees required to about 2,000.

Management

Cirque du Soleil has adopted a management style in its own image, that is, dynamic, vibrant, and imaginative. The organic nature of how it operates puts each employee in a position that allows him or her to contribute to a common work. Cirque du Soleil firmly believes that by appealing to everyone's intelligence all objectives are achievable. Also, communications are open and the moral authority that certain hierarchial titles could impose is almost non-existent. A core value of Cirque du Soleil's is respect for cultural diversity. Despite the continuous growth the company has experienced, it has always known how to ensure cohesion among employees and maintain a strong sense of belonging.

Challenges to be Met

Given its growth plans, both by the number of shows presented and the establishment of new commercial activities, Cirque du Soleil must apply itself to adapting its structure and above all to ensuring that its managers have the ability to support such development. Several managers who have grown up with Cirque du Soleil and who have thus acquired broad operating experience are having some difficulty moving to a strategic management mode. Given their extensive knowledge of how the Cirque operates, they too often remain occupied or preoccupied with operating questions, rather than investing their energy more in strategic planning. Also, given the increased number of tours planned, another problem that already exists is likely to get bigger. Because of the difficult touring conditions, such as the frequent relocations, the increased number of shows per week, and working conditions in general, the turnover rate among employees is very high. On average,

they work for the Cirque between 19 and 24 months, which creates a turnover rate of 18–22 percent. Despite the efforts made to reduce the inconveniences inherent in touring, problems remain. For example, the Cirque offers the services of a tutor to child performers and to the children of performers. However, because of the costs this would entail, this service cannot be offered to all the children of its personnel. Despite the advantageous salaries, Cirque du Soleil is experiencing some difficulties in retaining its touring personnel.

Finally, it is important to note that, in the touring shows and in International Headquarters in Montreal, the presence of many people of different nationalities, speaking different languages, is a challenge. Indeed, while the presence of Quebec or Canadian performers at International Headquarters and on tours is often secondary, having several nationalities greatly influences the quality of communications. And, depending on the cultural baggage of each person, the perception of the message communicated can differ greatly. Since cultural references are very divergent, what are innocuous gestures to some have unexpected implications for others. However, despite these difficulties in perception, Cirque du Soleil has always greatly valued cultural diversity and has always emphasized the richness it brings, rather than the differences it creates. Nonetheless, the Cirque du Soleil has to constantly manage stereotypes and prejudices. This situation is even more palpable at International Headquarters in Montreal since the performers who work there are passing through, either with the aim of learning a new number, or to take up training again following an injury. Also, people of the same nationality often remain among themselves without mixing much with other performers of different nationalities.

YOUR MANDATE

You have been given a mandate by Le Cirque du Soleil to propose solutions to the problems raised by the facts described. To do so, you must:

1. State your understanding of the situation at Cirque du Soleil.

2. Precisely determine the needs of Cirque du Soleil in the short and medium term.

3. Because of those needs, make provisions for the obstacles envisaged.

4. Finally, establish a plan of action by formulating possible solutions, taking into account the values transmitted by Cirque du Soleil.

Note: This case study was used in the 15th edition of *Excalibur, The Canadian University Tournament of Human Resources*.

SOURCE: www.rhri.org/Excalibur. Retrieved: March 2, 2004. Case is adapted from the website/*Effectif*, September/October 2001, pp. 12–14.

2

The Legal Context for Human Resource Management and Providing a Healthy and Safe Workplace

What Do I Need to Know? After reading this chapter, you should be able to:

1. Describe the legal framework for Human Resource Management in Canada.

2. Summarize the major federal and provincial laws impacting Human Resource Management.

3. Identify the agencies that enforce employment equality and privacy legislation and describe their roles.

4. Describe ways employers can avoid illegal discrimination and meet the duty to accommodate.

5. Define harassment and discuss how employers can eliminate or minimize it.

6. Explain the context for Occupational Health and Safety regulations.

7. Describe how Occupational Health and Safety regulations are enforced including employee rights and responsibilities.

8. Discuss ways employers promote worker safety and health.

Introduction

He's breaking barriers. Steven Fletcher is Canada's first quadriplegic MP. In 1996, Steven, a two-time Manitoba kayaking champion, was paralyzed from the neck down in a car collision with a moose. Elected in 2004, in a highly competitive constituency, Steven is creating change within Parliament.

Fletcher ran his campaign on increased access to post-secondary education, greater government accountability, and improving health care. One of Fletcher's immediate impacts will be directly on the House of Commons where aisles are too narrow and elevators too small for his motorized wheelchair. Many of the buildings are 75 to 140 years old and are not as accessible as one might expect. Because Fletcher needs help to perform the day-to-day aspects of his job—for example, turning the pages of a report, an aide will be by his side. But Steven is focused on his ability to contribute, "I made the decision to use what I have. What's important is from the neck up."

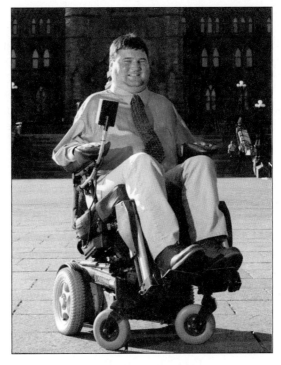

Steven Fletcher, Canada's first quadriplegic MP, is breaking down barriers within the House of Commons.

Heather Bradley, spokesperson for the House Speaker says, "We are working very closely with Mr. Fletcher to make the necessary arrangements for him to do his job as a parliamentarian." These accommodations will include not only building adaptations such as lifts and ramps, but also information technology needs such as wireless voice-activated dialing for his phone system and use of a head mouse for his computer. Although the focus initially is on accommodating Steven Fletcher's needs to allow him to do his job, his legacy will likely include creating awareness and improving the situation for many others. Steven adds, "let's lay the foundation so we'll see people in wheelchairs contributing...and it's natural."[1]

As we saw in Chapter 1, human resource management takes place in the context of the company's goals and society's expectations for how a company should operate. In Canada, the federal, provincial, and territorial governments have set some limits on how an organization can practise human resource management. Among these limits are requirements intended to prevent discrimination in hiring and employment practices and to protect the health and safety of workers while they are on the job. Questions about a company's compliance with these requirements can result in human rights complaints, lawsuits, and negative publicity that often cause serious problems for a company's success and survival. Conversely, a company that skillfully navigates the maze of regulations can gain an advantage over its competitors.

This chapter provides an overview of the ways government bodies regulate human resource management including workplace health and safety. It introduces you to major laws affecting employers in these areas, as well as the agencies charged with enforcing those laws. The chapter also discusses ways organizations can develop practices that ensure they are in compliance with the laws.

One point to make at the outset is that managers often want a list of do's and don'ts that will keep them out of legal trouble. Some managers rely on strict rules such as "Don't ever ask a female applicant if she is married," rather than learning the reasons behind those rules. Clearly, certain practices are illegal or at least inadvisable, and this chapter will provide guidance on avoiding such practices. However, managers who merely focus on how to avoid breaking the law are not thinking about how to be ethical or how to acquire and use human resources in the best way to carry out the company's mission. This chapter introduces ways to think proactively about the legal requirements for HRM including workplace health and safety.

LO1

The Legal Framework for Human Resource Management

Federal, provincial, and territorial governments in Canada all play an important role in creating the legal environment for human resource management. Approximately 90 percent of Canadian employers and their employees are covered by provincial and territorial legislation. The remaining 10 percent are covered by federal legislation. Table 2.1 summarizes the types of organizations which fall under federal versus provincial legislation.

Federal, provincial, and territorial employment-related laws tend to mirror one another, however, some differences exist. It is important for employers to ensure they are aware of and comply with all legal requirements. For organizations with workers in more than one province, territory, or industry it can be time-consuming and challenging to maintain compliance with this web of legal requirements. In addition, many proactive human resource departments and their organizations are moving beyond compliance and are recognizing the strategic importance of valuing the various goals pursued through the legislation, e.g., diversity, health and safety of employees, and privacy protection. Table 2.2 provides an overview of federal, provincial, and territorial human rights, employment standards, and health and safety laws in Canada.

TABLE 2.1

Summary of Federally versus Provincially Regulated Organizations

FEDERALLY REGULATED ORGANIZATIONS	PROVINCIALLY REGULATED ORGANIZATIONS
• Federal government departments, agencies, and Crown corporations • Canada Post and courier companies • Chartered banks • Airlines • Television and radio stations • Interprovincial communication and telephone companies • Interprovincial buses, railways, and trucking companies • Other federally regulated industries such as uranium, mining, grain elevators, flour and seed mills, and feed warehouses	• All other businesses not listed

SOURCE: *Anti-Discrimination Casebook*, p. 1, www.chrc-ccdp.ca/Legis&Poli Retrieved: February 18, 2004 and Human Resource Management Laws and Regulations Government of Canada, http://hrmanagement.gc.ca. Retrieved: February 18, 2004.

TABLE 2.2

Human Rights, Employment Standards, and Health and Safety Laws in Canada

JURISDICTION	HUMAN RIGHTS	EMPLOYMENT STANDARDS	HEALTH & SAFETY
Federal	Canadian Human Rights Act www.chrc-ccdp.ca	Canada Labour Code www.hrsdc.gc.ca	Canada Labour Code www.hrsdc.gc.ca
British Columbia	Human Rights Code www.ag.gov.bc.ca	Employment Standards Act www.gov.bc.ca	Workers Compensation Act www.gov.bc.ca
Alberta	Human Rights Citizenship and Multiculturalism Act www.albertahumanrights.ab.ca	Employment Standards Code www.gov.ab.ca	Occupational Health and Safety Act www.gov.ab.ca
Saskatchewan	Human Rights Code www.gov.sk.ca/shrc	Labour Standards Act www.gov.sk.ca	Occupational Health and Safety Act www.gov.sk.ca
Manitoba	Human Rights Code www.gov.mb.ca/hrc	Employment Standards Code www.gov.mb.ca	Workplace Safety and Health Act www.gov.mb.ca
Ontario	Human Rights Code www.ohrc.on.ca/english/code	Employment Standards Act www.gov.on.ca	Occupational Health and Safety Act and Workplace Safety and Insurance Act www.gov.on.ca
Quebec	Charter of Human Rights and Freedoms www.cdpdj.qc.ca	Labour Standards Act www.cnt.gouv.qc.ca	Act Respecting Occupational Health and Safety www.gouv.qc.ca
New Brunswick	Human Rights Act www.gnb.ca/hrc-cdp	Employment Standards Act www.gnb.ca	Occupational Health and Safety Act www.gnb.ca
Nova Scotia	Human Rights Act www.gov.ns.ca/humanrights	Labour Standards Code www.gov.ns.ca	Occupational Health and Safety Act www.gov.ns.ca
P. E. I.	Human Rights Act www.gov.pe.ca/humanrights	Employment Standards Act www.gov.pe.ca	Occupational Health and Safety Act www.gov.pe.ca
Newfoundland and Labrador	Human Rights Code www.gov.nl.ca/hrc	Labour Standards Act www.gov.nl.ca	Occupational Health and Safety Act www.gov.nl.ca
Yukon	Human Rights Act www.yhrc.yk.ca	Employment Standards Act www.gov.yk.ca	Occupational Health and Safety Act www.wcb.yk.ca
Northwest Territories	Human Rights Act www.assembly.gov.nt.ca/HumanRightsAct	Labour Standards Act www.gov.nt.ca	Occupational Health and Safety Regulations www.gov.nt.ca
Nunavut	Fair Practices Act www.cbsc.org/nunavut	Labour Standards Act www.gov.nu.ca	Workers' Compensation Act www.gov.nu.ca

Equality in Employment

discrimination
To treat someone differently or unfairly because of a personal characteristic.

direct discrimination
Policies or practices that clearly make a distinction on the basis of a prohibited ground.

FIGURE 2.1

Prohibited Grounds of Discrimination in Employment

Among the most significant efforts to regulate human resource management are those aimed at achieving equality in employment and eliminating discrimination. **Discrimination** means to "treat someone differently or unfairly because of a personal characteristic."[2]

All individuals have a right to an equal chance to be hired, keep a job, get a promotion, or receive other work benefit regardless of personal characteristics including race, colour, national or ethnic origin, religion, sexual orientation, age, marital status, sex, family status, physical or mental disability, or pardoned conviction.

Direct discrimination involves policies or practices that clearly make a distinction based on a prohibited ground (see Figure 2.1). **Indirect discrimination** involves policies or practices that appear to be neutral but have an adverse impact based on a prohibited ground. For example, requiring a job applicant to have a driver's licence appears to be applied equally to all applicants. However, the effect of this requirement is not neutral—someone who does not have a driver's licence because of suffering from epilepsy would not be able to apply for the job.[3] See Figure 2.2 for examples of discriminatory behaviour in employment.

Prohibited Ground	Federal	BC	AB	SK	MB	ON	QUE	NB	NS	PEI	NL	NWT	YK	NU
Race	*	*	*	*	*	*	*	*	*	*	*	*	*	*
National or ethnic origin	*	*	*	*	*	*	*	*	*	*	*	*	*	*
Colour	*	*	*	*	*	*	*	*	*	*	*	*	*	*
Religion or creed	*	*	*	*	*	*	*	*	*	*	*	*	*	*
Age	*	*	*	*	*	*	*	*	*	*	*	*	*	*
		19–64	18+	18–64		18–64					19–64			
Sex (including pregnancy & childbearing)	*	*	*	*	*	*	*	*	*	*	*	*	*	*
Sexual orientation	*	*	*	*	*	*	*	*	*	*	*	*	*	*
Marital status	*	*	*	*	*	*	*	*	*	*	*	*	*	*
Family status	*	*	*	*	*	*	*		*	*		*	*	*
Physical or mental disability (including dependence on drugs or alcohol)	*	*	*	*	*	*	*	*	*	*	*	*	*	*
Pardoned conviction	*	*				*	*				*			
Ancestry or place of origin		*	*	*	*	*		*				*	*	*
Political belief		*			*		*		*	*	*	*	*	
Source of income (social condition)		*	*	*	*		*		*	*		*		

SOURCES: From *Prohibited Grounds of Discrimination in Canada*, pp. 1–3, Canadian Human Rights Commission, 1998. Reproduced with the permission of the Minister of Public Works and Government Services Canada, 2004. www.chrc-ccdp.ca/discrimination/grounds-en.asp. Retrieved: December 6, 2004; www.ag.gov.bc.ca/programs/hrc/publications/ProtectDiscrimination.pdf. Retrieved: December 6, 2004; www.qp.gov.ab.ca/Documents/acts/H14.CFM. Retrieved: December 6, 2004; www.qp.gov.sk.ca/documents/English/Statutes/Statutes/S24-1.pdf. Retrieved: December 6, 2004; www.gov.mb.ca/hrc/english/publications/hr-code. Retrieved: December 6, 2004; www.ohrc.on.ca/english/publications/hr-code-guide_1.shtml#. Retrieved: December 6, 2004; www.cdpdj.qc.ca/en/human-rights/complaints.asp?noeud1=1&noeud2=3&cle=4#10. Retrieved: December 6, 2004; www.gnb.ca/hrc%2Dcdp/e/annual%2Dreport%2D2003%2D04%2Dnew%2Dbrunswick%2Dhuman%2Drights%2Dcommission.pdf. Retrieved: December 6, 2004; www.gov.ns.ca/legi/legc/statutes/humanrt.htm. Retrieved: December 6, 2004; www.gov.pe.ca/law/statutes/pdf/h-12.pdf. Retrieved: December 6, 2004; www.gov.nf.ca/hrc/Publications/code%203.htm#Section%209. Retrieved: December 6, 2004; www.yhrc.yk.ca/Human%20Rights%20in%20the%20Workplace.htm. Retrieved: December 6, 2004; www.assembly.gov.nt.ca/HumanRightsAct.pdf. Retrieved: December 6, 2004; www.cbsc.org/nunavut/english/search/display.cfm?Code=5035&Coll=NU_PROVBIS_E. Retrieved: December 6, 2004.

EXAMPLES OF DISCRIMINATORY BEHAVIOUR IN EMPLOYMENT

- Denying someone a job because of a disability that can be accommodated or doesn't affect job performance
- Internet or recorded telephone hate messages
- Firing an employee for filing a human rights complaint
- Including employment requirements not related to the job, e.g., asking for previous Canadian work experience

SOURCE: Adapted from *The Canadian Human Rights Act: A Guide*, pp. 2, 3, www.chrc-ccdp.ca/publications/chra_guide/ledp.asp. Retrieved: February 18, 2004.

FIGURE 2.2

Examples of Discriminatory Behaviour in Employment

Legislation In Canada

Canadian law recognizes the equality of people and prohibits discrimination in employment practices. Canadian law also requires employers to identify and remove barriers in employment.

The Charter of Rights and Freedoms (1982)

The Charter of Rights and Freedoms was the first constitutional recognition of the right to equality. The Charter identifies fundamental rights and freedoms including the right to equality (including the equality of men and women), Aboriginal peoples' rights, the right to seek employment anywhere in Canada, and the right to use either of Canada's official languages.[4]

The Official Languages Act (1988)

The Official Languages Act provides English and French-speaking Canadians equal opportunities in employment in federally regulated organizations.

The Employment Equity Act (1986)

The Employment Equity Act requires federally regulated employers as well as private sector contractors with more than 100 employees in Canada and with contracts valued at more than $200,000 to eliminate employment barriers to the four designated groups:

- Women
- Members of visible minorities ("persons other than Aboriginal peoples, who are non-Caucasian in race or non-white in colour")[5]
- Aboriginal peoples ("persons who are Indians, Inuit, or Metis")[6]
- Persons with disabilities ("persons who have a long-term or recurring physical mental, sensory, psychiatric or learning implement")[7]

See Table 2.3 for the representation of these four designated workforce groups.

By June 1 each year over 400 federally regulated employers (employers with 100+ employees) must submit a report outlining what they have done to improve the situation for the designated groups within their workforce. Employers also need to submit statistics including the representation of the designated groups in their workforce relative to the composition of the Canadian labour force. Employers receive ratings based on their results. Top ratings earned are "A's" and "B's" indicating superior to good performance. Less than average to poor performance is indicated with "C's" and "D's." A rating of "Z" indicates that an organization does not have any members of

LO2

indirect discrimination
Policies or practices that appear to be neutral but have an adverse impact based on a prohibited ground.

TABLE 2.3

Representation of the Designated Groups in the Canadian Workforce, 2002

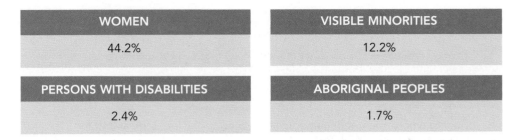

WOMEN	VISIBLE MINORITIES
44.2%	12.2%
PERSONS WITH DISABILITIES	ABORIGINAL PEOPLES
2.4%	1.7%

SOURCE: Annual Report Employment Equity Act, 2003, p. 3, www.hrsdc.gc.ca/en. Retrieved: July 13, 2004.

one or more of the designated group in its workforce. In addition, more organizations are integrating their employment equity plans into their business planning as a tool to achieve equality in their workforce and capitalize on the benefits of a diverse workforce. Employment Equity Vision Awards and Certificates of Merit are awarded annually to organizations based on criteria including results achieved, good faith efforts, innovativeness, and reasonable accommodation. In 2003 IBM Canada and Pelmorex Inc. (The Weather Network) received the Vision Award and Certificates of Merit were awarded to Shell Canada Ltd., Yanke Group, and the University of British Columbia.[8]

The Canadian Human Rights Act (1998)

Canadian Human Rights Act
Federal legislation that protects individuals from discrimination on the basis of 11 protected grounds.

The **Canadian Human Rights Act** is federal legislation that protects individuals from discrimination based on 11 prohibited grounds:

- Race
- National or ethnic origin
- Colour
- Religion
- Age
- Sex (including pregnancy and childbirth)
- Sexual orientation
- Marital status
- Family status
- Physical or mental disability (including dependence on alcohol or drugs)
- Pardoned criminal conviction[9]

Personal Information Protection and Electronic Documents Act (PIPEDA) (2004)

Personal Information Protection and Electronic Documents Act (PIPEDA)
Provides rules for how organizations can collect, use, or disclose information about you in the course of commercial activities.

The **Personal Information Protection and Electronic Documents Act (PIPEDA)** came into effect in three stages over a three-year period from 2001–2004 and provides rules for how organizations can "collect, use, or disclose information about you in the course of commercial activities."[10]

The Act's ten principles have implications for human resource departments and their responsibilities to safeguard employee privacy. Recent complaints to the federal Privacy Commissioner indicate that although employers can collect information on employees about performance, attendance, and potential for advancement there is little that an employer can keep from an employee.

In a recent case, an employee of Human Resources and Skills Development Canada demanded to see all of the information obtained about her during an assessment review. The employee wanted to see the notes made by the contractor hired to conduct the assessment. These notes contained feedback and comments from other employees. The federal Privacy Commissioner ruled the employee was entitled to this information and that employees cannot be promised confidentiality when they make statements about another person.[11] The "HR How To" box discusses some of the implications of PIPEDA.

HR HOW TO

Maintaining Legal Compliance When Collecting and Using Employee Information—PIPEDA

The implications to HRM of this new federal legislation are still being tested, however, the Act's ten principles serve as a guide to organizations and HR professionals as to how to maintain legal compliance when collecting and using employee information needed for administration and decision-making. HR professionals need to consider the following principles when collecting and using employee personal information in the course of all HR activities to avoid employee complaints.

1. Accountability
The organization is responsible for personal information it controls. Start by appointing a privacy officer(s).

2. Identifying Purpose
Before collecting information, the organization needs to identify why they are collecting the information and how it will be used. Conduct a "privacy audit" to determine what information is collected and why it is collected.

3. Consent
The organization is responsible for ensuring that consent is given. Consider what type of consent is needed for each

type of information based on criteria such as the sensitivity of the information.

4. Limiting Collection
Care must be taken to make sure that the collection of personal information is limited to what is needed for the stated purpose. Use a "reasonable person" test to determine what is considered appropriate.

5. Limiting Use, Disclosure, and Retention
Personal information cannot be used or disclosed to others without consent and information can only be retained to meet the stated purposes. Additional care must be taken when HR functions are outsourced. Create minimum and maximum retention times for information collected.

6. Accuracy
Information of employees must be current and correct. Keep information accurate and introduce a process to correct errors in a timely way.

7. Safeguards
Security protection needs to be put in place. Implement both technical and physical security measures to safeguard employee information.

8. Openness
Communicate privacy policies and practices. Consider developing training materials, brochures, or other means of communication about the organization's approach to privacy protection.

9. Individual Access
Be responsive to employees when they request access to information the organization holds about them. Have a method in place to deal with employee concerns about the accuracy and completeness of information.

10. Compliance Challenges
Individuals have the power to challenge what the organization does to comply with the principles just described. Be open to employee concerns and be willing to adapt policies and practices to ensure compliance with all aspects.

SOURCES:
www.privcom.gc.ca/information. Retrieved: March 21, 2004; Dianne Rinehart, "The ABC's of the New Privacy Legislation," *Small Business Canada Magazine*, Spring 2004, Vol. 6 No. 2, p. 7; "The 10 Principles of the Federal Privacy Law," *Canadian HR Reporter*, March 6, 2004, p. G7.

Employment Standards Legislation

Federal, provincial, and territorial laws are also in place to provide the minimum standards employees receive. Some of the areas covered include minimum wages, hours of work and overtime pay, annual vacations, statutory holidays, family-related leave (e.g., parental and adoption), and termination notice and pay requirements.

Each jurisdiction has relevant laws to provide minimum employment standards. Refer to Table 2.2 and its summary of the relevant employment standards legislation for each jurisdiction along with the addresses of searchable web links where detailed, specific information can be accessed.

Ontario has recently increased its emphasis on ensuring compliance—employers who violate the provincial Employment Standards Act could receive a $300 fine. This fine could be imposed for violations such as not paying wages on time, not giving employees vacation, or demanding employees work beyond the weekly hour limit.[12]

Pay Equity Act (1978)

pay equity
Principle of non-discrimination in wages that require men and women doing work of equal value to be paid the same.

Federally regulated employers are responsible for providing equal pay for work of equal value, or pay equity. **Pay equity** is a principle of non-discrimination in wages that requires men and women doing work of equal value to be paid the same. Most provinces and the Yukon, as well as Australia, Scandinavian countries, and many U.S. states have laws to ensure women and men working in female-dominated jobs, e.g., nursing, clerical, and retail sales are paid fairly. The four criteria usually applied are skill, effort, responsibility, and working conditions.

Pay equity legislation is intended to address the wage gap—the difference between the earnings of women working full-time versus the earnings of men working full-time. "In Canada, today, women working full-time still make an average of only 72 cents for every dollar earned by men, and this wage gap has narrowed by just 8 percent since the late 1960s."[13]

Statistics Canada reported the results of a study of 29 universities related to the salaries of male and female professors. The study revealed that "male university professors earned on average up to $17,300 more than female colleagues in 2003."[14] According to the Canadian Association of University Teachers (CAUT), one reason for the wage gap is that women are under-represented in the highest paying position of full professor. CAUT's analysis determined that in 2001, 85.9 percent of full professors were men versus 15.1 percent women.[15]

The pay equity system has been criticized for the overall lack of progress and the federal government has recently completed an extensive pay equity review process expected to result in a more proactive model.[16]

LO3

The Government's Role in Providing for Equality and Privacy Protection

At a minimum, employers must comply with the legal requirements of their jurisdictions. To enforce these laws, the federal government, for example, has the Canadian Human Rights Commission and the Privacy Commissioner of Canada.

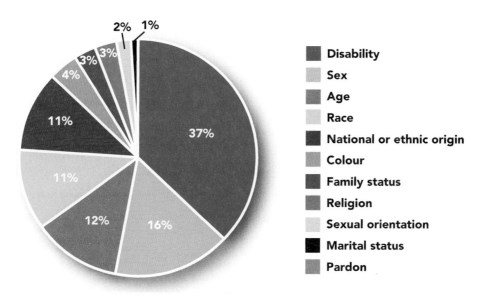

FIGURE 2.3

Types of Signed Complaints Filed with the Canadian Human Rights Commission

- Disability
- Sex
- Age
- Race
- National or ethnic origin
- Colour
- Family status
- Religion
- Sexual orientation
- Marital status
- Pardon

SOURCE: *Canadian Human Rights Commission Annual Report, 2003*, p. 14, Canadian Human Rights Commission, 2004. Reproduced with the permission of the Minister of Public Works and Government Services Canada, 2004; www.chrc-ccdp.ca/pdf/reports/2003Area.pdf. Retrieved: July 13, 2004.

In addition, the provinces and territories also have Human Rights Commissions (or a similar structure) to enforce the human rights legislation for their jurisdiction. For example, the **Canadian Human Rights Commission (CHRC)** provides individuals under federal jurisdiction a means to resolve complaints of discrimination (see Figure 2.3). The Canadian Human Rights Commission has the power to receive and address complaints based on the 11 prohibited grounds of discrimination outlined in the Canadian Human Rights Act. The CHRC tries to resolve complaints using mediation and conciliation, however, some complaints only get resolved by using a tribunal. Cases may also be ultimately appealed all the way to the Supreme Court of Canada for final resolution.

The Canadian Human Rights Commission is also responsible for auditing federally regulated employers to ensure compliance with the Employment Equity Act. Figure 2.4 provides a portion of a sample survey questionnaire used in the federal audit process. In addition, the CHRC enforces pay equity laws. Approximately 70,000 employees have obtained equal pay increases due to cases involving the CHRC. Some of the jobs where equal pay has been achieved are nurses and paramedics; librarians and historical researchers; and kitchen workers and janitors.[17]

Canadian Human Rights Commission (CHRC)
Provides individuals under federal jurisdiction a means to resolve complaints of discrimination.

The Privacy Commissioner of Canada

The Privacy Commissioner of Canada is responsible for ensuring compliance with the Personal Information Protection and Electronic Documents Act. The Privacy Commissioner has the power to investigate complaints and recommend solutions to employers. To ensure compliance, the Privacy Commissioner can publicly identify organizations violating individuals' privacy rights and take the complaint to the Federal Court of Canada. If unable to resolve the complaint, the court can order the organization to take specific actions and can also award damages.[18]

FIGURE 2.4

Employment Equity Audit: Excerpt from Survey Questionnaire

---

1. **WORKFORCE SURVEY & DATA SYSTEMS**

1.1 Has your organization conducted a self-identification survey of the entire workforce? .... ❐ Yes ❐ No ❐ In part

If so, in what year? _____ What was the return rate?* (___%) (*If no, go to section 2.*)

* The return rate is calculated by dividing the number of identifiable questionnaires which have been returned (completed or not) by the full population of the organization.

1.2 Do you have a process to invite new employees to self-identify? .... ❐ Yes ❐ No

If so, **please provide a copy of the self-identification package for new employees.**

1.3 If your survey took place more than one year ago, have the results been

updated? .... ❐ Yes ❐ No

If so, **please include a description of the update process and its frequency.**

1.4 Please provide a copy of the self-identification package including the questionnaire, any accompanying material or campaign communications, used at the time of the full survey. **Please include a description of the process, including any lead-up or follow-up strategy used.**

1.5 How do you store the information collected?   ❐ Manually   ❐ Electronically

Does this data system allow you to generate up-to-date representation data:

a) on the whole work force? .... ❐ Yes ❐ No ❐ In part

b) for each designated group? .... ❐ Yes ❐ No ❐ In part

c) by occupational group or category? .... ❐ Yes ❐ No ❐ In part

1.6 Please indicate the percentage of current employees for which a record of a self-identification questionnaire exists. _____

1.7 Do you collect data for designated groups on the following:

(*Please check all appropriate boxes*)

Hiring ❐   Applications ❐   Screening/Selection ❐

Promotions ❐   Terminations ❐   Salary ❐

2. **WORKFORCE ANALYSIS**

2.1 Has your organization conducted a workforce analysis? .... ❐ Yes ❐ No

(*If no, please go to section 3.*)

2.2 **Please provide a copy of the report on your workforce analysis** and, if not included in the report, a copy or description of the following:

a) the availability estimates and a description of how they were developed and calculated; .... Incl. ❐ Not avail. ❐

b) how appropriate geographic areas and occupational qualifications were considered in this process; .... Incl. ❐ Not avail. ❐

c) a copy of any background calculations and data (4-digit NOC group and regional) which were used to prepare the available estimates; .... Incl. ❐ Not avail. ❐

d) summary table(s) listing total workforce, representation and availability, and the gap, in actual numbers as well as percentages, by occupational group/category for all designated groups; Incl. ❐ Not avail. ❐

e) summary tables listing the results of the analysis of hires, promotions and terminations if applicable; .... Incl. ❐ Not avail. ❐

f) a description of the results of your analysis and its conclusions including identification of gaps. .... Incl. ❐ Not avail. ❐

2.3 Did your analysis include the following:

a) calculation of the **internal representation** of all designated groups in each occupational group/category .... ❐ Yes   ❐ No

b) development of **external representation/availability estimates** for all designated groups in each occupational group/category .... ❐ Yes   ❐ No

c) a **comparison of internal representation with external availability** to determine degree of under-representation (gap), if any, for each designated group in each occupational group/category .... ❐ Yes   ❐ No

2.4 In those occupational groups/categories where under-representation was found, have you done a comparative analysis of the affected designated groups in terms of:

a)   shares* of hiring/recruitment with external representation? .... ❐ Yes   ❐ No

b)   shares of promotions with internal representation? .... ❐ Yes   ❐ No

c)   shares* of terminations/separations with internal representation or termination/ separation rates* with those of non-designated group members? .... ❐ Yes   ❐ No

d)   clustering in the lower levels? .... ❐ Yes   ❐ No

* "Share" means the % of total hiring or promotions received by members of a particular designated group. "Rate" means the % of employees from a particular group who have been terminated over a defined period of time.

LO4

Employers' Role in Meeting Legal Requirements

Rare is the business owner or manager who wants to wait for the government to identify that his or her organization has failed to meet its legal requirements to treat employees fairly. Instead, out of motives ranging from concern for employee well-being to the desire to avoid costly lawsuits and negative publicity, most companies recognize the importance of complying with these laws. Often, management depends on the expertise of human resource professionals to help in identifying how to comply. These professionals can help organizations take steps to avoid discrimination and provide reasonable accommodation.

Avoiding Discrimination

How would you know if you had been discriminated against? Decisions about human resources are so complex that discrimination is often difficult to identify and prove. However, legal scholars and court rulings have arrived at some ways to show evidence of discrimination.

Differential Treatment

differential treatment
Differing treatment of individuals where the differences are based on a prohibited ground.

One sign of discrimination is **differential treatment**—differing treatment of individuals, where the differences are based on a prohibited ground of discrimination such as the individuals' race, colour, religion, sex, national origin, age, or disability status. For example, differential treatment would include hiring or promoting one person over an equally qualified person because of the individual's race. Suppose a company fails to hire women with school-age children (claiming the women will be frequently absent) but hires men with school-age children. In that situation, the women are victims of differential treatment, because they are being treated differently based on their sex.

To avoid complaints of differential treatment, companies can evaluate the questions and investigations they use in making employment decisions. These should be applied consistently. For example, if the company investigates conviction records of job applicants, it should investigate them for all applicants, not just for applicants from certain racial groups. Companies may want to avoid some types of questions altogether. For example, questions about marital status can cause problems, because interviewers may unfairly make different assumptions about men and women. (Common stereotypes about women have been that a married woman is less flexible or more likely to get pregnant than a single woman, in contrast to the assumption that a married man is more stable and committed to his work.)

bona fide occupational requirement (BFOR)
A necessary (not merely preferred) requirement for performing a job.

Is differential treatment ever legal? The courts have held that in some situations, a factor such as sex or race may be a **bona fide occupational requirement (BFOR),** that is, a necessary (not merely preferred) qualification for performing a job. A typical example is a job that includes handing out towels in a locker room. Requiring that employees who perform this job in the women's locker room be female is a BFOR. However, it is very difficult to think of many jobs where criteria such as sex and race are BFORs. In some cases, a core function of the job may be related to a protected ground. For example, a job may require a specified level of visual capability to be performed effectively and safely, thereby eliminating someone who does not meet this requirement. Employers should seek ways to perform the job so that these restrictions are not needed.

It is the employer's responsibility to prove the existence of a BFOR if any complaint of discrimination should arise. In the widely publicized *Meiorin* case from 1999, Tawny Meiorin, a female forest firefighter lost her job when she failed to meet a required aerobic fitness standard that had been established by the British Columbia Public Service Employee Relations Commission. This standard had been put in place as a minimum requirement for all firefighters. She lost her job after taking 49.4 seconds too long to complete a 2.5-km run.[19] She filed a complaint stating that the fitness standard discriminated against women because women usually have less aerobic capability than men. Although the employer argued the standard was a bona fide occupational requirement of the job, the Supreme Court of Canada ultimately ruled the standard was not a BFOR.[20] Ms. Meiorin was re-instated to her job and received compensation for lost wages and benefits.

The Duty to Accommodate

An employer has a duty to consider how an employee's characteristic such as disability, religion, or sex can be accommodated and to take action so that the employee can perform the job. This duty is referred to as the **duty to accommodate**.

The employer's duty to accommodate has been evolving since it became a part of human rights law in the 1980s. Accommodation frequently involves an employee with a disability. Employer awareness of the duty to accommodate has increased since the *Meiorin* case decision by the Supreme Court of Canada in 1999. The duty to accommodate is the employer's responsibility. Accommodation may even require that the employee perform another job within their capabilities.

In the context of religion, this principle recognizes that for some individuals, religious observations and practices may present a conflict with work duties, dress codes, or company practices. For example, some religions require head coverings, or individuals might need time off to observe the sabbath or other holy days, when the company might have them scheduled to work. When the employee has a legitimate religious belief requiring accommodation, the employee should demonstrate this need to the employer. Assuming that it would not present an undue hardship, employers are required to accommodate such religious practices. They may have to adjust schedules so that employees do not have to work on days when their religion forbids it, or they may have to alter dress or grooming requirements.

For employees with disabilities, accommodations also vary according to the individuals' needs. As shown in Figure 2.5, employers may restructure jobs, make facilities in the workplace more accessible, modify equipment, or reassign an employee to a job that the person can perform. In some situations, an individual with a disability may provide his or her own accommodation, which the employer allows, as in the case of a blind worker who brings a guide dog to work.

Preventing Harassment

Human Rights legislation prohibits **harassment** related to any of the protected grounds in their jurisdiction, e.g., race, colour, religion, sex, etc.. Human Rights legis-

duty to accommodate
An employer's duty to consider how an employee's characteristic such as disability, religion, or sex can be accommodated and to take action so the employee can perform the job.

harassment
Any behaviour that demeans, humiliates, or embarrasses a person and that a reasonable person should have known would be unwelcome.

LO5

FIGURE 2.5

Examples of Accommodations

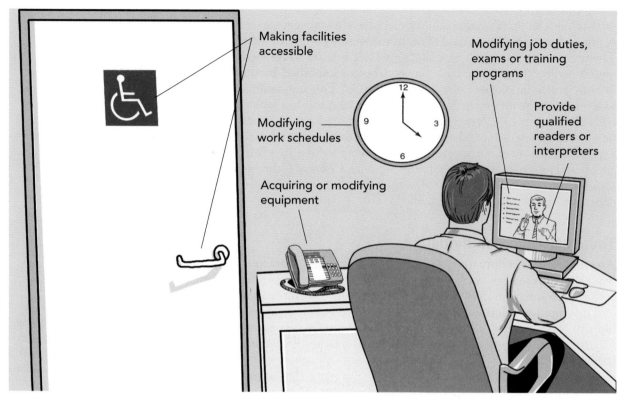

Restructuring a job and providing workplace accommodation

Note: Reasonable accommodations do *not* include hiring an unqualified person, lowering quality standards, or compromising coworkers' safety.

SOURCE: Equal Employment Opportunity Commission, "The ADA: Questions and Answers," www.eeoc.gov, January 15, 1997.

lation also prohibits all forms of harassment. Harassment is "any behaviour that demeans, humiliates, or embarrasses a person, and that a reasonable person should have known would be unwelcome."[21]

Seneca Colleges' Discrimination and Harassment Policy states: "It is the policy of Seneca College that all employees and students have a right to study in an environment that asserts the personal worth and dignity of each individual. In order to achieve this objective, Seneca College will not tolerate any form of discrimination and/or harassment in its employment, education, accommodation, or business. Every member of the College community has the right to file a compliant of discrimination/harassment."[22]

sexual harassment
Unwelcome behaviour that is of a sexual nature or is related to a person's sex.

Sexual harassment refers to unwelcome behaviour that is of a sexual nature or is related to a person's sex. Examples include:

- Question or discussion about a person's sexual life
- Comments about someone's sexual attractiveness (or unattractiveness)
- Continuing to ask for a date after being refused
- Writing sexually suggestive notes
- Telling a woman she should not be performing a particular job[23]

In general, the most obvious examples of sexual harassment involve *quid pro quo harassment*, meaning that a person makes a benefit (or punishment) contingent on an employee's submitting to (or rejecting) sexual advances. For example, a manager who promises a raise to an employee who will participate in sexual activities is engaging in quid pro quo harassment. Likewise, it would be sexual harassment to threaten to reassign someone to a less desirable job if that person refuses sexual favours.

A more subtle, and possibly more pervasive, form of sexual harassment is to create or permit a "hostile work environment." This occurs when someone's behaviour in the workplace creates an environment in which it is difficult for someone of a particular sex to work. Common complaints in sexual harassment lawsuits include claims that harassers ran their fingers through the plaintiffs' hair, made suggestive remarks, touched intimate body parts, posted pictures with sexual content in the workplace, and used sexually explicit language or told sex-related jokes. In Europe, employers can be liable for creating a hostile work environment if they fail to protect workers from receiving sexually explicit emails such as racy spam messages.[24]

Although a large majority of sexual harassment complaints received involve women being harassed by men, sexual harassment can affect anyone. Men have filed complaints that they were harassed by women, and in at least one case, a male employee won a lawsuit claiming sexual harassment by his male boss.[25]

To ensure a workplace free from harassment, organizations can follow some im-

BEST PRACTICES

Quebec's New Labour Law

Quebec's Labour Standards Division recently introduced a new law against workplace psychological harassment. This legislation, the first of its kind in North America, was based on a similar law introduced in France in 2002. The law is intended to improve workplace morale and result in improved productivity. The law defines psychological harassment as "any vexatious behaviour in the form of repeated and hostile or unwanted conduct, verbal comments, actions, or gestures that affect an employee's dignity, psychological, or physical integrity and that results in a harmful work environment for the employee."

Quebec employers are assessing their current policies and practices to ensure compliance with the new legislation that expands protection of workers from bullying bosses and co-workers. Under the new law, employers need to undertake the following pro-active measures:

- Provide a work environment that promotes respectful interpersonal communications

- Manage conflict quickly and effectively

- Consider providing specialized counselling services

Quebec's new law will raise awareness about an employee's right to an effective work environment where hostile or intimidating behaviour and abuse of power are not only unacceptable—but illegal. Although critics of the new law say that too much responsibility is placed on employers to manage behaviour in organizations, others say this new law will help change workplaces for the better.

SOURCE: Wallace Immen, "Quebec Squares Off Against Bullies," *The Globe and Mail*, May 26, 2004, pp. C1, C6. Reprinted with permission from *The Globe and Mail*.

portant steps. Federally regulated employees are required to develop an anti-harassment policy making it very clear that harassment will not be tolerated in the workplace. Second, all employees need to be made aware of the policy and receive training related to anti-harassment. In addition, the organization can develop a mechanism for reporting harassment in a way that encourages people to speak out. Finally, management can prepare to act promptly to discipline those who engage in harassment, as well as to protect the victims of harassment. The "Best Practices" box discusses Quebec's new law, the first of its kind in North America, which takes the elimination of harassment a step further by making it illegal to engage in psychological harassment.

Valuing Diversity

As we mentioned in Chapter 1, Canada is a diverse nation, and becoming more so. In addition, many Canadian companies have customers and operations in more than one country. Managers differ in how they approach the challenges related to this diversity. Some define a diverse workforce as a competitive advantage that brings them a wider pool of talent and greater insight into the needs and behaviours of their diverse customers. These organizations say they have a policy of *valuing diversity*.

The practice of valuing diversity has no single form; it is not written into law or business theory. Organizations that value diversity may actively work to meet employment equity goals, discussed earlier. Bell Canada speaks to the benefits of diversity: "Our business objectives, and our objectives for diversity and employment equity go hand in hand. And as we apply our considerable strengths to achieving our business goals with a strong diversity focus, we see no limits to what we are able to accomplish as individuals, as a company, and even as a nation."[26] They may have policies stating their value of understanding and respecting differences. Wal-Mart's website includes a statement that reinforces the company's folksy image along with its policy with regard to diversity: "All kinds of people work and shop at Wal-Mart—and we like it that way."[27] Organizations may try to hire, reward, and promote employees who demonstrate respect for others. They may sponsor training programs designed to teach employees about differences among groups. Whatever their form, these efforts are intended to make each individual feel respected. Also, these actions can support diversity by cultivating an environment in which individuals feel valued and able to perform to their potential.

LO6

Occupational Health and Safety

The protection of employee health and safety is regulated by the government. As outlined in Table 2.2, occupational health and safety legislation is in place for all jurisdictions. However, the effective management of health and safety in the workplace includes more than legal compliance. Increasingly, organizations are taking a strategic approach to occupational health and safety by adopting a values-based commitment to safe operations as a way to protect people. Additional benefits to business include cost savings by reducing worker injuries, fatalities, occupational disease, and property damage as well as improved employee relations and reliability and productivity improvement.[28]

Internal Responsibility System

In Canada, safety in the workplace is based on the foundation of an **internal responsibility system**. The internal responsibility system is a philosophy of occupational health and safety where employers and employees share responsibility for creating and maintaining safe and healthy work environments. Employer–employee partnerships are put in place to ensure compliance and create a culture of safety in the organization.[29]

Workplace Health and Safety Committees

Workplace health and safety committees are a key feature of the internal responsibility system. A workplace health and safety committee is a committee jointly appointed by the employer and employees at large (or union) to address health and safety issues in a workplace (see Figure 2.6). Under federal law, a workplace health and safety committee is required for each workplace that has 20 or more employees. The committee must consist of at least two persons and is required to meet at least nine times a year, at regular intervals, during normal working hours. The premise is that people who work in a particular workplace, know the most about hazards and unhealthy conditions.[30]

General and Specific Duties

Employers and supervisors have a duty to provide a safe workplace. At a minimum, supervisors must:

- Ensure that appropriate occupational health and safety policies and practices are in place
- Understand and follow policies and practices related to working safely
- Identify the need for training for employees and themselves
- Determine hazards that may exist and ensure employees are aware of these hazards
- Eliminate or at least reduce hazards
- Ensure employees comply with safety policies and practices[31]

internal responsibility system
Philosophy of occupational health and safety where employers and employees share responsibility for creating and maintaining safe and healthy work environments.

LO7

workplace health and safety committee
A committee jointly appointed by the employer and employees at large (the union) to address health and safety issues in a workplace.

POWER AND DUTIES OF A WORKPLACE HEALTH AND SAFETY COMMITTEE

- Consider and deal with health and safety complaints in a timely manner
- Participate in the development, implementation, and monitoring of programs to prevent workplace hazards and provide protective equipment, devices, and clothing
- Participate in safety inquiries, safety assessments, and ensure that effective records are kept
- Perform workplace inspections
- Be provided full access to all reports, studies, and tests related to the health and safety of workers

FIGURE 2.6

Power and Duties of a Workplace Health and Safety Committee

SOURCE: "Information on Occupational Health and Safety: 6B Workplace Health and Safety Committees," Government of Canada, http://info.load-otea.hrdc-drhc.gc.ca/publications/ohs/committees.pdf. Retrieved: February 25, 2004.

FIGURE 2.7

Federal Employer's Annual Hazardous Occurrence Report

Human Resources Development Canada | Développement des ressources humaines Canada

Year - Année

SCHEDULE - ANNEXE

CANADA OCCUPATIONAL SAFETY AND HEALTH REGULATIONS (Section 15.10)

RÈGLEMENT CANADIEN SUR LA SÉCURITÉ ET LA SANTÉ AU TRAVAIL (Article 15.10)

Page of - de

EMPLOYER'S ANNUAL HAZARDOUS OCCURRENCE REPORT - RAPPORT ANNUEL DE L'EMPLOYEUR CONCERNANT LES SITUATIONS COMPORTANT DES RISQUES

Employer identification number / Numéro d'identification de l'employeur	Address of work place / Adresse du lieu de travail	Number of disabling injuries / Nombre de blessures invalidantes	Number of deaths / Nombre de décès	Number of minor injuries / Nombre de blessures légères	Number of other hazardous occurrences / Nbre d'autres situations comportant des risques	Total number of employees / Nombre total d'employés	Number of office employees / Nombre d'employés de bureau	Total number of hours worked / Total des heures travaillées

GUIDE TO COMPLETION ON REVERSE SIDE
EXPLICATIONS AU VERSO

Submitting officer's name and title - Nom et titre de l'auteur du rapport	Signature	Date of submission - Date de présentation / Telephone - Téléphone ( ) -

NHQ/LAB 1009 (10-03) B

If this address is incorrect, please correct.

Si cette adresse est inexacte veuillez la corriger

Canada

SOURCE: "Human Resources and Skills Development Canada," Canada Occupational Safety and Health Regulations (Section 15.10) Employer's Annual Hazardous Occurrence Report. Reproduced with the permission of Her Majesty the Queen in Right of Canada 2005, http://www100.hrdc.gc.ca/indlab1009e.shtml.

Occupational Health & Safety Inspectors
Industrial

Apply your experience/knowledge gained in industrial processes/health-and-safety hazards/controls in one of these critical positions (11 bilingual). You will: enforce *Occupational Health and Safety Act*, regulations; conduct site inspections/investigations; write orders/reports; engage in enforcement activities, including prosecutions; promote safe work practices/working conditions with workers, unions, management (Internal Responsibility System). **Locations: Toronto East/Scarborough (11 positions) – File LBCR-21; Toronto West/Downsview (4) – File LBCR-25; Toronto North/Downsview (3) – File LBCR-28; Peel North/Mississauga (6) – File LBCR-32; York/Newmarket (3) – File LBCR-35; Durham/Oshawa (1) – File LBCR-39; Kingston (2) – File LBER-03; Peterborough (1) – File LBER-05; Ottawa East (1) – File LBER-07; Ottawa West (2) – File LBER-11; North Bay (1) – File LBNR-30; Sault Ste. Marie (1) – File LBNR-31; Sudbury East (1) – File LBNR-33; Thunder Bay/Dryden (1) – File LBNR-32; Timmins/South Porcupine (1) – File LBNR-27; Brant/Hamilton (2) – File LBWR-03; Hamilton (5) – File LBWR-06; Halton/Hamilton (2) – File LBWR-08; Kitchener-Waterloo/Waterloo (5) – File LBWR-10; London North (3) – File LBWR-12; London South (4) – File LBWR-14; Niagara/St. Catharines (4) – File LBWR-17; Windsor (2) – File LBWR-19. BILINGUAL POSITIONS: Toronto East/Scarborough (1) – File LBCR-22; Toronto West/Downsview (1) – File LBCR-26; Peel South/Mississauga (1) – File LBCR-30; Peel North/ Mississauga (1) – File LBCR-33; Ottawa East (2) – File LBER-08; Ottawa West (1) – File LBER-12; North Bay (1) – File LBNR-18; Timmins/South Porcupine (1) – File LBNR-23; Brant/Hamilton (1) – File LBWR-04; London South (1) – File LBWR-15.**

Qualifications: working knowledge of/practical experience in broad range of industrial processes, to identify, evaluate, control hazards associated with chemical/biological/physical agents; working knowledge of *Occupational Health and Safety Act*, regulations, standards, legislation re industrial/institutional workplaces; demonstrated ability to conduct investigations, enforce legislation, participate in court procedures, handle labour/management issues, resolve conflicts, use notebook technology in Windows environment; sound planning, organization, communication skills; experience writing clear, concise reports; ability to travel extensively and respond to after-hours calls; valid driver's licence. Candidates are required to be available for 7.25-hour work periods during days, evenings and some weekends. Bilingual positions also require proficiency in English and French.

Applicants who do not have the full range of practical experience in industrial processes, but have working knowledge typically acquired through a combination of practical experience and completion of relevant educational/training programs, may be considered on an underfill basis.

Salary range: $1,134 - $1,352 per week

Ontario is turning up its ability to monitor and enforce workplace health and safety by hiring 200 new enforcement positions in the Ministry of Labour.

SOURCE: *Financial Post*, August 4, 2004, p. FP8. © Queen's Printer for Ontario, 2004. Reproduced with permission.

Employers need to assess and be alert to workplace hazards and safety issues. Imperial Oil and ExxonMobil Canada introduced a safety initiative that forbids the use of cellphones while driving on company business. Imperial Oil's director of Safety, Health, and Environment, Jim Levins says, "since driving is one of the more hazardous tasks we do during a normal work day, this new initiative will help us all achieve our goal of zero injuries."[32]

Employers must keep records of work-related deaths, injuries, and hazardous occurrences and provide an annual summary of these records. Figure 2.7 provides a sample of the form federally regulated employers must complete annually.

Enforcement of Occupational Health and Safety Regulations

Enforcement responsibilities exist within the federal, provincial, and territorial governments. Occupational health and safety officers/inspectors have the authority to inspect workplaces and issue orders to employers and workers. Ontario is hiring 200 new health and safety inspectors which will almost double its enforcement staff. The Ontario government is planning to target 6,000 workplaces with poor safety records.[33] In some jurisdictions such as Nova Scotia and Ontario, safety officers/inspectors can issue tickets to people and organizations when these orders are not followed. In Nova Scotia, occupational health and safety officers can write tickets for up to $800 as a tool to ensure compliance.[34]

Bill C-45 (Westray Bill)
Amendment to the Criminal Code making organizations and anyone who directs the work of others criminally liable for safety offences.

In addition, the Criminal Code was amended in 2004 to create a legal duty on employers to ensure the safety of workers and the public. This amendment, **Bill C-45 or the Westray Bill**, named after the Nova Scotia mining disaster in 1992 that killed 26 workers, makes organizations and anyone who directs the work of others criminally liable for safety offences. Maximum fines were increased to $100,000 from $25,000 for less serious offences and provides an unlimited fine for more serious offences. Anyone who directs the work of others can also face serious charges—criminal conviction, a criminal record, and even life imprisonment for failing to provide for health and safety in the workplace.[35]

Employee Rights and Responsibilities

Although employers are responsible for protecting workers from health and safety hazards, employees have responsibilities as well. They have to follow safety rules and regulations governing employee behaviour. Employees also have a duty to report hazardous conditions.

Along with those responsibilities go certain rights. All Canadian workers have three fundamental rights that are protected by occupational health and safety legislation:

- *The right to know* about known or foreseeable hazards in the workplace
- *The right to participate* in identifying and resolving job-related safety and health problems
- *The right to refuse* dangerous work[36]

In federally regulated organizations, employees' right to refuse dangerous work was expanded in 2004 to include refusing work on the potential for risk versus existing danger. This expanded definition was put into practice in the precedent-setting *Verville v. Canada (Correctional Services)* case where maximum security prison guards at the Kent Penitentiary in British Columbia performed a work refusal when guards were prohibited from carrying handcuffs. Although Correctional Services Canada said availability of handcuffs at control posts was adequate, the judge ruled that employees can refuse work if there is a reasonable possibility of danger.[37]

Employees may file a complaint and request an inspection of the workplace, and their employers may not retaliate against them for complaining. Employees also have a right to receive information about any hazardous products they handle in the course of their jobs.

material safety data sheets (MSDSs)
Detailed hazard information concerning a controlled (hazardous) product.

The Workplace Hazardous Materials Information System or WHMIS is related to the worker's "right to know." WHMIS is implemented through coordinated federal, provincial, and territorial legislation to ensure that hazardous products are properly labelled, used, stored, handled, and disposed of safely.

Organizations must have **material safety data sheets (MSDSs)** for hazardous products that employees are exposed to. An MSDS form details the hazards associated with a chemical; the chemical's producer or importer is responsible for identifying

Annual Workplace Fatalities

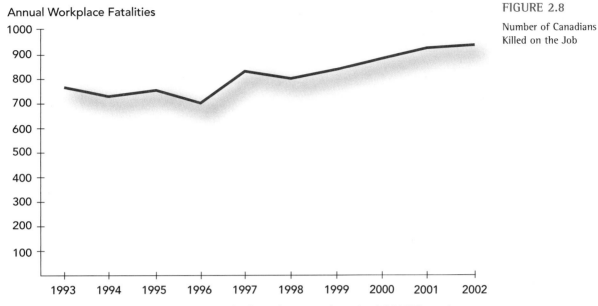

FIGURE 2.8

Number of Canadians Killed on the Job

SOURCE: Association of Workers' Compensation Boards of Canada, www.awcbc.org/english/NWISP_stats.htm. Retrieved: August 3, 2004.

these hazards and detailing them on the form. Employers must also ensure that all containers of hazardous chemicals are labelled with information about the hazards, and they must train employees in safe handling of the chemicals.

Impact of Occupational Health and Safety Legislation

Legislation has unquestionably succeeded in raising the level of awareness of occupational safety. However, as depicted in Figure 2.8, the number of Canadians killed on

E-HRM

Technology Enhancing Workplace Health and Safety

Access to information and resources is a key part of creating a safe and healthy workplace. Technology can provide new tools to employees to provide access to services and knowledge. Technology can come into play by providing links to reliable Internet sites for online information, briefing materials, best practices, statistics, safety assessments, presentations, and compliance information with national standards such as Workplace Hazardous Materials Information System (WHMIS). The official national WHMIS website is a comprehensive resource and source of information (www.hc-sc.gc.ca/hecs-sesc/whmis).

Online instruction can provide employees with information about preventative measures to reduce workplace accidents and injuries.

Technology also provides employees the ability to maintain accurate information about employees to ensure all legal requirements are met including analysis of hazards and accurate reporting of workplace accidents and injuries.

SOURCE: Jeff Koven, "Technology for a Healthy Workplace," *Canadian HR Reporter,* April 19, 2004, pp. 17, 21. © Copyright *Canadian HR Reporter,* April 19, 2004, by permission of Carswell, Toronto, Ontario, 1-800-387-5164, www.hrreporter.com.

the job has been increasing in recent years. For example, in Ontario, construction fatalities increased 50 percent in 2003.[38]

Many workplace accidents are a product of unsafe behaviours, not unsafe working conditions. Because legislation does not directly regulate employee behaviour, little behaviour change can be expected unless employees are convinced of the standards' importance.[39] This principle has been recognized by labour leaders. For example, Lynn Williams, president of the United Steelworkers, has noted, "We can't count on government. We can't count on employers. We must rely on ourselves to bring about the safety and health of our workers."[40]

Because conforming to the law alone does not necessarily guarantee their employees will be safe, many employers go beyond the letter of the law (see the "E-HRM" box). In the next section we examine various kinds of employer-initiated safety awareness programs that comply with legislation and, in some cases, exceed it.

LO8

Employer-Sponsored Health and Safety Programs

Many employers establish safety awareness programs to go beyond mere compliance with occupational health and safety regulations and attempt to instill an emphasis on safety. A safety awareness program has three primary components: identifying and communicating hazards, reinforcing safe practices, and promoting safety internationally.

Identifying and Communicating Job Hazards

job hazard analysis technique
Safety promotion technique that involves breaking down a job into basic elements, then rating each element for its potential for harm or injury.

technic of operations review (TOR)
Method of promoting safety by determining which specific element of a job led to a past accident.

Employees, supervisors, and other knowledgeable sources need to sit down and discuss potential problems related to safety. One method for doing this is the **job hazard analysis technique.**[41] With this technique, each job is broken down into basic elements, and each of these is rated for its potential for harm or injury. If there is agreement that some job element has high hazard potential, the group isolates the element and considers possible technological or behaviour changes to reduce or eliminate the hazard.

Another means of isolating unsafe job elements is to study past accidents. The **technic of operations review (TOR)** is an analysis method for determining which specific element of a job led to a past accident.[42] The first step in a TOR analysis is to establish the facts surrounding the incident. To accomplish this, all members of the work group involved in the accident give their initial impressions of what happened. The group must then, through discussion, come to an agreement on the single, systematic failure that most likely contributed to the incident, as well as two or three major secondary factors that contributed to it.

An analysis of jobs at Burger King, for example, revealed that certain jobs required employees to walk across wet or slippery surfaces, which led to many falls. Specific corrective action was taken based on analysis of where people were falling and what conditions led to those falls. Now Burger King provides mats at critical locations and has generally upgraded its floor maintenance. The company also makes slip-resistant shoes available to employees in certain job categories.[43]

To communicate with employees about job hazards, managers should talk directly with their employees about safety. Written communications also are important, because the written communication helps establish a "paper trail" that can later document due diligence and a history of the employer's concern regarding the job hazard.

Posters, especially if placed near the hazard, serve as a constant reminder, reinforcing other messages.

In communicating risk, managers should recognize that different groups of individuals may constitute different audiences. Research reported by Human Resources and Skills Development Canada indicates that younger workers (15–24 years) have a higher incidence of time-loss injuries than any other age group. In Ontario alone, "almost two young workers are injured every hour of every day and night, seven days a week, and it's often because of what they didn't know."[44] The employer's primary concern with respect to younger workers is to inform them. Training should include specific information about safe procedures, first aid, and any protective equipment related to the job.

Experienced employees need retraining to jar them from complacency about the real dangers associated with their work.[45] This is especially the case if the hazard in question poses a greater threat to older employees. For example, accidents that involve falling off a ladder are a greater threat to older workers than to younger ones. Over 20 percent of such falls lead to a fatality for workers in the 55 to 65 age group, compared with 10 percent for all other workers.[46]

Reinforcing Safe Practices

To ensure safe behaviours, employers should not only define how to work safely but reinforce the desired behaviour. One common technique for reinforcing safe practices is implementing a safety incentive program to reward workers for their support of and commitment to safety goals. Such programs start by focusing on monthly or quarterly goals or by encouraging suggestions for improving safety. Possible goals might include good housekeeping practices, adherence to safety rules, and proper use of protective equipment. Later, the program expands to include more wide-ranging, long-term goals. Typically, the employer distributes prizes in highly public forums, such as company or department meetings. Using merchandise for prizes, instead of cash, provides a lasting symbol of achievement. At Regina-based USF Water Group, the company is using a health and safety bingo. Bingo numbers are given out every day and employees can win a variety of prizes. If a lost-time accident occurs, the game board is erased and employees have to start over. Prizes include gift certificates, free lunches, and even a trip to Edmonton for an NHL game.[47] A good deal of evidence suggests that such incentive programs are effective in reducing the number and cost of injuries.[48]

Besides focusing on specific jobs, organizations can target particular types of injuries or disabilities, especially those for which employees may be at risk. For example, the National Society to Prevent Blindness estimates that 1,000 eye injuries occur every day in occupational settings.[49] Organizations can prevent such injuries through a combination of job analysis, written policies, safety training, protective eyewear, rewards and sanctions for safe and unsafe behaviour, and management support for the safety effort. Industries and occupational groups also provide overall organizational safety awards. DRG Resources Corporation, a national resource company, was the recipient of the BC and Yukon Chamber of Mines' Exploration and Safety Award. In 2003, DRG had no lost-day accidents in 24,800 hours of copper and gold exploration work.[50]

Promoting Safety Internationally

Given the increasing focus on international management, organizations also need to consider how to ensure the safety of their employees regardless of the nation in which they operate. Cultural differences may make this more difficult than it seems. For example, a study examined the impact of one standardized corporation-wide safety policy on employees in three different countries: the United States, France, and Argentina. The results of this study indicate that employees in the three countries interpreted the policy differently because of cultural differences. The individualistic, control-oriented culture of the United States stressed the role of top management in ensuring safety in a top-down fashion. However, this policy failed to work in Argentina, where the culture is more "collectivist" (emphasizing the group). Argentine employees tend to feel that safety is everyone's joint concern, so the safety programs needed to be defined from the bottom of the organization up.[51]

Summary

1. Describe the legal framework for Human Resource Management in Canada.

   Approximately 90 percent of Canadian employees are covered by provincial and territorial legislation. The remaining 10 percent are covered by federal legislation. Although jurisdictional differences exist, laws tend to mirror one another.

2. Summarize the major federal and provincial laws affecting Human Resource Management.

   Several Canadian laws create the foundation for equality in employment. The Charter of Rights and Freedoms (1982) identifies fundamental freedoms. The Official Languages Act (1988) provides equal opportunities for English and French-speaking Canadian. The Employment Equity Act (1986) was intended to eliminate employment barriers for four designated groups. Human Rights Acts protect individuals from discrimination related to prohibited grounds identified in the relevant federal, provincial, and territorial legislation. The Personal Information Protection and Electronic Documents Act (PIPEDA) (2004) provides rules about how organizations can collect, use, and disclose information about you. Employment Standards legislation deals with the minimum standards an employee will receive and the Pay Equity Act (1978) provides for equal pay for work of equal value.

3. Identify the agencies that enforce employment equality and privacy legislation and describe their roles.

   Human Rights Commissions are responsible for enforcing Human Rights legislation in their respective jurisdictions. The Canadian Human Rights Commission is responsible for enforcing the Employment Equity Act and the Pay Equity Act. The Privacy Commissioner of Canada is responsible for enforcing the Personal Information Protection and Electronic Documents Act (PIPEDA).

4. Describe ways employers can avoid illegal discrimination and meet the duty to accommodate.

   Employers can avoid discrimination by avoiding differential treatment of job applicants and employees. Organizations can develop and enforce practices and policies that demonstrate a high value placed on diversity. Employment equity initiatives may remove employment barriers to the designated groups. To provide accommodation, companies should recognize individuals' needs. Employers may need to make such accommodations as adjusting schedules or dress codes, making the workplace more accessible, or restructuring jobs.

5. Define harassment and discuss how employers can eliminate or minimize it.

   Harassment is any behaviour that demeans, humiliates, or embarrasses a person, and that a reasonable person should have known would be unwelcome. Sexual harassment is unwelcome behaviour that is of a sexual nature or is related to a person's sex. Organizations can prevent harassment by developing a policy that defines and forbids it, training employees to recognize and avoid this behaviour, and providing a means for employees to complain and be protected.

6. Explain the context for health and safety regulations in Canada.

   All jurisdictions in Canada have occupational health and safety legislation. Canada's approach to safety in the workplace is based on the internal responsibility system where both employers and employees are responsible for safety.

7. Describe how occupational health and safety regulations are enforced including employee rights and responsibilities.

   Employers and supervisors have a duty to provide a safe workplace. In addition, a recent amendment to the

Criminal Code (Bill C-45) has created a legal duty on employers to ensure the safety of workers. Employees also have responsibilities including following safety rules and reporting hazardous conditions.

8. Discuss ways employers promote worker safety and health.

Besides complying with occupational health and safety regulations, employers often establish safety awareness programs designed to instill an emphasis on safety. They may identify and communicate hazards through the job hazard analysis technique or the technic of operations review. They may adapt communications and training to the needs of different employees, such as differences in experience levels or cultural differences from one country to another. Employers may also establish incentive programs to reward safe behaviour.

Review and Discussion Questions

1. What are the major laws that impact Human Resource Management in your province or territory? Compare and contrast this legislation to the corresponding federal legislation.
2. How does the Personal Information Protection and Electronic Documents Act (PIPEDA) impact HRM?
3. What is the ground of discrimination most frequently cited in complaints to the Canadian Human Rights Commission? Why do you think this ground of discrimination is so frequently cited in discrimination complaints?
4. Have you ever experienced illegal discrimination in an employment situation? What could have the organization done to prevent this discrimination from occurring?
5. What is sexual harassment? What are some types of behaviour likely considered to be sexual harassment in a workplace?

6. "Organizations that value diversity are more likely to meet their employment equity goals." Do you agree or disagree with this statement? Why or why not?
7. What is the role of a workplace health and safety committee in reducing workplace accidents and injuries?
8. What effect will Bill C-45 (Westray Bill) likely have on supervisors' behaviours and attitudes related to workplace safety?
9. How can organizations motivate employees to promote safety and health in the workplace?
10. For each of the following occupations, identify at least one possible hazard and at least one action employees could take to minimize the risk of an injury or illness related to that hazard.
    a. Worker in a fast-food restaurant
    b. Computer programmer
    c. Worker in a special care home for seniors
    d. House painter

What's Your HR IQ?   www.mcgrawhill.ca/college/noe

The Online Learning Centre offers more ways to check what you've learned so far. Find experiential exercises as well as Test Your Knowledge Quizzes, Videos, and many other resources at www.mcgrawhill.ca/college/noe.

Case: Promote an Employee Whose Career was Damaged by Racism

A Classification Officer with the Correctional Service of Canada (CSC), Dr. Julius Uzoaba, was discriminated against because of his race and colour. Dr. Uzoaba worked with inmates to develop and recommend programs for them and to prepare reports for the National Parole Board, among others. He was one of the first Black Classification officers in the CSC.

Certain inmates, including some who had never met him, made negative comments about his work and signed a petition asking that he be taken off the job. A series of anonymous calls began, with the caller using racist names

and swearing at Dr. Uzoaba. CSC officials knew there were groups among the inmates who held overtly racist views. They heard that a threat had been made against Dr. Uzoaba, but did not inform him of it, a choice the Canadian Human Rights tribunal later called "shocking." The day after the threat, an inmate assaulted Dr. Uzoaba.

In evaluating Dr. Uzoaba's work, his managers relied on the statements and actions by inmates, which were partly motivated by racial bias. Managers used this material in giving him negative evaluations, and insisted that he no longer work with inmates. He was unable to find other suitable employment, and was without a job for several years. After an investigation, the case was heard by a Canadian Human Rights tribunal, which found the CSC had discriminated against Dr. Uzoaba. CSC managers should not have relied on racist comments by inmates or used these comments as evidence of poor work performance. By relying on these comments in his official performance evaluation, the CSC itself discriminated against Dr. Uzoaba. This tainted evaluation then followed Dr. Uzoaba and interfered with his securing new work, thus perpetuating the discrimination. The tribunal said that CSC management did not take effective action to protect its employees from racial harassment by inmates or staff members; it should have investigated and supported Dr. Uzoaba. Management's response was "wholly inadequate" and unfair.

As a remedy, the tribunal ordered that Dr. Uzoaba be rehired, at a level higher than his previous job. Based on the evidence, it was reasonable to conclude that he would have been promoted if the racism had not been a factor. It also ordered that the CSC apologize in writing, that Dr. Uzoaba receive three years' lost wages, and that he receive $5,000 (at the time, the top amount allowed in the Canadian Human Rights Act) for injury to his feelings and self-respect.

In reviewing the case, a Federal Court judge agreed with the tribunal that Dr. Uzoaba be awarded a job at the higher level. The Attorney General had argued that this remedy conflicted with the Public Service Employment Act, which contains specific provisions for promotions. The court ruled that the Canadian Human Rights Act takes precedence over the Public Service Employment Act and other legislation, and allows the tribunal to make such an award when the evidence supports it, which it did in this case.

SOURCE: Anti-Discrimination Casebook: Race, Colour, National, or Ethnic Origin, pp. 28, 29, Canadian Human Rights Commission, 2001. Reproduced with the permission of the Minister of Public Works and Government Services Canada, 2004; www.chrc-cdp.ca/Legis&Poli/AntiDiscrimination Casebook_RecueilDeDecisions/. Retrieved: February 18, 2004.

Questions
1. As discussed in this case, what is the employer's responsibility to prevent discrimination in the workplace?
2. Do you think the remedy provided to Dr. Uzoaba, as a victim of discrimination, was appropriate? Why or why not?

Case: The Voice of Sick Workers—Blayne Kinart 1946–2004

Blayne Kinart, a Sarnia, Ontario, millwright who had been exposed to deadly asbestos, wanted to raise public awareness of the plight of those who had been poisoned on the job.

To that end, Mr. Kinart allowed graphic and often intimate photographs of his emaciated body to be taken in the hope the images would give a higher profile to the illnesses that asbestos causes. Sarnia, a community that hosts Canada's largest petrochemical industrial complex, had become a slow-motion Bhopal for many of its workers. Mr. Kinart died of mesothelioma, a cancer caused by exposure to asbestos. He was 58.

"People who knew him as this big guy, powerful muscular guy, couldn't believe what they were witnessing," said Jim Brophy, who heads an occupational heath clinic in Sarnia. "This disease, transforms you physically. You look like you were just released from Auschwitz."

Mr. Kinart was born and grew up in Sarnia. He met his wife, Sandy, in grade school in the city, and he made his home and worked there. But Canada's Chemical Valley of refineries stretching along the St. Clair River had a darker side, a blue-collar tragedy of enormous proportions that he felt compelled to speak out about. About 3,000 workers there have registered with occupational health authorities over the past six years, complaining not only of mesothe-

lioma, but also an array of equally frightening illnesses, such as leukemia and brain cancer.

Mesothelioma, a cancer of the lining of the lungs and other internal organs, is an extremely painful illness with no known cure. The median survival time after diagnosis is only two years. The highest rates in Ontario—at more than four times the provincial average—are around Sarnia, according to figures from Cancer Care Ontario. Although the cancer is a relatively quick killer, it has a lengthy latency period. Those, like Mr. Kinart, who have recently become ill, received their premature death sentence in the 1960s and 1970s.

Mr. Brophy said the tragedy of Mr. Kinart's death is that it was preventable, had governments and industry taken asbestos seriously at that time. Until the 1980s, large amounts of asbestos were routinely used in the petrochemical industry as an insulating material by workers who had little in the way of the respirators and other protective equipment now mandatory when handling a dangerous carcinogen.

No one knows how many more workers will contract mesothelioma because of reductions in the amount of asbestos in use. The incident rate has risen about 65 percent over the past two decades and there are about 150 cases a year recorded in Ontario's cancer registry. The number of those afflicted is thought by occupational health experts to be higher than the official government statistics because the condition is often incorrectly diagnosed as lung cancer.

The only known cause of mesothelioma is asbestos, suggesting that most cases are caused by some kind of workplace exposure.

SOURCE: Martin Mittelstaedt, "The Voice of Sick Workers," *The Globe and Mail*, July 10, 2004, p. F10. Reprinted with permission from *The Globe and Mail*.

Questions

1. Who do you feel is responsible for Mr. Kinart's contracting mesothelioma? Why?
2. What is the role of the government in protecting workers from occupational diseases such as mesothelioma? What is the role of employers? Employees?

CBC VIDEO CASE: High Anxiety   CBC

Many North American employees are concerned about job loss due to offshoring and outsourcing. As thousands of jobs flood out of the U.S., fear and loathing of offshoring and outsourcing and the companies that send jobs to China and India is evident. Anxiety runs deep not only among employees who work in the manufacturing sector but among employees in other sectors as well. This anxiety has accelerated among the middle-class as better and better jobs are exported out of the country.

Canadians have tended to be less vocal so far because the outsourcing and offshoring trend has been slower to impact Canada. However, Canadian organizational examples show that more work will be outsourced to lower labour cost countries such as China in the future. For example, although an early production run of Mitel's latest telephone will likely be handled in Canada, ongoing production will take place in China where workers are paid one-tenth of Canadian salaries.

One Canadian manufacturer interviewed suggests that as lower-level jobs leave, ultimately "higher-skilled labour jobs will remain in Canada" and that jobs in North America will continue to "move upscale." However, fears and concerns are raised that the U.S. may plunge into "full scale protectionism" that could harm not only Canada's economy, but potentially even trigger a global recession.

SOURCE: Based on "High Anxiety," *CBC Venture* 918, March 14, 2004.

Questions

1. Would you be willing to pay more for a product to protect jobs in Canada? Why or why not?
2. The video suggests that although offshoring will result in the export of lower-skilled jobs, higher-skilled jobs will remain in Canada. Do you agree or disagree with this assessment? Why or why not?

Acquiring and Preparing Human Resources

Chapter **3**

Analyzing Work and Designing Jobs

What Do I Need to Know? After reading this chapter, you should be able to:

1. Summarize the elements of work flow analysis.

2. Describe how work flow is related to an organization's structure.

3. Define the elements of a job analysis, and discuss their significance for human resource management.

4. Explain how to obtain job analysis information.

5. Summarize recent trends in job analysis.

6. Describe methods for designing a job so that it can be done efficiently.

7. Identify approaches to designing a job to make it motivating.

8. Explain how organizations apply ergonomics to design safe jobs.

9. Discuss how organizations can plan for the mental demands of a job.

Introduction

The Software Human Resource Council (SHRC) is a nonprofit council that was established in 1992 to "address the human resource needs of the Canadian software sector."[1] One of the key aims of the SHRC is to "clarify job definitions for software workers."[2] The SHRC regularly receives calls from HR professionals complaining they are unable to find qualified candidates to fill vacant IT positions, said Paul Swinwood, president of the council.[3] The problem is that too many different definitions are being used to describe job requirements and qualifications, resulting in rejections of applicants actually having the needed skills. The extent of the problem was demonstrated in a new survey of the Canadian IT labour market, the National Survey of Information Technology Occupations, that involved more than 25,000 employers and 35,000 employees in both the private and public sectors.

"The study confirms that there is a lack of common understanding and definitions of what the IT jobs are," says Swinwood.[4] The SHRC has developed an occupational skills profile model that is a list of 25 IT occupations including more than 350 job titles. This Occupational Skills Profile Model (OSPM) was developed in response to the urgent need for standardized skills in the Canadian IT sector, educational institutions, and in the public sector. The OSPM is a human resource reference for IT occupations that allows jobs to be compared across industries. The model is available online in a searchable database available to SHRC members. In addition, a tool that allows you to assess your IT knowledge and skills against industry standards is available free on the SHRC's website (www.shrc.ca).

The council is striving to ensure that all IT employees and organizations that employ IT professionals are able to communicate by sharing a clear picture of employer expectations and employee competencies. The SHRC works closely with its sponsors, Human Resources and Skills Development Canada (HRSDC), Industry Canada, and the Treasury Board of Canada Secretariat, as well as its members from industry, educational institutions, and government. Member organizations include the Association of Canadian Community Colleges (ACCC), Canadian Association of Universities Continuing Education (CAUCE), Cognos Inc, Canadian Council of Professional Engineers (CCPE), General Dynamics Canada, Inco Ltd., and Telus.[5]

The ability to define IT jobs provides for the identification of the competencies required for success and they in turn help to narrow the field of people who will succeed in an IT career. Consideration of such elements is at the heart of analyzing work, whether in a small to medium-sized business, a multinational corporation, or the public sector.

This chapter discusses the analysis and design of work and, in doing so, lays out some considerations that go into making informed decisions about how to create and link jobs.

The Occupational Skills Profile Model (OSPM) is a human resource reference for IT occupations.

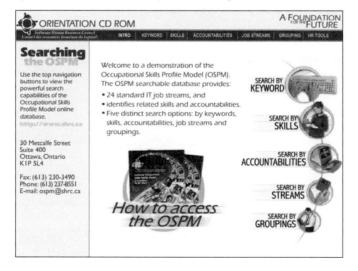

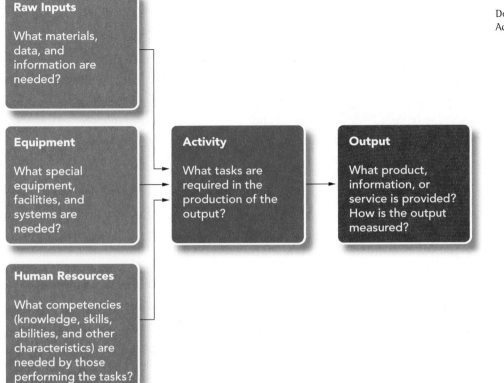

FIGURE 3.1

Developing a Work-Unit
Activity Analysis

The chapter begins with a look at the big-picture issues related to analyzing work flow and organizational structure. The discussion then turns to the more specific issues of analyzing and designing jobs. Traditionally, job analysis has emphasized the study of existing jobs in order to make decisions such as employee selection, training, and compensation. In contrast, job design has emphasized making jobs more efficient or more motivating. However, as this chapter shows, the two activities are interrelated.

work flow design
The process of analyzing the tasks necessary for the production of a product or service.

Work Flow in Organizations

Informed decisions about jobs take place in the context of the organization's overall work flow. Through the process of **work flow design,** managers analyze the tasks needed to produce a product or service. With this information, they assign these tasks to specific jobs and positions. (A **job** is a set of related duties. A **position** is the set of duties performed by one person. A school has many teaching *positions*; the person filling each of those positions is performing the *job* of teacher.) Basing these decisions on work flow design can lead to better results than the more traditional practice of looking at jobs individually.

job
A set of related duties.

position
The set of duties (job) performed by a particular person.

Work Flow Analysis

LO1

Before designing its work flow, the organization's planners need to analyze what work needs to be done. Figure 3.1 shows the elements of a work flow analysis. For each type

Firefighters work as a team. They and their equipment are the "inputs" (they do the work), and the "output" is an extinguished fire and the rescue of people and pets. In any organization or team, workers need to be cross-trained in several skills to create an effective team. If these firefighters are trained to do any part of the job, the chief can deploy them rapidly as needed.

of work, such as producing a product line or providing a support service (accounting, legal support, and so on), the analysis identifies the output of the process, the activities involved, and three categories of inputs: raw inputs (materials and information), equipment, and human resources.

Outputs are the products of any work unit, whether a department, team, or individual. An output can be as readily identifiable as a completed purchase order, an employment test, or a hot, juicy hamburger. An output can also be a service, such as transportation, cleaning, or answering questions about employee benefits. Even at an organization that produces tangible goods, such as computers, many employees produce other outputs, such as components of the computers, marketing plans, and building security. Work flow analysis identifies the outputs of particular work units. The analysis considers not only the amount of output but also quality standards. This attention to outputs has only recently gained attention among HR professionals. However, it gives a clearer view of how to increase the effectiveness of each work unit.

For the outputs identified, work flow analysis then examines the work processes used to generate those outputs. Work processes are the activities that members of a work unit engage in to produce a given output. Every process consists of operating procedures that specify how things should be done at each stage of developing the output. These procedures include all the tasks that must be performed in producing the output. Usually, the analysis breaks down the tasks into those performed by each person in the work unit. This analysis helps with design of efficient work systems by clarifying which tasks are necessary. Typically, when a unit's work load increases, the unit adds people, and when the work load decreases, some members of the unit may busy themselves with unrelated tasks in an effort to appear busy. Without knowledge of work processes, it is more difficult to identify whether the work unit is properly staffed. For example, Microsoft deliberately understaffs its product teams in "small bands of people with a mission." This approach ensures a lean organization and high levels of motivation.[6]

The final stage in work flow analysis is to identify the inputs used in the development of the work unit's product. As shown in Figure 3.1, these inputs can be broken down into the raw inputs (materials and knowledge), equipment, and human skills needed to perform the tasks. Makers of athletic shoes need nylon and leather, shoe-making machinery, and workers to operate the machinery, among other inputs. Nike and Reebok minimize the cost of inputs by subcontracting manufacturing to factories in countries where wages are low. In contrast, New Balance Athletic Shoes operates a factory in the U.S., where modern technology and worker training enable the company to afford North American workers. Teams of employees use automated equipment that operates over 20 sewing machines simultaneously. The employees are cross-trained in all tasks. The highly efficient factory produces shoes much faster than a typical shoe factory in China.[7]

LO2

Work Flow in Organizations

Besides looking at the work flow of each process, it is important to see how the work fits within the context of the organization's structure. Within an organization, units

Team-Based Jobs Put the Focus on Patient Care

One way medical facilities are improving patient care is to engage employees by organizing work around teams. At the internationally renowned Mayo Clinic based in Rochester, Minnesota, medicine has been practiced as an integrated team of professionals for almost a century. Patients come to the Mayo clinic for help with the diagnosis and treatment of challenging medical problems of all types. Mayo's expertise includes more than 2,800 staff physicians and scientists from 100 medical specialties and sub-specialties as well as approximately 2,000 residents, fellows, and temporary professionals and more than 40,000 allied health staff.

At the Mayo Clinic, a battle against cancer looks like this.... At 1 PM, support staffers line the walls of a tiny workroom on the 12th floor "with X-rays and test results from the current caseload. The space fills with a small crowd of cancer

specialists, surgeons, residents, and nurses. For the next three hours, this talented team will debate the condition and treatment of the day's patients. At Mayo, specialists don't just visit the patient; they swarm the patient as an integrated team, diagnosing a complex problem, proposing treatment—and often slotting the patient for surgery within 24 hours of the diagnosis."

Besides medicine, almost every aspect of Mayo's operation relies on consultation and collaboration. Three of the principles that define teamwork at Mayo include:
1. The patient's best interests guide treatment—a doctor can quickly add medical experts as well as social workers, or other advisers to best serve the patient.
2. "Teamwork is part of the culture." Teamwork is essential—it's not an option.
3. "The customer is part of the team." Patients are involved in their diagnosis and

treatment to the level of involvement they desire.

Mayo's list of medical accomplishments are far reaching and extensive including innovations in the fields of surgical procedures, rheumatoid arthritis, tuberculosis, cardiac treatments, diabetes, cancer, and transplant services. It is also noteworthy to consider that Mayo operates as a charitable, not-for profit organization where doctors are paid a set salary and benefactors contribute significantly to support state-of-the-art facilities, train future leaders in health care, and conduct research.

SOURCE: Paul Roberts, "The Agenda—Total Teamwork," *FastCompany*, Issue 23, April 1999, p. 148, www.fastcompany.com/magazine/23/totteam.html. Retrieved: April 14, 2004; www.mayoclinic.org/about/facts.html. Retrieved: April 21, 2004; www.mayoclinic.org/about/keydates.html. Retrieved: April 21, 2004.

and individuals must cooperate to create outputs. Ideally, the organization's structure brings together the people who must collaborate in order to efficiently produce the desired outputs. The structure may do this in a way that is highly centralized (that is, with authority concentrated in a few people at the top of the organizaton) or decentralized (with authority spread among many people). The organization may group jobs according to functions (for example, welding, painting, packaging), or it may set up divisions to focus on products or customer groups.

Although there is an infinite number of ways to combine the elements of an organization's structure, we can make some general observations about structure and work design. If the structure is strongly based on function, workers tend to have low authority and to work alone at highly specialized jobs. Jobs that involve teamwork or broad responsibility tend to require a structure based on divisions other than functions.

Writing a Job Description

Preparing a job description begins with gathering information from sources who can identify the details of performing a task. These sources may include persons already performing the job, the supervisor or team leader, or if the job is new, the managers who are creating the new position. Asking the purpose of the new position can provide insight into what the company expects this person to accomplish. Besides people, sources of information may include the company's human resource files, such as past job advertisements and job descriptions, as well as general sources of information about similar jobs, such as Human Resources and Skills Development Canada's National Occupational Classification (NOC) system (www.hrdc-drhc.gc.ca/noc).

There are several ways to gather information about the duties of a job:

- Employees can fill out a questionnaire that asks about what they do or complete a diary that details their activities over several days.

- A job analyst can visit the workplace and watch or videotape an employee performing the job. This method is most appropriate for jobs that are repetitive and involve physical activity.

- A job analyst can visit the workplace and ask an employee to show what the job entails. This method is most appropriate for clerical and technical jobs.

- A manager or supervisor can imagine what a well-done job would look like. What would the outputs be? Would customers feel the job holder had answered their questions fully and politely? Would a product be assembled correctly and in some quantity? Would coworkers have access to up-to-date information? The analyst can identify the activities necessary to create the outputs.

- A supervisor or job analyst can review company records related to performing the job—for example, work orders or summaries of customer calls. These records can show the kinds of problems a person solves in the course of doing a job.

After gathering such information, the next thing to do is list all the activities, then evaluate whether all of them or which ones are essential duties. One way to do this is to rate all the duties on a scale of 1 to 5, where 1 is most important. A rating scale also could rank the tasks according to how much time the person spends on them. Perhaps the ratings will show that some tasks are desirable but not essential. The tasks listed as essential duties on the job description should be only the ones that the job analysis identifies as essential.

Gathering information from many sources helps to verify which tasks are essential. Perhaps the job holder is aware of some activities that others do

When the goal is to engage employees, companies therefore need to set up structures and jobs that enable broad responsibility, such as jobs that involve employees in serving a particular group of customers or producing a particular product, rather than performing a narrowly defined function. The "Best Practices" box illustrates a way of applying this principle to health care.

Work design often emphasizes the analysis and design of jobs, as described in the remainder of this chapter. Although all of these approaches can succeed, each focuses on one isolated job at a time. These approaches do not necessarily consider how that single job fits into the overall work flow or structure of the organization. To use these techniques effectively, human resource professionals should also understand their or-not notice. Or on the other hand, perhaps the job holder performs activities that are not essential but are merely habits or holdovers from a time when they were essential. When different people analyzing a job come to different conclusions about which activities are essential, the person writing the job description should compare the listed activities with the company's goals and work flow to see which are essential. A group discussion also may help categorize tasks as essential, ideal, and unnecessary.

From these sources, the writer of the job description thus obtains the important elements of the description:

- *Title of the job*—The title should be descriptive and, if appropriate, indicate the job's level in the organization by using terms such as *junior, senior, assistant*, and *executive*.
- *Administrative information about the job*—Depending on the company's size and requirements, the job description may identify a division, department, supervisor's title, date of the analysis, name of the analyst, and other information for administering the company's human resource activities.
- *Summary of the job, focusing on its purpose and duties*—This summary should be brief and as specific as possible, including types of responsibilities, tools and equipment used, and level of authority (for example, the degree of authority and responsibility of the job holder—how much the person is supervised and how much the person supervises others or participates in teamwork).
- *Essential duties of the job*—These should be listed in order of importance to successful performance of the job and should include details such as physical requirements (for example, the amount of weight to be lifted), the persons with whom an employee in this job interacts, and the results to be accomplished.
- *Additional responsibilities*—The job description may have a section stating that the position requires additional responsibilities as requested by the supervisor.
- *Job specifications*—The specifications cover the knowledge, skills, abilities, and other characteristics required for a person to be qualified to perform the job successfully. These may appear at the end of the job description or as a separate document.

SOURCE: D. B. Bordeaux, "Writing Job Descriptions," *Motor Age*, November 2001, downloaded from Findarticles.com; "Job Descriptions and the ADA," HRNext, www.hrnext.com, downloaded March 7, 2002; "Simple Job Analysis," HRNext, www.hrnext.com, downloaded March 7, 2002; C. Joinson, "Refocusing Job Descriptions," *HR Magazine*, January 2001, downloaded from Findarticles.com.

ganization as a whole. Without this big-picture appreciation, they might redesign a job in a way that makes sense for the particular job but is out of line with the organization's work flow, structure, or strategy.

Job Analysis

LO3

To achieve high-quality performance, organizations have to understand and match job requirements and people. This understanding requires **job analysis,** the process of getting detailed information about jobs. Analyzing jobs and understanding what is required to carry out a job provide essential knowledge for staffing, training, perfor-

job analysis
The process of getting detailed information about jobs.

FIGURE 3.2

Sample Job Description

Part-Time Sales Associate

Position Responsibilities

- Provide fast, friendly service by actively seeking out customers to assess their needs and provide assistance

- Provide information on product features and know related items to sell an entire project

- Greet, qualify, recommend, and close every customer in the department and handle the basics in adjacent departments

- Maintain in-stock condition of assigned areas and ensure that it is clean, shoppable, and safe

SOURCE: Home Depot website, www.homedepot.com. Retrieved: April 17, 2004.

mance appraisal, and many other HR activities. For instance, a supervisor's evaluation of an employee's work should be based on performance relative to job requirements. In very small organizations, line managers may perform a job analysis, but usually the work is done by a human resource professional. A large company may have a compensation management department that includes job analysts. Organizations may also contract with firms that provide this service.

Job Descriptions

job description
A list of the tasks, duties, and responsibilities (TDRs) that a particular job entails.

An essential part of job analysis is the creation of job descriptions. A **job description** is a list of the tasks, duties, and responsibilities (TDRs) that a job entails. TDRs are observable actions. For example, a data entry job requires the job holder to enter data using a keyboard. If you were to observe someone in that position for a day, you would certainly see some keyboarding. When a manager attempts to evaluate job performance, it is most important to have detailed information about the work performed in the job (that is, the TDRs). This information makes it possible to determine how well an individual is meeting each job requirement.

A job description typically has the format shown in Figure 3.2. It includes the job title, a brief description of the TDRs, and a list of the essential duties with detailed specifications of the tasks involved in carrying out each duty. Although organizations may modify this format according to their particular needs, all job descriptions within an organization should follow the same format. This helps the organization make consistent decisions about such matters as pay and promotions. It also helps the organization show that it makes human resource decisions fairly.

Whenever the organization creates a new job, it needs to prepare a job description, using a process such as the one detailed in the "HR How To" box. Job descriptions should then be reviewed periodically (say, once a year) and updated as necessary. Performance appraisals can provide a good opportunity for updating job descriptions, as

E-HRM

Creating Job Descriptions Online

JobDescription.com offers HR professionals in companies large and small the means to access a library of thousands of jobs and write job descriptions online. An online template prompts the writer to answer questions about job qualifications, competencies required, physical demands, responsibilities, and work environment.

One-use applications as well as subscription-based services are available for immediate use and purchase. Besides the job description writing capabilities, interview questions as well as a job posting or advertisement are generated automatically on completion of the writing of the job description.

Another key feature of this online tool is the capability to "click (or call) for a live person" between the hours of 8 AM and 5 PM Monday to Friday.

SOURCE: www.jobdescription.com and www.hrtools.com. Retrieved: April 28, 2004.

the employee and supervisor compare what the employee has been doing against the details of the job description.

When organizations prepare many job descriptions, the process can become repetitive and time consuming. To address this challenge, a number of companies have developed software that provides forms into which the job analyst can insert details about the specific job. Typically, the job analyst would use a library of basic descriptions, selecting one that is for a similar type of job and then modifying it to fit the organization's needs. The "E-HRM" box features JobDescription.com, an online library of thousands of job descriptions.

Organizations should provide each newly hired employee a copy of his or her job description. This helps the employee to understand what is expected, but it shouldn't be presented as limiting the employee's commitment to quality and customer satisfaction. Ideally, employees will want to go above and beyond the listed duties when the situation and their abilities call for that. Many job descriptions include the phrase *and other duties as required* as a way to remind employees not to tell their supervisor, "But that's not part of my job."

Job Specifications

Whereas the job description focuses on the activities involved in carrying out a job, a **job specification** looks at the qualities of the person performing the job. It is a list of the **competencies**, i.e., knowledge, skills, abilities, and other characteristics that an individual must have to perform the job. *Knowledge* refers to factual or procedural information that is necessary for successfully performing a task. For example, this course is providing you with knowledge in how to manage human resources. A *skill* is an individual's level of proficiency at performing a particular task—that is, the capability to perform it well. With knowledge and experience, you could acquire skill in the task of preparing job specifications. *Ability*, in contrast to skill, refers to a more general enduring capability that an individual possesses. A person might have the ability to cooperate with others or to write clearly and precisely. Finally, *other characteristics* might be personality traits such as someone's persistence or motivation to achieve. Some jobs also have legal requirements, such as licensing or certification. Figure 3.3 is a set of sample job specifications for the job description in Figure 3.2.

job specification
A list of the competencies that an individual must have to perform a particular job.

competencies
Knowledge, skills, abilities, and other characteristics associated with effective job performance.

77

FIGURE 3.3

Sample Job
Specifications

Part-Time Sales Associate

Requirements

- Must be customer and team oriented and have the ability to handle difficult situations

- Must enjoy a fast paced environment

- Must be able to bend, stoop, reach, twist, lift, and be on your feet for extended periods of time

- Excellent communication skills

- This position is part-time and requires weekend availability

SOURCE: Home Depot website, www.homedepot.com. Retrieved: April 17, 2004.

In developing job specifications, it is important to consider all of the elements of the competencies. As with writing a job description, the information can come from a combination of people performing the job, people supervising or planning for the job, and trained job analysts. At Acxiom Corporation, job specifications are based on an analysis of employees' roles and competencies (what they must be able to do), stated in terms of behaviours. To reach these definitions, groups studied what the company's good performers were doing and looked for the underlying abilities. For example, according to Jeff Standridge, Acxiom's organizational development leader, they might ask a panel about a high-performing software developer, and panel members might identify the employee's knowledge of the Java and C++ programming languages. Then, Standridge says, the job analysts would probe for the abilities behind this knowledge: "When we asked, 'If Java becomes obsolete in five years, will this person no longer be successful?' the panel responded, 'Oh no, he'll update his skills and be great in the new language.' . . . The employee's strength was not just in his specific skills but in his ability to learn."[8]

In contrast to tasks, duties, and responsibilities, competencies are characteristics of people and are observable only when individuals are carrying out the TDRs of the job. Thus, if someone applied for a job requiring strong presentation skills, you could not simply look at the individual to determine whether he or she possessed strong presentation skills. However, you could assess the level of presentation skill by observing the person conduct a presentation as part of the hiring and selection process.

Accurate information about competencies is especially important for making decisions about who will fill a job. A manager attempting to fill a position

When a job entails working night shifts, job specifications should reflect this requirement. Some people who work at night experience emotional and physical stress. The organization needs to help these employees handle the challenges of night shift.

needs information about the characteristics required, and about the characteristics of each applicant. Interviews and selection decisions should therefore focus on competencies. In the earlier example of computer programming at Acxiom, the company would look for someone who knows the computer languages currently used, but also has a track record of taking the initiative to learn new computer languages as they are developed.

The identification of competencies is also being implemented widely in the public sector. The federal government has developed a Corporate Competency Profile for Middle Managers that identifies 14 leadership competencies. These competencies include detailed descriptions including the behaviours as well as the knowledge, skills, and abilities associated with each competency. Competencies identified for middle managers in the federal public sector include intellectual competencies (e.g., cognitive capacity); management competencies (e.g., team work); relationship competencies (e.g., communication); and personal competencies (e.g., stamina or stress resistance).[9]

Operations that need to run 24 hours a day have special job requirements. For example, shutting down certain equipment at night may be inefficient or may cause production problems, or some industries, such as security and health care, may have customers who demand services around the clock. Globalization often means that operations take place across many time zones, requiring management at all hours. When a job entails working night shifts, job specifications should reflect this requirement. For most people, working at night disrupts their normal functioning and may cause disorders such as fatigue, depression, and obesity. However, people show wide variability in how well they respond to working at night. Research has found that people who work well at night tend to prefer sleeping late in the morning and staying up late. They also tend to sleep easily at different times of day, like to take naps, and exercise regularly. When job specifications call for nighttime work, a person's ability to handle a nocturnal work life may be the most critical competency.[10]

Sources of Job Information

LO4

Information for analyzing an existing job often comes from incumbents, that is, people who currently hold that position in the organization. They are a logical source of information, because they are most acquainted with the details of the job. Incumbents should be able to provide very accurate information.

A drawback of relying solely on incumbents' information is that they may have an incentive to exaggerate what they do, to appear more valuable to the organization. Information from incumbents should therefore be supplemented with information from observers, such as supervisors. Supervisors should review the information provided by incumbents, looking for a match between what incumbents are doing and what they are supposed to do. Research suggests that incumbents may provide the most accurate estimates of the actual time spent performing job tasks, while supervisors may be more accurate in reporting information about the importance of job duties.[11]

The federal government also provides background information for analyzing jobs. Human Resources and Skills Development Canada working with Statistics Canada created the **National Occupational Classification (NOC)** to provide standardized sources of information about jobs in Canada's labour market. The NOC is a tool that uses a four-digit code to classify occupations based on the types and levels of skills required. The NOC classification system (www.hrdc-drhc.gc.ca/noc) supports the needs

National Occupational Classification (NOC)
Tool created by the federal government to provide a standardized source of information about jobs in Canada's labour market.

FIGURE 3.4

Excerpts from the
National Occupational
Classification Matrix
2001

OCCUPATIONAL DESCRIPTION GROUP 1 BUSINESS, FINANCE AND ADMINISTRATION OCCUPATIONS	
0 **Management Occupations**	Example: 012 Managers in Finance and Business Service
SKILL LEVEL A Occupations usually require university education	Major Group 11 PROFESSIONAL OCCUPATIONS IN BUSINESS AND FINANCE Example: 112 Human Resources and Business Services Professionals
SKILL LEVEL B Occupations usually require college education or apprenticeship training	Major Group 12 SKILLED ADMINISTRATIVE AND BUSINESS OCCUPATIONS Examples: 121 Clerical supervisors 123 Finance and Insurance Administrative Occupations
SKILL LEVEL C Occupations usually require secondary school and/or occupation-specific training	Major Group 14 CLERICAL OCCUPATIONS Example: 144 Administrative Support Clerks
SKILL LEVEL D On the job training usually provided for occupations	

SOURCE: Human Resources Development Canada, "National Occupational Classification Matrix, 2001," www23.hrdc-drhc.gc.ca/2001/e/generic/matrix.pdf. Retrieved: April 27, 2004. Reproduced with the permission of the Minister of Public Works and Government Services Canada, 2005.

Position Analysis Questionnaire (PAQ)

A standardized job analysis questionnaire containing 194 questions about work behaviours, work conditions, and job characteristics that apply to a wide variety of jobs.

of employers, individual job seekers, as well as career counsellors, statisticians, and labour market analysts by providing a consistent way to identify and interpret the nature of work. In total, more than 20,000 job titles are included in the classification.[12]

Other significant sources of information about jobs in Canada are organized according to the NOC classifications. For example, Job Futures (www.jobfutures.ca) provides information about occupational outlooks and the National Job Bank® (www.jobbank.gc.ca) is an electronic listing of jobs. Figure 3.4 provides excerpts from the NOC Classification Matrix to illustrate a sampling of jobs that relate to the "Business, Finance, and Administration Occupations" for the various skill levels classified in the NOC.

Position Analysis Questionnaire

After gathering information, the job analyst uses the information to analyze the job. One of the broadest and best-researched instruments for analyzing jobs is the **Position Analysis Questionnaire (PAQ).** This is a standardized job analysis questionnaire containing 194 items that represent work behaviours, work conditions, and job characteristics that apply to a wide variety of jobs. The questionnaire organizes these items into six sections concerning different aspects of the job:

1. *Information input*—Where and how a worker gets information needed to perform the job.
2. *Mental processes*—The reasoning, decision making, planning, and information-processing activities involved in performing the job.
3. *Work output*—The physical activities, tools, and devices used by the worker to perform the job.
4. *Relationships with other persons*—The relationships with other people required in performing the job.
5. *Job context*—The physical and social contexts where the work is performed.
6. *Other characteristics*—The activities, conditions, and characteristics other than those previously described that are relevant to the job.

The person analyzing a job determines whether each item on the questionnaire applies to the job being analyzed. The analyst rates each item on six scales: extent of use, amount of time, importance to the job, possibility of occurrence, applicability, and special code (special rating scales used with a particular item). The PAQ headquarters uses a computer to score the questionnaire and generate a report that describes the scores on the job dimensions.

Using the PAQ provides an organization with information that helps in comparing jobs, even when they are dissimilar. The PAQ also has the advantage that it considers the whole work process, from inputs through outputs. However, the person who fills out the questionnaire must have post-secondary-level reading skills, and the PAQ is meant to be completed only by job analysts trained in this method.[13] Also, the descriptions in the PAQ reports are rather abstract, so the reports may not be useful for writing job descriptions or redesigning jobs.

Task Analysis Inventory

Another type of job analysis method, the **task analysis inventory,** focuses on the tasks performed in a particular job. This method has several variations. In one, the task inventory–CODAP method, subject-matter experts such as job incumbents generate a list of the tasks performed in a job. Then they rate each task in terms of time spent on the task, frequency of task performance, relative importance, relative difficulty, and length of time required to learn the job. The CODAP computer program organizes the responses into dimensions of similar tasks.[14]

Task analysis inventories can be very detailed, including 100 or more tasks. This level of detail can be helpful for developing employment tests and criteria for performance appraisal. However, they do not directly identify competencies needed for success in a job.

Fleishman Job Analysis System

To gather information about worker requirements, the **Fleishman Job Analysis System** asks subject-matter experts (typically job incumbents) to evaluate a job in terms of the abilities required to perform the job.[15] The survey is based on 52 categories of abilities, ranging from written comprehension to deductive reasoning, manual dexterity, stamina, and originality. As in the example in Figure 3.5, the survey items are

task analysis inventory
Job analysis method that involves listing the tasks performed in a particular job and rating each task according to a defined set of criteria.

Fleishman Job Analysis System
Job analysis technique that asks subject-matter experts to evaluate a job in terms of the abilities required to perform the job.

FIGURE 3.5

Example of an Ability
from the Fleishman Job
Analysis System

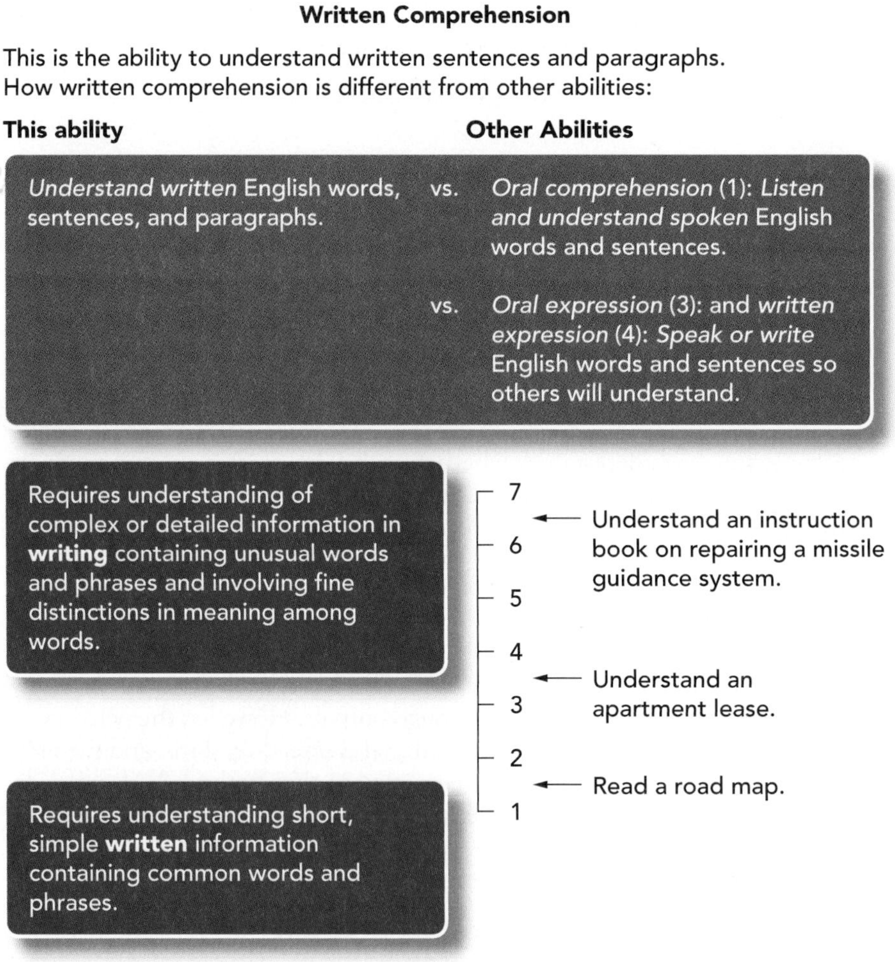

Written Comprehension

This is the ability to understand written sentences and paragraphs.
How written comprehension is different from other abilities:

This ability		Other Abilities
Understand written English words, sentences, and paragraphs.	vs.	*Oral comprehension* (1): *Listen and understand spoken* English words and sentences.
	vs.	*Oral expression* (3): and *written expression* (4): *Speak or write* English words and sentences so others will understand.

Requires understanding of complex or detailed information in **writing** containing unusual words and phrases and involving fine distinctions in meaning among words.

— 7
— 6   ← Understand an instruction book on repairing a missile guidance system.
— 5
— 4
— 3   ← Understand an apartment lease.
— 2
— 1   ← Read a road map.

Requires understanding short, simple **written** information containing common words and phrases.

SOURCE: E. A. Fleishman and M. D. Mumford, "Evaluating Classifications of Job Behavior: A Construct Validation of the Ability Requirements Scales," *Personnel Psychology* 44 (1991), pp. 523–76. The complete set of ability requirement scales, along with instructions for their use, may be found in E. A. Fleishman, *Fleishman Job Analysis Survey (F-JAS)* (Palo Alto, CA: Consulting Psychologists Press, 1992). Used with permission.

arranged into a scale for each ability. Each begins with a description of the ability and a comparison to related abilities. Below this is a seven-point scale with phrases describing extemely high and low levels of the ability. The person completing the survey indicates which point on the scale represents the level of the ability required for performing the job being analyzed.

When the survey has been completed in all 52 categories, the results provide a picture of the ability requirements of a job. Such information is especially useful for employee selection, training, and career development.

Importance of Job Analysis

Job analysis is so important to HR managers that it has been called the building block of everything that HR does.[16] The fact is that almost every human resource management program requires some type of information that is gleaned from job analysis:[17]

- *Work redesign*—Often an organization seeks to redesign work to make it more efficient or to improve quality. The redesign requires detailed information about the existing job(s). In addition, preparing the redesign is similar to analyzing a job that does not yet exist.
- *Human resource planning*—As planners analyze human resource needs and how to meet those needs, they must have accurate information about the levels of skill required in various jobs, so that they can tell what kinds of human resources will be needed.
- *Selection*—To identify the most qualified applicants for various positions, decision makers need to know what tasks the individuals must perform, as well as the necessary knowledge, skills, and abilities.
- *Training*—Almost every employee hired by an organization will require training. Any training program requires knowledge of the tasks performed in a job, so that the training is related to the necessary knowledge and skills.
- *Performance appraisal*—An accurate performance appraisal requires information about how well each employee is performing in order to reward employees who perform well and to improve their performance if it is below expectations. Job analysis helps in identifying the behaviours and the results associated with effective performance.
- *Career planning*—Matching an individual's skills and aspirations with career opportunities requires that those in charge of career planning know the skill requirements of the various jobs. This allows them to guide individuals into jobs in which they will succeed and be satisfied.
- *Job evaluation*—The process of job evaluation involves assessing the relative value of each job to the organization in order to set up fair pay structures. If employees do not believe pay structures are fair, they will become dissatisfied and may quit, or they will not see much benefit in striving for promotions. To put values on jobs, it is necessary to get information about different jobs and compare them.

The Royal Canadian Mounted Police (RCMP) has an automated resource, i.e., a database that identifies the functions and competency requirements of specific RCMP jobs. This automated resource integrates information about jobs to various HR functions. For example, this database links "Job Profiles," materials to help understand what the job is all about, with "Development Activities," which provide information about formal learning opportunities including workshops, online courses, and well as off-line resources such as articles and videos. By clicking on "Problem-Based Learning" you are linked to scenarios that test your skills and by linking to "Performance Management" employees and their supervisors can get assistance in determining competencies for further development.[18]

Job analysis is also important from a legal standpoint. As we saw in Chapter 2, governments impose requirements related to human rights and pay equity. Detailed, accurate, objective job specifications help decision makers comply with these requirements by keeping the focus on tasks and abilities. Employers have a legal obligation to eliminate discrimination against employees and prospective employees with disabilities. Job redesign may be required to consider the needs of the job applicant to ensure that accommodation is provided. When accommodation is discussed with the employee or job applicant it is important to use language that focuses on the person's abilities, rather than the person's disability. For example, ask all employees regardless of whether they have a disability, "will you require accommodation to perform this task?" rather than, "can you perform this task?"[19]

Besides helping human resource professionals, job analysis helps supervisors and other managers carry out their duties. Data from job analysis can help managers identify the types of work in their units, as well as provide information about the work flow process, so that managers can evaluate whether work is done in the most efficient way. Job analysis information also supports managers as they make hiring decisions, review performance, and recommend rewards.

LO5

Trends in Job Analysis

As we noted in the earlier discussion of work flow analysis, organizations are beginning to appreciate the need to analyze jobs in the context of the organization's structure and strategy. In addition, organizations are recognizing that today's workplace must be adaptable and is constantly subject to change. Thus, although we tend to think of "jobs" as something stable, they actually tend to change and evolve over time. Those who occupy or manage jobs often make minor adjustments to match personal preferences or changing conditions.[20] Indeed, although errors in job analysis can have many sources, most inaccuracy is likely to result from job descriptions being outdated. For this reason, job analysis must not only define jobs when they are created, but also detect changes in jobs as time passes. Competency requirements of a job may be more stable and long-lasting than the tasks, duties, and responsibilities associated with that specific job. In addition, an organization also requires specific competencies to be successful in a dynamic environment. Many organizations have developed a **competency framework** that identifies the competencies the entire organization requires to be successful. This competency framework is then used to assist in determining the competencies required by specific departments, teams, and jobs within the organization.

competency framework
Competencies the entire organization requires to be successful.

In today's world of rapidly changing products and markets, some observers have even begun to suggest that the concept of a "job" is obsolete. Some researchers and businesspeople have observed a trend they call *dejobbing*—viewing organizations as a field of work needing to be done, rather than as a set or series of jobs held by individuals. For example, at Amazon.com, HR director Scott Pitasky notes, "Here, a person might be in the same 'job,' but three months later be doing completely different work."[21] This means Amazon.com puts more emphasis on broad worker competencies ("entrepreneurial and customer-focused") than on detailed job descriptions ("HTML programming").

These changes in the nature of work and the expanded use of "project-based" organizational structures require the type of broader understanding that comes from an analysis of work flows. Because the work can change rapidly and it is impossible to rewrite job descriptions every week, job descriptions and specifications need to be

Amazon.com practices "dejobbing," or designing work by project rather than by jobs. What would appeal to you about working for a company organized like this?

flexible. At the same time, legal requirements (as discussed in Chapter 2) may discourage organizations from writing flexible job descriptions. So, organizations must balance the need for flexibility with the need for legal documentation. This presents one of the major challenges to be faced by HRM departments in the next decade. Many professionals are meeting this challenge with a greater emphasis on careful job design.

Job Design

Although job analysis, as just described, is important for an understanding of existing jobs, organizations also must plan for new jobs and periodically consider whether they should revise existing jobs. When an organization is expanding, supervisors and human resource professionals must help plan for new or growing work units. When an organization is trying to improve quality or efficiency, a review of work units and processes may require a fresh look at how jobs are designed.

These situations call for **job design,** the process of defining the way work will be performed and the tasks that a given job requires, or *job redesign*, a similar process that involves changing an existing job design. To design jobs effectively, a person must thoroughly understand the job itself (through job analysis) and its place in the larger work unit's work flow process (through work flow analysis). Having a detailed knowledge of the tasks performed in the work unit and in the job, a manager then has many alternative ways to design a job. As shown in Figure 3.6, the available approaches emphasize different aspects of the job: the mechanics of doing a job efficiently, the job's impact on motivation, the use of safe work practices, and the mental demands of the job.

job design
The process of defining the way work will be performed and the tasks that a given job requires.

Designing Efficient Jobs

If workers perform tasks as efficiently as possible, not only does the organization benefit from lower costs and greater output per worker, but workers should be less fatigued. This point of view has for years formed the basis of classical **industrial engineering,** which looks for the simplest way to structure work in order to maximize efficiency. Typically, applying industrial engineering to a job reduces the complexity of the work, making it so simple that almost anyone can be trained quickly and easily to perform the job. Such jobs tend to be highly specialized and repetitive.

In practice, the scientific method traditionally seeks the "one best way" to perform a job by performing time-and-motion studies to identify the most efficient movements for workers to make. Once the engineers have identified the most efficient sequence of motions, the organization should select workers based on their ability to do the job, then train them in the details of the "one best way" to perform that job. The company also should offer pay structured to motivate workers to do their best. (Chapter 9 discusses pay and pay structures.)

LO6

industrial engineering
The study of jobs to find the simplest way to structure work in order to maximize efficiency.

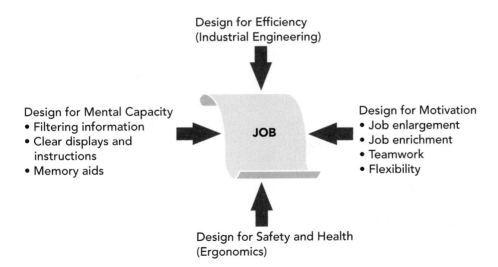

Design for Efficiency
(Industrial Engineering)

Design for Mental Capacity
• Filtering information
• Clear displays and instructions
• Memory aids

JOB

Design for Motivation
• Job enlargement
• Job enrichment
• Teamwork
• Flexibility

Design for Safety and Health
(Ergonomics)

FIGURE 3.6

Approaches to Job Design

Despite the logical benefits of industrial engineering, a focus on efficiency alone can create jobs that are so simple and repetitive that workers get bored. Workers performing these jobs may feel their work is meaningless. Hence, most organizations combine industrial engineering with other approaches to job design.

LO7

Designing Jobs That Motivate

Especially when organizations must compete for employees, depend on skilled knowledge workers, or need a workforce that cares about customer satisfaction, a pure focus on efficiency will not achieve human resource objectives. These organizations need jobs that employees find interesting and satisfying, and job design should take into account factors that make jobs motivating to employees.

The quest for meaningful work draws people to such career paths as teaching and public service. For example, when Patrick Bernhardt was laid off from his job as a marketing executive in an e-commerce start-up, he seized the chance to switch fields. Bernhardt became a computer science teacher and enrolled in evening classes. When he switched to this job, Bernhardt took a 50 percent pay cut, but he doesn't mind: "This is the hardest thing I've ever done, but the sense of satisfaction makes it worth it."[22]

A model that shows how to make jobs more motivating is the Job Characteristics Model, developed by Richard Hackman and Greg Oldham. This model describes jobs in terms of five characteristics:[23]

1. *Skill variety*—The extent to which a job requires a variety of skills to carry out the tasks involved.
2. *Task identity*—The degree to which a job requires completing a "whole" piece of work from beginning to end (for example, building an entire component or resolving a customer's complaint).
3. *Task significance*—The extent to which the job has an important impact on the lives of other people.
4. *Autonomy*—The degree to which the job allows an individual to make decisions about the way the work will be carried out.
5. *Feedback*—The extent to which a person receives clear information about performance effectiveness from the work itself.

FIGURE 3.7

Characteristics of a Motivating Job

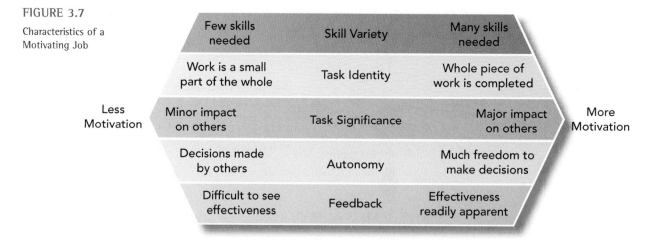

As shown in Figure 3.7, the more of each of these characteristics a job has, the more motivating the job will be, according to the Job Characteristics Model. The model predicts that a person with such a job will be more satisfied and will produce more and better work. This approach to designing jobs includes such techniques as job enlargement, job enrichment, self-managing work teams, flexible work schedules, and telework.

Job Enlargement

In a job design, **job enlargement** refers to broadening the types of tasks performed. The objective of job enlargement is to make jobs less repetitive and more interesting. Methods of job enlargement include job extension and job rotation.

Job extension is enlarging jobs by combining several relatively simple jobs to form a job with a wider range of tasks. An example might be combining the jobs of receptionist, typist, and file clerk into jobs containing all three kinds of work. This approach to job enlargement is relatively simple, but if all the tasks are dull, workers will not necessarily be more motivated by the redesigned job.

Job rotation does not actually redesign the jobs themselves, but moves employees among several different jobs. This approach to job enlargement is common among production teams. During the course of a week, a team member may carry out each of the jobs handled by the team. Team members might assemble components one day and pack products into cases another day. As with job extension, the enlarged jobs may still consist of repetitious activities, but with greater variation among those activities.

Job Enrichment

The idea of **job enrichment,** or engaging workers by adding more decision-making authority to their jobs, comes from the work of Frederick Herzberg. According to Herzberg's two-factor theory, individuals are motivated more by the intrinsic aspects of work (for example, the meaningfulness of a job) than by extrinsic rewards such as pay. Herzberg identified five factors he associated with motivating jobs: achievement, recognition, growth, responsibility, and performance of the entire job. Thus, ways to enrich a manufacturing job might include giving employees authority to stop production when quality standards are not being met and having each employee perform several tasks to complete a particular stage of the process, rather than dividing up the tasks among the employees. For a salesperson in a store, job enrichment might involve the authority to resolve customer problems, including the authority to decide whether to issue refunds or replace merchandise.

Self-Managing Work Teams

Instead of merely enriching individual jobs, some organizations engage employees by designing work to be done by self-managing work teams. As described in Chapter 1, these teams have authority for an entire work process or segment. Team members typically have authority to schedule work, hire team members, resolve problems related to the team's performance, and perform other duties traditionally handled by management. Teamwork can give a job such motivating characteristics as autonomy, skill variety, and task identity.

Because team members' responsibilities are great, their jobs usually are defined broadly and include sharing of work assignments. Team members may, at one time or

job enlargement
Broadening the types of tasks performed in a job.

job extension
Enlarging jobs by combining several relatively simple jobs to form a job with a wider range of tasks.

job rotation
Enlarging jobs by moving employees among several different jobs.

job enrichment
Engaging workers by adding more decision-making authority to jobs.

Employees who have enriched jobs and/or work in self-managed teams can be engaged and motivated when they have decision-making authority.

another, perform every duty of the team. The challenge for the organization is to provide enough training so that the team members can learn the necessary skills. Another approach, when teams are responsible for particular work processes or customers, is to assign the team responsibility for the process or customer, then let the team decide which members will carry out which tasks.

Teamwork can certainly make jobs more interesting, but teamwork's effectiveness is not guaranteed. Self-managing teams are most likely to accomplish their goals if they involve 6 to 18 employees who share the same technology (tools or ideas), location, and work hours. Such teams can be especially beneficial when a group's skills are relatively easy to learn (so that employees can readily learn one another's jobs) and demand for particular activities shifts from day to day (requiring flexibility). In addition, the job specifications should help the organization identify employees who will be willing and able to cooperate for the team's success. Such employees likely will have good problem-solving skills and be able to communicate well.

A study of work teams at a large financial services company found that the right job design was associated with effective teamwork.[24] In particular, when teams are self-managed and team members are highly involved in decision making, teams are more productive, employees more satisfied, and managers more pleased with performance. Teams also tend to do better when each team member performs a variety of tasks and when team members view their effort as significant.

Flexible Work Schedules

One way in which an organization can give employees some say in how their work is structured is to offer flexible work schedules. Depending on the requirements of the organization and the individual jobs, organizations may be able to be flexible in terms of when employees work. As introduced in Chapter 1, types of flexibility include flextime and job sharing. Figure 3.8 illustrates alternatives to the traditional 40-hour workweek.

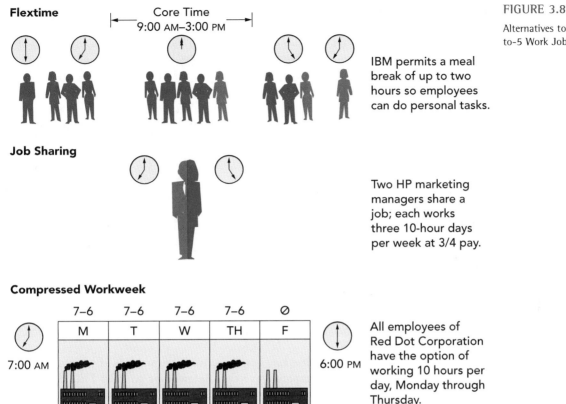

Flextime

Core Time
9:00 AM–3:00 PM

IBM permits a meal break of up to two hours so employees can do personal tasks.

Job Sharing

Two HP marketing managers share a job; each works three 10-hour days per week at 3/4 pay.

Compressed Workweek

7–6	7–6	7–6	7–6	∅
M	T	W	TH	F

7:00 AM

6:00 PM

All employees of Red Dot Corporation have the option of working 10 hours per day, Monday through Thursday.

FIGURE 3.8

Alternatives to the 8-to-5 Work Job

Flextime is a scheduling policy in which full-time employees may choose starting and ending times within guidelines specified by the organization. The flextime policy may require that employees be at work between certain hours, say, 10:00 AM and 3:00 PM. Employees work additional hours before or after this period in order to work the full day. One employee might arrive early in the morning in order to leave at 3:00 PM to pick up children after school. Another employee might be a night owl who prefers to arrive at 10:00 AM and work until 6:00, 7:00, or even later in the evening. A flextime policy also may enable workers to adjust a particular day's hours in order to make time for doctor's appointments, children's activities, hobbies, or volunteer work. A work schedule that allows time for community and family interests can be extremely motivating for some employees.

Job sharing is a work option in which two part-time employees carry out the tasks associated with a single job. Such arrangements can enable an organization to attract or retain valued employees who want more time to attend school or to care for family members. The job requirements in such an arrangement include the ability to work cooperatively and coordinate the details of one's job with another person.

Although not strictly a form of flexibility on the level of individual employees, another scheduling alternative is the *compressed workweek*. A compressed workweek is a schedule in which full-time workers complete their weekly hours in fewer than five days. For example, instead of working eight hours a day for five days, the employees could complete 40 hours of work in four 10-hour days. This alternative is most com-

flextime
A scheduling policy in which full-time employees may choose starting and ending times within guidelines specified by the organization.

job sharing
A work option in which two part-time employees carry out the tasks associated with a single job.

mon, but some companies use other alternatives, such as scheduling 80 hours over nine days (with a three-day weekend every other week) or reducing the workweek from 40 to 38 or 36 hours. Employees may appreciate the extra days available for leisure, family, or volunteer activities. An organization might even use this schedule to offer a kind of flexibility—for example, letting workers vote whether they want a compressed workweek during the summer months. This type of schedule has a couple of drawbacks, however. One is that employees may become exhausted on the longer workdays. Another is that if the arrangement involves working more than a specific number of hours during a week, Employment (Labour) Standards legislation may require the payment of overtime wages to nonsupervisory employees.

Telework

Flexibility can extend to work locations as well as work schedules. Before the Industrial Revolution, most people worked either close to or inside their own homes. Mass production technologies changed all this, separating work life from home life, as people began to travel to centrally located factories and offices. Today, however, skyrocketing prices for office space, combined with drastically reduced prices for portable communication and computing devices, seem ready to reverse this trend. The broad term for doing one's work away from a centrally located office is *telework* or telecommuting. Studies reveal that the cost savings from telework programs can top $8,000 per employee annually.

An example of a company that has benefited from telework is IBM, which initiated a program in which the company gave each teleworker an IBM ThinkPad notebook computer, printer, and extra home phone line. Marketing employees also were supplied with cellphones, pagers, faxes, and personal copiers. These workers, when not sharing office space at IBM headquarters, could use their equipment to work at home or at a customer's site. IBM found that teleworkers' productivity was higher than that of traditional workers, primarily because of the savings in commuting time and avoidance of distractions from coworkers. In addition, teleworkers were able to choose their most efficient times to work (sometimes very early in the morning or late at night) and were better able to fit work around personal obligations such as caring for a sick child. However, some teleworkers reported difficulty in maintaining the same level of teamwork and in separating home and work roles.[25]

Given the possible benefits, it is not surprising that telework is a growing trend. Definitions (and, therefore, statistics) differ, but the evidence suggests the trend is significant. Various companies, including Nortel Networks, Ontario Hydro, and Imperial Oil Ltd are among the large Canadian companies experimenting with telework.[26]

Saving commuting time and avoiding distractions, employees working at home or in a nontraditional workplace may be more productive. Would you like to work at home, or would you find it difficult to separate your home and work roles?

The president of the Canadian Telework Association estimates there are at least 1.5 million teleworkers in Canada but expects this number will soon grow to 2 million. Telework is also increasing around the world. A recent survey of global executives, conducted by the Economist Intelligence Unit for AT&T found that the number of companies where no one regularly works from home will drop from 46 percent last year to 20

FIGURE 3.9

Telework on the Rise
Around the World

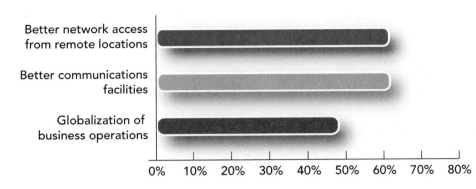

SOURCE: "Guide to HR Technology—On the Charts," *Canadian HR Reporter*, March 8, 2004, p. G3; Remote Working in the Net-Centric Organization. An AT&T survey and white paper in cooperation with the Economist Intelligence Unit. Copyright 2004.

percent next year.[27]   Figure 3.9 illustrates the driving forces that are causing the growth of telework.

Central British Columbia's Interior Health Authority delivers services to a region with difficult winter driving conditions, where in recent years a doctor and a nurse have been killed in motor vehicle accidents. Dr. David Stewart, urologist and chief of the department of surgery at the Royal Inland Hospital in Kamloops, is one of this growing number of Canadians accessing their workplace technologies from remote locations. Dr. Stewart uses a remote access system to examine X-ray images over the Internet while consulting with a local physician who can view the same image simultaneously. He can view patients' lab results and charts from his home computer before making his hospital rounds. As a result, Dr. Stewart has more time with his family, while the health authority, through accurate off-site diagnoses, reduces costs associated with unnecessary ambulance trips and hospital stays.[28]

Designing Ergonomic Jobs

LO8

The way people use their bodies when they work—whether toting heavy furniture onto a moving van or sitting quietly before a computer screen—affects their physical well-being and may affect how well and how long they can work. The study of the interface between individuals' physiology and the characteristics of the physical work environment is called **ergonomics.** The goal of ergonomics is to minimize physical strain on the worker by structuring the physical work environment around the way the human body works. Ergonomics therefore focuses on outcomes such as reducing physical fatigue, aches and pains, and health complaints.

Ergonomic job design has been applied in redesigning equipment used in jobs that are physically demanding. Such redesign is often aimed at reducing the physical demands of certain jobs so that anyone can perform them. In addition, many interventions focus on redesigning machines and technology—for instance, adjusting the height of a computer keyboard to minimize occupational illnesses, such as carpal tunnel syndrome. The design of chairs and desks to fit posture requirements is very important in many office jobs. One study found that having employees participate in an ergonomic redesign effort significantly reduced the number and severity of cumulative trauma disorders (injuries that result from performing the same movement over and over), lost production time, and restricted-duty days.[29]

ergonomics
The study of the interface between individuals' physiology and the characteristics of the physical work environment.

Ergonomically designed work equipment can minimize the strain on employees and lead to increased efficiencies.

Often, redesigning work to make it more worker-friendly also leads to increased efficiencies. For example, at International Truck and Engine Corporation, one of the most difficult aspects of truck production was pinning the axles to the truck frame. Traditionally, the frame was lowered onto the axle and a crew of six people, armed with oversized hammers and crowbars, forced the frame onto the axle. Because the workers could not see the bolts they had to tighten under the frame, the bolts were often fastened improperly, and many workers injured themselves in the process. After a brainstorming session, the workers and engineers concluded that it would be better to flip the frame upside down and attach the axles from above. The result was a job that could be done twice as fast by half as many workers, who were much less likely to make mistakes or get injured.[30]

Similarly, at a 3M plant, the company spent $60,000 on new ramps and forklifts specifically to help its aging workers lift crates filled with the company's product. The crates weighed over 125 pounds and were the source of numerous employee complaints. The result of this change in work processes was that productivity went up (expressed in terms of time to load trucks) and workers' compensation claims in the factory went to zero in the next year—down from an average of 20 over the last five years. These positive outcomes far outstripped the cost of the changes, again illustrating how a change aimed at improving the work from an ergonomic point of view often leads to cost savings as well.[31]

The Canadian Centre for Occupational Health and Safety identifies several workplace conditions that pose ergonomic hazards:[32]

- repetitive and forceful movements

- vibration

- temperature extremes

- awkward postures that arise from improper work methods

- improperly designed workstations, tools, and equipment

When jobs have these conditions, employers should be vigilant about opportunities to improve work design, for the benefit of both workers and the organization.

LO9

Designing Jobs That Meet Mental Capabilities and Limitations

Just as the human body has capabilities and limitations, addressed by ergonomics, the mind, too, has capabilities and limitations. Besides hiring people with certain mental skills, organizations can design jobs so that they can be accurately and safely performed given the way the brain processes information. Generally, this means reducing the information-processing requirements of a job. In these simpler jobs, workers may be less likely to make mistakes or have accidents. Of course, the simpler jobs also may be less motivating.

There are several ways to simplify a job's mental demands. One is to limit the amount of information and memorization that the job requires. Organizations can also provide adequate lighting, easy-to-understand gauges and displays, simple-to-operate equipment, and clear instructions. Often, employees try to simplify some of the mental demands of their own jobs by creating checklists, charts, or other aids. Finally, every job requires some degree of thinking, remembering, and paying attention, so for every job, organizations need to evaluate whether their employees can handle the job's mental demands.

Applying the perceptual approach to the job of cashier, electronic cash registers have simplified some aspects of this job. In the past, a cashier read the total price displayed by a cash register, received payment, then calculated any change due the customer. Today, most stores have cash registers that compute the change due and display that amount. The cash register display makes the job easier. However, some cashiers may have been proud of their ability to calculate change due, and for these people, the introduction of electronic cash registers may have reduced their job satisfaction. In this way, simplifying the mental demands of a job can also make it less interesting.

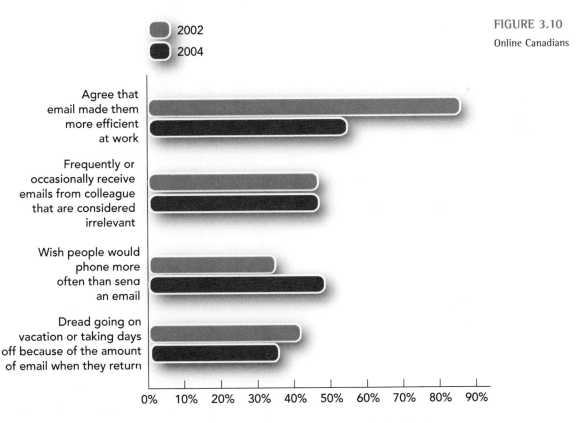

FIGURE 3.10

Online Canadians

SOURCE: "SPAM Volume Doubles," March 14, 2004, www.ipsos-na.com/news/pressrelease.cfm?id=2084. Retrieved: April 21, 2004.

Because of this drawback to simplifying jobs, it can be most beneficial to simplify jobs where employees will most appreciate having the mental demands reduced (as in a job that is extremely challenging) or where the costs of errors are severe (as in the job of a surgeon or air-traffic controller). A relatively recent source of complexity in many jobs is the need to process a daily flood of email messages. Canadian Internet users currently receive 197 emails each week on average, and approximately seven out of every ten of these emails are spam (electronic "junk mail"). This represents an increase of 60 percent from last year—the average Canadian Internet user receives almost 7,000 unsolicited emails in a year.[33] Many Canadians are concerned that the volume of email they receive is affecting their effectiveness. Figure 3.10 represents some findings from a recent study of online Canadians jointly conducted by Ipsos-Reid and Forge Marketing. It is clear that email has taken over a significant share of an 8-hour workday. Various studies estimate that office workers spend nearly an hour a day handling email, and top managers may spend four times that much handling their messages. Ferris Research, a U.S. market research firm, estimates that companies in Canada and the United States lose $10 billion in time deleting junk emails.[34]

Organizations take various steps to manage this challenge. Many have established policies—for example, limiting personal use of company email and restricting the number of Internet discussion groups to which employees may subscribe. Some companies delete email messages once a month. Another alternative is to install software that filters spam (electronic "junk mail"). Programs such as SpamKiller, Spam Buster, and Brightmail look for and block messages that match spam databases or have characteristics of spam. Of course, generators of spam continuously look for ways to evade these filters, so individual employees must develop ways of managing email, just as they have simplified other aspects of their jobs in the past.[35]

Summary

1. Summarize the elements of work flow analysis.
The analysis identifies the amount and quality of a work unit's outputs, which may be products, parts of products, or services. Next, the analyst determines the work processes required to produce these outputs, breaking down tasks into those performed by each person in the work unit. Finally, the work flow analysis identifies the inputs used to carry out the processes and produce the outputs.

2. Describe how work flow is related to an organization's structure.
Within an organization, units and individuals must cooperate to create outputs, and the organization's structure brings people together for this purpose. The structure may be centralized or decentralized, and people may be grouped according to function or into divisions focusing on particular products or customer groups. A functional structure is most appropriate for people who perform highly specialized jobs and hold relatively little authority. Employee engagement and teamwork succeed best in a divisional structure. Because of these links between structure and types of jobs, considering such issues improves the success of job design.

3. Define the elements of a job analysis, and discuss their significance for human resource management.
Job analysis is the process of getting detailed information about jobs. It includes preparation of job descriptions and job specifications. A job description lists the tasks, duties, and responsibilities of a job. Job specifications look at the qualities needed in a person performing the job. They list the competencies, i.e. knowledge, skills, abilities, and other characteristics that are required for successful performance of a job. Job analysis provides a foundation for carrying out many HRM responsibilities, including work redesign, human resource planning, employee selection and training, performance appraisal, career planning, and job evaluation to determine pay scales.

4. Tell how to obtain information for a job analysis.
Information for analyzing an existing job often comes from incumbents and their supervisors. The federal gov-

ernment provides background information about jobs in the National Occupational Classification (NOC). Job analysts, employees, and managers may complete a Position Analysis Questionnaire or task analysis inventory, or fill out a survey for the Fleishman Job Analysis System.

5. Summarize recent trends in job analysis.
Some organizations are "dejobbing," or viewing organizations in terms of a field of work needing to be done, rather than as a set or series of jobs. These organizations look for employees who can take on different responsibilities as the field of work changes. Organizations are also adopting project-based structures and teamwork, which also require flexibility and the ability to handle broad responsibilities.

6. Describe methods for designing a job so that it can be done efficiently.
The basic technique for designing efficient jobs is industrial engineering, which looks for the simplest way to structure work in order to maximize efficiency. Through methods such as time-and-motion studies, the industrial engineer creates jobs that are relatively simple and typically repetitive. These jobs may bore workers because they are so simple.

7. Identify approaches to designing a job to make it motivating.
According to the Job Characteristics Model, jobs are more motivating if they have greater skill variety, task identity, task significance, autonomy, and feedback about performance effectiveness. Ways to create such jobs include job enlargement (through job extension or job rotation) and job enrichment. In addition, self-managing work teams offer greater skill variety and task identity. Flexible work schedules and telework offer greater autonomy.

8. Explain how organizations apply ergonomics to design safe jobs.
The goal of ergonomics is to minimize physical strain on the worker by structuring the physical work environment around the way the human body works. Ergonomic design may involve modifying equipment to reduce the physical demands of performing certain jobs or redesigning the jobs themselves to reduce strain. Ergonomic design may target working conditions associated with ergonomic hazards including repetitive and forceful movements, vibration, temperature extremes, and awkward postures that arise from improper work methods and improperly designed workstations, tools, and equipment.

9. Discuss how organizations can plan for the mental demands of a job.
Employers may seek to reduce mental as well as physical strain. The job design may limit the amount of information and memorization involved. Adequate lighting, easy-to-read gauges and displays, simple-to-operate equipment, and clear instructions also can minimize mental strain. Computer software can simplify jobs—for example, by performing calculations or filtering out spam from relevant email. Finally, organizations can select employees with the necessary abilities to handle a job's mental demands.

Review and Discussion Questions

1. Assume you are the manager of a fast-food restaurant. What are the outputs of your work unit? What are the activities required to produce those outputs? What are the inputs?
2. Based on question 1, consider the cashier's job in the restaurant. What are the outputs, activities, and inputs for that job?
3. Consider the "job" of university or college student. Perform a job analysis on this job. What tasks are required in the job? What competencies are necessary to perform those tasks? Prepare a job description based on your analysis.
4. Discuss how the following trends are changing the skill requirements for managerial jobs in Canada:
   a. Increasing use of computers and the Internet.
   b. Increasing global competition.
   c. Increasing work-family conflicts.

5. How can a job analysis of each job in the work unit help a supervisor to do his or her job?
6. Consider the job of a customer service representative who fields telephone calls from customers of a retailer that sells online and through catalogues. What measures can an employer take to design this job to make it efficient? What might be some drawbacks or challenges of designing this job for efficiency?
7. How might the job in question 6 be designed to make it more motivating? Would these considerations apply to the manager's job in question 1?
8. What ergonomic considerations might apply to each of the following jobs? For each job, what kinds of costs would result from addressing ergonomics? What costs might result from failing to address ergonomics?
   a. A computer programmer.
   b. A FedEx delivery person.
   c. A child care worker.

9. The chapter states that modern electronics have eliminated the need for a store's cashiers to calculate change due on a purchase. How does this development modify the job description for a cashier? If you were a store manager, how would it affect the skills and qualities of job candidates you would want to hire? Does this change in mental processing requirements affect what you would expect from a cashier? How?

10. Consider a job you hold now or have held recently. Would you want this job to be redesigned to place more emphasis on efficiency, motivation, ergonomics, or mental processing? What changes would you want, and why? (Or why do you not want the job to be redesigned?)

What's Your HR IQ?   www.mcgrawhill.ca/college/noe

The Online Learning Centre offers more ways to check what you've learned so far. Find experiential exercises as well as Test Your Knowledge Quizzes, Videos, and many other resources at www.mcgrawhill.ca/college/noe.

Case: SiteSell Inc.—A Teleworking Company

SiteSell Inc. president Ken Evoy happily admits he doesn't have a clue what his employees do during the regular workday. He's never seen most of his customer support staff in the flesh, and considers his Australia-based programmer a good friend, despite having never met him. Indeed, Dr. Evoy only knows most of his 36 employees as a voice on the phone, or a name on an email. SiteSell sells Site Build It!, a product allowing small businesses and work-from-home types to get (and get noticed) online. According to Internet tracker, Alexa.com, SiteSell is ranked as one of the top 30 best business sites on the Web.

"I don't know whether my employee is working at four in the morning, or whether he's asleep at four in the morning" the intense, ever-smiling Dr. Evoy said. "All I measure is one thing: output."

Since its inception in 1998, SiteSell has been a teleworking—or telecommuting—company in the truest form of the term. The company, which sells Internet business development software, has no head office. Dr. Evoy directs business behind three gigantic plasma screens at his home in Hudson, about 45 minutes outside of Montreal.

He has none of the workaday hassles associated with your average nine-to-fiver. He doesn't wear a tie, he doesn't have to go outside in the minus 30-degree weather, and the only commuting he does is in his slippers—usually from the office to the kitchen.

SiteSell employees meanwhile, are scattered around the globe. There are software people in Australia, England, and France. In Kentucky, an employee works for the company's telemarketing and email sales—a department headed by an associate in the tiny Caribbean island of Anguilla. By not having an office, Dr. Evoy estimates that he saves nearly $800,000 a year. Employees supply their own computers and Internet connections. The regular staff meetings are done by conference calls and through a blizzard of emails.

His employees "would get chewed up in a big company," according to Dr. Evoy. "They're not game players, they're not politicians, they're not strokers. They're the kind of people who get taken advantage of in a big company. They're self-motivated, they work hard, they put out good quality work, [but] they don't self-promote very well. This doesn't count when it comes to teleworking. All that counts is quality and quantity of the work you put out. It speaks for itself, there can be no game playing."

As a purely telework-based company, SiteSell is somewhat of an anomaly in Canada, according to InnoVisions Canada, a telework consulting organization. "Most people have not clued in yet," said InnoVisions president Bob Fortier, noting that the lion's share of Canada's teleworkers work for larger, office-based companies."

SOURCE: Martin Patriquin, "Staff Get Along Without Meeting in Person," *Special to The Globe and Mail*—Telework, March 4, 2004, www.globeandmail.com. Retrieved: April 22, 2004 and www.Sitesellinc.com.

Questions

1. How does teleworking impact the tasks, duties, and responsibilities of jobs at SiteSell?

2. What are the benefits of telework to SiteSell? What are the benefits of telework to SiteSell employees?

3. As Site Sell continues to grow and add employees, does telework pose any challenges to human resource management? Suggest some ways SiteSell might meet these challenges.

Case: Mapping Competencies to Create a Job Profile for a Nurse Specialist

UK Health Departments have collaborated to develop a competency framework for Public Health Practice that will be used in four countries to develop the public health workforce. The Coronary Heart Disease National Workforce Competency Framework provides uniform language and clarification of skills to recognize and ensure transferability of competencies across the various disciplines.

The North Devon District Hospital, Barnstaple recently applied for funding of a specialized nursing unit as part of the coronary care unit to serve five hospitals in the area. In preparation, the hospital needed to identify the required duties and competency requirements for nurses employed in the District Hospital as well as for outreach nurses who will provide services to other hospitals and offer home visits to patients.

The National Framework provided an extensive schedule of job responsibilities to consider in developing the job duties of the coronary care nurses. Examples include:

- Contribute to the planning, implementation and evaluation of therapeutic programs to enable individuals to manage their behaviour
- Contribute to raising awareness of health issues
- Contribute to the support, care, and monitoring of patients undergoing clinical procedures
- Represent individuals' and families' interests when they are not able to do so themselves

The comprehensive framework of competencies included:

- IT skills
- Leadership
- Communication skills
- Customer focus
- Team working, including the emphasis on multi-disciplinary learning
- Customer focus
- Managing diversity

Job descriptions for the North Devon District Hospital's nurses in the new coronary care unit were created and mapped to the competency framework. These job descriptions provide detailed guidance to existing staff to determine required roles and to determine any required training or development needs to match the competencies required. In addition it is envisioned that this process will enable the team to provide a standardized level of quality and patient referral standards for the unit.

SOURCE: Adapted from "Public Health Practice National Competence Framework" and "Case Study: Service Development North Devon District Hospital, Barnstaple," www.skillsofrhealth.org.uk/. Retrieved: April 30, 2004.

Questions

1. What areas of HRM will likely be affected because of this job responsibility and competency identification initiative?
2. How would the developments discussed in the case influence the roles and responsibilities of HR professionals in the health system?
3. How would the developments discussed in the case influence the competency requirements of HR professionals in the health system?

4

Planning for and Recruiting Human Resources

1. Discuss how to plan for human resources needed to carry out the organization's strategy.

2. Determine the labour demand for workers in various job categories.

3. Summarize the advantages and disadvantages of ways to eliminate a labour surplus and avoid a labour shortage.

4. Describe recruitment policies organizations use to make job vacancies more attractive.

5. List and compare sources of job applicants.

6. Describe the recruiter's role in the recruitment process, including limits and opportunities.

Introduction

Would you meet the eligibility requirements to immigrate to Canada as a skilled worker? The Citizenship and Immigration Canada website (www.cic.gc.ca) provides a test to help potential immigrants assess whether they would meet the requirements to immigrate to Canada as a skilled worker. The passing grade is 75 points. Maximum

Weiling Qian, a systems engineer from China, left, and Agnes van Haeren, the human resource manager for Motorola Canada, who hired Ms. Qian as an intern under the Career Bridge program: "I began to look for a job but employment agents who saw my résumé said I needed Canadian experience," Ms. Qian says.

points for education—25 points—requires applicants to have at least 17 years of schooling and to hold a master's or Ph.D. degree (two bachelor's degrees earns 22 points; a college diploma earns 20 points). Other criteria include work experience in a skilled profession, language proficiency in English (or French), and age (10 points if you are 21 to 49 years old).[1]

Although Canada will require immigrants to fill various jobs and meet demand for skilled workers, internationally trained professionals face recruitment barriers. Ontario recently announced a $4-million program to assist internationally trained professionals in teaching, engineering, and health care gain access to jobs without duplicating education and training received outside Canada. One specific initiative, Career Bridge, provides employers in the Greater Toronto area with access to skilled, experienced immigrants in areas including information technology, engineering, and manufacturing.[2]

Trends and events that affect the economy create opportunities and problems in obtaining human resources. When customer demand rises (or falls), organizations may need more (or fewer) employees. When the labour market changes—say, when more people pursue post-secondary education or when a sizable share of the population retires—the supply of qualified workers may grow, shrink, or change in nature. Organizations recently have had difficulty filling information technology jobs because the demand for people with these skills outstrips the supply. To prepare for and respond to these challenges, organizations engage in *human resource planning*—defined in Chapter 1 as identifying the numbers and types of employees the organization will require to meet its objectives.

This chapter describes how organizations carry out human resource planning. In the first part of the chapter, we lay out the steps that go into developing and implementing a human resource plan. Throughout each section, we focus especially on recent trends and practices, including downsizing, employing temporary workers, and outsourcing. The remainder of the chapter explores the process of recruiting. We describe the process by which organizations look for people to fill job vacancies and the usual sources of job candidates. Finally, we discuss the role of recruiters.

LO1

The Process of Human Resource Planning

Organizations should carry out human resource planning so as to meet business objectives and gain an advantage over competitors. To do this, organizations need a clear idea of the strengths and weaknesses of their existing internal labour force. They also must know what they want to be doing in the future—what size they want the organization to be, what products and services it should be producing, and so on. This knowledge helps them define the number and kinds of employees they will need. Human resource planning compares the present state of the organization with its goals for the future, then identifies what changes it must make in its human resources to meet those goals. The changes may include downsizing, training existing employees in new skills, or hiring new employees.

These activities give a general view of HR planning. They take place in the human resource planning process shown in Figure 4.1. The process consists of three stages: forecasting, goal setting and strategic planning, and program implementation and evaluation.

Forecasting

forecasting
The attempts to determine the supply of and demand for various types of human resources to predict areas within the organization where there will be labour shortages or surpluses.

The first step in human resource planning is **forecasting,** as shown in the top portion of Figure 4.1. In forecasting, the HR professional tries to determine the supply of and demand for various types of human resources. The primary goal is to predict which areas of the organization will experience labour shortages or surpluses.

Forecasting supply and demand can use statistical methods or judgment. Statistical methods capture historic trends in a company's demand for labour. Under the right conditions, these methods predict demand and supply more precisely than a human forecaster can using subjective judgment. But many important events in the labour market have no precedent. When such events occur, statistical methods are of little use. To prepare for these situations, the organization must rely on the subjective judgments of experts. Pooling their "best guesses" is an important source of ideas about the future.

FIGURE 4.1

Overview of the Human Resource Planning Process

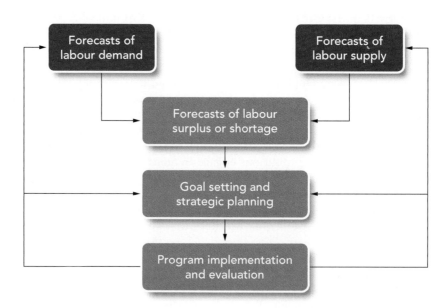

Forecasting the Demand for Labour

Usually, an organization forecasts demand for specific job categories or skill areas. After identifying the relevant job categories or skills, the planner investigates the likely demand for each. The planner must forecast whether the need for people with the necessary skills and experience will increase or decrease. There are several ways of making such forecasts.

At the most sophisticated level, an organization might use **trend analysis,** constructing and applying statistical models that predict labour demand for the next year, given relatively objective statistics from the previous year. These statistics are called **leading indicators**—objective measures that accurately predict future labour demand. They might include measures of the economy (such as sales or inventory levels), actions of competitors, changes in technology, and trends in the composition of the workforce. For example, a manufacturer of automobile parts that sells its product to automakers would use statistics on the auto industry, using the numbers from recent time periods to predict the demand for the company's product in a later time period.

Statistical planning models are useful when there is a long, stable history that can be used to reliably detect relationships among variables. However, these models almost always have to be complemented with subjective judgments of experts. There are simply too many "once-in-a-lifetime" changes to consider, and statistical models cannot capture them.

trend analysis
Constructing and applying statistical models that predict labour demand for the next year, given relatively objective statistics from the previous year.

leading indicators
Objective measures that accurately predict future labour demand.

Determining Labour Supply

Once a company has forecast the demand for labour, it needs an indication of the firm's labour supply. Determining the internal labour supply calls for a detailed analysis of how many people are currently in various job categories or have specific skills within the organization. The planner then modifies this analysis to reflect changes expected in the near future as a result of retirements, promotions, transfers, voluntary turnover, and terminations.

One type of statistical procedure that can be used for this purpose is the analysis of a **transitional matrix.** This is a chart that lists job categories held in one period and shows the proportion of employees in each of those job categories in a future period. It answers two questions: "Where did people who were in each job category go?" and "Where did people now in each job category come from?" Table 4.1 is an example of a transitional matrix.

transitional matrix
A chart that lists job categories held in one period and shows the proportion of employees in each of those job categories in a future period.

TABLE 4.1

Transitional Matrix: Example for an Auto Parts Manufacturer

2001	2004							
	(1)	(2)	(3)	(4)	(5)	(6)	(7)	(8)
(1) Sales manager	.95							.05
(2) Sales representative	.05	.60						.35
(3) Sales apprentice		.20	.50					.30
(4) Assistant plant manager				.90	.05			.05
(5) Production manager				.10	.75			.15
(6) Production assembler					.10	.80		.10
(7) Clerical							.70	.30
(8) Not in organization	.00	.20	.50	.00	.10	.20	.30	

This example lists job categories for an auto parts manufacturer. The jobs listed at the left were held in 2001; the numbers at the right show what happened to the people in 2004. The numbers represent proportions. For example, .95 means 95 percent of the people represented by a row in the matrix. The column headings under 2004 refer to the row numbers. The first row is sales managers, so the numbers under column (1) represent people who became sales managers. Reading across the first row, we see that 95 of the people who were sales managers in 2001 are still sales managers in 2004. The other 5 percent correspond to position (8), "Not in organization," meaning the 5 percent of employees who are not still sales managers have left the organization. In the second row are sales representatives. Of those who were sales reps in 2001, 5 percent were promoted to sales manager, 60 percent are still sales reps, and 35 percent have left the organization. In row (3), half (50 percent) of sales apprentices are still in that job, but 20 percent are now sales reps, and 30 percent have left the organization. This pattern of jobs shows a career path from sales apprentice to sales representative to sales manager. Of course, not everyone is promoted, and some of the people leave instead.

Reading down the columns provides another kind of information: the sources of employees holding the positions in 2004. In the first column, we see that most sales managers (95 percent) held that same job three years earlier. The other 5 percent were promoted from sales representative positions. Skipping over to column (3), half the sales apprentices on the payroll in 2004 held the same job three years before, and the other half were hired from outside the organization. This suggests that the organization fills sales manager positions primarily through promotions, so planning for this job would focus on preparing sales representatives. In contrast, planning to meet the organization's needs for sales apprentices would emphasize recruitment and selection of new employees.

Matrices such as this one are extremely useful for charting historical trends in the company's supply of labour. More important, if conditions remain somewhat constant, they can also be used to plan for the future. For example, if we believe that we are going to have a surplus of labour in the production assembler job category in the next three years, we can plan to avoid layoffs. Still, historical data may not always reliably indicate future trends. Planners need to combine statistical forecasts of labour supply with expert judgments. For example, managers in the organization may see that a new training program will likely increase the number of employees qualified for new openings. Forecasts of labour supply also should take into account the organization's pool of skills. Many organizations include inventories of employees' skills in an HR database. When the organization forecasts that it will need new skills in the future, planners can consult the database to see how many existing employees have those skills.

Besides looking at the labour supply within the organization, the planner should examine trends in the external labour market. The planner should keep abreast of labour market forecasts, including the size of the labour market, the unemployment rate, and the kinds of people who will be in the labour market. For example, we saw in Chapter 1 that the labour market is aging and that immigration is an important source of new workers. Important sources of data on the external labour market are available from Statistics Canada. Details and news releases (*The Daily*) are available at the Statistics Canada website (www.statcan.ca).

Determining Labour Surplus or Shortage

Based on the forecasts for labour demand and supply, the planner can compare the figures to determine whether there will be a shortage or surplus of labour for each job category. Determining expected shortages and surpluses allows the organization to plan how to address these challenges.

Japan's Matsushita Corporation has benefited from accurate forecasting. Much of Matsushita's revenues come from exporting, so a leading indicator for its labour demand is the value of the Japanese yen against other currencies. When the yen is high, sales in other countries tend to be low, because Matsushita's prices are relatively high. When the yen's value falls, Matsushita's prices in other currencies fall, so sales in other countries rise. Logically, when sales of Japanese products rise or fall, the demand for Japanese labour changes in the same direction. In 1988 Matsushita's planners accurately forecasted a large increase in the price of the yen, which could cause falling demand and an oversupply of Japanese labour. Rather than expanding in Japan, Matsushita opened "export centres," which designed and produced televisions and air conditioners in Malaysia, China, and the United States. When the yen's price rose as expected, Matsushita's export centres were very successful.[3] Meanwhile, Japanese companies that had failed to accurately predict labour demand had to lay off workers—an act almost unprecedented in Japan until that time.[4]

Goal Setting and Strategic Planning

LO3

The second step in human resource planning is goal setting and strategic planning, as shown in the middle of Figure 4.1. The purpose of setting specific numerical goals is to focus attention on the problem and provide a basis for measuring the organization's success in addressing labour shortages and surpluses. The goals should come directly from the analysis of labour supply and demand. They should include a specific figure

TABLE 4.2

HR Strategies for Addressing a Labour Shortage or Surplus

OPTIONS FOR REDUCING A SURPLUS		
OPTION	**SPEED OF RESULTS**	**AMOUNT OF SUFFERING CAUSED**
Downsizing	Fast	High
Pay reductions	Fast	High
Demotions	Fast	High
Transfers	Fast	Moderate
Work sharing	Fast	Moderate
Hiring freeze	Slow	Low
Natural attrition	Slow	Low
Early retirement	Slow	Low
Retraining	Slow	Low

OPTIONS FOR AVOIDING A SHORTAGE		
OPTION	**SPEED OF RESULTS**	**ABILITY TO CHANGE LATER**
Overtime	Fast	High
Temporary employees	Fast	High
Outsourcing	Fast	High
Retrained transfers	Slow	High
Turnover reductions	Slow	Moderate
New external hires	Slow	Low
Technological innovation	Slow	Low

indicating what should happen with the job category or skill area and a specific timetable for when the results should be achieved.

For each goal, the organization must choose one or more human resource strategies. A variety of strategies is available for handling expected shortages and surpluses of labour. The top of Table 4.2 shows major options for reducing an expected labour surplus, and the bottom of the table lists options for avoiding an expected labour shortage.

This planning stage is critical. The options differ widely in their expense, speed, and effectiveness. Options for reducing a labour surplus cause differing amounts of human suffering. The options for avoiding a labour shortage differ in terms of how easily the organization can undo the change if it no longer faces a labour shortage. For example, an organization probably would not want to handle every expected labour surplus by hiring new employees. The process is relatively slow and involves expenses to find and train new employees. Also, if the shortage becomes a surplus, the organization will have to consider laying off some of the employees. Layoffs involve another set of expenses, such as severance pay, and they are costly in terms of human suffering.

Another consideration in choosing an HR strategy is whether the employees needed will contribute directly to the organization's success. Organizations are most likely to benefit from hiring and retaining employees who provide an organizational **core competency**—that is, a set of knowledge and skills that provide the organization with a competitive advantage. These core competencies taken together form a competency framework as discussed in Chapter 3. At a store, for example, core competencies include choosing merchandise that shoppers want and providing shoppers with excellent service. For other work that is not associated with a core competency—say, cleaning the store and providing security—the organization may benefit from using HR strategies other than hiring full-time employees.

Organizations try to anticipate labour surpluses far enough ahead that they can freeze hiring and let natural attrition (people leaving on their own) reduce the labour force. Unfortunately for many workers, in the past decade, the typical way organizations have responded to a surplus of labour has been downsizing, which delivers fast results. Beyond the obvious economic impact, downsizing has a psychological impact that spills over and affects families, increasing the rates of divorce, child abuse, and drug and alcohol addiction.[5] To handle a labour shortage, organizations typically hire temporary employees or use outsourcing. Because downsizing, using temporary employees, and outsourcing are most common, we will look at each of these in greater detail in the following sections.

Downsizing

As we discussed in Chapter 1, **downsizing** is the planned elimination of large numbers of employees with the goal of enhancing the organization's competitiveness. Nortel Networks has gone through major downsizing worldwide. Nortel has cut approximately 60,000 jobs and is now only about one-third of it's former size.[6] Over 85 percent of the *Fortune* 1,000 firms downsized between 1987 and 2001, resulting in more than 8 million permanent layoffs. The jobs eliminated were not temporary losses due to downturns in the business cycle, but permanent losses resulting from changes in the competitive pressures faced by businesses today. In fact, eight out of every ten companies that underwent downsizing were earning a profit at the same time.[7]

core competency
A set of knowledge and skills that provide the organization with a competitive advantage.

downsizing
The planned elimination of large numbers of personnel with the goal of enhancing the organization's competitiveness.

The primary reason organizations engage in downsizing is to promote future competitiveness. According to surveys, they do this by meeting four objectives:

1. *Reducing costs*—Labour is a large part of a company's total costs, so downsizing is an attractive place to start cutting costs.
2. *Replacing labour with technology*—Closing outdated factories, automating, or introducing other technological changes reduces the need for labour. Often, the labour savings outweighs the cost of the new technology.
3. *Mergers and acquisitions*—When organizations combine, they often need less bureaucratic overhead, so they lay off managers and some professional staff members.
4. *Moving to more economical locations*—In recent years, British Columbia has been attractive to U.S. film and television production companies. Other moves, however, have shifted Canadian jobs to other countries. Celestica Inc. announced that it would close an electronics factory employing 700 people in the Montreal area. Celestica has been shifting operations from North America and Western Europe to low-cost Asian countries.[8]

Although the jury is still out on whether these downsizing efforts have enhanced performance, some indications are that the results have *not* lived up to expectations. According to a recent study of 52 *Fortune* 100 firms, most firms that announced a downsizing campaign showed worse, rather than better, financial performance in the years that followed.[9]

Why do so many downsizing efforts fail to meet expectations? There seem to be several reasons. First, although the initial cost savings give a temporary boost to profits, the long-term effects of an improperly managed downsizing effort can be negative. Downsizing leads to a loss of talent, and it often disrupts the social networks through which people are creative and flexible.[10] When Roche Holding acquired Syntex Corporation, half the Syntex jobs were eliminated. Most of the employees left voluntarily, taking advantage of a lucrative severance package that included two to three years of full compensation. Many felt that this downsizing strategy encouraged turnover among the best, most marketable scientists and managers.[11]

Also, many companies wind up rehiring. Downsizing campaigns often eliminate people who turn out to be irreplaceable. In one survey, 80 percent of the firms that had downsized wound up replacing some of the very people they had laid off. One senior manager of a *Fortune* 100 firm described a situation in which a bookkeeper making $9 an hour was let go. Later, the company realized she knew many things about the company that no one else knew, so she was hired back as a consultant—for $42 an hour.[12] Hiring back formerly laid-off workers has become so routine that many organizations track their laid-off employees, using software formerly used for tracking job applicants. If the organization ever faces a labour shortage, it can quickly contact these former workers and restore them to the payroll.[13]

Finally, downsizing efforts often fail because employees who survive the purge become self-absorbed and afraid to take risks. Motivation drops because any hope of future promotions—or any future—with the company dies. Many employees start looking for other employment opportunities. The negative publicity associated with a downsizing campaign can also

A Japanese worker passes by a laid-off white-collar worker in Tokyo's Hibiya park. The park is a common place for white-collar victims of downsizing to spend their days. Layoffs can be costly because of severance pay, and have severe repercussions in terms of human suffering.

hurt the company's image in the labour market, so it is harder to recruit employees later. The key to avoiding this kind of damage is to ensure that the need for the layoff is well explained and that procedures for carrying out the layoff are fair.[14] Although this advice may sound like common sense, organizations are often reluctant to provide complete information, especially when a layoff results from top-level mismanagement.[15]

Many problems with downsizing can be reduced with better planning. The "HR How To" box offers guidelines for carrying out downsizing. Still, downsizing hardly guarantees an increase in an organization's competitiveness. Organizations should more carefully consider using all the other avenues for eliminating a labour surplus (shown in Table 4.2). Many of these take effect slowly, so organizations must improve their forecasting or be stuck with downsizing as their only viable option.

Early-Retirement Programs

Another popular way to reduce a labour surplus is with an early-retirement program. As we discussed in Chapter 1, the average age of the Canadian workforce is increasing. But even though many baby boomers are approaching traditional retirement age, early indications are that this group has no intention of retiring soon.[16] Several forces fuel the drawing out of older workers' careers. First, the improved health of older people in general, combined with the decreased physical labour required by many jobs, has made working longer a viable option. Also, many workers fear their retirement savings and pension plans supplemented by the Canada Pension Plan will still not be enough to cover their expenses. Finally, protection from discrimination and the variations within Canada with respect to mandatory retirement ages have limited organizations' ability to induce older workers to retire. Under the pressures associated with an aging labour force, many employers try to encourage older workers to leave voluntarily by offering a variety of early-retirement incentives. The more lucrative of these programs succeed by some measures. Research suggests that these programs encourage lower-performing older workers to retire.[17] Sometimes they work so well that too many workers retire.

Many organizations are moving from early-retirement programs to phased-retirement programs. In a *phased-retirement program*, the organization can continue to enjoy the experience of older workers while reducing the number of hours that these employees work, as well as the cost of those employees. This option also can give older employees the psychological benefit of easing into retirement, rather than being thrust entirely into a new way of life.[18]

Employing Temporary Workers

While downsizing has been a popular way to reduce a labour surplus, the most widespread methods for eliminating a labour shortage are hiring temporary workers and outsourcing work. Temporary employment is popular with employers because it gives them flexibility they need to operate efficiently when demand for their products changes rapidly. Adecco Group, one of the world's largest staffing services companies, estimates that temporary staffing accounts for $140 billion of revenues worldwide.[19] Adecco has nearly 650,000 associates on payroll on an average day serving 100,000 clients from 5,800 offices worldwide. During the year, Adecco employs close to 4 million people.[20]·

In addition to flexibility, temporary employment offers lower costs. Using temporary workers frees the employer from many administrative tasks and financial burdens

Minimizing the Pain of Layoffs

Although layoffs are always painful, handling the task well can maintain employees' dignity and improve the organization's long-term health. Helen Drinan, chief executive officer of the Society for Human Resource Management, offers advice on minimizing the pain of layoffs. Here's what she recommends:

- *Communicate fully.* As soon as you know about layoffs, tell employees the news, in detail. First tell the people who will be laid off. Then tell the whole group what you are doing and why. If there's information you *don't* know, disclose that, too.
- *Involve managers to make choices.* The company's executives shouldn't decide precisely which people to lay off. People who are closer to the situation should be involved in such decisions.
- *Ask laid-off employees to leave immediately, but be humane about it.* It's probably unwise to let employees hang around for days, using the company's phones and computers. Still, you don't have to send over a security guard to usher the employees out of the building. Ways to be humane include offering to stay late and help pack personal belongings, providing an outplacement service, and offering to be a reference in the laid-off employee's job hunt.
- *Budget for layoffs.* Plan to give laid-off employees at least two weeks' severance pay, plus more based on years of employment. If possible, include outplacement services in the layoff budget.
- *Plan ahead.* Even when times are good, managers know that downsizing is often part of an organization's strategy. Drinan recommends the mental exercise of asking what you would do if the organization had to reduce its staff by 10 percent.

Why go to all this trouble for a change that is essentially about cutting costs? Quite simply, because even after layoffs, an organization still needs dedicated, talented people. In Drinan's words, "You want to treat [laid-off] people well, because this becomes an object lesson for everyone in your organization about how you treat employees."

SOURCE: Mike Hofman, "Five Rules for Making Layoffs Less Painful," *Inc.*, April 2001, pp. 97–98.

associated with being the "employer of record." The cost of employee benefits, including vacations, pension, life insurance, workers' compensation, and employment insurance, accounted for 40 percent of payroll expenses for permanent employees.

Agencies that provide temporary employees also may handle some of the tasks associated with hiring. Small companies that cannot afford their own testing programs often get employees who have been tested by a temporary agency.

Many temporary agencies train employees before sending them to employers. This reduces employers' training costs and eases the transition for the temporary worker and employer. When United Parcel Service (UPS) signed on with a temporary agency to supply data-entry personnel, the agency designed a computer screen that simulates those used at UPS. A temporary worker assigned to UPS must be able to enter data at a minimum speed on the simulated screens.[21]

Finally, temporary workers may offer benefits not available from permanent employees. Because the temporary worker has little experience at the employer's organi-

Companies such as Adecco offer organizations flexible staffing solutions to meet changing operational and business requirements.

zation, this person brings an objective point of view to the organization's problems and procedures. Also, a temporary worker may have a great deal of experience in other organizations.

To benefit from using temporary workers, organizations must overcome the disadvantages associated with this type of labour force. One drawback is that tension often exists between temporary and permanent employees. According to surveys, one-third of full-time employees perceive temporary workers as a threat to their own job security. Such an attitude can interfere with cooperation and, in some cases, lead to outright sabotage if the situation is not well managed.

One way organizations should manage this situation is to complete any downsizing efforts before bringing in temporary workers. Surviving a downsizing is almost like experiencing a death in the family. In this context, a reasonable time interval needs to occur before new temporary workers are introduced. Without the delay, the surviving employees will associate the downsizing effort (which was a threat) with the new temporary employees (who could be perceived as outsiders brought in to replace old friends). If an upswing in demand follows a downsizing effort, the organization should probably begin meeting its expanded demand for labour by granting overtime to core employees. If the demand persists, the organization will be more certain that the upswing will last and future layoffs will be unnecessary. The extended stretches of overtime will eventually tax the full-time employees, so they will accept using temporary workers to help lessen their load.

Organizations that use temporary workers must avoid treating them as second-class citizens. One way to do this is to ensure that the temporary agency provides temporaries with benefits that are comparable with those enjoyed by the organization's permanent workers. For example, one temporary agency, MacTemps, gives its workers long-term health coverage, full disability insurance, and complete dental coverage. This not only reduces the benefit gap between the temporary and permanent workers but also helps attract the best temporary workers in the first place.

Outsourcing

Instead of using a temporary employee to fill a single job, an organization might want a broader set of services. As discussed in Chapter 1, contracting with another organization to perform a broad set of services is called outsourcing.

A major reason outsourcing can save money is that the outside company specializes in the services and can benefit from economies of scale (the economic principle that producing something in large volume tends to cost less for each additional unit than producing in small volume). Several years ago, Ford Motor Company had a unit that processed applications for financing from people who wanted to buy Ford cars and trucks. Now Ford hands this work over to MCN Corporation, which can do the same job with fewer people than Ford had used. MCN's computers and staff are dedicated to processing data for Ford (and over 25 other companies). Their efficiency comes from a narrow focus on data entry and analysis, free from the need to produce automobiles. Outsourcing is logical when an organization lacks certain kinds of expertise and doesn't want to invest in developing that expertise.

Outsourcing in manufacturing often involves designing products in North America and shipping manufacturing responsibilities overseas, where production costs can be 10 to 60 percent less. Apple introduced a laptop computer produced by Sony, and Motorola set up equipment production centres in Hong Kong. In the service industry, data-entry jobs often are outsourced. Metropolitan Life Insurance has its medical claims analyzed in Ireland, where operating costs are about 35 percent less than in the United States. The labour forces of countries like China, India, Jamaica, and those of Eastern Europe are creating an abundant supply of labour for unskilled and low-skilled work. Figure 4.2 provides a comparison of international salaries and Canadian salaries for programmers.

Technological advances in computer networks and transmission have speeded up the outsourcing process and have helped it spread beyond manufacturing areas and low-skilled jobs. For companies that perform design engineering or software development, India is a fertile ground for outsourcing this type of work.

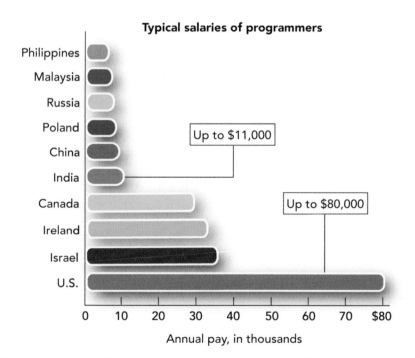

FIGURE 4.2

Wages in Many Countries are Significantly Lower than in Canada and the U.S.

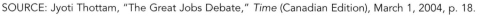

SOURCE: Jyoti Thottam, "The Great Jobs Debate," *Time* (Canadian Edition), March 1, 2004, p. 18.

Although outsourcing manufacturing may make good sense in the short term, it may hurt North American firms' competitiveness. Outsourcing reduces manufacturing costs, but companies eventually will have more and more difficulty designing products that apply innovations in technology. According to this argument, unrestrained outsourcing starts a downward spiral of more and more outsourcing until the organization no longer produces anything of value. Companies that manufacture goods develop their own design teams and compete directly and with a substantial competitive advantage.

Overtime and Expanded Hours

Organizations facing a labour shortage may be reluctant to hire employees, even temporary workers, or to commit to an outsourcing arrangement. Especially if the organization expects the shortage to be temporary, it may prefer an arrangement that is simpler and less costly. Under some conditions, these organizations may try to garner more hours from the existing labour force. Many employers opted for this strategy during the 1990s. As a result, 6 percent of the automobiles assembled in North America in 1997 resulted from overtime production—equivalent to the output of an additional four auto plants running on straight time (no overtime).[22]

A major downside of overtime is that the employer must pay nonmanagement employees additional pay above and beyond their normal wages for work done overtime. Even so, employers see overtime pay as preferable to the costs of hiring and training new employees. The preference is especially strong if the organization doubts that the current higher level of demand for its products will last long.

For a short time at least, many workers appreciate the added compensation for working overtime. Over extended periods, however, employees feel stress and frustration from working long hours. Overtime therefore is best suited for short-term labour shortages.

Implementing and Evaluating the HR Plan

For whatever HR strategies are selected, the final stage of human resource planning involves implementing the strategies and evaluating the outcomes. This stage is represented by the bottom part of Figure 4.1. When implementing the HR strategy, the organization must hold some individual accountable for achieving the goals. That person also must have the authority and resources needed to accomplish those goals. It is also important that this person issue regular progress reports, so the organization can be sure that all activities occur on schedule and that the early results are as expected.

In evaluating the results, the most obvious step is checking whether the organization has succeeded in avoiding labour shortages or surpluses. Along with measuring these numbers, the evaluation should identify which parts of the planning process contributed to success or failure.

Applying HR Planning to Employment Equity

As we discussed in Chapter 2, many organizations have a human resource strategy that includes employment equity to manage diversity or meet government requirements. Meeting employment equity goals requires that employers carry out an additional level of human resource planning aimed at those goals. In other words, besides looking at its overall workforce and needs, the organization looks at the representation of subgroups in its labour force—for example, the proportion of women and visible minorities.

Employment equity plans forecast and monitor the proportion of employees who are members of various protected groups (women, Aboriginal peoples, people with disabilities, and visible minorities). The planning looks at the representation of these employees in the organization's job categories and career tracks. The planner can compare the proportion of employees who are in each group with the proportion each group represents in the labour market. For example, the organization might note that in a labour market that consists of 20 percent visible minorities, 60 percent of its customer service employees are members of a visible minority. This type of comparison is called a **workforce utilization review.** The organization can use this process to determine whether there is any subgroup whose proportion in the relevant labour market differs substantially from the proportion in the job category.

If the workforce utilization review indicates that some group—for example, Aboriginal peoples—makes up 25 percent of the relevant labour market for a job category but that this same group constitutes only 5 percent of the employees actually in the job category at the organization, this is evidence of underutilization. That situation could result from problems in selection or from problems in internal movement (promotions or other movement along a career path). One way to diagnose the situation would be to use transitional matrices, such as the matrix shown in Table 4.1 earlier in this chapter. The federal public service is the largest employer in Canada with nearly 150,000 employees.[23] Figure 4.3 illustrates participation of its employment equity groups.

The steps in a workforce utilization review are identical to the steps in the HR planning process shown in Figure 4.1. The organization must assess current utilization patterns, then forecast how these are likely to change in the near future. If these analyses suggest the organization is underutilizing certain groups and if forecasts suggest this pattern is likely to continue, the organization may need to set goals and timetables for

workforce utilization review
A comparison of the proportion of employees in protected groups with the proportion that each group represents in the relevant labour market.

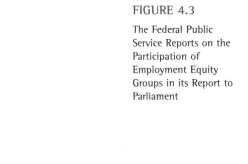

FIGURE 4.3

The Federal Public Service Reports on the Participation of Employment Equity Groups in its Report to Parliament

SOURCE: Adapted from Nurjehan Mawani, "The Federal Public Service: Opportunities for All Canadians," June 1, 2003, http://globeandmail.workopolis.com. Retrieved: February 17, 2004.

changing. The planning process may identify new strategies for recruitment or selection. The organization carries out these HR strategies and evaluates their success.

LO4

Recruiting Human Resources

As the first part of this chapter shows, it is difficult to always predict exactly how many (if any) new employees the organization will have to hire in a given year in a given job category. The role of human resource recruitment is to build a supply of potential new hires that the organization can draw on if the need arises. In human resource management, **recruiting** consists of any practice or activity carried on by the organization with the primary purpose of identifying and attracting potential employees.[24] It thus creates a buffer between planning and the actual selection of new employees (the topic of the next chapter).

Because of differences in companies' strategies, they may assign different degrees of importance to recruiting.[25] According to a 2004 survey of more than 400 human resource professionals conducted by Workopolis, 55 percent of respondents said, "recruiting/staff retention is as important to their business as profitability."[26] In general, however, all companies have to make decisions in three areas of recruiting: human resource policies, recruitment sources, and the characteristics and behaviour of the recruiter. As shown in Figure 4.4, these aspects of recruiting have different effects on whom the organization ultimately hires. Human resource policies influence the characteristics of the positions to be filled. Recruitment sources influence the kinds of job applicants an organization reaches. And the nature and behaviour of the recruiter affect the characteristics of both the vacancies and the applicants. Ultimately, an applicant's decision to accept a job offer—and the organization's decision to make the offer—depend on the match between vacancy characteristics and applicant characteristics.

recruiting
Any activity carried on by the organization with the primary purpose of identifying and attracting potential employees.

FIGURE 4.4

Three Aspects of Recruiting

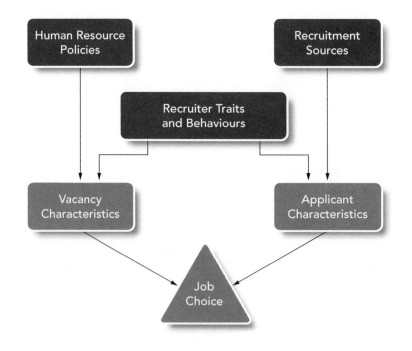

"Boomerang Employees" Bring Back Benefits for Employers

An employee who leaves a company to pursue other ventures and is later rehired is what has become known as a "boomerang employee." Many career experts say that, as competition for top talent intensifies, companies will open the door even wider to former top employees. "It'll be a growing trend because there's such a skills shortage, one that's only going to get worse," predicts Larry Gibbons, vice-president of human resources at Kinectrics Inc., an engineering and technical services company in Toronto that has rehired former employees.

Few companies go as far as Ernst and Young LLP to stay on good terms with former employees. Through its alumni relations program, the Toronto-based accounting firm actively cultivates a continuing connection with those who have moved on.

"We want to have a life-long relationship with our people, no matter where they are," says Colleen Albiston, E&Y's director of national marketing. About five years ago, the company decided to substantially beef up the alumni program. Ms. Albiston travelled the country, asking former employees what they would like provided by the company. Continuing education was a top request. Now former staffers have access to webcasts sponsored by E&Y that discuss developments in the accounting profession, such as regulatory changes. A newsletter is sent out a couple of times a year and several social events are held for former staff. When people leave the firm, they're given a password to access the alumni website, which includes a directory of current and former employees, updates on what former E&Y staff are doing, a place to post résumés and, not least a list of job vacancies at the company.

Encouraging former employees to consider E&Y again is definitely one of the aims of the program, Ms. Albiston says. "We wouldn't go aggressively recruiting someone but if there was a high performer showing an interest, we would look for the next opportunity for them to rejoin us." At E&Y, 13 percent of new hires last year were boomerangs, the previous year the figure was 15 percent. "It's something we'd like to see continue to grow," Albiston adds. "They always bring back a lot of assets and understand clients on a level they wouldn't if they'd spent their whole career focused on this side of the business."

One of the benefits of rehiring former staff is the positive message it sends about the firm to those starting out. Luana Comin-Sartor, senior manager of audit and assurance business services in Toronto, rejoined Ernst & Young in 1999, after a lengthy sojourn at Nortel Networks. Many of her younger colleagues seek out her advice about their own career prospects. "People see me as having a more objective view, because I did leave." She also gets calls from former employees thinking about returning.

The chance to recapture some of its talent isn't the only reason that E&Y puts so much effort into staying in touch. There are obvious business benefits for the consulting firm in maintaining a strong relationship with those who move on to other companies, which might need its services. "These are people we've trained, worked with, invested in," say Albiston. "Wherever they go, we'd like them to be an ambassador for the firm."

SOURCE: Ann Kerr, "Many Happy Returns" and "Accounting Firm Makes Sure to Stay in Touch with Past Staff," *The Globe and Mail*, June 30, 2004, p. C1.

Kelsey August has experienced the impact of this principle as she has struggled to find entry-level employees, including packers, shippers, and production workers, for her direct-marketing company, Lone Star Direct. Unskilled workers were just as happy to work for McDonald's and Wendy's, which were paying wages of $10 to $12 per hour. After such desperate efforts as hiring away the cashiers in stores where she shopped, August tried running a newspaper ad for part-time jobs. To August's surprise, a flood of applications poured in, mostly from women with children. Lone Star revised its human resource policies to suit this new group of employees, with benefits emphasizing flexible work hours and perks that appeal to young mothers. Many of these employees are high school dropouts, so Lone Star brings in instructors to help them prepare for their high school equivalency diplomas. The company also started paying a $200 bonus to employees who refer candidates—which enabled the company to cut its budget for job advertising.[27]

The remainder of this chapter explores these three aspects of recruiting: human resource policies, recruitment sources, and recruiter traits and behaviours.

Human Resource Policies

An organization's *human resource policies* are its decisions about how it will carry out human resource management, including how it will fill job vacancies. These policies influence the nature of the positions that are vacant. (The "Best Practices" box describes how firms actively cultivate a continuing connection to former employees.) According to the research on recruitment, it is clear that characteristics of the vacancy are more important than recruiters or recruiting sources for predicting job choice.[28] Several policies are especially relevant to recruitment:

- Recruiting existing employees to fill vacancies or hiring from outside the organization.
- Meeting or exceeding the market rate of pay.
- Emphasizing job security or the right to terminate employees.
- Images of the organization conveyed in its advertising.

Let's explore the impact of each of these policy areas.

Internal versus External Recruiting

Opportunities for advancement make a job more attractive to applicants and employees. Organizations with policies to "promote from within" try to fill upper-level vacancies by recruiting candidates internally—that is, finding candidates who already work for the organization. In a 2001 survey of students pursuing a master's degree in business administration (MBA), a policy of promotion from within was the students' top consideration when they were evaluating jobs at a company.[29]

As human resource policies, decisions about internal versus external recruiting affect the nature of jobs. As we will discuss later in the chapter, they also influence recruitment sources and the nature of applicants. For now, we will focus on the impact of these decisions as human resource policies. Promote-from-within policies signal to job applicants that the company provides opportunities for advancement, both for the present vacancy and for later vacancies created when people are promoted to fill higher-level vacancies.

McDonald's restaurants provide a good example of the virtues of promoting from within. McDonald's has a program with the goal of enabling low-income managers to buy franchises. Phil Hagans was once a cook at a McDonald's restaurant, who worked his way up, and thanks to his hard work and the McDonald's program for low-income employees, now owns two franchises. Hagans's restaurants not only turn a profit but also perform a valuable social function by providing needed employment and work experience.[30]

Lead-the-Market Pay Strategies

Pay is an important job characteristic for almost all applicants. Organizations have a recruiting advantage if their policy is to take a "lead-the-market" approach to pay—that is, pay more than the current market wages for a job. Higher pay can also make up for a job's less desirable features. For example, many organizations pay employees more for working midnight shifts than daytime shifts. (This practice is called paying a *shift differential*; we will take a closer look at these and other decisions about pay in Chapter 9.)

Increasingly, organizations that compete for applicants based on pay do so using forms of pay other than wages or salary. For example, a survey found that close to four out of ten employers used signing bonuses rather than higher wages to attract new hires. Almost two out of ten were using lucrative stock option plans (the right to buy company stock at a set price at a specified time).[31] Many employers prefer bonuses and stock options because, unlike wages and salary, they tend not to grow over time (as with a percent raise every year) and can be administered more flexibly. However, many job applicants are showing less interest in stock options. For example, as Nortel Networks' stock prices have declined and fluctuated dramatically, many employees have watched their stock lose much of its value.

Also, in reaction to the Enron and WorldCom experiences, many employees have become suspicious of the value of benefits tied to their company's stock. To attract top talent, employers are placing more emphasis on salary and more traditional benefits.

Recruitment Branding and Image Advertising

Recruitment branding, also known as internal branding, uses marketing techniques to attract and retain employees in the effort to become an "employer of choice." As the competition for top talent is expected to intensify during the next decade, employers are increasingly concerned they are able to attract and retain the most qualified recruits and to ensure that existing employees understand the company's goals and values. Recruitment branding may be as sophisticated as efforts to build consumer brands.[32]

For example, when an organization is recognized as one of "Canada's 50 Best Managed Companies" (www.canadas50best.com) the organization acquires the ability to use this well-known designation in various mediums, e.g., print, company website, etc., to support and enhance their recruitment efforts. This logo identifies to current and prospective employees that the organization is part of a prestigious group of Canadian employers who exemplify sound business practices in areas such as human resource management.

Advertising designed to create a generally favourable impression of the organization is called *image advertising*. Image advertising is particularly important for organizations in highly competitive labour markets that perceive themselves as having a bad image.[33]

When an organization is recognized as one of "Canada's 50 Best Managed Companies" they are likely to experience a dramatic increase in the number of résumés they receive.

The Canadian Forces includes three partners: the Army, the Navy, and the Air Force. The Canadian Forces actively promotes in the labour market to raise awareness of the types of career opportunities available as well as to portray a positive image of employment with the Canadian Forces. The Canadian Forces website promotes the career advantages offered such as subsidized training plans and recruitment allowances as well as targets specific groups within the overall labour market. For example, video testimonials are available at the Canadian Forces website (www.recruiting.forces.gc.ca) from women presently serving in the Army, the Air Force, and the Navy and a video produced in collaboration with the APN Aboriginal Peoples Network shows what life in the military is like from the perspective of Aboriginal young people.[34]

Whether the goal is to influence the perception of the public in general or specific segments of the labour market, job seekers form beliefs about the nature of the organizations well before they have any direct interviewing experience with these companies. Thus, organizations must assess their reputation in the labour market and correct any shortcomings they detect in people's actual image of them.[35]

LO5

Recruitment Sources

Another critical element of an organization's recruitment strategy is its decisions about where to look for applicants. The total labour market is enormous and spread over the entire globe. As a practical matter, an organization will draw from a small fraction of that total market. The methods the organization chooses for communicating its labour needs and the audiences it targets will determine the size and nature of the labour market the organization taps to fill its vacant positions.[36] A person who responds to a job advertisement on the Internet is likely to be different from a person responding to a sign hanging outside a factory. Figure 4.5 summarizes major sources from which organizations draw recruits. Each source has advantages and disadvantages.

Internal Sources

job posting
The process of communicating information about a job vacancy on company bulletin boards, in employee publications, on corporate intranets, and anywhere else the organization communicates with employees.

As we discussed with regard to human resource policies, an organization may emphasize internal or external sources of job applicants. Internal sources are employees who currently hold other positions in the organization. Organizations recruit existing employees through **job posting,** or communicating information about the vacancy on company bulletin boards, in employee publications, on corporate intranets, and anywhere else the organization communicates with employees. Managers also may identify candidates to recommend for vacancies. Policies that emphasize promotions and even lateral moves to achieve broader career experience can give applicants a favourable impression of the organization's jobs. The use of internal sources also affects what kinds of people the organization recruits.

For the employer, relying on internal sources offers several advantages.[37] First, it generates applicants who are well known to the organization. In addition, these applicants are relatively knowledgeable about the organization's vacancies, which minimizes the possibility they will have unrealistic expectations about the job. Finally, filling vacancies through internal recruiting is generally cheaper and faster than looking outside the organization.

CCL Industries, a Toronto manufacturing company, has provided leadership training to about 1,000 employees since 1992 to grow talent within the organization. This "leadership pool" is used to staff projects and assignments as well as prepare employees for additional responsibilities and challenges. In addition, CCL attributes this initiative to enhanced employee morale—employees feel valued because of the investment the company is making in them.[38]

Retailers tend to promote from within their organizations, a policy that is attractive to many workers.

External Sources

Despite the advantages of internal recruitment, organizations often have good reasons to recruit externally.[39] For entry-level positions and perhaps for specialized upper-level positions, the organization has no internal recruits from which to draw. Also, bringing in outsiders may expose the organization to new ideas or new ways of doing

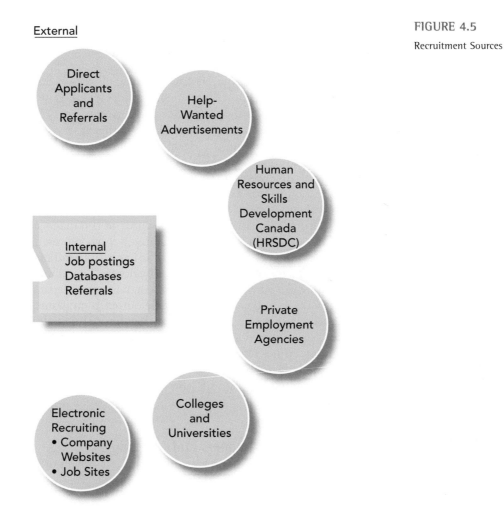

External

FIGURE 4.5

Recruitment Sources

Direct Applicants and Referrals

Help-Wanted Advertisements

Human Resources and Skills Development Canada (HRSDC)

Internal
Job postings
Databases
Referrals

Private Employment Agencies

Electronic Recruiting
• Company Websites
• Job Sites

Colleges and Universities

business. An organization that uses only internal recruitment can wind up with a workforce whose members all think alike and therefore may be poorly suited to innovation.[40] In order to attract a more diverse workforce, organizations often recruit through direct applicants and referrals, advertisements, employment agencies, schools, and websites. For example, the province of Quebec targets health care workers in France and Switzerland due to language requirements in addressing the shortage of doctors and nursing specialists.[41]

Direct Applicants and Referrals

direct applicants
People who apply for a vacancy without prompting from the organization.

Even without a formal effort to reach job applicants, an organization may hear from candidates through direct applicants and referrals. **Direct applicants** are people who apply for a vacancy without prompting from the organization. **Referrals** are people who apply because someone in the organization prompted them to do so. These two sources of recruits share some characteristics that make them excellent pools from which to draw.

referrals
People who apply for a vacancy because someone in the organization prompted them to do so.

One advantage is that many direct applicants are to some extent already "sold" on the organization. Most have done some research and concluded there is enough fit between themselves and the vacant position to warrant submitting an application, a process called *self-selection,* which, when it works, eases the pressure on the organization's recruiting and selection systems. A form of aided self-selection occurs with referrals. Many job seekers look to friends, relatives, and acquaintances to help find employment. Using these social networks not only helps the job seeker, but also simplifies recruitment for employers.[42] Current employees (who are familiar with the vacancy as well as the person they are referring) decide that there is a fit between the person and the vacancy, so they convince the person to apply for the job.

An additional benefit of using such sources is that it costs much less than formal recruiting efforts. Considering these combined benefits, referrals and direct applications are among the best sources of new hires. Some employers offer current employees financial incentives for referring applicants who are hired and perform acceptably on the job (for example, if they stay 180 days).[43] Other companies play off their good reputations in the labour market to generate direct applications. For example, minorities constitute about one-fourth of the managerial and professional employees at Avon Products, and this relatively high representation of visible minorities enhances Avon's ability to recruit other visible minority applicants. As Al Smith, Avon's director of managing diversity, notes, "I get a lot of résumés from people of all cultures and ethnicities because Avon has a good reputation." This takes the place of expensive and sometimes unreliable outreach programs.[44]

nepotism
The practice of hiring relatives.

The major downside of referrals is that they limit the likelihood of exposing the organization to fresh viewpoints. People tend to refer others who are like themselves. Furthermore, sometimes referrals contribute to hiring practices that are or that appear unfair, an example being **nepotism,** or the hiring of relatives. Employees may resent the hiring and rapid promotion of "the boss's son" or "the boss's daughter," or even the boss's friend.

Advertisements in Newspapers and Magazines

Open almost any newspaper or magazine and you can find advertisements of job openings. These ads typically generate a less desirable group of applicants than direct applications or referrals, and do so at greater expense. However, few employers can fill all their vacancies purely through direct applications and referrals, so they usually need to advertise. Also, an employer can take many steps to increase the effectiveness of recruitment through advertising.

The person designing a job advertisement needs to answer two questions:

1. What do we need to say?
2. To whom do we need to say it?

With respect to the first question, an ad should give readers enough information to evaluate the job and its requirements, so they can make a well-informed judgment about their qualifications. Providing enough information may require long advertisements, which cost more. The employer should evaluate the additional costs against the costs of providing too little information: Vague ads generate a huge number of applicants, including many who are not reasonably qualified or would not accept the job if they learned more about it. Reviewing all these applications to eliminate unsuitable applicants is expensive.

Specifying whom to reach with the message helps the advertiser decide where to place the ad. The most common medium for advertising jobs is the classified section of local newspapers. These ads are relatively inexpensive yet reach many people in a specific geographic area who are currently looking for work (or at least interested enough to be reading the classifieds). On the downside, this medium offers little ability to target skill levels. Typically, many of the people reading classified ads are either over- or underqualified for the position. Also, people who are not looking for work rarely read the classifieds. These people may include candidates the organization could lure from their current employers. For reaching a specific part of the labour market, including certain skill levels and more people who are employed, the organization may get better results from advertising in professional or industry journals. Some employers also advertise on television—particularly cable television.[45]

Human Resources and Skills Development Canada (HRSDC)

Human Resources and Skills Development Canada clients include both people looking for jobs and potential employers. Clients can access services without charge by mail, telephone, in person, and via the Internet. Specific program responsibilities of the HRSDC (www.hrsdc.gc.ca) include job creation partnerships designed to provide participants the opportunity to enhance job skills and acquire work experience. Employers post job advertisements in the Job Bank (www.jobbank.gc.ca), an electronic listing of jobs and receive financial assistance for hiring eligible participants.

Various links provide career information and resources to help job seekers prepare for their job search and to assist employers with their human resource management needs. Additional program responsibilities of the HRSDC include the Youth Employment Strategy, Aboriginal Human Resources Development Agreements, as well as administering the Canada Student Loan Program and the Employment Insurance Commision.

Private Employment Agencies

Private employment agencies provide assistance to employers in attracting quality applicants. Job seekers apply to the private employment agency and are usually screened for suitability. Private employment agencies differ significantly in the types of services provided. It is important for both job seekers and employers to research and assess thoroughly private agencies so as to work with the agency that will best meet their needs and expectations.

Private employment agencies provide their services for a fee. Usually these fees are paid by the employer for the service of receiving employee referrals. The staffing services business in Canada has grown into a $4-billion industry that places thousands of job seekers in full-time, temporary, and contract assignments.[46]

For managers or professionals, an employer may use the services of a type of private agency called an *executive search firm* (ESF). People often call these agencies "headhunters" because, unlike other employment agencies, they find new jobs for people almost exclusively already employed. For example, when BMW was preparing to open a new plant in the United States, it used an executive search firm to help "liberate" Allen Kinzer and Edwin Buker from Honda. These two executives were vice-presidents for Honda's U.S. operations, and by hiring them, BMW hoped to re-create Honda's success.[47]

For job candidates, dealing with executive search firms can be sensitive. Typically, executives do not want to advertise their availability, because it could trigger a negative reaction from their current employer. ESFs serve as a buffer, providing confidentiality between the employer and the recruit. That benefit may give an employer access to candidates it cannot recruit in other, more direct ways. EmploymentAgencies.ca is a free Internet directory of employment agencies and executive search firms. Alternatively, the *Directory of Canadian Recruiters* and the *Canadian Directory of Search Firms* are sources of information about private employment agencies. Both publications are provided for purchase, however, most libraries have copies available.[48]

Employing an executive search firm may be expensive because of direct and indirect costs. According to a 1997 survey, ESFs often charge one-third to one-half the salary of the executive who is eventually placed with the client.[49] Also, convincing a person to consider changing jobs requires that the employer offer something more attractive. A company in a growing industry may have to offer as much as 50 percent more than the executive's current pay.[50] The Canadian Forces offers various recruitment allowances for applicants who have specific qualifications. For example, signing bonuses are offered to qualified technicians, tradespeople, and engineers in amounts ranging from $10,000 to $40,000. Trained doctors are eligible for signing bonuses of $225,000.[51]

Due to competition for talent in Canada's pharmaceutical industry, Luc St-Pierre, vice-president of human resources for Pfizer Canada, states that signing bonuses for some candidates can "reach 10 to 25 percent of the salary."[52]

Universities and Colleges

Most universities and colleges have placement services that seek to help their graduates obtain employment. On-campus interviewing is the most important source of recruits for entry-level professional and managerial vacancies.[53] Organizations tend to focus especially on universities and colleges that have strong reputations in areas for which they have critical needs—say, chemical engineering or public accounting.[54] The recruiting strategy at 3M includes concentrating on 25 to 30 selected universities. The company has a commitment to those selected universities and returns to them each year with new job openings. HR professionals make sure that the same person works with the same university year in and year out, to achieve "continuity of contact."[55]

Many employers have found that successfully competing for the best students requires more than just signing up prospective graduates for interview slots. One of the best ways to establish a stronger presence on a campus is with a coooperative education or internship program. For example, Research in Motion (RIM) provides a variety of employment opportunities for students including four-month cooperative education placements. In addition to the opportunity to work for a leader in the mobile communications market, student employees are provided with a BlackBerry™.[56] These programs give an organization early access to potential applicants and let the organization assess their capabilities directly.

Another way of increasing the employer's presence on campus is to participate in university and college job fairs. In general, a job fair is an event where many employers gather for a short time to meet large numbers of potential job applicants. Although job fairs can be held anywhere (such as at a hotel or convention centre), campuses are ideal locations because of the many well-educated, yet unemployed, individuals who are there. Job fairs are an inexpensive means of generating an on-campus presence. They can even provide one-on-one dialogue with potential recruits—dialogue that would be impossible through less interactive media, such as newspaper ads. To support its student programs, Research in Motion employs a full-time "Campus Recruitment Specialist."[57]

Electronic Recruiting

The Internet has opened up new vistas for organizations trying to recruit talent. There are many ways to employ the Internet for recruiting. Increasingly, organizations are refining their use of this medium. The Internet has such a significant impact on recruitment that about 50 percent of all résumés are submitted electronically.[58] As shown in Figure 4.6, over one-third of HR executives responding to a 2001 survey indicated that electronic job boards were the most effective source of recruits for their organization.[59] As the "E-HRM" box on the following page describes, online recruiting also expands the labour market from which the organization can draw.

One of the easiest ways to get into "e-cruiting" is simply to use the organization's own website to solicit applications. Less than a quarter of the websites of the world's largest firms were using this approach in 1998, however, today it is becoming increasingly rare for any large organization to *not* be using this approach.

Providing a way to submit applications at the company website is not so successful for smaller and less well-known organizations, because fewer people are likely to visit

FIGURE 4.6

Sources of Recruits

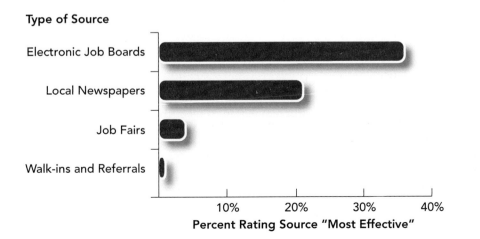

Type of Source

- Electronic Job Boards
- Local Newspapers
- Job Fairs
- Walk-ins and Referrals

10% 20% 30% 40%

Percent Rating Source "Most Effective"

Web Opens the Door to a Global Labour Market

The Internet's audience is a global one, so by definition, e-cruiting reaches an international labour market. An organization that posts a job on the World Wide Web might just hear from people as far away as Dublin or Sri Lanka. Some organizations regard this as an opportunity and develop recruitment strategies that target job seekers in other countries.

An obvious challenge in global recruiting is language differences. Aside from translation concerns, even websites targeting job seekers in English-speaking parts of the world such as Australia and Hong Kong need to adapt their English for local usages. Symbols or graphics as well as words have different meanings in different cultures, too. A thumb's-up gesture meant to signal a positive thought would be obscene in Sicily.

Countries also differ in terms of their recruitment laws and customs. Job candidates in Holland and France expect that employers will ask about such characteristics as age, gender, and marital status—questions that would violate human rights legislation if asked in Canada. In Germany, companies must give employees six months' notice before firing them, so recruiting methods should recognize the existence of German employees who know they will need a new job in a few months. Countries also vary in the degree to which they protect applicants' privacy. The European Union prohibits countries with "inadequate" privacy protection from transferring data outside the EU unless the data provider gives them permission.

Online recruiters also need to consider the values and expectations of job seekers. In contrast to North Americans, Europeans tend to be more reluctant to share information about themselves on the Internet—especially if they don't know who wants the information and how it will be used. These workers also are more likely to hunt for a job using an intermediary, such as an executive search firm.

How can recruiters plan for all these differences? A good place to start is to talk to recruiters and employees in the countries from which the organization hopes to draw job candidates. People who work for global advertising agencies and some HR consulting and Web consulting firms are also knowledgeable about communicating globally.

SOURCE: Anne Freedman, "The Web World-Wide," *Human Resource Executive*, March 6, 2002, pp. 44–48.

the website. These organizations may get better results by going to the national job board websites that are set up to attract job seekers, such as Monster.ca, Workopolis.com, and CanWest Media Works new website, www.working.canada.com, which attract a vast array of applicants. At these sites, job seekers submit standardized résumés. Employers can search the site's database for résumés that include specified key terms, and they can also submit information about their job opportunities, so that job seekers can search that information by key term. In 2004, Workopolis and Career Buider, a U.S.-based job board, teamed up to meet the needs of client organizations who recruit in both Canada and the U.S.[60] With both employers and job seekers submitting information to and conducting searches on them, these sites offer an efficient way to find matches between job seekers and job vacancies. However, a drawback is that the big job websites can provide too many leads of inferior quality because they are so huge and serve all job seekers and employers, not a select segment. In the words of an HR executive, "The last thing you need is to get a thousand résumés, 990 of which don't meet your needs."[61]

Because of this limitation of the large websites, smaller, more tailored websites called "niche boards" focus on certain industries, occupations, or geographic areas. Telecommcareers.net, for example, is a site devoted to, as the name implies, the telecommunications industry. Atlantic Canada's Career Beacon is a regional-based job board popular with applicants who live in Atlantic Canada and have no intention of relocating. The best evidence in favour of these niche boards is that the major websites are scrambling to create more focused subsections of their own.[62]

Technology such as recruitment software tools are assisting HR professionals to deal with the often overwhelming flood of applications received electronically. Chuck Allan, director of the HR-XML Consortium, a non-profit global organization that creates HRM data standards, describes developing technology that will provide jobseekers with a web address and a password. Job seekers would apply online by completing an assessment that provides pre-screening to the potential employer.[63] WestJet's online "Hiring Centre" requires job applicants to answer various questions and enter responses into mandatory fields on their online application forms. For example, applicants are asked: "What is your skill level with Microsoft Outlook?" on a scale ranging from "1" Beginner to "5" Advanced. In addition, specific information about skills, work location preferences, education/professional development, and salary/wage expectations provides a qualified pool of applicants for available job openings.[64]

Evaluating the Quality of a Source

In general, there are few rules that say what recruitment source is best for a given job vacancy. Therefore, it is wise for employers to monitor the quality of all their recruitment sources. One way to do this is to develop and compare **yield ratios** for each source.[65] A yield ratio expresses the percentage of applicants who successfully move from one stage of the recruitment and selection process to the next. For example, the organization could find the number of candidates interviewed as a percentage of the total number of résumés generated by a given source (that is, number of interviews divided by number of résumés). A high yield ratio (large percentage) means that the source is an effective way to find candidates to interview. By comparing the yield ratios of different recruitment sources, HR professionals can determine which source is the best or most efficient for the type of vacancy.

yield ratio
A ratio that expresses the percentage of applicants who successfully move from one stage of the recruitment and selection process to the next.

Another measure of recruitment success is the *cost per hire*. To compute this amount, find the cost of using a particular recruitment source for a particular type of vacancy. Then divide that cost by the number of people hired to fill that type of vacancy. A low cost per hire means that the recruitment source is efficient; it delivers qualified candidates at minimal cost.

To see how HR professionals use these measures, look at the examples in Table 4.3. This table shows the results for a hypothetical organization that used five kinds of recruitment sources to fill a number of vacancies. For each recruitment source, the table shows four yield ratios and the cost per hire. To fill these jobs, the best two sources of recruits were local universities and employee referral programs. Company websites generated the largest number of recruits (1,000 résumés). However, only 20 were judged acceptable, of which only half accepted employment offers, for a cumulative yield ratio of 10/1,000, or 1 percent. Recruiting at renowned universities generated highly qualified applicants, but relatively few of them ultimately accepted positions with the organization. Executive search firms produced the highest cumulative yield ratio. These generated only 20 applicants, but all of them accepted interview offers, most were judged acceptable, and 79 percent of these acceptable candidates took jobs

TABLE 4.3

Results of a Hypothetical Recruiting Effort

	RECRUITING SOURCE					
	LOCAL COLLEGE/ UNIVERSITY	RENOWNED COLLEGE/ UNIVERSITY	EMPLOYEE REFERRALS	NEWSPAPER AD	EXECUTIVE SEARCH FIRMS	COMPANY WEBSITE
Résumés generated	200	400	50	500	20	1,000
Interview offers accepted	175	100	45	400	20	40
Yield ratio	**87%**	**25%**	**90%**	**80%**	**100%**	**4%**
Applicants judged acceptable	100	95	40	50	19	20
Yield ratio	**57%**	**95%**	**89%**	**12%**	**95%**	**50%**
Accept employment offers	90	10	35	25	15	10
Yield ratio	**90%**	**11%**	**88%**	**50%**	**79%**	**50%**
Cumulative yield ratio	90/200 **45%**	10/400 **3%**	35/50 **70%**	25/500 **5%**	15/20 **75%**	10/1,000 **1%**
Cost	$30,000	$50,000	$15,000	$20,000	$90,000	$3,000
Cost per hire	**$333**	**$5,000**	**$428**	**$800**	**$6,000**	**$300**

with the organization. However, notice the cost per hire. The executive search firms charged $90,000 for finding these 15 employees, resulting in the largest cost per hire. In contrast, local colleges and universities and company websites provided modest yield ratios at the lowest cost per hire. Employee referrals provided excellent yield ratios at a slightly higher cost.

LO6

Recruiter Traits and Behaviours

As we showed in Figure 4.4, the third influence on recruitment outcomes is the recruiter, including this person's characteristics and the way he or she behaves. The recruiter affects the nature of both the job vacancy and the applicants generated. However, the recruiter often becomes involved late in the recruitment process. In many cases, by the time a recruiter meets some applicants, they have already made up their minds about what they desire in a job, what the vacant job has to offer, and their likelihood of receiving a job offer.[66]

Many applicants approach the recruiter with some skepticism. Knowing it is the recruiter's job to sell them on a vacancy, some applicants discount what the recruiter says, in light of what they have heard from other sources, such as friends, magazine articles, and professors. For these and other reasons, recruiters' characteristics and behaviours seem to have limited impact on applicants' job choices.

Characteristics of the Recruiter

Most organizations must choose whether their recruiters are specialists in human resources or are experts at particular jobs (that is, those who currently hold the same kinds of jobs or supervise people who hold the jobs). According to some studies, ap-

FIGURE 4.7

Recruits Who Were Offended by Recruiters

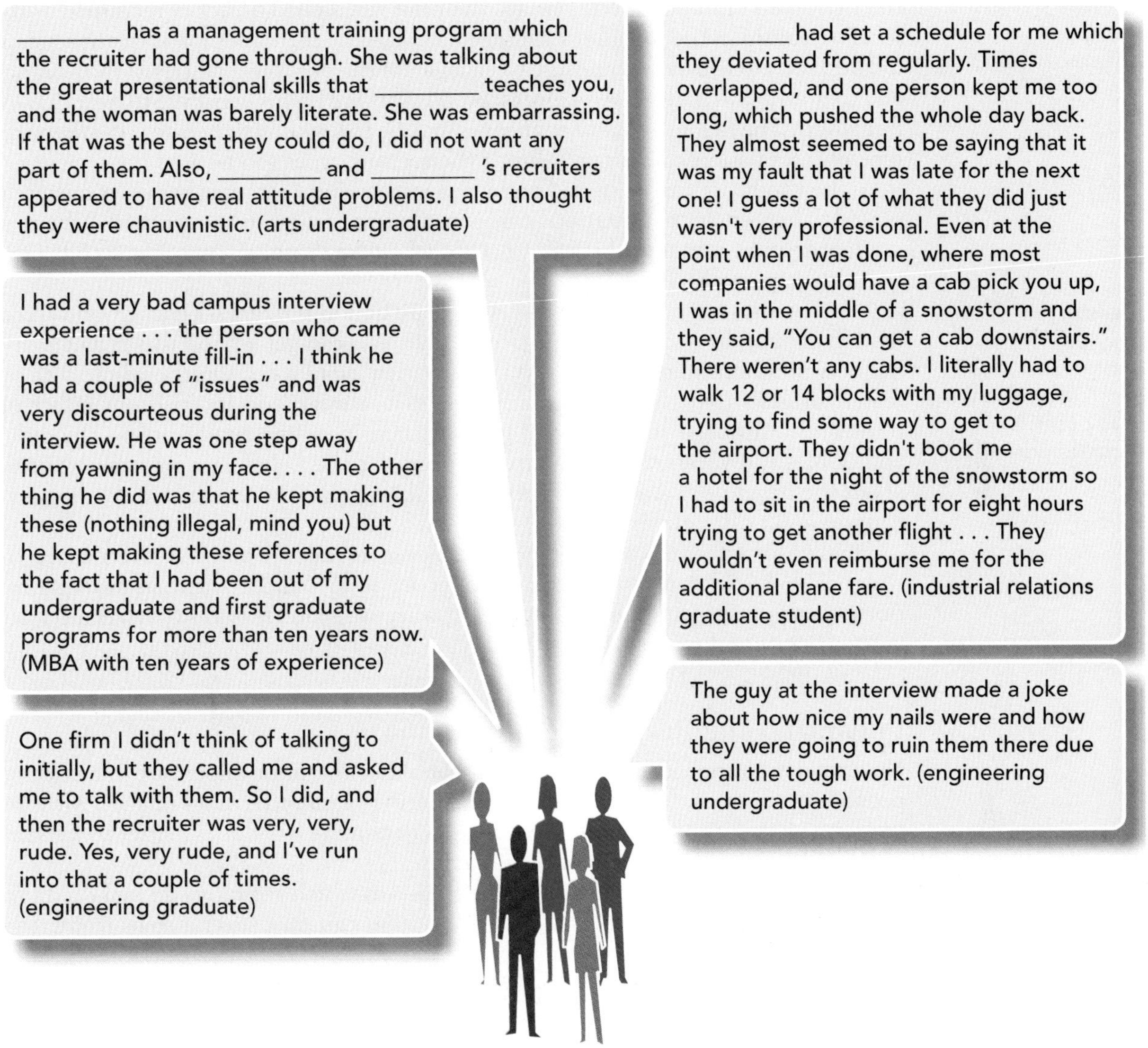

_____ has a management training program which the recruiter had gone through. She was talking about the great presentational skills that _____ teaches you, and the woman was barely literate. She was embarrassing. If that was the best they could do, I did not want any part of them. Also, _____ and _____ 's recruiters appeared to have real attitude problems. I also thought they were chauvinistic. (arts undergraduate)

I had a very bad campus interview experience . . . the person who came was a last-minute fill-in . . . I think he had a couple of "issues" and was very discourteous during the interview. He was one step away from yawning in my face. . . . The other thing he did was that he kept making these (nothing illegal, mind you) but he kept making these references to the fact that I had been out of my undergraduate and first graduate programs for more than ten years now. (MBA with ten years of experience)

One firm I didn't think of talking to initially, but they called me and asked me to talk with them. So I did, and then the recruiter was very, very, rude. Yes, very rude, and I've run into that a couple of times. (engineering graduate)

_____ had set a schedule for me which they deviated from regularly. Times overlapped, and one person kept me too long, which pushed the whole day back. They almost seemed to be saying that it was my fault that I was late for the next one! I guess a lot of what they did just wasn't very professional. Even at the point when I was done, where most companies would have a cab pick you up, I was in the middle of a snowstorm and they said, "You can get a cab downstairs." There weren't any cabs. I literally had to walk 12 or 14 blocks with my luggage, trying to find some way to get to the airport. They didn't book me a hotel for the night of the snowstorm so I had to sit in the airport for eight hours trying to get another flight . . . They wouldn't even reimburse me for the additional plane fare. (industrial relations graduate student)

The guy at the interview made a joke about how nice my nails were and how they were going to ruin them there due to all the tough work. (engineering undergraduate)

plicants perceive HR specialists as less credible and are less attracted to jobs when recruiters are HR specialists.[67] The evidence does not completely discount a positive role for HR specialists in recruiting. It does indicate, however, that these specialists need to take extra steps to ensure that applicants perceive them as knowledgeable and credible.

In general, applicants respond positively to recruiters whom they perceive as warm and informative. "Warm" means the recruiter seems to care about the applicant and to be enthusiastic about the applicant's potential to contribute to the organization. "Informative" means the recruiter provides the kind of information the applicant is seeking. The evidence of impact of other characteristics of recruiters—including their age, sex, and race—is complex and inconsistent.[68]

Behaviour of the Recruiter

Recruiters affect results not only by providing plenty of information, but by providing the right kind of information. Perhaps the most researched aspect of recruiting is the level of realism in the recruiter's message. Because the recruiter's job is to attract candidates, recruiters may feel pressure to exaggerate the positive qualities of the vacancy and to downplay its negative qualities. Applicants are highly sensitive to negative information. The highest-quality applicants may be less willing to pursue jobs when this type of information comes out.[69] But if the recruiter goes too far in a positive direction, the candidate can be misled and lured into taking a job that has been misrepresented. Then unmet expectations can contribute to a high turnover rate. When recruiters describe jobs unrealistically, people who take those jobs may come to believe that the employer is deceitful.[70]

realistic job preview
Background information about a job's positive and negative qualities.

Many studies have looked at how well **realistic job previews**—background information about jobs' positive and negative qualities—can get around this problem and help organizations minimize turnover among new employees. On the whole, the research suggests that realistic job previews have a weak and inconsistent effect on turnover.[71] Although recruiters can go overboard in selling applicants on the desirability of a job vacancy, there is little support for the belief that informing people about the negative characteristics of a job will "inoculate" them so that the negative features don't cause them to quit.[72]

Finally, for affecting whether people choose to take a job, but even more so, whether they stick with a job, the recruiter seems less important than an organization's human resource policies that directly affect the job's features (pay, security, advancement opportunities, and so on).

Enhancing the Recruiter's Impact

Nevertheless, although recruiters are probably not the most important influence on people's job choices, this does not mean recruiters cannot have an impact. Most recruiters receive little training.[73] If we were to determine what does matter to job candidates, perhaps recruiters could be trained in those areas.

Researchers have tried to find the conditions in which recruiters do make a difference. Such research suggests that an organization can take several steps to increase the positive impact that recruiters have on job candidates:

- Recruiters should provide timely feedback. Applicants dislike delays in feedback. They may draw negative conclusions about the organization (for starters, that the organization doesn't care about their application).
- Recruiters should avoid offensive behaviour. They should avoid behaving in ways that might convey the wrong impression about the organization.[74] Figure 4.7 quotes applicants who felt they had extremely bad experiences with recruiters. Their statements provide examples of behaviours to avoid.
- The organization can recruit with teams rather than individual recruiters. Applicants view job experts as more credible than HR specialists, and a team can include both kinds of recruiters. HR specialists on the team provide knowledge about company policies and procedures and ensure the integrity of the process, consistency, and compliance with Human Rights legislation.

Through such positive behaviour, recruiters can give organizations a better chance of competing for talented human resources. In the next chapter, we will describe how an organization selects the candidates that best meet its needs.

Summary

1. Discuss how to plan for human resources needed to carry out the organization's strategy.

    The first step in human resource planning is forecasting. Through trend analysis and good judgment, the planner tries to determine the supply of and demand for various human resources. Based on whether a surplus or a shortage is expected, the planner sets goals and creates a strategy for achieving those goals. The organization then implements its HR strategy and evaluates the results.

2. Determine the labour demand for workers in various job categories.

    The planner can look at leading indicators, assuming trends will continue in the future. Multiple regression can convert several leading indicators into a single prediction of labour needs. Analysis of a transitional matrix can help the planner identify which job categories can be filled internally and where high turnover is likely.

3. Summarize the advantages and disadvantages of ways to eliminate a labour surplus and avoid a labour shortage.

    To reduce a surplus, downsizing, pay reductions, and demotions deliver fast results but at a high cost in human suffering that may hurt surviving employees' motivation and future recruiting. Also, the organization may lose some of its best employees. Transferring employees and requiring them to share work are also fast methods and the consequences in human suffering are less severe. A hiring freeze or attrition is slow to take effect but avoids the pain of layoffs. Early-retirement packages may unfortunately induce the best employees to leave and may be slow to implement; however, they, too, are less painful than layoffs. Retraining can improve the organization's overall pool of human resources and maintain high morale, but it is relatively slow and costly.

    To avoid a labour shortage, requiring overtime is the easiest and fastest strategy, which can easily be changed if conditions change. However, overtime may exhaust workers and can hurt morale. Using temporary employees and outsourcing do not build an in-house pool of talent, but by these means staffing levels can be quickly and easily modified. Transferring and retraining employees require investment of time and money, but can enhance the quality of the organization's human resources; however, this may backfire if a labour surplus develops. Hiring new employees is slow and expensive but strengthens the organization if labour needs are expected to expand for the long term. Using technology as a substitute for labour can be slow to implement and costly, but it may improve the organization's long-term performance. New technology and hiring are difficult to reverse if conditions change.

4. Describe recruitment policies organizations use to make job vacancies more attractive.

    Internal recruiting (hiring from within) generally makes job vacancies more attractive because candidates see opportunities for growth and advancement. Lead-the-market pay strategies make jobs economically desirable. Due-process policies signal that employers are concerned about employee rights. Image advertising can give candidates the impression that the organization is a good place to work.

5. List and compare sources of job applicants.

    Internal sources, promoted through job postings, generate applicants who are familiar to the organization and motivate other employees by demonstrating opportunities for advancement. However, internal sources are usually insufficient for all of an organization's labour needs. Direct applicants and referrals tend to be inexpensive and to generate applicants who have self-selected; this source risks charges of unfairness, especially in cases of nepotism. Newspaper and magazine advertising reaches a wide audience and may generate many applications, although many are likely to be unsuitable. Employment agencies are inexpensive and typically have screened applicants. Private employment agencies charge fees but may provide many services. Another inexpensive channel is universities and colleges, which may give the employer access to top-notch entrants to the labour market. Electronic recruiting gives organizations access to a global labour market, tends to be inexpensive, and allows convenient searching of databases, however organizations may receive many applications from unqualified applicants.

6. Describe the recruiter's role in the recruitment process, including limits and opportunities.

    Through their behaviour and other characteristics, recruiters influence the nature of the job vacancy and the kinds of applicants generated. Applicants tend to perceive job experts as more credible than recruiters who are HR specialists. They tend to react more favourably to recruiters who are warm and informative. Recruiters should not mislead candidates. Realistic job previews are helpful, but have a weak and inconsistent effect on job turnover compared to personnel policies and actual job conditions. Recruiters can improve their impact by providing timely feedback, avoiding behaviour that contributes to a negative impression of the organization, and teaming up with job experts.

Review and Discussion Questions

1. Suppose an organization expects a labour shortage to develop in key job areas over the next few years. Recommend general responses the organization could make in each of the following areas:
   a. Recruitment.
   b. Training.
   c. Compensation (pay and employee benefits).
2. Review the sample transitional matrix shown in Table 4.1. What jobs experience the greatest turnover (employees leaving the organization)? How might an organization with this combination of jobs reduce the turnover?
3. In the same transitional matrix, which jobs seem to rely the most on internal recruitment? Which seem to rely most on external recruitment? Why?
4. Why do organizations combine statistical and judgmental forecasts of labour demand, rather than relying on statistics or judgment alone? Give an example of a situation in which each type of forecast would be inaccurate.
5. Some organizations have detailed employment equity plans, complete with goals and timetables, for women and visible minorities, yet have no formal human resource plan for the organization as a whole. Why might this be the case? What does this practice suggest about the role of human resource management in these organizations?
6. Give an example of a human resource policy that would help attract a larger pool of job candidates. Give an example of a human resource policy that would likely reduce the pool of candidates. Would you expect these policies to influence the quality as well as the number of applicants? Why or why not?
7. Discuss the relative merits of internal versus external recruitment. Give an example of a situation in which each of these approaches might be particularly effective.
8. List the jobs you have held. How were you recruited for each of these? From the organization's perspective, what were some pros and cons of recruiting you through these methods?
9. Recruiting people for jobs that require international assignments is increasingly important for many organizations. Where might an organization go to recruit people interested in such assignments?
10. A large share of HR professionals have rated e-cruiting as their best source of new talent. What qualities of electronic recruiting do you think contribute to this opinion?
11. How can organizations improve the effectiveness of their recruiters?

What's Your HR IQ?

www.mcgrawhill.ca/college/noe

The Online Learning Centre offers more ways to check what you've learned so far. Find experiential exercises as well as Test Your Knowledge Quizzes, Videos, and many other resources at www.mcgrawhill.ca/college/noe.

Case: Crystal Decisions Gets Creative Competing for Talent

Although Vancouver-based software firm, Crystal Decisions has offices in 25 locations around the world, "it's a modern day David" next to technological Goliaths such as Oracle or Microsoft. The media awards that Crystal Decisions has received include being on *Maclean's* magazine list of Canada's Top 100 employers and being voted by B.C. Business as the third-best company to work for in British Columbia. However, Matthew Handford, vice-president of HR, recognized that media awards such as these were not going to be enough to recruit the approximately 150 high skilled people they needed each quarter. Handford saw an opportunity to think of Crystal Decisions when they think of an innovative work environment. He established a sponsorship with the Rocky Mountain World Cup Race Team because mountain biking is a sport that attracts young professionals with education and backgrounds similar to the type of person Crystal wants to attract. To build the required organizational image and measure the value of the initiative, Handford created a position called talent brand manager within the HR department.

"This blending of marketing with human resources is a very smart move," says Kelli Gayford, a senior associate with executive search firm Korn/Ferry International in Vancouver. "Few companies can afford to build a talent brand, but particularly in the technical area where firms are new and don't have the heritage of a premium brand, it can really pay off."

To attract the needed undergraduate students, traditionally targeted at career fairs at renowned universities by companies such as Microsoft with wine and cheese functions or executive presentations, Crystal Decisions got creative. They screened unreleased extreme mountain bike videos, gave away jerseys, held raffles for bikes, and had race team members sign autographs and talk with the potential job seekers. The mountain bike team members have also participated in a recruiting dinner at the Hotel Vancouver, attended by 300 pre-screened employment candidates who also had the opportunity to meet and chat with senior managers and employees. Recruiters, employees, and their families and friends also attended one of the biggest races in the world, the UCI Mountain Bike World Cup. The objectives included raising awareness of the talent brand, increasing the recognition of Crystal Decisions

outside the company, and providing a benefit to employees attending the event. Of the 25,000 people present, recruiters found that 40 percent of the people they surveyed had a post-graduate education. In addition, current employee feedback that Crystal Decisions is a "phenomenal place to work" and has "great growth opportunities" helped organizers conclude the event was successful from all perspectives.

SOURCE: Eve Lazarus, "Ride Hire," *HR Professional Magazine*, February/March 2004, www.hrpao.org/Knowledge_Central/HR_Professional. Retrieved: March 28, 2004 and www.crystaldecisions.com.

Questions

1. Would you want to work for a company like Crystal Decisions? Why or why not?
2. Why was this recruiting initiative successful for Crystal Decisions? Would this recruiting initiative be successful for any organization? Why or why not?

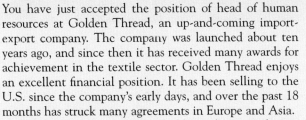

Excalibur Case: Golden Thread Company

You have just accepted the position of head of human resources at Golden Thread, an up-and-coming import-export company. The company was launched about ten years ago, and since then it has received many awards for achievement in the textile sector. Golden Thread enjoys an excellent financial position. It has been selling to the U.S. since the company's early days, and over the past 18 months has struck many agreements in Europe and Asia.

Golden Thread's main shareholder is also general manager of the company, an overworked individual with a strong entrepreneurial approach. There is often a need to conduct last-minute negotiations over the phone, but despite the pressure, the GM remains upbeat and pleased that business is doing so well.

The GM has asked you to give priority to settling the problem of recruiting an administrative assistant for him. He has had three since the beginning of the year, and they all left of their own accord. He is trying to understand what happened.

He adds that his previous assistant spent nearly eight years with the company, but left because of health prob-

lems. Since then, new assistants have come and gone through the revolving door. His former assistant had been entrusted with many responsibilities and challenges, including client relations and the authority to solve any problems that arose.

As you speak to the GM, he asserts his proficiency at selling a position to a skeptical candidate. You also find out that hefty payments were made to three different employment agencies over the past year.

NOTE: This case study was used in the 17th edition (2003) of *Excalibur, The Canadian University Tournament of Human Resources*

SOURCE: Richard Matte, CHRP, Matte groupe conseil, http://www.rhri.org/excalibur/en/case_study. Retrieved: May 16, 2004.

Questions

1. Summarize your understanding of the problem. Use no more than five lines.
2. In light of the information provided, what steps should be taken (at least four) to ensure the success of the recruitment process?

Chapter 5

Selecting Employees

What Do I Need to Know? After reading this chapter, you should be able to:

1. Identify the elements of the selection process.

2. Define ways to measure the success of a selection method.

3. Summarize the legal requirements for employee selection.

4. Compare the common methods used for selecting human resources.

5. Describe major types of employment tests.

6. Discuss how to conduct effective interviews.

7. Explain how employers carry out the process of making a selection decision.

Introduction

M&M Meat Shops Ltd. operates 388 stores across Canada selling an extensive range of frozen entrees, meat products, and desserts. Started as a family business in 1980, majority owner and CEO Mac Voisin attributes success to how it handles the selection of franchise holders. Voisin describes the selection of franchise holders as a "courting process" lasting several months.

Voisin explains, "twenty to thirty years ago, franchise companies didn't qualify their people. It used to be a joke that if you had a pulse and a cheque book, you could get a franchise." In contrast, M&M handles their selection process differently. M&M conducts extensive interviews and uses personality profile testing to select franchise holders. "We didn't want to let just anybody in here. We're as strong as our weakest link. We want strong people; we want them to be part of our team."[1]

Hiring decisions are about finding the people who will be a good fit with the job and the organization. Any organization that appreciates the competitive edge provided by good people must take the utmost care in choosing its members. The organization's decisions about selecting people are central to its ability to survive, adapt, and grow. Selection decisions become especially critical when organizations face tight labour markets or must compete for talent with other organizations in the same industry. If a competitor keeps getting the best applicants, the remaining companies must make do with who is left.

Mac Voisin, co-founder of M&M Meat Shops Ltd., values the importance of franchise-holder selection to the success of his company.

This chapter will familiarize you with ways to minimize errors in employee selection. The chapter starts by describing the selection process and how to evaluate possible methods for carrying out that process. It then takes an in-depth look at the most widely used methods: applications and résumés, employment tests, and interviews. The chapter ends by describing the process by which organizations arrive at a final selection decision.

Selection Process

LO1

Through **selection,** organizations make decisions about who will be chosen to fill job openings. Selection begins with the candidates identified through recruitment and attempts to reduce their number to the individuals best qualified to perform the available jobs. At the end of the process, the selected individuals are placed in jobs with the organization.

selection
The process through which organizations make decisions about who will be chosen to fill job openings.

The process of selecting employees varies considerably from organization to organization and from job to job. At most organizations, however, selection includes the steps illustrated in Figure 5.1. First, a human resource professional reviews the applications received to see which meet the requirements of the job. For candidates who meet the requirements, the organization administers tests and reviews work samples

FIGURE 5.1

Steps in the Selection Process

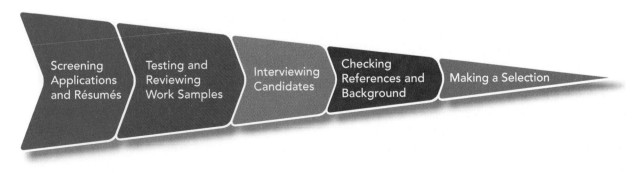

Screening Applications and Résumés → Testing and Reviewing Work Samples → Interviewing Candidates → Checking References and Background → Making a Selection

FIGURE 5.2

Criteria for Evaluating
Selection Methods

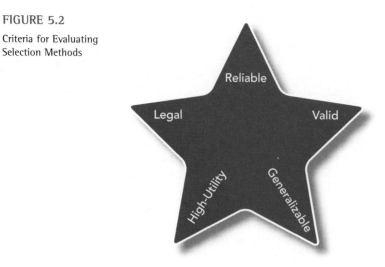

to assess the candidates' competencies. Those with the best capabilities are invited to the organization for one or more interviews. Often, supervisors and team members are involved in this stage of the process. By this point, the decision makers are beginning to form opinions about which candidates are most desirable. For the top few candidates, the organization should check references and conduct background checks to verify that the organization's information is correct. Then supervisors, teams, and other decision makers select a person to receive a job offer. In some cases, the candidate may negotiate with the organization regarding salary, benefits, and the like. If the candidate accepts the job, the organization places him or her in that job.

How does an organization decide which of these elements to use, and in what order? Some organizations simply repeat a selection process that is familiar. If members of the organization underwent job interviews, they conduct job interviews, asking familiar questions. However, what organizations *should* do is to create a selection process in support of its job descriptions and specifications. In Chapter 3, we explained that a job specification identifies the competencies required for successfully performing a job. The selection process should be set up in such a way that it lets the organization identify people who have the necessary competencies. When the Canadian Security and Intelligence Service (CSIS) hires Intelligence Officers, it looks for people who have specific experience, characteristics, and personal attributes. For example, CSIS wants people who are highly motivated and interested in the Service. The selection process for Intelligence Officers assesses these attributes during the suitability interview, an in-depth panel interview, and a psychological assessment. Candidates who survive the entire range of interviews and tests, not to mention the intensive security screening process, also spend time in an interview with CSIS executives.[2]

LO2

This kind of strategic approach to selection requires ways to measure the effectiveness of selection tools. From science, we have basic standards for this. The best selection methods will provide information that is reliable and valid and can be generalized to apply to the organization's group of candidates. In addition, selection should measure characteristics that have practical benefits for the organization. Finally, selection criteria must meet the legal requirements in effect where the organization operates. Figure 5.2 summarizes these criteria.

Reliability

The **reliability** of a type of measurement indicates how free that measurement is from random error.[3] A reliable measurement therefore generates consistent results. Assuming that a person's intelligence is fairly stable over time, a reliable test of intelligence should generate consistent results if the same person takes the test several times. Organizations that construct intelligence tests therefore should be able to provide (and explain) information about the reliability of their tests.

Usually, this information involves statistics such as *correlation coefficients*. These statistics measure the degree to which two sets of numbers are related. A higher correlation coefficient signifies a stronger relationship. At one extreme, a correlation coefficient of 1.0 means a perfect positive relationship—as one set of numbers goes up, so does the other. If you took the same vision test three days in a row, those scores would probably have nearly a perfect correlation. At the other extreme, a correlation of –1.0 means a perfect negative correlation—when one set of numbers goes up, the other goes down. In the middle, a correlation of 0 means there is no correlation at all. For example, the correlation between weather and intelligence would be at or near 0. A reliable test would be one for which scores by the same person (or people with similar attributes) have a correlation close to 1.0.

reliability
The extent to which a measurement generates consistent results.

Validity

For a selection measure, **validity** describes the extent to which performance on the measure (such as a test score) is related to what the measure is designed to assess (such as job performance). Although we can reliably measure such characteristics as weight and height, these measurements do not provide much information about how a person will perform most kinds of jobs. Thus, for most jobs height and weight provide little validity as selection criteria. One way to determine whether a measure is valid is to compare many people's scores on that measure with their job performance. For example, suppose people who score above 60 words per minute on a keyboarding test consistently get high marks for their performance in data-entry jobs. This observation suggests the keyboarding test is valid for predicting success in that job.

As with reliability, information about the validity of selection methods often uses correlation coefficients. A strong positive (or negative) correlation between a measure and job performance means the measure should be a valid basis for selecting (or rejecting) a candidate. This information is important, not only because it helps organizations identify the best employees, but also because organizations can ensure that their selection process is valid. Three ways of measuring validity are criterion-related, content, and construct validity.

validity
The extent to which performance on a measure (such as a test score) is related to what the measure is designed to assess (such as job performance).

Criterion-Related Validity

The first category, **criterion-related validity,** is a measure of validity based on showing a substantial correlation between test scores and job performance scores. In the example in Figure 5.3, a company compares two measures—an intelligence test and a university or college grade point average—with performance as research analyst. In the left graph, which shows the relationship between the intelligence test scores and job performance, the points for the 20 research analysts fall near the 45-degree line. The correlation coefficient is near .90 (for a perfect 1.0, all the points would be on the 45-degree line). In the graph at the right, the points are scattered more widely. The cor-

criterion-related validity
A measure of validity based on showing a substantial correlation between test scores and job performance scores.

FIGURE 5.3

Criterion-Related Measurements of a Student's Aptitude

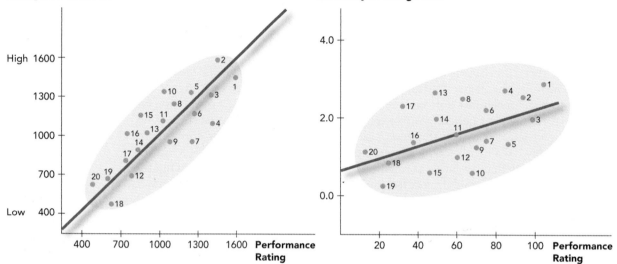

predictive
validation
Research that uses
the test scores of all
applicants and looks
for a relationship
between the scores
and future
performance of the
applicants who were
hired.

relation between university or college GPA and research analysts' performance is much lower. In this hypothetical example, the intelligence test is more valid than GPA for predicting success at this job.

Two kinds of research are possible for arriving at criterion-related validity:

1. **Predictive validation**—This research uses the test scores of all applicants and looks for a relationship between the scores and future performance. The researcher administers the tests, waits a set period of time, and then measures the performance of the applicants who were hired.
2. **Concurrent validation**—This type of research administers a test to people who currently hold a job, then compares their scores to existing measures of job performance. If the people who score highest on the test also do better on the job, the test is assumed to be valid.

concurrent
validation
Research that
consists of
administering a test
to people who
currently hold a job,
then comparing their
scores to existing
measures of job
performance.

Predictive validation is more time consuming and difficult, but it is the best measure of validity. Job applicants tend to be more motivated to do well on the tests, and their performance on the tests is not influenced by their firsthand experience with the job. Also, the group studied is more likely to include people who perform poorly on the test—a necessary ingredient to accurately validate a test.[4]

Content and Construct Validity

content validity
Consistency between
the test items or
problems and the
kinds of situations or
problems that occur
on the job.

Another way to show validity is to establish **content validity**—that is, consistency between the test items or problems and the kinds of situations or problems that occur on the job.[5] A test that is "content valid" exposes the job applicant to situations that are likely to occur on the job. It tests whether the applicant has the knowledge, skills, or ability, i.e., competencies to handle such situations.

For example, a general residential contracting firm needed to hire a construction superintendent.[6] This job involved organizing, supervising, and inspecting the work of many subcontractors. The tests developed for this position attempted to mirror the job. One test was a scrambled subcontractor test. The applicant had to take a random list of subcontractors (roofing, plumbing, electrical, and so on) and put them in the order that each firm should appear on the construction site. A second test measured recognition of construction errors. In this test, the applicant went into a shed that was specially constructed to have 25 common and expensive errors, including faulty wiring and upside-down windows. The applicant was supposed to record all the problems he or she could detect. The content of these tests so closely parallels the content of the job that it was safe to use test performance as the basis for predicting job performance.

The usual basis for deciding that a test has content validity is through expert judgment. Experts can rate the test items according to whether they mirror essential functions of the job. Because establishing validity is based on the experts' subjective judgments, content validity is most suitable for measuring behaviour that is concrete and observable.

For tests that measure abstract qualities such as intelligence or leadership ability, establishment of validity may have to rely on **construct validity.** This involves establishing that tests really do measure intelligence, leadership ability, or other such "constructs," as well as showing that mastery of this construct is associated with successful performance of the job. For example, if you could show that a test measures something called "mechanical ability," and that people with superior mechanical ability perform well as assemblers, then the test has construct validity for the assembler job. Tests that measure a construct usually measure a combination of behaviours thought to be associated with the construct.

construct validity
Capability of a test to measure a construct such as intelligence and the relationship of this construct to successful job performance.

Ability to Generalize

Along with validity in general, we need to know whether a selection method is valid in the context in which the organization wants to use it. A **generalizable** method applies not only to the conditions in which the method was originally developed—job, organization, people, time period, and so on. It also applies to other organizations, jobs, applicants, and so on. In other words, is a selection method that was valid in one context also valid in other contexts?

Researchers have studied whether tests of intelligence and thinking skills (called *cognitive ability*) can be generalized. The research has supported the idea that these tests are generalizable across many jobs. However, as jobs become more complex, the validity of many of these tests increases. In other words, they are most valid for complex jobs.[7]

generalizable
Valid in other contexts beyond the context in which the selection method was developed.

Practical Value

Not only should selection methods such as tests and interview responses accurately predict how well individuals will perform, they should produce information that actually benefits the organization. Being valid, reliable, and generalizable adds value to a method. Another consideration is the cost of using the selection method. Selection procedures such as testing and interviewing cost money. They should cost significantly less than the benefits of hiring the new employees. Methods that provide economic value greater than the cost of using them are said to have **utility.**

The choice of a selection method may differ according to the job being filled. If the job involves providing a product or service of high value to the organization, it is worthwhile to spend more to find a top performer. At a company where salespeople are responsible for closing million-dollar deals, the company will be willing to invest

utility
The extent to which something provides economic value greater than its cost.

TABLE 5.1

Guidelines for
Applications and
Interviews

SUBJECT	AVOID ASKING	PREFERRED
Name	• about name change: whether it was changed by court order, marriage, or other reason • maiden name	
Address	• for addresses outside Canada	• ask place and duration of current or recent address
Age	• for birth certificates, baptismal records, or about age in general	• ask applicants whether they are eligible to work under Canadian laws regarding age restrictions
Sex	• about pregnancy, child bearing plans, or child care arrangements	• ask applicant if the attendance requirements can be met
Marital status	• whether the applicant is single, married, divorced, engaged, separated, widowed, or living common-law • about the spouse's employment	• if transfer or travel is part of the job, the applicant can be asked whether he or she can meet these requirements • ask whether there are any circumstances that might prevent completion of a minimum service commitment
Family status	• number of children or dependants	• ask if the applicant would be able to work the required hours and, where applicable, overtime
National or ethic origin	• about birthplace, nationality of ancestors, spouse, or other relatives • whether born in Canada • for proof of citizenship	• ask if the applicant is legally entitled to work in Canada
Photographs	• for photo to be attached to applications or sent to interviewer before interview	
Religion	• about religious affiliation • for references from clergy	• explain the required work shift, and ask whether such a schedule poses problems for the applicant Note: accommodation of an employee's religious beliefs is the employer's duty
Disability	• for a list of all disabilities, limitations, or health problems	• ask whether the applicant has any condition that could affect ability to do the job Note: accommodation of an employee's disability is the employer's duty to the point of undue hardship
Pardoned conviction	• whether an applicant has ever been convicted • whether the applicant has a criminal record	• if bonding is a job requirement, ask whether the applicant is eligible
Sexual orientation	• about the applicant's sexual orientation	

Note: This table provides examples and is not intended as a complete listing of all guidelines. The examples are based on federal Human Rights legislation; some provincial laws vary and may affect these examples.

SOURCE: "A Guide to Screening and Selection in Employment," Canadian Human Rights Commission, February 2001, pp. 3–5, www.chrc-ccdp.ca/publications/employment_equity-en.asp. Retrieved: April 3, 2004. Reproduced with the permission of the Minister of Public Works and Government Services Canada, 2004.

more in selection decisions. At a fast-food restaurant, such an investment will not be worthwhile; the employer will prefer faster, simpler ways to select workers who ring up orders, prepare food, and keep the facility clean.

Legal Standards for Selection

LO3

Whether selecting a new employee or promoting an employee from within the organization, the selection process needs to be conducted in a way that avoids human rights complaints. For example, Human Rights legislation described in Chapter 2 has implications for the selection process.

- The interview needs to be conducted in a way that candidates can be assessed without drawing out information that is not relevant to the job being filled. As summarized in Table 5.1, the organization may not ask questions on an application form or in an interview that gathers information about a person's protected status, even indirectly. For example, asking candidates for the dates they attended high school could indirectly gather information about applicants' age.

- Interview notes are made by interviewers to help distinguish among candidates. Even if these notes are only used by the interviewers, they cannot include references to any prohibited ground of discrimination (for example, "Asian man, 40-ish" would be an inappropriate comment to include in interview notes).[8]

An important principle of selection is to combine several sources of information about candidates, rather than relying solely on interviews or a single type of testing. The sources should be chosen carefully to relate to the characteristics identified in the job description. When organizations do this, they are increasing the validity of the decision criteria. They are more likely to make hiring decisions that are fair and unbiased. They also are more likely to choose the best candidates.

Job Applications and Résumés

LO4

Nearly all employers gather background information on applicants at the beginning of the selection process. The usual ways of gathering background information are by asking applicants to fill out application forms and provide résumés. Organizations also verify the information by checking references and conducting background checks.

Asking job candidates to provide background information is inexpensive. The organization can get reasonably accurate information by combining applications and résumés with background checks and well-designed interviews.[9]

Application Forms

Asking each applicant to fill out an employment application is a low-cost way to gather basic data from many applicants. It also ensures that the organization has certain standard categories of information, such as mailing address and employment history, from each. Figure 5.4 is an example of an online application form for the Vice President, People position at WestJet.

Employment applications include areas for applicants to provide several types of information:

- *Contact information*—The employee's name, address, phone number, and email address.

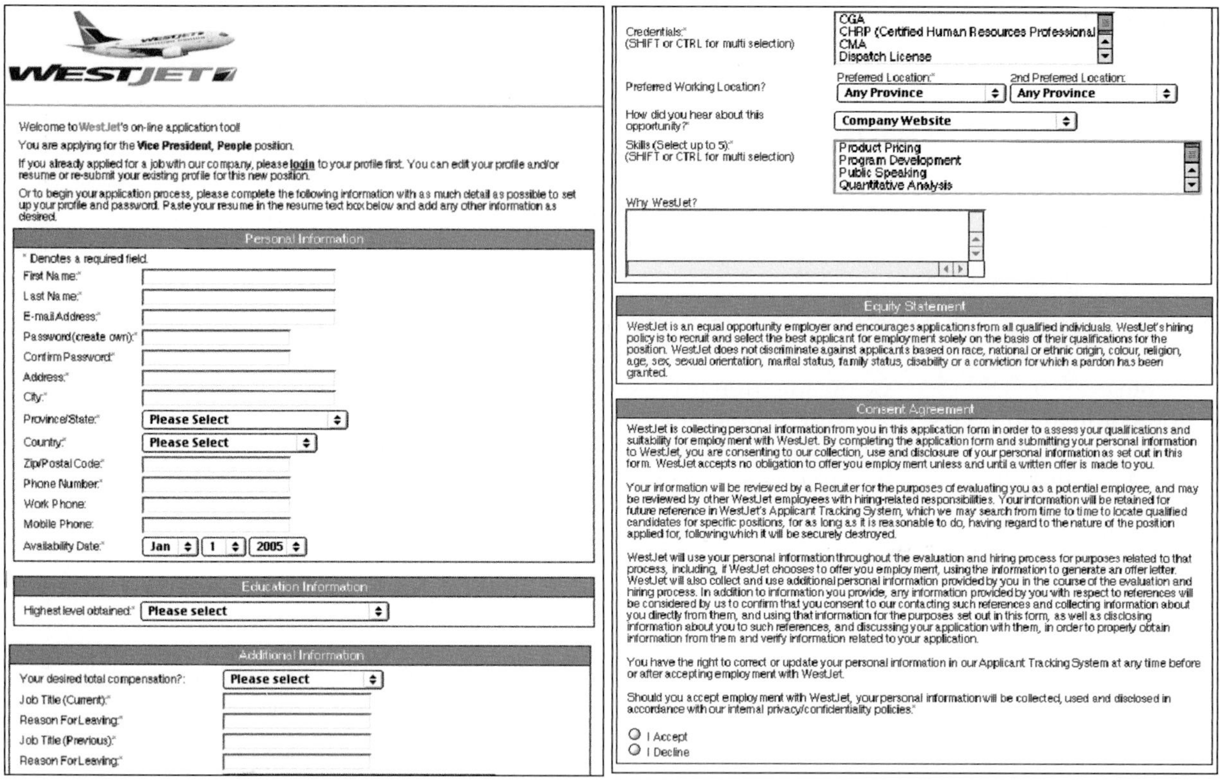

SOURCE: www.westjet.com. Retrieved: March 31, 2005.

FIGURE 5.4

WestJet's Online Application Form

- *Work experience*—Companies the applicant worked for, job titles, and dates of employment.
- *Educational background*—High school, college, and universities attended and degree(s) awarded.
- *Applicant's signature*—Signature or verification following a statement that the applicant has provided true and complete information.

The application form may include other areas for the applicant to provide additional information, such as specific work experiences, technical skills, or memberships in professional or trade associations. Also, including the date on an application is useful for keeping up-to-date records of job applicants. The application form should not request information that could violate Human Rights legislation. For example, questions about an applicant's birthplace, marital status, or number of children would be inappropriate.

By reviewing application forms, HR staff can identify which candidates meet minimum requirements for education and experience. They may be able to rank applicants—for example, giving applicants with ten years' experience a higher ranking than applicants with two years' experience. In this way, the applications enable the organization to narrow the pool of candidates to a number it can afford to test and interview.

Résumés

The usual way that applicants introduce themselves to a potential employer is to submit a résumé. An obvious drawback of this information source is that applicants control the content of the information, as well as the way it is presented. This type of information is therefore biased in favour of the applicant and (although this is unethical) may not even be accurate. However, this inexpensive way to gather information does provide employers with a starting point. Organizations typically use résumés as a basis for deciding which candidates to investigate further.

As with employment applications, an HR staff member reviews the résumés to identify candidates meeting such requirements including competencies, educational background, related work performed, and types of equipment the person has used. Because résumés are created by the job applicants (or the applicants have at least approved résumés created by someone they hire), they also may provide some insight into how candidates communicate and present themselves. Employers tend to decide against applicants whose résumés are unclear, messy, or contain mistakes. On the positive side, résumés may enable applicants to highlight accomplishments that might not show up in the format of an employment application. Review of résumés is most valid when the content of the résumés is assessed in terms of the criteria associated with successful job performance. Organizations are increasingly turning to applicant-tracking software to match job openings and applications and/or résumés. Applicant-tracking software is used to scan electronically-submitted applications and résumés to match applicant competencies with the requirements of jobs. Many organizations are expanding this capability by turning their websites into interactive career centres that can notify applicants when a job matching their qualifications becomes available.

References

Application forms often ask that applicants provide the names of several references. Applicants provide the names and contact information of former employers or others who can vouch for their abilities and past job performance. In some situations, the applicant may provide letters of reference written by those people. It is then up to the organization to have someone contact the references to gather information or verify the accuracy of the information provided by the applicant.

As you might expect, references are not an unbiased source of information. Most applicants are careful to choose references who will say something positive. In addition, former employers and others may be afraid that if they express negative opinions, they will be sued. Their fear is understandable. In the many thousands of lawsuits that have been filed over such matters, damage awards can run over $500,000.[10] Intuit Corporation, producer of Quicken software, gets around this problem by requiring as many as 12 letters of reference. Typically, the first two or three people listed provide glowing references, but people further down the list provide a fuller picture of the candidate.[11]

Usually the organization checks references after it has determined that the applicant is a finalist for the job. Contacting references for all applicants would be time-consuming, and it does pose some burden on the people contacted. Part of that burden is the risk of giving information that is seen as too negative or too positive. If the person who is a reference gives negative information, there is a chance the candidate will claim *defamation*, meaning the person damaged the applicant's reputation by

Checking out employees is a growth industry as more organizations conduct background checks on potential employees. Advanced technology has helped reduce costs and streamline the process.

making statements that cannot be proved truthful.[12] At the other extreme, if the person gives a glowing statement about a candidate, and the new employer later learns of misdeeds such as sexual misconduct or workplace violence, the new employer might sue the former employer for misrepresentation.[13]

Because such situations occasionally arise, often with much publicity, people who give references tend to give as little information as possible. Most organizations have policies that the human resource department will handle all requests for references and that they will only verify employment dates and sometimes the employee's final salary. In organizations without such a policy, HR professionals should be careful—and train managers to be careful—to stick to observable, job-related behaviours and to avoid broad opinions that may be misinterpreted. In spite of these drawbacks of references, the risks of not learning about significant problems in a candidate's past outweigh the possibility of getting only a little information. Potential employers should check references.

Background Checks

A background check is a way to verify that applicants are as they represent themselves to be. ADP Screening and Selection Services is a company that provides background checks on prospective employees. ADP found that more than half of candidates submitted false information—up from 40 percent in the previous year. These kinds of findings are prompting companies to increase their use of thorough background checks.[14] Also fuelling this growing use of background checks are applicants using complex and high-tech means to fraudulently impress employers. For example, candidates are paying computer hackers to insert their names into university and college class list databases and using websites that offer fake degrees and diplomas.[15]

Besides verifying résumés and employment history, education, and references, businesses are also checking for criminal records and personal credit histories. However, employers must keep in mind that before performing a background check they must get consent from the candidate. As discussed in Chapter 2, consent is needed to comply with Canada's Personal Information Protection and Electronic Documents Act (PIPEDA).[16]

To promote the industry and develop common standards, the National Association of Professional Background Screeners (NAPBS) was formed in 2004. During its first four months the NAPBS grew from 180 to 280 companies.[17]

LO5

Employment Tests and Work Samples

When the organization has identified candidates whose applications or résumés indicate they meet basic requirements, the organization continues the selection process with this narrower pool of candidates. Often, the next step is to gather objective data through one or more employment tests. These tests fall into two broad categories:

1. **Aptitude tests** assess how well a person can learn or acquire skills and abilities. In the realm of employment testing, the best-known aptitude test is the General Aptitude Test Battery (GATB).
2. **Achievement tests** measure a person's existing knowledge and skills. For example, some organizations use interactive tests to assess applicants' skills using software such as Access, Excel, PowerPoint, Word, or WordPerfect.

Employment tests may assess general abilities, such as physical strength, or specific skills, such as keyboarding speed. Some organizations also use personality tests to find applicants who have personality traits associated with successful job performance, as well as integrity tests to weed out dishonest candidates. In addition, drug testing and medical examinations try to ensure that candidates meet physical job requirements and will not be impaired on the job. Before using any test, organizations should investigate the test's validity and reliability. Besides asking the testing service to provide

aptitude tests
Tests that assess how well a person can learn or acquire skills and abilities.

achievement tests
Tests that measure a person's existing knowledge and skills.

HR HOW TO

Testing 101

Intelligence quotient

In use for about a century, we've all taken IQ tests in school. These are most often multiple-choice tests that determine how well you acquire verbal and mathematical knowledge, and how accurately you apply what you know.

Sample question: Which number does not belong: 4, 17, 18, 32? The answer is 17, the only odd number.

What it demonstrates: IQ score is based on an average. Scoring 100 means the person is technically higher than 50 percent of all people taking the test. An IQ of 130 is higher than 95 percent of the people taking the test.

Emotional intelligence

Based on research by psychologist Dr. Daniel Goleman, who claims a combination of self-awareness, empathy, and social skills is as important as factual knowledge in achieving success.

Sample question: Rate on a five-point scale from strongly agree to disagree: "Even when I do my best, I feel guilty about the things that didn't get done." Strongly agreeing indicates the person is a perfectionist, which an employer might prize, but it could also be seen as obsessive, which could affect ability to work with others.

What it shows: Proponents claim the combination of self-awareness, empathy and social skills these tests measure are vital to leadership.

Personality test

More than 100 tests are on the market that ask questions about anger, anxiety, pain, honesty, and integrity to rate a person's approach to life and relationships.

Sample question: Rate yourself on a five-point scale from strongly agree to disagree: I am a reliable worker; I can be careless at times; I tend to be disorganized.

What it measures: Traits, for instance, extroverted or introverted; agreeable or inflexible; creative or conservative.

SOURCE: Wallace Immen, "Testing 101," *The Globe and Mail*, January 26, 2005, p. C2. Reprinted with permission from *The Globe and Mail*.

this information, it is wise to consult more impartial sources of information, such as the ones identified in Table 5.2. The "HR How To" box discusses various types of employment tests.

Physical Ability Tests

Physical strength and endurance play less of a role in the modern workplace than in the past, thanks to the use of automation and current technology. Even so, many jobs still require certain physical abilities or psychomotor abilities (those connecting brain and body, as in the case of eye-hand coordination). When these abilities are essential to job performance or avoidance of injury, the organization may use physical ability tests. These evaluate one or more of the following areas of physical ability: muscular tension, muscular power, muscular endurance, cardiovascular endurance, flexibility, balance, and coordination.[18]

Although these tests can accurately predict success at certain kinds of jobs, they also tend to exclude women and people with disabilities. As a result, use of physical ability tests can make the organization vulnerable to human rights complaints. It is therefore important to be certain that the abilities tested for really are essential to job performance or that the absence of these abilities really does create a safety hazard.

Cognitive Ability Tests

Although fewer jobs require muscle power today, brainpower is essential for most jobs. Organizations therefore benefit from people who have strong mental abilities. **Cognitive ability tests**—sometimes called "intelligence tests"—are designed to measure such mental abilities as verbal skills (skill in using written and spoken language), quantitative skills (skill in working with numbers), and reasoning ability (skill in thinking through the answer to a problem). Many jobs require all of these cognitive skills, so employers often get valid information from general tests. The Public Service Commission of Canada uses the General Competency Test Level 1 (GCT1) to measure thinking skills (understanding written material, solving numerical problems, and drawing logical conclusions) for administrative support position selection decisions. The GCT2 is used to assess general cognitive abilities required

cognitive ability tests
Tests designed to measure such mental abilities as verbal skills, quantitative skills, and reasoning ability.

TABLE 5.2

Sources of Information about Employment Tests

Mental Measurements Yearbook	Descriptions and reviews of tests that are commercially available
Principles for the Validation and Use of Personnel Selection Procedures (Society for Industrial and Organizational Psychology)	Guide to help organizations evaluate tests
Standards for Educational and Psychological Tests (American Psychological Association)	Description of standards for testing programs
Tests: A Comprehensive Reference for Assessments in Psychology, Education, and Business	Descriptions of thousands of tests
Test Critiques	Reviews of tests, written by professionals in the field

Simulation Turns Recruitment into a Two-Way Street

Ken Church, the owner of Prudential Grand Valley Realty, a real estate firm in Kitchener, Ontario, is constantly on the lookout for new agents and competition for talent can be intense. Given its ambitious growth goals, recruitment and selection of new staff who would be top performers was one of his toughest challenges.

He started using job simulation as a selection tool. It's an online, video-based assessment that simulates the job of a real estate agent and gives candidates a realistic preview of what day-to-day life as a sales agent will be. It also evaluates the key skills required to succeed as an agent and

compiles that information for review to help make a better hiring decision.

"Since we've implemented this tool, we are getting way more recruiting leads and are seeing a higher quality of applicants," said Church. "It's no secret that attracting people into the real estate industry is tough, because they have no real way of knowing if they have what it takes to be successful. The simulation helps them make a more informed decision."

In the simulation, the recruit plays the role of an agent and gets to interact with virtual clients who are interested in buying or selling property. The

recruit is taken through the entire sales cycle from building rapport all the way to closing and must demonstrate the ability to handle objections, negotiate price, understand client needs, deal with personality clashes, and handle periodic rejection.

SOURCE: Igor Kotylar and Ravit Abelman, "Simulation Turns Recruitment into a Two-Way Street," *Canadian HR Reporter*, December 1, 2003, www.hrreporter.com. Retrieved: February 19, 2004. © Copyright *Canadian HR Reporter*, December 1, 2003, by permission of Carswell, Toronto, Ontario, 1-800-387-5164, www.hrreporter.com.

for officer level positions.[19] Many reliable tests are commercially available. The tests are especially valid for complex jobs and for those requiring adaptability in changing circumstances.[20]

Job Performance Tests and Work Samples

Many kinds of jobs require candidates that excel at performing specialized tasks, such as operating a certain machine, handling phone calls from customers, or designing advertising materials. To evaluate candidates for such jobs, the organization may administer tests of the necessary skills. Sometimes the candidates take tests that involve a sample of work, or they may show existing samples of their work. Examples of job performance tests include tests of keyboarding speed and *in-basket tests*. An in-basket test measures the ability to juggle a variety of demands, as in a manager's job. The candidate is presented with simulated emails and phone messages describing the kinds of problems that confront a person in the job. The candidate has to decide how to respond to these messages, and in what order. Examples of jobs for which candidates provide work samples include graphic designers and writers. The "E-HRM" box describes how job simulation is used as a selection tool in the real estate industry.

Pilots require high cognitive ability. Cognitive ability tests may be used to select individuals for such positions. What other positions might require some measure of an individual's ability to handle their complexities?

assessment centre
A wide variety of specific selection programs that use multiple selection methods to rate applicants or job incumbents on their management potential.

Tests for selecting managers may take the form of an **assessment centre**—a wide variety of specific selection programs that use multiple selection methods to rate applicants or job incumbents on their management potential. An assessment centre typically includes in-basket tests, tests of more general abilities, and personality tests. Combining several assessment methods increases the validity of this approach.

Job performance tests have the advantage of being job specific—that is, tailored to the kind of work done in a specific job. These tests therefore have a high level of validity, especially when combined with cognitive ability tests and a highly structured interview.[21] This advantage can become a disadvantage, however, if the organization wants to generalize the results of a test for one job to candidates for other jobs. Also, developing different tests for different jobs can become expensive. One way to save money is to prepare computerized tests that can be delivered online to various locations.

Personality Inventories

In some situations, employers may also want to know about candidates' personalities. For example, one way that psychologists think about personality is in terms of the "Big Five" traits: extroversion, adjustment, agreeableness, conscientiousness, and inquisitiveness (explained in Table 5.3). There is evidence that people who score high on conscientiousness tend to excel at work, especially when they also have high cognitive ability.[22] For people-related jobs like sales and management, extroversion and agreeableness also seem to be associated with success.[23]

The usual way to identify a candidate's personality traits is to administer one of the personality tests that are commercially available. The employer pays for the use of the test, and the organization that owns the test then scores the responses and provides a report about the test taker's personality. An organization that provides such tests should be able to discuss the test's validity and reliability. Assuming the tests are valid for the organization's jobs, they have advantages. However, Shawn Bakker a chartered psychologist at Psychometrics Canada, an Alberta firm that specializes in selection, cautions that personality tests were not designed for selection and work better for staff development purposes.[24]

Some people think they can identify personality traits by analyzing a person's handwriting. Research has not found a relationship between the results of handwriting analysis and job performance. However, handwriting analysis is a popular selection method in Europe. According to one estimate, eight out of ten companies in Western Europe use it in their selection process. North American organizations rarely use handwriting analysis, but in today's global business climate, HR professionals may want to know that it is common in other parts of the world.[25]

TABLE 5.3

Five Major Personality Dimensions Measured by Personality Inventories

1. Extroversion	Sociable, gregarious, assertive, talkative, expressive
2. Adjustment	Emotionally stable, nondepressed, secure, content
3. Agreeableness	Courteous, trusting, good-natured, tolerant, cooperative, forgiving
4. Conscientiousness	Dependable, organized, persevering, thorough, achievement-oriented
5. Inquisitiveness	Curious, imaginative, artistically sensitive, broadminded, playful

Honesty Tests, Alcohol and Drug Tests

No matter what employees' personalities may be like, organizations want employees to be honest and to behave safely. Some organizations are satisfied to assess these qualities based on judgments from reference checks and interviews. Others investigate these characteristics more directly through the use of tests.

Testing services have developed paper-and-pencil honesty (or integrity) tests. Generally these tests ask applicants directly about their attitudes toward theft and their own experiences with theft. Table 5.4 shows a sample of the items on such a test. Most of the research into the validity of these tests has been conducted by the testing companies, but evidence suggests they do have some ability to predict such behaviour as theft of the employer's property.[26]

As concerns about substance abuse and the harmful impacts of alcohol and drugs on employee safety and performance have grown, so has the use of alcohol and drug testing. As a measure of a person's past exposure to drugs, chemical testing is highly accurate. However, these tests are controversial for several reasons. Although breathalyzer tests can measure how much alcohol has been consumed and the person's level of impairment, current drug tests cannot measure impairment or assess if an employee is capable of performing the job.[27]

Employers considering the use of drug or alcohol tests should ensure that their testing programs conform to the Canadian Human Right Commission's drug and alcohol testing policy and all other relevant legal requirements. As discussed in Chapter 2, the Canadian Human Rights Act prohibits discrimination related to a disability and dependence on drugs or alcohol is considered a disability that must be accommodated to the point of undue hardship.

At least partially in response to cases brought before the Supreme Court of Canada and the Ontario Court of Appeals, the Canadian Human Rights Commission has updated its policy on drug testing and created a framework for alcohol testing. As a result, the following kinds of testing became unacceptable:

- Pre-employment drug tests
- Random drug tests
- Random alcohol tests for employees in jobs not considered "safety-sensitive"

Employers considering the use of alcohol or drug testing should get legal advice to make sure they can justify testing based on a bona fide occupational requirement.[28]

Medical Examinations

Especially for physically demanding jobs, organizations may wish to conduct medical examinations to see that the applicant can meet the job's requirements. Employers

TABLE 5.4

Sample Items from a Typical Honesty Test

1. It's OK to take something from a company that is making too much profit.
2. Stealing is just a way of getting your fair share.
3. When a store overcharges its customers, it's OK to change price tags on merchandise.
4. If you could get into a movie without paying and not get caught, would you do it?
5. Is it OK to go around the law if you don't actually break it?

SOURCE: "T or F? Honesty Tests," p. 104. Reprinted with permission, *Inc.* magazine, February 1992. © Copyright 1992 by Goldhirsh Group, Inc., 38 Commercial Wharf, Boston, MA 02110.

Interview Questions That Can Get Boffo Results

Behavioural interviewing is based on the premise that past behaviour is the best predictor of future behaviour. Behavioural interviewing offers at least a couple of key advantages relative to traditional methods:

- By focusing on the critical competencies or attributes most important to successful job performance, the interview has a valid basis for person-to-job matching.

- Because candidates are asked similar questions, the interviewer can make objective comparisons between candidates.

Here are five behavioural interview questions that are somewhat unexpected and are likely to produce revealing results:

1. "Tell us about a best-in-class standard or practice that you've introduced."

- This question can uncover results-orientation and may be adapted for less senior positions, e.g., "Tell us about a recent example of something you have done to improve your efficiency at work?"

2. "Describe a situation when a subordinate was able to change your mind on a particular course of action."

- This question is useful to uncover team leadership capabilities.

3. "Tell us about the most unpopular decision you have made."

- This question can tell you a lot about a candidate's leadership and negotiation skills.

4. "Describe a time when you were faced with a

challenging situation that involved balancing competing interests in your personal life with issues in the workplace."

- This question can uncover how employees effectively balance their work–life by using creative and innovative solutions.

5. "Describe a crisis situation and how you handled it."

- This question can provide key insights into the candidate's ability to assess and respond quickly.

Behavioural description interviews are flexible and can be applied and adapted to any situation or organization.

SOURCE: Sarah B. Hood, "Hire Echelon," *Canadian Business*, June 7–20, 2004, pp. 71–73.

---

may also wish to establish an employee's physical condition at the beginning of employment, so that there is a basis for measuring whether the employee has suffered a work-related disability later on. At the same time, as described in Chapter 2, organizations may not discriminate against individuals with disabilities who could perform a job with reasonable accommodations. Likewise, they may not use a measure of physical ability that discriminates against women, older workers, etc. unless those requirements are valid in predicting the ability to perform a job. Medical exams must be related to job requirements and may not be given until the candidate has received a conditional job offer. Therefore, organizations must be careful in how they use medical examinations. Many organizations make selection decisions first, then conduct the exams to confirm that the employee can handle the job, with any reasonable accommodations required. Limiting the use of medical exams in this way also holds down the cost of what tends to be an expensive process.

Interviews

LO6

Supervisors and team members most often get involved in the selection process at the stage of employment interviews. These interviews bring together job applicants and representatives of the employer to obtain information and evaluate the applicant's qualifications. While the applicant is providing information, he or she is also forming opinions about what it is like to work for the organization. Most organizations use interviewing as part of the selection process. In fact, this method is used more than any other.

Interviewing Techniques

An interview may be nondirective or structured. In a **nondirective interview,** the interviewer has great discretion in choosing questions to ask each candidate. For example, the interviewer might ask, "What is your greatest accomplishment in your current position?" The candidate's reply might suggest to the interviewer what other questions to ask. Often, these interviews include open-ended questions about the candidate's strengths, weaknesses, career goals, and work experience. Because nondirective interviews give the interviewer wide latitude, their reliability is not great. Also, interviewers do not necessarily ask valid questions. Inexperienced or poorly informed interviewers may ask questions that are irrelevant or even illegal.

To manage the risks of a nondirective interview, many organizations substitute the use of a **structured interview,** which establishes a set of questions for the interviewer to ask. Ideally, these questions are related to the requirements set out in the job description. They should cover the candidate's knowledge required to perform this type of job, his or her experience in handling job-related situations, and other job-related personal requirements such as willingness to travel, work overtime, or learn new skills. The interviewer asks questions from the list and is supposed to avoid asking questions that are not on the list. Some interviewers object to being limited in this way, but a list of well-written questions can provide more valid and reliable results.

Some of the best results of interviewing come from the use of **situational interviews.** In this type of structured interview, the interviewer describes a situation likely to arise on the job, then asks the candidate what he or she would do in that situation. Situational interviews have been shown to have high validity in predicting job performance.[29] A variation is the **behavioural interview,** in which the interviewer asks the candidate to describe how he or she handled a type of situation in the past. Questions about the candidates' actual experiences tend to have the highest validity.[30] This extensively used method is frequently referred to as "behaviourally-based" or "competency-based" interviewing.

When Andrew Kindler was a hiring manager, he used open-ended behavioural questions to good effect. When interviewing candidates for management positions, he would ask them to describe the most difficult ethical dilemma they had to solve at work. Kindler's objective was to learn about each candidate's ethics and problem-solving style. In one instance, a candidate for a position as the corporation's general counsel (an important legal position) said he had never encountered an ethical dilemma. Kindler quickly eliminated that candidate from consideration, on the grounds that "a lawyer who has never encountered an ethical dilemma doesn't have ethics."[31]

The "Best Practices" box examines specific questions to ask in an effective behavioural interview. BMO Financial Group has been using behavioural interviews since the early 1990s for almost every position it fills. BMO Financial Group views behavioural

nondirective interview
A selection interview in which the interviewer has great discretion in choosing questions to ask each candidate.

structured interview
A selection interview that consists of a predetermined set of questions for the interviewer to ask.

situational interviews
A structured interview in which the interviewer describes a situation likely to arise on the job, then asks the candidate what he or she would do in that situation.

behavioural interview
A structured interview in which the interviewer asks the candidate to describe how he or she handled a type of situation in the past.

When interviewing candidates, it's valid to ask about willingness to travel if that is part of the job. Interviewers might ask questions about previous business travel experiences and/or how interviewees handled situations requiring flexibility and self-motivation (qualities that would be an asset in someone who is travelling alone and solving business problems on the road).

panel interview
Selection interview in which several members of the organization meet to interview each candidate.

interviews as most effective for external candidates because internal candidates have existing performance reviews and have been through the process at some point. [32]

The common setup for either a nondirected or structured interview is for an individual (an HR professional or the supervisor for the vacant position) to interview each candidate face to face. However, variations on this approach are possible. In a **panel interview,** several members of the organization meet to interview each candidate. A panel interview gives the candidate a chance to meet more people and see how people interact in that organization. It provides the organization with the judgments of more than one person, to reduce the effect of personal biases in selection decisions. Panel interviews can be especially appropriate in organizations that use teamwork. At the other extreme, some organizations conduct interviews without any interviewers; they use a computerized interviewing process. The candidate enters replies to the questions interactively and results are submitted electronically. Such a format eliminates a lot of personal bias—along with the opportunity to see how people interact. Therefore, electronic interviews are useful for gathering objective data, rather than assessing people skills.

Advantages and Disadvantages of Interviewing

The wide use of interviewing is not surprising. People naturally want to see prospective employees firsthand. As we noted in Chapter 1, the top qualities that employers seek in new hires include communication skills and interpersonal skills. Talking face to face can provide evidence of these skills. Interviews can give insights into candidates' personalities and interpersonal styles. They are more valid, however, when they focus on job knowledge and skill.

Despite these benefits, interviewing is not necessarily the most accurate basis for making a selection decision. Research has shown that interviews can be unreliable, low in validity,[33] and biased against a number of different groups.[34] Interviews are also costly. They require that at least one person devote time to interviewing each candidate, and the applicants typically have to be brought to one geographic location. Interviews are also subjective, so they place the organization at greater risk of discrimination complaints by applicants who were not hired, especially if those individuals were asked questions not entirely related to the job.

Organizations can avoid some of these pitfalls.[35] Human resource staff should keep the interviews focused, structured, and standardized. The interview should concentrate on accomplishing a few goals, so that at the end of the interview, the organization has ratings on several observable measures, such as ability to express ideas. The interview should not try to measure abilities and skills—for example, intelligence—that tests can measure better. As noted earlier, situational and behavioural interviews are especially effective for doing this. Organizations can prevent problems related to subjectivity by training interviewers and using more than one person to conduct interviews. Training typically includes focusing on the recording of observable facts, rather than on making subjective judgments, as well as developing interviewers' awareness of their biases.[36] Levi Strauss provides for objectivity by ensuring that many different perspectives are included in selection decisions.[37]

Preparing to Interview

Organizations can reap the greatest benefits from interviewing if they prepare carefully. A well-planned interview should be standardized, comfortable for the participants, and focused on the job and the organization. The interviewer should have a quiet place in which to conduct interviews without interruption. This person should be trained in how to ask objective questions, what subject matter to avoid, and how to detect and handle his or her own personal biases or other distractions in order to fairly evaluate candidates.

The interviewer should have enough documents to conduct a complete interview. These should include a list of the questions to be asked, with plenty of space for recording the responses. When the questions are prepared, it is also helpful to determine how the answers will be assessed. For example, if questions are asked about how interviewees have handled certain situations, consider what responses are best in terms of meeting job requirements. If the job requires someone who develops new and creative solutions to problems, then a response that shows innovative behaviour would receive a higher score. The interviewer also should have a copy of the interviewee's employment application and résumé, to review before the interview and refer to during the interview. If possible, the interviewer should also have printed information about the organization and the job. Near the beginning of the interview, it is a good idea to go over the job specifications, organizational policies, and so on, so that the interviewee has a clearer understanding of the organization's needs.

The interviewer should schedule enough time to review the job requirements, discuss the interview questions, and give the interviewee a chance to ask questions. To close, the interviewer should thank the candidate for coming and provide information about what to expect—for example, that the organization will contact a few finalists within the next two weeks or that a decision will be made by the end of the week.

Selection Decisions

LO7

After reviewing applications, scoring tests, conducting interviews, and checking references, the organization needs to make decisions about which candidates to place in which jobs. In practice, most organizations find more than one qualified candidate to fill an open position. The selection decision typically combines ranking based on objective criteria along with subjective judgments about which candidate will make the greatest contribution.

How Organizations Select Employees

The selection decision should not be a simple matter of whom the supervisor likes best or which candidate will take the lowest offer. Rather, the people making the selection should look for the best fit between candidate and position. In general, the person's performance will result from a combination of ability and motivation. Often, the selection is a choice among a few people who possess the basic qualifications. The decision makers therefore have to decide which of those people have the best combination of ability and motivation to fit in the position and in the organization as a whole. Figure 5.5 illustrates an extreme example of such a candidate.

The usual process for arriving at a selection decision is to gradually narrow the pool of candidates for each job. This approach, called the **multiple-hurdle model,** is based on a process such as the one shown earlier in Figure 5.1. Each stage of the process is a hurdle, and candidates who overcome a hurdle continue to the next stage of the process. For example, the organization reviews applications and/or résumés of all candidates, conducts some tests on those who meet minimum requirements, conducts initial interviews with those who had the highest test scores, follows up with additional interviews or testing, and then selects a candidate from the few who survived this process. Another, more expensive alternative is to take most applicants through all steps of the process and then to review all the scores to find the most desirable candidates. With this alternative, decision makers may use a **compensatory model,** in which a very high score on one type of assessment can make up for a low score on another.

Whether the organization uses a multiple-hurdle model or conducts the same assessments on all candidates, the decision maker(s) needs criteria for choosing among qualified candidates. An obvious strategy is to select the candidates who score highest on tests and interviews. However, employee performance depends on motivation as well as ability. It is possible that a candidate who scores very high on an ability test might be "overqualified"—that is, the employee might be bored by the job the organization needs to fill, and a less-qualified employee might actually be a better fit. Similarly, a highly motivated person might learn some kinds of jobs very quickly, potentially outperforming someone who has the necessary skills. Furthermore, some or-

multiple-hurdle model
Process of arriving at a selection decision by eliminating some candidates at each stage of the selection process.

compensatory model
Process of arriving at a selection decision in which a very high score on one type of assessment can make up for a low score on another.

FIGURE 5.5

Fit for the Job
ZITS

Copyright © Zits Partnership. Reprinted with special permission of King Features Syndicate.

ganizations have policies of developing employees for career paths in the organization. Such organizations might place less emphasis on the skills needed for a particular job and more emphasis on hiring candidates who share the organization's values, show that they have the people skills to work with others in the organization, and are able to learn the skills needed for advancement.

Finally, organizations have choices about who will make the decision. Sometimes a supervisor makes the final decision, often alone. This person may couple knowledge of the job with a judgment about who will fit in best with others in the department. The decision could also be made by a human resource professional using standardized, objective criteria. Especially in organizations that value teamwork, selection decisions may be made by a work team or other panel of decision makers.

Communicating the Decision

The human resource department is often responsible for notifying applicants about the results of the selection process. When a candidate has been selected, the organization should communicate the offer to the candidate. The offer should include the job responsibilities, work schedule, rate of pay, starting date, and other relevant details. If placement in a job requires that the applicant complete a medical examination, the offer should state that contingency. The person communicating the offer should also indicate a date by which the candidate should reply with an acceptance or rejection of the offer. For some jobs, such as management and professional positions, the candidate and organization may negotiate pay, benefits, and work arrangements before they arrive at a final employment agreement.

The person who communicates this decision should keep accurate records of who was contacted, when, and for which position, as well as of the candidate's reply. The HR department and the supervisor also should be in close communication about the job offer. When an applicant accepts a job offer, the HR department must notify the supervisor, so that he or she can be prepared for the new employee's arrival.

Summary

1. Identify the elements of the selection process.
   Selection typically begins with a review of candidates' employment applications and résumés. The organization administers tests to candidates who meet requirements, and qualified candidates undergo one or more interviews. Organizations check references and conduct background checks to verify the accuracy of information provided by candidates. A candidate is selected to fill each vacant position. Candidates who accept offers are placed in the positions for which they were selected.

2. Define ways to measure the success of a selection method.
   One criterion is reliability, which indicates the method is free from random error, so that measurements are consistent. A selection method should also be valid, meaning that performance on the measure (such as a test score) is related to what the measure is designed to assess (such as job performance). Criterion-related validity shows a correlation between test scores and job performance scores. Content validity shows consistency between the test items or problems and the kinds of situations or problems that occur on the job. Construct validity establishes that the test actually measures a specified construct, such as intelligence or leadership ability, which is presumed to be associated with success on the job. A selection method also should be generalizable, so that it applies to more than one specific situation. Each selection method should have utility, meaning it provides economic value greater than its cost. Finally, selection methods should meet the legal requirements for employment decisions.

3. Summarize the legal requirements for employee selection.

   The selection process must comply with Human Rights legislation and be conducted in a fair and consistent manner. This means selection methods must be valid for job performance. Questions may not gather information about prohibited grounds, such as national or ethnic origin, family status, or religion, nor may the employer investigate a person's disability status.

4. Compare the common methods used for selecting human resources.

   Nearly all organizations gather information through employment applications and résumés. These methods are inexpensive, and an application form standardizes basic information received from all applicants. The information is not necessarily reliable, because each applicant provides the information. These methods are most valid when evaluated in terms of the criteria in a job description. References and background checks help to verify the accuracy of the information. Employment tests and work samples are more objective. To be legal, any test must measure abilities that actually are associated with successful job performance. Employment tests range from general to specific. General-purpose tests are relatively inexpensive and simple to administer. Tests should be selected to be related to successful job performance and avoid human rights violations. Interviews are widely used to obtain information about a candidate's interpersonal and communication skills and to gather more detailed information about a candidate's background. Structured interviews are more valid than unstructured ones. Situational interviews provide greater validity than general questions. Interviews are costly and may introduce bias into the selection process. Organizations can minimize the drawbacks through preparation and training.

5. Describe major types of employment tests.

   Physical ability tests measure strength, endurance, psychomotor abilities, and other physical abilities. They can be accurate but can discriminate and are not always job related. Cognitive ability tests, or intelligence tests, tend to be valid, especially for complex jobs and those requiring adaptability. They are a relatively low-cost way to predict job performance but have been challenged as discriminatory. Job performance tests tend to be valid but

are not always generalizable. Using a wide variety of job performance tests can be expensive. Personality tests measure personality traits such as extroversion and adjustment. Research supports their validity for appropriate job situations, especially for individuals who score high on conscientiousness, extroversion, and agreeableness. These tests are relatively simple to administer and generally meet legal requirements. Organizations may use paper-and-pencil honesty tests, which can predict certain behaviours, including employee theft. Some organizations may also administer alcohol and/or drug tests if a bona fide occupational requirement such as safety justifies it. Passing a medical examination may be a condition of employment, but to avoid discrimination against persons with disabilities, organizations usually administer a medical exam only after making a conditional job offer.

6. Discuss how to conduct effective interviews.

   Interviews should be focused, structured, and standardized. Interviewers should identify job requirements and create a list of questions related to the requirements. Interviewers should be trained to recognize their own personal biases and conduct objective interviews. Panel interviews can reduce problems related to interviewer bias. Interviewers should put candidates at ease in a comfortable place that is free of distractions. Questions should ask for descriptions of relevant experiences and job-related behaviours. The interviewers also should be prepared to provide information about the job and the organization.

7. Explain how employers carry out the process of making a selection decision.

   The organization should focus on the objective of finding the person who will be the best fit with the job and organization. This includes an assessment of ability and motivation. Decision makers may use a multiple-hurdle model in which each stage of the selection process eliminates some of the candidates from consideration at the following stages. At the final stage, only a few candidates remain, and the selection decision determines which of these few is the best fit. An alternative is a compensatory model, in which all candidates are evaluated with all methods. A candidate who scores poorly with one method may be selected if he or she scores very high on another measure.

Review and Discussion Questions

1. What activities are involved in the selection process? Think of the last time you were hired for a job. Which of those activities were used in selecting you? Should the organization that hired you have used other methods as well?

2. Why should the selection process be adapted to fit the organization's job specifications?

3. Choose two of the selection methods identified in this chapter. Describe how you can compare them in

terms of reliability, validity, ability to generalize, utility, and compliance with Human Rights legislation.

4. Why does predictive validation provide better information than concurrent validation? Why is this type of validation more difficult?

5. How does Human Rights legislation affect organizations' use of interviews?

6. Suppose your organization needs to hire several computer programmers, and you are reviewing résumés you obtained from an online service. What kinds of information will you want to gather from the "work experience" portion of these résumés? What kinds of information will you want to gather from the "education" portion of these résumés? What methods would you use for verifying or exploring this information? Why would you use those methods?

7. For each of the following jobs, select the two kinds of tests you think would be most important to include in the selection process. Explain why you chose those tests.
   a. City bus driver.
   b. Pharmaceutical sales representative.
   c. Member of a team that sells complex high-tech equipment to manufacturers.
   d. Member of a team that makes a component of the equipment in (c).

8. Suppose you are a human resource professional at a large retail chain. You want to improve the company's hiring process by standardizing interviews, so that every time someone is interviewed for a particular job category, that person answers the same questions. You also want to make sure the questions asked are relevant to the job and comply with Human Rights legislation. Think of three questions to include in interviews for each of the following jobs. For each question, state why you think it should be included.
   a. Cashier at one of the company's stores.
   b. Buyer of the stores' teen clothing line.
   c. Accounts payable clerk at company headquarters.

9. How can organizations improve the quality of their interviewing so that interviews provide valid information?

10. Some organizations set up a selection process that is long and complex. In some people's opinion, this kind of selection process not only is more valid but also has symbolic value. What can the use of a long, complex selection process symbolize to job seekers? How do you think this would affect the organization's ability to attract the best employees?

What's Your HR IQ?   www.mcgrawhill.ca/college/noe

The Online Learning Centre offers more ways to check what you've learned so far. Find experiential exercises as well as Test Your Knowledge Quizzes, Videos, and many other resources at www.mcgrawhill.ca/college/noe.

BusinessWeek Case

BusinessWeek It's Not Easy Making Pixie Dust

We are in the Utilidor—a series of tunnels below Disney World's Magic Kingdom theme park in Orlando. The tunnel complex is generally off-limits to outsiders, but not to 41 visiting managers whose companies have anted up $2,295 a head so they can learn about Walt Disney Company's approach to people management.

This underground city is a beehive of activity. Employees rush through the grey concrete tunnels, scrambling to put on costumes and assume their roles upstairs. Golf carts speed by with supplies. Makeup artists prepare an array of Cinderella and Snow White wigs.

Before coming to this $3^1/_2$-day seminar, I was skeptical. The program sounded like little more than a dream junket: three nights at the resort's most elegant hotel, plus four-day passes to Disney's theme parks. Besides, I thought, what could any manager possibly learn at Disney World? By the end of the first day's activities, however, my note pad was brimming with ideas and lessons dished out by Disney staff.

My colleagues, most of them human resource managers, take the program seriously. Most are facing a slew of challenges in need of Disney-style magic. A delivery manager at Anheuser-Busch Companies is trying to make his drivers more responsive to retailers. Personnel managers at a fast-growing bagel chain in Florida worry about maintaining standards as they beef up the chain's ranks. And an employee trainer at South Africa's state-owned transportation conglomerate is looking for ways to streamline the company's hiring process.

Disney's reputation for cleanliness, attention to detail, and helpful employees is what has drawn them here. "Everyone knows how wonderful Disney is, so you figure they must be doing something right," says Kathleen Scapini, who works for Multi-Media in West Hartford, Connecticut. That "something right" is what Disney refers to as the "pixie-dust" formula, with four key ingredients—employee selection, training, support, and benefits. Our seminar, "Disney's Approach to People Management," promises to reveal how the company motivates employees.

Instructors, called facilitators, tell us that we cannot count on Tinkerbell. "The solutions are not complicated," assures Jeff Soluri, a Disney instructor. "It's attention to detail and hard-nosed business practices that produce the magic."

If there is pixie dust, it starts with the hiring process. One of the first activities is a field trip to Disney's "casting centre," a Venetian-style castle where job candidates view a video before being interviewed. The short film informs job seekers about the company's strict appearance guidelines (one ring per hand and no tattoos, please) and the rigours of the work. By being blunt and detailed, Disney says, it's able to weed out incompatible candidates at the first crack.

The critical part of the process, though, is employee training. New hires, who average less than $10 an hour, are treated to a visual company history. They are told that they are not just employees but pivotal "cast members" in a "show." From street sweepers to monorail pilots, each cast member must go out of his way to make the resort seem *unreal*. No matter how tired workers are or how deeply guests may try their patience, they must never lose composure. To do so, the company tells its cast, is to risk alienating a guest, spoiling the illusion, and damaging Disney's standing in entertainment and American culture.

Between excursions, participants share what they have learned—and what they might use. Disney staffers with wireless microphones dart Oprah-like through a conference room seeking comments. They get plenty. John Lealos, the Anheuser-Busch manager, says he wants to incorporate more of an appreciative, team feel into his unit's corporate culture. "If we can get that kind of atmosphere at our company, the productivity will go up," he says. Hugo Strydom, the training manager at South Africa's Transit Ltd., intends to use a Disney-style orientation to weed out weak candidates in a major hiring blitz.

SOURCE: Antonio Fins, "It's Not Easy Making Pixie Dust," *BusinessWeek*, September 19, 1997.

Questions

1. This case reveals much about what Disney looks for in a job applicant as well as what it does (realistic job previews) to get unsuitable job candidates to remove themselves from the process. What characteristics would you expect Disney to be selecting for?
2. Based on the information given, what selection methods might be appropriate for further screening job applicants?
3. Why is selection an important part of a maintaining a competitive advantage at Disney? Would it be equally important at a bank? Why or why not?

Case: A Dozen First Impressions

McMaster University in Hamilton, Ontario, is Canada's third largest medical school. McMaster uses a screening method that requires medical school candidates to answer questions and dash from one room to the next when a bell rings.

This interviewing method was designed to enhance the quality of the selection process by getting an insight into the candidates' qualities related to the requirements of a medical career.

Traditional interviews for medical school involve interviews with a panel of professors. However, Chairman of Admissions, Dr. Harold Reiter explains, "It's hoped that by being able to differentiate which candidates are stronger in the desired personal qualities, we will be producing better physicians."

Applicants rotate through 12 mini-interviews that are exactly eight minutes long. They are given the chance to discuss one scenario or answer one question before having to move quickly to the next interview when a bell sounds. The mini-interviews focus on both ethical issues and realistic medical scenarios. For example, one mini-interview scenario requires applicants to answer a question about a patient who requests a faith healer after refusing traditional medical treatment. Another mini-interview requires applicants to confront a situation in which a law requires the physician to notify the police of treatment for a gunshot wound.

The use of these mini-interviews in the McMaster medical school's selection process takes the form of an assessment centre approach. This approach was put into place following three years of research into how to enhance the selection process. The medical school recently conducted these mini-interviews with 384 candidates in a two-week period to fill 138 available spots.

SOURCE: Anne Marie Owens, "Medical Schools Novel Entrance Test—12 Eight Minute Interviews," *National Post*, April 5, 2004, pp. A1, A5. Material reprinted with the express permission of The National Post Company, a CanWest Partnership.

Questions

1. In your opinion, does this selection method increase the validity of the selection process at McMaster's medical school? Why or why not?
2. What additional selection methods may be appropriate for the initial screening of medical school applicants (i.e., prior to the intensive mini-interview process)?
3. Would you prefer this interview process to a traditional panel interview? Why or why not?

VIDEO CASE

Manager's Hot Seat: Beck 'N Call

Most jobs start with an interview, whether it's conducted in person, by phone, or even online. Interpersonal dynamics can affect those interviews, so a human resource manager who is looking to develop a diverse workforce to meet company needs must be able to ask the right questions of a candidate and listen to the answers in an objective, controlled manner. The ultimate goal is to evaluate the candidate fairly and accurately so that he or she fits well with job requirements. As you'll see in the video, two managers for the Beck 'N Call company are interviewing two job applicants, and the way they conduct the interviews and evaluate the applicants will affect both the organization and the individuals—in the composition of the company's workforce and the way those employees later develop in their positions. Both racial and gender issues enter into play in this scenario.

The workforce is becoming increasingly diverse. Companies that want to grow and remain competitive need to utilize the talents, experiences, and knowledge of workers from different backgrounds and cultures. If they do not, they may miss a golden opportunity to reach a larger customer base. The interview should contain questions that allow the job applicant to respond and demonstrate his or her competencies in ways that are job related, not personal. Hunches and gut feelings should play but a tiny part in such an interview, because once a job applicant becomes an employee, it's the concrete evidence of performance that counts, not whether the interviewer and employee went to the same college or university or like the same sports teams.

Once employees are hired, it is important to give them opportunities to develop their skills and to advance. This practice not only enhances the employee–employer relationship but also boosts overall productivity of the company.

A firm like Beck 'N Call can do plenty to develop its workforce to its fullest potential: If the company hires one of the candidates in the videotaped interview, it can assign a mentor to the new hire to help her learn the ropes and identify ways to further her career within the organization.

Thus, an interview is much more important than a casual conversation about a job. It is the first step toward shaping an organization's future workforce. If it is conducted well, both parties win.

SOURCE: McGraw-Hill Higher Education: Manager's Hot Seat: Beck 'N Call.

Questions

1. Evaluate the interviewers in terms of their interviewing techniques and follow-up. Did either of the managers conduct their interviews with unfair or discriminating practices? Did they evaluate the best person for the job fairly and accurately? What could/should they have done differently?

2. Imagine that you were interviewing either of these candidates. How would you conduct your interview? Write four or five questions that you think should be asked to find the best applicant. Which candidate do you think you would hire, and why? (Be sure to think about long-term implications for both the employee and the organization.)

3. Think of your own experience in job interviews. Based on what you now know about interviewing, in what ways might you be able to improve your own techniques for participating in an interview as a job applicant?

Part 3

Developing Human Resources

Chapter **6**

Training Employees

What Do I Need to Know? After reading this chapter, you should be able to:

1. Discuss how to link training programs to organizational needs.

2. Explain how to assess the need for training.

3. Explain how to assess employees' readiness for training.

4. Describe how to plan an effective training program.

5. Compare widely used training methods.

6. Summarize how to implement a successful training program.

7. Evaluate the success of a training program.

8. Describe training methods for employee orientation and diversity management.

Introduction

Established in 1906, the PCL family of companies is the largest general contracting organization in Canada, and among the largest in the United States. The PCL College of Construction, unique to the construction industry, has a campus or private learning space in each operating centre. The goal is to communicate today's technology to employees and help prepare them for tomorrow's challenges, whether it's through self-directed learning activities, instructor-directed learning, or some other teaching or mentoring activity. PCL describes its strategy to be the employer of choice in the North American Construction industry as "They invest in us; we invest in them."[1] PCL is expanding its commitment to the College of Construction by building the $12-million Centennial Learning Centre to commemorate PCL's 100th anniversary in 2006. The 29,000-square foot addition to PCL's existing ten-acre business park in south Edmonton, will be home to the College of Construction.[2]

The College of Construction offers courses and learning materials that develop skills in five main areas:

- **Personal:** To enrich our personal abilities to learn, to communicate, and to organize ourselves.

- **Interpersonal:** To build on our skills to interact effectively with one another.

- **Leadership and Management:** To demonstrate and practise new methods for the management of our key resources: our people, our time, our materials/equipment, and our finances.

- **Technical:** To ensure that PCL employees have the appropriate opportunities to become and remain technically competent in key construction techniques, computer skills, and safety.

- **QUEST (skills for continuous improvement):** To help develop innovative ways for working that will help prepare PCL employees for the variety of challenges facing the organization now and in a more competitive, complex, and rapidly changing future.[3]

training

An organization's planned efforts to help employees acquire job-related competencies with the goal of applying these on the job.

Training consists of an organization's planned efforts to help employees acquire job-related competencies with the goal of applying these on the job. A training program may range from formal classes to one-on-one mentoring, and it may take place on the job or at remote locations. No matter what its form, training can benefit the organization when it is linked to organizational needs and when it motivates employees.

This chapter describes how to plan and carry out an effective training program. We begin by discussing how to develop effective training in the context of the organization's strategy. Next, we discuss how organizations assess employees' training needs. We then review training methods and the process of evaluating a training program. The chapter concludes by discussing some special applications of training: orientation of new employees and the management of diversity.

PCL's 29,000-square foot Centennial Learning Centre in Edmonton will house the College of Construction.

Training Linked to Organizational Needs   LO1

Workplace training is a key ingredient in the competitiveness of firms and ultimately of national competitiveness.[4] Rapid change, especially in the area of technology, requires that employees continually learn new skills, from the use of robots to collaboration on the Internet. The new psychological contract, described in Chapter 1, has created the expectation that employees invest in their own career development. Employees with this expectation will value employment at an organization that provides learning opportunities. Growing reliance on teamwork creates a demand for the ability to solve problems in teams, an ability that often requires formal training. Finally, the diversity of the Canadian population, coupled with the globalization of business, requires that employees be able to work well with people who are different from them. Successful organizations often take the lead in developing this ability.

How are Canadian firms investing in and supporting learning? How does Canada compare with other countries? The Conference Board of Canada explores these and other questions in its Training and Development Outlook—2003. The study reveals that Canadian firms continue to under-invest in learning and that Canada lags the United States and other countries in employee training, which could have serious adverse effects on long-term productivity as well as have serious ramifications for competitiveness—for both workers and markets— on the world stage.[5]

This survey of about 150 employers found that training remained relatively flat compared with previous years. Average training dollars represented 1.7 percent of payroll[6] (the average per capita direct expenditure on training and development across all industries in Canada is $838)[7] down from 2.0 percent in 2000.[8] Organizations surveyed indicated that an average of 30 percent of employees did not receive any formal training at all.[9] Overall, Canada has one of the lowest levels of participation in job-related continuing education and training of the leading developed

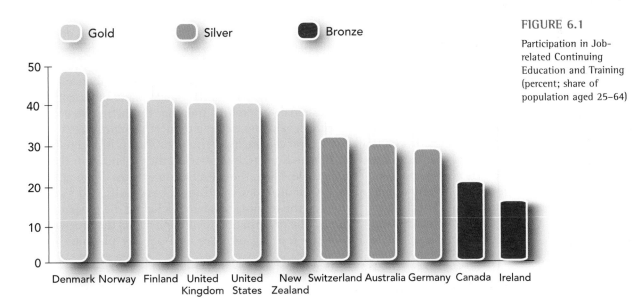

FIGURE 6.1

Participation in Job-related Continuing Education and Training (percent; share of population aged 25–64)

Note: Data for Sweden are not available.
SOURCE: "Performance and Potential 2003–04: Defining the Canadian Advantage: A Special Report by The Conference Board of Canada," October 2003, p. 31, www.conferenceboard.ca. Retrieved: March 2, 2004.

FIGURE 6.2

Stages of Instructional
Design

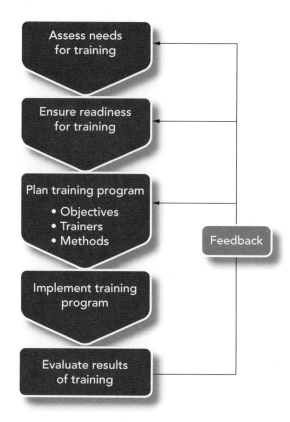

instructional design
A process of
systematically
developing training
to meet specified
needs.

countries in the world. Figure 6.1 illustrates how Canada's participation in job-related continuing education and training compares with other countries.[10]

With training so essential in modern organizations, it is important to provide training that is effective. An effective training program actually teaches what it is designed to teach, and it teaches skills and behaviours that will help the organization achieve its goals. Training programs may prepare employees for future positions in the organization, enable the organization to respond to change, reduce turnover, enhance worker safety, improve customer service and product design, and meet many other goals. To achieve those goals, HR professionals approach training through **instructional design**—a process of systematically developing training to meet specified needs.

A complete instructional design process includes the steps shown in Figure 6.2. It begins with an assessment of the needs for training—what the organization requires that its people know and be able to do. Next, the organization ensures that employees are ready for training in terms of their attitudes, motivation, basic skills, and work environment. The third step is to plan the training program, including the program's objectives, instructors, and methods. The organization then implements the program. Finally, evaluating the results of the training provides feedback for planning future training programs.

needs assessment
The process of
evaluating the
organization,
individual
employees, and
employees' tasks to
determine what
kinds of training, if
any, are necessary.

LO2

Needs Assessment

Instructional design logically should begin with a **needs assessment,** the process of evaluating the organization, individual employees, and employees' tasks to determine

FIGURE 6.3

Needs Assessment

what kinds of training, if any, are necessary. As this definition indicates, the needs assessment answers questions in the three broad areas shown in Figure 6.3:[11]

1. *Organization*—What is the context in which training will occur?
2. *Person*—Who needs training?
3. *Task*—What topics should the training cover?

The answers to these questions provide the basis for planning an effective training program.

A variety of conditions may prompt an organization to conduct a needs assessment. Management may observe that some employees lack basic skills or are performing poorly. Decisions to produce new products, apply new technology, or design new jobs should prompt a needs assessment, because these changes tend to require new skills. The decision to conduct a needs assessment also may be prompted by outside forces, such as customer requests or legal requirements.

The outcome of the needs assessment is a set of decisions about how to address the issues that prompted the needs assessment. These decisions do not necessarily include a training program, because some issues should be resolved through methods other than training. For example, suppose a company uses delivery trucks to transport anesthetic gases to medical facilities. A driver of one of these trucks mistakenly hooked up the supply line of a mild anesthetic from the truck to the hospital's oxygen system, contaminating the hospital's oxygen supply. This performance problem prompts a needs assessment. Whether or not the hospital decides to provide more training will depend partly on the reasons the driver erred. The driver may have hooked up the supply lines incorrectly because of a lack of knowledge about the appropriate line hookup, anger over a request for a pay raise being denied, or mislabeled valves for connecting the supply lines. Out of these three possibilities, only the lack of knowledge can be corrected through training. Other outcomes of a needs assessment might include plans for better rewards to improve motivation, better hiring decisions, and better safety precautions.

The remainder of this chapter discusses needs assessments and then what the organization should do when they indicate a need for training. The possibilities include offering existing training programs to more employees; buying or developing new training programs; and improving existing training programs. Before we consider the available training options, let's examine the elements of the needs assessment in more detail.

Organization Analysis

organization analysis
A process for determining the appropriateness of training by evaluating the characteristics of the organization.

Usually, the needs assessment begins with the **organization analysis.** This is a process for determining the appropriateness of training by evaluating the characteristics of the organization. The organization analysis looks at training needs in light of the organization's strategy, resources available for training, and management's support for training activities.

Training needs will vary depending on whether the organization's strategy is based on growing or shrinking its workforce, whether it is seeking to serve a broad customer base or focusing on the specific needs of a narrow market segment, and various other strategic scenarios. A company that is cutting costs with a downsizing strategy may need to train employees in job search skills. The employees who will remain following a downsizing may need cross-training so that they can handle a wider variety of responsibilities. An organization that concentrates on serving a niche market may need to continually update its employees on a specialized skills set. Transocean Offshore, a contractor that drills offshore oil wells for oil companies, focuses exclusively on deep-water drilling. Contracts for these jobs last four or five years, longer than contracts for other types of well drilling. Deep-water drilling also requires modern technology and new ships, such as the high-tech *Discoverer Enterprise*, which boasts numerous workstations, computer systems, and automated drilling systems. In contrast to most drilling companies, which merely provide safety training, Transocean must provide training for specialized job skills, as well as training for general rig safety.[12]

Even if training fits the organization's strategy, it can be viable only if the organization is willing to invest in this type of activity. Managers play a key role by supporting employees' needs and ensuring employees have opportunities to apply their competencies on the job.[13] Conversely, the managers will be most likely to support training if the people planning it can show that it will solve a significant problem or result in a significant improvement, relative to its cost. Managers appreciate training proposals with specific goals, timetables, budgets, and methods for measuring success.

Person Analysis

person analysis
A process for determining individuals' needs and readiness for training.

Following the organizational assessment, needs assessment turns to the remaining areas of analysis: person and task. The **person analysis** is a process for determining individuals' needs and readiness for training. It involves answering several questions:

- Do performance deficiencies result from a competency gap, i.e., a lack of knowledge, skill, or ability? (If so, training is appropriate; if not, other solutions are more relevant.)
- Who needs training?
- Are these employees ready for training?

The answers to these questions help the manager identify whether training is appropriate and which employees need training. In certain situations, such as the introduction of a new technology or service, all employees may need training. However, when needs assessment is conducted in response to a performance problem, training is not always the best solution.

The person analysis is therefore critical when training is considered in response to a performance problem. In assessing the need for training, the manager should identify all the variables that can influence performance. The primary variables are the person's ability and skills, his or her attitudes and motivation, the organization's input (including clear directions, necessary resources, and freedom from interference and distractions), performance feedback (including praise and performance standards), and positive consequences to motivate good performance. Of these variables, only ability and skills can be affected by training. Therefore, before planning a training program, it is important to be sure that any performance problem results from a deficiency in knowledge and skills. Otherwise, training dollars will be wasted, because the training is unlikely to have much effect on performance.

The person analysis also should determine whether employees are ready to undergo training. In other words, the employees to receive training not only should require additional knowledge and skill, but must be willing and able to learn. (After this discussion of the needs assessment, we will explore the topic of employee readiness in greater detail.)

Task Analysis

The third area of needs assessment is **task analysis,** the process of identifying the tasks and competencies (knowledge, skills, and behaviour) that training should emphasize. Usually, task analysis is conducted along with person analysis. Understanding shortcomings in performance usually requires knowledge about the tasks and work environment as well as the employee.

task analysis
The process of identifying the tasks and competencies that training should emphasize.

FIGURE 6.4

Sample Task Statement Questionnaire

Name _____ Date _____
Position _____

Instructions: Please rate each of the task statements according to three factors: the **importance** of the task for effective performance, how **frequently** the task is performed, and the degree of **difficulty** required to become effective in the task.

Use the following scales in making your ratings.

Importance
4 = Task is critical for effective performance.
3 = Task is important but not critical for effective performance.
2 = Task is of some importance for effective performance.
1 = Task is of no importance for effective performance.
0 = Task is not performed.

Frequency
4 = Task is performed once a day.
3 = Task is performed once a week.
2 = Task is performed once every few months.
1 = Task is performed once or twice a year.
0 = Task is not performed.

Difficulty
4 = Effective performance of the task requires extensive prior experience and/or training (12–18 months or longer).
3 = Effective performance of the task requires minimal prior experience and training (6–12 months).
2 = Effective performance of the task requires a brief period of prior training and experience (1–6 months).
1 = Effective performance of the task does not require specific prior training and/or experience.
0 = Task is not performed.

Task (circle the number from the scales above)	Importance	Frequency	Difficulty
1. Ensuring maintenance on equipment, tools, and safety controls	0 1 2 3 4	0 1 2 3 4	0 1 2 3 4
2. Monitoring employee performance	0 1 2 3 4	0 1 2 3 4	0 1 2 3 4
3. Scheduling employees	0 1 2 3 4	0 1 2 3 4	0 1 2 3 4
4. Using statistical software on the computer	0 1 2 3 4	0 1 2 3 4	0 1 2 3 4
5. Monitoring changes made in processes using statistical methods	0 1 2 3 4	0 1 2 3 4	0 1 2 3 4

To carry out the task analysis, the HR professional looks at the conditions in which tasks are performed. These conditions include the equipment and environment of the job, time constraints (for example, deadlines), safety considerations, and performance standards. These observations form the basis for a description of work activities, or the tasks required by the person's job. For a selected job, the analyst interviews employees and their supervisors to prepare a list of tasks performed in that job. Then the analyst validates the list by showing it to employees, supervisors, and other subject-matter experts and asking them to complete a questionnaire about the importance, frequency, and difficulty of the tasks. Figure 6.4 is an example of a task statement questionnaire. In this example, the questionnaire begins by defining categories that specify a task's importance, frequency, and difficulty. Then, for a production supervisor's job, the questionnaire lists five tasks. For each task, the subject-matter expert uses the scales to rate the task's importance, frequency, and difficulty.

The information from these questionnaires is the basis for determining which tasks will be the focus of the training. The person or committee conducting the needs assessment must decide what levels of importance, frequency, and difficulty signal a need for training. Logically, training is most needed for tasks that are important, frequent, and at least moderately difficult. For each of these tasks, the analysts must identify the competencies (knowledge, skills, and abilities) required to perform the task. This information usually comes from interviews with subject-matter experts, such as employees who currently hold the job.

LO3

Readiness for Training

readiness for training
A combination of employee characteristics and positive work environment that permit training.

Effective training requires not only a program that addresses real needs, but also a condition of employee readiness. **Readiness for training** is a combination of employee characteristics and positive work environment that permit training. The necessary employee characteristics include ability to learn the subject matter, favourable attitudes toward the training, and motivation to learn. A positive work environment is one that encourages learning and avoids interfering with the training program.

Employee Readiness Characteristics

Employees learn more from training programs when they are highly motivated to learn—that is, when they really want to learn the content of the training program.[14] Employees tend to feel this way if they believe they are able to learn, see potential benefits from the training program, are aware of their need to learn, see a fit between the training and their career goals, and have the basic skills needed for participating in the program. Managers can influence a ready attitude in a variety of ways. For example, they can provide feedback that encourages employees, establish rewards for learning, and communicate with employees about the organization's career paths and future needs.

Work Environment

Readiness for training also depends on two broad characteristics of the work environment: situational constraints and social support.[15] *Situational constraints* are the limits on training's effectiveness that arise from the situation or the conditions within the organization. Constraints can include a lack of money for training, lack of time for training or practicing, and failure to provide proper tools and materials for learn-

Understand the content of the training.
Know how training relates to what you need employees to do.
In performance appraisals, evaluate employees on how they apply training to their jobs.
Support employees' use of training when they return to work.
Ensure that employees have the equipment and technology needed to use training.
Prior to training, discuss with employees how they plan to use training.
Recognize newly trained employees who use training content.
Give employees release time from their work to attend training.
Explain to employees why they have been asked to attend training.
Give employees feedback related to skills or behaviour they are trying to develop.

TABLE 6.1

What Managers Should Do to Support Training

SOURCE: Based on A. Rossett, "That Was a Great Class, but . . . " *Training and Development,* July 1997, p. 21.

ing or applying the lessons of training. Conversely, trainees are likely to apply what they learn if the organization gives them opportunities to use their new skills and if it rewards them for doing so.[16]

Social support refers to the ways the organization's people encourage training, including giving trainees praise and encouraging words, sharing information about participating in training programs, and expressing positive attitudes toward the organization's training programs. Managers play an especially important role in providing social support. Besides offering positive feedback, they can emphasize the importance of training, show how training programs relate to employees' jobs, and provide opportunities for employees to apply what they learn. Table 6.1 summarizes some ways in which managers can support training. At the minimum, they should allow trainees to participate in training programs. At the other extreme, managers who not only encourage training but conduct the training sessions themselves are most likely to back up training by reinforcing new skills, providing feedback on progress, and giving trainees opportunities to practice.

Support can come from employees' peers as well as from supervisors and managers. The organization can formally provide peer support by establishing groups of employees who meet regularly to discuss their progress. Such a group might hold face-to-face meetings or communicate by email or over the organization's intranet, sharing ideas as well as encouragement. For example, group members can share how they coped with challenges related to what they have learned and how they obtained resources they needed for applying their training. Another way to encourage peer support is for the human resource department or others in the organization to publish a newsletter with articles relevant to training. The newsletter might include interviews with employees who successfully applied new skills. Finally, the organization can assign experienced employees as mentors to trainees, providing advice and support related to the training.

Planning the Training Program

LO4

When the needs assessment indicates a need for training and employees are ready to learn, the person responsible for training should plan a training program that directly

Extreme Hockey and Sport located in Regina, Saskatchewan, has developed a reputation for satisfied customers served by knowledgeable and dedicated employees. Management of this retail sports specialty store supports employee training through intensive product knowledge sessions that provide an environment that encourages employees to stay with the company.

relates to the needs identified. Planning begins with establishing objectives for the training program. Based on those objectives, the planner decides who will provide the training, what topics the training will cover, what training methods to use, and how to evaluate the training.

Objectives of the Program

Formally establishing objectives for the training program has several benefits. First, a training program based on clear objectives will be more focused and more likely to succeed. In addition, when trainers know the objectives, they can communicate them to the employees participating in the program. Employees learn best when they know what the training is supposed to accomplish. Finally, down the road, establishing objectives provides a basis for measuring whether the program succeeded, as we will discuss later in this chapter.

Effective training objectives have three components:

1. A statement of what the employee is expected to do (performance or outcome).
2. A statement of the quality or level of performance that is acceptable.
3. A statement of the conditions under which the trainee is expected to apply what he or she learned (for instance, physical conditions, mental stresses, or equipment failure).[17]

If possible, the objectives should include measurable performance standards. Suppose a training objective for a store's customer service training program is: "After training, the employee will be able to express concern to all irate customers with a brief (fewer than ten words) apology, only after the customer has stopped talking, and no matter how upset the customer is." Here, measures include the length and timing of the apology.

Finally, training objectives should identify any resources required to carry out the desired performance or outcome. This helps the organization ensure that employees will be able to apply what they have learned.

A related issue at the outset is who will participate in the training program. Some training programs are developed for all employees of the organization or all members of a team. Other training programs identify individuals who lack desirable skills or have potential to be promoted, then provide training in the areas of need that are identified for the particular employees. When deciding whom to include in training, the organization has to avoid illegal discrimination. The organization should not—intentionally or unintentionally—exclude anyone due to a prohibited ground of discrimination, e.g., sex, race, colour, ethnic background, sexual orientation, age, etc. During the training, all participants should receive equal treatment, such as equal opportunities for practice. In addition, the training program should provide accommodation for trainees with disabilities. The kinds of accommodations that are appropriate will vary according to the type of training and type of disability. One employee might need an alternative format for training materials, whereas another might need to have classroom instruction provided in a location accessible to wheelchairs.

In-House or Contracted Out?

An organization can provide an effective training program, even if it lacks expertise in training. Many companies and consultants provide training services to organizations. Colleges and technical institutes often work with employers to train employees in a variety of skills. When ESSO Resources needed power engineering certificate upgrading for employees at their Devon and Bonnie Glen plants, they called NAIT (The Northern Alberta Institute of Technology), located in Edmonton, Alberta. NAIT staff has delivered customized training to a diverse group of companies, including TELUS and the federal Department of National Defence.[18]

To select a training service, an organization can mail several vendors a *request for proposal (RFP)*, which is a document outlining the type of service needed, the type and number of references needed, the number of employees to be trained, the date by which the training is to be completed, and the date by which proposals should be received. A complete RFP also indicates funding for the project and the process by which the organization will determine its level of satisfaction. Putting together a request for proposal is time-consuming but worthwhile because it helps the organization clarify its objectives, compare vendors, and measure results.

Vendors that believe they are able to provide the services outlined in the RFP submit proposals that provide the types of information requested. The organization reviews the proposals to eliminate any vendors that do not meet requirements and to compare the vendors that do qualify. They check references and select a candidate, based on the proposal and the vendor's answers to questions such as those listed in Table 6.2.

The cost of purchasing training from a contractor can vary substantially. In general, it is much costlier to purchase specialized

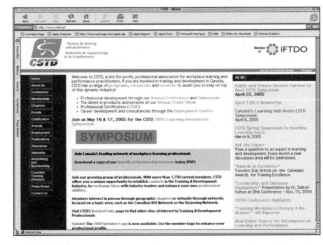

When organizations plan to outsource training, they can access information from associations such as the Canadian Society for Training and Development (an association of learning professionals). How can outsourcing training help organizations?

TABLE 6.2

Questions to Ask Vendors and Consultants

How much and what type of experience does your company have in designing and delivering training?
What are the qualifications and experiences of your staff?
Can you provide demonstrations or examples of training programs you have developed?
Would you provide references of clients for whom you worked?
What evidence do you have that your programs work?

SOURCE: Based on R. Zemke and J. Armstrong, "Evaluating Multimedia Developers," *Training*, November 1996, pp. 33–38. Adapted with permission. Lakewood Publications, Minneapolis, MN.

training that is tailored to the organization's unique requirements than to participate in a seminar or training course that teaches general skills or knowledge. According to estimates by consultants, preparing a training program can take 10 to 20 hours for each hour of instruction. Highly technical content that requires the developer to meet often with experts in the subject can take 50 percent longer.[19]

Even in organizations that send employees to outside training programs, someone in the organization may be responsible for coordinating the overall training program. Called *training administration*, this is typically the responsibility of a human resources professional. Training administration includes activities before, during, and after training sessions. The "HR How To" box describes what is involved in training administration.

Choice of Training Methods

Whether the organization prepares its own training programs or buys training from other organizations, it is important to verify that the content of the training relates directly to the training objectives. Such relevance to the organization's needs and objectives ensures that training money is well spent. Tying training content closely to objectives also improves trainees' learning, because it increases the likelihood that the training will be meaningful and helpful.

After deciding on the goals and content of the training program, planners must decide how the training will be conducted. As we will describe in the next section, a wide variety of methods are available. Training methods fall into the broad categories of presentation methods, hands-on methods, and group-building methods.[20]

With **presentation methods,** trainees receive information provided by instructors or via computers or other media. Trainees may assemble in a classroom to hear a lecture, or the material may be presented on videotapes, CD-ROMs, websites, or in workbooks. Presentations are appropriate for conveying facts or comparing alternative processes. Computer-based training methods tend to be less expensive than bringing trainees together in a classroom.

In contrast to presentation methods, **hands-on methods** actively involve the trainee in learning by trying out the behaviours being taught. Someone may help the trainee learn skills while on the job. Hands-on methods away from the job include simulations, games, role-plays, and interactive learning on computers. Hands-on training is appropriate for teaching specific skills and helping trainees understand how skills and behaviours apply to their jobs. These methods also help trainees learn to handle interpersonal issues, such as handling problems with customers.

presentation methods
Training methods in which trainees receive information provided by instructors or via computers or other media.

hands-on methods
Training methods which actively involve the trainee in trying out skills being taught.

group-building methods
Training methods in which trainees share ideas and experiences, build group identity, understand interpersonal relationships, and learn the strengths and weaknesses of themselves and their coworkers.

Administering a Training Program

For a training program to succeed, someone must be responsible for the nuts and bolts of the effort, from making sure there is an appropriate space to handling the paperwork. Usually, an organization's human resource department is responsible for this training administration. Carrying out that responsibility includes the following activities:

- *Communicate with employees.* The company intranet and postings are possible ways to inform employees about the organization's overall training program and specific learning events that are available. Messages should include the objectives as well as the topic of the training.
- *Enrol employees in courses and programs.* This may entail completing applications, registering employees for in-house training sessions, or ensuring employees have Internet access if course enrolment is available online.
- *Prepare and process pretests to be administered or materials to be reviewed before training begins.* The training administrator may be also asked to prepare materials for distribution during the course. Training materials may include handouts, videotapes, CD-ROMs, web links to review, etc.
- *Arrange the training facility.* The administrator may have to reserve a room, order refreshments, and make sure space is ready for the training session. The administrator ensures that trainees and trainer are not distracted by an uncomfortable room or missing items. Visual aids should be easy to see. The setup, including technology used, should be appropriate for the course objectives. If the course objectives call for group interaction, the room should be arranged to accommodate this.
- *Test equipment that will be used during the instruction.* In case of technology failure, the administrator should be prepared with backup resources.
- *Provide support during instruction.* The administrator should be accessible in case needs arise during a training session. Trainees should have full information about the schedule, including starting and finishing times and break times.
- *Distribute materials for evaluating the course*—for example, surveys or tests.
- *Provide for communication between the trainer and participants.* For example, if the trainer will handle follow-up questions via email, the administrator should ensure that trainees have the person's email address.
- *Maintain records of course completion.* Usually, this information goes in employees' files. The administrator should also keep records of the course evaluations. If the training is provided in-house, the records would include course materials.

SOURCE: Based on material in B. J. Smith and B. L. Delahaye, *How to Be an Effective Trainer*, 2nd ed. (New York: Wiley, 1987); M. Van Wart, N. J. Cayer, and S. Cook, *Handbook of Training and Development for the Public Sector* (San Francisco: Jossey-Bass, 1993).

Group-building methods help trainees share ideas and experiences, build group or team identity, understand how interpersonal relationships work, and get to know their own strengths and weaknesses and those of their coworkers. The various techniques available involve examining feelings, perceptions, and beliefs about the trainees' group. Participants discuss how to apply what they learn in the training program to the group's performance at work. Group-building methods are appropriate for establishing teams or work groups, or for improving their performance.

Training programs may use these methods alone or in combination. The methods used should be suitable for the course content and the learning abilities of the participants. The following section explores the options in greater detail.

LO5

Training Methods

A wide variety of methods is available for conducting training. Figure 6.5 shows the percentage of training delivered via the classroom (instructor-lead), learning technologies, and "other" delivery methods (e.g., self-paced instruction). Classroom training is the most widely used method. As more organizations use technology-based distribution methods for training it is estimated that training delivered via technology will significantly increase in coming years. Figure 6.6 illustrates the percentage of organizations using technology-based distribution methods in some aspect of training delivery.[21]

Classroom Instruction

At school, we tend to associate learning with classroom instruction, and that type of training is most widely used in the workplace, too. Classroom instruction typically involves an instructor leading a group. Instructors often use slides, discussions, case studies, question-and-answer sessions, and role playing. Actively involving trainees enhances learning.

When the course objectives call for presenting information on a specific topic to many trainees, classroom instruction is one of the least expensive and least time-consuming ways to accomplish that goal. Learning will be more effective if trainers enhance lectures with job-related examples and opportunities for hands-on learning.

Technology has expanded the notion of the classroom to classes of trainees scattered in various locations. With *distance learning*, trainees at different locations attend programs over phone and computer lines. Through audio- and videoconferencing, they can hear and see lectures and participate in discussions. Computers can enable participants to share documents as well. Satellite networks allow companies to link up with industry-specific and educational courses for which employees receive college credit and job certification. IBM, Digital Equipment, and Eastman Kodak are among

FIGURE 6.5

Delivery Methods as a Percentage of All Training Time

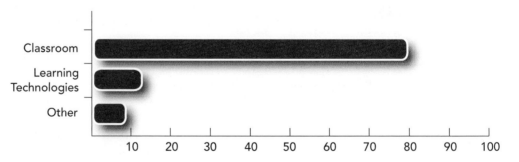

SOURCE: Adapted from Chart 9: Delivery Methods as a Percentage of All Training Time by Janice Cooney and Allison Cowan, *The Conference Board of Canada: Training and Development Outlook 2003: Canadian Organizations Continue to Under-Invest*, May 2003, p. 14, ISBN 0-88763-584-9.

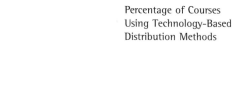

FIGURE 6.6

Percentage of Courses
Using Technology-Based
Distribution Methods

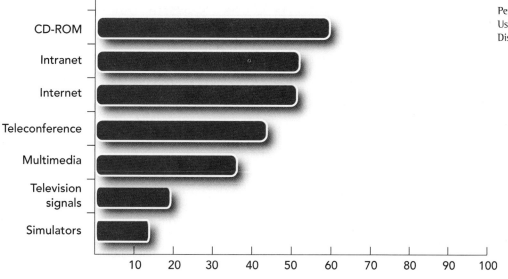

SOURCE: Adapted from Table 17: Percentage of Organizations Using Technology-Based Distribution Methods by Janice Cooney and Allison Cowan, *The Conference Board of Canada: Training and Development Outlook 2003: Canadian Organizations Continue to Under-Invest*, May 2003, p. 14, ISBN 0-88763-584-9.

the many companies that subscribe to the National Technological University, which broadcasts courses to a widely distributed audience of participants. Technical employees take these courses to obtain advanced degrees in engineering.[22] Distance learning provides many of the benefits of classroom training without the cost and time of travel to a shared classroom. The major disadvantage of distance learning is that interaction between the trainer and audience may be limited. To overcome this hurdle, distance learning usually provides a communications link between trainees and trainer. Also, on-site instructors or facilitators should be available to answer questions and moderate question-and-answer sessions.

Audiovisual Training

Presentation methods need not require that trainees attend a class. Trainees can also work independently, using course material prepared on audiotapes and videotapes or in workbooks. Audiovisual techniques such as slides and videos can also supplement classroom instruction.

Training with videotapes has been used for improving communications skills, interviewing skills, and customer service skills. Videotapes can also be effective for demonstrating how to follow procedures, such as welding methods. Morse-Brothers provides training to the drivers of its ready-mix trucks with a series of videos. A mentor-driver selects a weekly video, schedules viewing sessions, keeps attendance records, and guides a wrap-up discussion. The short (ten minutes or less) videos cover topics such as safe driving, avoidance of excessive idling, and observing product tests at job sites. The mentor-drivers are trained in leading the discussion that follows the video, including how to call attention to key learning points and relate the topics to issues the drivers encounter on the job.[23]

Users of audiovisual training often have some control over the presentation. They can review material and may be able to slow down or speed up the lesson. Videotapes and video clips on CD-ROM can show situations and equipment that cannot be easily demonstrated in a classroom. Another advantage of audiovisual presentations is that they give trainees a consistent presentation, not affected by an individual trainer's goals and skills. The problems associated with these methods may include their trying to present too much material, poorly written dialogue, overuse of features such as humour or music, and drama that distracts from the key points. A well-written and carefully produced video can overcome these problems.

Computer-Based Training

Although almost all organizations use classroom training, new technologies are gaining in popularity as technology improves and becomes less expensive. With computer-based training, participants receive course materials and instruction distributed over the Internet or on CD-ROM. Often, these materials are interactive, so participants can answer questions and try out techniques, with course materials adjusted according to participants' responses. Online training programs may allow trainees to submit questions via email and to participate in online discussions. Multimedia capabilities enable computers to provide sounds, images, and video presentations, along with text.

Computer-based training is generally less expensive than putting an instructor in a classroom of trainees. The low cost to deliver information gives the company flexibility in scheduling training, so that it can fit around work requirements. Training can be delivered in smaller doses, so material is easier to remember.[24] Finally, it is easier to customize computer-based training for individual learners.

FedEx uses a form of computer-based training called *interactive video*. With this format, a monitor presents a training program stored on videodisk or CD-ROM. Trainees use the keyboard or touch the monitor to interact with the program. The 25-disk curriculum includes courses on customer etiquette, defensive driving, and delivery procedures.[25] Employees decide what aspects of the training program they want to view. They can skip ahead when they feel competent or review topics when they believe they need to do so. The program gives trainees immediate feedback on their learning progress.

E-Learning

e-learning
Receiving training via the Internet or the organization's intranet.

Receiving training via the Internet or the organization's intranet is called **e-learning** or online learning. E-learning may bring together Web-based training, distance learning, virtual classrooms, and the use of CD-ROMs. Course content is presented with a combination of text, video, graphics, and sound. E-learning has three important characteristics. First, it involves electronic networks that enable the delivery, sharing, and updating of information and instruction. Second, e-learning is delivered to the trainee via computers with Internet access. Finally, it goes beyond traditional training objectives to offer tools and information that will help trainees improve performance. The system also may handle course enrolment, testing and evaluation of participants, and monitoring of progress. For example, Vancouver City Savings Credit Union (VanCity) has created DiscoverU, an e-learning tool that allows employees to map their career path and to create links between performance management, individual career development plans, and the corporate talent pool.[26]

Humanizing e-Learning

Some of Canada's biggest enterprises say online training improves employee access to valuable information—as long as companies make sure to mix some humanity with the technology.

Getting maximum value out of e-learning initiatives was the focus of a recent conference that brought together members of private and public sector organizations who shared stories on the challenges and benefits of their internal online training projects.

Rolling out a Web-based learning program for more than 60,000 employees in five time zones and two languages was a daunting task for the Hudson's Bay Company. The corporation also includes Zellers and Home Outfitters stores, and each chain carries many different items, making product

knowledge information important for its sales associates, said Jim Campbell, HBC's organizational management senior manager.

In the 1990s, HBC had introduced a robust computer-based training (CBT) system, but it was mainframe-based, Campbell said. The system was used until 2002, when it became clear that while most of the content stored on it was still relevant to the store's operation, the delivery mode was outdated.

HBC employees were also consistently asking for access to the CBT material from home, Campbell said. Taking the material onto the Web became an obvious choice. After a vendor search process and some difficulty figuring out how to price a solution that would be accessed numerous times by

anywhere from 60,000 to 70,000 users, a platform was developed. The company salvaged about 40 of its mainframe programs, and with the addition of about 140 more, it now has a training material database, accessible from any computer, says Campbell.

E-learning is not the be-all and end-all solution, Campbell added. His preferred approach is blended learning, where technology-assisted learning is integrated into more traditional training methods.

SOURCE: Monika Rola, "Don't Forget the Human Touch: Enterprises Swap Horror Stories and Best Practices with Their e-learning Initiatives," *Computing Canada*, April 25, 2003, www.findarticles.com. Retrieved: March 2, 2004.

With e-learning, trainees have a great deal of control. They determine what they learn, how fast they progress through the program, how much time they practise, and when they learn. E-learners also may choose to collaborate or interact with other trainees and experts. They may use the training system's links to other learning resources such as reference materials, company websites, and other training programs.

To enable organizations to bring together diverse computer-based training tools or authoring systems, a computer-managed instruction (CMI) system may be used.[27] For example, WebCT is a CMI system that is utilized in thousands of colleges and universities around the world to provide a flexible blend of e-learning and classroom-based teaching.[28]

Like other forms of computer-based learning, e-learning can reduce training costs and time. Trainees often appreciate the multimedia capabilities, which appeal to several senses, and the opportunity to actively participate in learning and apply it to situations on the job. The best e-learning combines the advantages of the Internet with the principles of a good learning environment. It takes advantage of the Web's dynamic na-

TABLE 6.3

Typical Jobs for Apprentices and Interns

APPRENTICESHIP	INTERNSHIP
Carpenter	Accountant
Electrician	Doctor
Electronics Technician	Engineer
Machinist	Journalist
Plumber	Lawyer
Welder	MBA

ture and ability to use many positive learning features, including hyperlinks to other training sites and content, control by the trainee, and ability for trainees to collaborate. As described in the nearby "Best Practices" box, some of the most successful uses of e-learning combine online resources integrated with more traditional training methods.

On-the-Job Training

on-the-job training (OJT)

Training methods in which a person with job experience and skill guides trainees in practising job skills at the workplace.

Although people often associate training with classrooms, much learning occurs while employees are performing their jobs. **On-the-job training (OJT)** refers to training methods in which a person with job experience and skill guides trainees in practising job skills at the workplace. This type of training takes various forms, including apprenticeships and internships.

An **apprenticeship** is a work-study training method that teaches job skills through a combination of on-the-job training and technical training.[29] The OJT component of an apprenticeship involves the apprentice assisting a certified journeyperson in the work place. Typically, the technical training is provided by local trade schools, high schools, community colleges, and technical institutes. On average, 85 percent of the apprentice's two to five year training is spent in the workplace, the rest is spent at a training institution.[30] Some apprenticeship programs are sponsored by individual companies, others by employee unions. Apprenticeship programs are usually administered by provincial and territorial government departments with support from advisory bodies such as apprenticeship and certification boards. To provide greater mobility across Canada for skilled workers, apprentices who have completed their training and certified journeypersons are able to obtain a "Red Seal" endorsement after completing an interprovincial standards exam that allows them to practice their trade anywhere in Canada.[31] For trainees, a major advantage of apprenticeship is the ability to earn an income while learning a trade, i.e., "earning while learning." In addition, training through an apprenticeship is usually effective because it involves hands-on learning and extensive practise.

apprenticeship

A work-study training method that teaches job skills through a combination of on-the-job training and technical training.

internship

On-the-job learning sponsored by an educational institution as a component of an academic program.

An **internship** is on-the-job learning sponsored by an educational institution as a component of an academic program. The sponsoring school works with local employers to place students in positions where they can gain experience related to their area of study. For example, summer internships have become an integral component of UBC's 15-month MBA program and a requirement of graduation.[32] See Table 6.3 for a listing of typical jobs for apprentices and interns.

co-operative education

A plan of higher education that incorporates paid work experience as an integral part of academic studies.

Co-operative education is a plan of higher education that incorporates paid work experience as an integral part of academic studies. Co-operative education is being readily accepted by government, business, and industry in Canada and throughout the world. Universities, colleges, technical schools, and high schools are offering co-op programs to thousands of students in a growing number of disciplines.[33]

To be effective, OJT programs should include several characteristics:

- The organization should issue a policy statement describing the purpose of OJT and emphasizing the organization's support for it.
- The organization should specify who is accountable for conducting OJT. This accountability should be included in the relevant job descriptions.
- The organization should review OJT practices at companies in similar industries.
- Managers and peers should be trained in OJT principles.
- Employees who conduct OJT should have access to lesson plans, checklists, procedure manuals, training manuals, learning contracts, and progress report forms.
- Before conducting OJT with an employee, the organization should assess the employees' level of basic skills.[34]

The OJT program at Borden's North American Pasta Division has many of these characteristics.[35] Borden's carefully selects, trains, and rewards the managers and peers who act as trainers. The train-the-trainer course involves classroom training as well as time on the manufacturing floor to learn how to operate machinery such as pasta machines and correctly teach other employees how to use the equipment. Trainees in the OJT program complete a checklist in which they verify that the trainer helped them learn the skills needed and used effective teaching techniques.

Simulations

A **simulation** is a training method that represents a real-life situation, with trainees making decisions resulting in outcomes that mirror what would happen on the job. Simulations enable trainees to see the impact of their decisions in an artificial, risk-free environment. They are used to teach production and process skills as well as management and interpersonal skills. At Motorola's Programmable Automation Literacy Lab, employees who may never have worked with computers or robots learn to operate them.[36] After completing a two-hour introduction to factory automation, trainees use a simulator to become familiar with the equipment by designing a product (a personalized memo holder). Success in simple exercises with the simulator increases trainees' confidence about working in an automated manufacturing environment.

simulation
A training method that represents a real-life situation, with trainees making decisions resulting in outcomes that mirror what would happen on the job.

Simulators must have elements identical to those found in the work environment. The simulator needs to respond exactly as equipment would under the conditions and response given by the trainee. For this reason, simulators are expensive to develop and need constant updating as new information about the work environment becomes available. Still, they are an excellent training method when the risks of a mistake on the job are great. Trainees do not have to be afraid of the impact of wrong decisions when using the simulator, as they would be with on-the-job training.

A recent development in simulations is the use of virtual reality technology. **Virtual reality** is a computer-based technology that provides an interactive, three-dimensional learning experience. Using specialized equipment or viewing the virtual model on a computer screen, trainees move through the simulated environment and interact with its components.[37] Devices relay information from the environment to the trainees' senses. For example, audio interfaces, gloves that provide a sense of touch, treadmills, or motion platforms create a realistic but artificial environment. Devices also communicate information about the trainee's movements to a computer. Virtual reality is a feature of the simulated environment of the advanced manufacturing courses in Motorola's Pager Robotic Assembly facility. Employees wear a head-

virtual reality
A computer-based technology that provides an interactive, three-dimensional learning experience.

mount display that lets them view a virtual world of lab space, robots, tools, and the assembly operation. The trainees hear the sounds of using the real equipment. The equipment responds as if trainees were actually using it in the factory.[38]

Business Games and Case Studies

Training programs use business games and case studies to develop employees' management skills. A case study is a detailed description of a situation that trainees study and discuss. Cases are designed to develop higher-order thinking skills, such as the ability to analyze and evaluate information. They also can be a safe way to encourage trainees to take appropriate risks, by giving them practice in weighing and acting on uncertain outcomes. There are many sources of case studies, including Harvard Business School, the Ivey School of Business, and McGraw-Hill publishing company.

With business games, trainees gather information, analyze it, and make decisions that influence the outcome of the game. For instance, Market Share, part of a marketing management course, requires participants to use strategic thinking (such as analyzing competitors) to increase their share of the market.[39] Games stimulate learning because they actively involve participants and mimic the competitive nature of business. A realistic game may be more meaningful to trainees than presentation techniques such as classroom instruction.

Training with case studies and games requires that participants come together to discuss the cases or the progress of the game. This requires face-to-face or electronic meetings. Also, participants must be willing to be actively involved in analyzing the situation and defending their decisions.

Behaviour Modelling

Research suggests that one of the most effective ways to teach interpersonal skills is through behaviour modelling.[40] This involves training sessions in which participants observe other people demonstrating the desired behaviour, then have opportunities to practise the behaviour themselves. For example, a training program could involve four-hour sessions, each focusing on one interpersonal skill, such as communicating or coaching. At the beginning of each session, participants hear the reasons for using the key behaviours, then they watch a videotape of a model performing the key behaviours. They practise through role-playing and receive feedback about their performance. In addition, they evaluate the performance of the model in the videotape and discuss how they can apply the behaviour on the job.

Experiential Programs

experiential programs
A teamwork and leadership training program based on the use of challenging, structured outdoor activities.

To develop teamwork and leadership skills, some organizations enrol their employees in a form of training called **experiential programs.** This type of program uses challenging, structured outdoor activities, which may include difficult sports such as dogsledding or mountain climbing. Other activities may be structured tasks like climbing walls, completing rope courses, climbing ladders, or making "trust falls" (in which each trainee stands on a table and falls backward into the arms of other group members). For example, Peak Performance™ is a company that offers experiential training programs to organizations including Microsoft, Smiland Paint, and a major health care organization.[41]

Do experiential programs work? The impact of these programs has not been rigorously tested, but participants report they gained a greater understanding of themselves and the ways they interact with their coworkers. One key to the success of such programs may be that the organization insist that entire work groups participate together. This encourages people to see, discuss, and correct the kinds of behaviour that keep the group from performing well. Organizations should make sure that the exercises are related to the types of skills employees need to develop. Experiential programs should end with a discussion of what happened during the exercise, what participants learned, and how they can apply what they learned to their work.[42]

Before requiring employees to participate in experiential programs, the organization should consider the possible drawbacks. Because these programs are usually physically demanding and often require participants to touch each other, companies face certain risks. Some employees may be injured or may feel that they were sexually harassed or that their privacy was invaded. Also, Human Rights and Employment Equity legislation (discussed in Chapter 2) raises questions about requiring employees with disabilities to participate in physically demanding training experiences.

Team Training

A possible alternative to experiential programs is team training, which coordinates the performance of individuals who work together to achieve a common goal. An organization may benefit from providing such training to groups when group members must share information and group performance depends on the performance of the individual group members. Examples include the military, power plants, and commercial airlines. In those work settings, much work is performed by crews, groups, or teams. Success depends on individuals' coordinating their activities to make decisions, perhaps in dangerous situations.

Ways to conduct team training include cross-training and coordination training.[43] In **cross-training,** team members understand and practise each other's skills so that they are prepared to step in and take another member's place. In a factory, for example, production workers could be cross-trained to handle all phases of assembly. This enables the company to move them to the positions where they are most needed to complete an order on time.

Coordination training trains the team in how to share information and decisions to obtain the best team performance. Both of these kinds of teams must monitor different aspects of equipment and the environment at the same time sharing information to make the most effective decisions.

Action Learning

Another form of group building, widely used in Europe, is **action learning.** In this type of training, teams or work groups get an actual problem, work on solving it, commit to an action plan, and are accountable for carrying out the plan.[44] Typically, 6 to 30 employees participate in action learning; sometimes the participants include customers and vendors. For instance, a group might include a customer that buys the product involved in the problem to be solved. Another arrangement is to bring together employees from various functions affected by the problem. Whirlpool used action learning to solve a problem related to importing compressors from Brazil. The company had to pay duties (import taxes) on the compressors. It was overpaying and

cross-training
Team training in which team members understand and prastice each other's skills so that they are prepared to step in and take another member's place.

coordination training
Team training that teaches the team how to share information and make decisions to obtain the best team performance.

action learning
Training in which teams get an actual problem, work on solving it and commit to an action plan, and are accountable for carrying it out.

One of the most important features of organizations today is teamwork. Experiential programs include team-building exercises like rope courses and wall climbing to help build trust and cooperation among employees.

General Motors.

"If the people who make the car don't fit together, the car won't either."

Welcome to the Excel training course. Before it's over, Saturn's Dennis Bowman will take these General Motors employees on a real adventure. They'll scale walls. Walk across high wires. Plunge backwards into the waiting arms of their coworkers. And take away some valuable lessons about trust, cooperation and seeing things from the other person's point of view. Developed by Saturn, Excel is now used throughout General Motors. It's turning out graduates who know the power of teamwork. Who go a little further to build quality automobiles. And who believe that the right way to treat a customer is the way you'd want to be treated yourself.

was trying to recover the overpayment. Members of the group responsible for obtaining the parts formed a team to implement Whirlpool's strategies for cost reduction and inventory control. Through action learning, they developed a process for recovering the overpayment, saving the company hundreds of thousands of dollars a year.

The effectiveness of action learning has not been formally evaluated. This type of training seems to result in a great deal of learning, however, and employees are able to apply what they learn because action learning involves actual problems the organization is facing. The group approach also helps teams identify behaviours that interfere with problem solving.

LO6

Implementing the Training Program: Principles of Learning

Learning permanently changes behaviour. For employees to acquire knowledge and skills in the training program and apply what they have learned in their jobs, the training program must be implemented in a way that applies what we know about how people learn. Researchers have identified a number of ways employees learn best.[45] Table 6.4 summarizes ways that training can best encourage learning. In general, effective training communicates learning objectives clearly, presents information in distinctive and memorable ways, and helps trainees link the subject matter to their jobs.

Employees are most likely to learn when training is linked to their current job experiences and tasks.[46] There are a number of ways trainers can make this link. Training sessions should present material using familiar concepts, terms, and examples. As far as possible, the training context—such as the physical setting or the images presented on a computer—should mirror the work environment. Along with physical elements, the context should include emotional elements. In the earlier example of training store employees to handle upset customers, the physical context is more relevant if it includes trainees acting out scenarios of employees dealing with unhappy customers. The role-play interaction between trainees adds emotional realism and further enhances learning.

To fully understand and remember the content of the training, employees need a chance to demonstrate and practise what they have learned. Trainers should provide ways to actively involve the trainees, have them practise repeatedly, and have them complete tasks within a time that is appropriate in light of the learning objectives. Practice requires physically carrying out the desired behaviours, not just describing them. Practice sessions could include role-playing interactions, filling out relevant forms, or operating machinery or equipment to be used on the job. The more the trainee practises these activities, the more comfortable he or she will be in applying the skills on the job. People tend to benefit most from practice that occurs over sev-

TABLE 6.4

Ways That Training Helps Employees Learn

TRAINING ACTIVITY	WAYS TO PROVIDE TRAINING ACTIVITY
Communicate the learning objective.	Demonstrate the performance to be expected. Give examples of questions to be answered.
Use distinctive, attention-getting messages.	Emphasize key points. Use pictures, not just words.
Limit the content of training.	Group lengthy material into chunks. Provide a visual image of the course material. Provide opportunities to repeat and practise material.
Guide trainees as they learn.	Use words as reminders about sequence of activities. Use words and pictures to relate concepts to one another and to their context.
Elaborate on the subject.	Present the material in different contexts and settings. Relate new ideas to previously learned concepts. Practise in a variety of contexts and settings.
Provide memory cues.	Suggest memory aids. Use familiar sounds or rhymes as memory cues.
Transfer course content to the workplace.	Design the learning environment so that it has elements in common with the workplace. Require learners to develop action plans that apply training content to their jobs. Use words that link the course to the workplace.
Provide feedback about performance.	Tell trainees how accurately and quickly they are performing their new skill. Show how trainees have met the objectives of the training.

SOURCE: Adapted from R. M. Gagne, "Learning Processes and Instruction," *Training Research Journal* 1 (1995/96), pp. 17–28.

eral sessions, rather than one long practice session.[47] For complex tasks, it may be most effective to practise a few skills or behaviours at a time, then combine them in later practice sessions.

Trainees need to understand whether or not they are succeeding. Therefore, training sessions should offer feedback. Effective feedback focuses on specific behaviours and is delivered as soon as possible after the trainees practise or demonstrate what they have learned.[48] One way to do this is to videotape trainees, then show the video while indicating specific behaviours that do or do not match the desired outcomes of the training. Feedback should include positive feedback when trainees show they have learned material, as well as guidance on how to improve.

Well-designed training helps people remember the content. Training programs need to break information into chunks that people can remember. Research suggests that people can attend to no more than four to five items at a time. If a concept or procedure involves more than five items, the training program should deliver information in shorter sessions or chunks.[49] Other ways to make information more memorable include presenting it with visual images and practising some tasks enough that they become automatic.

Workplace literacy is a relative rather than an absolute concept, involving prose, document, and quantitative capabilities in the languages in which business is conducted. Increasingly, organizations are recognizing the literacy skills that enabled employees to do their jobs effectively are no longer adequate in today's competitive

workplace literacy
Prose, document, and quantitative capabilities in the languages in which business is conducted.

marketplace.[50] A recent survey sponsored by the National Literacy Secretariat and Human Resources and Skills Development Canada found that "42 percent of Canadian workers have literacy skills below the level they need to succeed and perform well in most jobs."[51]

Palliser Furniture Ltd. employs an ethnically and linguistically diverse workforce and regards employees' basic skills as fundamental to business success. This Winnipeg-based manufacturer recently received an Award for Excellence in Workplace Literacy from the Conference Board of Canada in recognition of its workplace literacy contributions. Palliser provides employees with courses including English as a Second Language, Reading and Writing for Lead Hands, and various math modules to enhance employees' literacy skills, as they progress in employment and take on additional responsibilities that require advanced skills.[52]

LO7

Measuring Results of Training

After a training program ends, or at intervals during an ongoing training program, organizations should ensure that the training is meeting objectives. The stage to prepare for evaluating a training program is when the program is being developed. Along with designing course objectives and content, the planner should identify how to measure achievement of objectives. Depending on the objectives, the evaluation can use one or more of the measures shown in Figure 6.7.[53]

- **Reaction**—satisfaction with the program
- **Learning**— knowledge and skills gained
- **Behaviour**—behaviour changes
- **Results**— improvements in individual and organizational performance

The Conference Board of Canada reports that over 89 percent of organizations administer reaction-level training evaluations and that an increasing number of organizations are conducting learning, behaviour, and results-level training evaluations.[54]

The usual way to measure whether participants have acquired information is to administer tests on paper or electronically. Trainers or supervisors can observe whether participants demonstrate the desired competencies. Changes in company performance have a variety of measures, many of which organizations keep track of for preparing performance appraisals, annual reports, and other routine documents in order to demonstrate the final measure of success shown in Figure 6.7—results including return on investment (ROI).

Evaluation Methods

transfer of training
On-the-job use of competencies enhanced in training.

Evaluation of training should look for **transfer of training,** or on-the-job use of competencies enhanced in training. Transfer of training requires that employees actually learn the content of the training program and that the necessary conditions are in place for employees to apply what they learned. Thus, the assessment can look at whether employees have an opportunity to perform the skills related to the training.

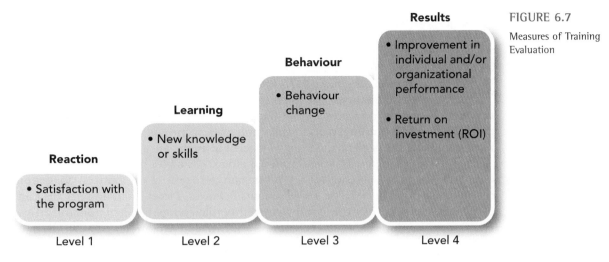

FIGURE 6.7

Measures of Training Evaluation

The organization can measure this by asking employees three questions about specific training-related tasks:

1. Do you perform the task?
2. How many times do you perform the task?
3. To what extent do you perform difficult and challenging learned tasks?

Frequent performance of difficult training-related tasks would signal great opportunity to perform. If there is low opportunity to perform, the organization should conduct further needs assessment and reevaluate readiness to learn. Perhaps the organization does not fully support the training activities in general or the employee's supervisor does not provide opportunities to apply new skills. Lack of transfer can also mean that employees have not learned the course material. The organization might offer a refresher course to give trainees more practice. Another reason for poor transfer of training is that the content of the training may not be important for the employee's job.

Assessment of training also should evaluate training *outcomes,* that is, what (if anything) has changed as a result of the training. The relevant training outcomes are the ones related to the organization's goals for the training and its overall performance. Possible outcomes include the following:

- Trainee and supervisor satisfaction with the training program (Reaction).
- Information such as facts, techniques, and procedures that trainees can recall after the training (Learning).
- Skills that trainees can demonstrate in tests or on the job (Behaviour).
- Changes in behaviour related to the content of the training, for example, concern for safety or tolerance of diversity (Behaviour).
- Improvements in individual, group, or company performance, for example, greater customer satisfaction, more sales, fewer defects (Results).

Training is a significant part of many organizations' budgets. Therefore, economic measures are an important way to evaluate the success of a training program. Businesses that invest in training want to achieve a high *return on investment*—the monetary benefits of the investment compared to the amount invested, expressed as a percentage. For example, IBM's e-learning program for new managers, Basic Blue, costs

$8,708 per manager.[55] The company has measured an improvement in each new manager's performance worth $415,000. That gives IBM a benefit of $415,000 − $8,708 = $406,292 for each manager. This is an extremely large return on investment: $406,292/$8,708 = 46.65, or 4,665 percent! In other words, for every $1 IBM invests in Basic Blue, it receives almost $47.

For any of these methods, the most accurate but most costly way to evaluate the training program is to measure performance, knowledge, or attitudes among all employees before the training, then to train only part of the employees. After the training is complete, the performance, knowledge, or attitudes are again measured, and the trained group is compared to the untrained group. A simpler but less accurate way to assess the training is to conduct a pre-test and post-test on all trainees, comparing their performance, knowledge, or behaviours before and after the training. This form of measurement does not rule out the possibility that change resulted from something other than training (for example, a change in the compensation system). The simplest approach is to use only a post-test. Of course, this type of measurement does not enable accurate comparisons, but it may be sufficient, depending on the cost and purpose of the training.

Applying the Evaluation

The purpose of evaluating training is to help with future decisions about the organization's training programs. Using the evaluation, the organization may identify a need to modify the training and gain information about the kinds of changes needed. The organization may decide to expand on successful areas of training and cut back on training that has not delivered significant benefits.

TD Bank Financial Group evaluates the effectiveness of training using both quantitative and qualitative measures. TD uses a comprehensive process that includes assessment of knowledge increase, on-the-job confidence, effectiveness of materials and methods, as well as the business impact of their training programs.[56]

LO8

Applications of Training

Two categories of training that have become widespread among North American companies are orientation of new employees and training in how to manage workforce diversity.

Orientation of New Employees

Many employees receive their first training during their first days on the job. This training is the organization's **orientation** program—its training designed to prepare employees to perform their job effectively, learn about the organization, and establish work relationships. Organizations provide for orientation because, no matter how realistic the information provided during employment interviews and site visits, people feel shock and surprise when they start a new job.[57] Also, employees need to become familiar with job tasks and learn the details of the organization's practices, policies, and procedures.

The objectives of orientation programs include making new employees familiar with the organization's rules, policies, and procedures. Table 6.5 summarizes the content of a typical orientation program. Such a program provides information about the

orientation
Training designed to prepare employees to perform their jobs effectively, learn about their organization, and establish work relationships.

TABLE 6.5

Content of a Typical
Orientation Program

Company-level information
Company overview (e.g., values, history, mission)
Key policies and procedures
Compensation
Employee benefits and services
Safety and accident prevention
Employee and union relations
Physical facilities
Economic factors
Customer relations

Department-level information
Department functions and philosophy
Job duties and responsibilities
Policies, procedures, rules, and regulations
Performance expectations
Tour of department
Introduction to department employees

Miscellaneous
Community
Housing
Family adjustment

SOURCE: J. L. Schwarz and M. A. Weslowski, "Employee Orientation: What Employers Should Know," *Journal of Contemporary Business Issues*, Fall 1995, p. 48. Used with permission.

overall company and about the department in which the new employee will be working. The topics include social as well as technical aspects of the job. Miscellaneous information helps employees from out of town learn about the surrounding community.

Orientation of new engineers at Pillsbury addresses these issues. Before being assigned to a production facility, engineers work for one year at headquarters. To provide orientation, Pillsbury assigns a senior engineer to serve as a mentor, showing the new engineer the technical resources available within the company. The mentor also helps the new engineer become familiar with the community and handle issues related to relocation. The new employees attend seminars at which engineers from various product divisions explain the role of engineering. New employees also meet key managers.[58]

At the Arthritis Foundation, new employee orientation combines an online learning course immediately upon employment and then live sessions that concentrate on skills development and group interaction. The results include reliable, easily updated, consistent, just-in-time content; new staff that are trained immediately on employment rather than waiting up to six months to journey to training; employees that come to live training with the needed knowledge base; and consistent delivery to a wider audience.[59]

Orientation programs may combine various training methods such as printed and audiovisual materials, classroom instruction, on-the-job training, and e-learning. Decisions about how to conduct the orientation depend on the type of material to be covered and the number of new employees, among other factors. The "E-HRM" box describes how some organizations are applying e-learning to orientation programs.

Diversity Training

In response to Human Rights and Employment Equity legislation and market forces, many organizations today are concerned about managing diversity—creating an inclusive environment that allows all employees to contribute to organizational goals and experience personal growth. This environment includes access to jobs as well as fair and positive treatment of all employees. Chapter 2 described how organizations manage diversity by complying with legal requirements. Besides these efforts, many

E-HRM

Getting Oriented Online

If you take a job with ChemConnect, don't expect to be greeted on your first day with a dry lecture from human resource employees. Rather, the online seller of chemicals and plastics offers an orientation via its intranet. The online orientation, titled "Tour de Chem," is a takeoff on the Tour de France bicycle race. Trainees use a computer mouse to manipulate the image of a bicycle to travel online through various scenarios. Clicking on the front wheel to move forward and on the rear wheel to move backward, trainees take a tour through company jargon, a menu of employee services and benefits, and background about ChemConnect's leaders. For each stage of the tour, one of those executives rides along—shown as a stick figure with a photo of the executive's head patched on top. The whole tour takes about 90 minutes.

The entertaining presentation keeps new hires engaged long after they might have nodded off in front of a benefits manual or lecture. The format also tells employees something about the company, says ChemConnect's vice-president of operations, Peter Navin. Navin, who is responsible for HRM, says, "If you look into a screen and see no creativity, you certainly get a sense of what you're joining."

No doubt, Jane Paradiso would applaud the Tour de Chem. Paradiso, leader of the recruiting solutions practice at the Watson Wyatt Worldwide consulting firm, says online orientations should be more than a video about the company plus a signup sheet for benefits. According to Paradiso, an online orientation should take advantage of the Internet's potential for communication. The orientation program should assign the new employee an email address and a password to the intranet, let the employee schedule lunch with his or her boss, set up a connection between the new employee and his or her mentor, and describe the organization's ethics policy, among other features. In fact, such a system could begin building the organization's relationship with new employees even before their first day on the job, assuming the organization gives out a password for the system.

That's what Pinnacle Decision Systems does. The consulting and software development company, sends new hires to a website it calls "HQ." There, the newly hired individuals can read policies and procedures, view the company's organization chart, or order business cards and company T-shirts. Thanks to these online services, employees are already acquainted with the company on their first day. During their first day at work, they meet with department heads to deepen their knowledge of the organization. Pinnacle believes that in-depth employee orientation and development require more than a virtual touch, however. Says Joanne Keller, Pinnacle's HR director, "We wouldn't want to lose the personal touch, where you pick up the clues of how the company really works and what's expected of you."

SOURCE: Tom Starner, "Welcome E-Board," *Human Resource Executive*, March 6, 2002, pp. 40–43.

organizations provide training designed to teach employees attitudes and behaviours that support the management of diversity. Training designed to change employee attitudes about diversity and/or develop skills needed to work with a diverse workforce is called **diversity training.** These programs generally emphasize either attitude awareness and change or behaviour change.

Programs that focus on attitudes have objectives to increase participants' awareness of cultural and ethnic differences, as well as differences in personal characteristics and physical characteristics (such as disabilities). These programs are based on the assumption that people who become aware of differences and their stereotypes about those differences will be able to avoid letting stereotypes influence their interactions with people. Many of these programs use videotapes and experiential exercises to increase employees' awareness of the negative emotional and performance effects of stereotypes and resulting behaviours on members of a diverse workforce. A risk of these programs is that they may actually reinforce stereotypes by focusing on differences rather than similarities among coworkers.[60] But it is generally held that greater awareness has a positive effect.

Programs that focus on behaviour aim at changing the organizational policies and individual behaviours that inhibit employees' personal growth and productivity. Sometimes these programs identify incidents that discourage employees from achieving their potential. Employees work in groups to discuss specific promotion opportunities or management practices that they believe were handled unfairly. Another approach is to teach managers and employees basic rules of behaviour in the workplace.[61] Trainees may be more positive about receiving this type of training than other kinds of diversity training.

Although many organizations have used diversity training, few have provided programs lasting more than a day, and few have researched their long-term effectiveness.[62] The existing evidence regarding diversity training does, however, suggest that some characteristics make diversity training more effective.[63] Most important, the training should be tied to business objectives, such as understanding customers. The support and involvement of top management, and the involvement of managers at all levels, also are important. Results from an employee survey at Pelmorex, the company that runs the Weather Network, showed more than 90 percent of employees feel the company values equity. Pelmorex offers training on non-discriminatory interviewing techniques, integrating new employees into the workplace, and accommodation strategies. Annual bonuses for managers are tied to promoting equity.[64] Diversity training should emphasize learning behaviours and skills, not blaming employees. Finally, the program should be well structured, connected to the organization's rewards for performance, and include a way to measure the success of the training.

diversity training
Training designed to change employee attitudes about diversity and/or develop skills needed to work with a diverse workforce.

Summary

1. Discuss how to link training programs to organizational needs.
   Organizations need to establish training programs that are effective. In other words, they teach what they are designed to teach, and they teach skills and behaviours that will help the organization achieve its goals. Organizations create such programs through instructional design. This process begins with a needs assessment. The organization then ensures readiness for training, including employee characteristics and organizational support. Next, the organization plans a training program, implements the program, and evaluates the results.

2. Explain how to assess the need for training.
   Needs assessment consists of an organization analysis, person analysis, and task analysis. The organization analysis determines the appropriateness of training by evaluating the characteristics of the organization,

including its strategy, resources, and management support. The person analysis determines individuals' needs and readiness for training. The task analysis identifies the tasks, knowledge, skills, and behaviours that training should emphasize. It is based on examination of the conditions in which tasks are performed, including equipment and environment of the job, time constraints, safety considerations, and performance standards.

3. Explain how to assess employees' readiness for training.
Readiness for training is a combination of employee characteristics and positive work environment that permit training. The necessary employee characteristics include ability to learn the subject matter, favourable attitudes toward the training, and motivation to learn. A positive work environment avoids situational constraints such as lack of money and time. In a positive environment, both peers and management support training.

4. Describe how to plan an effective training program.
Planning begins with establishing objectives for the training program. These should define an expected performance or outcome, the desired level of performance, and the conditions under which the performance should occur. Based on the objectives, the planner decides who will provide the training, what topics the training will cover, what training methods to use, and how to evaluate the training. Even when organizations purchase outside training, someone in the organization, usually a member of the HR department, often is responsible for training administration. The training methods selected should be related to the objectives and content of the training program. Training methods may include presentation methods, hands-on methods, or group-building methods.

5. Compare widely used training methods.
Classroom instruction is most widely used and is one of the least expensive and least time-consuming ways to present information on a specific topic to many trainees. It also allows for group interaction and may include hands-on practice. Audiovisual and computer-based training need not require that trainees attend a class, so they can reduce time and money spent on training. Computer-based training may be interactive and may provide for group interaction. On-the-job training methods such as apprenticeships, internships, and co-operative education give trainees first-hand experiences. A simulation represents a real-life situation, enabling trainees to see the effects of their decisions without dangerous or expensive consequences. Business games and case studies are other methods for practising decision-making skills. Participants need to come to-

gether in one location or collaborate online. Behaviour modelling gives trainees a chance to observe desired behaviours, so this technique can be effective for teaching interpersonal skills. Experiential programs provide an opportunity for group members to interact in challenging circumstances but may exclude members with disabilities. Team training focuses a team on achievement of a common goal. Action learning offers relevance, because the training focuses on an actual work-related problem.

6. Summarize how to implement a successful training program.
Implementation should apply principles of learning. In general, effective training communicates learning objectives, presents information in distinctive and memorable ways, and helps trainees link the subject matter to their jobs. Employees are most likely to learn when training is linked to job experiences and tasks. Employees learn best when they demonstrate or practise what they have learned and when they receive feedback that helps them improve. Trainees remember information better when it is broken into small chunks, presented with visual images, and practised many times. Consideration should also be given to ensuring employees have the required workplace literacy skills to succeed and perform well in their jobs.

7. Evaluate the success of a training program.
Training can be evaluated at four levels—reaction, learning, behaviour, and results. Evaluation of training should look for transfer of training by measuring whether employees are performing the tasks taught in the training program. Assessment of training also should evaluate training outcomes, such as change in attitude, ability to perform a new skill, and recall of facts or behaviours taught in the training program. Training should result in improvement in the group's or organization's outcomes, such as customer satisfaction or sales. An economic measure of training success is return on investment.

8. Describe training methods for employee orientation and diversity management.
Employee orientation is training designed to prepare new employees to perform their job effectively, learn about the organization, and establish work relationships. Organizations provide for orientation because, no matter how realistic the information provided during employment interviews and site visits, people feel shock and surprise when they start a new job, and they need to learn the details of how to perform the job. A typical orientation program includes information about the overall company and the department in which the new employee will be working, covering so-

cial as well as technical aspects of the job. Orientation programs may combine several training methods, from printed materials to on-the-job training to e-learning. Diversity training is designed to change employee attitudes about diversity and/or develop skills needed to work with a diverse workforce. Evidence regarding these programs suggests that diversity training is most effective if it is tied to business objectives, has management support, emphasizes behaviours and skills, and is well structured with a way to measure success.

Review and Discussion Questions

1. "Melinda!" bellowed Toran to the company's HR specialist, "I've got a problem, and you've got to solve it. I can't get people in this plant to work together as a team. As if I don't have enough trouble with our competitors and our past-due accounts, now I have to put up with running a zoo. You're responsible for seeing that the staff gets along. I want a training proposal on my desk by Monday." Assume you are Melinda.
   a. Is training the solution to this problem? How can you determine the need for training?
   b. Summarize how you would conduct a needs assessment.

2. How should an organization assess readiness for learning? In question 1, how do Toran's comments suggest readiness (or lack of readiness) for learning?

3. Assume you are the human resource manager of a small seafood company. The general manager has told you that customers have begun complaining about the quality of your company's fresh fish. Currently, training consists of senior fish cleaners showing new employees how to perform the job. Assuming your needs assessment indicates a need for training, how would you plan a training program? What steps should you take in planning the program?

4. Many organizations turn to e-learning as a less expensive alternative to classroom training. What are some other advantages of substituting e-learning for classroom training? What are some disadvantages?

5. Suppose the managers in your organization tend to avoid delegating projects to the people in their groups. As a result, they rarely meet their goals. A training needs analysis indicates that an appropriate solution is training in management skills. You have identified two outside training programs that are consistent with your goals. One program involves experiential programs, and the other is an interactive computer program. What are the strengths and weaknesses of each technique? Which would you choose? Why?

6. Consider your current job or a job you recently held. What types of training did you receive for the job? What types of training would you like to receive? Why?

7. A manufacturing company employs several maintenance employees. When a problem occurs with the equipment, a maintenance employee receives a description of the symptoms and is supposed to locate and fix the source of the problem. The company recently installed a new, complex electronics system. To prepare its maintenance workers, the company provided classroom training. The trainer displayed electrical drawings of system components and posed problems about the system. The trainer would point to a component in a drawing and ask, "What would happen if this component were faulty?" Trainees would study the diagrams, describe the likely symptoms, and discuss how to repair the problem. If you were responsible for this company's training, how would you evaluate the success of this training program?

8. In question 7, suppose the maintenance supervisor has complained that trainees are having difficulty troubleshooting problems with the new electronics system. They are spending a great deal of time on problems with the system and coming to the supervisor with frequent questions that show a lack of understanding. The supervisor is convinced that the employees are motivated to learn the system, and they are well qualified. What do you think might be the problems with the current training program? What recommendations can you make for improving the program?

9. Who should be involved in orientation of new employees? Why would it not be appropriate to provide employee orientation purely online?

10. Why do organizations provide diversity training? What kinds of goals are most suitable for such training?

What's Your HR IQ?

The Online Learning Centre offers more ways to check what you've learned so far. Find experiential exercises as well as Test Your Knowledge Quizzes, Videos, and many other resources at www.mcgrawhill.ca/college/noe.

Top 100 Employers Case: Learning Technologies in the Workplace—SaskTel

SaskTel is Saskatchewan's leading full-service telecommunications company. The company employs over 4,000 people, who work in more than 50 communities throughout the province. SaskTel conducts business through the Internet and develops e-business solutions for its customers. SaskTel's transition to an electronic environment put pressure on its employees to develop their computer literacy and e-business skills. Recognizing the opportunities the Internet affords for online training, the company aggressively uses technology to enhance learning in the workplace. SaskTel was recently the recipient of the Conference Board of Canada's Learning Technologies in the Workplace Award for demonstrating an innovative approach to its transition to an e-learning strategy.

SaskTel makes e-learning opportunities available to all of its employees, regardless of where they live. Employees can currently access over 450 online courses from work or home.

The employee barriers encountered during the transition included the difficulty for employees to make the connection between participating in e-learning and supporting SaskTel's e-business strategy and the need for call centre service representatives to develop a sales focus as well as a service focus. From a company perspective, SaskTel needed to measure the effectiveness of online learning including measuring performance gains made based on e-learning and developing line managers' project management skills including their ability to give timely and constructive feedback to employees regarding learning needs and performance. In addition, SaskTel wanted to ensure opportunities were provided to employees who had made use of online learning to apply, challenge, enhance, and reinforce their recently learned or honed skills.

Four keys to success for the company have been:

1. Building strategic awareness. Communicating the impact of technology-based changes on employees.

2. Soft launching the e-learning strategy. Offering online courses for four years before the launch of online learning provided SaskTel time to build up a repertoire of courses. In addition, line managers are encouraged to promote the benefits of e-learning.

3. Building a culture of engagement in e-learning. Making online learning fun, recognizing employee accomplishments and completion of online learning modules; and linking online learning back to employees' development plans.

4. Taking a broad approach to e-learning. Blending traditional and electronic approaches to teaching and learning according to what works best (e.g., online learning, classroom-lead learning, team meetings, etc.).

Some of the outcomes achieved include:

- approximately 50 percent of training at SaskTel is currently done online

- relevant portions of SaskTel's call centre curriculum are now being converted into online modules complete with pre- and post-assessment and opportunities for employee-learners to collaborate with each other

- SaskTel employees completed 5,480 online courses—on average, that is more than one course per employee

SaskTel's approach to implementing an e-learning training strategy may be used as a model by other organizations that are prepared to support a long-term cultural shift. SaskTel immersed its employees in online learning when its business was being transformed by the imperatives of e-business. SaskTel also integrated modular and course-based online learning with content conceived in a much more targeted way. For example, while their customers are on the telephone, call centre representatives can use quick links to obtain product and service information. In addition, self-directed online learning is also connected with help desk functions within the company.

SOURCE: Adapted from Kurtis Kitagawa, "Learning Technologies in the Workplace Award Winner 2002: SaskTel," (Ottawa: The Conference Board of Canada, 2002), www.conferenceboard.ca. Retrieved: February 28, 2004.

Questions

1. What considerations are needed for e-learning to be effective? Explain.

2. Because many organizations expect trainees to complete e-learning during breaks or outside work hours, online learning blurs the boundaries between training and work. Is this expectation realistic? Why or why not?

3. What measures can an organization take to improve employees' motivation to participate in e-learning?

Case: Wal–Mart Training Partnerships Let New Recruits Prove Their Value

When you enter Wal-Mart Canada's Agincourt store northeast of Toronto, chances are you will be greeted by Andrew. Andrew is friendly and outgoing. He knows everything that is going on in the store and is trained to perform many typical roles performed by retail staff, or associates, as Wal-Mart calls its employees. Andrew will direct you to the department with the goods you seek and he plays a critical troubleshooting role if a store emergency occurs. In fact, he has more formal training than most associates receive when they are hired.

By the way, Andrew has a disability.

Andrew has always known that he wanted to work in customer service, because he loves people. However, he encountered some difficulty in finding full-time work after leaving school. Now he is keen to perform well in his chosen career in retail. In fact, he is still slightly amazed to have passed numerous pre-screening hurdles to be accepted into the 24-week Wal-Mart Canada retail associate training program.

The retail associate training program is designed and managed by the Canadian Council on Rehabilitation and Work (CCRW) in partnership with federal and provincial governments. Goodwill Toronto is a key partner in training delivery.

The training program has been run for Wal-Mart in Toronto, Ottawa, and Vancouver several times since 1996, and plans are underway for a Halifax session. Local agencies attached to the program recruit extensively through local disability services networks. Rigorous pre-screening ensures that candidates are suited for the retail environment and Wal-Mart's unique culture. Wal-Mart is responsible for final selection from short-listed applicants and graduates are guaranteed jobs.

The first half of the program is classroom-based. Students learn about the retail business and about the "the Wal-Mart way." Curriculum also includes general skills, such as computer use, and soft skills like team-building and anger management. In the second half of the program, students are assigned to a particular store where they job-shadow and train in a number of associate roles. This was Andrew's favourite part of the program.

The program has provided a "win–win" for all involved. According to Wal-Mart's Darri Beaulieu, who has corporate responsibility for the program, the retention rate of graduates since courses began in 1996 is about 85 percent, which is remarkable in retail, where annual turnover can exceed 30 percent.

Diane Smith is the human resource manager at the Agincourt store. She and the store manager are the champions at the store level. Diane cites three keys to success:

1. Management support at the corporate and store levels

2. Good communication

3. Training

Canadian president and CEO, Dave Ferguson is an outspoken champion and a visible role model. He opens corporate training sessions and attends graduation ceremonies. The subject of integrating people with disabilities and providing the community with good customer service arises frequently.

As a result of short, regular training sessions on aspects of integrating people with disabilities into the store, as well as discussions at staff meetings, management and store associates are very well prepared and comfortable about working with a co-worker with a disability. Staff is also consulted on a regular basis on how to improve the training or any other aspect of the program that affects them. Store associates participate in hiring panels and act as sponsors, taking program participants under their wing and helping to train them.

The training program has benefited both Wal-Mart and its new associates with disabilities. Wal-Mart gains rigorously trained, enthusiastic recruits. The introduction of Andrew and two of his classmates to the Agincourt store has brought managers and many associates together in a common cause that has uniquely enhanced culture and spirit at the store. Wal-Mart has also earned a reputation as a community leader and employer of choice for people who want an opportunity to be recognized for their ability. People with disabilities like Andrew have a genuine opportunity for a meaningful, fulfilling, and sustainable career.

SOURCE: Ruth Wright, "Tapping the Talents of People with Disabilities: A Guide for Employers" in partnership with The Ministry of Citizenship—Government of Canada, The Conference Board of Canada 2001, p. 27, ISBN 0-88763-500-8, www.conference.board.ca. Retrieved: March 9, 2004.

Questions
1. What are the benefits of the training program to Wal-Mart?
2. What are the benefits of the training program to the new associates with disabilities?
3. What are the roles and requirements of the management team at Wal-Mart to ensure the ongoing success of this initiative?

7

Managing Employees' Performance

1. Identify the activities involved in performance management.

2. Discuss the purposes of performance management systems.

3. Define five criteria for measuring the effectiveness of a performance management system.

4. Compare the major methods for measuring performance.

5. Describe major sources of performance information in terms of their advantages and disadvantages.

6. Define types of rating errors and explain how to minimize them.

7. Explain how to provide performance feedback effectively.

8. Summarize ways to achieve performance improvement.

9. Discuss legal and ethical issues that affect performance management.

Introduction

Managing employees' performance in the Royal Canadian Mounted Police (RCMP) is a strategic process where supervisors play a key role. Supervisors are responsible for not only monitoring employee performance and giving feedback, but also taking on the role of "learning coach." This role involves:

- Determining the competencies needed to meet strategic and operational objectives

- Determining the strengths and gaps in employee competencies

- Working with employees to identify the right kinds of learning opportunities to develop needed competencies
- Assessing the effectiveness of employee performance
- Adjusting as needed
- Providing the process for employees to share learning
- Identifying and developing people with leadership potential[1]

Assessing employees' performance, as the RCMP does, is a central part of performance management. **Performance management** is the process of ensuring that employees' activities and outputs match the organization's goals. This process requires knowing what activities and outputs are desired, observing whether they occur, and providing feedback to help employees meet expectations. In the course of providing feedback, managers and employees may identify performance problems and establish ways to resolve those problems.

In this chapter we examine a variety of approaches to performance management. We begin by describing the activities involved in managing performance, then discuss the purpose of carrying out this process. Next, we discuss specific approaches to performance appraisal, including the strengths and weaknesses of each approach. We also look at various sources of performance information. The next section explores the kinds of errors that commonly occur during the assessment of performance, as well as ways to reduce those errors. Then we describe ways of giving performance feedback effectively and intervening when performance needs to improve. Finally, we summarize legal and ethical issues affecting performance management.

performance management
The process of ensuring that employees' activities and outputs match the organization's goals.

The Process of Performance Management

Traditional approaches to management have viewed **performance appraisal,** or the measurement of specified areas of an employee's performance, as the primary means of performance management. In the traditional approaches, the human resource department is responsible for setting up and managing a performance appraisal system. Managers conduct performance appraisals as one of their administrative duties. They tend to view the appraisals as a yearly ritual in which they quickly fill out forms and present the information to their employees, one by one. Appraisals include negative information (areas needing improvement), so the meetings for discussing performance appraisals tend to be uncomfortable for managers and employees alike. Often, managers feel they do not know how to evaluate performance effectively, and employees

performance appraisal
The measurement of specified areas of an employee's performance.

The RCMP has adopted a strategic approach to performance management where supervisors play a key role.

TABLE 7.1

Performance
Appraisal Problems
and Performance
Management
Solutions

PROBLEM	SOLUTION
Discourages teamwork	Make collaboration a criterion on which employees will be evaluated.
Evaluators are inconsistent or use different criterion and standards	Provide training for managers; have the HR department look for patterns on appraisals that suggest bias or over- or underevaluation; ensure employee's goals clearly align with team, departmental, and organizational goals.
Only valuable for very good or very poor employees	Evaluate specific behaviours or results to show specifically what employees need to improve.
Encourages employees to achieve short-term goals	Include both long-term and short-term goals in the appraisal process.
Manager has complete power over the employee	Managers should be appraised for how they appraise their employees.
Too subjective	Evaluate specific behaviour or results.
Produces emotional anguish	Focus on behaviour; do not criticize employees; conduct appraisal on time; ensure appraisal is linked to ongoing development of the employee.

SOURCE: Based on J. A. Siegel, "86 Your Appraisal Process?" *HR Magazine,* October 2000, pp. 199–202.

feel they are excluded from the process and that their contributions are not recognized.[2] The left side of Table 7.1 lists some of the criticisms that have been levelled against this style of performance management.

As indicated on the right side of Table 7.1, these problems can be solved through a more effective approach to performance management. Appraising performance need not cause the problems listed in the table. If done correctly, the process can provide valuable benefits to employees and the organization alike. For example, a performance management system can tell top performers that they are valued, encourage communication between managers and their employees, establish uniform standards for evaluating employees, and help the organization identify its strongest and weakest per-

FIGURE 7.1

Stages of the
Performance
Management Process

Managing Performance to Reinforce a High-Morale, High-Performance Workplace Culture

Technology services provider NexInnovations became independent of EDS in 2001 and today employs about 1,400 people across Canada. For the past few months the HR team at NexInnovations has been busy inventing a new performance management system.

Headquartered in Mississauga, Ontario, the firm knew they wanted something that would reinforce a high-morale, high-performance workplace culture. Most of all it clearly had to support the organization's corporate objectives and it had to be simple.

NexInnovations' six key corporate objectives served as the starting point for the creation of its performance management system. "We have gone to an objective-setting worksheet which basically is a grid with a bunch of boxes on it," Frank Price, Calgary-based vice-president of HR, explains. "We are literally making it that simple. We are going from left to right starting with corporate objectives, then business unit objectives, and then individual objectives and then your action plans and metrics that the individual has to do. Employees can see the corporate objectives

and their objectives linked together on the same sheet."

"Every single person in the organization will have one of those in the next four months," says Price. "Anybody (the president) walks up to, wherever he is in the country, should be able to say not only what one of the corporate objectives are but what they are doing right now and how it supports it."

SOURCE: "HR Leaders Talk," *Canadian HR Reporter*, February 10, 2003, www.hrreporter.com. Retrieved: February 12, 2005. © Copyright *Canadian HR Reporter*, February 10, 2003, by Carswell, Toronto, Ontario, 1-800-387-5164.

formers. According to the Hay Group, companies on its Global Most Admired list, which it prepares for *Fortune* magazine, have chief executive officers who understand that performance measurement helps the organization motivate people and link performance to rewards.[3] Many of these executives report that performance measurement encourages employees to cooperate and helps the company focus on smooth operations, customer loyalty, and employee development.

To meet these objectives, performance management extends beyond mere appraisals to include several activities. As shown in Figure 7.1, these are defining performance, measuring performance, and feeding back performance information. First, the organization specifies which aspects of performance are relevant to the organization. These decisions are based on the organization's environment and overall objectives, as well as job analysis, described in Chapter 3. Next, the organization measures the relevant aspects of performance by conducting performance appraisals. Finally, through performance feedback sessions, managers give employees information about their performance so they can adjust their behaviour to meet the organization's goals. When there are performance gaps, the feedback session should include efforts to identify and resolve the underlying problems. In addition, performance feedback can come through the organization's rewards, as described in Chapter 9.

Using this performance management process in place of the traditional performance appraisal routine helps managers and employees focus on the organization's goals. The "Best Practices" box describes how NexInnovations uses performance management to give a common focus to employees.

LO1

Computer software is available to help managers at various stages of performance management.[4] Software can help managers customize performance measurement forms. The manager uses the software to establish a set of performance standards for each job. The manager rates each employee according to the predetermined standards, and the software provides a report that compares the employee's performance to the standards and identifies the employee's strengths and weaknesses. Other software offers help with diagnosing performance gaps. This type of software asks questions—for example, Does the employee work under time pressure? The answers suggest reasons for performance problems and ways the manager can help the employee improve. These technological tools can also provide strategic analysis of an organization's or department's key performance indicators. A competency gap analysis report can then be generated to determine which of these skills the organization has and which ones it still needs.[5] In addition, PerformanceReview.com even offers managers online help with writing performance reviews. This service is offered as a single use or as an unlimited-use subscription.[6]

LO2

Purposes of Performance Management

Organizations establish performance management systems to meet three broad purposes: strategic, administrative, and developmental. *Strategic purpose* means effective performance management helps the organization achieve its business objectives. It does this by helping to link employees' behavior with the organization's goals. Performance management starts with defining what the organization expects from each employee. It measures each employee's performance to identify where those expectations are and are not being met. This enables the organization to take corrective action, such as training, incentives, or discipline. Performance management can achieve its strategic purpose only when measurements are truly aligned with the organization's goals and when the goals and feedback about performance are communicated to employees.

The *administrative purpose* of a performance management system refers to the ways in which organizations use the system to provide information for day-to-day decisions about salary, benefits, and recognition programs. Performance management can also support decision making related to employee retention, termination, and hiring or layoffs. Because performance management supports these administrative decisions, the information in a performance appraisal can have a great impact on the future of individual employees. Managers recognize this, which is the reason they may feel uncomfortable conducting performance appraisals when the appraisal information is negative and, therefore, likely to lead to a layoff, disappointing pay increase, or other negative outcome.

Finally, performance management has a *developmental purpose*, meaning that it serves as a basis for developing employees' competencies. Even employees who are meeting expectations can become more valuable when they hear and discuss performance feedback. Effective performance feedback makes employees aware of their strengths and of the areas in which they can improve. Discussing areas in which employees fall short can help the employees and their manager uncover the source of problems and identify steps for improvement. Although discussing shortcomings may feel uncomfortable, it is necessary when performance management has a developmental purpose.

Telus, the British Columbia-based communication company, was recently recognized by the American Society for Training and Development for its "growing for high performance" initiative that integrates performance management and the organization's learning systems. Telus has restructured its corporate learning function "so that it is more of a performance consulting organization. That basically means working together with the line groups to identify what are their performance gaps and then identify training or learning solutions to directly work toward closing those performance gaps," or taking performance that meets expectations and taking it to the next level.[7]

Criteria for Effective Performance Management

LO3

In Chapter 5, we saw that there are many ways to predict performance of a job candidate. Similarly, there are many ways to measure the performance of an employee. For performance management to achieve its goals, its methods for measuring performance must be effective. Selecting these measures is a critical part of planning a performance management system. Criteria that determine the effectiveness of performance measures include each measure's fit with the organization's strategy, its validity, its reliability, the degree to which it is acceptable to the organization, and the extent to which it gives employees specific feedback. These criteria are summarized in Figure 7.2.

A performance management system should ensure the organization's strategic goals are translated into specific unit, function, and individual goals and objectives. "By starting with the broadest organizational objectives and then drilling down through the functions that affect their achievement, employees can be reminded that all goals are interdependent across organizational units and levels. For example, an organizational objective to expand market penetration of a given product can be translated into specific goals for employees in sales, marketing, research and development, customer service, information technology, and training."[8] When an organization's strategy changes, human resource professionals should help managers assess how the performance management system should change to serve the new strategy.

FIGURE 7.2

Criteria for Effective
Performance Measures

FIGURE 7.3

Contamination and
Deficiency of a Job
Performance Measure

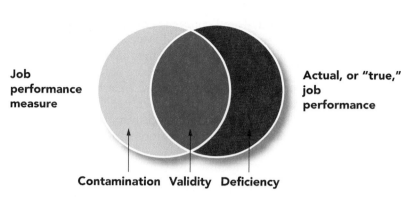

**Job
performance
measure**

**Actual, or "true,"
job
performance**

Contamination Validity Deficiency

As we discussed in Chapter 5, *validity* is the extent to which a measurement tool actually measures what it is intended to measure. In the case of performance appraisal, validity refers to whether the appraisal measures all the relevant aspects of performance and omits irrelevant aspects of performance. Figure 7.3 shows two sets of information. The circle on the left represents all the information in a performance appraisal; the circle on the right represents all relevant measures of job performance. The overlap of the circles contains the valid information. Information that is gathered but irrelevant is "contamination." Comparing salespeople based on how many calls they make to customers could be a contaminated measure. Making a lot of calls does not necessarily improve sales or customer satisfaction, unless every salesperson makes only well-planned calls. Information that is not gathered but is relevant represents a deficiency of the performance measure. For example, suppose a company measures whether employees have good attendance records but not whether they work efficiently. This limited performance appraisal is unlikely to provide a full picture of employees' contribution to the company. Performance measures should minimize both contamination and deficiency.

With regard to a performance measure, reliability describes the consistency of the results that the performance measure will deliver. *Interrater reliability* is consistency of results when more than one person measures performance. Simply asking a supervisor to rate an employee's performance on a scale of 1 to 5 would likely have low interrater reliability; the rating will differ depending on who is scoring the employees. *Test-retest reliability* refers to consistency of results over time. If a performance measure lacks test-retest reliability, determining whether an employee's performance has truly changed over time will be impossible.

Whether or not a measure is valid and reliable, it must meet the practical standard of being acceptable to the people who use it. For example, the people who use a performance measure must believe that it is not too time-consuming. Likewise, if employees believe the measure is unfair, they will not use the feedback as a basis for improving their performance.

Finally, a performance measure should communicate to employees what is expected of them and how they can meet those expectations. Being specific usually means the performance measure can be defined in quantitative terms. If a measure does not specify what an employee must do to help the organization achieve its goals, it does not support the strategy. If the measure fails to point out employees' performance gaps, they will not know how to improve.

Methods for Measuring Performance

LO4

Organizations have developed a wide variety of methods for measuring performance. A Conference Board of Canada study concluded that about 87 percent of all Canadian employers use some form of performance appraisal rating system.[9] Some methods rank each employee to compare employees' performance. Other methods break down the evaluation into ratings of individual competencies, behaviours, or results. Many organizations use a measurement system that includes a variety of the preceding measures.

Making Comparisons

The performance appraisal method may require the rater to compare one individual's performance with that of others. This method involves some form of ranking, in which some employees are the highest performers, some are average, and others are not meeting expectations. The usual techniques for making comparisons are simple ranking, forced distribution, and paired comparison.

Simple ranking requires managers to rank employees in their group from the highest performer to the lowest performer. In a variation of this approach, *alternation ranking,* the manager works from a list of employees. First, the manager decides which employee is the highest performer and crosses that person's name off the list. From the remaining names, the manager selects the lowest performing employee and crosses off that name. The process continues with the manager selecting the second highest, second lowest, third highest, and so on until all the employees have been ranked. The major downside of ranking involves validity. To state a performance measure as broadly as "highest" or "lowest" doesn't define what exactly is effective or ineffective about the person's contribution to the organization. Ranking therefore raises questions about fairness.

Another way to compare employees' performance is with the **forced-distribution method.** This type of performance measurement assigns a certain percentage of employees to each category in a set of categories. For example, the organization might establish the following percentages and categories:

- Exceptional—5 percent
- Exceeds expectations—25 percent
- Meets expectations—55 percent
- Room for improvement—10 percent
- Not acceptable—5 percent

The manager completing the performance appraisal would rate 5 percent of his or her employees as exceptional, 25 percent as exceeding standards, and so on. A forced-distribution approach works best if the members of a group really do vary this much in terms of their performance. It overcomes the temptation to rate everyone high in order to avoid conflict. However, a manager who does very well at selecting, motivating, and training employees will have a group of high performers. This manager would have difficulty assigning employees to the bottom categories. In that situation, saying that some employees require improvement or are "not acceptable" not only will be inaccurate, but will hurt morale.

The use of forced distribution is on the rise. A Conference Board of Canada performance management study reported that 25 percent of organizations responding

simple ranking
Method of performance measurement that requires managers to rank employees in their group from the highest performer to the lowest performer.

forced-distribution method
Method of performance measurement that assigns a certain percentage of employees to each category in a set of categories.

said they use some of the forced-distribution method and 4 percent are considering it in the next year.[10] Maple Leaf Foods, a Toronto-based food processing company, uses the forced-distribution method for assessing its 5,000 salaried employees. Wayne Johnson, vice-president of human resources explains, "A's make up the top 20 percent, B's the middle 70 percent, and C's the bottom 10 percent."[11]

paired-comparison method
Method of performance measurement that compares each employee with each other employee to establish rankings.

Another variation on rankings is the **paired-comparison method.** This approach involves comparing each employee with each other employee to establish rankings. Suppose a manager has five employees, Allen, Barbara, Caitlin, David, and Edgar. The manager compares Allen's performance to Barbara's and assigns one point to whichever employer is the higher performer. Then the manager compares Allen's performance to Caitlin's, then to David's, and finally to Edgar's. The manager repeats this process with Barbara, comparing her performance to Caitlin's, David's, and Edgar's. When the manager has compared every pair of employees, the manager counts the number of points for each employee. The employee with the most points is considered the top-ranked employee. Clearly, this method is time-consuming if a group has more than a handful of employees. For a group of 15, the manager must make 105 comparisons.

In spite of the drawbacks, ranking employees offers some benefits. It counteracts the tendency to avoid controversy by rating everyone favourably or near the centre of the scale. Also, if some managers tend to evaluate behaviour more strictly (or more leniently) than others, a ranking system can erase that tendency from performance scores. Therefore, ranking systems can be useful for supporting decisions about how to distribute pay raises or layoffs. Some ranking systems are easy to use, which makes them acceptable to the managers who use them. A major drawback of rankings is that they often are not linked to the organization's goals. Also, a simple ranking system leaves the basis for the ranking open to interpretation. In that case, the rankings are not helpful for employee development and may hurt morale or result in legal challenges.

Rating Individuals

Instead of focusing on arranging a group of employees from highest to lowest, performance measurement can look at each employee's performance relative to a uniform set of standards. The measurement may evaluate employees in terms of competencies believed necessary for success in the job or in the organization. These measurements may identify whether employees have *behaved* in desirable ways, such as closing sales or completing assignments. The performance management system must identify the desired competencies, then provide a form on which the manager can rate the employee. Typically, the form includes a rating scale, such as a scale from 1 to 5, where 1 is the worst performance and 5 is the best.

graphic rating scale
Method of performance measurement that lists competencies and provides a rating scale for each competency; the employer uses the scale to indicate the extent to which an employee displays each competency.

Rating Competencies

The most widely used method for rating competencies is the **graphic rating scale.** This method lists competencies and provides a rating scale for each. The employer uses the scale to indicate the extent to which the employee being rated displays the behaviours associated with each competency. The rating scale may provide points to circle (as on a scale going from 1 for poor to 5 for excellent), or it may provide a line representing a range of scores, with the manager marking a place along the line. Figure 7.4 shows an example of a graphic rating scale that uses a set of ratings from 1 to 5. A drawback of this approach is that it leaves to the particular manager the decisions about what is "exceptional client service" or "exceeds expectations for teamwork" or "counter-productive interpersonal skills." The result is low reliability, because managers are likely to arrive at different judgments.

To avoid this problem, some organizations use **mixed-standard scales,** which use several statements describing each competency to produce a final score for that competency. The manager scores the employee in terms of how the employee compares to each statement. Consider the sample mixed-standard scale in Figure 7.5 on page 203. To create this scale, the organization determined that the relevant competencies are initiative, client orientation, and relations with others. For each competency, sentences were written to describe a person having a high level of that competency, a medium level, and a low level. The sentences for the traits were rearranged so that the nine statements about the three traits are mixed together. The manager who uses this scale reads each sentence, then indicates whether the employee performs above (+), at (0), or below (–) the level described. The key in the middle section of Figure 7.5 tells how to use the pluses, zeros, and minuses to score performance. Someone who excels at every level of performance (pluses for high, medium, and low performance) receives a score of 7 for that competency. Someone who fails to live up to every description of performance (minuses for high, medium, and low) receives a score of 1 for that competency. The bottom of Figure 7.5 calculates the scores for the ratings used in this example.

Assessing competencies is the most popular way to measure performance in organizations. In general, competency-based performance methods are easy to develop and can be applied to a wide variety of jobs and organizations. If the organization is careful to identify which competencies are associated with high performance, and to define them carefully on the appraisal form, these methods can be reliable and valid. However, appraisal forms often fail to meet this standard. In addition, measurement of competencies is often not linked to the organization's strategy. Furthermore, employees tend perhaps rightly to be defensive about receiving a mere numerical rating on some com-

mixed-standard scales
Method of performance measurement that uses several statements describing each competency to produce a final score for that competency.

FIGURE 7.4

Example of a Graphic Rating Scale

The following areas of performance are significant to most positions. Indicate your assessment of performance on each dimension by circling the appropriate rating.

COMPETENCY	RATING				
	EXCEPTIONAL	EXCEEDS EXPECTATIONS	MEETS EXPECTATIONS	BELOW EXPECTATIONS	COUNTER-PRODUCTIVE
Client service	4	3	2	1	0
Communication skills	4	3	2	1	0
Judgment	4	3	2	1	0
Managerial skill	4	3	2	1	0
Professionalism	4	3	2	1	0
Teamwork	4	3	2	1	0
Interpersonal skills	4	3	2	1	0
Initiative	4	3	2	1	0
Creativity	4	3	2	1	0
Problem solving	4	3	2	1	0

petency. How would you feel if you were told you scored 2 on a 5-point scale of initiative or communication skill? The number might seem arbitrary, and it doesn't tell you how to improve.

Rating Behaviours

One way to support a competency-based approach to performance is to assess employees' behaviour. To rate behaviours, the organization begins by defining which behaviours are associated with success on the job. Which kinds of employee behaviour help the organization achieve its goals? The appraisal form asks the manager to rate an employee in terms of each of the identified behaviours.

critical-incident method
Method of performance measurement based on managers' records of specific examples of the employee behaving in ways that are either effective or ineffective.

One way to rate behaviours is with the **critical-incident method.** This approach requires managers to keep a record of specific examples of the employee behaving in ways that are either effective or ineffective. Here's an example of a critical incident in the performance evaluation of an appliance repairperson:

> A customer called in about a refrigerator that was not cooling and was making a clicking noise every few minutes. The technician prediagnosed the cause of the problem and checked his truck for the necessary parts. When he found he did not have them, he checked the parts out from inventory so that the customer's refrigerator would be repaired on his first visit and the customer would be satisfied promptly.

This incident provides evidence of the employee's knowledge of refrigerator repair and concern for efficiency and customer satisfaction. Evaluating performance in this specific way gives employees feedback about what they do well and what requires improvement. The manager can also relate the incidents to how the employee is helping the company achieve its goals. Keeping a daily or weekly log of critical incidents requires significant effort, however, and managers may resist this requirement. Also, critical incidents may be unique, so they may not support comparisons among employees.

behaviourally anchored rating scale (BARS)
Method of performance measurement that rates behaviour in terms of a scale showing specific statements of behaviour that describe different levels of performance.

A **behaviourally anchored rating scale (BARS)** builds on the critical incident approach. The BARS method is intended to define competency dimensions specifically, using statements of behaviour that describe different levels of the competency.[12] (The statements are "anchors" of the competency levels.) The scale in Figure 7.6 shows various competency levels for "listening, understanding, and responding." The statement at the top (rating 4) describes the highest level of listening, understanding, and responding. The statement at the bottom describes behaviour associated with ineffective or counter-productive performance. These statements are based on data about past performance. The organization gathers many critical incidents representing effective and ineffective performance, then classifies them from most to least effective. When experts about the job agree the statements clearly represent levels of a competency, they are used as anchors to guide the rater. Although BARS can improve interrater reliability, this method can bias the manager's memory. The statements used as anchors can help managers remember similar behaviours, at the expense of other critical incidents.[13]

organizational behaviour modification (OBM)
A plan for managing the behaviour of employees through a formal system of feedback and reinforcement.

Another approach to assessment builds directly on a branch of psychology called *behaviourism*, which holds that individuals' future behaviour is determined by their past experiences—specifically, the ways in which past behaviours have been reinforced. People tend to repeat behaviours that have been rewarded in the past. Providing feedback and reinforcement can therefore modify individuals' future behaviour. Applied to behaviour in organizations, **organizational behaviour modification (OBM)** is a plan for managing the behaviour of employees through a formal system

FIGURE 7.5

Example of a Mixed-Standard Scale

Three competencies being assessed:	Levels of performance in statements:
Initiative (INTV)	High (H)
Client Orientation (CLO)	Medium (M)
Relations with others (RWO)	Low (L)

Instructions: Please indicate next to each statement whether the employee's performance is above (+), equal to (0), or below (−) the statement.

INTV	H	1.	This employee is a real self-starter. The employee always takes the initiative and his/her supervisor never has to prod this individual.	+
CLO	M	2.	Although this employee has some difficulty anticipating client needs, s/he is usually friendly and approachable.	+
RWO	L	3.	This employee has a tendency to get into unnecessary conflicts with other people.	0
INTV	M	4.	While generally this employee shows initiative, occasionally his/her supervisor must prod him/her to complete work.	+
CLO	L	5.	This employee frequently needs assistance in handling customer requests.	+
RWO	H	6.	This employee is on good terms with everyone. S/he can get along with people even when s/he does not agree with them.	−
INTV	L	7.	This employee has a bit of a tendency to sit around and wait for directions.	+
CLO	H	8.	This employee creates and maintains long-term client relationships.	−
RWO	M	9.	This employee gets along with most people. Only very occasionally does s/he have conflicts with others on the job, and these are likely to be minor.	−

Scoring Key:

	STATEMENTS		SCORE
HIGH	MEDIUM	LOW	
+	+	+	7
0	+	+	6
−	+	+	5
−	0	+	4
−	−	+	3
−	−	0	2
−	−	−	1

Example score from preceding ratings:

	STATEMENTS			SCORE
	HIGH	MEDIUM	LOW	
Initiative	+	+	+	7
Client orientation	−	+	+	5
Relations with others	−	−	0	2

of feedback and reinforcement. Specific OBM techniques vary, but most have four components:[14]

1. Define a set of key behaviours necessary for job performance.
2. Use a measurement system to assess whether the employee exhibits the key behaviours.
3. Inform employees of the key behaviours, perhaps in terms of goals for how often to exhibit the behaviours.
4. Provide feedback and reinforcement based on employees' behaviour.

OBM techniques have been used in a variety of settings. For example, a community health agency used OBM to increase the rates and timeliness of critical job behaviours by showing employees the connection between job behaviours and the agency's accomplishments.[15] This process identified job behaviours related to administration, record keeping, and service provided to clients. Feedback and reinforcement improved staff performance. OBM also increased the frequency of safety behaviours in a processing plant.[16]

Behavioural approaches such as organizational behaviour modification and rating scales can be very effective. These methods can link the company's goals to the specific behaviour required to achieve those goals. Behavioural methods also can generate specific feedback, along with guidance in areas requiring improvements. As a result, these methods tend to be valid. The people to be measured often help in developing the measures, so acceptance tends to be high as well. When raters are well trained, reliability also tends to be high. However, behavioural methods do not work as well for complex jobs in which it is difficult to see a link between behaviour and results or there is more than one good way to achieve success.[17]

FIGURE 7.6

BARS Rating Dimension: Customer Service Representative

Competency: Listening, Understanding, and Responding

"Is the desire and ability to understand and respond effectively to other people from diverse backgrounds. It includes the ability to understand accurately and respond effectively to both spoken and unspoken or partly expressed thoughts, feelings, and concerns of others."

BEHAVIOURAL LEVEL		INTERPRETIVE GUIDE
Anticipates and plans for future interactions	4	Did the employee understand the underlying reasons for a person's behaviour?
Understands and responds to underlying issues	3	Did the employee use knowledge of the person's perspectives and concerns when responding?
Listens and responds to unexpressed emotions	2	Did the employee solicit input, paraphrase the individual's words, mirror body language, and tone of voice?
Listens and responds to expressed emotions	1	Did the employee ask questions and respond to others' feelings or concerns?
Provides inappropriate information or service	0	Did the employee demonstrate ineffective or counter-productive behaviours? (e.g., displayed boredom or lack of empathy, interrupted the client, etc.)

SOURCE: Adapted from "Manager's HR Toolkit," BC Public Service Agency, www.hrtoolkit.gov.bc.ca/staffing. Retrieved: February 16, 2005.

Measuring Results

Performance measurement can focus on managing the objective, measurable results of a job or work group. Results might include sales, costs, or productivity (output per worker or per dollar spent on production), among many possible measures. Two of the most popular methods for measuring results are measurement of productivity and management by objectives.

Productivity is an important measure of success, because getting more done with a smaller amount of resources (money or people) increases the company's profits. Productivity usually refers to the output of production workers, but it can be used more generally as a performance measure. To do this, the organization identifies the products—set of activities or objectives—it expects a group or individual to accomplish. At a repair shop, for instance, a product might be something like "quality of repair." The next step is to define how to measure production of these products. For quality of repair, the repair shop could track the percentage of items returned because they still do not work after a repair and the percentage of quality-control inspections passed. For each measure, the organization decides what level of performance is desired. Finally, the organization sets up a system for tracking these measures and giving employees feedback about their performance in terms of these measures. This type of performance measurement can be time-consuming to set up, but research suggests it can improve productivity.[18]

Management by objectives (MBO) is a system in which people at each level of the organization set goals in a process that flows from top to bottom, so employees at all levels are contributing to the organization's overall goals. These goals become the standards for evaluating each employee's performance. An MBO system has three components:[19]

1. Goals and objectives should be "SMART":
   - **S**pecific—precise behaviour or outcome is identified
   - **M**easurable—stated in quantifiable terms
   - **A**chievable—challenging but achievable
   - **R**elevant—within the employee's control and is important to the organization
   - **T**imed—there is a defined completion date
   The goals listed in the second column of Table 7.2 provide two examples for a Human Resource Vice-President.
2. Managers and their employees work together to set the goals.
3. The manager gives objective feedback through the rating period to monitor progress toward the goals. The two right-hand columns in Table 7.2 are examples of feedback given after one year.

MBO can have a very positive effect on an organization's performance. In 70 studies of MBO's performance, 68 showed that productivity improved.[20] The productivity gains tended to be greatest when top management was highly committed to MBO. Also, because staff members are involved in setting goals, it is likely that MBO systems effectively link individual employees' performance with the organization's overall goals.

management by objectives (MBO)
A system in which people at each level of the organization set goals in a process that flows from top to bottom, so employees at all levels are contributing to the organization's overall goals; these goals become the standards for evaluating each employee's performance.

A coach/trainer provides feedback to team members or students, just as managers give feedback to their employees. Feedback provides information about what you're doing well and how you can change to improve. Feedback can contribute to a feeling of achievement.

TABLE 7.2

Management by
Objectives: Two
Goals for a Human
Resource Vice-
President

KEY RESULT AREA	OBJECTIVE	% COMPLETE	ACTUAL PERFORMANCE
Human Resource strategy linked to business goals	92 percent employee retention for the period January 1 – December 31, 2005	103%	95 percent employee retention in 2005
Motivated and productive HR team	100 percent of HR employees receive a documented performance review by December 31, 2005	100%	100 percent of HR employees have a written performance review that was completed by December 31, 2005

SOURCE: Adapted from "Vice-President Human Resources Example Performance Plan,"
www.zigonperf.com/resources/examples/hrvp.asp. Retrieved: July 15, 2004.

In general, evaluation of results can be less subjective than other kinds of performance measurement. This makes measuring results highly acceptable to employees and managers alike. Results-oriented performance measurement is also relatively easy to link to the organization's goals. However, measuring results has problems with validity, because results may be affected by circumstances beyond each employee's performance. Also, if the organization measures only final results, it may fail to measure significant aspects of performance that are not directly related to those results. If individuals focus only on aspects of performance that are measured, they may neglect significant skills or behaviours. For example, if the organization measures only productivity, employees may not be concerned enough with customer service. The outcome may be high efficiency (costs are low) but low effectiveness (sales are low, too).[21] Finally, focusing strictly on results does not provide guidance on how to improve. If baseball players are in a hitting slump, simply telling them that their batting average is .190 may not improve their hitting. The coach would help more by providing feedback about how or what to change (for instance, taking one's eye off the ball or dropping one's shoulder).[22]

balanced scorecard
An organizational approach to performance management that integrates strategic perspectives including financial, customer, internal processes, and learning and growth.

The **balanced scorecard** is an organizational approach to performance management that integrates strategic perspectives including financial, customer, internal processes, and learning and growth. Robert Kaplan and David Norton developed this widely adopted approach. The basic idea is that managers are encouraged to go beyond meeting just traditional financial targets and recognize the importance of other goals such as customer and employee satisfaction.[23] A chapter-ending case examines implementation of the balanced scorecard in a financial services company.

LO5

Sources of Performance Information

All the methods of performance measurement require decisions about who will collect and analyze the performance information. To qualify for this task, a person should have an understanding of the job requirements and the opportunity to see the employee doing the job. The traditional approach is for managers to gather information about their employees' performance and arrive at performance ratings. However, many sources are possible. As illustrated in Figure 7.7, possibilities of information sources include managers, peers, direct reports, self, and customers.

Using just one person as a source of information poses certain problems. People tend to like some people more than others, and those feelings can bias how an employee's efforts are perceived. Also, one person is likely to see an employee in a limited number of situations. A supervisor, for example, cannot see how an employee behaves when the supervisor is not there—for example, when a service technician is at the customer's facility. To get as complete an assessment as possible, some organizations combine information from most or all of the possible sources, in what is called a multi-rater or **360-degree feedback.** The "E-HRM" box describes how online 360-degree feedback has improved performance management at Sandy Hill Community Health Centre in Ottawa.

The John Molson School of Business at Montreal's Concordia University conducted a recent study to learn about the experiences of 101 large Canadian organizations with 360-degree feedback programs. The study found that 43 percent of the organizations surveyed used 360-degree feedback. Companies are using 360-degree feedback because of advantages including increased measurement accuracy and perceived fairness. Respondents also identified challenges such as resistance from individuals because of concerns about the process being time-, cost-, and energy-consuming, trust issues including anonymity of feedback, and the need to ensure a clear purpose and link to organizational strategy are in place before implementing 360-degree feedback.[24]

360-degree feedback
Performance measurement that combines information from the employee's managers, peers, direct reports, self, and customers.

Managers

The most-used source of performance information is the employee's manager. It is usually safe for organizations to assume that supervisors have extensive knowledge of the job requirements and that they have enough opportunity to observe their employees. In other words, managers possess the basic qualifications for this responsibility. Another advantage of using managers to evaluate performance is that they have an incentive to provide accurate and helpful feedback, because their own success depends so much on their employees' performance.[25] Finally, when managers try to observe employee behaviour or discuss performance issues in the feedback session, their feedback can improve performance, and employees tend to perceive the appraisal as accurate.[26]

Still, in some situations, problems can occur with using supervisors as the source of performance information. For employees in some jobs, the supervisor does not have enough opportunity to observe the employee performing job duties. A sales manager

FIGURE 7.7

Sources of Performance Information

E-HRM

Paperless Performance Appraisal

Sandy Hill Community Health Centre (SHCHC) in downtown Ottawa decided its approach to performance appraisals was "time consuming, labour intensive, and lethal to forests everywhere." Although the 360-degree approach was valued by both management and staff, managers were overwhelmed with the administrative burden.

Initially, a performance appraisal reference group was assembled with leadership from the centre's HR officer. This group created a new competency-based performance evaluation tool, however the paper format still created confidentiality concerns when distributed through internal mail. In addition, the appraisal process created a large volume of paper that was described as a "literal stumbling block."

Matthew Garrison, the HR director at SHCHC researched and sampled approximately two dozen different Web-based performance appraisal tools in the effort to find an online tool that would meet SHCHC's needs. He ultimately found a UK-based application called Quask that allowed their organization to design a form that could be completed online using a secure website. The software also provided SHCHC the flexibility it required to choose not only the content of the performance appraisal but also customize the rating scale that would be used to assess employees.

The new software application compiles performance assessments for each employee and provides the employee's manager with a summary of results for each question. The reporting format is flexible enough to allow results to be easily imported into a database, spreadsheet, or HTML application. A pilot of the new online performance evaluation tool was completed and additional enhancements such as drop-down menus were added to make the tool more user-friendly. With approval from SHCHC's management team, the technology was incorporated into their intranet and the system became fully functional.

According to Matthew Garrison, "The ability to conduct performance reviews online provides us with information that we would not have been able to gather through traditional paper means." Garrison also hopes to take the next step to add the performance appraisal data to their Human Resources Information System (HRIS). The executive director of the SHCHC, David Gibson, also describes the ability of the new performance appraisal system to assess not only people but also to assess the effectiveness and efficiency of the centre's programs and processes. The goal is to measure "progress in meeting strategic goals and objectives, gather and analyze performance data, and then use this data to drive improvements in our organization and successfully translate strategy into action."

By implementing the new online performance evaluation software, the SHCHC has already met several key objectives including improving the efficiency of the performance process, saving management and staff time, and maintaining a 360-degree approach.

SOURCE: Dave Silverstone, "Paperless Performance Reviews," *HR Professional*, February 2005, www.hrpao.org/HRPAO/Knowledge Centre/HRProfessional/newscluster/ Paperless+Performance+Reviews.htm. Retrieved: February 19, 2005.

with many outside salespeople cannot be with the salespeople on many visits to customers. Even if the sales manager does make a point of travelling with salespeople for a few days, they are likely to be on their best behaviour while the manager is there. The manager cannot observe how they perform at other times.

Peers

Another source of performance information is the employee's peers or coworkers. Peers are an excellent source of information about performance in a job where the supervisor does not often observe the employee. Examples include law enforcement and sales. For these and other jobs, peers may have the most opportunity to observe the employee in day-to-day activities. Peers have expert knowledge of job requirements. They also bring a different perspective to the evaluation and can provide extremely valid assessments of performance.[27]

Peer evaluations obviously have some potential disadvantages. Friendships (or rivalries) have the potential to bias ratings. Research, however, has provided little evidence that this is a problem.[28] Another disadvantage is that when the evaluations are done to support administrative decisions, peers are uncomfortable with rating employees for decisions that may affect themselves. Generally, peers are more willing to participate in reviews to be used for employee development.[29]

Direct Reports

For evaluating the performance of managers, direct reports are an especially valuable source of information. Direct reports—the people reporting to the manager—often have the best chance to see how well a manager treats employees.

Direct report evaluations have some potential problems because of the power relationships involved. Direct reports are reluctant to say negative things about the person to whom they report; they prefer to provide feedback anonymously. Managers, however, have a more positive reaction to this type of feedback when the employees are identified. When feedback forms require that the direct reports identify themselves, they tend to give the manager higher ratings.[30] Another problem is that when managers receive ratings from direct reports, the employees have more power, so managers tend to emphasize employee satisfaction, even at the expense of productivity. This issue arises primarily when the evaluations are used for administrative decisions. Therefore, as with peer evaluations, direct report evaluations are most appropriate for developmental purposes. To protect employees, the process should be anonymous and use at least three employees to rate each manager.

Self

No one has a greater chance to observe the employee's behaviour on the job than does the employee himself or herself. Self-ratings are rarely used alone, but they can contribute valuable information. A common approach is to have employees evaluate their own performance before the feedback session. This activity gets employees thinking about their performance. Areas of disagreement between the self-appraisal and other evaluations can be fruitful topics for the feedback session. Employee self-assessment offers a way to balance power in a process that tends to be manager-dominated. Areas of disagreement between the self-rating and the manager's rating should be used to create dialogue and reach mutual agreement during the feedback session.[31]

The obvious problem with self-ratings is that individuals have a tendency to inflate assessments of their performance. Especially if the ratings will be used for administrative decisions, exaggerating one's contributions has practical benefits. Also, social psychologists have found that, in general, people tend to blame outside circumstances for their failures while taking a large part of the credit for their successes.

Supervisors can soften this tendency by providing frequent feedback, but because people tend to perceive situations this way, self-appraisals are not appropriate as the basis for administrative decisions.[32]

Customers

Service industries continue to account for significant job growth. Services are often produced and consumed on the spot—so, the customer is often the only person who directly observes the service performance, and therefore, the customer may be the best source of performance information.

Many companies in service industries have introduced customer evaluations of employee performance. Marriott Corporation provides a customer satisfaction card in every room and mails surveys to a random sample of its hotel customers. Whirlpool's Consumer Services Division conducts both mail and telephone surveys of customers after factory technicians have serviced their appliances. These surveys allow the company to evaluate an individual technician's customer-service behaviours while in the customer's home. Many organizations also use mystery-shopper services. Tell Us About Us, a Winnipeg-based company, was recently contracted for a seven-figure, multi-year deal to provide customer evaluations at 5,500 Dunkin Donuts, Baskin-Robbins, and Togo's in Canada and the U.S.[33]

Using customer evaluations of employee performance is appropriate in two situations.[34] The first is when an employee's job requires direct service to the customer or linking the customer to other services within the organization. Second, customer evaluations are appropriate when the organization is interested in gathering information to determine what products and services the customer wants. That is, customer evaluations contribute to the organization's goals by enabling HRM to support the organization's marketing activities. In this regard, customer evaluations are useful both for evaluating an employee's performance and for helping to determine whether the organization can improve customer service by making changes in HRM activities such as training or compensation.

The weakness of using customer feedback for performance measurement is the expense. Many organizations therefore limit the information gathering to short periods once a year.

LO6

Errors in Performance Measurement

As we noted in the previous section, one reason for gathering information from several sources is that performance measurements are not completely objective, and errors can occur. People observe behaviour, and they have no practical way of knowing all the circumstances, intentions, and outcomes related to that behaviour, so they interpret what they see. In doing so, observers make a number of judgment calls, and in some situations may even distort information on purpose. Therefore, fairness in rating performance and interpreting performance appraisals requires that managers understand the kinds of distortions that commonly occur.

Types of Rating Errors

Several kinds of errors and biases commonly influence performance measurements. Usually people make these errors unintentionally, especially when the criteria for measuring performance are not very specific.

Similar to Me

A common human tendency is to give a higher evaluation to people we consider similar to ourselves. Most of us tend to think of ourselves as effective. If others seem to be like us in some way—physical characteristics, family or economic background, attitudes, or beliefs—we expect them to be effective as well. Research has demonstrated that this effect, called the **similar-to-me error,** is strong. One unfortunate result (besides inaccuracy) is that when similarity is based on characteristics such as race or sex, the decisions may be discriminatory.[35]

Errors in Distribution

Raters often tend to use only one part of a rating scale—the low scores, the high scores, or the middle of the range. Sometimes a group of employees really do perform equally well (or poorly). In many cases, however, similar ratings for all members of a group are not an accurate description of performance, but an error in distribution. When a rater inaccurately assigns high ratings to all employees, this error is called **leniency.** When a rater incorrectly gives low ratings to all employees, holding them to unreasonably high standards, the resulting error is called **strictness.** Rating all employees as somehow "average" or in the middle of the scale is called the **central tendency.**

These errors pose two problems. First, they make it difficult to distinguish among employees rated by the same person. Decisions about promotions, job assignments, and so on are more difficult if employees all seem to be performing at the same level. Second, these errors create problems in comparing the performance of individuals rated by different raters. If one rater is lenient and the other is strict, employees of the strict rater will receive significantly fewer rewards than employees of the lenient rater. The rewards are not tied to actual performance but are to some degree erroneous.

Halo and Horns

Another common problem is that raters often fail to distinguish among different aspects of performance. Consider a research lab that hires chemists. A chemist who expresses herself very well may appear to have greater knowledge of chemistry than a chemist with poor communication skills. In this example, a rater could easily fail to distinguish between communication skills and scientific skills.

This type of error can make a person look better, or worse, overall. When the rater reacts to one positive performance aspect by rating the employee positively in all areas of performance, the bias is called the **halo error.** As in the example of the chemist who communicates well, giving the impression of overall intelligence. In contrast, when the rater responds to one negative aspect by rating an employee low in other aspects, the bias is called the **horns error.** Suppose an employee sometimes arrives to work late. The rater takes this as a sign of lack of motivation, lack of ambition, and inability to follow through with responsibility—an example of the horns error.

When raters make halo and horns errors, the performance measurements cannot provide the specific information needed for useful feedback. Halo error signals that no aspects of an employee's performance need improvement, possibly missing opportunities for employee development. Horns error tells the employee that the rater has a low opinion of the employee. The employee is likely to feel defensive and frustrated, rather than motivated to improve.

similar-to-me error
Rating error of giving a higher evaluation to people who seem similar to oneself.

leniency error
Rating error of assigning inaccurately high ratings to all employees.

strictness error
Rating error of giving low ratings to all employees, holding them to unreasonably high standards.

central tendency
Incorrectly rating all employees at or near the middle of a rating scale.

halo error
Rating error that occurs when the rater reacts to one positive performance aspect by rating the employee positively in all areas of performance.

horns error
Rating error that occurs when the rater responds to one negative aspect by rating an employee low in other aspects.

Ways to Reduce Errors

Training can reduce rating errors.[36] Raters can be trained how to avoid rating errors.[37] Prospective raters watch video segments with story-lines designed to lead them to make specific rating errors. After rating the fictional employees in the video segments, raters discuss their rating decisions and how such errors affected their rating decisions. Training programs offer tips for avoiding the errors in the future.

Another training method for raters focuses not on errors in rating, but on the complex nature of employee performance.[38] Raters learn to look at many aspects of performance that deserve their attention. Actual examples of performance are studied to bring out various performance dimensions and the standards for those dimensions. The objective of this training is to help raters evaluate employees' performance more thoroughly and accurately.

Political Behaviour in Performance Appraisals

Unintentional errors are not the only cause of inaccurate performance measurement. Sometimes the people rating performance distort an evaluation on purpose, to advance their personal goals. This kind of appraisal politics is unhealthy especially because the resulting feedback does not focus on helping employees contribute to the organization's goals. High-performing employees who are rated unfairly will become frustrated, and low-performing employees who are overrated will be rewarded rather than encouraged to improve. Therefore, organizations try to identify and discourage appraisal politics.

Several characteristics of appraisal systems and company culture tend to encourage appraisal politics. Appraisal politics are most likely to occur when raters are accountable to the employee being rated, the goals of rating are not compatible with one another, performance appraisal is directly linked to highly desirable rewards, top executives tolerate or ignore distorted ratings, and senior employees tell newcomers company "folklore" that includes stories about distorted ratings.

Political behaviour occurs in every organization. Organizations can minimize appraisal politics by establishing an appraisal system that is fair. Some ways to promote fairness are to involve managers and employees in developing the system, use consistent standards for evaluating different employees, require that feedback be timely and complete, allow employees to challenge their evaluation, and communicate expectations about performance standards, evaluations, and rewards.[39] The organization can also help managers give accurate and fair appraisals by training them to use the appraisal process, encouraging them to recognize accomplishments that the employees themselves have not identified, and fostering a climate of openness in which employees feel they can be honest about their weaknesses.[40]

LO7

Giving Performance Feedback

Once the manager and others have measured an employee's performance, this information must be given to the employee. Only after the employee has received feedback can he or she begin to plan how to improve performance. Although the feedback stage of performance management is essential, it may be uncomfortable to managers and employees. Delivering feedback feels to the manager as if he or she is standing in judgment of others—a role few people enjoy. Receiving criticism feels even worse. Fortunately, managers can do much to smooth the feedback process and make it effective.

Scheduling Performance Feedback

Performance feedback should be a regular, expected management activity. The practice or policy at many organizations is to give formal performance feedback once a year. But annual feedback is not enough. One reason is that managers are responsible for dealing with performance gaps as soon as they occur. If the manager notices a problem with an employee's behaviour in June, but the annual appraisal is scheduled for November, the employee will miss months of opportunities for improvement.

Another reason for frequent performance feedback is that feedback is most effective when the information does not surprise the employee. If an employee has to wait for up to a year to learn what the manager thinks of his work, the employee will wonder whether he is meeting expectations. Employees should instead receive feedback so often that they know what the manager will say during their annual performance review.

Preparing for a Feedback Session

Managers should be well prepared for each formal feedback session. The manager should create the right context for the meeting. The location should be neutral. If the manager's office is the site of unpleasant conversations, a conference room may be more appropriate. In announcing the meeting to an employee, the manager should describe it as a chance to discuss the role of the employee, the role of the manager, and relationship between them. Managers should also say (and believe) that they would like the meeting to be an open dialogue.

Managers should also enable the employee to be well prepared. The manager should ask the employee to complete a self-assessment ahead of time. The self-assessment requires employees to think about their performance over the past rating period and to be aware of their strengths and weaknesses, so they can participate more fully in the

When giving performance feedback, do it in an appropriate meeting place. Meet in a setting that is neutral and free of distractions. What other factors are important for a feedback session?

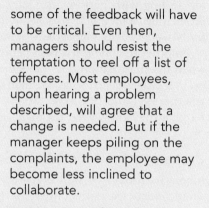

Delivering Performance Feedback

Effective performance feedback communicates information that encourages and enhances performance. Here are some guidelines for communicating feedback to achieve those purposes:

Make feedback a common practice. Feedback should be timely so the employees understand what behaviours and performance outcomes it relates to. This means feedback should not be limited to formal appraisals. To be effective, feedback should be daily and weekly.

Reinforce effective performance. People often think of performance feedback as criticism and problem solving. But the purpose of the session is to give accurate feedback. Accuracy requires recognizing good performance as well as poor performance. By reinforcing good performance, the manager encourages the employee to continue that behaviour. Talking about the good as well as the areas for improvement also makes the feedback credible.

Focus on problem solving, not punishing. When there are performance issues, the feedback should be designed to launch a problem-solving discussion, not to make the employee feel bad. Using feedback as a punishment just causes employees to become defensive and ignores the cause of the problem. The manager should therefore work with the employee to identify the cause of the problem and reach an agreement on how to solve it.

Talk about behaviour and results, not about personalities. Especially when feedback involves the need for performance improvement, it is essential for the manager's words to distinguish between the person and his or her behaviours. Saying "You're not motivated" or "You're lazy" tends to make the employee defensive and angry. These assumptions about the employee's attitudes and feelings may or may not be true. Better: "You did not meet the deadline that you agreed to."

Keep criticism to a minimum. In the case of an individual who performs below expectations, some of the feedback will have to be critical. Even then, managers should resist the temptation to reel off a list of offences. Most employees, upon hearing a problem described, will agree that a change is needed. But if the manager keeps piling on the complaints, the employee may become less inclined to collaborate.

Agree to specific goals and a follow-up meeting. Goal setting is essential. It is one of the most effective ways to create a motivational environment for employees. Focus on behaviours, knowledge, and skills that are within the employee's control. Discussions about needed improvements should end with an agreement on what the employee will do differently and by what date. Then the manager and employee should agree on a date to review the employee's progress toward this goal. Setting a date gives the employee added incentive to work on achieving the goal.

SOURCE: M. London, *Job Feedback: Giving, Seeking, and Using Feedback for Performance Improvement* (Mahwah, NJ: Lawrence Erlbaum Associates, 1997).

discussion. Even though employees may tend to overstate their accomplishments, the self-assessment can help the manager and employee identify areas for discussion. When the purpose of the assessment is to define areas for development, employees may actually understate their performance. Also, differences between the manager's and the employee's rating may be fruitful areas for discussion.

Conducting the Feedback Session

During the feedback session, managers can take any of three approaches. In the "tell-and-sell" approach, managers tell the employees their ratings and then justify those ratings. In the "tell-and-listen" approach, managers tell employees their ratings and then let the employees explain their side of the story. In the "problem-solving" approach, managers and employees work together to solve performance problems in an atmosphere of respect and encouragement. Not surprisingly, research demonstrates that the problem-solving approach is superior. Perhaps surprisingly, most managers rely on the tell-and-sell approach.[41] Managers can improve employee satisfaction with the feedback process and improve performance by creating two-way communication, by letting employees voice their opinions and discuss performance goals.[42] The "HR How To" box provides some additional suggestions for conducting an effective feedback session.

Performance Improvement

LO8

When performance evaluation indicates that an employee's performance is below expectations, the feedback process should launch an effort to address the performance gap. Even when the employee is meeting current standards, the feedback session may identify areas in which the employee can improve in order to contribute more to the

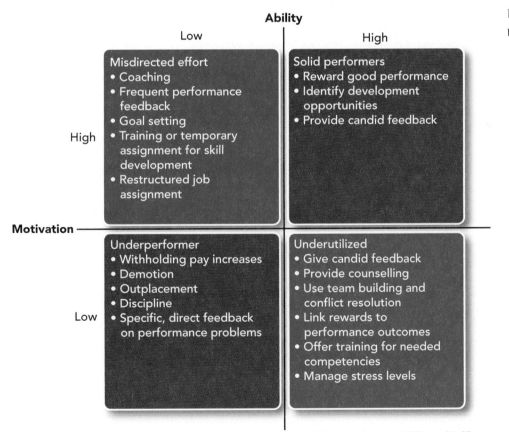

FIGURE 7.8

Improving Performance

SOURCE: Based on M. London, Job Feedback (Mahwah, N.J.: Lawrence Erlbaum Associates, 1997), pp. 96, 97. Used by permission.

organization in a current or future job. In sum, the final feedback stage of performance management involves identifying areas for improvement and ways to improve performance in those areas.

As shown in Figure 7.8, the most effective way to improve performance varies according to the employee's ability and motivation. In general, when employees have high levels of ability and motivation, they perform at or above expectations. But when they lack ability, motivation, or both, corrective action is needed. The type of action called for depends on what the employee lacks.

To determine an employee's ability level, the manager should consider whether the employee has the competencies needed to perform the job effectively. Sometimes lack of ability is an issue when an employee is new or the job has changed. When a motivated employee lacks knowledge, skills, or abilities in some area, there are a number of ways to help the employee improve. The manager may offer coaching, training, and more detailed feedback. Sometimes it is appropriate to restructure the job so that its demands no longer exceed the employee's abilities.

To determine an employee's level of motivation, managers need to consider whether the employee is holding a job he or she wants. A belief that pay and other rewards are too small can also hurt motivation. Sometimes personal problems are such a distraction that they interfere with motivation. Managers with an unmotivated employee can explore ways to demonstrate that the employee is being treated fairly and rewarded adequately. The solution may be as simple as delivering more positive feedback (praise). Employees may also benefit from a referral for counselling or help with stress management.

Employees whose performance is below expectations because they have neither the motivation nor the ability to perform the job may not be a good fit for the position. Performance may improve if the manager directs their attention to the significance of the problem by withholding rewards or by providing specific feedback. If employees do not respond by improving their performance, the organization may have to discipline or terminate these underperformers.

As a rule, employees who combine high ability with high motivation are solid performers. As Figure 7.8 indicates, managers should by no means ignore these employees on the grounds of leaving well enough alone. Rather, such employees are likely to appreciate opportunities for further development. Rewards and direct feedback help to maintain these employees' high motivation levels.

LO9

Legal and Ethical Issues in Performance Management

In developing and using performance management systems, human resource professionals need to ensure that these systems meet legal requirements, such as the avoidance of discrimination related to any of the prohibited grounds and protecting employees' privacy.

Legal Requirements for Performance Management

Because performance measures play a central role in decisions about pay, promotions, and discipline, employment-related legal challenges may be directed at an organization's performance management system. Legal challenges related to performance management usually involve charges of illegal discrimination or unjust dismissal.

Claims often allege that the performance management system discriminated against employees on the basis of one of the protected grounds identified in human rights legislation such as age or sex. Many performance measures are subjective, and measurement errors, such as those described earlier in the chapter, can easily occur.

With regard to lawsuits filed on the grounds of unjust dismissal, the usual claim is that the person was dismissed for reasons besides the ones that the employer states. Health Canada recently fired three veterinary scientists who have attracted international attention for their public criticism of Canada's drug approval process and the use of drugs such as growth hormones in cattle. The scientists disclosed they were terminated for "insubordination," however, the scientists' union, the Professional Institute of Public Servants, is likely to argue that the firings were a way to punish the employees for blowing the whistle.[43] In this type of situation, courts generally focus on the employer's performance management system, looking to see whether the dismissal could have been based on poor performance. To defend itself, the employer would need a performance management system that provides evidence to support its employment decisions.

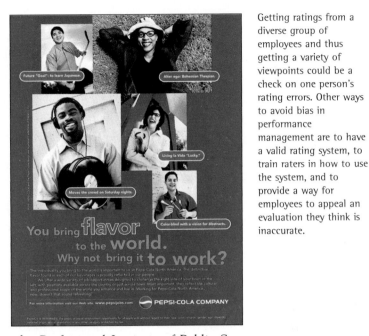

Getting ratings from a diverse group of employees and thus getting a variety of viewpoints could be a check on one person's rating errors. Other ways to avoid bias in performance management are to have a valid rating system, to train raters in how to use the system, and to provide a way for employees to appeal an evaluation they think is inaccurate.

FIGURE 7.9

How Employees are Monitored in the Workplace

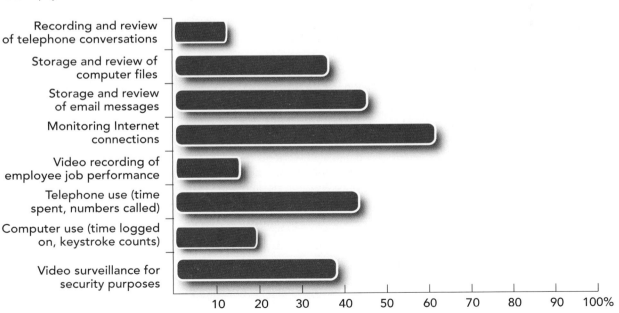

SOURCE: : "Employee Monitoring Practices—A 2002 Survey of More than 1,600 Large American Employers by the American Management Association Reveals How Employees are being Monitored in the Workplace," *Canadian HR Reporter*, March 8, 2004, p. 2.

To protect against both kinds of legal challenges, it is important to have a performance management system based on valid job analyses, as described in Chapter 3, with the requirements for job success clearly communicated to employees. Performance measurement should evaluate behaviours or results, based on objective criteria. The organization should use multiple raters (including self-appraisals) and train raters in how to use the system. The organization should provide for a review of all performance ratings by upper-level managers and set up a system for employees to appeal when they believe they were evaluated unfairly. Along with feedback, the system should include a process for coaching or training employees to help them improve, rather than simply dismissing poor performers.

Employee Monitoring and Employee Privacy

Computer technology and other types of employee monitoring now support many performance management systems. Organizations often store records of employees' performance ratings, disciplinary actions, and work-rule violations in electronic databases. Many companies use personal computers to monitor productivity and other performance measures electronically.[44] As shown in Figure 7.9, organizations are using a variety of methods to monitor employees. According to a recent survey, 77.7 percent of employers used some form of employee monitoring.[45] For example, at a General Electric customer service centre, agents answer over 14,000 telephone inquiries per day. The agents' calls are recorded and reviewed to help the agents improve customer service.

Organizations need to consider how employees react to this type of performance measurement. Monitoring provides detailed, accurate information, but employees may find it demoralizing, degrading, and stressful. They are more likely to accept employee monitoring if the organization explains its purpose and links it to help in improving performance. As discussed in Chapter 2, the federal Personal Information Protection and Electronic Documents Act (PIPEDA) has implications for performance management. For example, organizations are required to ensure that personal information including an employee's performance review is securely protected, retained only for a specified time, and accessible to the employee.

Summary

1. Identify the activities involved in performance management.

Performance management is the process through which managers ensure that employees' activities and outputs contribute to the organization's goals. The organization begins by specifying which aspects of performance are relevant to the organization. Next, the organization measures the relevant aspects of performance through performance appraisal. Finally, in performance feedback sessions, managers provide employees with information about their performance so they can modify their behaviour to meet the organization's goals. Feedback includes efforts to identify and solve problems.

2. Discuss the purposes of performance management systems.

Organizations establish performance management systems to meet three broad purposes. Effective performance management helps the organization with strategic purposes, that is, meeting business objectives. It does this by helping to link employees' behaviour with the organization's goals. The administrative purpose of performance management is to provide information for day-to-day decisions about salary, benefits, recognition, and retention or termination. The developmental purpose of performance management is using the system as a basis for developing employees' competencies.

3. Define five criteria for measuring the effectiveness of a performance management system.

   Performance measures should fit with the organization's strategy by supporting its goals and culture. Performance measures should be valid, so they measure all the relevant aspects of performance and do not measure irrelevant aspects of performance. These measures should also provide interrater and test-retest reliability, so that appraisals are consistent among raters and over time. Performance measurement systems should be acceptable to the people who use them or receive feedback from them. Finally, a performance measure should specifically tell employees what is expected of them and how they can meet those expectations.

4. Compare the major methods for measuring performance.

   Performance measurement may use ranking systems such as simple ranking, forced distribution, or paired comparisons to compare one individual's performance with that of other employees. These methods may be time-consuming, and they will be seen as unfair if actual performance is not distributed in the same way as the ranking system requires. However, ranking counteracts some forms of rater bias and helps distinguish employees for administrative decisions. Other approaches involve rating employees' attributes, behaviours, or outcomes. Rating competencies is relatively simple but not always valid, unless behaviours are specifically defined. Rating behaviours requires a great deal of information, but these methods can be very effective. They can link behaviours to goals, and ratings by trained raters may be highly reliable. Rating results, such as productivity or achievement of objectives, tends to be less subjective than other kinds of rating, making this approach highly acceptable. Validity may be a problem because of factors outside the employee's control. This method also tends not to provide much basis for determining how to improve. Use of a balanced scorecard is a widely used strategic approach.

5. Describe major sources of performance information in terms of their advantages and disadvantages.

   Performance information may come from an employee's self-appraisal and from appraisals by the employee's manager, employees, peers, and customers. Using only one source makes the appraisal more subjective. Organizations may combine many sources into a 360-degree performance appraisal. Gathering information from each employee's supervisor may produce accurate information, unless the supervisor has little opportunity to observe the employee. Peers are an excellent source of information about performance in a job where the supervisor does not often observe the employee. Disadvantages are that friendships (or rival-ries) may bias ratings and peers may be uncomfortable with the role of rating a friend. Direct reports often have the best chance to see how a manager treats employees. Employees may be reluctant to contribute candid opinions about a supervisor unless they can provide information anonymously. Self-appraisals may be biased, but they do come from the person with the most knowledge of the employee's behaviour on the job, and they provide a basis for discussion in feedback sessions, opening up fruitful comparisons and areas of disagreement between the self-appraisal and other appraisals. Customers may be an excellent source of performance information, although obtaining customer feedback tends to be expensive.

6. Define types of rating errors and explain how to minimize them.

   People observe behaviour often without a practical way of knowing all the relevant circumstances and outcomes, so they necessarily interpret what they see. A common tendency is to give higher evaluations to people we consider similar to ourselves. Other errors involve using only part of the rating scale: Giving all employees ratings at the high end of the scale is called leniency error. Rating everyone at the low end of the scale is called strictness error. Rating all employees at or near the middle is called central tendency. The halo error refers to rating employees positively in all areas because of strong performance observed in one area. The horns error is rating employees negatively in all areas because of weak performance observed in one area. Ways to reduce rater error are training raters to be aware of their tendencies to make rating errors and training them to be sensitive to the complex nature of employee performance so they will consider many aspects of performance in greater depth. Politics also may influence ratings. Organizations can minimize appraisal politics by establishing a fair appraisal system, involving managers and employees in developing the system, allowing employees to challenge evaluations, communicating expectations, and fostering a climate of open discussion.

7. Explain how to provide performance feedback effectively.

   Performance feedback should be a regular, scheduled management activity, so that employees can correct problems as soon as they occur. Managers should prepare by establishing a neutral location, emphasizing that the feedback session will be a chance for discussion and asking the employee to prepare a self-assessment. During the feedback session, managers should strive for a problem-solving approach and encourage employees to voice their opinions and discuss performance goals. The manager should look for opportunities to reinforce desired behaviour and should limit criticism. The discussion should focus on behaviour and results rather than on personalities.

8. Summarize ways to achieve performance improvement. For an employee who is motivated but lacks ability, the manager should provide coaching and training, give detailed feedback about performance, and consider restructuring the job. For an employee who has ability but lacks motivation, the manager should investigate whether outside problems are a distraction and if so, refer the employee for help. If the problem has to do with the employee not feeling appreciated or rewarded, the manager should try to meet the employee's needs and evaluate whether additional pay and other rewards are appropriate. For an employee lacking both ability and motivation, the manager should consider whether the employee is a good fit for the position. Specific feedback or withholding rewards may spur improvement, or the employee may have to be demoted or terminated. Solid employees who are high in ability and motivation will continue so and may be able to contribute even more if the manager provides appropriate direct feedback, rewards, and opportunities for development.

9. Discuss legal and ethical issues that affect performance management.
Lawsuits related to performance management usually involve charges of discrimination or unjust dismissal. Managers must make sure that performance management systems and decisions treat employees equally, without regard to their age, sex, or other protected grounds. Organizations can do this by establishing and using valid performance measures and by training raters to evaluate performance accurately. A system is more likely to be legally defensible if it is based on behaviours and results, and if multiple raters evaluate each person's performance. The system should include a process for coaching or training employees to help them improve, rather than simply dismissing poor performers. An ethical issue of performance management is the use of employee monitoring. This type of performance measurement provides detailed, accurate information, but employees may find it demoralizing, degrading, and stressful. They are more likely to accept it if the organization explains its purpose, and links it to help in improving performance.

Review and Discussion Questions

1. How does a complete performance management system differ from the use of annual performance appraisals?
2. Give two examples of an administrative decision that would be based on performance management information. Give two examples of developmental decisions based on this type of information.
3. How can involving employees in the creation of performance standards improve the effectiveness of a performance management system? (Consider the criteria for effectiveness shown in Figure 7.2.)
4. Consider how you might rate the performance of three instructors from whom you are currently taking a course. (If you are currently taking only one or two courses, consider this course and two you recently completed.)
   a. Would it be harder to *rate* the instructors' performance or to *rank* their performance? Why?
   b. Write three items to use in rating the instructors—one each to rate them in terms of an attribute, a behaviour, and an outcome.
   c. Which measure in (b) do you think is most valid? Most reliable? Why?
   d. Many educational institutions use questionnaires to gather data from students about their instructors' performance. Would it be appropriate to use the data for administrative decisions? Developmental decisions? Other decisions? Why or why not?
5. Imagine that a pet supply store is establishing a new performance management system to help employees provide better customer service. Management needs to decide who should participate in measuring the performance of each of the store's salespeople. From what sources should the store gather information? Why?
6. Would the same sources be appropriate if the store in question 5 will use the performance appraisals to support decisions about which employees to promote? Explain.
7. Suppose you were recently promoted to a supervisory job in a company where you have worked for two years. You genuinely like almost all your coworkers, who now report to you. The only exception is one employee, who dresses more formally than the others and frequently tells jokes that embarrass you and the other workers. Given your preexisting feelings for the employees, how can you measure their performance fairly and effectively?
8. Continuing the example in question 7, imagine that you are preparing for your first performance feedback

session. You want the feedback to be effective—that is, you want the feedback to result in improved performance. List five or six steps you can take to achieve your goal.

9. Besides giving employees feedback, what steps can a manager take to improve employees' performance?

10. Suppose you are a human resource professional helping to improve the performance management system of a company that sells and services office equipment. The company operates a call centre that takes calls from customers who are having problems with their equipment. Call centre employees are supposed to verify that the problem is not one the customer can easily handle (for example, equipment that will not operate because it has come unplugged). Then, if the problem is not resolved over the phone, the employ-

ees arrange for service technicians to visit the customer. The company can charge the customer only if a service technician visits, so performance management of the call centre employees focuses on productivity—how quickly they can complete a call and move on to the next caller. To measure this performance efficiently and accurately, the company uses employee monitoring.

a. How would you expect the employees to react to the monitoring? How might the organization address the employees' concerns?

b. Besides productivity in terms of number of calls, what other performance measures should the performance management system include?

c. How should the organization gather information about the other performance measures?

What's Your HR IQ?   www.mcgrawhill.ca/college/noe

The Online Learning Centre offers more ways to check what you've learned so far. Find experiential exercises as well as Test Your Knowledge Quizzes, Videos, and many other resources at www.mcgrawhill.ca/college/noe.

Case: The Trials and Tribulations of Performance Appraisal at Ford

Many companies, including Ford Motor Company, General Electric, Microsoft, and Hewlett-Packard, use a method of performance measurement called a forced-ranking system. With this method, employees are ranked as above, at, or below average, and the system requires that a certain percentage of employees fall into each category. For example, at General Electric, managers must place 20 percent of employees in the top category, 70 percent in the middle, and 10 percent in the bottom category. Typically, the bottom 10 percent receive no bonuses and may be terminated. At some companies using forced ranking, morale is poor, and some employees have filed lawsuits.

In spite of these drawbacks, Ford began using a forced-ranking system in the belief that it would help the company build a younger, more diverse management team able to succeed with new technology and rapid change. Forced rankings would serve as a way to change corporate culture by removing poor performers. (This was not Ford's first effort to remove poor performers. In the late 1990s, Ford offered a package of benefits to salaried employees who resigned or retired early. Managers were directed to tell candidates for this program that management believed they should resign or retire.)

Ford called its forced-ranking system the Performance Management Process. The process involved grading Ford's

1,800 middle managers with an A, B, or C, with 10 percent of managers receiving a C. Managers who received a C for one year received no bonus. Two years at the C level meant possible demotion and termination.

After Ford began using its Performance Management Process, a number of employees filed complaints, pressuring the company to change. In two separate legal challenges, 57 employees charged that the performance management system discriminated against older employees. A relatively large proportion of Ford's older workers received Cs.

Ford responded by abandoning the major elements of the Performance Management Process, including the practice of assigning a C to 10 percent of managers. The company modified the system because it had harmed teamwork and morale. Under the modified system, only 5 percent of managers are to receive the lowest grade. In addition, the names of the rankings have changed. In place of A, B, and C grades, the rankings are now called Top Achiever, Achiever, and Improvement Required. Employees ranked as requiring improvement receive counselling to help them improve their performance.

In the time since Ford acknowledged the problems and modified the system, the company's CEO Jacques Nasser resigned, as did the head of human resources. The new CEO, William Clay Ford Jr., inherited the job of resolving the legal challenges.

SOURCE: M. Boyle, "Performance Reviews: Perilous Curves Ahead," *Fortune*, May 28, 2001, pp. 187–88; N. Shirouzu, "Ford Stops Using Letter Rankings to Rate Workers," *The Wall Street Journal*, July 11, 2001, pp. B1, B4; N. Shirouzu, "Nine Ford Workers File Bias Suit Saying Ratings Curb Older Staff," *The Wall Street Journal*, February 15, 2001, p. B14; N. Shirouzu and J. B. White, "Ford Assesses Job Ratings Amid Bias Suit," *The Wall Street Journal*, July 9, 2001, pp. A3, A14; T. D. Schellhardt and S. K. Goo, "At Ford, Buyout Plan Has a Twist," *The Wall Street Journal*, July 22, 1998, pp. B1, B6; N. Shirouzu, "Ford Is in Talks on Settling Bias Lawsuits," *The Wall Street Journal*, November 2, 2001, p. A4.

Questions

1. Why did Ford use a forced-distribution system for measuring performance? What problems did the system cause?
2. Ford modified its forced-distribution system but did not abandon it. What might be some advantages and disadvantages of its decision?
3. What changes or practices do you recommend to improve performance management at Ford?

Case: Implementing the Balanced Scorecard

Arran Ltd. is a U.K. multi-divisional retail financial services company. Arran Ltd. first introduced the balanced scorecard concept in the mid 1990s as a performance management system for its retail division. This approach was picked because Arran Ltd. needed "better sources of management and performance information" and "better ways of rewarding management performance."

The balanced scorecard was primarily used for management control purposes and consisted of standardized operational performance measurements. Many of these performance measurements had been used prior to introducing balanced scorecards. The general manager was supportive and expanded the use of balanced scorecards to each individual within the division. For example, both managers and front-line employees such as cashiers had their performance assessed using the same standardized measures. This provided continuity throughout the whole retail division.

The retail division's approach to balanced scorecards was viewed to be a success and implementation was extended to other divisions within the company. It was felt that the use of the balanced scorecard approach provided a clear, organized approach to present a diverse array of performance measures.

Arran Ltd. relied heavily on performance management software to get relevant and timely information to decision-makers. Information was gathered and performance data was reported and used by managers daily. Although this worked well initially, the system and software proved to be inflexible and difficulties and delays were experienced in changing elements or performance measures. In addition, the main focus of the balanced scorecards shifted primarily to financial measures and as a result did not support other aspects of performance that were strategically relevant to Arran Ltd.'s organizational success.

NOTE: The identity of the organization discussed in this case has been disguised.

SOURCE: Ian Cobbold, Consultant, 2GC Active Management Limited, "Balanced Scorecard Case Study—Arran Ltd." in *Implementing the Balanced Scorecard—Lessons and Insights from a Financial Services Firm*, (Maidenhead, UK: 2GC Limited, 2001), www.2gc.co.uk/pdf/2GC-Arran.pdf. Retrieved: July 22, 2004.

Questions

1. What benefits did the use of balanced scorecards offer Arran Ltd. initially?
2. What performance measures (in addition to financial) would be important to Arran Ltd.?
3. Suggest some ways that Arran Ltd. could enhance their balanced scorecard performance management system.

Chapter **8**

Developing Employees for Future Success

What Do I Need to Know? After reading this chapter, you should be able to:

1. Discuss how development is related to training and careers.

2. Identify the methods organizations use for employee development.

3. Describe how organizations use assessment of personality type, work behaviors, and job performance to plan employee development.

4. Explain how job experiences can be used for developing skills.

5. Summarize principles for setting up successful mentoring programs.

6. Tell how managers and peers develop employees through coaching.

7. Identify the steps in the process of career management.

8. Discuss how organizations are meeting the challenges of the "glass ceiling," succession planning, and dysfunctional managers.

Introduction

The managers at Irving Oil, Ltd. a family-owned company known for its tankers, truck stops, and refinery towers, are telling stories and painting with watercolours as they learn to lead. The St. John-based company has teamed up with the workplace learning provider, Forum Corporation to teach leadership skills to managers.

For many years, managers at Irving Oil have traditionally focused on corporate values that include a business strategy based on a rewarding working environment that

Irving managers, from left, Kevin Scott, Tanya Chapman, Daniel Goodwin, and Greg Bambury: "We wanted to be explicit about our people strategy and talk about it in the same way that we often talk about our marketing strategy and our financial strategy," Mr. Bambury says.

shuns the use of job titles and stresses the importance of relationships with its staff, suppliers, and customers.

Irving Oil began as a single service station in 1924 and has become an icon of Atlantic highways and operates Canada's largest refinery. Top executive, Kenneth Irving and a group of seven executives formed the first group to go through the program and decided the development would be an investment in the company's people.

Greg Bambury, head of human resources says, "Irving Oil has been successful for a long time because of a deliberate strategy of knowing who is going to do what." "We wanted to be explicit about our people strategy and talk about it in the same way that we often talk about our marketing strategy and our financial strategy"

Although it is hard to measure the full impact of this leadership development initiative, Saint John refinery employees have been giving the company a higher rating for leadership in recent surveys. Irving Oil recently received a Human Resources Innovation Award from Atlantic Canada Human Resources Awards (ACHRA) for its Mutual Value Promise (MVP) program that includes a wide range of learning and development opportunities for employees and managers.[1] In addition, Irving was recently named North American refiner of the year by Hart Publications, a major energy sector publisher based in the United States. Irving is the first Canadian company to receive this annual reward, which examines a refiner's environmental performance, ability to produce clean fuel, and investment in facilities and employees.[2]

As we noted in Chapter 1, employees' commitment to their organization depends on how their managers treat them. To "win the war for talent" managers must be able to identify high-potential employees, make sure the organization uses the talents of these people, and reassure them of their value, so that they do not become dissatisfied and leave the organization. Managers also must be able to listen. Although new employees need strong direction, they expect to be able to think independently and be treated with respect. In all these ways, managers provide for **employee development**—the combination of formal education, job experiences, relationships, and assessment of personality and competencies to help employees

employee development
The combination of formal education, job experiences, relationships, and assessment of personality and competencies to help employees prepare for the future of their careers.

prepare for the future of their careers. Human resource management establishes a process for employee development that prepares employees to help the organization meet its goals.

This chapter explores the purpose and activities of employee development. We begin by discussing the relationships among development, training, and career management. Next, we look at development approaches, including formal education, assessment, job experiences, and interpersonal relationships. The chapter emphasizes the types of competencies that are strengthened by each development method, so employees and their managers can choose appropriate methods when planning for development. The third section of the chapter describes the steps of the career management process, emphasizing the responsibilities of employee and employer at each step of the process. The chapter concludes with a discussion of special challenges related to employee development—succession planning, the so-called glass ceiling, and dysfunctional managers.

Training, Development, and Career Management

LO1

Organizations and their employees must constantly expand their competencies to meet customer needs and compete in today's demanding and rapidly changing business environment. More and more companies operate globally, requiring that employees understand different cultures and customs. More companies organize work in terms of projects or customers, rather than specialized functions, so employees need to acquire a broad range of technical and interpersonal skills. Many companies expect employees at all levels to perform roles once reserved for management. Organizations are required to provide development opportunities to employees without regard to prohibited grounds of discrimination discussed in Chapter 2, including characteristics such as sex, race, ethnic origin, and age. In this climate, organizations are placing greater emphasis on training and development. To do this, organizations must understand the relationship of development to training and career management.

Development and Training

The definition of development indicates that it is future oriented. Development implies learning that is not necessarily related to the employee's current job.[3] Instead, it prepares employees for other positions in the organization and increases their ability to move into jobs that may not yet exist.[4] Development also may help employees prepare for changes in their current jobs, such as changes resulting from new technology, work

	TRAINING	DEVELOPMENT
Focus	Current	Future
Use of work experiences	Low	High
Goal	Preparation for current job	Preparation for changes
Participation	Required	Voluntary

TABLE 8.1

Training versus Development

designs, or customers. So development is about preparing for change and achieving one's full potential in the form of new jobs, new responsibilities, or new requirements.

In contrast, training traditionally focuses on helping employees improve performance of their current jobs. Many organizations have focused on linking training programs to business goals. In these organizations, the distinction between training and development is more blurred. Table 8.1 summarizes the traditional differences.

Development for Careers

The concept of a career has changed in recent years. In the traditional view, a career consists of a sequence of positions within an occupation or organization.[5] For example, an academic career might begin with a position as a sessional instructor. It continues with appointment to faculty positions such as assistant professor, then associate professor, and finally full professor. An engineer might start as a staff engineer, then with greater experience earn promotions to the positions of advisory engineer, senior engineer, and vice president of engineering. In these examples, the career resembles a set of stairs from the entry to a profession or organization to the senior levels.

Changes such as downsizing, restructuring, bankruptcy, and growth have become the norm in the modern business environment. As this has happened, the concept of career has become more fluid. The new concept of a career is often referred to as a **protean career**—that is, a career that frequently changes based on changes in the person's interests, abilities, and values and in the work environment. For example, an engineer might decide to take a sabbatical from her position to work in a management role with the United Way for a year. The purpose of this change could be to develop her managerial skills and evaluate whether she likes managerial work more than engineering. As in this example, the concept of a protean career assumes that employees will take major responsibility for managing their careers. This concept is consistent with the modern *psychological contract* we described in Chapter 1. In place of the traditional expectation of job security and advancement within a company, today's employees need to take control over their careers and personal responsibility for managing their careers. They look for organizations that will support them by providing development opportunities and flexible work arrangements so they can pursue their goals.

In this environment, employees need to develop new skills, rather than rely on an unchanging base of knowledge. This need results from employers' efforts to respond to customer demands. The types of knowledge that an employee needs have changed.[6] The traditional career requires "knowing how," or having the appropriate skills and knowledge to provide a particular service or product. Such knowledge and skills remain important, but a protean career also requires that employees "know why" and "know whom." Knowing why means understanding the employer's business and culture in order to apply knowledge and skills in a way that contributes to the business. Knowing whom means developing relationships that contribute to the employer's success—for example, connections with vendors, suppliers, community members, customers, or industry experts. Learning these categories of knowledge requires more than formal courses and training programs. Rather, the employee must build relationships and obtain useful job experiences.

These relationships and experiences often take an employee along a career path that is far different from the traditional steps upward through an organization or profession. Although such careers will not disappear, more employees will follow a spiral career path in which they cross the boundaries between specialties and organizations. As organizations provide for employee development (and as employees take control

protean career
A career that frequently changes based on changes in the person's interests, abilities, and values and in the work environment.

of their own careers), they will need a pair of opportunities. First, employees need to determine their interests, competencies, and areas for development. Second, based on that information, employees seek the development experiences that will likely involve jobs and relationships as well as formal courses. As discussed later in the chapter, organizations can meet these needs through a system for *career management* or *development planning*. Career management helps employees select development activities that prepare them to meet their career goals. It helps employers select development activities in line with its human resource needs.

Employee development includes building relationships with key vendors, suppliers, or community members that contribute to career success.

Approaches to Employee Development

LO2

Ricard Peddie, president and CEO of Toronto-based Maple Leaf Sports and Entertainment (MLSE), views developing employees as a legacy. "They say universities are judged by the quality of their alumni. I think that can also be said about business."[7]

To operate the business side of the Toronto Maple Leafs and the Toronto Raptors, MLSE employs about 350 people. In recent years, leadership development has been a major focus in the company. The MLSE philosophy to leadership development involves cross-functional and stretch assignments, extensive training and development, and succession planning. MLSE's approach to developing leaders has not gone unnoticed. For example, two former employees developed by MLSE are now vice-presidents with the Florida Panthers. Reddie takes pride in hearing, "Boy, that is quite a little factory up in Toronto that creates great sports entertainment leaders."[8]

FIGURE 8.1

The Four Approaches to Employee Development

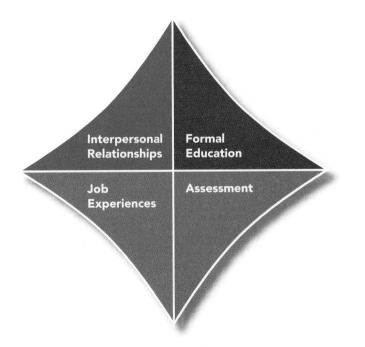

As at MLSE, employee development often focuses on managers, but development is useful for all levels of employees. For example, a restaurant manager could give waiters feedback as part of their performance appraisals. At the same time, the manager could ask the waiters to think of ways to improve their performance and invite them to state goals, such as roles they desire to hold in the future. In this way, the performance management process can support employee development.

The many approaches to employee development fall into four broad categories: formal education, assessment, job experiences, and interpersonal relationships.[9] Figure 8.1 summarizes these four methods. Many organizations combine these approaches.

Formal Education

Organizations may support employee development through a variety of formal educational programs, either at the workplace or off-site. These may include workshops designed specifically for the organization's employees, short courses offered by consultants, colleges or universities, and executive MBA programs (which enrol participants to meet on weekends or evenings to earn a master's degree in business administration). These programs may involve lectures by business experts, business games and simulations, experiential programs, and meetings with customers. Chapter 6 described most of these training methods, including their pros and cons.

Many companies, including SaskTel, IBM, BMO, and KPMG LLP, operate training and development centres that offer in-house training. GE's Management Development Institute teaches courses in manufacturing and sales marketing, and advanced management training.[10] New employees may take the professional development program, with courses emphasizing preparation for a specific career path. Courses in the executive development program emphasize strategic thinking, leadership, integration of the functional specialties, global competition, and customer satisfaction. Tuition is paid by the employee's business unit.

Universities including Queen's, the University of Western Ontario, the University of Alberta, and UBC as well as colleges including Humber, Conestoga, Durham, Seneca, and Grant MacEwan offer management and professional development programs to organizations. A growing number of companies and educational institutions are also using distance learning (discussed in Chapter 6) to reach their audiences. For example, Queen's Executive MBA program is offered in cities across Canada using interactive multi-point video-conferencing.[11] The "E-HRM" box details how IBM is using the Web for its management development program.

Another trend in formal education is for employers and the education provider to create short courses with content designed specifically for the audience. An example of this type of customized learning is Toronto's University Health Network's leadership development program that was developed with the help of the Rotman School of Management.[12] For almost a decade, BMO has offered an MBA program on company time. Participants meet for week-long sessions at the bank's learning centre on the outskirts of Toronto with professors from Dalhousie who fly in to deliver each of the 16 modules that comprise the program.[13]

Education may also supplement formal courses with other types of development activities. Avon Products offers its Passport Program to employees thought to have potential to be general managers.[14] To learn Avon's global strategy, they meet for each session in a different country. The program brings a team of employees together for

E-Learning Helps Build Management Talent at IBM

To compete successfully, companies need to identify employees with managerial talent and help managers become more effective. To attract and retain talented employees, companies must offer training and development opportunities. This can be challenging for a company such as IBM whose employees are geographically dispersed and dealing with many demands. IBM's solution is to apply its e-commerce expertise to its development programs.

IBM's "Basic Blue for Managers" program uses e-learning and face-to-face classroom experiences. The program helps managers understand their responsibilities in managing performance, employee relations, diversity, and multicultural issues. It moves the learning of all basic management skills to the Web, using classroom experiences for more complex management issues. It also gives managers and their bosses greater responsibility for development, while the company provides support in the form of unlimited access to development activities and support networks.

The learning model has four levels:

1. *Management quick views*— These provide practical information on over 40 common management topics related to how to conduct business, leadership and management competencies, productivity, and HRM issues.
2. *Interactive learning modules and simulations*—Interactive simulations emphasize people and task management. Employees learn by viewing videos; interacting in scenarios involving difficult employee situations; deciding how to deal with a problem, issue, or request; and getting feedback on their decisions. Case studies also are available for review.
3. *Collaborative learning*—The learner can connect on IBM's intranet with tutors, team members, customers, or other learners to discuss problems, issues, and approaches to share learning.
4. *Learning labs*—Five-day class workshops build on the learning acquired during the previous phases of

e-learning. The workshops emphasize peer learning and the development of a learning community. Through challenging activities and assignments, managers gain increased awareness of themselves, their work teams, and IBM.

The program recognizes the roles of the manager's supervisor as coach, supporter, and role model. This person provides coaching and feedback, on-the-job learning experiences, assessment of the manager's development needs and progress, and help in completing individual development plans.

IBM believes that e-learning combined with the classroom environment lets managers participate in self-directed learning, try out skills in a low-risk environment, and gain access to communities of learning and just-in-time learning. Combining the advantages of e-learning with classroom experiences and support from the manager's supervisor creates a superior development program.

SOURCE: N. Lewis and P. Orton, "The Five Attributes of Innovative E-Learning," *Training and Development*, June 2000, pp. 47–51.

six-week periods spread over 18 months. University faculty and consultants give participants general background of a functional area. The team then works with Avon senior executives on a country project, such as how to enter a new market. The teams present their projects to Avon's top managers.

LO3

Assessment

assessment
Collecting information and providing feedback to employees about their behaviour, communication style, or skills.

Another way to provide for employee development is **assessment**—collecting information and providing feedback to employees about their behaviour, communication style, or skills.[15] Information for assessment may come from the employees, their peers, managers, and customers. The most frequent uses of assessment are to identify employees with managerial potential to measure current managers' strengths and weaknesses. Organizations also use assessment to identify managers with potential to move into higher-level executive positions. Organizations that assign work to teams may use assessment to identify the strengths and weaknesses of individual team members and the effects of the team members' decision-making and communication styles on the team's productivity.

For assessment to support development, the information must be shared with the employee being assessed. Along with that assessment information, the employee needs suggestions for correcting skill weaknesses and for using skills already learned. The suggestions might be to participate in training courses or develop skills through new job experiences. Based on the assessment information and available development opportunities, employees should develop action plans to guide their efforts at self-improvement.

It is increasingly recognized that excellent technical skills are not enough for individuals or organizations to be successful. "Strong people skills are equally important to attracting clients, building lasting relationships with both clients and colleagues, and expanding business."[16] As a result, organizations vary in the methods and sources of information they use in developmental assessment. Many organizations appraise performance. Organizations with sophisticated development systems may use psychological tests to measure employees' skills, personality types, and communication styles. They may collect self, peer, and manager ratings of employees' behaviour and style of working with others. Assessment of emotional intelligence (EQ) increases an employee's self-awareness and facilitates their development with respect to intrapersonal and interpersonal skills, adaptability, and handling of stress.[17] Other tools used for these assessment methods include the Myers-Briggs Type Indicator, assessment centres, the Benchmarks assessment, performance appraisal, and 360-degree feedback.

Myers–Briggs Type Indicator®

Myers-Briggs Type Indicator (MBTI)
Psychological test that identifies individuals' preferences for source of energy, means of information gathering, way of decision making, and lifestyle, providing information for team building and leadership development.

The most popular psychological test for employee development is the **Myers-Briggs Type Indicator (MBTI).** This test, taken by millions of people each year, identifies individuals' preferences for source of energy, means of information gathering, way of decision making, and lifestyle. The results of the test provide information for team building and leadership development. The test consists of more than 100 questions about how the person feels or prefers to behave in different situations (such as "Are you usually a good 'mixer' or rather quiet and reserved?" and so forth). The MBTI is based on the work of Carl Jung, noted psychologist who believed that differences in individuals' behaviour result from their degree of extroversion–introversion and from their psychological makeup across several other dimensions. The test described these differences and individuals' preferences in the four areas:

1. The *energy* dimension indicates where individuals gain interpersonal strength and vitality, measured as their degree of introversion or extroversion. Extroverts (E) gain energy through interpersonal relationships. Introverts (I) gain energy by focusing on inner thoughts and feelings.

TABLE 8.2

Personality Types Used in the Myers-Briggs Type Indicator Assessment

	SENSING TYPES (S)		INTUITIVE TYPES (N)	
	THINKING (T)	**FEELING (F)**	**FEELING (F)**	**THINKING (T)**
Introverts (I) Judging (J)	**ISTJ** Quiet, serious, earn success by thoroughness and dependability. Practical, matter-of-fact, realistic, and responsible. Decide logically what should be done and work toward it steadily, regardless of distractions. Take pleasure in making everything orderly and organized—their work, their home, their life. Value traditions and loyalty.	**ISFJ** Quiet, friendly, responsible, and conscientious. Committed and steady in meeting their obligations. Thorough, painstaking, and accurate. Loyal, considerate, notice and remember specifics about people who are important to them, concerned with how others feel. Strive to create an orderly and harmonious environment at work and at home.	**INFJ** Seek meaning and connection in ideas, relationships, and material possessions. Want to understand what motivates people and are insightful about others. Conscientious and committed to their firm values. Develop a clear vision about how best to serve the common good. Organized and decisive in implementing their vision.	**INTJ** Have original minds and great drive for implementing their ideas and achieving their goals. Quickly see patterns in external events and develop long-range explanatory perspectives. When committed, organize a job and carry it through. Skeptical and independent, have high standards of competence and performance—for themselves and others.
Perceiving (P)	**ISTP** Tolerant and flexible, quiet observers until a problem appears, then act quickly to find workable solutions. Analyze what makes things work and readily get through large amounts of data to isolate the core of practical problems. Interested in cause and effect, organize facts using logical principles, value efficiency.	**ISFP** Quiet, friendly, sensitive, and kind. Enjoy the present moment, what's going on around them. Like to have their own space and to work within their own time frame. Loyal and committed to their values and to people who are important to them. Dislike disagreements and conflicts, do not force their opinions or values on others.	**INFP** Idealistic, loyal to their values and to people who are important to them. Want an external life that is congruent with their values. Curious, quick to see possibilities, can be catalysts for implementing ideas. Seek to understand people and to help them fulfill their potential. Adaptable, flexible, and accepting unless a value is threatened.	**INTP** Seek to develop logical explanations for everything that interests them. Theoretical and abstract, interested more in ideas than in social interaction. Quiet, contained, flexible, and adaptable. Have unusual ability to focus in depth to solve problems in their area of interest. Skeptical, sometimes critical, always analytical.
Extroverts (E) Perceiving (P)	**ESTP** Flexible and tolerant, they take a pragmatic approach focused on immediate results. Theories and conceptual explanations bore them—they want to act energetically to solve the problem. Focus on the here-and-now, spontaneous, enjoy each moment that they can be active with others. Enjoy material comforts and style. Learn best through doing.	**ESFP** Outgoing, friendly, and accepting. Exuberant lovers of life, people, and material comforts. Enjoy working with others to make things happen. Bring common sense and a realistic approach to their work, and make work fun. Flexible and spontaneous, adapt readily to new people and environments. Learn best by trying a new skill with other people.	**ENFP** Warmly enthusiastic and imaginative. See life as full of possibilities. Make connections between events and information very quickly, and confidently proceed based on the patterns they see. Want a lot of affirmation from others, and readily give appreciation and support. Spontaneous and flexible, often rely on their ability to improvise and their verbal fluency.	**ENTP** Quick, ingenious, stimulating, alert, and outspoken. Resourceful in solving new and challenging problems. Adept at generating conceptual possibilities and then analyzing them strategically. Good at reading other people. Bored by routine, will seldom do the same thing the same way, apt to turn to one new interest after another.
Judging (J)	**ESTJ** Practical, realistic, matter-of-fact. Decisive, quickly move to implement decisions. Organize projects and people to get things done, focus on getting results in the most efficient way possible. Take care of routine details. Have a clear set of logical standards, systematically follow them and want others to also. Forceful in implementing their plans.	**ESFJ** Warmhearted, conscientious, and cooperative. Want harmony in their environment, work with determination to establish it. Like to work with others to complete tasks accurately and on time. Loyal, follow through even in small matters. Notice what others need in their day-by-day lives and try to provide it. Want to be appreciated for who they are and for what they contribute.	**ENFJ** Warm, empathetic, responsive, and responsible. Highly attuned to the emotions, needs, and motivations of others. Find potential in everyone, want to help others fulfill their potential. May act as catalysts for individual and group growth. Loyal, responsive to praise and criticism. Sociable, facilitate others in a group, and provide inspiring leadership.	**ENTJ** Frank, decisive, assume leadership readily. Quickly see illogical and inefficient procedures and policies, develop and implement comprehensive systems to solve organizational problems. Enjoy long-term planning and goal setting. Usually well informed, well read, enjoy expanding their knowledge and passing it on to others. Forceful in presenting their ideas.

2. The *information-gathering* preference relates to the preparations individuals make before taking decisions. Individuals with a Sensing (S) preference tend to gather the facts and details to prepare for a decision. Intuitives (N) tend to focus less on the facts and more on possibilities and relationships among them.

3. In *decision making,* individuals differ in the amount of consideration they give to their own and others' values and feelings, as opposed to the hard facts of a situation. Individuals with a Thinking (T) preference try always to be objective in making decisions. Individuals with a Feeling (F) preference tend to evaluate the impact of the alternatives on others, as well as their own feelings; they are more subjective.

4. The *lifestyle* preference describes an individual's tendency to be either flexible or structured. Individuals with a Judging (J) preference focus on goals, establish deadlines, and prefer to be conclusive. Individuals with a Perceiving (P) preference enjoy surprises, are comfortable with changing a decision, and dislike deadlines.

The alternatives for each of the four dimensions result in 16 possible combinations, the personality types summarized in Table 8.2. Of course people are likely to be mixtures of these types; but the point of the test is that certain types predominate in individuals.

As a result of their psychological types, people develop strengths and weaknesses. For example, individuals who are Introverted, Sensing, Thinking, and Judging (known as ISTJs) tend to be serious, quiet, practical, orderly, and logical. They can organize tasks, be decisive, and follow through on plans and goals. As a consequence, however—that is, by not having the opposite preferences (Extroversion, Intuition, Feeling, and Perceiving)—ISTJs have several weaknesses. They may have difficulty responding to unexpected opportunities, appear to their colleagues to be too task-oriented or impersonal, and make decisions too fast.

Applying this kind of information about employees' preferences or tendencies helps organizations understand the communication, motivation, teamwork, work styles, and leadership of the people in their groups. For example, salespeople or executives who want to communicate better can apply what they learn about their own personality styles and the way other people perceive them. For team development, the MBTI can help teams match team members with assignments based on their preferences and thus improve problem solving.[18] The team could assign brainstorming (idea-generating) tasks to employees with an Intuitive preference and evaluation of the ideas to employees with a Sensing preference.

Research on the validity, reliability, and effectiveness of the MBTI is inconclusive.[19] People who take the MBTI find it a positive experience and say it helps them change their behaviour. MBTI scores appear to be related to one's occupation; that is, people in the same occupation tend to have the same or similar personality types. Analysis of managers' scores in North America, England, Latin America, and Japan found that a large majority of managers are ISTJ, INTJ, ESTJ, or ENTJ. However, MBTI scores are not necessarily stable over time. Studies in which the MBTI was administered at two different times found that as few as one-fourth of those who took the test were classified as exactly the same type the second time. Still, the MBTI is a valuable tool for understanding communication styles and the ways people prefer to interact with others. It is not appropriate for measuring job performance, however, or as the only means of evaluating promotion potential.

Assessment Centres

At an **assessment centre,** multiple raters or evaluators (assessors) evaluate employees' performance on a number of exercises.[20] An assessment centre is usually an off-site location such as a conference centre. Usually 6 to 12 employees participate at one time. The primary use of assessment centres is to identify whether employees have the personality characteristics, administrative skills, and interpersonal skills needed for managerial jobs. Organizations also use them to determine whether employees have the skills needed for working in teams.

The types of exercises used in assessment centres include leaderless group discussions, interviews, in-baskets, and role plays.[21] In a **leaderless group discussion,** a team of five to seven employees is assigned a problem and must work together to solve it within a certain time period. The problem may involve buying and selling supplies, nominating an employee for an award, or assembling a product. Interview questions typically cover each employee's work and personal experiences, skill strengths and weaknesses, and career plans. In-basket exercises, discussed as a selection method in Chapter 5, simulate the administrative tasks of a manager's job, using a large number of documents and emails for the employee to handle. In role plays, the participant takes the part of a manager or employee in a situation involving the skills to be assessed. For example, a participant might be given the role of a manager who must discuss performance problems with an employee, played by someone who works for the assessment centre. Other exercises in assessment centres might include interest and

assessment centre
An assessment process in which multiple raters or evaluators (assessors) evaluate employees' performance on a number of exercises, usually as they work in a group at an off-site location.

leaderless group discussion
An assessment centre exercise in which a team of five to seven employees is assigned a problem and must work together to solve it within a certain time period.

TABLE 8.3

Skills Related to Success as a Manager

Resourcefulness	Can think strategically, engage in flexible problem solving, and work effectively with higher management.
Doing whatever it takes	Has perseverance and focus in the face of obstacles.
Being a quick study	Quickly masters new technical and business knowledge.
Building and mending relationships	Knows how to build and maintain working relationships with coworkers and external parties.
Leading subordinates	Delegates to employees effectively, broadens their opportunities, and acts with fairness toward them.
Compassion and sensitivity	Shows genuine interest in others and sensitivity to employees' needs.
Straightforwardness and composure	Is honourable and steadfast.
Setting a developmental climate	Provides a challenging climate to encourage employees' development.
Confronting difficult employee situations	Acts decisively and fairly when dealing with difficult employee situations.
Team orientation	Accomplishes tasks through managing others.
Balance between personal life and work	Balances work priorities with personal life so that neither is neglected.
Decisiveness	Prefers quick and approximate actions to slow and precise ones in many management situations.
Self-awareness	Has an accurate picture of strengths and weaknesses and is willing to improve.
Hiring talented staff	Hires talented people for the team.
Putting people at ease	Displays warmth and a good sense of humour.
Acting with flexibility	Can behave in ways that are often seen as opposites.

SOURCE: Adapted with permission from C. D. McCauley, M. M. Lombardo, and C. J. Usher, "Diagnosing Management Development Needs: An Instrument Based on How Managers Develop," *Journal of Management* 15 (1989), pp. 389–403.

aptitude tests to evaluate an employee's vocabulary, general mental ability, and reasoning skills. Personality tests may be used to determine employees' ability to get along with others, tolerance for uncertainty, and other traits related to success as a manager or team member.

The assessors are usually managers who have been trained to look for employee behaviours that are related to the skills being assessed. Typically, each assessor observes and records one or two employees' behaviours in each exercise. The assessors review their notes and rate each employee's level of skills (for example, 5 = high level of leadership skills, 1 = low level of leadership skills). After all the employees have completed the exercises, the assessors discuss their observations of each employee. They compare their ratings and try to agree on each employee's rating for each of the skills.

As we mentioned in Chapter 5, research suggests that assessment centre ratings are valid for predicting performance, salary level, and career advancement.[22] Assessment centres may also be useful for development because of the feedback that participants receive about their behaviours, skill strengths, and weaknesses.[23] Some organizations, including Eastman Kodak, offer employees training courses and development activities related to the skills evaluated in the assessment centre.

Benchmarks

Benchmarks
A measurement tool that gathers ratings of a manager's use of skills associated with success in managing.

A development method that focuses on measuring management skills is an instrument called **Benchmarks.** This measurement tool gathers ratings of a manager's use of skills associated with success in managing. The items measured by Benchmarks are based on research into the lessons that executives learn in critical events of their careers.[24] Items measure the 16 skills and perspectives listed in Table 8.3, including how well managers deal with employees, acquire resources, and create a productive work climate. Research has found that managers who have these skills are more likely to receive positive performance evaluations, be considered promotable, and be promoted.[25]

To provide a complete picture of managers' skills, the managers' supervisors, their peers, and the managers themselves all complete the instrument. The results include a summary report, which the organization provides to the manager so he or she can see the self-ratings in comparison to the ratings by others. Also available with this method is a development guide containing examples of experiences that enhance each skill and ways successful managers use the skill.

Performance Appraisals and 360-Degree Feedback

As we stated in Chapter 7, *performance appraisal* is the process of measuring employees' performance. This information can be useful for employee development under certain conditions.[26] The appraisal system must tell employees specifically about their performance problems and ways to improve their performance. Employees must gain a clear understanding of the differences between current performance and expected performance. The appraisal process must identify causes of any performance gap and develop plans for improving performance. Managers must be trained to deliver frequent performance feedback and must monitor employees' progress in carrying out their action plans.

A recent trend in performance appraisals, also discussed in Chapter 7, is *360-degree feedback*—performance measurement by the employee's supervisor, peers, direct reports, and customers. Often the feedback involves rating the individual in terms of work-related behaviours. For development purposes, the rater would identify an area

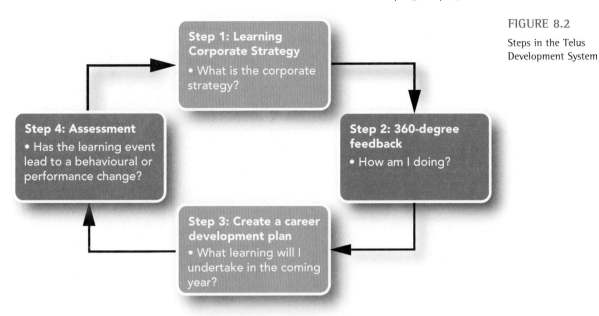

FIGURE 8.2

Steps in the Telus
Development System

SOURCE: "Telus Awarded for Development System," *Canadian HR Reporter*, March 8, 2004, p. 16.

of behaviour as a strength of that employee or an area requiring further development. The results presented to the employee show how he or she was rated on each item and how self-evaluations differ from other raters' evaluations. The individual reviews the results, seeks clarification from the raters, and sets specific development goals based on the strengths and weaknesses identified.[27]

However, the 360-degree feedback is often viewed as more successful when used for development purposes rather than for performance appraisal. Consider how Telus uses development planning with 360-degree feedback. As illustrated in Figure 8.2, Telus uses a four-step process that encourages all employees to create a development plan with objectives for learning and performance. This process relies on 360-degree feedback as a critical step.[28]

Job Experiences

Most employee development occurs through **job experiences**[29]—the combination of relationships, problems, demands, tasks, and other features of an employee's jobs. Using job experiences for employee development assumes that development is most likely to occur when the employee's skills and experiences do not entirely match the skills required for the employee's current job. To succeed, employees must stretch their skills. In other words, they must learn new skills, apply their skills and knowledge in new ways, and master new experiences.[30] For example, companies that want to prepare employees to expand overseas markets are assigning them to a variety of international jobs.

Most of what we know about development through job experiences comes from a series of studies conducted by the Center for Creative Leadership.[31] These studies asked executives to identify key career events that made a difference in their managerial styles and the lessons they learned from these experiences. The key events included job assignments (such as fixing a failed operation), interpersonal relationships (getting along with supervisors), and types of transitions (situations in which the

LO4

job experiences
The combination of relationships, problems, demands, tasks, and other features of an employee's jobs.

Working outside one's home country is one of the most important job experiences that can develop an employee for a career in the global economy.

manager at first lacked the necessary background). Through job experiences like these, managers learn how to handle common challenges, prove themselves, lead change, handle pressure, and influence others.

The usefulness of job experiences for employee development varies depending on whether the employee views the experiences as positive or negative sources of stress. When employees view job experiences as positive stressors, the experiences challenge them and stimulate learning. When they view job experiences as negative stressors, employees may suffer from high levels of harmful stress. Of the job demands studied, managers were most likely to experience negative stress from creating change and overcoming obstacles (adverse business conditions, lack of management support, lack of personal support, or a difficult boss). Research suggests that all of the job demands except obstacles are related to learning.[32] Organizations should offer job experiences that are most likely to increase learning, and they should consider the consequences of situations that involve negative stress.

Although the research on development through job experiences has focused on managers, line employees also can learn through job experiences. Organizations may, for example, use job experiences to develop skills needed for teamwork, including conflict resolution, data analysis, and customer service. These experiences may occur when forming a team and when employees switch roles within a team. Effem Inc., the organization that makes consumer products including Mars chocolate bars employs about 500 people in Canada. Effem's approach to career development starts "at recruitment when associates are not hired for 'The Job' but assessed for their potential to transfer into different roles."[33]

Various job assignments can provide for employee development. The organization may enlarge the employee's current job or move the employee to different jobs. Lateral moves include job rotation, transfer, or temporary assignment to another organization. The organization may also use downward moves or promotions as a source of job experience. Figure 8.3 summarizes these alternatives.

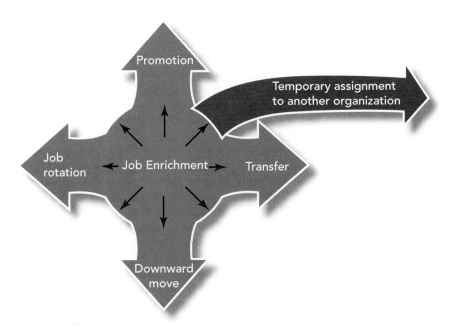

FIGURE 8.3

How Job Experiences Are
Used for Employee
Development

Job Enrichment

Job enrichment involves adding challenges or new responsibilities to employees' current jobs. Examples include completing a special project, switching roles within a work team, or researching new ways to serve customers. An engineering employee might join a task force developing new career paths for technical employees. The work on the project could give the engineer a leadership role through which the engineer learns about the company's career development system while also practising leadership skills to help the task force reach its goals. In this way, job enrichment not only makes a job more interesting, but also creates an opportunity for employees to develop new competencies.

Job Rotation

Another job design technique that can be applied to employee development is *job rotation,* moving employees through a series of job assignments in one or more functional areas. At Purdy's Chocolates in British Columbia, employees are provided development opportunities. Plant workers are given the chance to run a shift to see if they have the potential to replace a lead hand or become a warehouse manager in the future.[34] Greyhound Financial Corporation has high-potential managers participate in its job rotation program, known as "muscle-building."[35] Greyhound puts managers in departments where they have to perform tasks different from those they performed in the past. The managers maintain their titles and compensation levels while moving through the assignments, which have varying status.

Job rotation helps employees gain an appreciation for the company's goals, increases their understanding of different company functions, develops a network of contacts, and improves problem-solving and decision-making competencies.[36] Job rotation also helps employees increase their salary and earn promotions faster. At RBC Financial Group, 12,000 of the bank's 70,000 employees move to new positions through internal job postings each year.[37] Zabeen Hirji, RBC's senior vice-president of human resources, says, "job hopping helps employees provide better customer service because they learn about different areas of the company."[38] However, job rotation poses some problems for employees and the organization. Knowing they will be rotated to another job may give the employees a short-term perspective on problems and their solutions. Employees may feel less satisfied and motivated because they have difficulty developing specialized skills and leave the position too soon to fulfill any challenging assignments. The rotation of employees through a department may hurt productivity and increase the workload of those who remain after employees are rotated out. Job rotation is most likely to succeed when it meets certain conditions:[39]

- Job rotation is used for developing competencies as well as gaining experience for management careers.
- Employees understand specifically what competencies rotation is to develop.
- The organization uses job rotation for all levels and types of employees.
- Job rotation is linked with the career management process so employees know what development needs each assignment addresses.
- The organization manages the timing of rotations to maximize their benefits and minimize their costs.
- All employees have equal opportunities for job rotation, without facing discrimination due to their ethnic origin, sexual orientation, age, etc.

Transfers, Promotions, and Downward Moves

Most companies use upward, downward, and lateral moves as an option for employee development. In a **transfer,** the organization assigns an employee to a position in a different area of the company. Transfers do not necessarily increase job responsibilities or compensation. They are usually lateral moves, that is, moves to a job with a similar level of responsibility. They may involve relocation to another part of the country or even to another country.

Relocation can be stressful because of the demands of moving, especially when family members are affected. People have to find new housing, shopping, health care, and leisure facilities, and they often lack the support of nearby friends and family. These stresses come at the same time the employee must learn the expectations and responsibilities associated with the new position. Because transfers can provoke anxiety, many companies have difficulty getting employees to accept them. Employees most willing to accept transfers tend to be those with high career ambitions, a belief that the organization offers a promising future, and a belief that accepting the transfer will help the company succeed.[40]

A **downward move** occurs when an employee is given less responsibility and authority. The organization may demote an employee because of poor performance or move the employee to a lower-level position in another function so that the employee can develop different skills. The temporary cross-functional move is the most common way to use downward moves for employee development. For example, engineers who want to move into management often take lower-level positions, such as shift supervisor, to develop their management skills.

Many employees have difficulty associating transfers and downward moves with development; these changes may feel more like forms of punishment. Employees often decide to leave an organization rather than accept such a change, and then the organization must bear the costs of replacing those employees. Employees will be

transfer
Assignment of an employee to a position in a different area of the company, usually in a lateral move.

downward move
Assignment of an employee to a position with less responsibility and authority.

more likely to accept transfers and downward moves as development opportunities if the organization provides information about the change and its possible benefits and involves the employee in planning the change. Employees are also more likely to be positive about such a recommendation if the organization provides clear performance objectives and frequent feedback. Employers can encourage an employee to relocate by providing financial assistance with the move, information about the new location and job, and help for family members, such as identifying schools, child-care and elder-care options, and job search assistance for the employee's spouse.[41]

A **promotion** involves moving an employee into a position with greater challenges, more responsibility, and more authority than in the previous job. Usually promotions include pay increases. Because promotions improve the person's pay, status, and feelings of accomplishment, employees are more willing to accept promotions than lateral or downward moves. Even so, employers can increase the likelihood that employees will accept promotions by providing the same kind of information and assistance that are used to support transfers and downward moves. Organizations can more easily offer promotions if they are profitable and growing. In other conditions, opportunities for promoting employees may be limited.

promotion
Assignment of an employee to a position with greater challenges, more responsibility, and more authority than in the previous job, usually accompanied by a pay increase.

Temporary Assignments with Other Organizations

In some cases, an employer may benefit from the skills an employee can learn at another organization. The employer may encourage the employee to participate in an **externship**—a full-time temporary position at another organization. Mercer Management, a consulting firm, uses externships to develop employees who want experience in a specific industry.[42] Mercer Management promises to employ the externs after their assignments end. One employee with several years' experience as a Mercer consultant became vice-president of Internet services for Binney and Smith, the maker of Crayola crayons. He had been consulting on an Internet project for Binney and Smith and wanted to implement his recommendations, rather than just give them to the client and move on to another project. He started working at Binney and Smith while remaining employed by Mercer Management, though his pay comes from Binney and Smith. Mercer believes that employees who participate in its externship program will remain committed to the consulting firm because they have a chance to learn and grow professionally without the demands of a job search.

externship
Employee development through a full-time temporary position at another organization.

Temporary assignments can include a **sabbatical**—a leave of absence from an organization to renew or develop skills. Employees on sabbatical often receive full pay and benefits. Sabbaticals let employees get away from the day-to-day stresses of their jobs and acquire new skills and perspectives. Sabbaticals also allow employees more time for personal pursuits such as writing a book or spending more time with family members. Morningstar, which tracks and reports the performance of mutual funds, provides a six-week paid sabbatical every four years for all employees.[43] A Morningstar manager who had recently been promoted to the role of exhibit/conference manager waited an extra year before taking his sabbatical. He spent half his sabbatical on the beach in California and another three weeks pursuing his passion for modern dance. How employees spend their sabbaticals varies from company to company. Some employees may work for a nonprofit service agency; others may study at a college or university or travel and work on special projects in international subsidiaries of the company.

sabbatical
A leave of absence from an organization to renew or develop skills.

Interpersonal Relationships

Employees can also develop skills and increase their knowledge about the organization and its customers by interacting with a more experienced organization member. Two types of relationships used for employee development are mentoring and coaching.

LO5

mentor

An experienced, productive senior employee who helps develop a less experienced employee (a protégé/mentee).

Mentors

A **mentor** is an experienced, productive senior employee who helps develop a less experienced employee, called the *protégé* or *mentee*. Most mentoring relationships develop informally as a result of interests or values shared by the mentor and protégé. According to research, the employees most likely to seek and attract a mentor have certain personality characteristics: emotional stability, ability to adapt their behaviour to the situation, and high needs for power and achievement.[44] Mentoring relationships also can develop as part of the organization's planned effort to bring together successful senior employees with less experienced employees.

One major advantage of formal mentoring programs is that they ensure access to mentors for all employees. An advantage is that participants in a company-sponsored mentoring program know what is expected of them.[45] However, in an artificially created relationship, mentors may have difficulty providing counselling and coaching.[46] Mentoring programs tend to be most successful when they are voluntary and participants understand the details of the program. Rewarding managers for employee development also is important, because it signals that mentoring and other development activities are worthwhile. In addition, the organization should carefully select mentors based on their interpersonal and technical competencies, train them for the role, and evaluate whether the program has met its objectives. The "HR How To" box offers tips for setting up an effective mentoring program.

Bell Canada's mentoring program, "Mentor Match," has been recognized as one of the best. Mentor Match is open to employees at all levels and uses an online cross-functional mentoring program. Protégés/mentees browse a pool of possible mentors

TABLE 8.4

Advantages of Mentoring Programs

FOR PROTÉGÉS/MENTEES	FOR MENTORS
• Breaks down "silos" throughout the organization	• Maintains a pulse on the organization by keeping regular contact and communication with employees
• Increases communication	
• Supports continuous learning throughout all levels of the organization	• Enhances interpersonal and leadership competencies
• Enhances career development and growth	
• Improves employee satisfaction and engagement	
• Fosters a culture where employees support and help one another	

SOURCE: Adapted from "Mentoring—Low Cost, Big Benefits," The Conference Board of Canada, www.conferenceboard.ca/humanresource/mentoring-inside.htm. Retrieved: February 24, 2005.

Setting Up a Mentoring Program

Mentoring is most effective if it is part of a well-planned program that supports the organization's goals. The effective use of mentoring can be a key strategic advantage for organizations competing in a knowledge-based economy. The following are tips for introducing a mentoring program:

- Keep it simple and accessible. Provide all employees with access to the program and make the process easy to follow.

- Formalize the partnership through a written agreement to identify the frequency and length of meetings, and the goals of each participant.

- Build a solid pool of mentors before launching the program, so protégés/mentees have a wide selection of potential partners.

- Ensure senior executives are active participants. For example, 29 Bell Canada executives at the vice-president level or higher have mentoring partners.

- Generate and sustain interest in the program with effective communication.

- Link mentoring to human resource processes.

SOURCE: Adapted from "Mentoring—Low Cost, Big Benefits," The Conference Board of Canada, www.conferenceboard.ca/human resource/mentoring-inside.htm. Retrieved: February 24, 2005.

using a search tool. A list of suitable mentors is generated based on the profile of the protégé/mentee. From a strategic perspective, Mentor Match is expected to improve employee retention, enhance performance and productivity, and accelerate the development of employees. Because it is fully automated, Mentor Match can track data and generate results such as sign-up statistics. All the necessary mentoring tools such as mentoring agreements, suggestions, and templates are available online.[47]

Mentors and protégés/mentees can both benefit from a mentoring relationship. Table 8.4 summarizes the advantages of mentoring programs to both protégés/mentees and mentors. Protégés/mentees receive career support, including coaching, protection, sponsorship, challenging assignments, and visibility among the organization's managers. They also receive benefits of a positive relationship—a friend and role model who accepts them, has a positive opinion toward them, and gives them a chance to talk about their concerns. Employees with mentors are also more likely to be promoted, earn higher salaries, and have more influence within their organization.[48] Acting as a mentor gives managers a chance to develop their interpersonal skills and increase their feelings that they are contributing something important to the organization. Working with the protégé/mentee on technical matters such as new research in the field may also increase the mentor's technical knowledge. When General Electric became involved in e-commerce, it used younger employees with Web expertise to mentor older managers. As the veterans became more familiar with the Internet, their young mentors became more comfortable working with senior managers and developed their business expertise.[49]

So that more employees can benefit from mentoring, some organizations use *group mentoring programs*, which assign four to six protégés/mentees to a successful senior employee. A potential advantage of group mentoring is that protégés can learn from each other as well as from the mentor. The leader helps protégés/mentees understand the organization, guides them in analyzing their experiences, and helps them clarify

Pat Quinn has a top reputation as a coach who has helped teams and individuals become champions. Career coaches motivate employees, help them develop their skills, and provide feedback for improvement.

career directions. Each member of the group may complete specific assignments, or the group may work together on a problem or issue.

Coaching

LO6

coach
A peer or manager who works with an employee to provide a source of motivation, help him or her develop skills, and provide reinforcement and feedback.

A **coach** is a peer or manager who works with an employee to provide a source of motivation, help him or her develop skills, and provide reinforcement and feedback. Coaches may play one or more of three roles:[50]

1. Working one-on-one with an employee, as when giving feedback.
2. Helping employees learn for themselves—for example, helping them find experts and teaching them to obtain feedback from others.
3. Providing resources such as mentors, courses, or job experiences.

William Gray, president of Corporate Mentoring Solutions Inc. and former UBC professor, draws a distinction between mentoring and coaching. Gray describes mentoring as developing the "whole person" and coaching involves developing a specific skill set.[51]

Best Buy, a consumer-electronics retailer, has invested nearly $10 million on coaches for all top managers.[52] Once a month, top executives spend a few hours with an industrial psychologist who helps them work through leadership issues. One manager discussed with his coach how to balance the needs of some of the managers who worked for him with the company's business needs. His managers were more comfortable focusing on traditional store retailing at a time when the company needed a focus on competition on the Internet. The manager being coached needed to learn how to lead his team and push new ideas without squelching team members.

LO7

Systems for Career Management

Employee development is most likely to meet the organization's needs if it is part of a human resource system of career management. In practice, organizations' career

FIGURE 8.4

Steps and Responsibilities in the Career Management Process

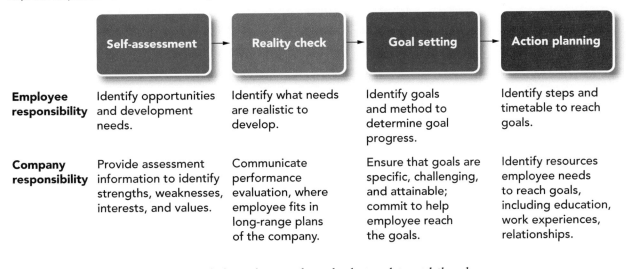

	Self-assessment	Reality check	Goal setting	Action planning
Employee responsibility	Identify opportunities and development needs.	Identify what needs are realistic to develop.	Identify goals and method to determine goal progress.	Identify steps and timetable to reach goals.
Company responsibility	Provide assessment information to identify strengths, weaknesses, interests, and values.	Communicate performance evaluation, where employee fits in long-range plans of the company.	Ensure that goals are specific, challenging, and attainable; commit to help employee reach the goals.	Identify resources employee needs to reach goals, including education, work experiences, relationships.

management systems vary. Some rely heavily on informal relationships, while others are sophisticated programs. As shown in Figure 8.4, a basic career management system involves four steps: self-assessment, reality check, goal setting, and action planning. At each step, both the employee and the organization have responsibilities. The system is most likely to be beneficial if it is linked to the organization's objectives and needs, has support from top management, and is created with employee participation.[53] Human resource professionals can also contribute to the system's success by ensuring that it is linked to other HR practices such as performance management, training, and recruiting.

A recent Conference Board of Canada survey revealed that 78 percent of participating organizations have a formal career development planning process. As illustrated in Figure 8.5, almost half of these organizations say that both the employee and the organization share responsibility for an employee's career development plan.[54]

FIGURE 8.5

Responsibility for Employee's Career Development Plan (percentage of respondents)

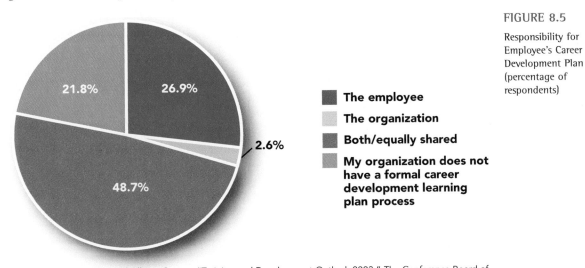

21.8%   26.9%

2.6%

48.7%

- ■ **The employee**
- ■ **The organization**
- ■ **Both/equally shared**
- ■ **My organization does not have a formal career development learning plan process**

SOURCE: Janice Cooney and Allison Cowan, "Training and Development Outlook 2003," The Conference Board of Canada, p. 16, ISBN 0-88763-584-9.

Self-Assessment

self-assessment The use of information by employees to determine their career interests, values, aptitudes, and behavioural tendencies.

In discussing the methods of employee development, we highlighted several assessment tools. Such tools may be applied to the first stage of career development, **self-assessment.** This is the use of information by employees to determine their career interests, values, aptitudes, and behavioural tendencies. The employee's responsibility is to identify opportunities and development needs. The organization's responsibility is to provide assessment information for identifying strengths, weaknesses, interests, and values.

Self-assessment tools often include psychological tests such as the Myers-Briggs Type Inventory (described earlier in the chapter), the Strong-Campbell Interest Inventory, and the Self-Directed Search. The Strong-Campbell Inventory helps employees identify their occupational and job interests. The Self-Directed Search identifies employees' preferences for working in different kinds of environments—sales, counselling, and so on. Tests may also help employees identify the relative value they place on work and leisure activities. Self-assessment tools can include exercises such as the one in Figure 8.6. This type of exercise helps an employee consider his or her

FIGURE 8.6

Sample Self-Assessment Exercise

Step 1: Where am I?
Examine current position of life and career.
Think about your life from past and present to the future. Draw a time line to represent important events.

Step 2: Who am I? What are my accomplishments?
Examine different roles.
- What am I good at?
- How would you describe yourself?
- Describe times when you have said to yourself, "Well done!"

Step 3: Where would I like to be, and what would I like to happen?
Begin setting goals.
Consider your life from present to future. Write an autobiography answering these questions:
- What do you want to have accomplished?
- What milestones do you want to achieve?
- What do you want to be remembered for?

Step 4: An ideal year in the future
Identify resources needed.
Consider a one-year period in the future. Answer these questions:
- If you had unlimited resources, what would you do?
- What would the ideal environment look like?
- Does the ideal environment match Step 3?

Step 5: An ideal job
Create current goal.
In the present, think about an ideal job for you with your available resources. Describe your role, resources, and type of training or education needed.

Step 6: Career by objective inventory
Summarize current situation.
- What gets you excited each day?
- What do you do well? What are you known for?
- What do you need to achieve your goals?
- What could interfere with reaching your goals?
- What should you do now to move toward reaching your goals?
- What is your long-term career objective?

SOURCE: Based on J. E. McMahon and S. K. Merman, "Career Development," in *The ASTD Training and Development Handbook*, 4th ed., ed. R. L. Craig (New York: McGraw-Hill, 1996), pp. 679–97. Reproduced with permission.

current career status, future plans, and the fit between the career and the employee's current situation and resources. Some organizations provide counsellors to help employees in the self-assessment process and to interpret the results of psychological tests.

Completing the self-assessment can help employees identify a development need. This need can result from gaps between current skills or interests and the type of work or position the employee has or wants. Ford Motor Company has a career management system that provides this type of information.[55] Ford's system, which it calls the Personal Development Roadmap (PDR), is a Web-based resource that lets marketing, sales, and service employees plan their own personal and professional development. Employees visit PDR on Ford's intranet, where they complete a profile each year.

Reality Check

In the next step of career management, the **reality check,** employees receive information about their competencies and where these assets fit into the organization's plans. The employee's responsibility is to identify what skills she or he could realistically develop in light of the opportunities available. The organization's responsibility is to communicate the performance evaluation and the opportunities available to the employee, given the organization's long-range plans. Opportunities might include promotions and transfers. Some organizations develop and communicate **career paths**—the identified pattern or progression of jobs or roles within an organization to provide clarity about how an employee may progress into more senior positions. Career paths may include a wide variety of jobs or may provide specific information related to cumulative responsibilities for a managerial, technical, or professional career. Career path information can also enhance the discussion of opportunities between employees and their managers by providing consistent language related to how jobs and roles are defined in the organization.[56] Figure 8.7 provides information about career paths in Building Operations at PCL.

reality check
Information employers give employees about their competencies and where these assets fit into the organization's plans.

career path
The identified pattern or progression of jobs or roles within an organization.

FIGURE 8.7
Career Paths—Building Operations at PCL

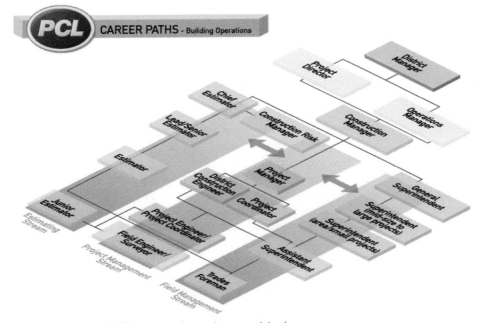

SOURCE: www.pcl.com/html/homesection/careers/career_path.html.

Usually the employer conducts the reality check as part of a performance appraisal or as the feedback stage of performance management. In well-developed career management systems, the manager may hold separate discussions for performance feedback and career development. At Ford, the Personal Development Roadmap helps employees identify areas for development by comparing their annual profiles with the expected skill levels for their job group.

Goal Setting

Based on the information from the self-assessment and reality check, the employee sets short- and long-term career objectives. These goals usually involve one or more of the following categories:

- Desired roles, such as becoming a team leader within three years.
- Level of competency—for example, to use one's budgeting skills to improve the unit's cash flow problems.
- Work setting—for example, to move to corporate marketing within two years.
- Skill acquisition, such as learning how to use the company's human resource information system.

As in these examples, the goals should be SMART (specific, measurable, achievable, relevant, and timed) as discussed in Chapter 7. It is the employee's responsibility to identify the goal and the method of determining her or his progress toward each goal.

Usually the employee discusses the goals with his or her manager. The organization's responsibility is to help the employee reach the goal. At Ford, the PDR system does this by helping employees identify areas on which to focus development and recommending development opportunities offered by the company. The PDR has also identified specific leadership behaviours associated with Ford's business success—for example, innovation and desire to serve—and helps employees focus on developing these behaviours.

Action Planning

During the final step, employees prepare an action plan for how they will achieve their short- and long-term career goals. The employee is responsible for identifying the steps and timetable to reach the goals. The employer should identify resources needed, including courses, work experiences, and relationships.

Action plans may involve any one or a combination of the development methods discussed earlier in the chapter—training, assessment, job experiences, or the help of a mentor or coach. The approach used depends on the particular developmental needs and career objectives. For example, suppose the program manager in an information systems department uses feedback from performance appraisals to determine that greater knowledge of project management software is needed. The manager plans to increase that knowledge by reading articles (formal education), meeting with software vendors, and contacting the vendors' customers to ask them about the software they have used (job experiences). The manager and his supervisor agree that six months will be the target date for achieving the higher level of knowledge through these activities.

The outcome of action planning often takes the form of a career development plan. Figure 8.8 is an example of a development plan for a product manager. Devel-

FIGURE 8.8

Career Development Plan

Name: **Title:** Project Manager   **Immediate Manager:**

Competencies
Please identify your three greatest strengths and areas for improvement.
Strengths
- Strategic thinking and execution (confidence, command skills, action orientation)
- Results orientation (creating a motivating work environment, perseverance)
- Spirit for winning (building team spirit, customer focus, respect colleagues)

Areas for Improvement
- Patience (tolerance of people or processes and sensitivity to pacing)
- Written communications (ability to write clearly and succinctly)
- Overly ambitious (too much focus on successful completion of projects rather than developing relationships with individuals involved in the projects)

Career Goals
Please describe your overall career goals.
- **Long-term:** Accept positions of increased responsibility to a level of general manager (or beyond). The areas of specific interest include but are not limited to product and brand management, technology and development, strategic planning, and marketing.
- **Short-term:** Continue to improve my skills in marketing and brand management while utilizing my skills in product management, strategic planning, and global relations.

Next Assignments
Identify potential next assignments (including timing) that would help you develop toward your career goals.
- Manager or director level in planning, development, product, or brand management. Timing estimated to be Spring 2007.

Training and Development Needs
List both training and development activities that will either help you develop in your current assignment or provide overall career development.
- Master's degree classes will allow me to practise and improve my written communications skills. The dynamics of my current position, teamwork, and reliance on other individuals allow me to practise patience and to focus on individual team members' needs along with the success of the project.

Employee _____   **Date** _____
Immediate Manager _____   **Date** _____
Mentor _____   **Date** _____

---

opment plans usually include descriptions of strengths and weaknesses, career goals, and development activities for reaching each goal. Ford's PDR helps employees create an annual development plan. It recommends education (Ford classes and seminars), exploration (activities outside the company), and/or experiences (job assignments and other on-the-job opportunities) geared toward meeting each employee's particular development needs. Employees also can enrol in suggested courses on Ford's intranet.

LO8

Development-Related Challenges

A well-designed system for employee development can help organizations face three widespread challenges: the glass ceiling, succession planning, and dysfunctional behaviour by managers.

The Glass Ceiling

As we mentioned in Chapter 1, women and other members of the employment equity target groups are rare in the top level of Canadian corporations. According to a study conducted by Catalyst, only 12 percent of corporate officers in Canada are held by women (690 out of 5,746 corporate officers).[57] Observers of this situation have noted that it looks as if an invisible barrier is keeping these individuals from reaching the top jobs, a barrier that has come to be known as the **glass ceiling.** The glass ceiling is likely caused by a lack of access to training programs, appropriate developmental job experiences, and developmental relationships such as mentoring.[58] According to research, women and men have equal access to job experiences involving transitions or creating change.[59] But male managers receive significantly more assignments involving great responsibility (high stakes, managing business diversity, handling external pressure) than female managers of similar ability and managerial level. Also, female managers report experiencing more challenge due to lack of personal support (which, as we saw earlier in the chapter, is related to harmful stress). With regard to developmental relationships, women and visible minorities often have trouble finding mentors. They may not participate in the organization's, profession's, or community's "old boys' network." Also, managers in the organization may prefer to interact with people who have similar status or may avoid interacting with certain people because of discomfort or negative stereotypes.[60]

Organizations can use development systems to help break through the glass ceiling. Managers making developmental assignments need to carefully consider whether stereotypes are influencing the types of assignments men and women receive. A formal process for regularly identifying development needs and creating action plans can make these decisions more objective. The "Best Practices" box describes the steps that Procter & Gamble is taking to break the glass ceiling.

Another organization that is actively working to eliminate the glass ceiling is Deloitte & Touche, an accounting, tax, and consulting firm with offices throughout North America.[61] Deloitte & Touche had been experiencing high turnover of talented women, so it set up a task force chaired by the company's chief executive officer to analyze the problem and develop recommendations. The task force gathered data by having every management professional in the company attend a workshop designed to explore how attitudes about gender affected the work environment. The workshops included discussions, videos, and case studies, such as one case in which two promising candidates, one male and one female, with identical skills were evaluated. The workshops also focused on how work assignments were allocated. The workshops found differences in the ways men and women were evaluated and in the kinds of assignments they were given, based on managers' assumptions about men and women. As a result, Deloitte & Touche began to rethink how assignments were given, to make sure women had opportunities for highly visible assignments. The company started a formal process for career planning for women and men and began offering networking events at which women could meet successful female partners and high-

glass ceiling
Circumstances resembling an invisible barrier that keep most women and other members of the employment equity target groups from attaining the top jobs in organizations.

Procter & Gamble Selling Women on Careers

Procter & Gamble is famous for its ability to sell products like Tide detergent and Pampers diapers to women. Until recently, it was much less successful in bringing women into its management ranks. No women sat on P&G's executive committee, and few executives were female. A study of employee turnover found that two of every three high-performing employees who left the company were women. P&G has a policy of promoting from within, so retaining and promoting high performers is important for filling the company's top ranks.

To uncover the reasons women were leaving rather than moving up, P&G conducted interviews and surveys. The results showed that women felt they had a consensus-building management style that was not valued; rather, P&G executives favoured quick, aggressive decision making. Career planning was not openly discussed, so women reported they didn't know where they stood with the company, and women (more than male employees) were uncomfortable with the feeling that they were not valued. Women also expressed an interest in flexible schedules so that they could put in the long hours required for success and still meet other demands on their time.

To apply these results, P&G created a task force to study the career path of the brand manager, the major route to executive-level jobs. The team set goals to lower the turnover rate among women and to achieve 40 percent women at each level of brand management.

The task force also developed a mentoring program, which it named Mentor Up. As the name suggests, the Mentor Up program directs the mentoring relationship in an unusual direction: The mentors are mid-level or junior female managers with at least a year's experience as good performers in the job. The protégés are senior-level male executives. Mentoring is intended to raise the executives' awareness of women's work-related issues. The female managers are matched with senior managers, based on their responses to a questionnaire. These protégés and mentors attend an orientation session that includes a panel discussion by past participants in the program and a series of exercises probing women's workplace issues and reasons for success at P&G. Mentors are required to meet with their protégés at least once every two months.

Mentors and protégés receive discussion guides designed to help them conduct a beneficial dialogue when they meet. For example, one discussion guide asked the mentoring pairs to explore the keys to success and failure for women and men in company leadership positions. The discussion guides also include questions designed to uncover feelings about occasions when women feel valued. The mentors and protégés answer the questions independently, then discuss their responses. By noticing similarities and differences in their answers, they can identify ways people like to be recognized.

The Mentor Up program has frequently raised two issues: the barriers that women face in balancing work and personal demands; and differences that mentoring pairs notice in the ways men and women manage people and make decisions. One of the program's biggest benefits has been that mentors and protégés have shared advice and perspectives and feel comfortable using each other to test new ideas. The junior managers also appreciate their exposure to top executives. The program has reduced the turnover rate of female managers by 25 percent, making it similar to turnover among male managers.

SOURCE: Based on T. Parker-Pope, "Inside P&G, a Pitch to Keep Women Employees," *The Wall Street Journal*, September 9, 1998, pp. B1, B6; D. Zielinski, "Mentoring Up," *Training*, October 2000, pp. 136–40.

level managers. Deloitte & Touche began measuring turnover and promotion rates and linking rewards to meeting career development objectives. Through these changes, the company improved its retention of women, and reducing turnover has saved $250 million in hiring and training costs.

Succession Planning

succession planning
The process of identifying and tracking high-potential employees who will be able to fill top management positions when they become vacant.

Organizations have always had to prepare for the retirement of their leaders, but the need is more intense than ever. The aging of the workforce means that a greater share of employees are reaching retirement age. Many organizations are fuelling the trend by downsizing through early-retirement programs. As positions at the top of organizations become vacant, many organizations have determined that their middle managers are fewer and often unprepared for top-level responsibility. This situation has raised awareness of the need for **succession planning**—the process of identifying and tracking high-potential employees who will be able to fill top management positions when they become vacant. Forty-five percent of Purdy's Chocolates' employees will be eligible to retire in a decade. Because Purdy's prefers to promote from within they are developing a succession plan to deal with future retirements of store managers from their 48 retail-store chains in Alberta and British Columbia.[62]

Succession planning offers several benefits.[63] It forces senior management to regularly and thoughtfully review the company's leadership talent. It assures that top-level management talent is available. It provides a set of development experiences that managers must complete to be considered for top management positions, so the organization does not promote managers before they are ready. Succession planning systems also help attract and retain ambitious managerial employees by providing development opportunities.

Succession planning focuses on *high-potential employees*, that is, employees the organization believes can succeed in higher-level business positions such as general manager of a business unit, director of a function (such as marketing or finance), or chief executive officer.[64] A typical approach to development of high-potential employees is to have them complete an individual development program including education, executive mentoring and coaching, and rotation through job assignments. Job assignments are based on the successful career paths of the managers whom the high-potential employees are preparing to replace. High-potential employees may also receive special assignments, such as making presentations and serving on committees and task forces. Research shows that an effective program for developing high-potential employees has three stages:[65]

1. *Selection of high-potential employees*—Organizations may select outstanding performers and employees who have completed academic programs, such as earning a master's degree in business administration. They may also use the results of psychological tests and assessment centres.
2. *Developmental experiences*—As employees participate in developmental experiences, the organization identifies those who succeed in the experiences. The organization looks for employees who continue to show qualities associated with success in top jobs, such as communication skills, leadership talent, and willingness to make sacrifices for the organization. Employees who display these qualities continue to be considered high-potential employees.

3. *Active involvement with the* CEO—High-potential employees seen by top management as fitting into the organization's culture and having personality characteristics necessary for representing the company become actively involved with the chief executive officer. The CEO exposes these employees to the organization's key people and gives them a greater understanding of the organization's culture. The development of high-potential employees is a slow process. Reaching stage 3 may take 15 to 20 years.

When American Express Financial Services wanted to develop leaders for expansion of the business, the company established a process for succession planning.[66] The process forecasts how many and what kinds of leaders the company will need over the next two years, assesses the talents of current employees, and develops employees identified as having management talent. Vice-presidents recommend talented employees to participate in assessment programs that measure leadership and basic managerial skills. Employees receive personalized development plans for improving their weaknesses in knowledge, skill, or experiences. Top managers monitor their progress and provide coaching as needed.

At some organizations, succession planning systems identify a few potential managers for each position. This limited approach allows the organization to target development activities to the most talented managers, but it may not prepare enough managers to fill vacant positions. High-potential employees who are not on the short list for managerial jobs may leave. American Express's approach avoids this problem by identifying many qualified leaders, which builds commitment to the company.

Dysfunctional Managers

A manager who is otherwise competent may engage in some behaviours that make him or her ineffective or even "toxic"—someone who stifles good ideas and drives away employees. These dysfunctional behaviours include insensitivity to others, inability to be a team player, arrogance, poor conflict management skills, inability to meet business objectives, and inability to adapt to change.[67] For example, suppose a manager has great depth of technical knowledge and has excellent ability in keeping two steps ahead of competitors. But the manager is abrasive and aggressive with employees and peers and has a leadership style that discourages employees from contributing their ideas. This manager is likely to have difficulty motivating employees and may alienate people inside and outside the organization. Some of these dysfunctional manager behaviours are illustrated humourously in the popular "Dilbert" comic strip, shown in Figure 8.9.

When a manager is an otherwise valuable employee and is willing to improve, the organization may try to help him or her change the dysfunctional behaviour. The usual ways to help with development include assessment, training, and counselling. The organization may enrol the manager in a program designed specifically to help managers with dysfunctional behaviour, such as the Individual Coaching for Effectiveness (ICE) program. The ICE program includes diagnosis, coaching, and support activities, which are tailored to each manager's needs.[68] Psychologists conduct the diagnosis, coach and counsel the manager, and develop action plans for implementing new skills on the job.

FIGURE 8.9

Dysfunctional Managers

DILBERT

BY SCOTT ADAMS

DILBERT © United Feature Syndicate. Reprinted by permission.

During diagnosis, the psychologist collects information about the manager's personality, skills, and interests. The information comes from psychological tests and interviews with the manager, his or her supervisor, and colleagues. The psychological tests help the psychologist determine whether the manager will be able to change the dysfunctional behaviour. For example, change will be difficult if the manager is extremely defensive. If the diagnosis indicates the manager can benefit from the program, the manager and supervisor work with the psychologist to set specific developmental objectives.

During the coaching phase of the program, the manager receives information about the target skills or behaviour. This may include principles of effective communication or teamwork, tolerance of individual differences in the workplace, or conducting effective meetings. Next, the manager participates in behaviour modelling training, described in Chapter 6. The manager also receives psychological counselling to overcome beliefs that may interfere with learning the desired behaviour.

The support phase of the ICE program creates conditions to ensure that the manager can use the new behaviours and skills on the job. The manager's supervisor gives the manager and psychologist feedback about the manager's progress in using the new skills and behaviours. The psychologist and manager identify situations in which the manager may tend to rely on dysfunctional behaviour. The coach and manager also develop action plans that outline how the manager should try to use new behaviours in daily work activities.

The effectiveness of this kind of program has not yet been thoroughly studied. Still, research suggests that managers who participate in programs like ICE improve their skills and are less likely to be terminated.[69] This suggests that organizations can benefit from offering development opportunities to valuable employees with performance problems, not just to star performers.

Summary

1. **Discuss how development is related to training and careers.**
Employee development is the combination of formal education, job experiences, relationships, and assessment of personality and abilities to help employees prepare for the future of their careers. Training is more focused on improving performance in the current job, but training programs may support employee development. In modern organizations, the concept of a career is fluid—a protean career that changes along with changes in a person's interests, abilities, and values and changes in the work environment. To plan and prepare for a protean career requires active career management, which includes planning for employee development.

2. **Identify the methods organizations use for employee development.**
Organizations may use formal educational programs at the workplace or off-site, such as workshops, college and university programs, company-sponsored training, or programs offered by independent institutions. Organizations may use the assessment process to help employees identify strengths and areas requiring further development. Assessment can help the organization identify employees with managerial potential or identify areas in which teams need to develop. Job experiences help employees develop by stretching competencies as they meet new challenges. Interpersonal relationships with a more experienced member of the organization—often in the role of mentor or coach—can help employees develop their understanding of the organization and its customers.

3. **Describe how organizations use assessment of personality type, work behaviours, and job performance to plan employee development.**
Organizations collect information and provide feedback to employees about their behaviour, communication style, and skills. The information may come from the employees, their peers, managers, and customers. Many organizations use performance appraisals as a source of assessment information. Appraisals may take the form of 360-degree feedback. Some organizations use psychological tests designed for this purpose, including the Myers-Briggs Type Indicator and the Benchmarks assessment. Assessment centres combine a variety of methods to provide assessment information. Managers must share the assessments, along with suggestions for improvement.

4. **Explain how job experiences can be used for developing skills.**
Job experiences contribute to development through a combination of relationships, problems, demands, tasks, and other features of an employee's jobs. The assumption is that development is most likely to occur when the employee's skills and experiences do not entirely match the competencies required for the employee's current job, so employees must stretch to meet the demands of the new assignment. The impact varies according to whether the employee views the experience as a positive or negative source of stress. Job experiences that support employee development may include job enrichment, job rotations, transfers, promotions, downward moves, and temporary assignments with other organizations.

5. **Summarize principles of successful mentoring programs.**
A mentor is an experienced, productive senior employee who helps develop a less experienced employee. Although most mentoring relationships develop informally, organizations can link mentoring to development goals by establishing a formal mentoring program. A formal program also provides a basis for ensuring that all eligible employees are included. Mentoring programs tend to be most successful when they are voluntary and participants understand the details of the program. The organization should reward managers for employee development, carefully select mentors based on interpersonal and technical skills, train them for the role, and evaluate whether the program has met its objectives.

6. **Tell how managers and peers develop employees through coaching.**
A coach is a peer or manager who works with an employee to motivate the employee, help him or her develop skills, and provide reinforcement and feedback. Coaches should be prepared to take on one or more of three roles: working one-on-one with an employee, helping employees learn for themselves, and providing resources, such as mentors, courses, or job experiences.

7. **Identify the steps in the process of career management.**
First, during self-assessment, employees use information to determine their career interests, values, aptitudes, and behavioural tendencies, looking for opportunities and areas needing development. Self-assessment tools often include psychological tests or exercises that ask

about career status and plans. The second step is the reality check, during which the organization communicates information about the employee's skills and knowledge and how these fit into the organization's plan. The employee then sets goals and discusses them with his or her manager, who ensures that the goals are specific, challenging, and attainable. Finally, the employee works with his or her manager to create an action plan for development activities that will help the employee achieve the goals.

8. Discuss how organizations are meeting the challenges of the "glass ceiling," succession planning, and dysfunctional managers.

   The glass ceiling is a barrier that has been observed preventing women and other members of the employment equity target groups from achieving top jobs in an organization. Development programs can ensure that these employees receive access to development resources such as coaches, mentors, and developmental job assignments. Succession planning ensures that the organization prepares qualified employees to fill management jobs as managers retire. It focuses on applying employee development to high-potential employees. Effective succession planning includes methods for selecting these employees, providing them with developmental experiences, and getting the CEO actively involved with employees who display qualities associated with success as they participate in the developmental activities. For dysfunctional managers who have the potential to contribute to the organization, the organization may offer development targeted at correcting the areas of dysfunction. Typically, the process includes collecting information about the manager's personality, skills, and interests; providing feedback, training, and counseling; and ensuring that the manager can apply new, functional behaviours on the job.

Review and Discussion Questions

1. How does development differ from training? How does development support career management in modern organizations?
2. What are the four broad categories of development methods? Why might it be beneficial to combine all of these methods into a formal development program?
3. Recommend a development method for each of the following situations, and explain why you chose that method.
   a. An employee recently promoted to the job of plant supervisor is having difficulty motivating employees to meet quality standards.
   b. A sales manager annoys salespeople by directing every detail of their work.
   c. An employee has excellent leadership skills but lacks knowledge of the financial side of business.
   d. An organization is planning to organize its production workers into teams for the first time.
4. A company that markets sophisticated business management software systems uses sales teams to help customers define needs and to create systems that meet those needs. The teams include programmers, salespeople who specialize in client industries, and software designers. Occasionally sales are lost as a result of conflict or communication problems among team members. The company wants to improve the effectiveness of these teams, and it wants to begin with assessment. How can the teams use 360-degree feedback and psychological tests to develop?
5. In an organization that wants to use work experiences as a method of employee development, what basic options are available? Which of these options would be most attractive to you as an employee? Why?
6. Many employees are unwilling to relocate because they like their current community and family members prefer not to move. Yet preparation for management requires that employees develop new skills, strengthen areas of weakness, and be exposed to new aspects of the organization's business. How can an organization change an employee's current job to develop management skills?
7. Many people feel that mentoring relationships should occur naturally, in situations where senior managers feel inclined to play that role. What are some advantages of setting up a formal mentoring program, rather than letting senior managers decide how and whom to help?
8. What are the three roles of a coach? How is a coach different from a mentor? What are some advantages of using someone outside the organization as a coach? Some disadvantages?
9. Why should organizations be interested in helping employees plan their careers? What benefits can companies gain? What are the risks?
10. What are the manager's roles in a career management system? Which role do you think is most difficult for the typical manager? Which is the easiest role? List reasons why managers might resist becoming involved in career management.
11. What is the glass ceiling? What are the possible consequences to an organization that has a glass ceiling? How can employee development break the glass ceil-

ing? Can succession planning help with this problem? Explain.

12. Why might an organization benefit from giving employee development opportunities to a dysfunctional manager, rather than simply dismissing the manager? Do these reasons apply to nonmanagement employees as well?

Case: Lawyers Nurture Their Own As Never Before

When Borden Ladner Gervais recruits "baby lawyers" to the firm, it immediately enrols them in an intensive development program—BLG 101—to bring them up to speed on client relationship skills, basic practice skills, even office politics, says Ken Bagshaw, a senior partner in the firm's Vancouver office and chairman of its national professional excellence committee.

But these professional development opportunities are not just restricted to the newcomers. Canadian law firms, in their quest for a competitive edge, are nurturing their own as never before—in a Type-A way. An increasing number of firms are now turning their focus to developing lawyers throughout their careers, right up to the senior partnership level.

BLG 301 sends all third-year associates on a retreat, where the transaction lawyers are schooled in negotiation techniques and "how to run a deal," while the litigation lawyers work on their presentation and cross-examination strategies. The firm books empty courtrooms at Toronto's Osgoode Hall for the occasion and brings in acting coaches for some of the sessions. "Acting skills are a valuable thing for litigation lawyers," Mr. Bagshaw says.

BLG 501 is for senior associates being developed for the position of partner. Senior associates are coached in the leadership and business development skills they will need to manage staff and attract new clients to the firm. To help its lawyers track their progress, the firm has developed BLG Blueprints. Customized to each practice area, the program provides associates with a detailed plan of the skills and experiences they are expected to have at the various stages of their careers—from first year to admission to partnership.

As daunting as all this might sound, other major law firms are moving in the same direction. Baker and McKenzie is putting the finishing touches on a career-path planner that will clearly outline "here's where you are, here's where you are going, here's what you have to do to get there" says Stewart Saxe, a Toronto-based partner in the international law firm. The Ogilvy Renault variation is called Passport, says Christian Beaudry, the firm's Montreal-based partner in charge of professional development and knowledge management. The reason is simple: Today's law school graduates are demanding nothing less, according to Magnus Verbrugge, a recently named partner in Borden Ladner's Vancouver office and an ultramarathon runner in his spare time.

SOURCE: Virginia Galt, "Lawyers Nurture Their Own As Never Before," *The Globe and Mail*—Globe Careers, June 9, 2004, p. C1. Reprinted with permission from *The Globe and Mail*.

Questions

1. What benefits do the development programs discussed in the case offer to employees (i.e., lawyers)? To the law firms?
2. Suggest some ways the law firms could enhance these programs with other employee development activities.
3. What if the development programs lead some lawyers to decide they should leave the company to pursue their career objectives elsewhere? Does that make the programs unwise? How might the law firms address this risk?

Case: Career Change—Setting a Different Course

For Carolyn Weaver, the epiphany came in a crowded office elevator. A colleague, who had worked for the company her entire career, told Weaver that several of their fellow riders were also "lifers." "All of a sudden my heart started palpitating and I had that moment when you just go, 'I'm in the wrong place. I'm going to end up a lifer and before you know it my life is going to be done,'" Weaver said. So she quit. Six years later, the 33-year-old has gone from direct marketing specialist at IBM Corp. to creator and host of Fine Print, a television series on books that is now in its third season. Weaver admits she didn't know the first thing about TV when she started. But like many who have left steady jobs and paycheques to pursue their passions, she didn't let that lack of knowledge stand in her way.

Changing careers takes flexibility, hard work, and determination. Despite financial risk and emotional upheaval, many workers who have changed course say it's a small price to pay for happiness. But the choice to do something different is sometimes less deliberate than Weaver's.

In 2001, Parmjit Parmar was laid off from Sun Microsystems Inc. in Toronto as the technology boom went bust. She looked for another job for a few months, but soon a friend who owned a marketing communications company asked her for some help. Now, the 43-year-old former business development specialist runs her own marketing and public relations company. "I've always had that entrepreneurial streak when you just make it happen," said Parmar. Her company, Montana Ridge Enterprises, has been operating for less than two years, but clients already include University of Toronto Press, Ruth's Hemp Foods, and author Douglas Glover. Parmar attributes her success to the 14 years she spent as a computer consultant at the beginning of her career. "It's tough at the beginning," she said. "There's so much to learn and at the same time, that's never stopped me, because I think my brain was trained that way," she added. "When you work as a consultant, you're working in so many different lines of business."

Parmar took seminars, read books, and cold-called people to ask for information interviews. She also joined networking groups such as the Toronto Board of Trade. The money was slow to come at first. "That's tough. You have to pay cash for everything," she said. And although her salary is growing with the business, the real payoff is less tangible. "I feel so much happier as a person," Parmar said. "And people who knew me from four years ago, five years ago, say, 'I can't believe the difference in you,' be-cause they see I feel very empowered." "And I know that if I keep that state of mind, the money will follow, and it is starting to grow that way."

Weaver's path from computer employee to TV host wasn't a straight one. In fact, she didn't know what she wanted to do when she first quit her job at IBM. But one day when she was home sick with the flu and channel-surfing, she hatched her idea. She made some phone calls and pitched her show to Rogers Television. The pitch was successful, but she still had to raise the money. After loads of rejections, she lined up a potential sponsor but the deal was contingent on a top Canadian author agreeing to appear on her show. The whole plan hung in the balance. An impromptu pitch to Margaret Atwood at a book signing didn't pan out. So Weaver and her mother arrived unannounced at Alistair MacLeod's office at the University of Windsor. The award-winning author agreed to appear on the show, and Weaver hasn't looked back.

"Within a certain range, there's so much possibility," said Weaver, who has since developed several other television shows. "I think sometimes when people feel unhappy or stuck or frustrated in their careers, sometimes you need to step back and really ask yourself, "What are the things about this job that I love? And what are the things about this job that I don't love, and are those things big enough for me to consider thinking about alternatives?"

SOURCE: Ann Perry, "Setting a Different Course," April 5, 2004, www.workopolis.com/serlet/Content/torontostar/2004045. Retrieved: April 13, 2004. Reprinted with permission of Torstar Syndication Services.

Questions

1. Is there anything Carolyn Weaver's employer could have done to support her development and retain her as an employee? In your answer, please include specific references to the four approaches to employee development discussed in the text.

2. Choose one of the individuals described in the case and identify how she applied the steps outlined in the career management process. Did she fully execute each step?

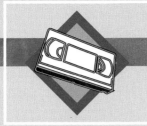

Crash 'N' Burn

"Crashing cars, motorcycle stunt men, and flaming walls of fire. All in a day's work for an entrepreneur who plans to give up his day job for his dream job." Ralph Moore, 32 years old, uses two cellphones to try to keep up with his Monday–Thursday kitchen installation business and his Friday–Sunday business staging demolition derbies and motorcycle and stunt car thrill shows for town fairs. He plans to give up the kitchen installation business and focus full-time on his "Destruction Productions" and "Edge Motor Sports."

Ralph leads a frantic existence in the meantime. Several of his kitchen projects are behind schedule and his weekends are spent coping with travel, weather, financial, logistical, and employee issues as he attempts to expand his business and make money. This weekend, Ralph and his crew are scheduled to appear in five events, in four different towns.

Ralph is trying to do it all—run the business side, including negotiating with event coordinators, training and managing employees, while also doing whatever it takes to make sure the show goes on. In this segment, Ralph takes on the job of clown when one of his employees is a no-show and almost sets himself on fire while lighting a barricade. Although some events are more successful than others, Ralph is determined to find partners to help achieve his goal to expand the business. Ralph takes the first step by quitting his day job installing kitchens.

On to marriage and 13 derbies in three days in Phoenix, Arizona.

SOURCE: Based on "Crash 'N' Burn," CBC *Venture* #909, January 11, 2004.

Questions
1. Based on your knowledge of the Myers-Briggs Type Indicator (MBTI), what psychological type do you expect Ralph Moore to be?
2. Using Figure 8.8 as a guide, prepare a Career Development Plan for Ralph Moore.
   a. What are Ralph's greatest strengths? Areas for improvement?
   b. What are Ralph's long and short-term career goals?
   c. What are Ralph's training and development needs?
3. Would a career as an entrepreneur be appealing to you? Why or why not?

Part 4

Compensating and Rewarding Human Resources

Chapter 9

Total Rewards

Chapter

9

Total Rewards

What Do I Need to Know? After reading this chapter, you should be able to:

1. Discuss how organizations implement a "total rewards" approach to compensating and rewarding employees.

2. Identify the kinds of decisions and influences involved in providing base pay to employees.

3. Describe alternatives to job-based pay.

4. Describe how organizations recognize individual, team, and organizational performance through the use of incentives.

5. Discuss the role of benefits and services as part of employee total rewards.

6. Summarize the types of employee benefits and services offered by employers.

7. Discuss the importance of effectively communicating the organization's approach to total rewards.

8. Discuss issues related to compensating and rewarding executives.

Introduction

Since late 2002, Markham Ontario-based business automation software company In-Systems has been transforming its employee compensation and rewards system through the adoption of a total rewards approach. Some parts of the total rewards package may be considered intangibles, but Laurie McRae, vice-president of Human Resources, says the goal is to turn those intangibles into hard data.

The guiding philosophy is: anything that employees take into account when considering the value of working at InSystems is part of the total rewards package. The shift to total rewards at InSystems was precipitated by an employee survey in late 2002. "The (employee satisfaction) scores weren't low, but then again I have some lofty goals for employee satisfaction," McRae says. The survey also revealed a few areas of the traditional rewards programs that could, in the minds of employees stand some improvement. "They made comments about our incentive plan, about the way it was designed and structured. From their perspective it was too complex," she says. Employees wanted high performance to be recognized, but it often wasn't clear why some employees were getting incentives while others weren't. "They wanted to see these types of direct financial awards really differentiate high performance, so people who were high performers could get more sizable rewards." Employees only singled out a few issues for improvement, but McRae wanted to re-examine everything that comprised the employee value proposition. "You have to step back and say we need to balance the cost and the effectiveness of these programs. We have to manage it as a whole portfolio."

Laurie McRae, vice-president of HR at InSystems, says HR needs to bundle and market employee offerings.

Before then, compensation and rewards were managed in isolation. Therefore, it was difficult for employees to understand exactly what they were getting from their employer. After recognizing improvements were possible, and with the objective of ultimately improving corporate performance, the HR team set to work with external help to overhaul employee rewards. "We went right back to the drawing board," says McRae. A new job evaluation methodology was created to ease market salary comparisons, a retirement savings program was introduced for the first time, incentive programs were tweaked, and new recognition programs introduced. A total rewards package also makes it easier for employees to make comparisons when other opportunities arise. She is confident that the InSystems total rewards package is strong enough that when employees have a full picture of everything they get from InSystems, they won't easily be lured away.[1]

Like InSystems, many organizations are recognizing the strategic value of adopting a comprehensive approach to compensating and rewarding employees, frequently referred to as **total rewards**. Figure 9.1 shows the types of specific outcomes and rewards people may obtain from work.

From the employer's view, compensation and rewards are powerful tools for meeting the organization's goals. Organizations such as InSystems and RBC are redefining

LO1

total rewards
Comprehensive approach to compensating and rewarding employees.

FIGURE 9.1

Total Rewards in
Exchange for Work

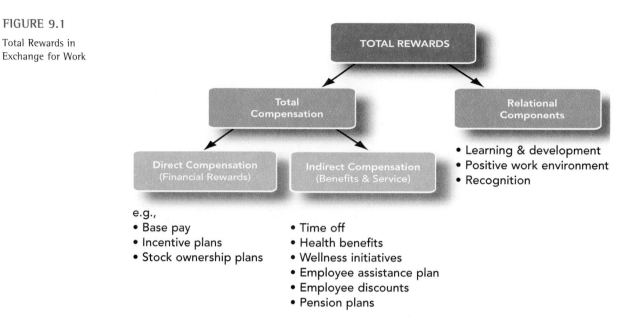

SOURCE: Adapted from George T. Milkovich and Jerry M. Newman, *Compensation*, 6th edition, Irwin McGraw-Hill, ISBN 0-256-26906-8, p. 7. Reprinted with permission from The McGraw-Hill Companies, Inc.

their approaches to employee compensation and benefits to also take into account the relational elements identified in the right side of Figure 9.1.[2] Organizations with this total rewards approach create a "total value proposition" for current and prospective employees. Because compensation and rewards have a major impact on employee attitudes and behaviours, total rewards influence which kinds of employees are attracted to (and remain with) the organization. According to a recent Watson Wyatt survey on strategic rewards and pay practices, Canadian companies cited the primary reason for developing a total rewards strategy was to align rewards with the business strategy. As shown in Figure 9.2, other reasons Canadian companies take a total rewards approach is to focus employees on business goals, enforce consistent pay practices, optimize how reward dollars are used, and control costs.[3]

Employees care about policies affecting their compensation and rewards because the policies affect the employee's income, well-being, and security. Also, employees consider compensation and rewards a sign of status and success. They attach great importance to compensation and rewards when they evaluate their relationship and satisfaction with their employers. As the workforce becomes increasingly diverse, the definition of what employees expect in exchange for their work will become increasingly complex. As a result, although this chapter addresses total rewards, the primary emphasis will be on forms of **total compensation**, i.e., direct and indirect compensation including base pay, benefits, and services. Chapters 6 and 8 discussed learning and development opportunities provided employees and Chapter 12 will discuss the "relational" components of total rewards in the context of creating a high performance and motivational work environment.

This chapter opens by describing the role of **direct compensation**, all types of financial rewards and tangible benefits and services employees receive as part of their employment, and defines the kinds of influences on managers making pay level decisions. We describe methods of evaluating jobs and market data to develop effective pay structures. Next, we look at the elements of incentive pay systems. The

total compensation
All types of financial rewards and tangible benefits and services employees receive as part of their employment.

direct compensation
Financial rewards employees receive in exchange for their work.

FIGURE 9.2

Why Firms Develop a Total Rewards Strategy

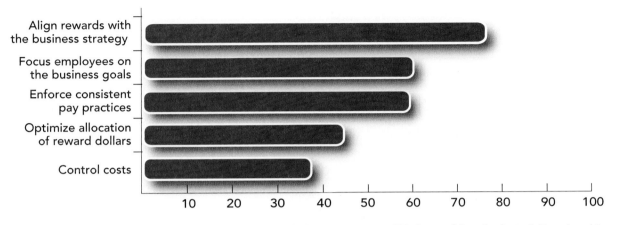

SOURCE: Strategic Rewards in Canada: Building the Optimal Reward Plan—Watson Wyatt's 2004 Survey of Canadian Strategic Rewards and Pay Practices in "Why Firms Develop a Total Rewards Strategy," *Canadian HR Reporter*, February 14, 2005, p. R5.

many kinds of incentive pay fall into three broad categories: incentives linked to individual, group, or organizational performance. Choices from these categories should consider not only their strengths and weaknesses, but also their fit with the organization's goals. This chapter also looks at **indirect compensation**, the benefits and services employees receive in exchange for their work, including the important role that benefits and services play. The chapter also covers why and how organizations should effectively communicate with employees about their total rewards Finally, this chapter looks at an issue also of importance to organizational performance—executive compensation. In summary, Figure 9.3 provides an illustration of how total rewards are allocated in 294 organizations surveyed by the Conference Board of Canada in 2005.

indirect compensation
The benefits and services employees receive in exchange for their work.

Decisions about Base Pay

Because pay is important both in its effect on employees and on account of its cost, organizations need to plan what they will pay employees in each job. An unplanned approach, in which each employee's pay is independently negotiated, will likely result in unfairness, dissatisfaction, and rates that are either overly expensive or so low that positions are hard to fill. Organizations therefore make decisions about two aspects of pay structure: job structure and pay level. **Job structure** consists of the relative pay for different jobs within the organization. It establishes relative pay among different functions and different levels of responsibility. For example, job structure defines the difference in pay between an entry-level accountant and an entry-level assembler, as well as the difference between an entry-level accountant, the accounting department manager, and the organization's comptroller. **Pay level** is the average amount (including wages, salaries, and incentives) the organization pays for a particular job. Together, job structure and pay levels establish a **pay structure** that helps the organization achieve goals related to employee motivation, cost control, and the ability to attract and retain talented human resources.

The organization's job structure and pay levels are policies of the organization, rather than the amount a particular employee earns. For example, an organization's

LO2

job structure
The relative pay for different jobs within the organization.

pay level
The average amount (including wages, salaries, and bonuses) the organization pays for a particular job.

pay structure
The pay policy resulting from job structure and pay-level decisions.

FIGURE 9.3

The Total Rewards Dollar

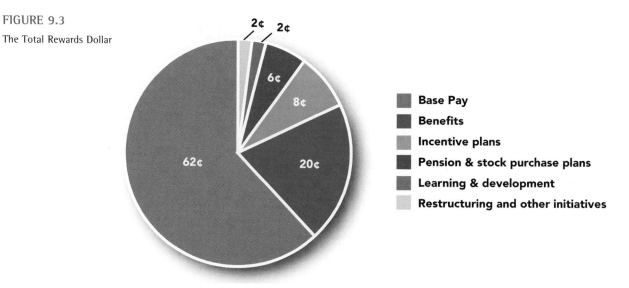

SOURCE: "Compensation Planning Outlook 2005, Conference Board of Canada," *Canadian HR Reporter*, February 14, 2005, p. R5.

pay structure could include the range of pay that a person may earn in the job of entry-level accountant. An individual accountant could be earning an amount anywhere within that range. Typically, the amount a person earns depends on the individual's qualifications, accomplishments, and experience. The individual's pay may also depend partly on how well the organization performs.

Especially in an organization with hundreds or thousands of employees, it would be impractical for managers and the human resource department to make an entirely unique decision about each employee's pay. The decision would have to weigh so many factors that this approach would be expensive, difficult, and often unsatisfactory. Establishing a pay structure simplifies the process of making decisions about individual employees' pay by grouping together employees with similar jobs. Human resource professionals develop this pay structure based on legal requirements, market forces, and the organization's goals, such as attracting a high-quality workforce and meeting principles of fairness.

Legal Requirements

All of an organization's decisions about compensation should comply with the applicable laws. Although these laws differ between federal, provincial, and territorial jurisdictions, a common core of legal requirements exists.

Human Rights Legislation

Under Human Rights legislation, described in Chapter 2, employers may not base differences in pay on an employee's age, sex, race, or other prohibited grounds of discrimination. Any differences in pay must instead be tied to such business-related considerations as job responsibilities or performance. Job descriptions, job structures, and pay structures can help organizations demonstrate that they are upholding these laws.

Employment/Labour Standards Acts

The Canada Labour Code and the relevant provincial and territorial laws include minimum requirements for wages, hours of work, overtime pay, vacation, statutory holidays, as well as other specific provisions. Executives, professionals, administrative, and outside sales employees are usually considered "exempt" employees and are not eligible for certain provisions such as overtime pay that "non-exempt" employees receive.

Two employees who do the same job cannot be paid different wages because of gender, race, or age. It would be illegal to pay these two employees differently because one is male and the other is female. Only if there are differences in their experience, skills, seniority, or job performance are there legal reasons why their pay might be different.

Pay Equity Acts

As discussed in Chapter 2, pay equity legislation exists federally and in several provincial jurisdictions and attempts to address the wage gap between female and male-dominated jobs and ensure that jobs of equal value within the organization receive similar rates of pay. Organizations use job evaluation (described later in the chapter) to establish the worth of an organization's jobs in terms of such criteria as their difficulty and their importance to the organization. The employer then compares the evaluation points awarded to each job with the pay for each job. If jobs have the same number of evaluation points, they should be paid equally. If they are not, pay of the lower-paid job is raised to meet the comparable worth of the male-dominated job.

Economic Influences on Pay

An organization cannot make spending decisions independent of the economy. Organizations must keep costs low enough that they can sell their products profitably, yet they must be able to attract workers in a competitive labour market. Decisions about how to respond to the economic forces of product markets and labour markets limit an organization's choices about pay structure.

Product Markets

Pressure to be globally competitive influences compensation and rewards. Companies increasingly recognize that increases in employees' pay needs to be linked to corresponding increases in productivity. To protect Canadian jobs from being outsourced to nations with lower labour costs, organizations are also focusing on cost containment.[4] Organizations under pressure to cut labour costs may respond by reducing staff levels, freezing pay levels, postponing hiring decisions, or requiring employees to bear more of the cost of benefits such as insurance premiums.

Pay Level: Deciding What to Pay

Although legal requirements and economic influences limit organizations' choices about pay levels, there is a range within which organizations can make decisions.[5] The size of this range depends on the details of the organization's competitive environment. If many workers are competing for a few jobs, employers will have more choice. Similarly, employers can be more flexible about pay policies if they use technology and work design to get better results from employees than their competitors do.

When organizations have a broad range in which to make decisions about pay, they can choose to pay at, above, or below the rate set by market forces. Economic theory holds that the most profitable level, all things being equal, would be at the market rate. Often, however, all things are *not* equal from one employer to another. For instance, an organization may gain an advantage by paying above the market rate if it uses the higher pay as one means to attract top talent and then uses these excellent employees' knowledge to be more innovative, produce higher quality, or work more efficiently.

This approach is based on the view of employees as resources. Higher pay may be an investment in superior human resources. Having higher labour costs than your competitors is not necessarily bad if you also have the best and most effective workforce, which produces more products of better quality. Pay policies are one of the most important human resource tools for encouraging desired employee behaviours and discouraging undesired behaviours. Therefore, organizations must evaluate pay as more than a cost, but also as an investment that can generate returns in attracting, retaining, and motivating a high-quality workforce. For this reason, paying above the going rate may be advantageous for an organization that involves employees or that cannot closely watch employees (as with repair technicians who travel to customers). Those employers might use high pay to attract and retain top candidates and to motivate them to do their best because they want to keep their high-paying jobs.[6]

Of course, employers do not always have this much flexibility. Some companies are under intense pressure to charge low prices for their products, and some companies are trying to draw workers from a pool that is too small to satisfy all employers' needs.

When a segment of the labour market is laid off, it adds to the number of people available to work and places less pressure on employers to offer high pay.

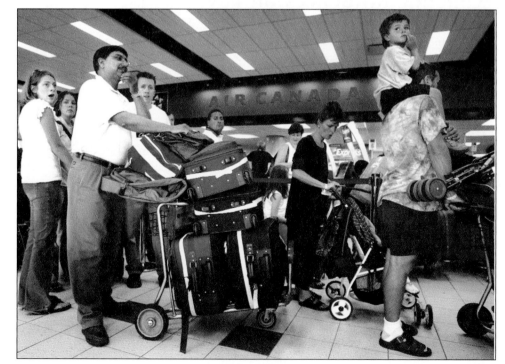

Gathering Information about Market Pay

To compete for talent, organizations use **benchmarking,** a procedure in which an organization compares its own practices against those of successful competitors. Benchmarking involves the use of pay surveys. These provide information about the going rates of pay at competitors in the organization's product and labour markets. An organization can conduct its own surveys, but the federal government and other organizations make a great deal of data available already.

For example, the federal government's Job Futures website (www.jobfutures.ca) provides average hourly earnings data for occupations listed in the National Occupational Classification (NOC) discussed in Chapter 3. Many industry, trade, and professional groups also collect wage and salary data. Employers should check with the relevant groups to see what surveys are available. Consulting firms also will provide data, including the results of international surveys, and can tailor data to the organization's particular needs.

Human resource professionals need to determine whether to gather data focusing on particular industries or on job categories. Industry-specific data are especially relevant for jobs with skills that are specific to the type of product. For jobs with skills that can be transferred to companies in other industries, surveys of job classifications will be more relevant.

benchmarking
A procedure in which an organization compares its own practices against those of successful competitors.

Employee Judgments about Pay Fairness

In developing a pay structure, it is important to keep in mind employees' opinions about fairness. If employees perceive their pay as unfair they may experience pay dissatisfaction and be less motivated to achieve organizational goals.

Judging Fairness

Employees evaluate their pay relative to the pay of other employees. Social scientists have studied this kind of comparison and developed *equity theory* to describe how people make judgments about fairness.[7] According to equity theory, people measure outcomes such as pay in terms of their inputs. For example, an employee might think of her pay in terms of her master's degree, her 12 years of experience, and her 60-hour workweeks. To decide whether a level of pay is equitable, the person compares her ratio of outcomes and inputs with other people's outcome/input ratios, as shown in Figure 9.4. The person in the previous example might notice that an employee with less education or experience is earning more than she is (unfair) or that an employee who works 80 hours a week is earning more (fair). In general, employees compare their pay and contributions using several considerations:

- What they think employees in other organizations earn for doing the same job.
- What they think other employees holding different jobs within the organization earn for doing work at the same or different levels.
- What they think other employees in the organization earn for doing the same job as theirs.

The ways employees respond to their impressions about equity can have a great impact on the organization. Typically, if employees see their pay as equitable, their attitudes and behaviour continue unchanged. If employees see themselves as receiving an advantage, they usually rethink the situation to see it as merely equitable. But if em-

FIGURE 9.4

Opinions about Fairness:
Pay Equity

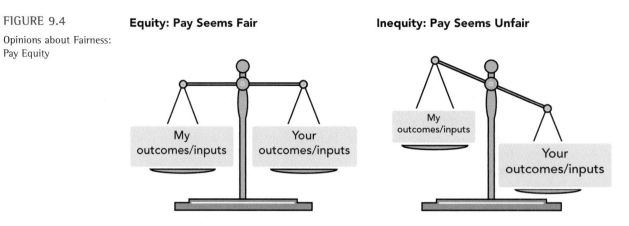

Equity: Pay Seems Fair

My outcomes/inputs

Your outcomes/inputs

Inequity: Pay Seems Unfair

My outcomes/inputs

Your outcomes/inputs

ployees conclude that they are underrewarded, they are likely to make up the difference in one of three ways. They might put forth less effort (reducing their inputs), find a way to increase their outcomes (for example, stealing), or withdraw by leaving the organization or refusing to cooperate. Employees' beliefs about fairness also influence their willingness to accept transfers or promotions. For example, if a job change involves more work, employees will expect higher pay.

Job Structure: Relative Value of Jobs

Along with market forces and principles of fairness, organizations consider the relative contribution each job should make to the organization's overall performance. In general, an organization's top executives have a great impact on the organization's performance, so they tend to be paid much more than entry-level workers. Executives at the same level of the organization—for example, the vice-president of marketing and the vice-president of information systems—tend to be paid similar amounts. Creation of a pay structure requires that the organization develop an internal structure showing the relative contribution of its various jobs.

job evaluation
An administrative procedure for measuring the relative internal worth of the organization's jobs.

One typical way of doing this is with a **job evaluation,** an administrative procedure for measuring the relative worth of the organization's jobs. Usually, the organization does this by assembling and training a job evaluation committee, consisting of people familiar with the jobs to be evaluated. The committee often includes a human resource specialist and, if its budget permits, may hire an outside consultant.

To conduct a job evaluation, the committee identifies each job's *compensable factors*, meaning the characteristics of a job that the organization values and chooses to pay for. As shown in Table 9.1, an organization might consider the effort required and skill requirements of people performing computer-related jobs. Other compensable factors might include working conditions and responsibility. Based on the job attributes defined by job analysis (discussed in Chapter 3), the jobs are rated for each factor. The rater assigns each factor a certain number of points, giving more points to factors when they are considered more important and when the job requires a high level of that factor. Often the number of points comes from one of the *point manuals* published by trade groups and management consultants. If necessary, the organization can adapt the scores in the point manual to the organization's situation or even develop its own point manual. As in the example in Table 9.1, the scores for each factor are totalled to arrive at an overall evaluation for each job.

TABLE 9.1

Job Evaluation of Three Jobs

JOB TITLE	COMPENSABLE FACTORS				TOTAL
	SKILL	EFFORT	RESPONSIBILITY	WORKING CONDITIONS	
Data entry clerk	20	40	20	30	110
Computer programmer	80	60	50	20	210
Systems analyst	110	70	70	20	270

Job evaluations provide the basis for decisions about relative internal worth, i.e., value of the job within the organization. According to the sample assessments in Table 9.1, the job of systems analyst is worth more to this organization than the job of data entry clerk. Therefore, the organization would be willing to pay significantly more for the work of a systems analyst than it would for the work of a data entry clerk.

The organization may limit its pay survey to jobs evaluated as *key jobs*. These are jobs that have relatively stable content and are common among many organizations, so it is possible to obtain survey data about what people earn in these jobs. Organizations can make the process of creating a pay structure more practical by defining key jobs. Research for creating the pay structure is limited to the key jobs that play a significant role in the organization. Pay for the key jobs can be based on survey data, and pay for the organization's other jobs can be based on the organization's job structure. A job with a higher evaluation score than a particular key job would receive higher pay than that key job.

Pay Structure: Putting It All Together

As we described in the first section of this chapter, the pay structure reflects decisions about how much to pay (pay level) and the relative value of each job (job structure). The organization's pay structure should reflect what the organization knows about market forces, as well as its own unique goals and the relative contribution of each job to achieving the goals. By balancing this external and internal information, the organization's goal is to set levels of pay that employees will consider motivating. Organizations typically apply the information by establishing some combination of pay rates, pay grades, and pay ranges. Within this structure, they may state the pay in terms of a rate per hour, commonly called an **hourly wage;** a rate of pay for each unit produced, known as a **piecework rate;** or a rate of pay per month or year, called a **salary.**

hourly wage
Rate of pay for each hour worked.

piecework rate
Rate of pay for each unit produced.

salary
Rate of pay for each week, month or year worked.

Pay Rates

If the organization's main concern is to match what people are earning in comparable jobs, the organization can base pay directly on market research into as many of its key jobs as possible. To do this, the organization looks for survey data for each job title. If it finds data from more than one survey, it must weight the results based on their quality and relevance. The final number represents what the competition pays. In light of that knowledge, the organization decides what it will pay for the job.

FIGURE 9.5

Pay Policy Lines

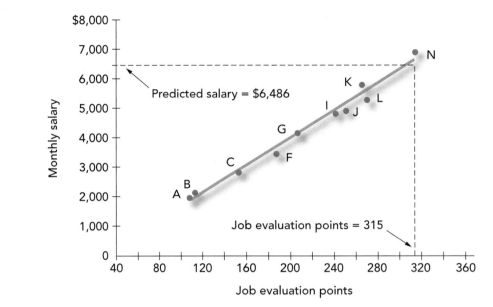

The next step is to determine salaries for the nonkey jobs, for which the organization has no survey data. Instead, the person developing the pay structure creates a graph like the one in Figure 9.5. The vertical axis shows a range of possible pay rates, and the horizontal axis measures the points from the job evaluation. The analyst plots points according to the job evaluation and pay rate for each key job. Finally, the analyst fits a line, called a **pay policy line,** to the points plotted. (This can be done statistically on a computer, using a procedure called regression analysis.) Mathematically, this line shows the relationship between job evaluation and rate of pay. Using this line, the analyst can estimate the market pay level for a given job evaluation. Looking at the graph gives approximate numbers, or the regression analysis will provide an equation for calculating the rate of pay.

pay policy line
A graphed line showing the mathematical relationship between job evaluation points and pay rate.

The pay policy line reflects the pay structure in the market, which does not always match rates in the organization (see key job F in Figure 9.5). Survey data may show that people in certain jobs are actually earning significantly more or less than the amount shown on the pay policy line. For example, some kinds of expertise are in short supply. People with that expertise can command higher salaries, because they can easily leave one employer to get higher pay somewhere else. Suppose, in contrast, that local businesses have laid off many warehouse employees. Because so many of these workers are looking for jobs, organizations may be able to pay them less than the rate that job evaluation points would suggest.

When job structure and market data conflict in these ways, organizations have to decide on a way to resolve the two. One approach is to stick to the job evaluations and pay according to the employees' worth to the organization. Organizations that do so will be paying more or less than they have to, so they will likely have more difficulty competing for customers or employees. A way to moderate this approach is to consider the importance of each position to the organization's goals.[8] If a position is critical for meeting the organization's goals, paying more than competitors pay may be worthwhile.

At the other extreme, the organization could base pay entirely on market forces. However, this approach also has some practical drawbacks. One is that employees may conclude that pay rates are unfair. Two vice-presidents or two supervisors will expect to receive similar pay because their responsibilities are similar. If the differences between their pay are large, because of different market rates, the lower-paid employee will likely be dissatisfied. Also, if the organization's development plans include rotating managers through different assignments, the managers will be reluctant to participate if managers in some departments receive lower pay. Organizations therefore must weigh all the objectives of their pay structure to arrive at suitable rates.

Pay Grades

A large organization could have hundreds or even thousands of different jobs. Setting a pay rate for each job would be extremely complex. Therefore, many organizations group jobs into **pay grades**—sets of jobs having similar worth or content, grouped together to establish rates of pay. For example, the organization could establish five pay grades, with the same pay available to employees holding any job within the same grade.

A drawback of pay grades is that grouping jobs will result in rates of pay for individual jobs that do not precisely match the levels specified by the market and the organization's job structure. Suppose, for example, that the organization groups together its senior accountants (with a job evaluation of 255 points) and its senior systems analysts (with a job evaluation of 270 points). Surveys might show that the market rate of pay for systems analysts is higher than that for accountants. In addition, the job evaluations give more points to systems analysts. Even so, for simplicity's sake, the organization pays the same rate for the two jobs because they are in the same pay grade. The organization would have to pay more than the market requires for accountants or pay less than the market rate for systems analysts (so it would probably have difficulty recruiting and retaining them).

pay grades
Sets of jobs having similar worth or content, grouped together to establish rates of pay.

Pay Ranges

Usually, organizations want some flexibility in setting pay for individual jobs. They want to be able to pay the most valuable employees the highest amounts and to give rewards for performance, as described in the next chapter. Flexibility also helps the organization balance conflicting information from market surveys and job evaluations. Therefore, pay structure usually includes a **pay range** for each job or pay grade. In other words, the organization establishes a minimum, maximum, and midpoint of pay for employees holding a particular job or a job within a particular pay grade or band. Employees holding the same job may receive somewhat different pay, depending on where their pay falls within the range.

A typical approach is to use the market rate or the pay policy line as the midpoint of a range for the job or pay grade. The minimum and maximum values for the range may also be based on market surveys of those amounts. Figure 9.6 shows an example of pay ranges based on the pay policy line in Figure 9.5. Notice that the jobs are grouped into five pay grades, each with its own pay range. In this example, the range is widest for employees who are at higher levels in terms of their job evaluation points. That is because the performance of these higher-level employees will likely have more effect on the organization's performance, so the organization needs more latitude to reward them. For instance, as discussed earlier, the organization may want to select a higher point in the range to attract an employee who is more critical to achieving the organization's goals.

pay ranges
A set of possible pay rates defined by a minimum, maximum, and midpoint of pay for employees holding a particular job or a job within a particular pay grade or band.

FIGURE 9.6

Sample Pay Grade Structure

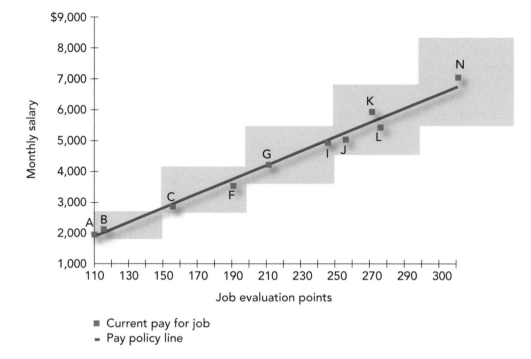

Usually pay ranges overlap somewhat, so that the highest pay in one grade is somewhat higher than the lowest pay in the next grade. Overlapping ranges gives the organization more flexibility in transferring employees among jobs, because transfers need not always involve a change in pay. On the other hand, the less overlap, the more important it is to earn promotions in order to keep getting raises. Assuming the organization wants to motivate employees through promotions (and assuming enough opportunities for promotion are available), the organization will want to limit the overlap from one level to the next.

When the organization develops a pay structure, it may find that a few employees are being paid at rates that are above or below the range for their jobs. For example, an employee with exceptionally high seniority might earn above his range. Rates above the range are often called **red-circle rates.** In some cases, employees earning red-circle rates would receive no pay increases until they receive a promotion or until cost-of-living adjustments raise the pay range to include their pay rate. At the other extreme are **green-circle rates,** that is, rates below the pay range for a job. These employees usually would receive raises when the pay structure is put into practice; otherwise, their current pay rate signals that they are being paid less than their worth to the organization.

red-circle rate
Pay at a rate that falls above the pay range for the job.

green-circle rate
Pay at a rate that falls below the pay range for the job.

LO3

Alternatives to Job–Based Pay

The traditional and most widely used approach to developing a pay structure focuses on setting pay for jobs or groups of jobs.[9] This emphasis on jobs has some limitations. The precise definition of a job's responsibilities can contribute to an attitude that some activities "are not in my job description," at the expense of flexibility, innovation, quality, and customer service. Organizations may avoid change because it requires repeating the time-consuming process of creating job descriptions and related paperwork. Another change-related problem is that when the organization needs a new set of competencies, the existing pay structure may be rewarding the wrong behaviours. Finally, a pay structure that rewards employees for winning promotions may discourage them from gaining valuable experience through lateral career moves.

Organizations have responded to these problems with a number of alternatives to job-based pay structures. Some organizations have found greater flexibility through **broadbanding,** or reducing the number of levels in the organization's job structure. By combining more assignments into a single layer, organizations give managers more flexibility in making assignments and awarding pay increases. These broader groupings often are called *broad bands*. IBM recently changed from a pay structure with 5,000 job titles and 24 salary grades to one with 1,200 jobs and 10 bands. When IBM began using broad bands, it replaced its point-factor job evaluation system with an approach based on matching jobs to descriptions. Broad bands reduce the opportunities for promoting employees, so organizations that eliminate layers in their job descriptions must find other ways to reward employees.

broadbanding
Reducing the number of levels in the organization's job structure.

Another way organizations have responded to the limitations of job-based pay has been to move away from the link to jobs and toward pay structures that reward employees based on their competencies.[10] **Competency-based pay systems** are pay structures that set pay according to the employees' level of skill or knowledge and what they are capable of doing. Paying for competencies makes sense at organizations where changing technology requires employees to continually widen and deepen their knowledge. For example, modern machinery often requires that operators know how to program and monitor computers to perform a variety of tasks. Competency-based pay also supports efforts to involve employees and enrich jobs because it encourages employees to add to their knowledge so they can make decisions in many areas. In this way, competency-based pay helps organizations become more flexible and innovative. More generally, competency-based pay can encourage a climate of learning and adaptability and give employees a broader view of how the organization functions. These changes should help employees use their knowledge and ideas more productively. A field study of a manufacturing plant found that changing to a competency-based pay structure led to better quality and lower labour costs.[11]

competency-based pay systems
Pay structures that set pay according to the employees' levels of skill or knowledge and what they are capable of doing.

Of course, competency-based pay has its own disadvantages.[12] It rewards employees for acquiring skills but does not provide a way to ensure that employees can use their new skills. The result may be that the organization is paying employees more for learning skills that the employer is not benefiting from. The challenge for HRM is to design work so that the work design and pay structure support one another. Also, if employees learn skills very quickly, they may reach the maximum pay level so quickly that it will become difficult to reward them appropriately. Competency-based pay does not necessarily provide an alternative to the bureaucracy and paperwork of traditional pay structures, because it requires records related to skills, training, and knowledge acquired.

Incentive Pay

LO4

The first part of this chapter discussed the framework for total rewards and setting pay for jobs. Now we focus on using pay to recognize and reward employees' contributions to the organization's success.

incentive pay
Forms of pay linked to an employee's performance as an individual, group member, or organization member.

In contrast to decisions about pay structure, organizations have wide discretion in setting performance-related pay, called **incentive pay.** Organizations can tie incentive pay to individual performance, profits, or many other measures of success. They select incentives based on their costs, expected influence on performance, and fit with the organization's broader HR and company policies and goals. These decisions are significant. A study of 150 organizations found that the way organizations paid employees was strongly associated with their level of profitability.[13]

Along with wages and salaries, many organizations offer *incentive pay*—that is, pay specifically designed to energize, direct, or influence employees' behaviour. According to the 2004 Annual Canadian Salary Survey conducted by Watson Wyatt Worldwide, 86 percent of organizations indicated they used short-term incentives in 2003.[14] Incentive pay is influential because the amount paid is linked to certain predefined behaviours or outcomes. For example, an organization can pay a salesperson a *commission* for closing a sale, or the members of a production department can earn a *bonus* for meeting a monthly production goal. Usually, these payments are in addition to wages and salaries. Knowing they can earn extra money for closing sales or meeting departmental goals, the employees often try harder or get more creative than they might without the incentive pay. In addition, the policy of offering higher pay for higher performance may make an organization attractive to high performers when it is trying to recruit and retain these valuable employees.[15]

For incentive pay to motivate employees to contribute to the organization's success, the pay plans must be well designed. According to a recent study by Hewitt Associates, a global HR consulting firm, approximately 83 percent of companies using incentive pay say "this approach is only somewhat successful or not successful at all."[16] In designing incentive pay plans, organizations should consider whether the pay encourages the kinds of behaviour that are most needed, whether employees believe they have the ability and resources to meet the performance standards, and whether they value the rewards and think the pay plan is fair. These principles are summarized in Figure 9.7.

Since incentive pay is linked to particular outcomes or behaviours, the organization is encouraging them to demonstrate those desired outcomes and behaviours. As obvious as that may sound, the implications are more complicated. If incentive pay is extremely rewarding, employees may focus on only the performance measures re-

FIGURE 9.7

Principles of Effective Incentive Pay Plans

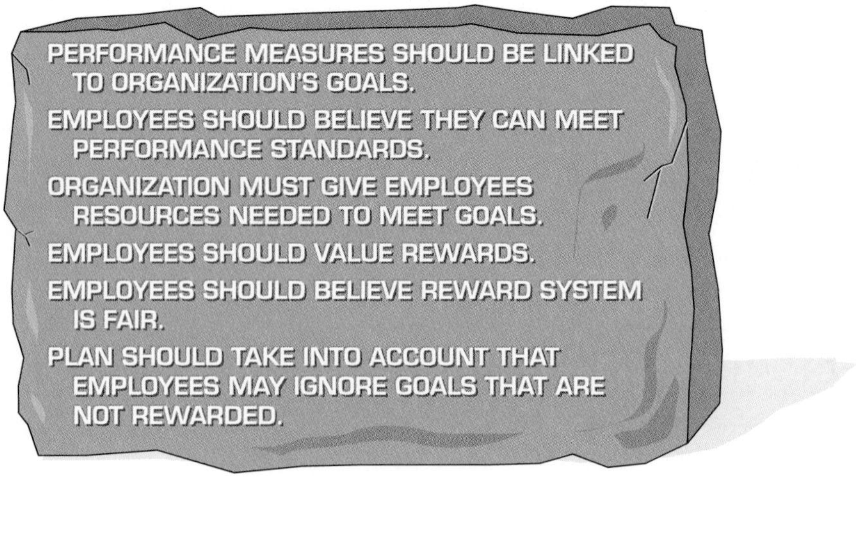

- PERFORMANCE MEASURES SHOULD BE LINKED TO ORGANIZATION'S GOALS.
- EMPLOYEES SHOULD BELIEVE THEY CAN MEET PERFORMANCE STANDARDS.
- ORGANIZATION MUST GIVE EMPLOYEES RESOURCES NEEDED TO MEET GOALS.
- EMPLOYEES SHOULD VALUE REWARDS.
- EMPLOYEES SHOULD BELIEVE REWARD SYSTEM IS FAIR.
- PLAN SHOULD TAKE INTO ACCOUNT THAT EMPLOYEES MAY IGNORE GOALS THAT ARE NOT REWARDED.

warded under the plan and ignore measures that are not rewarded. Suppose an organization pays managers a bonus when employees are satisfied; this policy may interfere with other management goals. A manager who doesn't quite know how to inspire employees to do their best might be tempted to fall back on overly positive performance appraisals, letting work slide in order to keep everyone happy. Similarly, many call centres pay employees based on how many calls they handle, as an incentive to work quickly and efficiently. However, speedy call handling does not necessarily foster good customer relationships. Gallup Organization depends on good relationships to keep the people in its research samples from hanging up on its telephone pollsters, so its incentive pay is based on customer evaluations, rather than number of calls.[17] As we will see in this chapter, organizations may combine a number of incentives so employees do not focus on one measure to the exclusion of others.

Employees must also believe they have the ability and resources to meet the performance standards. For rewards to be motivating, employees have to believe they can earn them. As we will discuss in the section on rewards for organizational performance, this is a challenge in the case of incentives based on an organization's profits or stock price. Employees at lower levels of the organization may doubt that they have much influence over these performance measures. Therefore, these incentives likely will not have much effect on these employees' behaviour, at least in large companies. For the same reason, if organizations want to reward employees for meeting goals, they must give the employees access to the resources needed for meeting those goals. If rewards are tied to customer satisfaction, for example, employees must be engaged to satisfy customers.

Other attitudes that influence the success of incentive pay include whether employees value the rewards and think the pay plan is fair. Most, if not all, employees value pay, but it is important to remember that earning money is not the only reason people try to do a good job. As we have discussed in other chapters (see Chapters 3, 7 and 12), people also want interesting work, appreciation for their efforts, flexibility, and a sense of belonging to the work group—not to mention the inner satisfaction of work well done. Therefore, a complete plan for compensating and rewarding employees has many components, from pay to work design to developing managers so they can exercise positive leadership.

With regard to the fairness of incentive pay, equity theory explains how employees form judgments about the fairness of a pay structure. The same process applies to judgments about incentive pay. In general, employees compare their efforts and rewards with other employees', considering a plan to be fair when the rewards are distributed according to what the employees contribute.

We will now identify elements of incentive pay systems. We consider each option's strengths and limitations with regard to these principles. The many kinds of incentive pay fall into three broad categories: incentives linked to individual, group, or organizational performance. Choices from these categories should consider not only their strengths and weaknesses, but also their fit with the organization's goals. The choice of incentive pay may affect not only the level of motivation, but also the kinds of employees who are attracted to and stay with the organization. For example, there is some evidence that organizations with team-based rewards will tend to attract employees who are more team-oriented, while rewards tied to individual performance make an organization more attractive to those who think and act independently, as individuals.[18]

FIGURE 9.8

Types of Pay for Individual Performance

| Piecework Rates (Straight or Differential) | Standard Hours Plan | Merit Pay | Performance Bonus | Sales Commissions |

Pay for Individual Performance

Organizations may reward individual performance with incentives such as piecework rates, standard hour plans, merit pay, individual bonuses, and sales commissions. These alternatives are summarized in Figure 9.8.

Piecework Rates

As an incentive to work efficiently, some organizations pay production workers a piecework rate, a wage based on the amount they produce. This rate is often paid in addition to employees' base pay. The amount paid per unit is set at a level that rewards employees for above-average production volume. For example, suppose that on average, assemblers can finish ten components in an hour. If the organization wants to pay its average assemblers $8 per hour, it can pay a piecework rate of $8/hour divided by ten components/hour, or $.80 per component. An assembler who produces the average of ten components per hour earns an amount equal to $8 per hour. An assembler who produces 12 components in an hour would earn $.80 × 12, or $9.60 each hour.

In one study, the use of piece rates increased production output by 30 percent—more than any other motivational device evaluated.[19] An obvious advantage of piece rates is the direct link between how much work the employee does and the amount the employee earns. This type of pay is easy to understand and seems fair to many people, if they think the production standard is reasonable. In spite of their advantages, piece rates are relatively rare for several reasons.[20] Most jobs, including those of managers, have no physical output, so it is hard to develop an appropriate performance measure. This type of incentive is most suited for very routine, standardized jobs with output that is easy to measure. For complex jobs or jobs with hard-to-measure outputs, piecework plans do not apply very well. Also, unless a plan is well designed to include performance standards, it may not reward employees for focusing on quality or customer satisfaction if it interferes with the day's output. (See Figure 9.9.)

FIGURE 9.9

How Incentives Sometimes "Work"

SOURCE: DILBERT reprinted by permission of United Features Syndicate, Inc.

Standard Hour Plans

Another quantity-oriented incentive for production workers is the **standard hour plan,** an incentive plan that pays workers extra for work done in less than a preset "standard time." The organization determines a standard time to complete a task, such as tuning up a car engine. If the mechanic completes the work in less than the standard time, the mechanic receives an amount of pay equal to the wage for the full standard time. Suppose the standard time for tuning up an engine is two hours. If the mechanic finishes a tune-up in 1½ hours, the mechanic earns two hours' worth of pay in 1½ hours. Working that fast over the course of a week could add significantly to the mechanic's pay.

In terms of their pros and cons, standard hour plans are much like piecework plans. They encourage employees to work as fast as they can, but not necessarily to care about quality or customer service. Also, they only succeed if employees want the extra money more than they want to work at a pace that feels comfortable.

standard hour plan
An incentive plan that pays workers extra for work done in less than a preset "standard time."

Merit Pay

Almost all organizations have established some program of **merit pay**—a system of linking pay increases to ratings on performance appraisals. (Chapter 7 described the content and use of performance appraisals.) Merit pay is most common for management and professional employees.

An advantage of merit pay is that it provides a method for rewarding performance in all of the dimensions measured in the organization's performance management system. If that system is appropriately designed to measure all the important job behaviours, then the merit pay is linked to the behaviours the organization desires. This link seems logical, although so far there is little research showing the effectiveness of merit pay.[21]

A drawback of merit pay, from the employer's standpoint, is that it can quickly become expensive. Managers at a majority of organizations rate most employees' performance in the top two categories (out of four or five).[22] Therefore, the majority of employees are eligible for the biggest merit increases, and their pay rises rapidly. This cost is one reason that some organizations have established guidelines about the percentage of employees that may receive the top rating, as discussed in Chapter 7.

merit pay
A system of linking pay increases to ratings on performance appraisals.

Another drawback of merit pay is that it makes assumptions that may be misleading. Rewarding employees for superior performance ratings assumes that those ratings depend on employees' ability and motivation. But performance may actually depend on forces outside the employee's control, such as managers' rating biases, the level of cooperation from coworkers, or the degree to which the organization gives employees the authority, training, and resources they need. Under these conditions, employees will likely conclude that the merit pay system is unfair.

Quality guru W. Edwards Deming also criticizes merit pay for discouraging teamwork. In Deming's words, "Everyone propels himself forward, or tries to, for his own good, on his own life preserver. The organization is the loser."[23]

Performance Bonuses

Like merit pay, performance bonuses reward individual performance, but bonuses are not rolled into base pay. The employee must re-earn them during each performance period. In some cases, the bonus is a one-time reward. Bonuses may also be linked to objective performance measures, rather than subjective ratings. Bonuses for individual performance can be extremely effective and give the organization great flexibility in deciding what kinds of behaviour to reward.

Sales Commissions

commissions
Incentive pay calculated as a percentage of sales.

A variation on piece rates and bonuses is the payment of **commissions,** or pay calculated as a percentage of sales. For instance, a furniture salesperson might earn commissions equaling 6 percent of the price of the furniture the person sells during the

Many salespeople in the auto industry earn a straight commission, meaning that 100% of their pay comes from commission instead of a salary. What type of individual might enjoy a job like this?

Using Incentives to Motivate Salespeople

During the recent economic boom, employers scrambled to keep good salespeople by putting together the most generous package of pay and benefits. A thornier problem is how to keep the sales reps motivated when demand slows down and profits tumble. Here are some ideas from several companies.

Set performance goals that are clear and achievable. If salespeople have to fill a quota before they earn a commission or bonus, make sure the quota is realistic for the current economic climate. Or pay an incentive for meeting a fraction of the goal. Provide training to help salespeople meet their quotas.

Establish adjustable goals related to market conditions. *The New York Times* has a "push goal" for its advertising sales force. Teams that meet the goal earn a preset bonus. The size of the goal depends on business conditions. At times, business has been so good that teams have met the push goal before year-end. When that happens, the *Times* creates additional push goals, so there is an incentive to keep selling.

Along with commissions, offer daily and weekly rewards tied to activities. Typical examples are number of customers visited and prospects phoned. These incentives, known as *activity-based pay,* can encourage salespeople to build customer relationships, preparing for a time when they are ready to start spending again. Rewards can be as inexpensive as $20 or lunch at a local restaurant.

Supplement pay incentives with nonpay motivation. Tom Salonek, founder of a software development company called Intertech Software (www.intertechsoftware.com), uses a personal touch. He revived an earlier practice of visiting key customers along with his sales reps, and he starts each day with what he calls a "15-minute huddle." Every morning at 7:25, Salonek and the sales associates dial the company's conference call centre and share their experiences of the day before.

Offer a choice. Business consulting firm Artis & Associates offers bigger potential rewards to salespeople willing to shoulder more of the risk. Salespeople have two alternatives. They can accept a straight commission at a higher rate or a small salary plus commission at a lower rate. The rates are set so that the salespeople on straight commission have the potential to earn more than their colleagues earning a salary.

SOURCE: S. Greco, "Sales: What Works Now," *Inc.*, February 2002, pp. 52–59.

period. Selling a $2,000 sofa would add $120 to the salesperson's commissions for the period. At most organizations today, commissions range from 5 percent to 20 percent of sales.[24] In a growth-oriented organization, sales commissions need not be limited to salespeople. Many of the technical experts at Scientific & Engineering Solutions are eligible for commissions and bonuses tied to the profitability of the sales they help to close. The "HR How To" box provides additional suggestions for incentive pay.

Pay for Group Performance

Employers may address the drawbacks of individual incentives by including group incentives in the organization's compensation plan. To win group incentives, employees must cooperate and share knowledge so that the entire group can meet its performance targets. As shown in Figure 9.10, common group incentives include gainsharing, bonuses, and team awards.

Gainsharing

gainsharing
Group incentive program that measures improvements in productivity and effectiveness and distributes a portion of each gain to employees.

Organizations that want employees to focus on efficiency may adopt a **gainsharing** program, which measures increases in productivity and effectiveness and distributes a portion of each gain to employees. For example, if a factory enjoys a productivity gain worth $30,000, half the gain might be the company's share. The other $15,000 would be distributed among the employees in the factory. Knowing that they can enjoy a financial benefit from helping the company be more productive, employees supposedly will look for ways to work more efficiently and improve the way the factory operates.

Gainsharing addresses the challenge of identifying appropriate performance measures for complex jobs. Even for simpler jobs, setting acceptable standards and measuring performance can be complicated. Gainsharing frees employees to determine how to improve their own and their group's performance. It also broadens employees' focus beyond their individual interests. But in contrast to profit sharing, discussed later, it keeps the performance measures within a range of activity that most employees believe they can influence. Organizations can enhance the likelihood of a gain by providing a means for employees to share knowledge and make suggestions, as we will discuss later in this chapter.

Gainsharing is most likely to succeed when organizations provide the right conditions. Among the conditions identified, the following are among the most common:[25]

- Management commitment.
- Need for change or strong commitment to continuous improvement.
- Management acceptance and encouragement of employee input.
- High levels of cooperation and interaction.
- Employment security.

FIGURE 9.10

Types of Pay for Group Performance

Gainsharing   Bonuses   Team Awards

Happy sales staff look forward to getting their one-time bonus cheques, along with most of The Brick's 5,700 employees across Canada.

- Information sharing on productivity and costs.
- Goal setting.
- Commitment of all involved parties to the process of change and improvement.
- Performance standard and calculation that employees understand and consider fair and that is closely related to managerial objectives.
- Employees who value working in groups.

The Brick, the Edmonton-based furniture chain, recently surprised and delighted its employees by announcing a one-time bonus to almost all of its 5,700 Canadian employees. The bonuses will be based on years of service and were announced by the Brick's chairman, Bill Comrie, "(Comrie) knows its the people around him who helped make him who he is." "He wants all of his team to be winners."[26]

Group Bonuses and Team Awards

In contrast to gainsharing plans, which typically reward the performance of all employees at a facility, bonuses for group performance tend to be for smaller work groups.[27] These bonuses reward the members of a group for attaining a specific goal, usually measured in terms of physical output. Team awards are similar to group bonuses, but they are more likely to use a broad range of performance measures, such as cost savings, successful completion of a project, or even meeting deadlines.

Both types of incentives have the advantage that they encourage group or team members to cooperate so that they

Group members that meet a sales goal or a product development team that meets a deadline or successfully launches a product may be rewarded with a bonus for group performance. What are some advantages and disadvantages of group bonuses?

can achieve their goal. However, depending on the reward system, competition among individuals may be replaced by competition among groups. Competition may be healthy in some situations, as when groups try to outdo one another in satisfying customers. On the downside, competition may also prevent necessary cooperation among groups. To avoid this, the organization should carefully set the performance goals for these incentives so that concern for costs or sales does not obscure other objectives, such as quality, customer service, and ethical behaviour.

Pay for Organizational Performance

Two important ways organizations measure their performance are in terms of their profits and their stock price. In a competitive marketplace, profits result when an organization is efficiently providing products that customers want at a price they are willing to pay. Stock is the owners' investment in a corporation; when the stock price is rising, the value of that investment is growing. Rather than trying to figure out what performance measures will motivate employees to do the things that generate high profits and a rising stock price, many organizations offer incentive pay tied to those organizational performance measures. The expectation is that employees will focus on what is best for the organization.

These organization-level incentives can motivate employees to align their activities with the organization's goals. Linking incentives to the organization's profits or stock price exposes employees to a high degree of risk. Profits and stock price can soar very high very fast, but they can also fall, e.g., Nortel Networks. The result is a great deal of uncertainty about the amount of incentive pay each employee will receive in each period. Therefore, these kinds of incentive pay are likely to be most effective in organizations that emphasize growth and innovation, which tend to need employees who thrive in a risk-taking environment.[28]

Profit Sharing

profit sharing
Incentive pay in which payments are a percentage of the organization's profits and do not become part of the employees' base salary.

Under **profit sharing,** payments are a percentage of the organization's profits and do not become part of the employees' base salary. Organizations use profit sharing for a number of reasons. It may encourage employees to think more like owners, taking a broad view of what they need to do in order to make the organization more effective. They are more likely to cooperate and less likely to focus on narrow self-interests. Also, profit sharing has the practical advantage of costing less when the organization is experiencing financial difficulties. If the organization has little or no profit, this incentive pay is small or nonexistent, so employers may not need to rely as much on layoffs to reduce costs.[29]

An organization setting up a profit-sharing plan should consider what to do if profits fall. If the economy slows and profit-sharing payments disappear along with profits, employees may become discouraged or angry. Consider the case of the Du Pont Fibres Division, which linked a portion of employees' pay to the division's profits.[30] Under the plan, employees' base salary was about 4 percent lower than salaries for similar employees in other Du Pont divisions unless the Fibres Division reached 100 percent of its profit goal. If the division reached its profit goal, its employees' earnings would match that of employees in other divisions; if the division exceeded its profit goal, its employees would earn substantially more. In the first year, the division exceeded its goal, and employees earned slightly more than their counterparts in other divisions. In the next year, profits fell significantly, and employees' pay fell below that of other divisions. The Fibres Division eliminated the profit-sharing plan and returned to the original fixed salaries. One way to avoid this kind of problem is to design profit-sharing plans to reward employees for high profits but not penalize them when profits fall. This solution may be more satisfactory to employees but does not offer the advantage of reducing labour costs without layoffs during economic downturns.

Given the limitations of profit-sharing plans, one strategy is to use them as a component of a pay system that includes other kinds of pay more directly linked to individual behaviour. This increases employees' commitment to organizational goals while addressing concerns about fairness.

Stock Ownership

While profit-sharing plans are intended to encourage employees to "think like owners," a stock ownership plan actually makes employees part owners of the organization. Like profit sharing, employee ownership is intended as a way to encourage employees to focus on the success of the organization as a whole. The drawbacks of stock ownership as a form of incentive pay are similar to those of profit sharing. Specifically, it may not have a strong effect on individuals' motivation. Employees may not see a strong link between their actions and the company's stock price, especially in larger organizations. The link between pay and performance is even harder to appreciate because the financial benefits mostly come when the stock is sold—typically when the employee leaves the organization.

Ownership programs usually take the form of *stock options* or *employee stock ownership plans*. These are illustrated in Figure 9.11.

Stock Options

One way to distribute stock to employees is to grant them **stock options**—the right to buy a certain number of shares of stock at a specified price. (Purchasing the stock is called *exercising* the option.) Suppose that in 2005 a company's employees received options to purchase the company's stock at $10 per share. The employees will benefit if the stock price rises above $10 per share, because they can pay $10 for something (a share of stock) that is worth more than $10. If in 2010 the stock is worth $30, they can exercise their options and buy stock for $10 a share. If they want to, they can sell their stock for the market price of $30, receiving a gain of $20 for each share of stock. Of course, stock prices can also fall. If the 2010 stock price is only $8, the employees would not bother to exercise the options.

stock options
Rights to buy a certain number of shares of stock at a specified price.

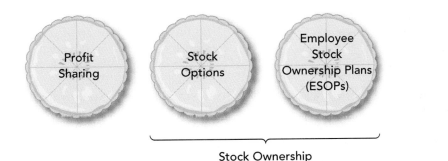

FIGURE 9.11

Types of Pay for Organizational Performance

Traditionally, organizations have granted stock options to their executives. In recent years, many organizations pushed eligibility for options further down in the organization's structure. The share of companies granting stock options to at least half of their employees has grown from less than one-quarter to more than half. Wal-Mart and PepsiCo are among the large companies that have granted stock options to employees at all levels. Stock options were a popular way to lure employees to Internet start-ups during the last decade. Stock values were rising so fast during the 1990s that options were extremely rewarding for a time. But when stock prices tumbled in the current decade, options lost their attractiveness as a way to reward employees at all levels.

Some studies suggest that organizations perform better when a large percentage of top and middle managers are eligible for long-term incentives such as stock options. This evidence is consistent with the idea of encouraging employees to think like owners.[31] It is not clear whether these findings would hold up for lower-level employees. They may see much less opportunity to influence the company's performance in the stock market.

Recent scandals have drawn attention to another challenge of using stock options as incentive pay. As with other performance measures, employees may focus so much on stock price that they lose sight of other goals, including ethical behaviour. Ideally, managers would bring about an increase in stock price by adding value in terms of efficiency, innovation, and customer satisfaction. But there are other, unethical ways to increase stock price by tricking investors into thinking the organization is more valuable and more profitable than it actually is. Hiding losses and inflating the recorded value of revenues are just two of the ways some companies have boosted stock prices, enriching managers until these misdeeds come to light. The bankruptcy of World-Com demonstrated on a massive scale that the short-term benefits of an inflated stock price may not be in a company's long-term best interests. Criticism has also been aimed at Nortel Networks former CEO, John Roth, who received stock option grants that "allowed him to walk away fabulously wealthy while millions of Canadians tossed their retirement plans in the fire."[32]

employee stock ownership plan (ESOP)
An arrangement in which the organization distributes shares of stock to all its employees by placing it in a trust.

Many companies now have an employee stock ownership plan (ESOP). What are some of the benefits and drawbacks of ESOPs?

Employee Stock Ownership Plans

While stock options are most often used with top management, a broader arrangement is the **employee stock ownership plan (ESOP)**. In an ESOP, the organization distributes shares of stock to its employees by placing the stock into a trust managed on the employees' behalf. Employees receive regular reports on the value of their stock, and when they leave the organization, they may sell the stock to the organization or (if it is a publicly traded company) on the open market.

For example, WestJet's Share Purchase Program enables WestJetters to receive up to 20 percent of their salaries in WestJet shares. Shares can be purchased as common shares or can be directed into RRSPs with WestJet matching the employee's contributions.[33]

ESOPs are the most common form of employee ownership. ESOPs raise a number of issues. On the negative side, they carry a significant risk for employees. Problems with the company's performance therefore can take away significant value from the ESOP. Many companies set up ESOPs to hold retirement funds, so these risks directly affect employees' retirement income.

Still, ESOPs can be attractive to employers. Along with tax and financing advantages, ESOPs give employers a way to build pride in and commitment to the organization. Employees have a right to participate in votes by shareholders (if the stock is registered on a national exchange, such as the TSX).[34] This means employees participate somewhat in corporate-level decision making. Still, the overall level of participation in decisions appears to vary significantly among organizations with ESOPs. Some research suggests that the benefits of ESOPs are greatest when employee participation is greatest.[35]

Balanced Scorecard

As the preceding descriptions indicate, any form of incentive pay has advantages and disadvantages. For example, relying exclusively on merit pay or other individual incentives may produce a workforce that cares greatly about meeting those objectives but competes to achieve them at the expense of cooperating to achieve organizational goals. Relying heavily on profit sharing or stock ownership may increase cooperation but do little to motivate day-to-day effort or to attract and retain top individual performers. Because of this, many organizations design a mix of pay programs. The aim is to balance the disadvantages of one type of incentive pay with the advantages of another type.

One way of accomplishing this goal is to design a balanced scorecard—a combination of performance measures directed toward the company's long- and short-term goals and used as the basis for awarding incentive pay. A corporation would have financial goals to satisfy its stockholders (owners), quality- and price-related goals to satisfy its customers, efficiency goals to ensure better operations, and goals related to acquiring skills and knowledge for the future to fully tap into employees' potential. Different jobs would contribute to those goals in different ways. For example, an engineer could develop products that better meet customer needs and can be produced more efficiently. The engineer could also develop knowledge of new technologies, in order to contribute more to the organization in the future. A salesperson's goals would include measures related to sales volume, customer service, and learning about product markets and customer needs. Organizations customize their balanced scorecards according to their markets, products, and objectives. The scorecards of a company that is emphasizing low costs and prices would be different from the scorecards of a company emphasizing innovative use of new technology.

Not only does the balanced scorecard combine the advantages of different incentive-pay plans, it helps employees understand the organization's goals. By communicating the balanced scorecard to employees, the organization shows employees information about what its goals are and what it expects employees to accomplish.

Tellabs, which provides communication service products around the world, uses a balanced scorecard. The company tracks performance measures such as revenue growth, customer satisfaction, time to market for new products, and employee satisfaction.[36] Each department has objectives that support the goals on the scorecard. Every employee has a bonus plan; bonuses are tied to performance as measured by the objectives. The company conducts quarterly meetings at which employees learn how their performance will be evaluated according to the scorecard. The company also makes this information available on its intranet.

Processes That Make Incentives Work

Communication and employee participation can contribute to a belief that the organization's pay structure is fair. In the same way, the process by which the organization creates and administers incentive pay can help it use incentives to create a motivational work environment. The monetary rewards of gainsharing, for example, can substantially improve productivity,[37] but the organization can set up the process to be even more effective. In a study of an automotive parts plant, productivity rose when the gainsharing plan added employee participation in the form of monthly meetings with managers to discuss the gainsharing plan and ways to increase productivity. A related study asked employees what motivated them to participate actively in the plan (for example, by making suggestions for improvement). According to employees, other factors besides the pay itself were important—especially the ability to influence and control the way their work was done.[38]

Participation in Decisions

Employee participation in pay-related decisions can be part of a general move toward employee involvement. If employees are involved in decisions about incentive pay plans and employees' eligibility for incentives, the process of creating and administering these plans can be more complex.[39] There is also a risk that employees will make decisions that are in their interests, at the expense of the organization's interests. However, employees have hands-on knowledge about the kinds of behaviour that can help the organization perform well, and they can see whether individuals are displaying that behaviour.[40] Therefore, in spite of the potential risks, employee participation can contribute to the success of an incentive plan. This is especially true when monetary incentives encourage the monitoring of performance and when the organization fosters a spirit of trust and cooperation.

Providing Employee Benefits and Services

Hewitt Associates signals to its employees that it cares about them, body, mind, and spirit. Employees participate in plans that help them pay for medical, dental, and vision care expenses, stop-smoking programs, and care expenses for sick children. Employees who travel on business can receive reimbursement for overnight dependant care and overnight care for their pets. Employees enjoy paid time off for vacations and holidays, plus additional "Splash" time off in their fifth year of service and every five years after that. Through the LifeWorks referral service, Hewitt employees can find help with family, education, legal, and financial issues. A tuition reimbursement program pays 85 percent of employees' tuition for approved courses. The company also encourages employees to participate in charitable activities. Employees who wish to volunteer time in their communities can recive up to two days of paid time off. These and other benefits attract qualified employees and keep them loyal to Hewitt.[41]

Like Hewitt's employees, employees at almost every organization receive more than dollars and cents in exchange for their efforts. They also receive a package of **employee benefits and services**—compensation in forms other than cash. Besides the use of corporate fitness centres, examples include paid vacation time, employer-paid health insurance, and pension plans, among a wide range of possibilities.

The following section describes the content of an employee benefits and services package and the way organizations administer these employee benefits and services. We begin by discussing the important role of benefits as a part of employee compensation.

employee benefits and services
Compensation in forms other than cash.

The Role of Employee Benefits and Services

LO5

As a part of the total rewards provided to employees, benefits and services serve functions similar to pay. Benefits contribute to attracting, retaining, and motivating employees. Different employees look for different types of benefits and services. Employers need to examine their benefits and services package regularly to see whether they still meet employees' needs and expectations. At the same time, benefits packages are more complex than pay structures, so benefits are harder for employees to understand and appreciate. Even if employers spend large sums on benefits and services, if employees do not understand how to use them or why they are valuable, the cost of the benefits will be largely wasted.[42] Employers need to communicate effectively so that the benefits succeed in motivating employees.

Employees have come to expect that benefits will help them maintain economic security. Canada Pension/Quebec Pension, company pension plans, and retirement savings plans help employees prepare for their retirement. Insurance plans help to protect employees from unexpected costs such as prescription drugs. This important role of benefits is one reason that some benefits are subject to government regulation. Benefits, such as Employment Insurance, are required by law.

Even though many kinds of benefits are not required by law, they have become so common that today's employees expect them. Many employers find that attracting qualified workers requires them to provide health and retirement benefits of some sort. A large employer without such benefits would be highly unusual and would have difficulty competing in the labour market. A 2004 national survey conducted by Ipsos-Reid found that Canadian employees value their health benefits: "72 percent of 1503 Canadians polled, said they would choose their plan over annual payments of up to $8,000."[43] However, health benefit costs are a concern to Canadian employers. The Conference Board of Canada recently reported that health benefits in 2003 represented over 6 percent of payroll, up from 3.2 percent in 1990.[44]

Like other forms of compensation and rewards, benefits impose significant costs. The number one concern of Canadian employee benefit specialists, according to Deloitte's *Top five benefit priorities for 2004*, is managing the health and welfare costs of benefits plans. This has been the top concern for each of the past five years the survey has been conducted. Besides the direct costs of offering the plan, other cost concerns include providing for the coverage of new prescription drugs, maintaining some form of cost-sharing with employees, and educating employees to value and use available plans effectively.[45] An organization managing its labour costs must pay careful attention to the cost of its employee benefits.

Overall, employers are concerned about balancing various issues related to benefits and services provided to employees. Several forces have made benefits and services a significant part of compensation packages. One is that laws require employers to provide certain benefits, such as contributions to Canada Pension Plan and Employment Insurance. Also, tax laws can make benefits favourable. For example, employees do not pay income taxes on most benefits they receive, but they pay income taxes on cash compensation. Therefore, an employee who receives a $1,000 raise "takes home" less than the full $1,000, but an employee who receives an additional $1,000 worth of benefits receives the full benefits. Another cost advantage of paying benefits is that employers, especially large ones, often can get a better deal on insurance or other programs than employees can obtain on their own. Finally, some employers assemble creative benefits packages that set them apart in the competition for talent. Examples include Hewitt Associates, described in the Introduction, and CUETS, described in a case at the end of this chapter.

LO6

Benefits and Services Required by Law

Governments require various forms of security to protect workers from the financial hardships of being out of work. In general, the Canada Pension Plan/Quebec Pension Plan provides support for retired workers, Employment Insurance assists workers who are unemployed involuntarily, and workers' compensation provides benefits and services to workers injured on the job. Employers must also provide unpaid leave for certain family and medical needs. Because these benefits are required by law, employers cannot gain an advantage in the labour market by offering them, nor can they design the nature of these benefits. Rather, the emphasis must be on complying with the details of the law.

Canada Pension Plan (CPP)/Quebec Pension Plan (QPP)
A contributory, mandatory plan that provides retirement pensions, disability benefits, and survivor benefits.

Canada Pension Plan (CPP)/Quebec Pension Plan (QPP)

The **Canada Pension Plan (CPP)** and the **Quebec Pension Plan (QPP)** (in Quebec), were established in 1966 and cover all workers in Canada that are age 18 and older and have annual income exceeding $3,500. CPP/QPP is a mandatory **contributory plan** that provides retirement pensions, disability benefits, and survivor benefits.

contributory plan
All costs of the plan are funded by employees, employers, and the plan's own investments.

Workers who meet eligibility requirements receive the retirement benefits according to their age and earnings history. If they elect to begin receiving benefits at age 65, they can receive full benefits, or if eligible to begin receiving benefits at age 60, they receive benefits at a permanently reduced level. For example, if the individual elects to commence their pension at age 60, they will receive 30 percent less than they would receive if they started receiving their pension at age 65. In 2004, the maximum monthly CPP benefit was $814.17.

Employment Insurance (EI)
A federally mandated program to provide temporary financial assistance to unemployed Canadians.

Employment Insurance (EI)

Employment Insurance (EI) provides temporary financial assistance to unemployed workers who have lost their jobs through no fault of their own, while they look for another job or upgrade their skills. Coverage is also extended to eligible workers who are sick, are pregnant, or are caring for a newborn or adopted child. In addition, EI can assist employees when they are caring for a gravely ill family member.

Workers' Compensation

Decades ago, workers who suffered work-related injury or illness had to bear the cost unless they won a lawsuit against their employer. Those who sued often lost the case because of the defences available to employers. Today, the provinces have passed **Workers' Compensation Acts**, which help workers with the expenses resulting from job-related accidents and illnesses.[46] These laws operate under a principle of *no-fault liability*, meaning that an employee does not need to show that the employer was grossly negligent in order to receive compensation, and the employer is protected from lawsuits. The employer loses this protection if it intentionally contributes to a dangerous workplace. The benefits fall into three major categories:

Workers' compensation laws are intended to protect the incomes of workers injured on the job, without the workers having to sue or the employers having to admit responsibility.

1. Wage loss benefits
2. Medical services
3. Rehabilitative services

Compensation varies from province to province but is typically 80 percent of the worker's earnings before the disability. The benefits are tax free, however, the person receiving the benefits must report them to the Canada Revenue Agency.

Workers' compensation is entirely funded by employers—neither workers nor the government contribute. The amount employers pay depends on the industry and kinds of occupations involved as well as the size of the employer's payroll. Organizations can minimize the cost of this benefit by keeping workplaces safe and making employees and their managers conscious of safety issues, as discussed in Chapter 2. Benefits continue as long as the employee is unable to work.

Workers' Compensation Acts
Provincial programs that provide benefits to workers who suffer work-related injuries or illnesses.

Optional Benefits Programs

Other types of benefits are optional. These include various kinds of insurance, retirement plans, and paid leave. Part-time workers often receive fewer benefits than full-time employees. The most widely offered benefits are paid leave for vacations and holidays (that exceed the legally required minimums specified in Employment/Labour Standards legislation), life and medical insurance, and retirement plans. In general, benefits packages at smaller companies are more limited than at larger companies. The extent to which the employer pays for the benefit varies widely among organizations. Some organizations require employees to pay a significant percentage of the premiums for insurance plans such as dental coverage. Other organizations pick up 100 percent of the premiums.

Benefits such as health insurance usually extend to employees' dependants. Today, to ensure an employer does not face a charge of discrimination where the relevant jurisdiction includes sexual orientation and/or marital status as a protected ground of discrimination, employers cover domestic partners. Typically, a domestic partner is an adult non-relative who lives with the employee in a relationship defined as permanent and financially interdependent.

As organizations continue to contain the increasing costs of providing employee benefits a variety of alternatives may be considered. As outlined in Table 9.2 many Canadian organizations are considering increasing employee contributions (premiums) or increasing deductibles and/or requiring co-payment of associated costs. Microsoft Corp. recently made changes to its benefits package including reduction in stock purchase discounts, annual vacation cuts, and changes to the drug benefit plan.[47] According to Wendy Poirier, a consultant at Towers Perrin in Calgary, "companies across North America are cutting employee benefits as part of a survival strategy adopted to cope with a tough economy."[48]

Paid Leave

Employment/Labour Standards legislation outlines minimum vacation entitlements and paid holidays. Many employers provide vacation and holidays in addition to the minimum legislated requirements. Some organizations also offer additional days off for personal reasons or to contribute their time to a charitable organization.

Sick leave programs pay employees for days not worked because of illness. The amount of sick leave is often based on length of service, so that it accumulates over time—for example, one day added to sick leave for each month of service. Employers must decide how many sick days to grant and whether to let them continue accumulating year after year. If sick days accumulate without limit, employees can "save" them in case of disability. If an employee becomes disabled, the employee can use up the accumulated sick days, receiving full pay rather than smaller payments from disability insurance, discussed later. Some employers let sick days accumulate for only a year, and unused sick days "disappear" at year-end. This may provide an unintended incentive to use up sick days. Some healthy employees may call in sick near the end of the year so that they can obtain the benefit of the paid leave before it disappears. Employers may counter this tendency by paying employees for some or all of their unused sick days at year-end or when the employees retire or resign.

An organization's policies for time off may include other forms of paid and unpaid leave. For a workforce that values flexibility, the organization may offer paid *personal days*, days off that employees may schedule according to their personal needs, with the supervisor's approval. Typically, organizations offer a few personal days in addition to sick leave. *Floating holidays* are paid holidays that vary from year to year. The organization may schedule floating holidays so that they extend a Tuesday or Thursday

TABLE 9.2

Keeping the Lid on Benefits

Respondents from survey of 130 Canadian organizations were asked what cost reduction measures they are using or considering. The following table provides their answers, in percentages:

BENEFIT	IN 2004	BEING CONSIDERED	NOT BEING CONSIDERED
Eliminated or reduced coverage	7	15	78
Increased employee contributions	20	18	62
Increased deductible and/or co-payments	17	18	65
Implementation or expansion of a disability management program	14	21	65

SOURCE: Hewitt Associates, "HR's Cost Control," *Canadian HR Reporter*, May 31, 2004, p. 2.

holiday into a long weekend. Organizations may also give employees discretion over the scheduling of floating holidays. Employers should establish policies for leaves without pay—for example, leaves of absence to pursue nonwork goals or to meet family needs. Unpaid leave is an employee benefit because the employee usually retains seniority and benefits during the leave.

Group Insurance

As we noted earlier, rates for group insurance are typically lower than for individual policies. Also, insurance benefits are not subject to income tax, as wages and salaries are. When employees receive insurance as a benefit, rather than higher pay so they can buy their own insurance, employees can get more for their money. Because of this, most employees value group insurance. The most common types of insurance offered as employee benefits are medical, life, and disability insurance.

Medical Insurance

For many employees, the most important benefit is medical insurance. The policies typically cover medical expenses that are incurred over and above provincially funded medical coverage. Some employers offer additional coverage, such as dental care, vision care, and prescription drug programs.

Organizations' health benefit costs rose to more than 6 percent of payroll in 2003 up from 3.2 percent of payroll in 1990. Much of the increase is due to soaring prescription drug costs and organizations are facing heavy resistance from employees (and unions) when considering or implementing cost-containment measures.[49] Some organizations are passing the rising costs of health care premiums to consumers. In 2004, Starbucks Corp. raised their prices by US 11 cents a cup in North America, the first increase since August 2000, citing higher costs for coffee and health insurance as the reason for the increase.[50]

Health Spending Accounts. Another alternative to traditional employer-provided insurance is a **health spending account**, also known as a medical savings account, in which an employer puts aside a specific amount of money per employee to cover health-related costs. Employees decide what health care services they will purchase with their allocation. Major insurers, such as Great-West Life, administer the health spending account, usually for a fixed percentage fee. Health spending accounts are particularly attractive to small companies because the cost to the employer for employee benefits and administration is capped.[51]

health spending account
A specific amount of money set aside per employee by the employer to cover health-related costs.

Wellness Programs. Another way to lower the cost of health insurance is to reduce employees' need for health care services. Employers may try to do this by offering an **employee wellness program,** a set of communications, activities, and facilities designed to change health-related behaviours in ways that reduce health risks. Typically, wellness programs aims at specific health risks, such as high blood pressure, high cholesterol levels, smoking, and obesity, by encouraging preventive measures such as exercise and good nutrition. However, many organizations are adopting an integrated strategic approach to wellness that promotes a corporate culture to support employees in taking responsibility for their health and overall wellness. "It is about providing employees with the tools to give them control," notes Suzanne Fergusson, a corporate

employee wellness program
A set of communications, activities, and facilities designed to change health-related behaviours in ways that reduce health risks.

Dofasco Inc. operates a 100-acre recreational facility park in Hamilton, Ontario for employees, retirees, and their families. These facilities include double NHL-size ice surfaces, a twin gymnasium complex, track, golf driving range, mini-putt, tennis courts, kids' playground, and baseball diamonds. Can you think of other organizations that offer other unique benefits and services?

health and wellness specialist with Ottawa-based MDS Nordion.[52]

Organizations that place a strategic emphasis on corporate wellness achieve economic benefits including reduced injury and disability insurance costs, enhanced productivity and service, and reduced costs due to a reduction in employee absenteeism and turnover.[53]

Wellness programs are either passive or active. Passive programs provide information and services, but no formal support or motivation to use the program. Examples include health education (such as lunchtime courses) and fitness facilities. These programs are passive because they rely on employees to identify the services they need and act on their own to obtain the services, such as participating in classes. Active wellness programs assume that behaviour change requires support and reinforcement along with awareness and opportunity. These programs provide for outreach and follow-up. For example, the program may include counsellors who tailor programs to individual employees' needs, take baseline measurements (for example, blood pressure and weight), and take follow-up measures for comparison to the baseline. Active programs often set goals and provide symbolic rewards as individuals make progress toward meeting their goals. In general, passive health education programs cost less than active wellness programs.[54] All these variations have had success in reducing risk factors associated with cardiovascular disease (obesity, high blood pressure, smoking, lack of exercise), but the follow-up method is most successful.

Life Insurance

Employers may provide life insurance to employees or offer the opportunity to buy coverage at low group rates. With a *term life insurance* policy, if the employee dies during the term of the policy, the employee's beneficiaries receive a payment called the death benefit. In policies purchased as an employee benefit, the usual death benefit is twice the employee's yearly pay. The policies may provide additional benefits for accidental death and dismemberment. Along with a basic policy, the employer may give employees the option of purchasing additional coverage, usually at a nominal cost.

Disability Insurance

Employees risk losing their incomes if a disability makes them unable to work. Disability insurance provides protection against this loss of income. Typically, **short-term disability insurance** provides benefits for six months or less. **Long-term disability insurance** provides benefits after that initial period, potentially for the rest of the disabled employee's life. Disability payments are a percentage of the employee's salary—typically 50 to 70 percent. Payments under short-term plans may be higher. Often the policy sets a maximum amount that may be paid each month. Because its limits make it more affordable, short-term disability coverage is offered by more employers. Fewer than half of employers offer long-term plans. An additional key issue facing disability management programs is the increasing number of multiple issue (psychological and medical) claims, resulting in increased organizational costs.

In planning an employee benefits package, the organization should keep in mind that CPP and QPP includes some long-term disability benefits. To manage benefits costs, the employer should ensure that the disability insurance is coordinated with CPP/QPP and any other programs that help workers who become disabled.

Retirement Plans

Employers have no obligation to offer retirement plans beyond the protection of CPP/QPP security, but most offer some form of pension or retirement savings plan. About half of employees working for private businesses (that is, nongovernment jobs) have employer-sponsored retirement plans. These plans are most common for higher-earning employees. Among employees earning the top one-fifth of incomes, almost three-quarters have a pension plan, and about one out of six employees in the bottom fifth have pensions.[55] Retirement plans may be **contributory plans,** meaning they are funded by contributions from the employer and employee, or **noncontributory plans,** meaning all the contributions come from the employer. As illustrated in Figure 9.12, 88 percent of organizations offer at least one type of pension plan, and many offer both.

Defined Benefit Plans

Employers have a choice of using retirement plans that define the amount to be paid out after retirement or plans that define the amount the employer will invest each year. A defined benefit plan guarantees a specified level of retirement income. Usually the amount of this defined benefit is calculated for each employee based on the employee's years of service, age, and earnings level (for example, the average of the employee's five highest-earnings years). These calculations typically result in pension payments that may provide 70 percent of pre-retirement income for a long-service employee. Using years of service as part of the basis for calculating benefits gives employees an incentive to stay with the organization as long as they can, so it can help to reduce voluntary turnover.

For employees under federal legislation, defined benefit plans must meet the funding requirements of the Pension Benefits Act for employees under federal legislation. With a defined benefit plan, the employer sets up a pension fund to invest the contributions. The employer and/or employee must contribute enough for the plan to cover all the benefits to be paid out to retirees. Defined benefit plans are intended to protect employees from the risk that the pension fund will not earn as much as expected. If the pension fund earns less than expected, the employer is required to make

short-term disability insurance
Insurance that pays a percentage of a disabled employee's salary as benefits to the employee for six months or less.

long-term disability insurance
Insurance that pays a percentage of a disabled employee's salary after an initial period and potentially for the rest of the employee's life.

contributory plan
Retirement plan funded by contributions from the employer and employee.

noncontributory plan
Retirement plan funded entirely by contributions from the employer.

defined benefit plan
Pension plan that guarantees a specified level of retirement income.

FIGURE 9.12

Defined Benefit Pension Plans Still as Prevalent as Defined Contribution Pension Plans

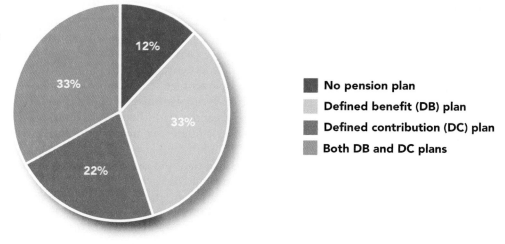

- ■ **No pension plan**
- □ **Defined benefit (DB) plan**
- ■ **Defined contribution (DC) plan**
- ■ **Both DB and DC plans**

SOURCE: Conference Board of Canada, Compensation Planning Outlook, 2004 in "On the Charts," *Canadian HR Reporter*, May 31, 2004, p. G5.

up the difference from other sources. However, a recent study warns that six out of ten defined benefit pension plans in Canada are under-funded, with $160 billion needed to cover the shortfall. For example, both Air Canada and Stelco Inc. have recently faced significant shortfalls.[56]

Defined Contribution Plans

defined contribution plan
Retirement plan in which the employer sets up an individual account for each employee and specifies the size of the investment into that account.

An alternative to defined benefits is a **defined contribution plan,** which sets up an individual account for each employee and specifies the size of the investment into that account, rather than the amount to be paid out upon retirement. The amount the retiree receives will depend on the account's performance. These plans free employers from the risks that investments will not perform as well as expected. They put the responsibility for wise investing squarely on the shoulders of each employee. A defined contribution plan is also easier to administer. Considering the advantages to employers, it is not surprising that a growing share of retirement plans are defined contribution plans, especially at relatively small organizations.

When retirement plans make individual employees responsible for investment decisions, the employees need information about retirement planning. Retirement savings plans often give employees much control over decisions about when and how much to invest.

Defined contribution plans also offer an advantage to employees in today's highly mobile workforce. They do not penalize employees for changing jobs. With these plans, retirement earnings are less related to the number of years an employee stays with a company.

phased retirement
A gradual transition into full retirement by reducing hours or job responsibility.

An additional issue facing employers' approaches to retirement plans is a growing interest in **phased retirement**, a gradual transition into full retirement by reducing hours or job responsibility.[57] Employers are facing an increasing demand for phased retirement programs from employees, however regulatory barriers such as mandatory retirement age laws pose barriers to implementation.

Family-Friendly Benefits and Services

As employers have recognized the inportance of employees' need to balance their work and outside commitments including the care of family members, pursuit of education, personal development, and volunteer activities, many have implemented "family-friendly" HR practices. Options such as flextime and telework were discussed in Chapter 3. In addition, some organizations provide benefits and services including child and/or elder care, maternity leave top-up, and adoption assistance. For example, The University Health Network, Canada's largest health care employer provides on-

Many organizations provide an extensive range of family friendly benefits and services. What types of benefits and services would help to alleviate stress at the workplace?

site subsidized day care, top-up to 75 percent of salary for the first 25 weeks of maternity leave, telecommuting, and flextime.[58] Ernst & Young LLP's family friendly benefits include access to a nearby daycare facility onsite, maternity leave salary top up for 100 percent for the first 17 weeks of leave, and adoption benefits of up to $5,000 per child in addition to telecommuting, flextime, and reduced summer hours.[59]

Statistics Canada recently released the results of the study related to the "sandwich generation"—approximately 712,000 Canadians with the dual responsibility of raising children and providing care for aging parents or relatives. Due to the aging of the baby boomers and their delay in having children the sandwich generation is expecting to grow, resulting in increased stress and demands on employees.[60] Some employers have responded by providing benefits and services including access to counselling, flexible schedules, referral services, and access to information and other resources available in the community or region.

The value of these family-friendly benefits accrue to not only employees but to employers as well in the form of increased productivity, enhanced commitment, and reduced stress.[61]

An organization should not take lightly the decision to staff its own child-care facility. Such an operation is costly and involves important liability concerns. At the same time, the results of this type of benefit, in terms of reducing absenteeism and enhancing productivity, have been mixed. Some organizations have simply offered day care to follow a trend in employee benefits, rather than to address the needs of specific employees.[62] One large North American corporation found that less than 2 percent of its workforce used a flexible spending account the company offered as its main child-care benefit. Organizations can avoid such wasted benefits by conducting a thorough needs analysis before selecting programs to offer.[63] The "Best Practices" box describes CIBC's (and other organizations') approach to providing backup child care.

Other Benefits

The scope of possible employee benefits is limited only by the imagination of the organization's decision makers. Figure 9.13 outlines emerging benefits expected to be the most popular over the next few years. Organizations have developed a wide vari-

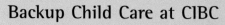
Backup Child Care at CIBC

Over the past decade, progressive Canadian employers have been providing benefits to help parents balance their work and family responsibilities. According to Human Resources and Skills Development Canada, the number of employer-supported child-care centres in Canada nearly doubled between 1991 and 2000. Yet most employers are still reluctant to get involved with child-care benefits. However, some employers are providing backup child care as an alternative to investing in full-time regular child-care centres. Backup services are available for employees when their primary or regular child care is unavailable, when schools are closed, during maternity/paternity transition or when there is an increase in work demands. Backup child care enables employers to provide a less-expensive, high-impact service while receiving a significant return on investment. Absences due to personal and family responsibilities are two to three times higher among employees with preschool children under six years, according to Statistics Canada figures. Backup child care is a solution to such absenteeism and the employee stress it creates.

Two years ago, CIBC opened Canada's first dedicated backup child-care centre located at company headquarters in downtown Toronto. Recently, the backup child-care centre was identified as an innovative benefit by the Canadian Association for Mental Illness, which honoured CIBC with the Mental Health in the Workplace Award. CIBC's backup centre is free to employees, and CIBC reported they saved more than 2,500 days of absenteeism in 2003 because of the centre.

Other organizations provide backup child care within existing full-time centres. At Husky Injection Molding Systems, parents needing emergency or temporary child care can contact the firms' on-site child-care centre to access a space. Another alternative for delivering backup child care is the use of drop-in care centres, for example, VanCity, British Columbia's credit union, purchased a space at a child-care centre near its head office for employees to use in emergencies, or to provide in-home emergency care.

The business case for employer-supported backup child-care solutions is solid. When employees can be at work, focused, stress-free, and guilt-free they are more committed, more engaged and more satisfied.

SOURCE: John Marvin and Nora Spinks, "Backup Child Care: Canada's New Employee Benefit," *Canadian HR Reporter*, November 8, 2004, p. 19.

ety of benefits to meet the needs of employees and to attract and keep the kinds of workers who will be of value to the organization. Traditional extras include subsidized cafeterias, on-site health care for minor injuries or illnesses, and moving expenses for newly hired or relocating employees. Stores and manufacturers may offer employee discounts on their products.

To encourage learning and attract the kinds of employees who wish to develop their knowledge and skills, many organizations offer *tuition reimbursement* programs. A typical program covers tuition and related expenses for courses that are relevant to the employee's current job or future career at the organization. Employees are reimbursed for these expenses after they demonstrate they have completed an approved course.

Especially for demanding, high-stress jobs, organizations may look for benefits that help employees put in the necessary long hours and alleviate stress. Recreational ac-

FIGURE 9.13

Emerging Benefits

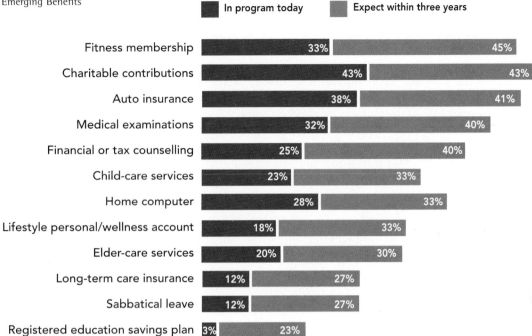

SOURCE: Hewitt Associates, "Happy Shareholders, Happy Employees," *Canadian HR Reporter*, February 10, 2004, p. G9.

tivities such as on-site basketball courts or company-sponsored softball teams provide for social interaction as well as physical activity. Ernst and Young LLP offers employees who are working out of town for extended periods access to video conferencing for virtual family get-togethers.[64]

Selecting Employee Benefits

Although the government requires certain benefits, employers have wide latitude in creating the total benefits package they offer employees.[65] Decisions about which benefits to include should take into account the organization's goals, its budget, and the expectations of the organization's current employees and those it wishes to recruit in the future. Employees have come to expect certain things from employers. An organization that does not offer the expected benefits will have more difficulty attracting and keeping talented workers. Also, if employees believe their employer feels no commitment to their welfare, they are less likely to feel committed to their employer.

Organization's Objectives

A logical place to begin selecting employee benefits is to establish objectives for the benefits package. This helps an organization select the most effective benefits and monitor whether the benefits are doing what they should. Unfortunately, research suggests that most organizations do not have written benefits objectives.

Intuit Canada, the Edmonton-based company that develops small business, accounting, and tax software, Quicken, offers employees a set of benefits intended to attract and retain loyal and high-performing employees. The bottom line for Glenn McGillvray, senior human resources specialist at Intuit, is attracting and retaining the best people. "Top notch people in any specific field have a lot of choices. So we want to make sure we are the choice they're going to make and this is the type of place they want to work."[66] McGillivray adds that turnover is low at Intuit, "fluctuating between 3 and 6 percent."[67] Intuit Canada picks up 100 percent of most health and benefit plan premiums, offers stock options and an employee stock purchase plan, pays 100 percent of Alberta Health Care Benefit premiums, reimburses home Internet access, supplies interest free loans to purchase computer equipment, includes towel service in the on-site gym and fitness centre, and provides nap rooms.[68]

Employees' Expectations and Values

To meet employees' expectations about benefits and services, it can be helpful to see what other organizations offer. Employers should also consider that the value employees place on various benefits is likely to differ from one employee to another. At a broad level, basic demographic factors such as age and sex can influence the kinds of benefits employees want. An older workforce is more likely to be concerned about

E-HRM

Instant Information at Everyone's Fingertips— Canada Post

Canada Post has 70,000 employees spread across every province and territory. Until recently, Canada Post had been using a home-grown technology system that was only accessible by a handful of HR professionals. Line managers had no instant access to basic information on their employees. If a manager needed to know how many vacation days a particular employee was entitled to, he/she usually had to pick up the phone or navigate an unfriendly, unreliable patchwork of systems.

Now Canada Post is on the leading edge of HR technology.

One of the most useful features of the new system at Canada Post is self-service for both employees and managers. Through self-service, Canada Post has been able to decentralize its HR data collection and maintenance, putting information at the fingertips of every employee.

Managers can now access everything about the organization on their computers, including:

- How much employees are being paid
- What leave days employees have
- What benefits they are entitled to

With self-service, every employee across the country can log on to:

- Change an address
- Change banking information
- View benefits entitlement
- View vacation time

Canada Post employees can access self-service through computers at work or through their home Internet connection.

SOURCE: Todd Humber, "Through Wind, and Sleet and the Internet," *Guide to HR Technology—Supplement to Canadian HR Reporter*, November 8, 2004, pp. G1, G8.

(and use) medical coverage, life insurance, and pensions. A workforce with a high percentage of employees in their 20s–40s may care more about disability or family leave. Young, unmarried men and women often place more value on pay than on benefits. However, these are only general observations; organizations should check which considerations apply to their own employees and identify more specific needs and differences. One approach is to use surveys to ask employees about the kinds of benefits they value. The survey should be carefully worded to not raise employees' expectations by seeming to promise all the benefits asked about at no cost to the employee.

The choice of benefits may influence current employees' satisfaction and may also affect the organization's recruiting, in terms of both the ease of recruiting and the kinds of employees attracted to the organization.

Flexible Benefits

Organizations can address differences in employees' needs and engage their employees by offering **flexible benefits plans** in place of a single benefits package for all employees. These plans, often called flexible benefits or "flex benefits," offer employees a set of alternatives from which they can choose the types and amounts of benefits they want. The plans vary. Some impose minimum levels for certain benefits, such as health care coverage; some allow employees to receive money in exchange for choosing a "light" package; and some let employees pay extra for the privilege of receiving more benefits. For example, some plans let employees give up vacation days for more pay or to purchase extra vacation days in exchange for a reduction in pay.

Flexible benefits plans have a number of advantages.[69] The selection process can make employees more aware of the value of the benefits, particularly when the plan assigns each employee a sum of money to allocate to benefits. Also, the individual choice in a flexible benefits plan enables each employee to match his or her needs to the company's benefits, increasing the plan's actual value to the employee. Superior Propane, a Calgary-based Canadian marketer of propane and appliances, switched to a flex benefits plan for its 1,800 employees. Terry Gill, vice-president of human resources, says that Superior Propane changed to flex benefits to "attract a more diverse group of employees to fit in with our new performance-based culture. We realized that most employees wanted opportunity and choice—a 'one-size-fits-all' plan wouldn't work."[70]

A drawback of flexible benefits plans is that they have a higher administrative cost, especially in the design and start-up stages. Organizations can avoid some of the higher cost, however, by using software packages and standardized plans that have been developed for employers wishing to offer flexible benefits. Another possible drawback is that employee selection of benefits will increase rather than decrease costs because employees will select the kinds of benefits they expect to need the most. For example, an employee expecting to need a lot of dental work is more likely to sign up for a dental plan. The heavy use of the dental coverage would then drive up the employer's premiums for that coverage. Costs can also be difficult to estimate when employees select their benefits. Organizations frequently respond by requiring employees to share in the costs of benefits.

flexible benefits plan
A benefits plan that offers employees a set of alternatives from which they can choose the types and amounts of benefits they want.

Communicating Total Rewards to Employees   LO7

"Communication is often a weak link. An average program well-communicated will do better than an outstanding program poorly communicated."[71] A comprehensive communications strategy is required to help employees understand the total value the organization is investing in its approach to compensating and rewarding employees. This is essential so that total rewards can achieve their objectives including focusing employees on organizational goals, attracting and retaining employees, and creating a motivating environment.

Because they interact with their employees each day, managers play a significant role in communication The HR department should prepare them to explain to their employees why the organization's approach to compensating and rewarding employees is designed as it is and to determine whether employee concerns indicate a need for change. Employees are interested in their compensation and rewards and they need a great deal of detailed information. It follows that technology such as the Internet and supporting databases can play a significant role. More employers are using technology to provide employees with tools and information related to both communication and administration of employee compensation and rewards. According to a recent survey, 56 percent of employers communicate benefit plan details to employees online, up from 30 percent in 2001.[72] The "E-HRM" feature discusses how Canada Post is using technology to provide employees with information related to compensation and rewards.

In fact, employees and job applicants often lack a clear sense of the market value of total rewards that an organization offers. For example, research asking employees about their benefits has shown that employees significantly underestimate the cost and value of their benefits.[73] Probably a major reason for their lack of knowledge is a lack of communications from employers. When New Brunswick Power teamed up with its union to communicate the benefits of the move to a flexible benefits plan, the objective was to "get the message out to workers that this was their plan, they owned it, and they needed to get an understanding of how it worked." The company provided training sessions, and gave every employee a video to take home and watch and discuss with their families. Employees' move to flex benefits was optional. In the first year of implementation 18 percent of employees had elected flex benefits, by 2003, 68 percent of employees had made the transition.[74]

Employers have many options for communicating information about benefits. To increase the likelihood that employees will receive and understand the messages, employers can combine several media, such as videos, brochures, question-and-answer meetings, online total rewards statements, intranet pages, memos, presentations, and email. An investment of creativity in employee communication can reap great returns in the form of committed, satisfied employees, and the achievement of organizational objectives.

LO8

Executive Compensation and Rewards

The media have drawn public attention to the issue of executive compensation and rewards. The issue attracts notice because of the very high pay that the top executives of major North American companies have received in recent years. A significant part of executive compensation comes in the form of company stock. For example, Peter Godsoe, recently retired chairman of the Bank of Nova Scotia, received $1.35 million in salary and a $2.6 million bonus in his final year with the company. In total, however, he will have amassed approximately $122 million worth of shares and securities in the company after 37 years of service. In addition, he will receive an annual pension of $2.5 million.[75]

Although high amounts like this apply to only a small proportion of the total workforce, the issue of executive pay is relevant to pay structure in terms of equity theory.

Overall, executive compensation and rewards are complicated due to the increased number of items included, e.g., direct pay, short and long-term incentives, stock options, as well as benefits and services. As a result, many senior executives ask financial experts to help them compare the value of their total compensation when considering employment offers.[76] Top executives help to set the tone or culture of the organization, and employees at all levels are affected by behaviour at the top. As a result, the equity of executive compensation and rewards can affect more employees than, say, equity among warehouse workers or sales clerks. Labour leaders also express concerns about perceived inequities in executive pay relative to employees. For example, CAW, the union representing CN employees, cited high executive pay as a contributing factor to a recent strike that saw striking employees receive a 3 percent annual wage increase.[77]

Executive Incentives

Because executives have a much stronger influence over the organization's performance than other employees do, incentive pay for executives warrants special attention. Assuming that incentives influence performance, decisions about incentives for executives should have a great impact on how well the executives and the organization perform. Along with overall pay levels for executives, organizations need to create incentive plans for this small but important group of employees.

To encourage executives to develop a commitment to the organization's long-term success, executive compensation often combines short-term and long-term incentives. *Short-term incentives* include bonuses based on the year's profits, return on investment, or other measures related to the organization's goals. Sometimes, to gain tax advantages, the actual payment of the bonus is deferred (for example, by making it part of a retirement plan). *Long-term incentives* include stock options and stock purchase plans. The rationale for these long-term incentives is that executives will want to do what is best for the organization because that will cause the value of their stock to grow.

According to a recent study released by Watson Wyatt Worldwide, "CEOs of high-performing Canadian companies earned significantly more compensation than their counterparts at low-performing organizations."[78] This study concluded that a strong link exists between an organization's financial performance and executive compensation. Companies that provided above median increases in total direct compensation for executives (i.e., base salary plus annual bonuses, and long-term incentives including stock option rewards) also "provided significantly higher performance for their shareholders."[79]

However, although the Royal Bank of Canada missed several key performance goals, Gord Nixon, chief executive still received $7.75 million in compensation (salary, incentive payments, and additional benefits) in 2004. Although his bonus was cut by 18 percent to $1.35 million from $1.65 million from the previous year, Mr. Nixon's salary reportedly increased 16 percent to $1.36 million from $1.15 million.[80] Scott Hand, chief executive of Inco Ltd., the world's second largest producer of nickel, made $6.1 million in 2003. Mr. Hand's total 2003 compensation included approximately $853,000 in salary and benefits and $1.3 million in bonuses and incentives. The balance came from cashing in stock options during a year when Inco's stock rose 87 percent due to high prices for nickel.[81]

A corporation's shareholders—its owners—want the corporation to encourage managers to act in the owners' best interests. They want managers to care about the company's profits and stock price, and incentive pay can encourage this interest. One way to achieve these goals is to tie a large share of executives' pay to performance. Another study has found that relying on such long-term incentives is associated with greater profitability.[82] In Canada, 96 percent of companies offer their executives stock options.[83]

Performance Measures for Executives

The balanced-scorecard approach is useful in designing executive pay. Whirlpool, for example, has used a balanced scorecard that combines measures of whether the organization is delivering value to shareholders, customers, and employees. These measures are listed in Table 9.3. Similarly, at Eastman Kodak, the CEO's bonus has been based on the satisfaction of shareholders, customers, and employees. In one year, for example, only shareholder satisfaction received a "strong" rating relative to the year before, so chief executive George Fisher's annual bonus was reduced by $290,000. However, Fisher's total compensation was mostly based on stock options, so it remained high, at $5.5 million. The next year Fisher agreed to a new contract that tied even more of his bonus to the three criteria.[84]

Regulators and shareholders have pressured companies to do a better job of linking executive pay and performance. The Ontario Securities Commission requires companies to disclose executive compensation levels and the company's performance relative to that of compensation.[85] These reporting requirements shine a light on situations where executives of poorly performing companies receive high pay, so companies feel more pressure to link pay to performance.

Ethical Issues

Incentive pay for executives lays the groundwork for significant ethical issues. When an organization links pay to its stock performance, executives need the ethical backbone to be honest about their company's performance even when dishonesty or clever shading of the truth offers the tempting potential for large earnings. As recent scandals involving WorldCom, Enron, Nortel Networks, and other companies have shown, the results can be disastrous when unethical behaviour comes to light.

Among these issues is one we have already touched on in this chapter: the difficulty of setting performance measures that encourage precisely the behaviour desired.

TABLE 9.3

Balanced Scorecard for Whirlpool Executives

TYPE OF VALUE CREATION	MEASURES
Shareholder value	Economic value added
	Earnings per share
	Cash flow
	Total cost productivity
Customer value	Quality
	Market share
	Customer satisfaction
Employee value	High-performance culture index
	High-performance culture deployment
	Training and development diversity

SOURCE: E. L. Gubman, *The Talent Solution* (New York: McGraw-Hill, 1998).

In the case of incentives tied to stock performance, executives may be tempted to inflate the stock price in order to enjoy bonuses and valuable stock options. Although four Nortel executives are returning cash bonuses worth US $8.6 million, they are keeping lucrative stock options received when corporate profits were over-stated.[86]

A related issue when executive pay includes stock or stock options is insider trading. When executives are stockholders, they have a dual role as owners and managers. This places them at an advantage over others who want to invest in the company. An individual, a pension fund, or other investors have less information about the company than its managers do—for example, whether product development is proceeding on schedule, whether a financing deal is in the works, and so on. An executive who knows about these activities could therefore reap a windfall in the stock market by buying or selling stock based on knowledge about the company's future. Although regulators place strict limits on this "insider trading," some executives have violated these limits. In the worst cases executives have sold stock, secretly knowing their company was failing, before the stock price collapsed. The losers are the employees, retirees, and other investors who hold the now-worthless stock.

As recent news stories have reminded us, linking pay to stock price can reward unethical behaviour, at least in the short term and at least in the minds of a handful of executives. Yet, given the motivational power of incentive pay, organizations cannot afford to abandon incentives for their executives. These temptations are among the reasons that executive positions demand individuals who maintain high ethical standards.

As well as legally required benefits and the benefits extended to other employees in the organization, executives often receive extra benefits and services. These executive benefits and services may include such far-reaching benefits as use of corporate aircraft, company-provided or subsidized homes, memberships and tickets to sporting and cultural events, in addition to benefits such as company cars, cellphones, home computers, PDAs, sabbaticals, and extended vacations. For example, at Price Waterhouse Coopers, partners receive an extra three weeks of vacation every fifth year.[87]

Summary

1. Discuss how organizations implement a "total rewards" approach to compensating and rewarding employees.
   Many organizations are recognizing the strategic value of taking a comprehensive approach to compensating and rewarding employees. This "total rewards" approach frequently involves creating a value proposition for current and prospective employees that clearly identifies direct compensation elements such as base pay and incentives; indirect compensation such as benefits and services; and relational components including learning and development and the work environment itself. Canadian companies take a total rewards approach to attract and retain valued employees and improve capacity to meet organizational goals.

2. Identify the kinds of decisions and influences involved in providing base pay to employees.
   Organizations make decisions to define a job structure, or relative pay for different jobs within the organization. They establish relative pay for different functions and different levels of responsibility for each function. Organizations must also establish pay levels, or the average paid for the different jobs. These decisions are based on the organization's goals, market data, legal requirements, and principles of fairness. Together job structure and pay level establish a pay structure policy.

   Organizations typically begin with a job evaluation to measure the relative worth of their jobs. A job evaluation committee identifies each job's compensable factors and rates each factor. The organization then creates a pay structure that includes pay grades or pay ranges for each job in the organization.

3. Describe alternatives to job-based pay.
   To obtain more flexibility, organizations may reduce the levels in the organization's job structure. This process of delayering or broadbanding involves creating broad bands of jobs within pay ranges. Other organizations reward employees according to their com-

petencies. They establish competency-based pay systems, or structures that set pay according to the employees' level of knowledge and what they are capable of doing. This encourages employees to be more flexible and adapt to changing technology. However, if the organization does not also provide systems in which employees can apply new skills, it may be paying them for skills they do not actually use.

4. Describe how organizations recognize individual, team, and organizational performance through the use of incentives.

Incentive pay is tied to individual performance, profits, or other measures of success. Organizations select forms of incentive pay to energize, direct, or influence employees' behaviour. Employees must value the rewards, have the resources they need to meet the standards, and believe the pay plan is fair. Organizations may recognize individual performance through such incentives as piecework rates, merit pay, sales commissions, and bonuses for meeting individual performance objectives. Common group incentives include gainsharing, bonuses, and team awards. Incentives for meeting organizational objectives include profit sharing and stock ownership.

5. Discuss the role of benefits and services as a part of employee total rewards.

Like pay, benefits and services help employers attract, retain, and provide a source of motivation for employees. The variety of possible benefits and services also helps employers tailor their offerings to attract the right types of employees. Employees expect at least a minimum level of benefits, and providing more than the minimum helps an organization compete in the labour market. Benefits and services are also a significant expense, but employers provide benefits and services because employees value them and many are required by law.

6. Summarize the types of employee benefits and services offered by employers.

Employers must contribute to the Canada Pension Plan/Quebec Pension Plan, Employment Insurance, and Workers' Compensation. In addition, employers offer various kinds of insurance, retirement plans, and paid leave. Due to the increasing costs of providing employee benefits, many Canadian organizations are seeking ways to hold back the costs. Many employers have responded to work–life role conflicts by offering family-friendly benefits. Organizations need to establish objectives and select benefits that support those objectives. Flexible benefits are a means to give employees control over the benefits they receive.

7. Discuss the importance of effectively communicating the organization's approach to total rewards.

A comprehensive communications strategy is needed to help employees understand and value all the components in an organization's approach to total rewards. Managers and the human resource department share responsibility for this important requirement. Technology can provide employees access to information and other tools associated with administration of compensation and rewards. Employers have many options for communicating information about total rewards including online or printed rewards statements, presentations, videos, meetings, brochures, intranets, memos, and email. Using a combination of media increases employees' understanding.

8. Discuss issues related to compensating and rewarding executives.

Executive compensation has drawn public scrutiny because top executive compensation is much higher than average workers' pay. Chief executive officers have an extremely large impact on the organization's performance, but critics complain that when performance falters, executive pay does not decline as fast as the organization's profits or stock price. In addition, executive pay usually combines long-term and short-term incentives as well as additional benefits and services not provided to all employees. Incentives and additional benefits and services should be motivating but also meet standards for equity. Performance measures should encourage behaviour that is in the organization's best interests, including ethical behaviour. Executives need to follow ethical standards that prevent them from engaging in insider trading or deceptive practices designed to manipulate the organization's stock price.

Review and Discussion Questions

1. Some individuals evaluate prospective employers' job offers based only on direct pay considerations. What additional factors should be considered when evaluating job offers from employers?

2. Why might an organization choose to pay employees more than the market rate? Why might it choose to pay less? What are the consequences of paying more or less than the market rate?

3. What are the advantages of establishing pay ranges, rather than specific pay levels, for each job? What are the drawbacks of this approach?

4. Suppose a small start-up business wants to establish a competency-based pay structure? What would be some advantages of this approach? List the issues the company should be prepared to address in setting up this system. Consider the kinds of information you will need and the ways employees may react to the new pay structure.

5. With some organizations and jobs, pay is primarily wages or salaries, and with others, incentive pay is more important. For each of the following jobs, state whether you think the pay should emphasize base pay (wages and salaries) or incentive pay (bonuses, profit sharing, and so on). Give a reason for each.
   a. An accountant at a manufacturing company
   b. A salesperson for a software company
   c. A mechanic for a major airline

6. Why do some organizations link incentive pay to the organization's overall performance? Is it appropriate to use stock performance as an incentive for employees at all levels? Why or why not?

7. Why do employers provide employee benefits, rather than providing all compensation in the form of pay and letting employees buy the services they want?

8. Of the benefits discussed in this chapter, list the ones you consider essential, i.e., the benefits you would require in any job offer. Why are these benefits important to you?

9. Why is it important to communicate information about total rewards? Suppose you work in the HR department of a company that has decided to add new elements to its total rewards—dental and vision care plus an increased budget to support learning and development opportunities for all employees. How would you recommend communicating this change? What information should your messages include?

10. Do you think executive compensation is too high? Why or why not?

What's Your HR IQ? www.mcgrawhill.ca/college/noe

The Online Learning Centre offers more ways to check what you've learned so far. Find experiential exercises as well as Test Your Knowledge Quizzes, Videos, and many other resources at www.mcgrawhill.ca/college/noe.

Excalibur Case: Smith Rubber

EXCALIBUR

Located in the Eastern Townships region of Quebec, Smith Rubber grew from a small family-owned business into a medium-sized company. The organization is now facing a great deal of competition within Quebec and across North America. Its success has always been tied to its ability to compete with Japanese and Mexican companies that also supply the automobile industry.

Steve Smith Jr. is now president of Smith Rubber. At the time of his promotion some years ago, the company was not unionized. During this period he wondered how to best recognize employees and reward their performance while encouraging them to increase productivity. He hesitated about increasing wages because he feared losing his competitive edge if his fixed costs rose.

Three years ago, Smith Rubber had a particularly good year in terms of sales and profits. As a result, Steve thought that a Christmas bonus would be the best way to reward employees. In fact, he told David Sanders, his human resource manager, "There is nothing like cold hard cash to make employees work harder." He set out his bonus system as follows:

Compensation	Bonus
$30,000 and under	$2,500
$30,001–$35,000	$3,000
$35,001–$40,000	$3,500
$40,001–$45,000	$4,000
$45,001–$50,000	$4,500
$50,001 or higher	10% of salary

The bonuses were a hit. Many employees thanked the president personally. Moreover, in February, David Sanders received many positive comments from supervisors, saying that employees were working harder.

The following year there was a slump in the automobile industry, and competitors abroad made dramatic cuts in their costs by using robots in their assembly lines. It was difficult for Smith Rubber to compete and sales dropped by 5 percent, while profits plunged by 15 percent. Steve decided he could not offer the same bonuses as the previous year. The company, therefore, set out the following plan:

Compensation	Bonus
$30,000 and under	$1,250
$30,001–$35,000	$1,500
$35,001–$40,000	$1,750
$40,001–$45,000	$2,000
$45,001–$50,000	$2,250
$50,001 or higher	5% of salary

This time around, David Sanders did not receive any favourable comments from supervisors on the subject of increased productivity. In fact, he asked Jim Rolland, a supervisor, how employees had reacted.

Jim: To tell you the truth, morale is low. Many people worked hard this year. Some of them were hoping to get the same bonus, or even more. So they bought Christmas presents with the old bonus in mind. When they got the letter from the president telling them that he had cut their bonuses in half, they were in a sour mood and lost their motivation. Some of my employees have never been so unproductive.

David: But that's not right. We never even had bonuses before. They should have been happy just getting something this year.

Jim: That's not how they see it.

David Sanders decided that he would not discuss the matter with Steve for fear of upsetting him.

Eleven months passed, bringing increased stagnation. Sales were steady, but not on par with the levels of previous years. Profits were modest, and the board of directors cut the dividend. On December 1, Steve had a meeting with David and told him, "David, I don't know how I can pay out any bonuses this year. Do you think we can hold back without damaging the morale of our troops?"

Note: This case study was used in the 17th edition (2003) of *Excalibur, The Canadian University Tournament of Human Resources*.

SOURCE: Richard Matte, CHRP, Matte groupe conseil, www.rhri.org/excalibur.

Questions

You are David Sanders:

1. What would you advise Steve Smith to do? (two lines)

2. What are the pros and cons of the proposed bonus plan? (at least three)

3. What would have been the right approach from the outset of the plan? (no more than five lines)

Case: Wellness Program Symbolic for Saskatchewan Company

For the first 14 years of its corporate existence dating back to 1981, Regina-based CUETS focused on the challenges of bringing competitive and reliable electronic transaction services, including a complete MasterCard product suite, to a ready cardholder market within the national credit union system. During this time, technology issues were central to the business strategy and most of the other key components of a well-developed organization were in the developmental stages. The organization was typical of many successful start-ups, with a strong entrepreneurial bent and record of growth, reaching 100 employees and $25 million in annual revenue.

With the appointment of new CEO Stan Kuss in 1995, attention turned to developing the organizational infrastructure, establishing a partnership relationship with a distribution network of 500 credit unions, and gaining ground in the increasingly competitive product development, marketing, and sales areas. The first strategic plan was entitled "A Bias for Action," a precursor to a pronounced cultural shift in the organization.

From the outset, Kuss recognized the human resources infrastructure was almost non-existent, and the few policies, programs and processes that were in place were not well aligned with the organization's strategic direction. Among these was a seldom used wellness program that provided services in fitness, weight loss, smoking cessation, and nutrition counselling. The most commonly cited flaw of the program was that it involved converting accumulated sick leave hours into credits, which could be used for YMCA memberships. To reach the level required for an annual membership, a person needed to accumulate the equivalent of four years of sick-free employment, which for most people would take seven to eight years. In a rapidly growing company with many new employees this was, in effect, saying that the vast majority would not be eligible for several years. Demographically, the average age within the organization was in the low 30s, with 70 percent of the workforce female.

Acting on the feedback from employee opinion surveys, Kuss had the program redesigned, with the express direction to remove the barriers to participation. The new program featured some improvements to nutrition counselling, weight loss and smoking cessation services, and major changes to the support provided for physical fitness.

Starting on their first day, each employee was now eligible for a company-paid YMCA membership, provided he or she made the commitment to use the YMCA facilities at least four times each month. As well, individual fitness assessments were also provided and corporate funding was made available to support various company sports teams and events.

"The feedback was outstanding, both from relative newcomers and longtime employees. To many, it signalled a change in the way management viewed its human resources, especially since these changes were made on the heels of a number of other progressive policy changes," recalls Kuss.

Since that time, the program has flourished along with the company, usage is high, and prospective new employees often cite the wellness program as one key attraction to working at CUETS. To many, it's not about the actual program—the wellness program is simply an indicator that the company is progressive and prepared to make strong investments in its workforce.

Still, the program is not without its critics, says Kuss. "Some employees oppose the 'use it or lose it' program feature, which we consider necessary to ensure the program meets its objectives. Some others believe other fitness facilities—and a myriad of other past time endeavours that could be deemed 'wellness'—should also be covered."

Kuss is also cognizant of the growing cost of the program. "We've got 500 employees now and usage continues to rise, so what started as a relatively small commitment is now an investment of more than $60,000 annually."

SOURCE: Robert Lane, vice-president, Human Resources and Corporate Support, CUETS.

Questions

1. Is the new wellness program design aligned with the company's strategic direction?
2. When designing employee benefits, how do you decide to invest in one area such as wellness versus making additional investment in base salaries, variable compensation, or other total compensation elements such as insured benefits?
3. What are some of the challenges that might emerge if the company decided to take a broader view of "wellness" in its funding commitments?
4. If you could give advice to Stan Kuss, what changes, if any, would you recommend? Why?

CBC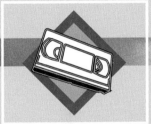
VIDEO CASE

Work–Life Balance

CBC *Venture* explores a crisis in the Canadian workforce—a crisis that is costly to business in terms of absenteeism, health costs, and lost productivity. Canadians are under more stress than ever. From children to work to parents—the list of Canadians' responsibilities is growing—and so are workers' stress levels. A major study, "Voice of Canadians," represents the views of 33,000 Canadians from coast-to-coast and reveals that Canada's workforce is cracking under the strain of balancing work, family, and lifestyle responsibilities. For example, more employees are working 50-hour weeks, health care benefit costs are growing, and absenteeism is a $3-billion annual drain on the Canadian economy.

There is some hope that corporate Canada is waking up to the costs of over-work and is recognizing that finding balance between work and life is a way to attract and retain employees. However, concerns are expressed that although many organizations talk about human capital and the importance of balancing work and family, disconnects between words and actions exist in many organizations.

SOURCE: Based on "Work–Life Balance," CBC *Venture* 863, January 19, 2003.

QUESTIONS

1. What concerns did employees express about using the family-friendly benefits and services offered by employers?
2. Do you expect to utilize employer-provided family-friendly benefits and services during your career? Why or why not?
3. Describe the work environment at Davies-Howe Partners, the law firm in the video. How does the work environment contribute to the success of their law firm? How important is work environment relative to pay and incentives when choosing an employer? Why?

Part 5

Meeting Other HR Goals

Chapter **10**

Collective Bargaining and Labour Relations

What Do I Need to Know? After reading this chapter, you should be able to:

1. Define unions and labour relations and their role in organizations.
2. Identify the labour relations goals of management, labour unions, and society.
3. Summarize laws and regulations that affect labour relations.
4. Describe the union organizing process.
5. Explain how management and unions negotiate collective agreements.
6. Summarize the practice of collective agreement administration.
7. Describe more cooperative approaches to labour-management relations.

Introduction

Wal-Mart Canada Corp. dealt a decisive blow to union forces, announcing it will shut down the first Wal-Mart store to successfully certify in North America in almost a decade. "We honestly were hoping we could avoid this—it's a sad day for us," Wal-Mart spokesperson Andrew Pelletier said of the decision to shutter the four-year-old outlet in Jonquiere, Que., which the retailer says was losing money. "Despite nine days of meeting with the union over more than a three-month period, we have been unsuccessful in reaching an agreement that would allow the store to operate efficiently and, ultimately, profitably."

Six applications for union certification at Wal-Mart Canada stores are pending or under appeal in three provinces

"We're all in shock," said one employee reached the next day at the Jonquiere store. Michael Fraser, the United Food and Commercial Workers Union president, was not available for comment. The store's 190 workers will be offered "generous" severance packages and career counselling," Mr. Pelletier said.

While the big-box giant has never before closed a store in this country for economic reasons, the news does not come as a surprise. The announcement of the closure of the Jonquiere store was the latest event in a longstanding fight between the world's biggest retailer and unions determined to organize the corporation's workers throughout North America. Wal-Mart insists it does not promote an anti-union agenda. "We bargained in good faith," Mr. Pelletier said.

However, union organizers and some industry analysts say otherwise. "Wal-Mart, like a lot of other companies with a non-unionized workforce, is scared to death of unions," said David Abella, an analyst at New-York based Rochdale Investment Management. Even if they could manage that store with the union, it could lead to a domino effect across Canada and the United States. The UFCW scored a minor victory recently when a Saskatchewan appeal overturned a decision barring the province's labour board from accessing internal Wal-Mart documents, among them one titled, "Wal-Mart: A Manager's Tool Box to Remaining Union-Free." Jonquiere's certification was viewed as a big win for the UFCW, one that has not been realized since 1996, when the Ontario Labour Relations Board unionized a Wal-Mart in Windsor, Ontario. The store was later decertified after a high-profile campaign by anti-union employees, which included allegations of union misconduct.

"Shutting down the Jonquiere store for any reason is completely legal," said Anil Verna, a professor of industrial relations at the University of Toronto. "Any business can open or close as they see fit. Most of the time it is about whether the operations are profitable or not. In this case, the timing kind of looks suspicious, but not knowing the numbers for the store, it's difficult to make a conclusive inference that [unionization] had anything to do with it."[1]

This chapter explores human resource activities in organizations where employees belong to unions or where employees are seeking to organize unions. We begin by formally defining unions and labour relations, then describe the history and scope and impact of union activity. We next summarize government laws and regulations affecting unions and labour relations. The following three sections detail types of activities involving unions: union organizing, collective agreement negotiation, and collective agreement administration. Finally, we identify ways in which unions and management are working together in arrangements that are more cooperative than the traditional labour-management relationship.

LO1

Role of Unions and Labour Relations

In Canada today, most workers act as individuals to select jobs that are acceptable to them and to negotiate pay, benefits, flexible hours, and other work conditions. Especially when there is stiff competition for labour and employees have hard-to-replace skills, this arrangement produces satisfactory results for most employees. At times, however, workers have believed their needs and interests do not receive enough consideration from management. One response by workers is to act collectively by forming and joining labour **unions,** organizations formed for the purpose of representing their members' interests and resolving conflicts with employers.

Unions have a role because some degree of conflict is inevitable between workers and management.[2] For example, managers can increase profits by lowering workers' pay, but workers benefit in the short-term if lower profits result because their pay is higher. Still, this type of conflict is more complex than a simple trade-off, such as wages versus profits. Rising profits can help employees by driving up profit sharing or other benefits, and falling profits can result in layoffs and a lack of investment. Although employers can use programs like profit sharing to help align employee interests with their own, some remaining divergence of interests is inevitable. Labour unions represent worker interests and the collective bargaining process provides a way to manage the conflict. In other words, through systems for hearing complaints and negotiating agreements, unions and managers resolve conflicts between employers and employees.

As unionization of workers became more common, universities and colleges developed training in how to manage union-management interactions.[3] This specialty, called **labour relations,** emphasizes skills that managers and union leaders can use to foster effective labour-management cooperation, minimize costly forms of conflict (such as strikes), and seek win-win solutions to disagreements. Labour relations involves three levels of decisions:[4]

1. *Labour relations strategy*—For management, the decision involves whether the organization will work with unions or develop (or maintain) nonunion operations. This decision is influenced by outside forces such as public opinion and competition. For unions, the decision involves whether to resist changes in how unions relate to the organization or accept new kinds of labour-management relationships.

2. *Negotiating contracts*—As we will describe later in the chapter, collective agreement negotiations in a union setting involve decisions about pay structure, job security,

unions
Organizations formed for the purpose of representing their members' interests in dealing with employers.

labour relations
Field that emphasizes skills managers and union leaders can use to minimize costly forms of conflict (such as strikes) and seek win-win solutions to disagreements.

work rules, workplace safety, and many other issues. These decisions affect workers' and the employer's situation for the term of the contract.

3. *Administering collective agreements*—These decisions involve day-to-day activities in which union members and the organization's managers may have disagreements. Issues include complaints of work rules being violated or workers being treated unfairly in particular situations. A formal grievance procedure is typically used to resolve these issues.

Later sections in this chapter describe how managers and unions carry out the activities connected with these levels of decisions, as well as the goals and legal constraints affecting these activities.

National and International Unions

Most union members belong to a national or international union. Figure 10.1 shows the membership of the largest national unions in Canada. Half of these have memberships of over 200,000 workers.

These unions may be either craft or industrial unions. The members of a **craft union** all have a particular skill or occupation. Examples include the International Brotherhood of Electrical Workers for electricians and the United Brotherhood of Painters and Allied Trades for painters. Craft unions are often responsible for training their members through apprenticeships and for supplying craft workers to employers. For example, an employer would send requests for electricians to the union, which would decide which electricians to send out. In this way, craft workers may work for many employers over time but have a constant link to the union. A craft union's bargaining power depends greatly on its control over the supply of its workers.

In contrast, **industrial unions** consist of members who are linked by their work in a particular industry. Examples include the United Steelworkers of America and the Communications Energy and Paperworkers Union of Canada. Typically, an industrial union represents many different occupations. Membership in the union is the result of working for a particular employer in the industry. Changing employers is less common than it is among craft workers, and employees who change employers remain members of the same union only if they happen to move to other employers covered by that union. Another difference is that whereas a craft union may restrict the number of skilled crafts people—say, carpenters—to maintain higher wages, industrial unions try to organize as many employees in as wide a range of skills as possible.

Most national unions are affiliated with the **Canadian Labour Congress (CLC).** The CLC is not a labour union but an association that seeks to advance the shared interests of its member unions

craft union
Labour union whose members all have a particular skill or occupation.

industrial union
Labour union whose members are linked by their work in a particular industry.

Canadian Labour Congress (CLC)
An association that seeks to advance the shared interests of its member unions at the national level.

Kenneth Georgetti, president of the Canadian Labour Congress (CLC), works with his organization to improve the lives of working families and to bring economic justice to the workplace. Most national unions are affiliated with the CLC.

FIGURE 10.1

Largest Unions in Canada and their Affiliations

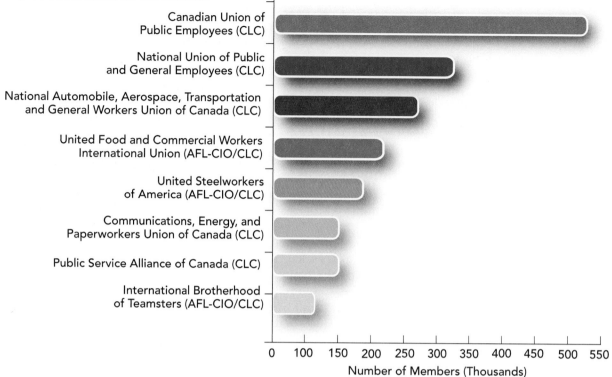

SOURCE: Social Development Canada website, www.sdc.gc.ca/asp/gateway.asp?hr=en/lp/wid/06union_member. Retrieved: November 5, 2004. Reproduced with the permission of the Minister of Public Works and Government Services, 2005.

at the national level, much as the Chamber of Commerce does for its member employers. Approximately 3 million workers are affiliated with the CLC. An important responsibility of the CLC is to represent labour's interests in public policy issues such as labour law, social equality, economic policy, and occupational safety and health. The organization also provides information and analysis that member unions can use in their activities. Some international unions, e.g., International Brotherhood of Teamsters are also associated with the **American Federation of Labor and Congress of Industrial Organizations (AFL-CIO)**, which advances member interests at the international level, i.e., headquartered in the U.S. but with members in Canada.

American Federation of Labor and Congress of Industrial Organizations (AFL-CIO)
An association that seeks to advance the shared interests of its member unions at the international level.

Local Unions

Most national unions consist of multiple local units. Even when a national union plays the most critical role in negotiating the terms of a collective bargaining agreement, negotiation occurs at the local level for work rules and other issues that are locally determined. In addition, administration of the agreement largely takes place at the local union level. As a result, most day-to-day interaction between labour and management involves the local union.

Membership in the local union depends on the type of union. For an industrial union, the local may correspond to a single large facility or to a number of small facilities. In a craft union, the local may cover a city or a region.

Typically, the local union elects officers, such as president, vice-president, and treasurer. The officers may be responsible for contract negotiation, or the local may form a bargaining committee for that purpose. When the union is engaged in bargaining, the national union provides help, including background data about other settlements, technical advice, and the leadership of a representative from the national office.

Individual members participate in local unions in various ways. At meetings of the local union, they elect officials and vote on resolutions to strike. Most of workers' contact is with the **union steward,** an employee elected by union members to represent them in ensuring that the terms of the agreement are enforced. The union steward helps to investigate complaints and represents employees to supervisors and other managers when employees file grievances alleging contract violations.[5] When the union deals with several employers, as in the case of a craft union, a *business representative* performs some of the same functions as a union steward. Because of union stewards' and business representatives' close involvement with employees, it is to management's advantage to cultivate positive working relationships with them.

union steward
An employee elected by union members to represent them in ensuring that the terms of the collective agreement are enforced.

History and Trends in Union Membership

Labour unions have existed in Canada as early as 1812. Unionism in Canada had early ties to Britain, as tradesmen active in the British trade union movement immigrated to Canada and settled in the Maritimes. The first national labour organization, a forerunner of the Canadian Labour Congress, was formed in 1873. During the early 1900s labour activities escalated as workers demanded better wages, shorter workdays, and improved working conditions. Strikes involving large numbers of workers were frequent, with the Winnipeg General Strike in 1919 being one of the largest. As labour politics developed, unionization was supported by the Co-operative Commonwealth Federation (CCF Party), which later became the New Democratic Party (NDP). Collective bargaining was first recognized in 1937. Post-World War II, U.S. unions began to spread into Canada and influenced Canada's labour legislation. Unionization levels continued to grow in both the private and public sectors until the mid 1990s despite pressures on unions that labour costs had not kept pace with productivity.[6]

Union membership in Canada peaked in 1994, reaching 36.1 percent of employees.[7] The total number of unionized employees has increased from 2.8 million in 1977 to over 4 million in 2003,[8] however, this growth did not keep up with increased employment. As a result, the rate of unionization has gradually declined to 31.1 percent of employees.[9]

As illustrated in Figure 10.2, union membership is concentrated in public-sector jobs (70 percent), and education, health care, and social services (62 percent). Manufacturing is also highly unionized. Among the least unionized sectors are retail trade (16 percent), financial services (9 percent) and the food and accommodation industry (9 percent).

Figure 10.3 on page 317 illustrates the significant variation in rates of union membership among the provinces. Quebec (40 percent) and Newfoundland (39 percent) have the highest rates of unionization. Alberta (24 percent) and Ontario (28 percent) have the lowest rates of union density. Unionization also varies by firm size. Unionization is the most common in large organizations.

The decline in union membership has been attributed to several factors.[10] The factor that seems to be cited most often is change in the structure of the economy. Much recent job growth has occurred among women and youth in the service sector of the economy, while union strength has traditionally been among urban blue-collar workers, especially middle-aged workers.

FIGURE 10.2

Union Membership Concentrated in Public-Sector Jobs

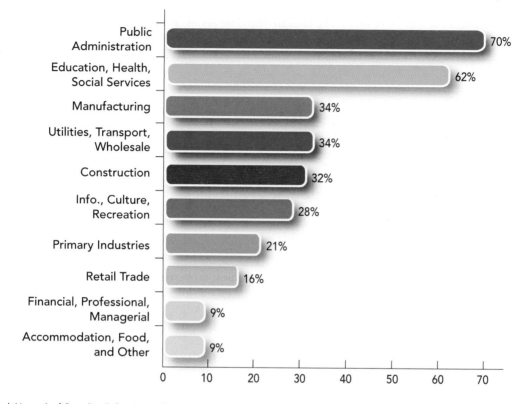

SOURCE: Work Network of Canadian Policy Research Networks, www.jobquality.ca/indicator_e/enlarge/uni001cc.htm. Retrieved: November 5, 2004.

Another force working against union membership is management efforts against union organizing. In a survey, almost half of large employers said their most important labour goal was to be union-free. Efforts to control costs have contributed to employer resistance to unions.[11] On average, unionized workers receive higher pay than their nonunionized counterparts, and the pressure is greater because of international competition. In the past, union membership across an industry such as automobiles or steel resulted in similar wages and work requirements for all competitors. Today, North American producers must compete with companies that have entirely different pay scales and work rules, often placing the North American companies at a disadvantage. Another way in which management may contribute to the decline in union membership is by adopting human resource practices that increase employees' commitment to their job and employer. Competition for scarce human resources can lead employers to offer much of what employees traditionally sought through union membership. Government regulations, too, can make unions seem less important. Stricter regulation in such areas as workplace safety and human rights leaves fewer areas in which unions can show an advantage over what employers must already offer.

Unions have made strategic decisions in recent years to organize the growing private-service sector. This sector includes workers employed in hotels, home care agencies, and offices. Often, these employees are women. This extension of union activity into the service sector has been one reason for the most significant transformation in

FIGURE 10.3

Union Density Highest in Newfoundland and Quebec

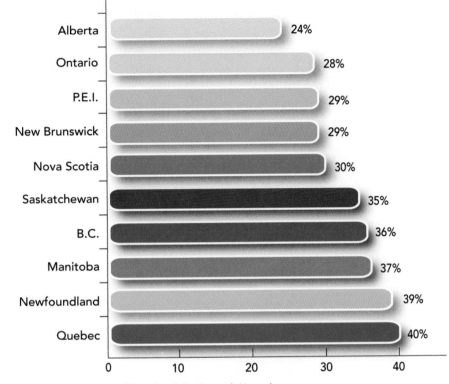

SOURCE: Work Network of Canadian Policy Research Networks,
www.jobquality.ca/indicator_e/enlarge/uni001cc.htm. Retrieved: November 5, 2004.

union membership, i.e., the mix of men and women. In 1977, women represented only 12 percent of total union membership. By 2003, women's share had quadrupled to 48 percent. Other reasons for the increase in women membership in unions can be attributed to the increasing:

- number of women in the paid workforce
- number of women in the highly unionized public sector
- unionization of part-time employees (many of whom are women)
- number of women employed in non-traditional male-dominated occupations and industries.[12]

Unions active in organizing workers in the private-service sector include the United Steelworkers of America (USWA), which organized Pinkerton's security guards, and the Canadian Autoworkers (CAW), which organized more than 50 Kentucky Fried Chicken outlets in British Columbia.[13] The CAW is also recruiting the 4,000 clergy of the United Church to unionize. Rev. David Galston, a member of the organizing committee says, "We think it can bring a lot of professionalism and accountability to the church and its clergy."[14] Galston adds, "clergy want safe working conditions, including everything from proper fire escapes to formal protections from congregants who have been known to harass, stalk and assault ministers. They also want more say in their pay and benefits."[15]

FIGURE 10.4

Union Membership Rates and Coverage in Selected Countries

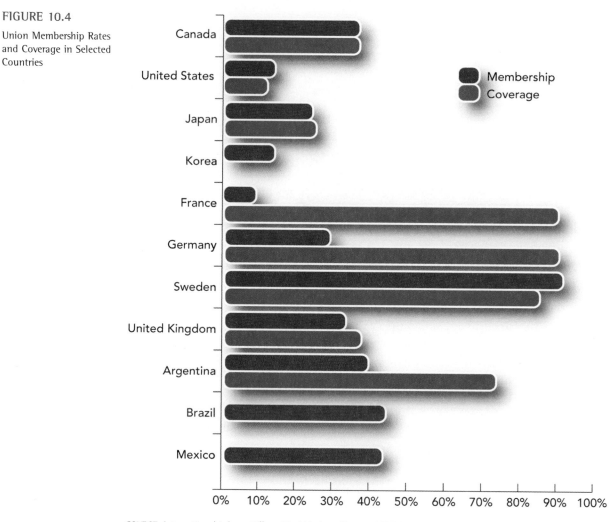

SOURCE: International Labour Office, *World Labour Report, 1997–98* (most current report at time of writing) (Geneva, Switzerland).

As Figure 10.4 indicates, the percentage of Canadian workers who belong to unions, although much higher than in the U.S., is lower than in many countries. More dramatic is the difference in "coverage"—the percentage of employees whose terms and conditions of employment are governed by a union contract, whether or not the employees are technically union members. In Western Europe, it is common to have coverage rates of 80 to 90 percent, so the influence of labour unions far outstrips what membership levels would imply.[16] Also, employees in Western Europe tend to have a larger formal role in decision making than in Canada. This role, including worker representatives on boards of directors, is often mandated by the government. But as markets become more and more global, pressure to cut labour costs and increase productivity is likely to be stronger in every country. Unless unions can help companies improve productivity or organize new production facilities opened in lower-wage countries, union influence may decline in countries where it is now strong.

Impact of Unions on Company Performance

Organizations are concerned about whether union organizing and bargaining will hurt their performance, in particular, unions' impact on productivity, profits, and stock performance. Researchers have studied the general relationship between unionization and these performance meas-

Harley-Davidson and the International Association of Machinists and Aerospace Workers have cooperated to produce good results. In general, though, companies wishing to become more competitive need to continually monitor their labour relations strategies.

ures. Through skillful labour relations, organizations can positively influence outcomes.

There has been much debate regarding the effects of unions on productivity.[17] The view that unions decrease productivity is based on work rules and limits on workloads set by union contracts and production lost to such union actions as strikes and work slowdowns. At the same time, unions can have positive effects on productivity.[18] They can reduce turnover by giving employees a route for resolving problems.[19] Unions emphasize pay systems based on seniority, which remove incentives for employees to compete rather than cooperate. The introduction of a union also may force an employer to improve its management practices and pay greater attention to employee ideas.

Although there is evidence that unions have both positive and negative effects on productivity, most studies have found that union workers are more productive than nonunion workers. Are highly productive workers more likely to form unions, or does a union make workers more productive? The answer is unclear. In theory, if unions caused greater productivity, we would expect union membership to be rising, not falling as it has been.[20]

Even if unions do raise productivity, a company's profits and stock performance may still suffer if unions raise wage and benefits costs by more than the productivity gain. On average, union members receive higher wages and more generous benefits than nonunion workers, and evidence shows that unions have a large negative effect on profits. Also, union coverage tends to decline faster in companies with a lower return to shareholders.[21] In summary, companies wishing to become more competitive must continually monitor their labour relations strategy.

These studies look at the average effects of unions, not at individual companies or innovative labour relations. Some organizations can report success stories in labour relations. Harley-Davidson, for example, has developed a cooperative relationship with the International Association of Machinists and Aerospace Workers (IAM).[22] The two parties negotiated a contract that provides for employment security and joint labour-management decision making in many areas. The company shares technical and financial information and expects a high level of participation in improving productivity and satisfying customers. The IAM's Lou Kiefer explains, "We know that if we increase productivity and lower costs, we're not working ourselves out of a job."

Goals of Each Group

LO2

Resolving conflicts in a positive way is usually easiest when the parties involved understand each other's goals. Although individual cases vary, we can draw some general conclusions about the goals of labour unions and management. Society, too, has goals for labour and business, given form in the laws regulating labour relations.

Goals of Management

Management goals are to increase the organization's profits. Managers tend to prefer options that lower costs and raise output. When deciding whether to discourage employees from forming a union, a concern is that a union will create higher costs for wages and benefits, as well as raise the risk of work stoppages. Managers may also fear that a union will make managers and workers into adversaries or limit management's discretion in making business and employment decisions.

When an employer has recognized a union, management's goals continue to emphasize restraining costs and improving output. Managers continue to prefer to keep the organization's operations flexible, so they can adjust activities to meet competitive challenges and customer demands. Therefore, in their labour relations managers prefer to limit increases in wages and benefits and to retain as much control as they can over work rules and schedules. In addition, globalization and the need to compete with lower-cost competitors influences management's goals to remain competitive and productive.

Goals of Labour Unions

In general, labour unions have the goals of obtaining pay and working conditions that satisfy their members and of giving members a voice in decisions that affect them. Traditionally, they obtain these goals by gaining power in numbers. The more workers who belong to a union, the greater the union's power. More members translates into greater ability to halt or disrupt production. Larger unions also have greater financial resources for continuing a strike; the union can help to make up for the wages the workers lose during a strike. The threat of a long strike—stated or implied—can make an employer more willing to meet the union's demands.

In 2003, Statistics Canada found that unionized workers received on average, hourly earnings 26 percent higher than the average non-union worker did. Union membership has an even greater impact on part-time workers. Unionized part-time workers averaged 65 percent higher earnings than non-union part-time workers.[23]

Unions typically want to influence the *way* pay and promotions are determined. Unlike management, which tries to consider employees as individuals so that pay and promotion decisions relate to performance differences, unions try to build group solidarity and avoid possible arbitrary treatment of employees. To do so, unions try to have any pay differences based on seniority, on the grounds that this measure is more objective than performance evaluations. As a result, where workers are represented by a union, it is common for all employees in a particular job classification to be paid at the same rate. As well as working to advance the interests of members, unions often engage in **social unionism**, i.e., activities intended to influence social and economic policies of government. For example, CAW, Canada's largest private-sector union is actively involved in anti-racism programs, creating safer workplaces for LGBT (lesbian, gay, bisexual, and transgender) union members, and supporting work and family balance initiatives. Buzz Hargrove, national president of CAW, was recently featured in the *Financial Post* describing CAW's unanimous endorsement of fighting anti-Semitism through far-reaching local activities including offering reward money for tips leading to the arrest and conviction of people committing anti-Semitic hate crimes.[24]

social unionism
Social unionism involves activities intended to influence social and economic policies of government.

However, the survival and security of a union ultimately depends on its ability to ensure a regular flow of new members and member dues to support the services it provides. In 1946, Supreme Court of Canada Justice Ivan Rand brought down a significant decision that affected union financial security in Canada. The case came about as part of an arbitrated settlement of the labour dispute between the Ford Motor Company and the United Auto Workers. The **Rand Formula** is a union security provision that makes the payment of labour union dues mandatory even if the worker is not a member of the union. The rationale for the principle was that every employee benefits from union representation.[25] Unions typically place high priority on negotiating two types of contract provisions with an employer that are critical to a union's security and viability: checkoff provisions and provisions relating to union membership or contribution.

Under a **checkoff provision,** the employer, on behalf of the union, automatically deducts union dues from employees' paycheques.

The strongest union security arrangement is a **closed shop,** under which a person must be a union member before being hired or the **union shop,** an arrangement that requires an employee to join the union within a certain time after beginning employment.

These provisions are ways to address unions' concern about "free riders"—employees who benefit from union activities without belonging to a union. By law, all members of a bargaining unit, whether union members or not, must be represented by the union. If the union must offer services to all bargaining unit members but some of them are not dues-paying union members, the union may not have enough financial resources to operate successfully.

Goals of Society

The activities of unions and management take place within the context of society, with society's values driving the laws and regulations that affect labour relations. As long ago as the late 1800s and early 1900s, industrial relations scholars saw unions as a way to make up for individual employees' limited bargaining power.[26] At that time, clashes between workers and management could be violent, and many people hoped that unions would replace the violence with negotiation. Since then, observers have expressed concern that unions in certain industries have become too strong, achieving their goals at the expense of employers' ability to compete or meet other objectives. Overall, however, societal goals for government include ensuring that neutral rules exist to ensure balance is maintained between the powers of unions and employers. For example, Ontario is introducing sweeping labour law changes intended to "restore greater fairness and balance to labour relations in Ontario."[27]

Rather than being left to the activities of unions and management, many societal goals are also enforced through laws and regulations. As discussed in Chapter 2, human rights, pay equity, employment equity, privacy and other types of legislation determine how workers are treated by their employers. In addition, as we will see in the next section, a set of laws and regulations also exists to give workers the right to choose to join unions.

Laws and Regulations Affecting Labour Relations

LO3

The laws and regulations pertaining to labour relations affect unions' size and bargaining power, so they significantly affect the degree to which unions, management, and society achieve their varied goals. These laws and regulations set limits on union

Rand Formula Union security provision that makes payment of labour union dues mandatory even if the worker is not a member of the union.

checkoff provision Requirement that the employer, on behalf of the union, automatically deducts union dues from employees' paycheques.

closed shop Union security arrangement under which a person must be a union member before being hired.

union shop Union security arrangement that requires employees to join the union within a certain amount of time after beginning employment.

The Ontario Labour Relations Board's (OLRB) Interactive Website

HR professionals can now access a comprehensive range of tools and resources on a self-service basis. The OLRB has advanced the use of technology to clients and stakeholders through the implementation of an interactive website. *OLRB Online* provides access to the full text of OLRB decisions from January 1, 2000 (as well as some prior decisions) from their link to the Canadian Legal Information Institute (www.canlii.org/on/cas/onlrb/). The OLRB website also provides access to key processes such as rules of procedure, making an application, mediation, and adjudication. The OLRB also provides access to its bi-monthly collection of significant decisions as well as featured "decisions of interest."

In addition, all forms that relate to labour relations in Ontario are made accessible, either alphabetically or by application, in html, pdf, and Word formats. For example, all forms, information bulletins, and schedules related to certification of a union in the construction industry are grouped to ensure clients and stakeholders can retrieve all relevant forms and information from a single point of self-directed contact.

SOURCES: Ontario Labour Relations Board website, www.olrb.gov.on.ca; "A Look Ahead—Technology at the OLRB" OLRB Annual Report 2000-2001, p. 42, www.olrb.gov.on.ca/english/Public.htm. Retrieved: November 6, 2004; Canadian Legal Information Institute website, www.canlii.org/on/cas/onlrb/.

structure and administration and the ways in which unions and management interact.

Canada's overall labour relations legal framework is decentralized and relatively complex. Since a ruling of the Supreme Court of Canada in 1925, responsibility for labour relations is primarily a provincial/territorial responsibility. Which organizations fall under federal vs. provincial/territorial legislation was discussed in Chapter 2. Federally regulated private-sector employees are regulated by the Canada Labour Code (Part 1—Industrial Relations). In addition, private-sector employees in Nunavut, the Yukon, and the Northwest Territories are also regulated by the Canada Labour Code. Each province and territory has its own distinct labour laws. Each jurisdiction, i.e., federal, provincial, and territorial, also have laws governing public-sector employees. There are additional labour statutes that apply to specific occupations, e.g., teachers, law enforcement officers, firefighters, and hospital employees. The Human Resources and Skills Development Canada website provides links to all industrial relations legislation in Canada (www.hrsdc.gc.ca).

Although some differences exist among jurisdictions, the main features of labour legislation in Canada can be summarized as follows:

unfair labour practice
A prohibited conduct of an employer, union, or individual under the relevant labour legislation.

- Methods to certify a union which will represent a group of employees
- Requirement of the employer to recognize the union chosen by the majority of its employees and to accept the union as the employees' exclusive representative for bargaining purposes
- Responsibility to bargain in good faith with the intention to reach an agreement

Avoiding Unfair Labour Practices

A common core of labour legislation prohibits employers, unions, and individuals from engaging in unfair labour practices. Each jurisdiction in Canada has specific provisions dealing with unfair labour practices by management. Here are some of the most common examples of unfair labour practices that management must avoid:

- Interfering in the formation of a union or contributing to it financially (although, there have been allowances for the providing of an office for the union to conduct business and for paid leave for union officials conducting union business)

- Discriminating against an employee because the individual is or is not a member of a union

- Discriminating against an employee because the individual chooses to exercise rights granted by labour law

- Intimidating or coercing an employee to become or not become a member of a union

Unfair labour practices by unions are also prohibited. While each jurisdiction has laws regulating union conduct, important examples of unfair labour practices that unions must avoid include:

- Seeking to compel an employer to bargain collectively with the union if the union is not the certified bargaining agent

- Attempting at the workplace and during working hours to persuade an employee to become or not become a union member

- Intimidating, coercing, or penalizing an individual because he or she has filed a complaint or testified in any proceeding pursuant to the relevant labour law

- Engaging in, encouraging, or threatening illegal strikes

- Failing to represent employees fairly

SOURCE: Schwind, Das, and Wager, *Canadian Human Resource Management*, 7th ed. (Toronto: McGraw-Hill Ryerson, 2005), p. 604.

- Requirement of the employer to deduct union dues from employees
- Minimum length of a collective agreement (at least one year)
- Regulation of strike and lockout activities
- Creation of a labour relations board (or specialized tribunal) to interpret and enforce the labour laws in their jurisdiction
- Prohibition of identified **unfair labour practices** by management and labour (See the "HR How To" box.)

There is a **Labour Relations Board (LRB)** (or similar structure) in each jurisdiction that serves as a specialized quasi-judicial tribunal with authority to interpret and enforce the labour laws in their jurisdiction. The **Canada Industrial Relations Board (CIRB)** has jurisdiction for federally regulated employees as well as private-sector employees in Nunavut, the Yukon, and the Northwest Territories. As described in the "E-HRM" feature, the Ontario Labour Relations Board offers access to tools and resources on its interactive website.

Labour Relations Board (LRB)
A specialized tribunal with authority to interpret and enforce the labour laws in their jurisdiction.

Canada Industrial Relations Board (CIRB)
Quasi-judicial tribunal responsible for the interpretation and enforcement of the Canada Labour Code (Part I—Industrial Relations).

Prevention of Unfair Labour Practices

When someone believes that an unfair labour practice has taken place, he or she may file a complaint with the appropriate Labour Relations Board for the jurisdiction. There are deadlines for filing complaints. For example, the deadline for filing a complaint with the Canada Industrial Relations Board (CIRB) for employees falling under the Canada Labour Code, is no later than the 90th day after the individual knew or, in the Board's opinion should have known, of the events in question.[28] All parties are provided a copy of the complaint and the process usually involves the Labour Relations Board conducting a preliminary investigation to determine if the complaint has merit and if it may be possible for the parties to resolve the complaint themselves. If the Labour Relations Board finds the complaint has merit and determines the complaint cannot be resolved through the parties, the Labour Relations Board will conduct a formal hearing with the parties present. Either the case can be dismissed at this point or the Labour Relations Board has the authority to issue cease-and-desist orders to halt unfair labour practices. If the union or employer does not comply with the Labour Relations Board order, the order can be referred to a court of law for enforcement.

LO4

Union Organizing

Unions begin their involvement with an organization's employees by conducting an organizing campaign. To meet its objectives, a union needs to convince a majority of workers that they should receive better pay or other employment conditions and that the union will help them do so. The employer's objectives will depend on its strategy—whether it seeks to work with a union or convince employees that they are better off without union representation.

The Process of Organizing

The organization process begins with a membership application. Union representatives contact employees, present their message about the union, and invite them to sign an application for membership. By signing the application and paying a nominal fee in some jurisdictions (e.g., for private-sector employees under federal jurisdiction the fee is $5) the employee indicates they want the union to represent them.

When the necessary number of employees have signed membership applications, the union will apply to the appropriate Labour Relations Board for certification. Requirements differ among jurisdictions. For example, if your employer is in the private sector and falls under federal jurisdiction the local can be certified without a vote if more than 50 percent of employees sign applications. If fewer than 50 percent of employees signed application forms, the Canada Industrial Relations Board will conduct an election among the employees. For the union to be certified, at least 35 percent of employees in the work group must vote and more than 50 percent of these voting employees must vote in favour of unionizing.[29] Social Development Canada's website (www.sdc.gc.ca) discusses the specific application requirements for union certification in the various jurisdictions in Canada.

Management Strategies

Sometimes an employer will recognize a union after a majority of employees have signed membership applications. More often, there is a hotly contested election campaign. During the campaign, unions try to persuade employees that their wages, ben-

WHAT TO DO:
Report any direct or indirect signs of union activity to a core management group.
Deal with employees by carefully stating the company's response to pro-union arguments. These responses should be coordinated by the company to maintain consistency and to avoid threats or promises. Take away union issues by following effective management practices all the time:
Deliver recognition and appreciation.
Solve employee problems.
Protect employees from harassment or humiliation.
Provide business-related information.
Be consistent in treatment of employees.
Accommodate special circumstances where appropriate.
Ensure due process in performance management.
Treat all employees with dignity and respect.
WHAT TO AVOID:
Threatening employees with harsher terms and conditions of employment or employment loss if they engage in union activity.
Interrogating employees about pro-union or anti-union sentiments that they or others may have or reviewing union authorization cards or pro-union petitions.
Promising employees that they will receive favourable terms or conditions of employment if they forgo union activity.
Spying on employees known to be, or suspected of being, engaged in pro-union activities.

SOURCE: J. A. Segal, "Unshackle Your Supervisors to Stay Union Free," *HRMagazine*, June 1998, pp. 177–84.

efits, treatment by employers, and chances to influence workplace decisions are too poor or small and that the union will be able to obtain improvements in these areas. Management typically responds with its own messages providing an opposite point of view. Management messages say the organization has provided a valuable package of wages and benefits and has treated employees well. Management also argues that the union will not be able to keep its promises but will instead create costs for employees, such as union dues and lost income during strikes.

Employers use a variety of methods to avoid unionization in organizing campaigns.[30] Their efforts range from hiring consultants to distributing leaflets and letters to presenting the company's viewpoint at meetings of employees. Some management efforts go beyond what the law permits, especially in the eyes of union organizers. This impression is supported by an increase in charges of employer unfair labour practices and awards of back pay since the late 1960s.[31] Why would employers break the law? One explanation is that the consequences, such as reinstating workers with back pay, are small compared to the benefits.[32] If coercing workers away from joining a union saves the company the higher wages, benefits, and other costs of a unionized workforce, management may feel an incentive to accept costs like back pay.

Supervisors have the most direct contact with employees. Thus, as Table 10.1 indicates, it is critical that they establish good relationships with employees even before there is any attempt at union organizing. Supervisors also must know what *not* to do if a union drive takes place. They should be trained in the legal principles discussed earlier in this chapter.

Decertifying a Union

Union members' right to be represented by unions of their own choosing also includes the right to vote out an existing union. The action is called *decertifying* the union. Decertification follows the same process as a representation election. An application to decertify a union may not be acted upon during a legal strike or lockout. In some jurisdictions (e.g., Ontario) when a collective agreement is in place, decertification applications may only be filed during specified "open periods." Laws in some jurisdictions require the employer to post and annually circulate information related to union decertification.

LO5

Collective Bargaining

collective bargaining
Negotiation between union representatives and management representatives to arrive at an agreement defining conditions of employment for the term of the agreement and to administer that agreement.

When a union has been certified, that union represents employees during contract negotiations. In **collective bargaining,** a union negotiates on behalf of its members with management representatives to arrive at a contract defining conditions of employment for the term of the contract and to resolve differences in the way they interpret the contract. Typical collective agreements include provisions for pay, benefits, work rules, and resolution of workers' grievances. Table 10.2 shows typical provisions negotiated in collective agreements.

Collective bargaining differs from one situation to another in terms of *bargaining structure*—that is, the range of employees and employers covered by the contract. An agreement may involve a narrow group of employees in a craft union or a broad group in an industrial union. Agreements may cover one or several facilities of the same employer, or the bargaining structure may involve several employers. Many more interests must be considered in collective bargaining for an industrial union with a bargaining structure that includes several employers than in collective bargaining for a craft union in a single facility.

The majority of collective agreement negotiations take place between unions and employers that have been through the process before. In the typical situation, management has come to accept the union as an organization it must work with. The situation can be very different when a union has just been certified and is negotiating its first collective agreement.

TABLE 10.2

Typical Provisions in Collective Agreements

Rights of parties	Recognition of union security • Union membership • Union security • Leave for union business • Restrictions on contracting out Management rights to test • Drug and alcohol testing • Intelligence and aptitude testing • Electronic surveillance • Internet/telephone monitoring • Medical examinations • Other tests Employee rights/security • Harassment • Employment Equity Program • Assistance programs, e.g., substance abuse

Organization of work	Technological change • Advance notice • Obligation to provide training, instruction, or retraining • Layoff protection • Wage protection • Special leaves, severance pay, and/or retirement offers Distribution of work • Flexibility in work assignment • Job rotation • Semi-autonomous work groups or teams • Job sharing
Labour relations	Labour relations • Grievance procedures • Bargaining method or approach • Application of the agreement • Job evaluation (position evaluation) • Joint committees • Participation (other than committees)
Education, training and development	Education, training, and employee development • Leave • Reimbursement for tuition fees and books • Multi-skilling, i.e., flexibility for the employee • Contribution to a training fund • Apprenticeship programs
Conditions of work	Work schedule • Normal hours of work • Type of work schedules • Special provisions Overtime • Clause limiting the use of overtime • Compensatory days in lieu of pay (banking) • Overtime pay • Meal allowance (overtime) Job security and termination • No layoffs while the agreement is in effect • Layoffs by seniority • Bumping rights • Retention of seniority • Work sharing (reduction in hours to avoid layoffs) • Education/training with pay • Supplementary employment insurance benefit Pay • Cost of living allowance • Wage guarantees Leaves and vacations • Paid holidays • Annual vacation • Family leave • Paid sick leave plan Benefits • Private group insurance plans • Pension plans (funding, administration) Provisions relating to part-time workers • Maximum hours of work normally allowed • Ratio of part-time to full-time workers • Holidays, vacations, sick leave, benefits, pension plan, seniority

SOURCE: "Collective Agreement Provisions," Human Resources and Skills Development website, www.hrsdc.gc.ca. Retrieved: November 2, 2004. Reproduced with the permission of the Minister of Public Works and Government Services, 2005.

As part of its programming, the Labour Relations Board British Columbia makes available a free-of-charge information session that is offered to an employer or union either jointly or separately as requested to help reach a first collective agreement.[33] Due to the recognized difficulties associated in reaching a first agreement, the legislation in some jurisdictions provides a process to ensure a first agreement can be reached. Under the Canada Labour Code, the federal Minister of Labour can direct the Canada Industrial Relations Board to establish the terms and conditions of a first collective agreement for the parties. This process would require the use of arbitration, which is discussed later in the chapter.[34]

Bargaining over New Collective Agreements

Clearly, the outcome of collective agreement negotiations can have important consequences for labour costs, productivity, and the organization's ability to compete. Therefore, unions and management need to prepare carefully for collective bargaining. Preparation includes establishing objectives for the agreement, reviewing the old agreement, gathering data (such as compensation paid by competitors and the company's ability to survive a strike), predicting the likely demands to be made, and establishing the cost of meeting the demands.[35] This preparation can help negotiators develop a plan for how to negotiate. Different situations and goals call for different approaches to bargaining, such as the following alternatives proposed by Richard Walton and Robert McKersie:[36]

- *Distributive bargaining* divides an economic "pie" between two sides—for example, a wage increase means giving the union a larger share of the pie.
- *Integrative (mutual-gains) bargaining* looks for win-win solutions, or outcomes in which both sides benefit. If the organization's labour costs hurt its performance, integrative bargaining might seek to avoid layoffs in exchange for work rules that improve productivity.
- *Attitudinal structuring* focuses on establishing a relationship of trust. The parties are concerned about ensuring that the other side will keep its part of any bargain.
- *Intraorganizational bargaining* addresses conflicts within union or management groups or objectives, such as between new employees and workers with high seniority or between cost control and reduction of turnover.

The collective bargaining process may involve any combination of these alternatives.

Negotiations go through various stages.[37] In the earliest stages, many more people are often present than in later stages. On the union side, this may give all the various internal interest groups a chance to participate and voice their goals. Their input helps communicate to management what will satisfy union members and may help the union achieve greater solidarity. At this stage, union negotiators often present a long list of proposals, partly to satisfy members and partly to introduce enough issues that they will have flexibility later in the process. Management may or may not present proposals of its own. Sometimes management prefers to react to the union's proposals.

During the middle stages of the process, each side must make a series of decisions, even though the outcome is uncertain. How important is each issue to the other side? How likely is it that disagreement on particular issues will result in a strike? When and to what extent should one side signal its willingness to compromise?

In the final stage of negotiations, pressure for an agreement increases. Public negotiations may be only part of the process. Negotiators from each side may hold one-on-one meetings or small-group meetings where they escape some public relations pressures. A neutral third party may act as a go-between or facilitator. In some cases, bargaining breaks down as the two sides find they cannot reach a mutually acceptable agreement. The outcome depends partly on the relative bargaining power of each party. That power, in turn, depends on each party's ability to withstand a strike, which costs the workers their pay during the strike and costs the employer lost production and possibly lost customers.

When Bargaining Breaks Down

The intended outcome of collective bargaining is an agreement with terms acceptable to both parties. If one or both

Failing to reach a contract under collective bargaining can result in a strike or boycott. Here actor Rob Schneider encourages the public to boycott Procter & Gamble products because the company used nonunion workers in its commercials in place of striking members of the Screen Actors Guild.

sides determine that negotiation alone will not produce such an agreement, bargaining breaks down. To bring this impasse to an end, the union may strike, or the parties may bring in outside help to resolve their differences.

FIGURE 10.5
Number of Strikes and Lockouts

Legend:
Canada
United States
Japan
United Kingdom

(Graph: Number of Strikes and Lockouts vs. Year, 1993–2001, y-axis 0 to 500)

SOURCE: Adapted from Statistics Canada website, www.statcan.ca/english/Pgdb/labor30a.htm. Retrieved: October 30, 2004.

FIGURE 10.6

Workdays Not Worked Due to Strikes and Lockouts (Thousands)

	CANADA	UNITED STATES	JAPAN	UNITED KINGDOM
1993	1516.7	3981.2	116.0	649.0
1994	1606.9	5021.5	85.4	278.0
1995	1516.6	5771.2	77.0	415.0
1996	3342.2	4888.6	42.8	1303.3
1997	3568.8	4497.1	110.2	234.7
1998	2441.0	5115.7	101.5	282.4
1999	2445.7	1995.8	87.1	241.8
2000	1661.6	2014.9	35.1	498.8
2001	2231.1	1151.3	29.1	525.1

SOURCE: Adapted from Statistics Canada website, www.statcan.ca/english/Pgdb/labor30a.htm. Retrieved: October 30, 2004.

Strikes and Lockouts

strike

A collective decision by union members not to work or to slow down until certain demands or conditions are met.

A **strike** is a collective decision of the union members not to work or to slow down until certain demands or conditions are met. The union members vote, and if the majority favours a strike, they all go on strike at that time or when union leaders believe the time is right. Strikes are typically accompanied by *picketing*—the union stations members near the worksite with signs indicating the union is on strike. During the strike, the union members do not receive pay from their employer, but the union may be able to make up for some of the lost pay. The employer loses production unless it can hire replacement workers, and even then, productivity may be reduced. Often, other unions support striking workers by refusing to cross their picket line—for example, refusing to make deliveries to a company during a strike. A **lockout** on the other hand, is initiated by the employer. A lockout is a closure of a place of employment or refusal of the employer to provide work as a way to compel employees to agree to certain demands or conditions.

lockout

A closure of a place of employment or refusal of the employer to provide work as a way to compel employees to agree to certain demands or conditions.

Although the vast majority of labour-management negotiations do not result in a strike or lockout, Figure 10.5 shows Canada has a relatively high number of strikes and lockouts compared to other countries. However, the number of strikes does not tell the whole story due to the impact of small vs. large strikes. As shown in Figure 10.6, Canada also loses a significant number of workdays due to strikes and lockouts relative to other countries. Not only do workers lose wages and employers lose production, but the negative experience of a strike or lockout can make future interactions more difficult. For example, there has been "a string of problems in recent months between Air Canada and its unions, which were forced to absorb $1-billion worth of labour concessions during the airline's restructuring."[38] When strikes or lockouts do occur, the conduct of each party during the strike can do lasting harm to labour-management relations. Violence by either side or threats of job loss or actual job loss because jobs went to replacement workers can make future relations difficult.

Alternatives to Strikes and Lockouts

Because strikes and lockouts are so costly and risky, unions and employers generally prefer other methods for resolving conflicts. Three of the most common alternatives are mediation, conciliation, and arbitration. All of these rely on a neutral third party, who usually is appointed by the federal or provincial Minister of Labour.

Strikers demonstrate a heated reaction to people crossing their picket line at Aliant's main office in St John.

The least formal and most widely used of these procedures is **mediation.** In this procedure, a mediator hears the views of both sides and facilitates the negotiation process. The mediator has no formal authority to impose a resolution, so a strike remains a possibility. In a survey studying negotiations between unions and large businesses, mediation was used in almost four out of ten negotiation efforts.[39]

Conciliation, most often used for negotiations with governmental bodies, typically reports on the reasons for the dispute, the views and arguments of both sides, and (sometimes) a recommended settlement, which the parties may decline. The public nature of these recommendations may pressure the parties to reach a settlement. Even if they do not accept the conciliator's recommended settlement, the hope of this process is that the conciliator will identify or frame issues in a way that makes agreement easier. Sometimes merely devoting time to this process gives the parties a chance to reach an agreement. In most jurisdictions in Canada, conciliation is mandatory before a strike or lockout can be called. Again, however, there is no guarantee that a strike or lockout will be avoided.

The most formal type of outside intervention is **arbitration,** under which an arbitrator or arbitration board determines a settlement that is *binding*, meaning the parties have to accept it. There is wide acceptance of "rights arbitration," which focuses on enforcing or interpreting agreement terms, but arbitration in the writing of collective agreements or setting of agreement terms has traditionally been reserved for special circumstances such as negotiations between unions and government agencies, where strikes may be illegal or especially costly. Occasionally, arbitration has also been used with businesses in situations where strikes have been extremely damaging. Arbitration is uncommon in the private sector and one reason is the general opinion that union and management representatives are in the best position to resolve conflicts themselves, because they are closer to the situation than an arbitrator can be. A notable exception is in the case of first agreement arbitration, mentioned previously in the context of ensuring a first collective agreement is reached in a timely manner.

mediation
Conflict resolution procedure in which a mediator hears the views of both sides and facilitates the negotiation process but has no formal authority to dictate a resolution.

conciliation
Conflict resolution procedure in which a third party to collective bargaining reports the reasons for a dispute, the views and arguments of both sides, and possibly a recommended settlement, which the parties may decline.

arbitration
Conflict resolution procedure in which an arbitrator or arbitration board determines a binding settlement.

LO6

Collective Agreement Administration

Although the process of negotiating a collective agreement (including the occasional strike) receives the most publicity, other union-management activities occur far more often. Bargaining over a new contract typically occurs only about every three years, but administering labour agreements goes on day after day, year after year. The two activities are linked, of course. Vague or inconsistent language in the agreement can make administering the agreement more difficult. The difficulties can create conflict that spills over into the next round of negotiations.[40] Events during negotiations—strikes, the use of replacement workers, or violence by either side—also can lead to difficulties in working successfully under a conflict.

Collective agreement administration includes carrying out the terms of the agreement and resolving conflicts over interpretation or violation of the agreement. Under a labour agreement, the process for resolving these conflicts is called a **grievance procedure.** This procedure has a key influence on success in collective agreement administration. A grievance procedure may be started by an employee or discharged employee who believes the employer violated the agreement or by a union representative on behalf of a group of workers or union representatives.

For grievances launched by an employee, a typical grievance procedure follows the steps shown in Figure 10.7. The grievance may be settled during any of the four steps. In the first step, the employee talks to his or her supervisor about the problem. If this conversation is unsatisfactory, the employee may involve the union steward in further discussion. The union steward and employee decide whether the problem has been resolved and, if not, whether it is an agreement violation. If the problem was not resolved and does seem to be an agreement violation, the union moves to step 2, putting the grievance in writing and submitting it to a line manager. The union steward meets with a management representative to try to resolve the problem. Management consults with the industrial relations staff and puts its response in writing too at this second stage. If step 2 fails to resolve the problem, the union appeals the grievance to top line management and representatives of the industrial relations staff. The union may involve more local or national officers in discussions at this stage (see step 3 in Figure 10.7). The decision resulting from the appeal is put into writing. If the grievance is still not resolved, the union may decide (step 4) to appeal the grievance to an arbitrator. If the grievance involves a discharged employee, the process may begin at step 2 or 3, however, and the time limits between steps may be shorter. Grievances filed by the union on behalf of a group may begin at step 1 or step 2.

The majority of grievances are settled during the earlier steps of the process. This reduces delays and avoids the costs of arbitration. If a grievance does reach arbitration, the arbitrator makes the final ruling in the matter.

From the point of view of employees, the grievance procedure is an important means of getting fair treatment in the workplace. Its success depends on whether it provides for all the kinds of problems that are likely to arise (such as how to handle a business slowdown), whether employees feel they can file a grievance without being punished for it, and whether employees believe their union representatives will follow through. Too many grievances may indicate a problem—for example, the union members or line supervisors do not understand how to uphold the collective agreement or have no desire to do so. At the same time, a very small number of grievances

grievance procedure
The process for resolving union–management conflicts over interpretation or violation of a collective agreement.

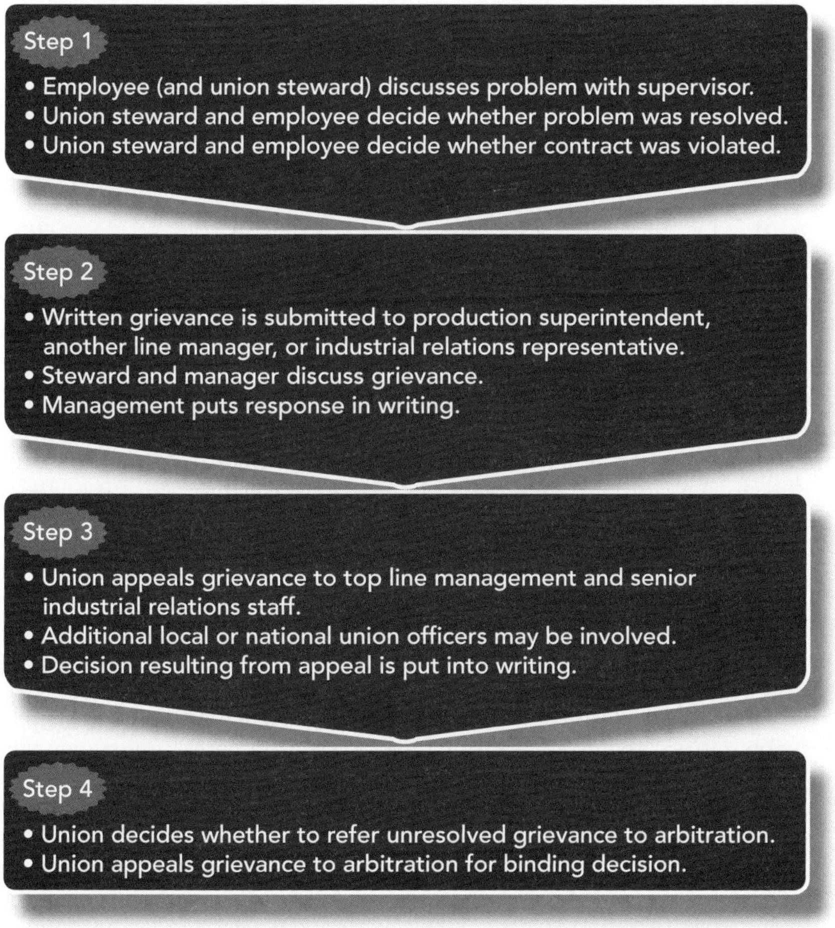

FIGURE 10.7

Steps in an Employee-
Initiated Grievance
Procedure

Step 1
- Employee (and union steward) discusses problem with supervisor.
- Union steward and employee decide whether problem was resolved.
- Union steward and employee decide whether contract was violated.

Step 2
- Written grievance is submitted to production superintendent, another line manager, or industrial relations representative.
- Steward and manager discuss grievance.
- Management puts response in writing.

Step 3
- Union appeals grievance to top line management and senior industrial relations staff.
- Additional local or national union officers may be involved.
- Decision resulting from appeal is put into writing.

Step 4
- Union decides whether to refer unresolved grievance to arbitration.
- Union appeals grievance to arbitration for binding decision.

SOURCE: Adapted from T. A. Kochan, *Collective Bargaining and Industrial Relations* (Homewood, IL: Richard D. Irwin, 1980), p. 395; J. A. Fossum, *Labour Relations* (Boston: McGraw-Hill/Irwin, 2002), pp. 448–52.

may also signal a problem. A very low grievance rate may suggest a fear of filing a grievance, a belief that the system does not work, or a belief that employees are poorly represented by their union.

Labour–Management Cooperation

LO7

The traditional understanding of union-management relations is that the two parties are adversaries, meaning each side is competing to win at the expense of the other. There have always been exceptions to this approach. And since at least the 1980s, there seems to be wider acceptance of the view that greater cooperation can increase employee commitment and motivation while making the workplace more flexible.[41] Also, evidence suggests that employees who worked under traditional labour relations systems and then under the new, more cooperative systems prefer the cooperative approach.[42]

Cooperation between labour and management may feature employee involvement in decision making, self-managing employee teams, joint labour-management committees, broadly defined jobs, and sharing of financial gains and business information with employees.[43] The search for a win-win solution requires that unions and their members understand the limits on what an employer can afford in a competitive marketplace. Finding common ground may be part of an ongoing trend at least in parts of the private sector. As outlined in the Conference Board of Canada's 2005 Industrial Relations Outlook: "Many unions recognize they have a stake in their organizations' competitiveness."[44]

For example, Bombardier Inc. and the union representing Montreal-area workers have reached a deal aimed at ensuring that Bombardier Aerospace will build its new series of C-Series passenger jets in the province (other locations in the running for the new plant that would employ 2,500 workers were Toronto, Belfast in Northern Ireland, and New Mexico).[45] Union members have voted in favour of a six-year labour agreement that includes reducing overtime costs by using flextime scheduling and accepting a one-year wage freeze.[46] Although some may say the union members provided concessions to management, others argue the agreement is a mutual-gains solution, i.e., jobs in the aerospace industry are retained in Quebec. The "Best Practices" box describes The City of Toronto's collaborative efforts.

Without the union's support, efforts at employee involvement are less likely to survive and less likely to be effective if they do survive.[47] Unions have often resisted employee involvement programs, precisely because the programs try to change workplace relations and the role that unions play. Union leaders have often feared that such programs will weaken unions' role as independent representatives of employee interests.

An effective day-to-day relationship between labour and management is critical to achieving cooperation. In an adversarial type of environment, union-management communication consists of dealing with grievances, however a cooperative model requires effective communication, trust, and mutual respect as the foundation for the day-to-day relationship. Many management and union leaders recognize that new approaches are needed to handle mutual concerns. "A sense of shared purpose is required to increase the effectiveness of the organization"[48] and methods are needed to benefit from the insights and skills of employees. Joint labour-management committees provide a relatively flexible approach to labour-management cooperation in the workplace.

Over the past two decades, the use of joint labour-management committees has been growing. More than 80 percent of labour and management respondents to a recent study conducted by the Conference Board of Canada and resulting in "The Canadian Industrial Relations System Current Challenges and Future Options Re-

TABLE 10.3

Most Common Joint Labour-Management Committees

MOST COMMON JOINT LABOUR-MANAGEMENT COMMITTEES
1. Pay, benefits, pensions
2. Business issues/updates
3. General labour relations
4. Training/apprenticeships
5. Job evaluation/classifications/postings
6. Operations/technology
7. Hours of work/scheduling

SOURCE: Judith Lendvay-Zwicki, Conference Board Document "The Canadian Industrial Relations System: Current Challenges and Future Options," April 2004, p. 17, www.conferenceboard.ca. Retrieved: April 19, 2004.

Building a New Model for Labour Relations

The stench of garbage steaming in the sun may have long faded from the streets of Toronto, but not so the memory of the rancid labour relations that brought city services to a halt two years ago. As the City of Toronto heads into collective bargaining with two CUPE locals, it's hoping to replace that taint with a new reputation. It's a reputation for collaboration and trust that the city has tried to establish through interest bargaining with the city's 3,000 firefighters. "The record was clear. Labour relations weren't working in the City of Toronto," said Bill Adams. Brought in as the city's director of employee and labour relations in 2002, Adams had a mandate to clean up the mess that labour relations had become.

When he arrived, both CUPE locals representing the city's workers had walked off the job in quick succession in 1999 and 2002. Workers in the second, two-week strike were ordered back to work and to resume collective bargaining with arbitrator Tim Armstrong. Outside that process, the two CUPE locals had another 3,300

grievances before arbitration.

After 35 years in labour relations, first as a union representative and then in public-sector management, Adams has long been disenchanted with much of traditional, adversarial labour relations. "In traditional collective bargaining, the side with the most power rules. The adversarial approach doesn't take into consideration the other party's needs," said Adams. Each side looks after its needs, "and what we wind up with is a third-party solution to everything."

To start cleaning up the labour relations' mess in Toronto, Adams first had to look for "a pilot" opportunity to try out the new interest-based approach. He found it with the firefighters. The city's 3,000 firefighters, prevented by law from striking, were chalking up 125 days in arbitration just to work out the collective agreement. The opportunity for change came when a new fire chief was appointed, just around the time the firefighters' association elected Scott Marks as its new president. Together

with Adams' arrival, the change in leadership marked an opportunity to turn the page.

The city applied for a $100,000 grant from the Labour-Management Partnership Program, a federal program mandated to help both sides work out innovative approaches. Although there were ultimately a number of rough spots in the collaborative process, a key gesture on the part of Adams—providing an interim wage settlement while bargaining was in process—showed that a different labour relations environment was now in place.

For the city, peace with the firefighters is just one milestone; the tougher goal is still ahead. At this point, it appears that the CUPE local representing outside workers is not interested in a collaborative approach, given the lack of trust between the union and the administration.

SOURCE: Uyen Vu, "Building a New Model for Labour Relations in T.O.," *Canadian HR Reporter,* September 13, 2004, pp. 1, 13. © Copyright Canadian HR Reporter, September 13, 2004, by permission of Carswell, Toronto, Ontario, 1-800-387-5164, www.hrreporter.com.

port 2004" reported that they have experience in using joint labour-management committees. The most common issues that these joint labour-management committees deal with are summarized in Table 10.3.

Employers build cooperative relationships by the way they treat employees—with respect and fairness, in the knowledge that attracting talent and minimizing turnover are in the employer's best interests. "In the end we must look for opportunities to create a more collaborative culture in Canadian workplaces to ensure the long-term sustainability of our businesses."[49]

Summary

1. Define unions and labour relations and their role in organizations.

A union is an organization formed for the purpose of representing its members in resolving conflicts with employers. Labour relations is the management specialty emphasizing skills that managers and union leaders can use to minimize costly forms of conflict and to seek win-win solutions to disagreements. Unions—often locals belonging to national and/or international organizations—engage in organizing, collective bargaining, and contract administration with businesses and government organizations. In Canada, union membership has declined marginally from a peak in 1994. Unionization is associated with more generous compensation and higher productivity but lower profits. Unions may reduce a business's flexibility and economic performance.

2. Identify the labour relations goals of management, unions, and society.

Management goals are to increase the organization's profits. Managers generally expect that unions will make these goals harder to achieve. Unions have the goal of obtaining pay and working conditions that satisfy their members. They obtain these results by gaining power in numbers. Society's values have included the hope that the existence of unions will replace conflict or violence between workers and employers with fruitful negotiation.

3. Summarize laws and regulations that affect labour relations.

Canada's overall labour relations legal framework is decentralized with responsibility for labour relations shared between the federal, provincial, and territorial governments. However, a common core of labour legislation exists that includes prohibiting unfair labour practices by management and labour. Labour Relations Boards or similar quasi-judicial tribunals exist within each jurisdiction to administer and enforce labour laws.

4. Describe the union-organizing process.

Organizing begins when union representatives contact employees and invite them to sign a membership application. When the required numbers of employees have signed membership applications, the union will apply to their appropriate Labour Relations Board for certification. Requirements for certification differ among federal, provincial, and territorial jurisdictions.

5. Explain how management and unions negotiate collective agreements.

Negotiations take place between representatives of the union and the management bargaining unit. The majority of negotiations involve parties that have been through the process before. The process begins with preparation, including research into the other side's strengths and demands. In the early stages of negotiation, many more people are present than at later stages. The union presents its demands, and management sometimes presents demands as well. Then the sides evaluate the demands and the likelihood of a strike. In the final stages, pressure for an agreement increases, and a neutral third party may be called on to help reach a resolution. If bargaining breaks down, the impasse may be broken with a strike, lockout, mediation, conciliation, or arbitration.

6. Summarize the practice of collective agreement administration.

Collective agreement administration is a daily activity under the collective agreement. It includes carrying out the terms of the agreement and resolving conflicts over interpretation or violation of the agreement. Conflicts are resolved through a grievance procedure. Typically, the grievance procedure begins with an employee talking to his or her supervisor about the problem and possibly involving the union steward in the discussion. If this does not resolve the conflict, the union files a written grievance with a line manager, and union and management representatives meet to discuss the problem. If this effort fails, the union appeals the grievance to top line management and the industrial relations staff. If the appeal fails, the union may appeal the grievance to an arbitrator.

7. Describe more cooperative approaches to labour-management relations.

In contrast to the traditional view that labour and management are adversaries, some organizations and unions work more cooperatively. Cooperation may feature employee involvement in decision making, self-managing employee teams, joint labour-management committees, broadly defined jobs, and sharing of financial gains and business information with employees. Cooperative labour relations seem to contribute to an organization's success.

Review and Discussion Questions

1. Why do employees join unions? Did you ever belong to a union? If you did, do you think union membership benefited you? If you did not, do you think a union would have benefited you? Why or why not?

2. Why do managers at most companies prefer that unions not represent their employees? Can unions provide benefits to an employer? Explain.

3. How has union membership in Canada changed over the past few decades? How does union membership in Canada compare with union membership in other countries? How might these patterns in union membership affect the HR decisions of an international company?

4. What legal responsibilities do employers have regarding unions? What are the legal requirements affecting unions?

5. Suppose you are the HR manager for a chain of clothing stores. You learn that union representatives have been encouraging the stores' employees to sign an ap-

plication for membership. What events can follow in this process of organizing? Suggest some ways that you might respond in your role as HR manager.

6. If the parties negotiating a collective agreement are unable to reach a settlement, what actions can resolve the situation?

7. Why are most negotiations settled without a strike or lockout? Under what conditions might management choose to accept a strike?

8. What are the usual steps in a grievance procedure? What are the advantages of resolving a grievance in the first step? What skills would a supervisor need so grievances can be resolved in the first step?

9. The "Best Practices" box in the chapter gives an example of union-management cooperation in The City of Toronto. What does the employer gain from this effort? What do workers gain? Do you think the cooperative effort eliminates the union's role for The City of Toronto? Explain.

What's Your HR IQ? www.mcgrawhill.ca/college/noe

The Online Learning Centre offers more ways to check what you've learned so far. Find experiential exercises as well as Test Your Knowledge Quizzes, Videos, and many other resources at www.mcgrawhill.ca/college/noe.

BusinessWeek Case

BusinessWeek A World of Sweatshops

If you tour Tong Yang Indonesia (TYI) shoe factory, an 8,500-worker complex of hot, dingy buildings outside Jakarta, company president Jung Moo Young will show you the improvements he has made in the past two years. He did so to satisfy his biggest customer, Reebok International, accused by activists of using sweatshops.

Last year Jung bought machinery to apply a water-based solvent to glue on shoe soles instead of toluene, which may be hazardous to workers. He installed a ventilation system after Reebok auditors found the old one inadequate. TYI bought new chairs with backs, so that its young seamstresses have some support while seated at their machines, and bought back braces for 500 workers who do heavy lifting. In all, TYI, which has $100 million in annual sales, spent $2 million to satisfy Reebok. But to Jung's surprise, it was a sound investment. "We should make it all back after

three years," he says. "The workers are more productive, and the new machinery is more efficient."

TYI's efforts show how much progress Western consumer goods companies can make in cleaning up sweatshop conditions. In the early 1990s, many companies adopted codes of conduct requiring contractors to fix harsh or abusive conditions. Several companies—such as Reebok, Nike, and Liz Claiborne—have begun enforcing their codes in the past year or two.

More than a dozen companies have joined efforts to create an industrywide system for verifying that consumer goods sold in North America are made under humane conditions. The most ambitious effort involves the Fair Labour Association, which grew out of a U.S. presidential task force of companies and human rights groups. It plans to send outside monitors to factories worldwide to ensure they meet minimum standards on everything from health and safety to workers' rights to join unions.

The problem is that such conscientious companies are the exceptions. Although many multinationals operate facilities in Asia and Latin America that are run as well as any in the West, most still buy from factories where practices are appalling. The claims of many companies that they adhere to labour codes are no more than window-dressing.

Then there are the tougher issues that even companies such as Reebok haven't yet grappled with. How can companies respect workers' rights to collectively bargain in China, for instance, where free unions are banned and the country's own labour laws often aren't enforced? Nor have most Western companies improved wages, which are often below what even governments like Indonesia's define as enough to support a family.

Investigators for labour and human rights groups estimate that Asia and Latin America have thousands of sweatshops, which force employees to work 16-hour days and cheat them out of already meagre wages. "It would be extremely generous to say that even 10 percent of [Western companies charged with abuses] have done anything meaningful about labour conditions," says S. Prakash Sethi, a Baruch College business professor. Price hikes in North American retail garments have lagged inflation since 1982, and Asian factory owners complain they are under intense pressure to squeeze out costs.

Liz Claiborne's attempt to improve conditions at a factory in Guatemala shows how hard it is for companies to clean up sweatshops. In 1998 the U.S. apparel giant began working with the Commission for the Verification of Corporate Codes of Conduct (Coverco) to monitor one of its suppliers, a Korean-owned factory near Guatemala City. Coverco found a litany of problems, beginning with workers' claims that they didn't receive proper overtime payments or promised production bonuses. Workers lacked adequate protection when handling hazardous chemicals. Toilets and canteens were unsanitary. Some managers screamed at workers and pressured those who complained to resign. Many workers said they were denied time off for doctors' appointments. Coverco says the plant is slowly improving under Liz Claiborne's pressure.

The inability to form free unions means that workers often lack power to make much beyond subsistence wages. The Modas Uno Korea plant in a Guatemala City suburb stopped paying workers on time in August 2000 and fired 22 who complained to the Labour Ministry. That September, workers stormed the plant demanding back pay—and the company relented. Workers who stayed on said they were offered sewing machines instead of severance pay when the factory shut down in early October.

Workers' pay, even if it's better than average for the country, is still pitiful considering the nearly 40 percent profit margins (profit as a percent of expenses) Nike and Reebok earn before taxes. TYI pays about 22 cents an hour, just over Indonesia's minimum wage. It gets around $13 for every pair of shoes it makes for Reebok, paying only $1 for labour. Still, TYI says that after paying for materials and overhead, its margins are just 10 percent. It can't just hike its price to Reebok. "They look for suppliers who sell for the lowest price," says a TYI manager.

Given the huge oversupply of cheap labour in many developing nations, more widespread gains in the workplace are unlikely until workers can organize unions to demand changes—or unless there is a system to punish violators of international codes.

SOURCE: "A World of Sweatshops," *BusinessWeek Online*, November 6, 2000, www.businessweek.com.

Questions

1. What would you expect to happen if the workers in this case were able to join unions?
2. What might happen to a shoe company like Reebok if it began to sell union-made shoes?
3. Would you be willing to pay more for shoes made under better working conditions? Explain.

Case: NHL Officially Cancels 2004–05 Season

National Hockey League commissioner Gary Bettman officially cancelled the 2004–05 season on February 17, 2005 after the league and the union were unable to reach a labour agreement and prevent hockey from becoming the first professional sport to cancel an entire season.

"When I stood before you last September, I said NHL teams will not play again until our economic problems had been solved. As I stand before you today, it is my sad duty to announce that because the solution has not yet been attained, it is no longer practical to conduct even an abbreviated season," Mr. Bettman said from a Times Square hotel yesterday. Although there were indications of room for further negotiations—the two sides were separated in their salary cap proposition by U.S. $6.5 million—the league ultimately decided the financial rift was too wide and there was too little time left to play what was left of the 2004–05 NHL season.

"I think this is a tragedy," Mr. Bettman said. "It's a tragedy for the fans and a tragedy for the players. Their careers are short. This is money and opportunity that they'll never get back. I hope at the end of this, they feel it was worth it because I don't see how it plays out that way."

In Toronto, NHL Players' Association head Bob Goodenow, who rebuffed the NHL's final offer late on Tuesday, was defiant. "I had hoped we would never see the NHL owners and commissioner do the unthinkable and cancel the entire season," he said, "unfortunately they did exactly that." "We've said all along that players don't want to earn a dollar more or a dollar less than they're worth. The players wanted to reach a fair agreement but never had a negotiating partner to work with," he said. "If you want to talk about greed I suggest you ask that to the other side."

Despite making headway in labour talks, the two sides were unable to compromise on a final salary cap figure. In a frantic exchange of letters, in the days prior to the cancellation of the season, the NHLPA offered to accept an individual team payroll cap of U.S. $49 million, which was a dramatic about-face for players who had consistently said they would sit out as much as three seasons to avoid playing under the restrictive cap system.

The sport's best known former player, Wayne Gretzky, a managing partner with the Phoenix Coyotes, told ESPN from Arizona: "There's a lot of people that are darn disappointed in the National Hockey League at this point in time." "I don't know if we realize the falling out that we have created in the National Hockey League to the fans of our game throughout North America," Mr. Gretzky said. "When we do come back to work and when this thing does get resolved, we've got a lot of work ahead of us to win back a lot of people."

SOURCES: Allan Woods, "NHL Officially Cancels Season," *National Post*. February 17, 2005, pp. A1, A4. Material reprinted with express permission of: "The National Post Company," a CanWest Partnership.

Questions
1. Use a website such as www.cbc.ca/sports to provide a brief timeline of the significant dates in this high-profile labour dispute.
2. What approach to collective bargaining, as discussed in the chapter, was used by the NHL owners and players? What other approach(es) would perhaps have been more effective? Why?
3. Are there any long-term implications to the NHL owners or players as a result of this labour-management conflict?

Chapter 11

Managing Human Resources Globally

1. Summarize how the growth in international business activity affects human resource management.

2. Identify the factors that most strongly influence HRM in international markets.

3. Discuss how differences among countries affect HR planning at organizations with international operations.

4. Describe how companies select and train human resources in a global labour market.

5. Discuss challenges related to compensating and rewarding employees from other countries.

6. Explain how employers prepare managers for international assignments and for their return home.

Introduction

Research in Motion (RIM) is a leading designer, manufacturer, and marketer of innovative wireless solutions for the worldwide mobile communications market. RIM's portfolio of award-winning products is used by thousands of organizations around the world and includes the BlackBerry® wireless platform, software development tools, and software/hardware licensing agreements. Founded in 1984 and based in Waterloo, Ontario, RIM operates offices in North America, Europe, and Asia Pacific. A search of the "Job Opportunities" area of RIM's website provides some insight about the globalization of

Co-CEOs Mike Lazaridis and Jim Balsillie of Research in Motion. RIM has offices in Europe, Asia Pacific, and the U.S.

its business structure and operations. For example, at the time of this writing, 195 job openings were listed for RIM's worldwide operations. Job openings included a Technical Sales Representative in Brussels, a Reference Guide Coordinator in Waterloo, a Software Test Specialist in Issaquah, Washington, a Technical Account Manager in New Delhi, and an Employee Health and Safety Advisor in Egham, England.[1]

According to a survey of almost 3,000 line executives and HR executives from 12 countries, international competition is the number one factor affecting human resource management. The globalization of business structures and globalization of the economy ranked fourth and fifth, respectively.[2] Business decisions such as whether to enter foreign markets or set up operations in other countries are complex, and in the course of moving and executing them many human resource issues surface.

This chapter discusses the HR issues that organizations must address in a world of global competition. We begin by describing how the global nature of business is affecting human resource management in modern organizations. Next, we identify how global differences among countries affect the organization's decisions about human resources. In the following sections we explore HR planning, selection, training, and compensation practices in international settings. Finally, we examine guidelines for managing employees sent on international assignments.

LO1

HRM in a Global Environment

The environment in which organizations operate is rapidly becoming a global one. More and more companies are entering international markets by exporting their products, building facilities in other countries, and entering into alliances with foreign companies. At the same time, companies based in other countries are investing and setting up operations in Canada. Indeed, most organizations now function in the global economy. The HRM function needs to continuously re-examine its role in supporting this expanding pace of business globalization. This requires HRM to:

- align HRM processes and functions with global requirements.
- adopt a global mindset including a thorough understanding of the global environment and the impact on managing people worldwide.
- enhance its own capabilities and competencies to become a business partner in acting on global business opportunities.[3]

What is behind the trend toward expansion into global markets? Foreign countries can provide a business with new markets in which there are millions or billions of new customers; developing countries often provide such markets, but developed countries do so as well. Companies set up operations overseas because they can operate with lower labour costs. As discussed in Chapter 1, outsourcing jobs to lower-cost nations will continue to increase.

Global activities are simplified and encouraged by trade agreements among nations; for example, most countries in Western Europe belong to the European Union and have begun to share a common currency, the euro. Canada, Mexico, and the United States have encouraged trade among themselves with the North American Free Trade Agreement (NAFTA). The World Trade Organization (WTO) resolves trade disputes among more than 100 participating nations.

As these trends and arrangements encourage international trade, they increase and change the demands on human resource management. According to a recent study from Hewitt Associates, a global human resources consulting firm, organizations must do a better job of addressing human capital costs and issues.[4] Organizations with customers or suppliers in other countries need employees who understand those customers or suppliers. Organizations that operate facilities in foreign countries need to understand the laws and customs that apply to employees in those countries. They may have to prepare managers and other employees to take international assignments. They have to adapt their human resource plans and policies to different settings. Even if some practices are the same worldwide, the company now has to communicate them to its international workforce. A variety of international activities require managers to understand HRM principles and practices prevalent in global markets.

Employees in an International Workforce

When organizations operate globally, their employees are very likely to be citizens of more than one country. Employees may come from the employer's home country, a host country, or a third country. The **home country** is the country in which the organization's headquarters is located. For example, Canada is the home country of Fairmont Hotels and Resorts, because Fairmont's headquarters are in Toronto. A Fairmont employee who is a Canadian citizen and works at Fairmont's headquarters or one of its Canadian properties is therefore a *home-country national*.

A **host country** is a country (other than the home country) in which an organization operates a facility. Barbados is a host country of Fairmont because Fairmont has operations there. Any Barbadian workers hired to work at Fairmont's Barbados property would be *host-country nationals*, that is, employees who are citizens of the host country.

A **third country** refers to a country that is neither the home country nor the host country. (The organization may or may not have a facility in the third country.) In

home country
The country in which an organization's headquarters is located.

host country
A country (other than the home country) in which an organization operates a facility.

third country
A country that is neither the home country nor the host country of an employer.

FIGURE 11.1

Levels of Global Participation

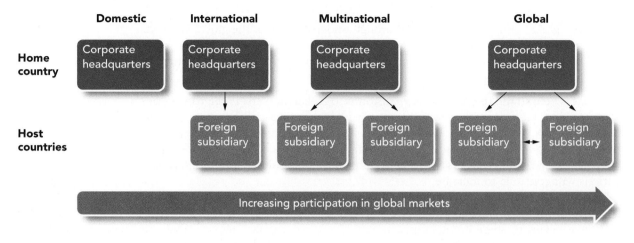

the example of Fairmont's operations in Barbados, the company could hire an Australian manager to work there. The Australian manager would be a *third-country national* because the manager is neither from the home country (Canada) nor from the host country (Barbados).

When organizations operate globally, they must decide whether to hire home-country nationals, host-country nationals, or third-country nationals for the overseas operations. Usually, they hire a combination of these. In general, employees who take assignments in other countries are called **expatriates.** In the Fairmont example, the Canadian and Australian managers working in Barbados would be expatriates during those assignments.

expatriates
Employees who take assignments in other countries.

The extent to which organizations use home-country, host-country, or third-country nationals varies. According to one study, Japanese firms with overseas operations use Japanese (home-country) managers for their foreign assignments relatively often.[5] European and U.S. companies are less likely to emphasize home-country nationals. (In the same study, HRM practices emphasizing the use of managers from the home country were associated with more HRM problems.)

Employers in the Global Marketplace

Just as there are different ways for employees to participate in international business—as home-country, host-country, or third-county nationals—so there are different ways for employers to do business globally, ranging from simply shipping products to customers in other countries to transforming the organization into a truly global one, with operations, employees, and customers in many countries. Figure 11.1 shows the major levels of global participation.

Most organizations begin by serving customers and clients within a domestic marketplace. Typically, a company's founder has an idea for serving a local, regional, or national market. The business must recruit, hire, train, and compensate employees to produce the product, and these people usually come from the business owner's local labour market. Selection and training focus not only on employees' technical abilities but also on other competencies such as interpersonal skills. Pay levels reflect local labour conditions. If the product succeeds, the company might expand operations to other domestic locations, and HRM decisions become more complex as the organization draws from a larger labour market and needs systems for training and engaging employees in several locations. As the employer's workforce grows, it is also likely to become more diverse. Even in small domestic organizations, a significant share of workers may be immigrants. In this way, even domestic companies are affected by issues related to the global economy.

As organizations grow, they often begin to meet demand from customers in other countries. The usual way that a company begins to enter foreign markets is by *exporting,* or shipping domestically produced items to other countries to be sold there. For example, Loewen, the Manitoba-based manufacturer of premium doors and windows, is hiring aggressively to meet growing demand for its products in the luxury home markets of Florida, Texas, and Georgia.[6] Eventually, it may become economically desirable to set up operations in one or more foreign countries. An organization that does so becomes an **international organization.** The decision to participate in international activities raises a host of HR issues, including the basic question of whether a particular location provides an environment where the organization can successfully acquire and manage human resources. Canada's largest hardware retailer, Canadian Tire, has had an office in Hong Kong for 25 years. Canadian Tire also has offices in Seoul, Taipei, and recently expanded into Shanghai.[7] CN Rail recently opened its first offices in China "to try and capture a larger share of the growing freight market for Canadian commodities shipped to China as well as consumer goods coming from China to North America."[8] The Bank of Nova Scotia has taken over the fourth largest bank in El Salvador, a Central American country of 6.6 million people, and will merge Banco de Comercio (assets of U.S. $1.1 billion) with Scotiabank El Salvador. Scotiabank also owns the seventh largest bank in Mexico and the largest bank in the Caribbean.[9]

While international companies build one or a few facilities in another country, **multinational companies** expand on a broader scale. They build facilities in a number of different countries as a way to keep production and distribution costs to a minimum. In general, when organizations become multinationals, they move production facilities from relatively high-cost locations to lower-cost locations. The lower-cost locations may have lower average wage rates, or they may reduce distribution costs by being nearer to customers. The HRM challenges faced by a multinational company are similar but larger than those of an international organization, because more countries are involved. More than ever, the organization needs to hire managers who can function in a variety of settings, give them necessary training, and provide flexible compensation systems that take into account the different pay rates, tax systems, and costs of living from one country to another.

At the highest level of involvement in the global marketplace are **global organizations.** These flexible organizations compete by offering top products tailored to segments of the market while keeping costs as low as possible. A global organization locates each facility based on the ability to effectively, efficiently, and flexibly produce a product or service, using cultural differences as an advantage. Rather than treating differences in other countries as a challenge to overcome, a global organization treats different cultures as equals. It may have multiple headquarters spread across the globe, so decisions are more decentralized. BP is one of the largest global energy companies. BP, with global sales and operating revenues of $233 billion, employs 103,700 employees worldwide and BP Canada Energy Company, headquartered in Calgary, Alberta, employs more than 1,400 Canadians.[10] This type of organization needs HRM practices that encourage flexibility and are based on an in-depth knowledge of differences among countries. In the wake of the $6-billion merger of historic brewers, Mol-

international organization
An organization that sets up one or a few facilities in one or a few foreign countries.

multinational company
An organization that builds facilities in a number of different countries in an effort to minimize production and distribution costs.

global organization
An organization that chooses to locate a facility based on the ability to effectively, efficiently, and flexibly produce a product or service, using cultural differences as an advantage.

transnational HRM system
Type of HRM system that makes decisions from a global perspective, includes managers from many countries, and is based on ideas contributed by people representing a variety of cultures.

son (Canada) and Adolph Coors Co. (U.S.), 11 executives are quitting. Leaving Molson are its chief strategy officer, chief legal officer, chief people officer, chief accounting officer, and vice-president for global rewards. Leaving Coors are its chief financial officer, chief revenue officer, chief people officer, regional vice-president for sales, and vice-president for corporate excellence. Company spokesperson Sylvia Morin puts a positive tone on the loss of these key executives: "an event like today can be looked at as an opportunity to re-create a team to assure cohesiveness."[11] Global organizations must be able to recruit, develop, retain, and use managers who can get results across national boundaries.

A global organization needs a **transnational HRM system**[12] that features decision making from a global perspective, managers from many countries, and ideas contributed by people from a variety of cultures. Decisions that are the outcome of a transnational HRM system balance uniformity (for fairness) with flexibility (to account for cultural and legal differences). This balance and the variety of perspectives should work together to improve the quality of decision making. The participants from various countries and cultures contribute ideas from a position of equality, rather than the parent country's culture dominating.

LO2

Factors Affecting HRM in International Markets

Whatever their level of global participation, organizations that operate in more than one country must recognize that the countries are not identical and differ in terms of many factors. To simplify this discussion, we focus on four major factors: culture, education, economic systems, and political-legal systems. These influences on human resource management are shown in Figure 11.2.

FIGURE 11.2

Factors Affecting Human Resource Management in International Markets

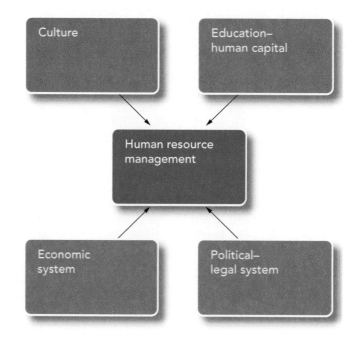

Culture

By far the most important influence on international HRM is the culture of the country in which a facility is located. *Culture* is a community's set of shared assumptions about how the world works and what ideals are worth striving for.[13] Cultural influences may be expressed through customs, languages, religions, and so on.

Culture is important to HRM for two reasons. First, it often determines the other three international influences. Culture can greatly affect a country's laws, because laws often are based on the culture's definitions of right and wrong. Culture also influences what people value, so it affects people's economic systems and efforts to invest in education.

Even more important for understanding human resource management, culture often determines the effectiveness of various HRM practices. Practices that are effective in Canada, for example, may fail or even backfire in a country with different beliefs and values.[14] Consider the five dimensions of culture that Geert Hofstede identified in his classic study of culture:[15]

1. *Individualism/collectivism* describes the strength of the relation between an individual and other individuals in the society. In a culture that is high in individualism, such as Canada, Great Britain, and the Netherlands, people tend to think and act as individuals rather than as members of a group. People in these countries are expected to stand on their own two feet, rather than be protected by the group. In a culture that is high in collectivism, such as Colombia, Pakistan, and Taiwan, people think of themselves mainly as group members. They are expected to devote themselves to the interests of the community, and the community is expected to protect them when they are in trouble.

2. *Power distance* concerns the way the culture deals with unequal distribution of power and defines the amount of inequality that is normal. In countries with large power distances, including India and the Philippines, the culture defines it as normal to maintain large differences in power. In countries with lower power distances, such as Denmark and Israel, people try to eliminate inequalities. One way to see differences in power distance is in the way people talk to one another. In the high-power-distance countries of Mexico and Japan, people address one another with titles (Señor Smith, Smith-san). At the other extreme, in Canada, in most situations people use one another's first names—behaviour that would be disrespectful in other cultures.

3. *Uncertainty avoidance* describes how cultures handle the fact that the future is unpredictable. High uncertainty avoidance refers to a strong cultural preference for structured situations. In countries such as Greece and Portugal, people tend to rely heavily on religion, law, and technology to give them a degree of security and clear rules about how to behave. In countries with low uncertainty avoidance, including Singapore and Jamaica, people seem to take each day as it comes.

4. *Masculinity/femininity* is the emphasis a culture places on practices or qualities that have traditionally been considered masculine or feminine. A "masculine" culture is a culture that values achievement, money making, assertiveness, and competition. A "feminine" culture is one that places a high value on relationships, service, care for the weak, and preserving the environment. In this model, Germany and Japan are examples of masculine cultures, and Sweden and Norway are examples of feminine cultures.

FIGURE 11.3

Five Dimensions of Culture

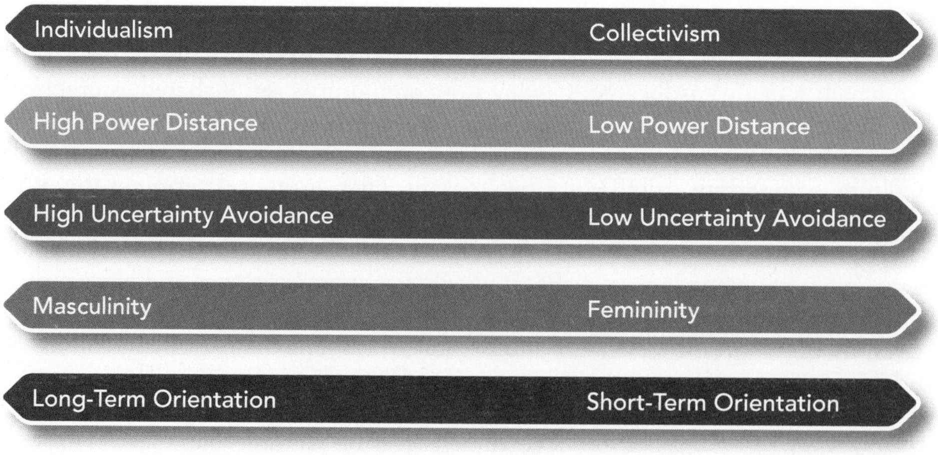

Individualism	Collectivism
High Power Distance	Low Power Distance
High Uncertainty Avoidance	Low Uncertainty Avoidance
Masculinity	Femininity
Long-Term Orientation	Short-Term Orientation

SOURCE: G. Hofstede, "Dimensions of National Cultures in Fifty Countries and Three Regions," in *Expectations in Cross-Cultural Psychology*, eds. J. Deregowski, S. Dziurawiec, and R. C. Annis (Lisse, Netherlands: Swets and Zeitlinger, 1983); G. Hofstede, "Cultural Constraints in Management Theories," *Academy of Management Executive* 7 (1993), pp. 81–90.

5. *Long-term/short-term orientation* suggests whether the focus of cultural values is on the future (long term) or the past and present (short term). Cultures with a long-term orientation value saving and persistence, which tend to pay off in the future. Many Asian countries, including Japan and China, have a long-term orientation. Short-term orientations, as in the cultures of Canada, Russia, and West Africa, promote respect for past tradition, and for fulfilling social obligations in the present. Figure 11.3 summarizes these five cultural dimensions.

Such cultural characteristics as these influence the ways members of an organization behave toward one another, as well as their attitudes toward various HRM practices. For instance, cultures differ strongly in their opinions about how managers should lead, how decisions should be handled, and what motivates employees. In Germany, managers achieve their status by demonstrating technical skills, and employees look to managers to assign tasks and resolve technical problems. In the Netherlands, managers focus on seeking agreement, exchanging views, and balancing the interests of the people affected by a decision.[16] Clearly, differences like these would affect how an organization selects and trains its managers and measures their performance.

Cultures strongly influence the appropriateness of HRM practices. For example, the extent to which a culture is individualist or collectivist will affect the success of a compensation program. Compensation tied to individual performance may be seen as fairer and more motivating by members of an individualist culture; a culture favouring individualism will be more accepting of great differences in pay between the organization's highest- and lowest-paid employees. Collectivist cultures tend to have much flatter pay structures.

Job design aimed at employee involvement can be problematic in cultures with high "power distance." In a Mexican slipper-manufacturing plant, an effort to expand the decision-making authority of production workers stumbled when the workers balked at doing what they saw as the supervisor's proper responsibility.[17] Realizing they had moved too quickly, the plant's managers narrowed the scope of the workers' decision-making authority so they could adapt to the role. On the other hand, a factor in favour of involvement at that plant was the Mexican culture's high collectivism. The workers liked discussing team-related information and using the information to benefit the entire team. As in this example, a culture does not necessarily rule out a particular HRM practice, such as employee involvement, but it should be a consideration in deciding how to carry out the practice.

Finally, cultural differences can affect how people communicate and how they coordinate their activities. In collectivist cultures, people tend to value group decision making, as in the previous example. When a person raised in an individualistic culture must work closely with people from a collectivist culture, communication problems and conflicts often occur. People from the collectivist culture tend to collaborate heavily and may evaluate the individualistic person as unwilling to cooperate and share information with them. Cultural differences in communication affected the way an agricultural company embarked on employee involvement at its facilities in the U.S. and Brazil.[18] Employee involvement requires information sharing, but in Brazil, high power distance leads employees to expect managers to make decisions, so they do not desire information that is appropriately held by managers. Involving the Brazilian employees required involving managers directly in giving and sharing information to show that this practice was in keeping with the traditional chain of command. Also, because uncertainty avoidance is another aspect of Brazilian culture, managers explained that greater information sharing would reduce uncertainty about their work. At the same time, greater collectivism in Brazil made employees comfortable with the day-to-day communication of teamwork. The individualistic U.S. employees needed to be sold more on this aspect of employee involvement.

Because of these challenges, organizations must prepare managers to recognize and handle cultural differences. They may recruit managers with knowledge of other cultures or provide training, as described later in the chapter. For expatriate assignments, organizations may need to conduct an extensive selection process to identify individuals who can adapt to new environments.

Education and Skill Levels

Countries also differ in the degree to which their labour markets include people with education and skills of value to employers. As discussed in Chapter 1, Canada suffers from a shortage of skilled workers in many occupations, and the problem is expected to increase. On the other hand, the labour markets in many countries are very attractive because they offer high skills and low wages.

Educational opportunities also vary from one country to another. In general, spending on education is greater per student in high-income countries than in poorer countries.[19] In the Netherlands, government funding of school systems allows students to go all the way through graduate school without paying.[20] Similarly, the free education provided to citizens in the former Soviet bloc resulted in a highly educated workforce, in spite of the region's economic difficulties. Some Third World countries, such as Nicaragua and Haiti, have relatively low educational levels because those countries have not invested in education.

Companies with foreign operations locate in countries where they can find suitable employees. The education and skill levels of a country's labour force affect how and the extent to which companies want to operate there. In countries with a poorly educated population, companies will limit their activities to low-skill, low-wage jobs. In Ireland, a high rate of post-secondary education, along with a strong work ethic and high unemployment, attracted employers looking for skilled workers, high productivity, and low turnover.[21]

Economic System

A country's economic system whether capitalist or socialist, as well as the government's involvement in the economy through taxes or compensation, price controls, and other activities, influences human resource management practices in a number of ways.

As with all aspects of a region's or country's life, the economic system and culture are likely to be closely tied, providing many of the incentives or disincentives for developing the value of the labour force. Socialist economic systems provide ample opportunities for educational development because the education system is free to students. At the same time, socialism may not provide economic rewards (higher pay) for increasing one's education. In capitalist systems, students bear more of the cost of their education, but employers reward those who invest in education.

The health of an economic system affects human resource management. In developed countries with great wealth, labour costs are relatively high. Such differences show up in compensation systems and in recruiting and selection decisions.

In general, socialist systems take a higher percentage of each worker's income as the worker's income increases. Capitalist systems tend to let workers keep more of their earnings. In this way, socialism redistributes wealth from high earners to the poor, while

Students at the University of Warsaw in Poland are provided with a government-supported education. In general, former Soviet bloc countries tend to be generous in funding education, so they tend to have highly educated and skilled labour forces. Countries such as Canada and the United States generally leave higher education up to individual students to pay for, but the labour market rewards students who earn a college diploma or university degree.

capitalism apparently rewards individual accomplishments. In any case, since the amount of take-home pay a worker receives after taxes may thus differ from country to country, in an organization that pays two managers in two countries $100,000 each, the manager in one country might take home more than the manager in the other country. Such differences make pay structures more complicated when they cross national boundaries, and they can affect recruiting of candidates from more than one country.

Political-Legal System

A country's political-legal system—its government, laws, and regulations—strongly impinges on human resource management. The country's laws often dictate the requirements for certain HRM practices, such as training, compensation, selection, and labour relations. As we noted in the discussion of culture, the political-legal system arises to a large degree from the culture in which it exists, so laws and regulations reflect cultural values.

For example, Canada has been a leader in eliminating discrimination in the workplace. Because the value of diversity is important in Canadian culture, legal safeguards such as Human Rights laws discussed in Chapter 2 exist, which affect hiring and other HRM decisions. As a society, Canada also has strong beliefs regarding the fairness of pay systems. Thus, Pay Equity legislation (discussed in Chapter 2), provides for equal pay for work of equal value. Other laws and regulations dictate much of the process of negotiation between unions and management. All these are examples of laws and regulations that affect the practice of HRM in Canada. When Canadian companies employ workers in other countries, the workers are usually covered by the employment laws in their own countries. Employment laws in many countries offer workers less protection than Canadian legislation provides.

Laws and regulations in other countries reflect the norms of their cultures. In Germany employees have a legal right to "codetermination" at the level of the company, facility, and individual. At the company level, an organization's employees have direct influence on the important decisions that affect them, such as large investments or new strategies. This influence comes from employee representatives on each company's supervisory council. At the level of each facility, codetermination exists through work councils. The councils have no rights in the economic management of the company, but they can influence HRM policies on issues such as working hours, payment methods, hirings, and transfers. Finally, at the individual level, employees have contractual rights, such as the right to read their employee files and the right to be informed about how their pay is calculated.[22]

As this example suggests, an organization that expands internationally must gain expertise in the host country's legal requirements and ways of dealing with its legal system, often leading organizations to engage an international relocation consulting firm or hire one or more host-country nationals to help in the process. Some countries have laws requiring that a certain percentage of the employees of any foreign-owned subsidiary be host-country nationals, and in the context of our discussion here, this legal challenge to an organization's HRM may hold an advantage if handled creatively.

Human Resource Planning in a Global Economy   LO3

As economic and technological change creates a global environment for organizations, human resource planning is involved in decisions about participating as an exporter or as an international, multinational, or global company. Even purely domestic companies may draw talent from the international labour market. For example, the Academy of Learning, an Edmonton-based college, is setting up a recruitment and training office in Caracas to help Canadian employers find foreign tradespeople and prepare them for jobs in Canada. In 2002, 18,000 Venezuelan oil workers were laid off from the state oil company and the Academy of Learning is interested in these foreign-trained workers because they already possess work experience.[23] As organizations consider decisions about their level of international activity, HR professionals should provide information about the relevant human resource issues, such as local market pay rates and labour laws. When organizations decide to operate internationally or globally, human resource planning involves decisions about where and how many employees are needed for each international facility.

In Chapter 4, we saw that human resource planning includes decisions to hire and lay off workers to prepare for the organization's expected needs. Compared with other countries, Canada allows employers wide latitude in reducing their workforce, giving Canadian employers the option of hiring for peak needs, then laying off employees if needs decline. Other governments place more emphasis on protecting workers' jobs. European countries tend to be very strict in this regard.

Until recently, Japanese law and culture supported the concept of "lifetime employment," but this practice is changing to help companies weather a difficult recession.[24] HR planning at Japanese companies now includes more decisions to shrink or close Japanese facilities in favour of production elsewhere. At its peak in the mid-1990s, Nissan Motor Company's Murayama plant was a symbol of Japanese automaking efficiency, producing almost a half million cars a year. A few years later, Nissan closed the plant, displacing all 5,000 workers. As Nissan was closing plants in Japan, it was expanding production of its Maxima sedan in North America and planning a new factory to produce minivans and sport utility vehicles. The company's home market was weak, and demand for its product was strong in North America, so the decisions made economic sense. Producing in North America keeps transportation costs down and protects the company from shifts in the relative value of the dollar and yen. As can be easily imagined, many HR issues come into play in consequence of and especially in planning for such shifts, in both home country and host country.

LO4

Selecting Employees in a Global Labour Market

Many companies such as Fairmont have headquarters in Canada plus facilities in locations around the world. To be effective, employees in Fairmont's Mexico operations must understand that region's business and social culture. Organizations often meet this need by hiring host-country nationals to fill most of their foreign positions.[25] A key reason is that a host-country national can more easily understand the values and customs of the local workforce than someone from another part of the world can. Also, training for and transporting families to foreign assignments is more expensive than hiring people in the foreign country. Employees may be reluctant to take a foreign assignment because of the difficulty of relocating internationally. Sometimes the move requires the employee's spouse to quit a job, and some countries will not allow the employee's spouse to seek work, even if jobs might be available.

Even so, organizations fill many key foreign positions with home-country or third-country nationals. Sometimes a person's technical and human relations skills outweigh the advantages of hiring locally. In other situations, such as the shortage of North American knowledge workers, the local labour market simply does not offer enough qualified people. At organizations located where needed skills are in short supply, hiring immigrant employees may be part of an effective recruitment and selection strategy.[26]

Whether the organization is hiring immigrants or selecting home-country or third-country nationals for international assignments, some basic principles of selection apply. Selection of employees for international assignments should reflect criteria that have been associated with success:

Qualities associated with success in foreign assignments are the ability to communicate in the foreign country, flexibility, enjoying a challenging situation, and support from family members. What would persuade you to take an international assignment?

- Competency in the employee's area of expertise
- Ability to communicate verbally and nonverbally in the foreign country
- Flexibility, tolerance of ambiguity, and sensitivity to cultural differences
- Motivation to succeed and enjoyment of challenges
- Willingness to learn about the foreign country's culture, language, and customs
- Support from family members[27]

In research conducted a number of years ago, the factor most strongly influencing whether an employee completed a foreign assignment was the comfort of the employee's spouse and family.[28] Personality may also be important. Research has found successful completion of international assignments to be most likely among employees who are extroverted (outgoing), agreeable (cooperative and tolerant), and conscientious (dependable and achievement oriented).[29]

Qualities of flexibility, motivation, agreeableness, and conscientiousness are so important because of the challenges involved in entering another culture. The emotions that accompany an international assignment tend to follow a cycle like that in Figure 11.4.[30] For a month or so after arriving, the foreign worker enjoys a "honeymoon" of fascination and euphoria as the employee enjoys the novelty of the new culture and compares its interesting similarities to or differences from the employee's own culture. Before long, the employee's mood declines as he or she notices more unpleasant differences and experiences feelings of isolation, criticism, stereotyping, and even hostility. As the mood reaches bottom, the employee is experiencing **culture shock,** the

culture shock
Disillusionment and discomfort that occur during the process of adjusting to a new culture.

FIGURE 11.4

Emotional Cycle Associated with a Foreign Assignment

SOURCE: Adapted from C. Lachnit, "Low-Cost Tips for Successful Inpatriation," *Workforce*, August 2001, p. 44.

disillusionment and discomfort of ideas that occur during the process of adjusting to a new culture and its norms, values, and perspectives. Eventually, if employees persist and continue learning about their host country's culture, they develop a greater understanding and a support network. As the employee's language skills and comfort increase, the employee's mood should improve as well. Eventually, the employee reaches a stage of adjustment in which he or she accepts and enjoys the host country's culture.

Even if the organization determines that the best candidate for a position is someone from another country, employers often have difficulty persuading candidates to accept foreign assignments. Not only do the employee and employee's family have to contend with culture shock, but the employee's spouse commonly loses a job when an employee makes an international move. Some organizations solve this problem with a compromise: the use of **virtual expatriates,** or employees who manage an operation abroad without locating permanently in that country.[31] They take frequent trips to the foreign country, and when they are home, they use technologies such as videoconferencing and electronic collaboration tools to stay in touch. An assignment as a virtual expatriate may be less inconvenient to family members and less costly to the employer. The arrangement does have disadvantages. Most notably, by limiting personal contact to sporadic trips, the virtual expatriate will likely have a harder time building relationships.

The "E-HRM" box features how Fairmont Hotels and Resorts uses the Web to recruit employees.

virtual expatriates
Employees who manage an operation abroad without permanently locating in the country.

E-HRM

Fairmont Hotels and Resorts—Recruiting Online

Fairmont Hotels and Resorts, headquartered in Toronto, is North America's largest luxury hotel management company. Employing approximately 18,000 employees, Fairmont Hotels and Resorts has 41 unique, upscale properties located throughout Canada, the United States, Bermuda, Barbados, Mexico, and the United Arab Emirates. Fairmont's website (www.fairmont.com) provides a wealth of information about its luxury properties to attract not only guests but also prospective employees. Career opportunity links are grouped into four categories:

- U.S. Mexico, Bermuda, Barbados
- Canada
- United Arab Emirates
- Student Work Experience Program (SWEP)

Both Canadian and international jobs are linked to the electronic job board, www.monster.ca, which provides job applicants with a range of interactive capabilities and job search resources. The Student Work Experience Program (SWEP) is targeted to community college and university hospitality students and provides links to specific properties including employee vignettes that provide perspectives from program participants. Vignettes titled "A Day in the Life" provide photos of the property, employees and other information of interest to prospective employees. By recruiting online, Fairmont Hotels and Resorts is able to attract qualified applicants from anywhere in the world to meet its human resource needs.

SOURCE: www.fairmont.com. Retrieved: September 23, 2004.

Training and Developing a Global Workforce

In an organization whose employees come from more than one country, some special challenges arise with regard to training and development: (1) Training and development programs should be effective for all participating employees, regardless of their background. (2) When organizations hire employees to work in a foreign country or transfer them to another country, the employer needs to provide the employees with training in how to handle the challenges associated with working in the foreign country.

Training Programs for an International Workforce

Developers of effective training programs for an international workforce must ask certain questions.[32] The first is to establish the objectives for the training and its content. Decisions about the training should support those objectives. The developers should next ask what training techniques, strategies, and media to use. Some will be more effective than others, depending on the learners' language and culture, as well as the content of the training. For example, in preparation Canadian employees might expect to discuss and ask questions about the training content, whereas employees from other cultures might consider this level of participation to be disrespectful, so for them some additional support might be called for. Language differences will require translations and perhaps a translator at training activities. Next, the developers should identify any other interventions and conditions that must be in place for the training to meet its objectives. For example, training is more likely to meet its objectives if it is linked to performance management and has the full support of management. Finally, the developers of a training program should identify who in the organization should be involved in reviewing and approving the training program.

The plan for the training program must consider international differences among trainees. For example, economic and educational differences might influence employees' access to and ability to use Web-based training. Cultural differences may influence whether they will consider it appropriate to ask questions and whether they

CULTURAL DIMENSION	IMPACT ON TRAINING
Individualism	Culture high in individualism expects participation in exercises and questioning to be determined by status in the company or culture.
Uncertainty avoidance	Culture high in uncertainty avoidance expects formal instructional environments. Less tolerance for impromptu style.
Masculinity	Culture low in masculinity values relationships with fellow trainees. Female trainers less likely to be resisted in low-masculinity cultures.
Power distance	Culture high in power distance expects trainer to be expert. Trainers expected to be authoritarian and controlling of session.
Time orientation	Culture with a long-term orientation will have trainees who are likely to accept development plans and assignments.

TABLE 11.1

Effects of Culture on Training Design

SOURCE: Based on B. Filipczak, "Think Locally, Act Globally," *Training*, January 1997, pp. 41–48.

expect the trainer to spend time becoming acquainted with employees or to get down to business immediately. Table 11.1 provides examples of how cultural characteristics can affect training design. These differences may call for extra planning and creativity on the part of the training program's developer. To meet the needs of trainees in China, for instance, the training program should take into account that culture's high power distance.[33] The instructor needs to encourage audience feedback, perhaps by inviting the group's senior member to speak. If the instructor gives other trainees a chance to forward questions to this person, they can avoid embarrassing a high-status participant by asking a better question. Also, extra time is needed to prepare translations and practice delivering presentations with a translator.

Cross-Cultural Preparation

cross-cultural preparation
Training to prepare employees and their family members for an assignment in a foreign country.

When an organization selects an employee for a position in a foreign country, it must prepare the employee for the foreign assignment. This kind of training is called **cross-cultural preparation,** preparing employees to work across national and cultural boundaries, and it often includes family members who will accompany the employee on the assignment. The training is necessary for all three phases of an international assignment:

1. Preparation for *departure*—language instruction and an orientation to the foreign country's culture.
2. The *assignment* itself—some combination of a formal program and mentoring relationship to provide ongoing further information about the foreign country's culture.
3. Preparation for the *return* home—providing information about the employee's community and home-country workplace (from company newsletters, local newspapers, and so on).

Methods for providing this training may range from lectures for employees and their families to visits to culturally diverse communities.[34] Employees and their families may also spend time visiting a local family from the country where they will be working. In many organizations, cross-cultural training is mandatory. In the later section on managing expatriates, we provide more detail about cross-cultural preparation.

Global Employee Development

At global organizations, international assignments are a part of many career paths. The organization benefits most if it applies the principles of employee development in deciding which employees should be offered jobs in other countries. Career development helps expatriate and inpatriate employees make the transitions to and from their assignments and helps the organization apply the knowledge the employees obtain from these assignments. An example of a company with a strong program for global employee development is Deloitte, described in the "Best Practices" box.

Performance Management across National Boundaries

The general principles of performance management may apply in most countries, but the specific methods that work in one country may fail in another. Therefore, organizations have to consider legal requirements, local business practices, and national cultures when they establish performance management methods in other countries.

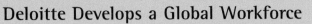

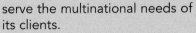

BEST PRACTICES

Deloitte Develops a Global Workforce

Deloitte is an accounting and consulting firm whose 95,000 employees work in 700 offices located in 140 different countries around the world. An organization like that has the human resources to know the ins and outs of international business—but only if it gives employees international experience. Deloitte does just that with its Global Development Program.

The Global Development Program, based on a curriculum developed by the human resource department, identifies midcareer employees in Deloitte's worldwide locations and assigns them to work in other countries. HR coordinators work with applicants to identify countries that offer experiences likely to be relevant to future work in the applicants' own countries. Often, employees wind up working with the same multinational client but in another country where that client operates. Through the program, these employees learn the languages, business practices, and cultures of the countries where they are assigned. They also have plenty of opportunity to interact with other expatriate employees.

For example, Fabian Gomez left Mexico for a year and a half at Deloitte's New York office. When he returned to León, a city northwest of Mexico City, Gomez was well prepared to serve an international clientele as an audit partner. Explains Gomez, "A lot of our business is serving Mexican subsidiaries of international companies, and the executives usually come from other places" as far from Mexico as Japan.

Hundreds of employees and Deloitte offices in 50 countries participate in the Global Development Program. Executives give the program some of the credit for the firm's growth in global revenue. The company expects further benefits down the road, as Deloitte increases its ability to serve the multinational needs of its clients.

The participants praise the program, too. Gomez says, "People are very excited about [the Global Development Program], because they know that if they have international experience, both they and the company are going to get ahead."

Canadian Pam McLaughlin trained with a Big Four firm and qualified with Deloitte's Ottawa office in September 2002. Six weeks later, Pam joined Deloitte's Bermuda office as an audit senior with the insurance group. Pam was promoted to manager in July 2004 and is serving one of Bermuda's largest insurance clients. Pam is an active participant in softball and sailing and is a volunteer little-league coach on the weekends.

SOURCES: P. J. Kiger, "How Deloitte Builds Global Expertise," *Workforce*, June 2002, pp. 62–64, 66; "Looking for a New Experience?" *Leader-Post*, March 5, 2005, p. D1.

Differences may include which behaviours are rated, how and the extent to which performance is measured, who performs the rating, and how feedback is provided.[35]

For example, National Rental Car uses a behaviourally based rating scale for customer service representatives. To measure the extent to which customer service representatives' behaviours contribute to the company's goal of improving customer service, the scale measures behaviours such as smiling, making eye contact, greeting customers, and solving customer problems. Depending on the country, different behaviours may be appropriate. In Japan, culturally defined standards for polite behaviour include the angle of bowing as well as proper back alignment and eye contact. In Ghana and many other African nations, appropriate measures would include behaviours that reflect loyalty and repaying of obligations as well as behaviours related to following regulations and procedures.

The extent to which managers measure performance may also vary from one country to another. In rapidly changing regions, such as Southeast Asia, the organization may have to update its performance plans more often than once a year.

Not every culture values the independence and freedom from surveillance that North American workers and managers desire. Ito-Yokado, the Japanese company that controls 7-Eleven convenience stores in that country, has installed cash registers that let headquarters monitor every time a sale is made and the frequency with which managers use the system's analytical tools to track product sales.[36]

Feedback is another area in which differences can occur. Employees around the world appreciate positive feedback, but Canadian employees are much more used to direct feedback than are employees in other countries. In Mexico managers are expected to provide positive feedback before focusing the discussion on behaviours the employee needs to improve.[37] At the Thai office of Singapore Airlines, managers resisted giving negative feedback to employees because they feared this would cause them to have bad karma, contributing to their reincarnation at a lower level in their next life.[38] The airlines therefore allowed the managers to adapt their feedback process to fit local cultures.

LO5

Compensating and Rewarding an International Workforce

Chapter 9 explained that total compensation includes decisions about pay structure, incentive pay, and employee benefits and services. All these decisions become more complex when an organization has an international workforce.

Pay Structure

As Figure 11.5 shows, market pay structures can differ substantially across countries. For example, compared with the labour market in Germany, the markets in Mexico and Hong Kong provide much lower pay levels overall. The latter two labour markets also exhibit less of a pay difference for jobs requiring greater skill and education.

Differences such as these create a dilemma for global companies: Should pay levels and differences reflect what workers are used to in their own countries? Or should they reflect the earnings of colleagues in the country of the facility, or earnings at the company headquarters? For example, should a German engineer posted to Mexico be paid according to the standard in Germany or the standard in Mexico? If the standard is Frankfurt, the engineers in Mexico will likely see the German engineer's pay as unfair. If the standard is Mexico, the company will likely find it impossible to persuade a German engineer to take an assignment in Mexico. Typically, companies have resolved this dilemma by linking pay and benefits more closely to those of the employee's home country. However, evidence suggests this link is slowly weakening and now depends more on the nature and length of the foreign assignment.[39]

These decisions affect a company's costs and ability to compete. The average hourly labour costs in industrialized countries such as Canada, the United States, Germany, and Japan are far higher than these costs in newly industrialized countries such as Mexico, Hong Kong, and Korea.[40] As a result, we often hear that Canadian labour costs are too high to allow Canadian companies to compete effectively unless

FIGURE 11.5

Hourly Compensation Costs for Production Workers in Manufacturing in Ten Countries

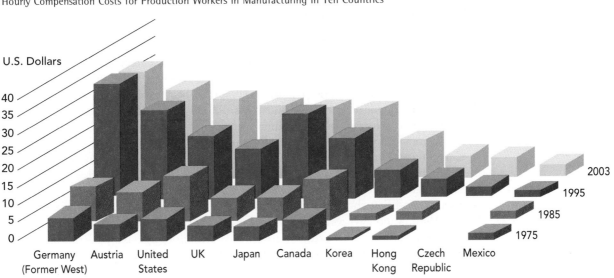

SOURCE: "Hourly Compensation Costs in U.S. Dollars for Production Workers in Manufacturing, 31 Countries or Areas and Selected Economic Groups, Selected Years, 1975–2003," U.S. Department of Labor, Bureau of Labor Statistics, November 2004, www.bls.gov/news.release/pdf/ichcc.pdf. Retrieved: March 21, 2005.

the companies shift operations to low-cost foreign subsidiaries. That conclusion over-simplifies the situation for many companies. Merely comparing wages ignores differences in education, skills, and productivity.[41] If an organization gets more or higher-quality output from a higher-wage workforce, the higher wages may be worth the cost. Besides this, if the organization has many positions requiring highly skilled workers, it may need to operate in (or hire immigrants from) a country with a strong educational system, regardless of labour costs. Finally, labour costs may be outweighed by other factors, such as transportation costs or access to resources or customers.

At the same time, the challenge of competing with organizations in low-wage countries can be very difficult. China, for example, has invested in vocational schools, which provide training for skilled factory jobs. Chinese universities graduate a much larger share of engineers than Canadian universities. These schools are flooding the Chinese labour market with talent, so that even as high-tech manufacturing spreads to many Chinese cities, the need for workers is easy to fill. For Chinese workers, even experienced engineers, the result is that pay is growing but remains low compared to rates in other countries. An example is Li Guangxiang, a senior engineer and assistant manager at a Flextronics International computer parts factory, who earns just $10,000 a year.[42]

Incentive Pay

Besides setting a pay structure, the organization must make decisions with regard to incentive pay, such as bonuses and stock options. International labour laws vary. For example, in Mexico, profit-shar-

A large number of journalists found shelter in the old building of the French nongovernmental organization in Afghanistan. Taking an overseas assignment, especially in a harsh or potentially dangerous climate, requires the challenge of adjusting to life in a new country, so many companies pay employees higher salaries to compensate for this hardship.

ing is mandatory. Employers are required by law to distribute 10 percent of pre-tax earnings among employees other than senior managers.[43] Although stock options became a common form of incentive pay in North America during the 1990s, European businesses did not begin to embrace this type of compensation until the end of that decade. European companies with North American operations have felt the greatest pressure to join the stock option "club."[44] For instance, executives at Alcatel, a French manufacturer of telecommunications equipment, recently realized they needed to broaden the scope of their compensation when they began to acquire North American firms such as Canada's Newbridge Networks. Afraid that failure to offer stock options would result in a loss of qualified employees, Alcatel announced a plan that would award options to over one-third of its engineers and middle managers.

Canada and Europe differ in the way they award stock options. European companies usually link the options to specific performance goals, such as the increase in a company's share price compared with that of its competitors. German law actually requires this, and British firms such as Barclays are beginning to enforce stricter guidelines. Belgium and Switzerland still discourage the use of stock options by imposing high taxes on this form of compensation. Italy and Norway have passed laws and tax changes that make stock options more attractive to employers and employees. As competition in European labour markets increases, experts predict that companies not offering options will have a harder time recruiting the best employees.

Employers are adding incentives to compensate employees working in high-risk parts of the world such as the Middle East. A recent study conducted by Watson Wyatt, found that many companies are offering added incentives to reward staff for working in high-risk areas.[45]

Employee Benefits and Services

As in Canada, compensation packages in other countries include benefits and services. Decisions about benefits and services must take into account the laws of each country involved, as well as employees' expectations and values in those countries. Some countries require paid parental leave, and some countries, in addition to

FIGURE 11.6

Normal Annual Hours Worked in Manufacturing Relative to Canada

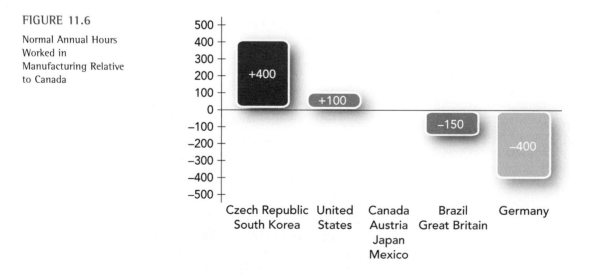

SOURCE: *Key Indicators of the Labor Market 2001–2002* (Geneva, Switzerland: International Labor Office, 2001).

Canada, have nationalized health care systems, which would affect the value of private health insurance in a compensation package. Pension plans are more widespread in parts of Western Europe than in Canada, the United States, or Japan. Over 90 percent of workers in Switzerland have pension plans, as do all workers in France. Among workers with pension plans, Canadian workers are significantly less likely to have defined benefit plans than workers in Japan or Germany.

Paid vacation, discussed in Chapter 9, tends to be more generous in Western Europe than in North America. Figure 11.6 compares the number of hours the average manufacturing employee works in various countries. Of these countries, only in the Czech Republic, South Korea, and the United States do manufacturing workers put in more hours than Canadian workers—up to 400 more hours per year. In Brazil, Great Britan, and Germany, the norm is to work 150 to 400 hours less than a Canadian worker over the course of a year.

International Labour Relations

In some industries, unions are forming global labour alliances. For example, the United Steelworkers of America and Mexico's Miners and Metalworkers Union (250,000 members) want to create a coalition of metals and mining industry unions throughout the western hemisphere.[46]

Companies that operate across national boundaries will increasingly need to work with unions in more than one country. Organizations establish policies and goals for labour relations, overseeing labour agreements, and monitoring labour performance (for example, output and productivity).[47] The day-to-day decisions about labour relations are usually handled by each foreign subsidiary. The reason is that labour relations on an international scale involve differences in laws, attitudes, and economic systems, as well as differences in negotiation styles.

At least in comparison with European organizations, North American organizations exert more centralized control over labour relations in the various countries where they operate.[48] Management therefore must recognize differences in how various countries understand and regulate labour relations. For example, in North America, collective bargaining usually involves negotiations between a union local and an organization's management, but in Sweden and Germany, collective bargaining generally involves negotiations between an employers' organization and a union representing an entire industry's employees.[49] Legal differences range from who may form a union to how much latitude an organization is allowed in laying off workers. In China, for example, efforts at economic reform have resulted in many thousands of layoffs. In the spring of 2002, as many as 20,000 workers at a time have rallied to protest layoffs by PetroChina, angry that early-retirement packages did not include expected medical insurance and social security payments. The workers resort to public protest because the country's legal and economic system allows only government-controlled unions and does not provide them with recourse when the government does not support their position.[50] In Germany, because labour representatives participate on companies' boards of directors, the way management handles labour relations can affect a broad range of decisions.[51] Management therefore has an incentive to build cooperative relationships.

International labour relations must also take into account that negotiations between labour and management take place in a different social context, not just different economic and legal contexts. Cultural differences that affect other interactions come into play in labour negotiations as well. Negotiators will approach the process differently depending on whether the culture views the process as primarily cooperative or competitive and whether it is local practice to negotiate a deal by starting with the specifics or agreeing on overall principles.[52] Working with host-country nationals can help organizations navigate such differences in negotiation style.

Managing Expatriates

At some point, most international and global organizations assign managers to foreign posts. These assignments give rise to significant human resource challenges, from selecting managers for these assignments to preparing them, compensating them, and helping them adjust to a return home. In a global marketplace, expatriate assignments are important, but evidence suggests that North American companies have not yet learned to select and use expatriates. Out of every hundred expatriates, between 16 and 40 return before their assignment is complete, a rate about two to three times that of foreign nationals.[53] Other research found that between one-third and one-half of expatriates perform at a level that, according to employers' evaluations, is either ineffective or marginally effective.[54]

Selecting Expatriate Managers

The challenge of managing expatriate managers begins with determining which individuals in the organization are most capable of handling an assignment in another country. Expatriate managers need technical competence in the area of operations, in part to help them earn the respect of employees. In the past and at many organiza-

TABLE 11.2

Topics for Assessing Candidates for Global Assignments

Motivation
- Investigate reasons and degree of interest in wanting to be considered.
- Determine desire to work abroad, verified by previous concerns such as personal travel, language training, reading, and association with foreign employees or students.
- Determine whether the candidate has a realistic understanding of what working and living abroad requires.
- Determine the basic attitudes of the spouse/partner toward an overseas assignment.

Health
- Determine whether any medical problems of the candidate or candidate's family might be critical to the success of the assignment.
- Determine whether the candidate is in good physical and mental health.

Language ability
- Determine potential for learning a new language.
- Determine any previous language(s) studied or oral ability (judge against language needed on the overseas assignment).
- Determine the ability of the spouse/partner to meet the language requirements.

Family considerations
- How many moves have been made in the past among different cities or internationally?
- What problems were encountered?
- How recent was the last move?

TABLE 11.2 Concluded

Family considerations (*continued*)
- What is the spouse/partner's goal in this move?
- What family responsibilities, e.g., child care, elder care does the candidate have?
- Are there any special adjustment problems that you would expect?
- How is each member of the family reacting to this possible move?
- Do special educational problems exist within the family?

Resourcefulness and initiative
- Can the candidate make and stand by decisions and judgments?
- Does the candidate have the intellectual capacity to deal with several dimensions simultaneously?
- Is the candidate able to reach objectives and produce results with whatever people and facilities are available, regardless of the limitations and barriers that might arise?
- Is the candidate able to operate without a clear definition of responsibility and authority on a foreign assignment?
- Will the candidate be able to explain the aims and company philosophy to the local managers and workers?
- Does the candidate possess sufficient self-discipline and self-confidence to overcome difficulties or handle complex problems?
- Can the candidate work without supervision?
- Can the candidate operate effectively in a foreign environment without normal communications and supporting services?

Adaptability
- Is the candidate sensitive to others, open to the opinions of others, cooperative, and able to compromise?
- What are the candidate's reactions to new situations, and efforts to understand and appreciate differences?
- Is the candidate culturally sensitive, aware, and able to relate across the culture?
- Does the candidate understand his own culturally derived values?
- How does the candidate react to criticism?
- What is the candidate's understanding of the government system?
- Will the candidate be able to make and develop contacts with peers in the foreign country?
- Does the candidate have patience when dealing with problems?
- Is the candidate resilient; can he or she bounce back after setbacks?

Career planning
- Does the candidate consider the assignment more than a temporary overseas trip?
- Is the move consistent with the candidate's career goals and aspirations?
- Is the employee's career planning realistic?
- What is the candidate's basic attitude toward the company?
- Is there any history or indication of interpersonal problems with this employee?

Financial
- Are there any current financial and/or legal considerations that might affect the assignment?
- Are financial considerations negative factors? Will undue pressures be brought to bear on the employee or family as a result of the assignment?

SOURCE: Adapted from D. M. Noer, *Multinational People Management,* pp. 55–57. Copyright © 1989 by the Bureau of National Affairs, Inc., Washington, DC, 20037.

tions even today, technical competence has been almost the only basis upon which companies have selected expatriate managers.[55] Of course, many other skills are also necessary for success in any management job, especially one that involves working overseas. Depending on the nature of the assignment and the culture where it is located, the organization should consider each candidate's skills, learning style, and approach to problem solving.[56]

A successful expatriate manager must be sensitive to the host country's cultural norms, flexible enough to adapt to those norms, and strong enough to survive the culture shock of living in another culture. In addition, if the manager has a family, the family members must be able to adapt to a new culture. Adaptation requires three kinds of skills:[57]

1. Ability to maintain a positive self-image and feeling of well-being
2. Ability to foster relationships with the host-country nationals
3. Ability to perceive and evaluate the host country's environment accurately

In a study that drew on the experience of people holding international assignments, expatriates told researchers that the most important qualities for an expatriate manager are, in order of importance, family situation, flexibility and adaptability, job knowledge and motivation, relational skills, and openness to other cultures.[58] To assess candidates' ability to adapt to a new environment, interviews should address topics such as the ones listed in Table 11.2. The interviewer should be certain to give candidates a clear and complete preview of the assignment and the host-country culture. This helps the candidate evaluate the assignment and consider it in terms of his or her family situation, so the employer does not violate the employee's privacy.[59]

A final issue with regard to selecting expatriates is the use of women in international assignments. For a long time, many firms believed that women would have little success as managers in countries where women have not traditionally been promoted to management positions (such as in Japan and other Asian countries). In spite of this view, some organizations have taken a chance on female managers, and evidence suggests the original assumption was wrong. Robin Abrams, working for Apple Computer in Hong Kong, found that nobody cares whether "you are wearing trousers or a skirt if you have demonstrated core competencies." Some female expatriates' experience has been that the novelty of being a woman in a group of men gives them an extra sort of credibility with host-country nationals. With such successes, organizations began rapidly increasing the share of women assigned to foreign countries.[60] The percentage of female expatriates is currently 18 percent of the overall expatriate population.[61]

Of course, selection decisions are not just about finding employees who can do the job; the organization needs to select people who *want* an expatriate assignment. It is nothing new that many people are reluctant to move to a foreign country. Since the terrorist attacks of September 2001 and the subsequent war on terrorism, however, the reluctance of some employees has grown, because they fear being targets of terrorism or civil unrest. However, despite the risks, many multinational companies plan to maintain their operations in high-risk areas. More than 80 respondents to a recent Watson Wyatt survey said they "have no plans to reduce the number of employees working in affected areas in the long term. However, some businesses may rely more heavily on business trips as opposed to permanent residence in affected regions, at least in the short term."[62] They should prepare evacuation plans in case of emergency and should tell the employees about those plans. However, according to a recent study, only 40 percent of employers surveyed have implemented a formal evacuation policy.[63] Employers should provide strong channels of communication for expatriate workers, as well as access to employee assistance plans (EAPs). Above all, they should ensure that employees are well trained for their assignments, prepared for the culture, and knowledgeable about the transportation and geography in their host country, so that they do not unintentionally draw negative attention to themselves or expose themselves unduly. Finally, employers should take a global perspective that recognizes the present heightened anxiety felt by all—"inpatriates" (foreign workers in Canada) as well as expatriates.

Preparing Expatriates

LO6

Once the organization has selected a manager for an overseas assignment, it is necessary to prepare that person through training and development. Because expatriate success depends so much on the entire family's adjustment, the employee's spouse should be included in the preparation activities. Employees selected for expatriate assignments already have job-related skills, so preparation for expatriate assignments often focuses on cross-cultural training—that is, training in what to expect from the host country's culture. The general purpose of cross-cultural training is to create an appreciation of the host country's culture so expatriates can behave appropriately.[64] Paradoxically, this requires developing a greater awareness of one's own culture, so that the expatriate manager can recognize differences and similarities between the cultures and, perhaps, home-culture biases.

On a more specific level, cross-cultural training for foreign assignments includes the details of how to behave in business settings in another country—the ways people behave in meetings, how employees expect managers to treat them, and so on. As an example, Germans value promptness for meetings to a much greater extent than do Latin Americans—and so on. How should one behave when first meeting one's business counterparts in another culture? The "outgoing" personality style so valued in North America may seem quite rude in other parts of the world.[65]

Employees preparing for a foreign assignment also need information about such practical matters as housing, schools, recreation, shopping, and health care facilities in the country where they will be living. This is a crucial part of the preparation.

Communication in another country often requires a determined attempt to learn a new language. Some employers try to select managers who speak the language of the host country, and a few provide language training. Most companies assume that employees in the host country will be able to speak the host country's language. Even if this is true, host country nationals are not likely to be fluent in the home country's language, so language barriers remain. The "HR How To" box provides suggestions for cross-cultural training.

Along with cross-cultural training, preparation of the expatriate should include career development activities. Before leaving for a foreign assignment, expatriates should discuss with their managers how the foreign assignment fits into their career plans and what types of positions they can expect upon their return. This prepares the expatriate to develop valuable skills during the overseas assignment and eases the return home when the assignment is complete.

When the employee leaves for the assignment, the preparation process should continue.[66] Employees need a chance to discuss their experiences with other expatriates, so they can learn from their failures and successes. The organization may provide a host-country mentor or "assimilator" to help expatriates understand their experiences. Successful expatriates tend to develop a bicultural or multicultural point of view, so as they spend more time in the host country, the value of their connections to other expatriates may actually increase.

Cross-Cultural Training for Expatriates and Their Families

When an employee on an international assignment fails to meet performance expectations, it is often due to difficulties the employee's family has experienced in adjusting to the host country. Cross-cultural training for individual expatriates and their families should be incorporated as a standardized preparatory tool for a successful international assignment. The following are some implementation recommendations:

1. Cross-cultural training should be considered a necessary and mandatory process.

2. The location of training should be determined based on the needs of the entire family. Organizations need to be flexible with respect to the best location for the training, i.e., home or host country.

3. The depth of training is key. Cross-cultural training needs to be done with care. Cross-cultural training needs to be planned and delivered at the appropriate depth.

4. Families need to be fully included in the training process.

5. International human resource professionals need to be clear about the training priorities and objectives and communicate them clearly to the expatriate and their family prior to and during the learning events.

SOURCE: Adapted from Allon Bross, Adrienne Churchill, and Judi Zifkin, "Cross-Cultural Training: Issues to Consider during Implementation," *Canadian HR Reporter*, June 5, 2000, www.hrreporter.com. Retrieved: March 3, 2004. © Copyright *Canadian HR Reporter*, June 5, 2000, by permission of Carswell, Toronto, Ontario, 1-800-387-5164, www.hrreporter.com.

Compensating and Rewarding Expatriates

One of the greatest challenges of managing expatriates is determining the compensation package. Most organizations use a *balance sheet approach* to determine the total amount of the package. This approach adjusts the employee's compensation so that it gives the employee the same standard of living as in the home country plus extra pay for the inconvenience of locating globally. As shown in Figure 11.7, the balance sheet approach begins by determining the purchasing power of compensation for the same type of job in the employee's own country—that is, how much a person can buy, after taxes, in terms of housing, goods and services, and a reserve for savings. Next, this amount is compared with the cost (in dollars, for a Canadian company) of these same expenses in the foreign country. In Figure 11.7, the greater size of the second column means the costs for a similar standard of living in the foreign country are much higher in every category except the reserve amount. For the expatriate in this situation, the employer would pay the additional costs, as shown by the third column. Finally, the expatriate receives additional purchasing power from premiums and incentives. Because of these added incentives, the expatriate's purchasing power is more than what the employee could buy at home with the salary for an equivalent job. (Compare the fourth column with the first.) In practice, allowances for hardship and higher costs can more than double total compensation.[67]

After setting the total pay, the organization divides this amount into the four components of a total compensation package. First, there is a base salary. Determining the base salary is complex because different countries use different currencies (dollars, yen, euros, and so on). The exchange rate—the rate at which one currency may be ex-

FIGURE 11.7

The Balance Sheet for
Determining Expatriate
Compensation

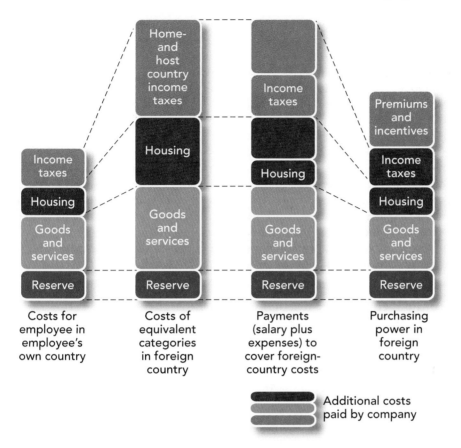

Costs for employee in employee's own country

Costs of equivalent categories in foreign country

Payments (salary plus expenses) to cover foreign-country costs

Purchasing power in foreign country

Additional costs paid by company

SOURCE: C. Reynolds, "Compensation of Overseas Personnel," in *Handbook of Human Resource Administration*, 2nd ed., J. J. Famularo, ed. (New York: McGraw-Hill, 1986), p. 51. Reprinted with permission.

changed for another—constantly shifts in response to a host of economic forces, so the real value of a salary in terms of dollars is constantly changing. Also, as discussed earlier, the base salary may be comparable to the pay of other managers at headquarters or comparable to other managers at the foreign subsidiary. Because many organizations pay a salary premium as an incentive to accept an overseas assignment, expatriates' salaries are often higher than pay for staying at headquarters.

A second component of total pay is a *tax equalization allowance*. Companies have different systems for taxing income, and in some countries, tax rates are higher than in Canada. Usually, the employer of an expatriate withholds the amount of tax to be paid in the parent country, then pays all of the taxes due in the country where the expatriate is working.

A third component, benefits, presents additional challenges. Most of these have to do with whether an employee can use the same benefits in the foreign country. For example, if an expatriate has been contributing to a pension plan in Canada, does this person have a new pension in the foreign country? Or can the expatriate continue to contribute to the Canadian pension plan? Similarly, health benefits may involve receiving care at certain health facilities. While the person is abroad, does the same health plan cover services received in the foreign country? In one case, flying an employee back to Canada for certain procedures actually would have cost less than having the procedures done in the country where the person was working. But the company's health plans did not permit this alternative.

An employer may offer expatriates additional benefits to address the problem of uprooting the spouse when assigning an employee overseas. Pfizer, a pharmaceutical company, provides a $10,000 allowance that the spouse can use in many different ways.[68] A person in the foreign country helps the spouse with professional development and locating educational or other resources. In countries where the spouse is allowed to work, Pfizer tries to find him or her a job within the company. Pfizer also provides cross-cultural counselling and language assistance and tries to connect the family with the area's expatriate community.

The final component of the total compensation packages is some set of allowances to make a foreign assignment more attractive. Cost-of-living allowances make up the differences in expenses for day-to-day needs. Housing allowances ensure that the expatriate can maintain the same standard of living as in Canada. Education allowances reimburse expatriates who pay tuition for their children to attend private schools. Relocation allowances cover the expenses of making the move to the foreign country, including transportation, shipping or storage of possessions, and expenses for temporary housing until the employee can rent or purchase a home.

Helping Expatriates Return and Minimizing Turnover

repatriation
The process of preparing expatriates to return home from a foreign assignment.

As the expatriate's assignment nears its end, the human resource department faces a final challenge: helping the expatriate make the transition back to his or her home country. The process of preparing expatriates to return home from a foreign assignment is called **repatriation.** Companies are increasingly discussing repatriation/reentry with expatriates. Presently, 86 percent of organizations discuss repatriation with employees up from only 48 percent in 1995.[69] Often, repatriation issues are discussed, at least informally, even before the candidate accepts an international assignment. Reentry is not as simple as it might sound. Culture shock takes place in reverse. The experience has changed the expatriate, and the company's and expatriate's home culture have changed as well. Also, because of differences in economies and compensation levels, a returning expatriate may experience a decline in living standards. The standard of living for an expatriate in many countries includes maid service, a limousine, private schools, and clubs.

Companies are increasingly making efforts to help expatriates through this transition and take steps to ensure expatriates stay with the company after their return. Expatriates are more likely to stay with a company that provides them opportunities to use their international experience.[70] Two activities help the process along: communication and validation.[71] Communication refers to the expatriate receiving information and recognizing changes while abroad. The more the organization keeps in contact with the expatriate, the more effective and satisfied the person will be upon return. The expatriate plays a role in this process as well. Expatriates should work at maintaining important contacts in the company and industry. Communication related to performance and career development before and during the international assignment also should help the employee return to a choice of positions that are challenging and interesting. Validation means giving the expatriate recognition for the international service when this person returns home. Expatriates who receive family repatriation support and recognition from colleagues and top managers for their international service and future contribution have fewer troubles with reentry than those whose contributions are disregarded. Validation should also include planning for how the returning employee will contribute to the organization. What skills will this person bring back? What position will he or she fill? The new skills may be much more than knowledge of a particular culture. For example, the person may have learned how to lead or negotiate with a diverse group of people.[72]

Monsanto, a large agricultural, chemical, and pharmaceutical company, has an extensive repatriation program that begins long before the expatriate returns. Before the employee begins an international assignment, the employee and the sending and receiving managers develop an agreement that expresses their understanding of the assignment, including its fit with the company's business objectives and employee's career path. When the assignment is nearing its end, Monsanto gives expatriates information about the potential culture shock that can accompany the return home, as well as information about possible changes in family members, friends, and the office environment. Repatriating employees also share their experiences with associates, managers, and employees. A few months after the expatriate has returned, he or she holds "debriefing" sessions with several colleagues to help work through difficulties. According to Monsanto, this program makes the company more competitive in benefiting from international assignments. Not only does the process help employees return home, it helps their colleagues better understand different cultural issues and business environments.[73]

Summary

1. Summarize how the growth in international business activity affects human resource management.

   More and more companies are entering international markets by exporting and operating foreign facilities. Organizations therefore need employees who understand customers and suppliers in other countries. They need to understand local laws and customs and be able to adapt their plans to local situations. To do this organizations may hire a combination of home-country, host-country, and third-country nationals. They may operate on the scale of an exporter or an international, global, or multinational organization. A global organization needs a transnational HRM system, which makes decisions from a global perspective, includes managers from many countries, and is based on ideas contributed by people representing a variety of cultures.

2. Identify the factors that most strongly influence HRM in international markets.

   By far the most important influence is the culture of each market—its set of shared assumptions about how the world works and what ideals are worth striving for. A culture has the dimensions of individualism/collectivism, high or low power distance, high or low uncertainty avoidance, masculinity/femininity, and long-term or short-term orientation. Countries also differ in the degree to which their labour markets include people with education and skills of value to employers. Another influence on international HRM is the foreign country's political-legal system—its government, laws, and regulations. Finally, a country's economic system, capitalist or socialist, as well as the government's involvement in the country's economy, such as through taxes and price controls, is a strong factor determining HRM practices.

3. Discuss how differences among countries affect HR planning at organizations with international operations.

   As organizations consider decisions about their level of international activity, HR professionals should provide information about the relevant human resource issues. When organizations decide to operate internationally or globally, HR planning involves decisions about where and how many employees are needed for each international facility. Some countries limit employers' ability to lay off workers, so organizations would be less likely to staff for peak periods. Other countries allow employers more flexibility in meeting human resource needs. HRM professionals need to be conversant with such differences.

4. Describe how companies select and train human resources in a global labour market.

   Many organizations with international operations fill most positions with host-country nationals. These employees can more easily understand the values and customs of the local workforce, and hiring locally tends to be less expensive than moving employees to new locations. Organizations also fill foreign positions with home-country and third-country nationals who have human relations skills associated with success in international assignments. They also may use "virtual expatriates," who do not go abroad for an extended period. When sending employees on international assignments, organizations prepare the employees (and often their families) through cross-cultural training. Before the assignment, the training provides instruction in the other country's language and culture. During the assignment, there is communication with the home country and mentoring. For the return home the employer provides further training.

5. Discuss challenges related to compensating and rewarding employees from other countries.
Pay structures can differ substantially among countries in terms of pay level and the relative worth of jobs. Organizations must decide whether to set pay levels and differences in terms of what workers are used to in their own countries or in terms of what employees' colleagues earn at headquarters. Typically, companies have resolved this dilemma by linking pay and benefits more closely to those of the employee's country, but this practice may be weakening so that it depends more on the nature and length of the foreign assignment. These decisions affect the organization's costs and ability to compete, so organizations consider local labour costs in their location decisions. Along with the basic pay structure, organizations must make decisions regarding incentive pay, such as bonuses and stock options. Laws may dictate differences in benefit packages, and the value of benefits will differ if a country requires them or makes them a government service.

6. Explain how employers prepare managers for international assignments and for their return home.
When an organization has selected a manager for an international assignment, it must prepare the person for the experience. In cross-cultural training the soon to-be expatriate learns about the foreign culture he or she is heading to, and studies her or his own home-country culture as well for insight. The trainee is given a detailed briefing on how to behave in business settings in the new country. Along with cross-cultural training, preparation of the expatriate should include career development activities to help the individual acquire valuable career skills during the international assignment and at the end of the assignment to handle repatriation successfully. Communication of changes at home and validation of a job well done abroad help the expatriate through the repatriation process.

Review and Discussion Questions

1. Identify the home country, host country(ies), and third country(ies) in the following example: A global soft-drink company called Cold Cola has headquarters in Halifax, Nova Scotia. It operates production facilities in the United States, and in Jakarta, Indonesia. The company has assigned a manager from Moncton to head the U.S. facility and a manager from Hong Kong to manage the Jakarta facility.

2. What are some HRM challenges that arise when a Canadian company expands from domestic markets by exporting? When it changes from simply exporting to operating as an international company? When an international company becomes a global company?

3. In recent years, many North American companies have invested in Russia and sent Canadian managers there in an attempt to transplant North American-style management. According to Hofstede (see Figure 11.3), Canadian culture has low power distance, uncertainty avoidance, and long-term orientation and high individuality and masculinity. Russia's culture has high power distance and uncertainty avoidance, low masculinity and long-term orientation, and moderate individuality. In light of what you know about cultural differences, how well do you think Canadian managers can succeed in each of the following North American-style HRM practices? (Explain your reasons.)

   a. Selection decisions based on extensive assessment of individual abilities.
   b. Appraisals based on individual performance.
   c. Systems for gathering suggestions from workers.
   d. Self-managing work teams.

4. Besides cultural differences, what other factors affect human resource management in an organization with international operations?

5. Suppose you work in the HR department of a company that is expanding into a country where the law and culture make it difficult to lay off employees. How should your knowledge of that difficulty affect human resource planning for the overseas operations?

6. Why do multinational organizations hire host-country nationals to fill most of their foreign positions, rather than sending expatriates for most jobs?

7. Suppose an organization decides to improve collabouration and knowledge sharing by developing an intranet to link its global workforce. It needs to train employees in several different countries to use this system. List the possible cultural issues you can think of that the training program should take into account.

8. For an organization with operations in three different countries, what are some advantages and disadvantages of setting compensation according to the labour markets in the countries where the employees live

and work? What are some advantages and disadvantages of setting compensation according to the labour market in the company's headquarters? Would the best arrangement be different for the company's top executives and its production workers? Explain.

9. What abilities make a candidate more likely to succeed in an assignment as an expatriate? Which of these abilities do you have? How might a person acquire these abilities?

What's Your HR IQ?

www.mcgrawhill.ca/college/noe

The Online Learning Centre offers more ways to check what you've learned so far. Find experiential exercises as well as Test Your Knowledge Quizzes, Videos, and many other resources at www.mcgrawhill.ca/college/noe.

Case: Foreign Assignments Increasing, Along with Employee Resistance

Canadians are working outside the country in increasing numbers. Data from the 2001 Census show that more than 68,000 Canadians had a place of work outside the country, an increase of about 20 percent from the 1996 Census. In addition, as Canada continues to play a growing role in an expanding global marketplace, there is every expectation the need for Canadian talent to work abroad will grow.

In the Canadian Employee Relocation Council's most recent *Survey of Corporate Relocation Policies*, more than two-thirds of the 88 firms surveyed had transferred staff overseas in 2003, a 14-percent increase from 2001. In the same survey, family issues ranked as the number one challenge for an overseas assignment.

While working in foreign lands may hold appeal, it is clearly not for everybody. There are many barriers to overcome for both the organization and its employees when it comes to a foreign posting. Partly in response to the personal realities that individuals are coping with as well as to rapidly changing business opportunities, shorter-term assignments, lasting from six months to three years, are becoming more common.

Whether it's a short- or long-term assignment, many of the challenges remain the same: getting the right people in the right job, at the right place, and at the right time.

Today, most Canadian families have both parents working, and there are more than 7.3 million women in the labour force, so when it comes to taking on a foreign assignment, it's no surprise that family issues are top of mind. Statistics Canada also reports a 40-percent increase in the number of female managers since 1990. Today, their careers are an even more important consideration than perhaps was the case ten or so years ago. The bottom line: Moving is a far more complex undertaking than ever before.

"Moving people is a very expensive undertaking for the company," says Sue Irwin, responsible for international HR and relocations with ConocoPhillips Canada in Cal-

gary. "It can cost three times as much to move somebody from say Houston than it does to hire a local person in Calgary and so it has to be the right fit."

Irwin manages a portfolio of both inpatriates (people coming to work in Canada) as well as expatriates. "While shorter-term assignments meet business needs, they also provide the much-needed career development and experience to the best talent in the organization," she says. "And it's not just about getting the right technical talent. Equally important is the ability to work with people with varied skill sets and from different backgrounds." All are critical skills on the global stage.

Terri Lynn Oliver, international HR advisor with Siemens Canada, notes that at Siemens, "the selection of high potentials (for assignment) is part of the overall corporate approach for succession planning and career development."

With a global workforce of 420,000, of which 6,600 are in Canada, there is no shortage of foreign opportunities. At Siemens the process for selection is structured and the company maintains a pool of potential talent to draw from as opportunities arise. The challenge from a corporate perspective, says Oliver, is managing the expectation and linking the move to a strategic objective. "People want to know, 'What position will I come back to?' In most situations it's impossible to give a guarantee about opportunities on the completion of the assignment. And so people will often opt for the domestic promotion."

When it comes to individuals accepting an assignment, family and career issues dominate. "The spouse's career is a major consideration particularly on a longer assignment," says Oliver. "Schooling is also a challenge and Siemens tries to be innovative for both its inpatriates and expatriates in finding workable solutions within budget."

Schooling issues are echoed by Irwin who adds, "There are many students in gifted and extracurricular programs, people just don't want to uproot their families."

Thomas Vulpe, with the Canadian Foreign Service Institute, an agency within the Department of Foreign Affairs and International Trade, says family issues can predict the successful completion of an international assignment.

"Various studies have shown family issues to be the single most important issue in early repatriation," he says. These subtleties may not be readily apparent before the move, but culture shock and the inability to work in a foreign location can often be too much for the trailing spouse, leading to an early return.

"Companies are becoming more concerned about these soft issues," says Mike Watters, vice-president of sales with moving firm Allied International. These are not just Canadian problems, he adds. He tells the story of the wife of a French company executive who was "abandoned" in the Toronto-area, without access to any support. "She couldn't speak a word of English and left saying it was the worst two years of her life."

While family issues are the main barriers to individuals taking on a foreign assignment, safety is an escalating concern. Canada is a safe country to live and raise a family. Many of the countries where Canadians are working are becoming more dangerous it seems with each passing day.

"One of the key parts of safety training for foreign-aid workers in hot spots like Columbia, Bolivia, and Afghanistan, includes looking under their vehicles with a mirror to check for bombs," Vulpe says. Not a pleasant routine as you're also trying to comfort children who are used to walking to school. These issues are compounded by the fact the "megalopolises where people are being posted are becoming more polluted, and access to quality health care is a concern. Ten years ago it wasn't such a big issue, but today it's a big decision," he adds.

Perhaps that's why Terri Lynn Oliver says, "flexibility to shorten an assignment and planning for the worst," are a key part in the development of any foreign assignment.

SOURCE: Stephen Cryne, "Foreign Assignments Increasing, Along with Employee Resistance," *Canadian HR Reporter*, September 27, 2004, www.hrreporter.com. Retrieved: April 15, 2005. © Copyright *Canadian HR Reporter*, September 27, 2004, by permission of Carswell, Toronto, Ontario, 1-800-387-5164, www.hrreporter.com.

Questions

1. What are some of the human resource challenges associated with relocating employees to jobs and work assignments outside Canada?
2. Would you be interested in working outside Canada? Why or why not? If you would consider working outside Canada at some point in your career, at what life/career stage would a global assignment be most appealing?

Case: Human Resource Management in a World with Terrorism

As we have seen in this chapter, human resource management cannot function apart from world events. Certainly the link was made tragically clear during and after the events of September 11, 2001. Terrorists (allegedly part of Osama bin Laden's al-Qaida network) hijacked four U.S. planes, then crashed two of them into the World Trade Centre's twin towers and one into the Pentagon. (The fourth crashed in a field after passengers scuffled with the hijackers.) After no response to U.S. warnings that the Taliban government in Afghanistan must turn over bin Laden and his deputies, the United States and United Kingdom began military action against the Taliban and al-Qaida in Afghanistan. Bombing in that country started on October 7, 2001.

As of the writing of this chapter, we do not know what the ultimate result of the ongoing war on terrorism will be. But we do know that the terrorist attacks and the U.S. war on terrorism have intensified the challenges faced by multinational companies. The impact is especially strong for global companies that must manage employees from a variety of nationalities and religions, and do so across many countries.

First, North American companies doing business internationally must recognize that many parts of the world have the potential to become hostile territory. Particularly sensitive areas include countries where many citizens hold the opinion that the bombings of Afghanistan were hostile to their religion. In these parts of the world, companies must manage their workforce in light of the greater risk to their security. Many of these employees were afraid, and some asked to return to their home countries. Accounting giant KPMG surveyed HR executives about the impact of terrorism, and some said that at least half their expatriate workforce had asked to return home. Those most likely to request a return home were employees working in high-risk countries such as Egypt and Pakistan.

Before September 11, 2001, many of these employees had lived relatively normal lives, free from security concerns. Recent threats and terrorist acts have shattered that sense of security. Expatriate assignments are more risky in the eyes of many employees.

One result of these issues is that compensation for expatriates is likely to rise. Candidates for international jobs are more likely to look for help in paying for housing that offers security as well as the comforts of home. Many may ask for more frequent trips home to be with family as well.

Another challenge is that companies with global workforces must manage across boundaries that are more nationalistic. While many U.S. citizens have felt united in actions they justify as a valid response to an act of war, many citizens of other countries consider the U.S. military response as an act of aggression.

SOURCE: E. Tahmincioglu, "Opportunities Mingle with Fear Overseas," *New York Times*, October 24, 2001, p. G1.

Questions

1. Give an example of how the experience of the September 11 attacks and the U.S. war on terrorism might affect each of the HRM functions of recruiting, training, and compensating employees for a global company.

2. Do the issues in question 1 differ depending on the countries where employees are located? (For example, would the issues and HRM practices have the same effect on employees in Germany, Colombia, and Saudi Arabia?) Explain.

3. The case points out that although people in different parts of the world condemn terrorism, they do not necessarily view events in the same context. For a global or international organization, what challenges to HRM do these different viewpoints present?

Creating and Maintaining High-Performance Organizations

1. Define high-performance work systems and identify the elements of such a system.

2. Summarize the outcomes of a high-performance work system.

3. Describe the conditions that create a high-performance work system.

4. Explain how human resource management can contribute to high performance.

5. Discuss the role of HRM technology in high-performance work systems.

6. Summarize ways to measure the effectiveness of human resource management.

Introduction

"It is the world's most spectacular and unifying event. Literally billions of people stop what they're doing to watch it. The attention of those billions will focus on British Columbia and Canada as we celebrate the Vancouver 2010 Olympic & Paralympic Games. The planning and staging of this extraordinary event will require the harmonized efforts and passions of thousands of people. It will become an intricate, split second ballet of planning, construction, revenue generation, relationship building, co-

VANCOUVER 2010

The Vancouver Organizing Committee for the 2010 Olympic & Paralympic Games has a mandate of high performance and the Senior Vice President, Human Resources has a key role to play.

DO SOMETHING EXTRAORDINARY FOR CANADA AND THE WORLD.

Senior Vice President, Human Resources

In an organization that aims to spread its values across the world, you will become an advocate in the creation of a culture that focuses on performance, inclusion, fellowship and celebration. The ultimate HR generalist, you will bring the leadership and stewardship to the recruitment of talented people who believe passionately and professionally in the Olympic ideas. Generate a human resource plan. Create a flexible and scalable infrastructure that accommodates best practices in employee relations, compensation, and performance measurement. As you've done throughout your career you will be a leader by example in a large, complex and results-first organization.

A PASSION FOR WHAT THE OLYMPIC RINGS REPRESENT

---

ordination, and leadership. It will attract the best and the brightest as the clock ticks down to the opening ceremonies, then twenty-seven days of unprecedented athletic achievement, international goodwill, arts and cultural events. It will be the time of our lives!"[1]

To achieve this mandate of high performance, the leadership team of the Vancouver Organizing Committee for the 2010 Olympic & Paralympic Games (Vancouver 2010) was looking for a Senior Vice President, Human Resources. Vancouver 2010 requires an infrastructure that will provide for best practices in employee relations, compensation, and performance measurement to bring out the best in the employees and in the volunteers. This senior human resource executive will play a key role in creating a high performance culture.

Although few occupy roles as visible as Vancouver 2010's Senior Vice President, Human Resources, HR professionals are increasingly engaged in strategic roles responsible for creating and maintaining high-performance organizations.

This chapter summarizes the role of human resource management in creating an organization that achieves a high level of performance. We begin with a definition of *high-performance work systems* and a description of these systems' elements and outcomes. Next, we identify the conditions that contribute to high performance. We explain how the various HRM functions can contribute to high performance. Finally, we introduce ways to measure the effectiveness of human resource management.

LO1

high-performance work system
An organization in which technology, organizational structure, people, and processes all work together to give an organization an advantage in the competitive environment.

High-Performance Work Systems

The challenge facing managers today is how to make their organizations into high-performance work systems, in which technology, organizational structure, people, and processes all work together to give an organization an advantage in the competitive environment. To function as a high-performance work system, each of these elements must fit well with the others in a smoothly functioning whole. Many manufacturers use the latest in processes including flexible manufacturing technology and just-in-time inventory control (meaning parts and supplies are automatically restocked as needed), but of course, these processes do not work on their own; they must be run by qualified people. Organizations need to determine what kinds of people fit their needs, and then locate, train, and motivate those special people.[2] According to research, organizations that introduce integrated high-performance

SGCI, the Sackville, New Brunswick-based marketing communications company, serves diverse and highly successful clients including Aliant Mobility, Mount Allison University, and Pizza Delight and has a legendary reputation for providing a caring, appreciative, family-oriented environment.

work practices usually experience increases in productivity and long-term financial performance.3

Creating a high-performance work system contrasts with traditional management practices. In the past, decisions about technology, organizational structure, and human resouces were treated as if they were unrelated. An organization might acquire a new information system, restructure jobs, or add an office in another country without considering the impact on its people.4 More recently, managers have realized that success depends on how well all the elements work together.

SGCI, a marketing communications company based in Sackville, New Brunswick (www.sgcicom.com), is an example of an organization that has effectively integrated all the elements of a high-performance work system. Harvey Gilmour, director of Development, Acadia University describes SGCI as a "collection of wonderfully creative individuals, working as a team. They have supported Acadia University since 1995 with work that has been unparalleled. We know—we have tested their quality of work, dedication to their client, their enthusiasm, willingness to go the extra mile and their philanthropy—against many others in New Brunswick and Nova Scotia. SGCI always comes out ahead. We rely on SGCI greatly and they share in our success at Acadia."5 SGCI's work environment is described by Nelson Cabral, creative director, "We work in a house that we fill with family. We have a chef. Egos are rare but sentiment is frequent."6

Elements of a High-Performance Work System

As shown in Figure 12.1, in a high-performance work system, the elements that must work together include organizational structure, task design, people (the selection, training, and development of employees), reward systems, and information systems, and human resource management plays an important role in establishing all these.

Organizational structure is the way the organization groups its people into useful divisions, departments, and reporting relationships. The organization's top management

FIGURE 12.1

Elements of a High-Performance Work System

makes most decisions about structure, for instance, how many employees report to each supervisor and whether employees are grouped according to the functions they carry out or the customers they serve. Such decisions affect how well employees coordinate their activities and respond to change. In a high-performance work system, organizational structure promotes cooperation, learning, and continuous improvement.

Task design determines how the details of the organization's necessary activities will be grouped, whether into jobs or team responsibilities. In a high-performance work system, task design makes jobs efficient while encouraging high quality results. In Chapter 3, we discussed how to carry out this HRM function through job analysis and job design.

The right *people* are a key element of high-performance work systems. HRM has a significant role in providing people who are well suited and well prepared for their jobs. Human resource professionals help the organization recruit and select people with the needed qualifications. Training, development, and career management ensure that these people are able to perform their current and future jobs with the organization.

Reward systems contribute to high performance by encouraging people to strive for objectives that support the organization's overall goals. Reward systems include the performance measures by which employees are judged, the methods of measuring performance, and the incentive pay and other rewards linked to success. Human resource management plays an important role in developing and administering reward systems, as we saw in Chapters 7 through 9.

The final element of high-performance work systems is the organization's *information systems*. Managers make decisions about the types of information to gather and the sources of information. They also must decide who in the organization should have access to the information and how they will make the information available. Modern information

In a high-performance work system, all the elements—people, technology, and organizational structure—work together for success.

systems, including the Internet, have enabled organizations to share information widely. HR departments take advantage of this technology to give employees access to information about benefits, training opportunities, job openings, and more, as we will describe later in this chapter.

Outcomes of a High-Performance Work System

LO2

Consider the practices of steel minimills. Some of these mills have strategies based on keeping their costs below competitors' costs; low costs let them operate at a profit while winning customers with low prices. Other steel minimills focus on "differentiation," meaning they set themselves apart in some way other than low price—for example, by offering higher quality or unusual product lines. Research has found that the minimills with cost-related goals tend to have highly centralized structures, so managers can focus on controlling through a tight line of command. These organizations have low employee participation in decisions, relatively low wages and benefits, and pay highly contingent on performance.[7] At minimills that focus on differentiation, structures are more complex and decentralized, so authority is more spread out. These minimills encourage employee participation and have higher wages and more generous benefits. They are high-performance work systems. In general, these differentiator mills enjoy higher productivity, lower scrap rates, and lower employee turnover than the mills that focus on low costs.

Outcomes of a high-performance work system thus include higher productivity and efficiency. These outcomes contribute to higher profits. A high-performance work system may have other outcomes, including high product quality, great customer satisfaction, and low employee turnover. Some of these outcomes meet intermediate goals that lead to higher profits (see Figure 12.2). For example, high quality contributes to

FIGURE 12.2

Outcomes of a High-Performance Work System

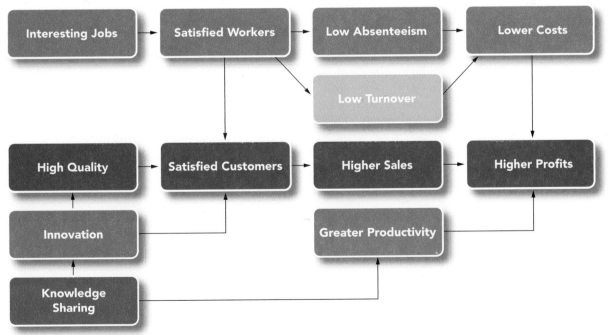

customer satisfaction, and customer satisfaction contributes to growth of the business. Likewise, improving productivity lets the organization do more with less, which satisfies price-conscious customers and may help the organization win over customers from its competitors. Other ways to lower cost and improve quality are to reduce absenteeism and turnover, providing the organization with a steady supply of experienced workers. In the previous example of minimills, some employers keep turnover and scrap rates low. Meeting those goals helps the minimills improve productivity, which helps them earn more profits.

In a high-performance work system, the outcomes of each employee and work group contribute to the system's overall high performance. The organization's individuals and groups work efficiently, provide high-quality goods and services, and so on, and in this way, they contribute to meeting the organization's goals. When the organization adds or changes goals, people are flexible and make changes as needed to meet the new goals.

LO3

Conditions that Contribute to High Performance

Certain conditions underlie the formation of a high-performance work system. Common practices in high-performing organizations, such as those involving rewards, employee involvement, and jobs with variety, contribute to high performance by giving employees skills, incentives, knowledge, autonomy—as well as satisfaction and engagement—conditions associated with high performance. Finally, managing employee turnover and discipline effectively and engaging in ethical behaviour are necessary conditions of high performance because they contribute to good long-term relationships with employees, customers, and the public.

Teamwork and Involvement

Today's organizations involve employees. They expect employees to make more decisions about how they perform their jobs. One of the most popular ways to involve employees is to design work so that it is performed by teams. On a work team, employees bring together various skills and experiences to produce goods or provide services. The organization may charge the team with making decisions traditionally made by managers, such as hiring team members and planning work schedules. Teamwork and involvement contribute to high performance when they improve job satisfaction and give the organization fuller use of employees' ideas and expertise. At Cognos Inc., an Ottawa-based software company, managers worldwide are required to attend workshops on how to recognize individual achievements and keep employees challenged and motivated to stay. According to Beverly Kaye, a California-based author and consultant whose theories form the basis of the Cognos program, the most consistent reason that people left their previous job was "my boss was a jerk." When asked, "What do you mean by jerk?" most of the responses came down to "lack of appreciation, or their manager's desire to always be in control."[8]

For employee involvement to succeed, managers must serve in linking and coordinating roles[9] and providing the team with the resources it needs to carry out its work. The manager should help the team and its members interact with employees from other departments or teams and should make sure communication flows in both directions—the manager keeps the team updated on important issues and ensures that the team shares information and resources with others who need it. Along with these efforts at coordination, the team's manager should help team members resolve problems as needed. To provide such help, the manager may have to refer team members to resources outside the team or organization.

Knowledge Sharing

For the last decade, managers have been interested in creating a **learning organization,** that is, an organization in which people continually expand their capacity to achieve the results they desire.[10] The people in a learning organization are constantly learning. Their learning results from monitoring the business environment, taking in information, making decisions, and making changes in the organization based on what they learn. An organization's information systems, discussed later in this chapter, have an important role in making this learning activity possible. Information systems capture knowledge and make it available even after individual employees who provided the knowledge have left the organization. Ultimately, people are the essential ingredients in a learning organization. They must be committed to learning and willing to share what they have learned. A learning organization has the key features identified in Figure 12.3: continuous learning, generating and sharing of knowledge, thinking that is critical and systematic, a culture that values learning, encouraging flexibility and experimentation, and appreciating the value of each employee.

    Continuous learning is each employee's and each group's ongoing efforts to gather information and apply the information to their decisions. In many organizations, the process of continuous learning is aimed at improving quality. To engage in continuous learning, employees must understand the entire work system they participate in, the relationships among jobs, their work units, and the organization as a whole. Employees who continuously learn about their work system are adding to their ability to improve performance.

learning organization
An organization in which people continually expand their capacity to achieve the results they desire.

continuous learning
Each employee's and each group's ongoing efforts to gather information and apply the information to their decisions in a learning organization.

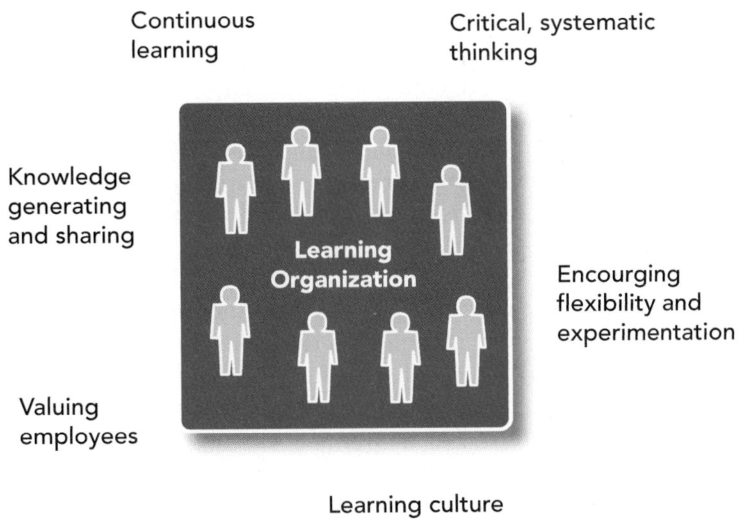

FIGURE 12.3

Key Features of a Learning Organization

Continuous learning

Critical, systematic thinking

Knowledge generating and sharing

Learning Organization

Encourging flexibility and experimentation

Valuing employees

Learning culture

SOURCE: Adapted from M. A. Gephart, V. J. Marsick, M. E. Van Buren, and M. S. Spiro, "Learning Organizations Come Alive," *Training and Development* 50 (1996), pp. 34–45.

Knowledge is most valuable to the organization when it is *shared*. Therefore, to create a learning organization, one challenge is to shift the focus of training away from merely teaching skills and toward a broader focus on generating and sharing knowledge.[11] In this view, training is an investment in the organization's human resources; it increases employees' value to the organization. Also, training content should be related to the organization's goals. Human resource departments can support the creation of a learning organization by planning training programs that meet these criteria, and they can help to create systems for creating, capturing, and sharing knowledge.

Critical, systemic thinking occurs when organizations encourage employees to see relationships among ideas and to test assumptions and observe the results of their actions. Reward systems can be set up to encourage employees and teams to think in new ways.

A *learning culture* is an organizational culture in which learning is rewarded, promoted, and supported by managers and organizational objectives. This culture may be reflected in performance management systems and pay structures that reward employees for gathering and sharing more knowledge. A learning culture creates the conditions in which managers encourage *flexibility* and *experimentation*. The organization should encourage employees to take risks and innovate, which means it cannot be quick to punish ideas that do not workout as intended.

Finally, in a learning organization, *employees are valued*. The organization recognizes that employees are the source of its knowledge. It therefore focuses on ensuring the development and well-being of each employee.

Employee Satisfaction and Engagement

A condition underpinning any high-performance organization is that employees experience job satisfaction—they experience their jobs as fulfilling or allowing them to fulfill important values. Research supports the idea that employees' job satisfaction and job performance are related.[12] Higher performance at the individual level should contribute to higher performance for the organization as a whole. One study looked at job satisfaction in teachers and the overall performance of their schools.[13] It found a significant link between teachers' satisfaction and their schools' performance according to a variety of measures, including students' behaviour and academic achievement. More recently, a study by Watson Wyatt Worldwide found that companies with high employee commitment (which includes employees' satisfaction with their jobs and the company) enjoyed higher total returns to shareholders, a basic measure of a company's financial performance.[14] An extensive study by Sears also demonstrated a link between employee satisfaction and profits. The Sears study showed that when "employees felt good about their jobs and the company, their behaviour with customers was more positive. Sears found that if a store increased its employee satisfaction score by five measuring units in a quarter, the following quarter its customer satisfaction score would go up by 2 percent. This in turn would lead to a revenue growth of half a percent above the national average." Satisfied employees produce more revenue—that's something that gets the attention of executives.[15]

There are a number of ways organizations can promote job satisfaction. They include making jobs more interesting, setting clear and challenging goals, and providing valued rewards that are linked to performance in a performance management system that employees consider fair.

As discussed in Chapter 1 some organizations are moving beyond concern with mere job satisfaction and are trying to foster employees' engagement. "An organization's capacity to manage employee engagement is closely related to its ability to achieve superior results. That's the conclusion of a new compilation of data from Hewitt Associates that makes the strongest link yet between engaged employees and business success."[16] An analysis of the Hewitt Associates Employee Engagement and Best Employer Database of 1,500 companies over a four-year period showed that companies with high engagement levels had markedly higher total shareholder return (TSR) than those with low employee engagement. Specifically companies with 60 percent to 100 percent employee engagement achieved an average TSR of 24.2 percent. With engagement scores of 49 percent to 60 percent, TSR dropped off to 9.1 percent. Companies with engagement below 25 percent suffered negative TSR.[17]

Research has found that teachers' job satisfaction is associated with high performance of the schools where they teach. What are other ways in which organizations can promote and foster employee satisfaction and engagement?

Measuring Employee Satisfaction and Engagement

The usual way to measure satisfaction or engagement is with a survey. A systematic, ongoing program of employee surveys should be part of the organization's human resource strategy. This allows the organization to monitor trends and prevent voluntary turnover. For example, if satisfaction with promotion opportunities has been falling over several years, the trend may signal a need for better career management (a topic of Chapter 8). An organizational change, such as a merger, also might have important consequences. In addition, ongoing surveys give the organization a way to measure whether new policies improve job satisfaction and employee engagement. Organizations can also compare results from different departments to identify groups with successful practices that may apply elsewhere in the organization. Another benefit is that some scales provide data that organizations can use to compare themselves to others in the same industry. This information will be valuable for creating and reviewing human resource policies that enable organizations to attract and retain employees in a competitive job market. Finally, conducting surveys gives employees a chance to be heard, so the practice itself can contribute to employee satisfaction.

To obtain a survey instrument, an excellent place to begin is with one of the many established scales. The validity and reliability of many satisfaction scales have been tested, so it is possible to compare the survey instruments. The main reason for the organization to create its own scale would be that it wants to measure satisfaction with aspects of work that are specific to the organization (such as satisfaction with a particular wellness initiative).

Some satisfaction scales measure general satisfaction, using broad questions such as "All in all, how satisfied are you with your job?"[18] Some scales avoid language altogether, relying on pictures. The faces scale in Figure 12.4 is an example of this type of measure. Other scales exist for measuring more specific aspects of satisfaction. For example, the Pay Satisfaction Questionnaire (PSQ) measures satisfaction with specific aspects of pay, such as pay levels, structure, and raises.[19]

Conducting opinion surveys is not something an organization should take lightly. Especially when the program is new, surveys often raise employees' expectations. The

FIGURE 12.4

Example of a Simplified, Nonverbal Measure of Job Satisfaction

Job Satisfaction from the Faces Scale
Consider all aspects of your job. Circle the face that best describes your feelings about your job in general.

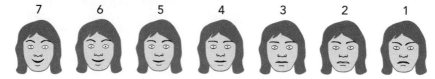

SOURCE: The faces were adapted from R. B. Dunham and J. B. Herman and published in the *Journal of Applied Psychology* 60 (1975), pp. 629–31. Copyright 1975 by the American Psychological Association. Adapted with permission.

organization should therefore be ready to act on the results. At the Canadian division of the Swiss pharmaceutical company, Hoffman-La Roche Ltd., comments from employee surveys are quickly acted on. For example, based on the surveys, a holiday-hours program was recently set up, giving full-time employees an extra day off on long weekends. This attention to employees recently earned Hoffman-LaRoche one of the top spots on Hewitt Associates' list of the 50 Best Employers in Canada.[20]

HR HOW TO

Measuring Worker Engagement

To identify the elements of worker engagement, Gallup conducted hundreds of focus groups and many thousands of worker interviews in all kinds of organizations, and at all levels, in most industries, and in many countries. The result was 12 key employee expectations that, when satisfied, form the foundation of strong feelings of engagement.

These are Gallup's 12 questions:
- Do you know what is expected of you at work?
- Do you have the materials and equipment you need to do your work right?
- At work, do you have the opportunity to do what you do best every day?
- In the last seven days, have you received recognition or praise for doing good work?
- Does your supervisor, or someone at work, seem to care about you as a person?
- Is there someone at work who encourages your development?
- At work, do your opinions seem to count?
- Does the mission/purpose of your company make you feel your job is important?
- Are your associates (fellow employees) committed to doing quality work?
- Do you have a best friend at work?
- In the last six months, has someone at work talked to you about your progress?
- In the last year, have you had opportunities at work to learn and grow?

The 12 engagement questions are answered by employees on a scale of one to five, based on their weak or strong agreement. The process also involves a feedback methodology for improving engagement by creating a factual base for discussion and debate of the causes behind the numbers. In this way, it yields actionable input from staff and mangers for changes in behaviour, attitudes, policies, and processes. Follow-up surveys are conducted to track long-term progress—or backsliding—on the 12 questions.

SOURCE: John Thackray "Feedback for Real" March 15, 2001 http://gmj.gallup.com/content/default.asp?ci=811. Retrieved: November 28, 2004.

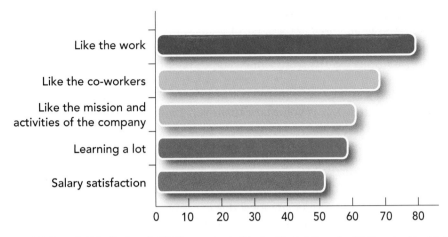

FIGURE 12.5

Top Five Reasons Why
Employees Will Stay

SOURCE: Ipsos-Reid for Workopolis (2001) appearing in "On the Charts," *Canadian HR Reporter*, May 17, 2004, p. G3.

However, critics describe the traditional employee satisfaction feedback process as: "The individual has his or her moment of self-expression, a fleeting participation in the great collective search for truth, then silence, nada, frustration as the status quo prevails."[21] As a result, the Gallup Organization set about to create a better employee feedback process that linked the elements of employee engagement to improved business outcomes, e.g., sales growth, productivity, customer loyalty, and the generation of value.[22] The "HR How To" box identifies questions used for measuring employee engagement.

In spite of surveys and other efforts to retain employees, some employees inevitably will leave the organization. This presents another opportunity to gather information for retaining employees: the **exit interview**—a meeting of the departing employee with the employee's supervisor and/or a human resource specialist to discuss the employee's reasons for leaving. A well-conducted exit interview can uncover reasons why employees leave and perhaps set the stage for some of them to return.[23] HR professionals can help make exit interviews more successful by arranging for the employee to talk to someone from the HR department (rather than the departing employee's supervisor) in a neutral location.[24] Questions should start out open-ended and general, to give the employee a chance to name the source of the dissatisfaction.

A recruiter armed with information about what caused a specific person to leave may be able to negotiate a return when the situation changes. And when several exiting employees give similar reasons for leaving, management should consider whether this indicates a need for change. Most white-collar workers feel their job responsibilities are what ultimately cause them to decide to stay with an organization. Figure 12.5 illustrates the results of a recent Ipsos-Reid study of 1,000 full-time white-collar workers in Canada and what matters the most when it comes to retention. Ultimately in the war for talent, the best way to manage retention is to engage in a battle for every valued employee, even when it looks as if the battle has been lost.

exit interview
A meeting of a departing employee with the employee's supervisor and/or a human resource specialist to discuss the employee's reasons for leaving.

Managing Voluntary and Involuntary Turnover

Organizations must try to ensure that good performers want to stay with the organization and that employees whose performance is chronically low are encouraged—or forced—to leave. Both of these challenges involve *employee turnover*, that is, em-

involuntary turnover
Turnover initiated by an employer (often with employees who would prefer to stay).

voluntary turnover
Turnover initiated by employees (often when the organization would prefer to keep them).

ployees leaving the organization. When the organization initiates the turnover (often with employees who would prefer to stay), the result is **involuntary turnover.** Examples include terminating an employee for theft or laying off employees during a downturn. Most organizations use the word *termination* to refer only to a discharge related to a discipline problem, but some organizations call any involuntary turnover a termination. When the employees initiate the turnover (often when the organization would prefer to keep them), it is **voluntary turnover.** Employees may leave to retire or to take a job with a different organization.

In general, organizations try to avoid the need for involuntary turnover and to minimize voluntary turnover, especially among top performers. Both kinds of turnover are costly, as summarized in Table 12.1. Replacing workers is expensive, and new employees need time to learn their jobs. In addition, people today are more ready to take legal action against a former employer if they feel they were unfairly dismissed. The prospect of workplace violence also raises the risk associated with discharging employees. Effective human resource management can help the organization minimize both kinds of turnover, as well as carry it out effectively when necessary. Despite a company's best efforts at selection, training, and compensation, some employees will fail to meet performance requirements or will violate company policies. When this happens, organizations need to apply a discipline program that could ultimately lead to discharging the individual.

For a number of reasons, discharging employees can be very difficult. First, the decision has legal aspects that can affect the organization. Historically, if the organization and employee do not have a specific employment contract, the employer or employee may end the employment relationship at any time. This is the *employment-at-will doctrine*, described in Chapter 4. This doctrine has eroded significantly, however. Employees who have been terminated sometimes sue their employers for wrongful dismissal. In cases of wrongful dismissal, the courts may award employees significant financial settlements. Publicity associated with the proceedings may also be embarrassing or harmful to the employer's reputation. Employment/Labour Standards laws in each of the federal, provincial, and territorial jurisdictions set out the legal minimum requirements that employers must follow when terminating or laying off employees. No notice or compensation is needed if the employee quit or retired, the employee had been employed for less than the required minimum (usually three months), the employee was employed on an "on-call" basis or if the employee was terminated for "just cause." Examples of "just cause" or dismissal that are considered serious violations of the employment relationship are dishonesty; willful disobedience to a supervisor, and failure to comply with known policies or procedures or meet performance requirements.[25]

Employers have a right to terminate workers for reasons other than for "just cause," however, they must provide notice, termination pay, or severance pay as prescribed in Employment/Labour Standards legislation. **Termination pay** is a lump sum payment equal to the regular wages for a regular work week that an employee would have earned

termination pay
A lump sum payment equal to the regular wages for a regular work week that an employee would have earned during the notice period.

TABLE 12.1
Costs Associated with Turnover

INVOLUNTARY TURNOVER	VOLUNTARY TURNOVER
Recruiting, selecting, and training replacements	Recruiting, selecting, and training replacements
Lost productivity	Lost productivity
Lawsuits	Loss of talented employees
Workplace violence	

during the notice period. **Severance pay** is compensation that recognizes the employee's years of service and compensates the employee for loss of job-related earnings.[26] Employers cannot avoid paying termination or severance pay by attempting to force an employee to resign. **Constructive dismissal** occurs when the employer makes a significant change to a worker's condition of employment. Examples may include changing the employee's hours of work, authority, travel requirements, or other elements that may cause the employee to feel they have no choice but to resign.

Sometimes terminations may occur because the organization determines that for economic reasons it must close a facility. An organization that plans such a broad-scale layoff must consult with their Employment/Labour Standards office to ensure that all the requirements for their jurisdiction are handled appropriately. An organization should also seek legal advice before implementing a mass termination.

Along with the financial risks of dismissing an employee, there are issues related to personal safety. Distressing as it is that some former employees go to the courts, even more problematic are the employees who react to a termination decision with violence. Violence in the workplace has become a major organizational problem. Workplace homicide is the fastest-growing form of murder.[27] Although any number of organizational actions or decisions may incite violence among employees, the "nothing else to lose" aspect of an employee's dismissal makes the situation dangerous.

Because of the critical financial and personal risks associated with employee dismissal, it is easy to see why organizations must develop a standardized, systematic approach to discipline and discharge. These decisions should not be left solely to the discretion of individual managers or supervisors. Policies that can lead to employee separation should be based on principles of justice and law, and they should allow for various ways to intervene.

Employees form conclusions about the system's fairness based on the system's outcomes and procedures and the way managers treat employees when carrying out those procedures. Figure 12.6 summarizes these principles as outcome fairness, procedural justice, and interactional justice. Outcome fairness involves the ends of a discipline process, while procedural and interactional justice focus on the means to those ends.

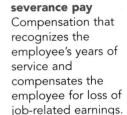

severance pay
Compensation that recognizes the employee's years of service and compensates the employee for loss of job-related earnings.

constructive dismissal
Occurs when the employer makes a significant change to a worker's condition of employment.

FIGURE 12.6

Principles of Justice

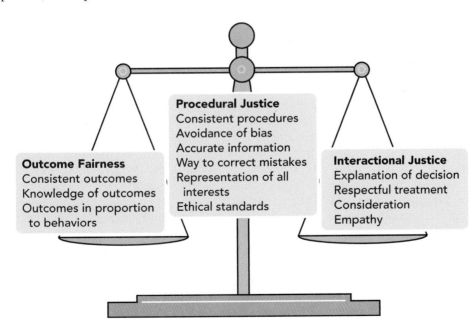

Outcome Fairness
Consistent outcomes
Knowledge of outcomes
Outcomes in proportion
  to behaviors

Procedural Justice
Consistent procedures
Avoidance of bias
Accurate information
Way to correct mistakes
Representation of all
  interests
Ethical standards

Interactional Justice
Explanation of decision
Respectful treatment
Consideration
Empathy

outcome fairness
A judgment that the consequences given to employees are just.

People's perception of **outcome fairness** depends on their judgment that the consequences of a decision to employees are just. As shown in Figure 12.6, one employee's consequences should be consistent with other employees' consequences. Organizations promote outcome fairness when they clearly communicate policies regarding the consequences of inappropriate behaviour. Finally, the outcome should be proportionate to the behaviour. Terminating an employee for being late to work, especially if this is the first time the employee is late, would seem out of proportion to the offence in most situations. Employees' sense of outcome fairness usually would reserve loss of a job for the most serious offences.

procedural justice
A judgment that fair methods were used to determine the consequences an employee receives.

People's perception of **procedural justice** is their judgment that fair methods were used to determine the consequences an employee receives. Figure 12.6 shows six principles that determine whether people perceive procedures as fair. The procedures should be consistent from one person to another, and the manager using them should suppress any personal biases. The procedures should be based on accurate information, not rumours or falsehoods. The procedures should also be correctable, meaning the system includes safeguards, such as channels for appealing a decision or correcting errors. The procedures should take into account the concerns of all the groups affected—for example, by gathering information from employees, customers, and managers. Finally, the procedures should be consistent with prevailing ethical standards, such as concerns for privacy and honesty.

interactional justice
A judgment that the organization carried out its actions in a way that took the employee's feelings into account.

A perception of **interactional justice** is a judgment that the organization carried out its actions in a way that took the employee's feelings into account. It is a judgment about the ways that managers interact with their employees. A disciplinary action meets the standards of interactional justice if the manager explains to the employee how the action is procedurally just. The manager should listen to the employee. The manager should also treat the employee with dignity and respect and should empathize with the employee's feelings. The precedent-setting Supreme Court case of *Wallace v. United Grain Growers* (1997) sent a clear message that employers must act fairly and respectfully when handling an employee termination. The *Wallace* case gave judges a legal precedent to award employees additional notice or damages if the employer treats an employee callously or unfairly during termination.

The issue of off-the-job behaviour is also of concern to employers. One of the chapter-ending cases explores a recent case where an employer terminated an employee for an off-the-job role the employee accepted. Employers are frequently concerned if a worker's off-the-job behaviour could affect the organization's business or reputation in some way. Violet Legere, a YMCA-YWCA employee ran into her colleague and neighbour at a grocery store. They had been on opposing sides of a bitter environmental dispute in the community. The colleague, who was with her four-year old daughter, approached Legere and said "Hi." Legere lost it and told the colleague, "You f*** right off." Shortly after this incident, she was dismissed from her job at the YMCA-YWCA where she was responsible for running an after-school program. The employer said she had cursed in front of children and this violated the Y's code of conduct. However, a New Brunswick Court of Queen's Bench judge ruled in Legere's favour and concluded that Legere had exercised her right to free speech and the phrase she used was just an intense way of saying, "go away."[28]

outplacement counselling
A service in which professionals try to help dismissed employees manage the transition from one job to another.

An employee who has been discharged is likely to feel angry and confused about what to do next. If the person feels there is nothing to lose and nowhere else to turn, the potential for violence or a lawsuit is greater than most organizations are willing to tolerate. This concern is one reason many organizations provide **outplacement counselling,** which tries to help dismissed employees manage the transition from one job to another.

Some organizations have their own staff for conducting outplacement counselling. Other organizations have contracts with outside providers to help with individual cases. Either way, the goals for outplacement programs are to help the former employee address the psychological issues associated with losing a job—grief, depression, and fear—while at the same time helping the person find a new job.

Employee Discipline

Organizations look for methods of handling problem behaviour that are fair, legal, and effective. A popular principle for responding effectively is the **hot-stove rule.** According to this principle, discipline should be like a hot stove: The glowing or burning stove gives warning not to touch. Anyone who ignores the warning will be burned. The stove has no feelings to influence which people it burns, and it delivers the same burn to any touch. Finally, the burn is immediate. Like the hot stove, an organization's discipline should give warning and have consequences that are consistent, objective, and immediate.

The principles of justice suggest that the organization prepare for problems by establishing a formal discipline process in which the consequences become more serious if the employee repeats the offence. Such a system is called **progressive discipline.** A typical progressive discipline system identifies and communicates inappropriate behaviours and responds to a series of offences with the actions shown in Figure 12.7—verbal and then written warnings, temporary suspension, and finally, termination. This process fulfills the purpose of discipline by teaching employees what is expected of them and creating a situation in which employees must try to do what is expected. It seeks to prevent inappropriate behaviour (by publishing rules) and to correct, rather than merely punish, inappropriate behaviour.

Such procedures may seem exasperatingly slow, especially when the employee's misdeeds hurt the team's performance. In the end, however, if an employee must be discharged, careful use of the procedure increases other employees' belief that the organization is fair and reduces the likelihood that the employee will take legal action (or at least that the employee will win in court). For situations in which inappropriate behaviour is dangerous, the organization may establish a stricter policy, even terminating an employee for the first offence. In that case, it is especially important to communicate the procedure—not only to ensure fairness, but also to prevent the dangerous inappropriate behaviour.

Creating a formal discipline process is a primary responsibility of the human resource department. The HR professional should consult with supervisors and managers to identify inappropriate behaviours and establish rules and consequences for violating the rules. The rules should cover disciplinary problems such as the ones identified in Table 12.2. For each infraction, the HR professional would identify a se-

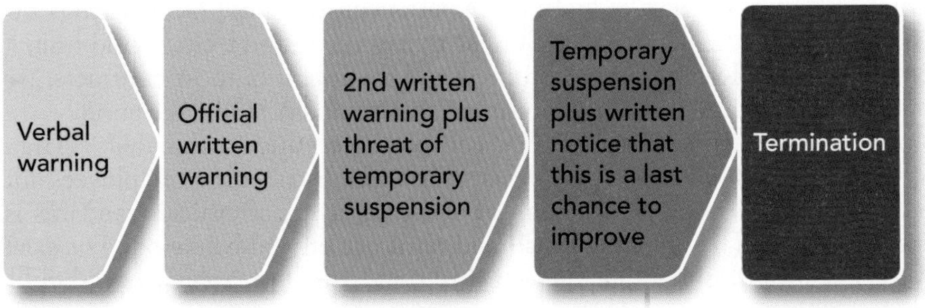

hot-stove rule
Principle of discipline that says discipline should be like a hot stove, giving clear warning and following up with consistent, objective, immediate consequences.

progressive discipline
A formal discipline process in which the consequences become more serious if the employee repeats the offence.

FIGURE 12.7

Progressive Discipline Responses

TABLE 12.2

Common Problems
Requiring Discipline

Tardiness
Absenteeism
Unsafe work practices
Poor quantity or quality of work
Sexual harassment of coworkers
Theft of company property
Cyberslacking (surfing the Internet at work)

ries of responses, such as those in Figure 12.7. In addition, the organization must communicate these rules and consequences in writing to every employee. Ways of publishing rules include presenting them in an employee handbook, posting them on the company's intranet, and displaying them on a bulletin board. Supervisors should be familiar with the rules, so that they can discuss them with employees and apply them consistently.

Along with rules and a progression of consequences for violating the rules, a progressive discipline system should have requirements for documenting the rules, offences, and responses.

As we noted in the earlier discussion of procedural justice, the discipline system should provide an opportunity to hear every point of view and to correct errors. Before discussing and filing records of inappropriate behaviour, it is important for the supervisor to investigate the incident. The employee should be made aware of what he or she is said to have done wrong and should have an opportunity to present his or her version of events. Anyone who witnessed the misdeed also should have a chance to describe what happened. In general, employees who belong to a union have a right to the presence of a union representative during a formal investigation interview if they request representation.[29]

Ethics

In the long run, a high-performance organization meets high ethical standards. Ethics, defined in Chapter 1, establishes fundamental principles for behaviour, such as honesty and fairness. Organizations and their employees must meet these standards if they are to maintain positive long-term relationships with their customers and their community.

Ethical behaviour is most likely to result from values held by the organization's leaders combined with systems that promote ethical behaviour. Charles O. Holliday Jr., the chairman and chief executive officer of DuPont Company, is an example of an executive who cares about ethics. For Holliday, ethics is a matter of behaving in ways that promote trust: "Just saying you're ethical isn't very useful. You have to earn trust by what you do every day."[30] Holliday experienced this kind of leadership himself when he first joined DuPont. The CEO at that time, Dick Heckert, told him, "This company lives by the letter of its contracts and the intent of those contracts," speaking with such conviction that he imprinted the lesson on Holliday's mind.

A number of organizational systems can promote ethical behaviour.[31] These include a written code of ethics that the organization distributes to employees and expects them to use in decision making. Publishing a list of ethical standards is not enough, however. The organization should reinforce ethical behaviour. For example, performance measures should include ethical standards. The organization should provide channels employees can use to ask questions about ethical behaviour or to seek help if they are expected to do something they believe is wrong. Organizations also can provide training in ethical decision making.

As these examples suggest, ethical behaviour is a human resource management concern. The systems that promote ethical behaviour include such HRM functions as training, performance management, and discipline policies. In today's business climate, ethical behaviour also can affect recruiting. Recent high profile scandals involving fraudulent accounting practices and executive fraud have hastened the collapse of some companies and put thousands of employees out of work. Job candidates want to avoid employers whose misdeeds might cost them their jobs and their reputations. Many job candidates have asked recruiters how well their organizations promote ethical behaviour.[32]

Many organizations are developing and clarifying expectations for ethical behaviour. For example, CIBC clearly defines its requirements for employee behaviour in its "Code of Conduct"[33] and director behaviour in a "Code of Ethics"[34] The most common ethics initiatives undertaken by Canadian businesses are providing a secure forum for employees to report unethical behaviour and implementing ethics training according to a recent CEO/Business Leader Poll by COMPAS in the *Financial Post*.[35]

Boeing Co. chief executive officer Harry Stonecipher was recently asked to quit over an affair with a female executive at Boeing. Stonecipher had been the champion of a far-reaching new code of conduct that stated, "Employees will not engage in conduct or activity that may raise questions as to the company's honesty, impartiality, reputation or otherwise cause embarrassment to the company."[36] In Boeing's zero-tolerance environment, company officials were concerned the 68-year-old married father and grandfather's affair might embarrass the company.

HRM'S Contribution to High Performance

LO4

Management of human resources plays a critical role in determining companies' success in meeting the challenges of a rapidly changing, highly competitive environment.[37] Compensation, staffing, training and development, performance management, and other HRM practices are investments that directly affect employees' motivation and ability to provide products and services that are valued by customers. A study by Watson Wyatt Worldwide found that significant improvements in major HR practices, including reward systems, recruitment, and employee retention, led to significant increases in the value of a company's stock.[38]

Research suggests that it is more effective to improve HRM practices as a whole than to focus on one or two isolated practices, such as the organization's pay structure or selection system.[39] Also, to have the intended influence on performance, the HRM practices must fit well with one another and the organization as a whole.[40] The "Best Practices" box discusses the business case for corporate volunteerism.

Job Design

For the organization to benefit from teamwork and employee involvement, jobs must be designed appropriately. Often, a high-performance work system places employees in work teams where employees collaborate to make decisions and solve problems. A good example of this approach to job design is GE Fanuc Automation North America, a joint venture between General Electric Company and FANUC Ltd.

Doing Good Helps You Do Well at Work

Lesley Brown, an executive with Investors Group Inc. in Toronto, recently traded in her cellphone and high heels for a hammer and steel-toed work boots to help build some townhomes in suburban Toronto. Ms. Brown and 13 colleagues from the mutual fund giant didn't mind working through drizzling rain and cold winds for a day that might otherwise have been spent in a warm office because they were volunteering side by side for a worthy cause—helping Habitat for Humanity erect affordable housing for low-income people.

"It's a double win," says Ms. Brown, vice-president of financial services for the Ontario region at Investors Group. "Not only are we doing something good, but we are doing something that further connects the bond between the people in the office." Such corporate volunteerism is gaining momentum in Canada as more companies understand the business case for participating in charitable work.

Doing good for others also means doing good for themselves and their employees by helping to develop a variety of staff skills-from team-building to leadership. Companies are also finding that corporate volunteerism helps to boost morale and loyalty, and can give them an edge in both recruiting and retaining talent.

Company-sponsored efforts can range from allowing employees to modify their work hours or take time off without pay for community service to a more generous practice of permitting staff to do volunteer work on company time, also known as "release time." As more companies choose the latter option, they are going a step further by sending teams of employees out together to work for charities for up to several days a year. According to management consultant Linda Graff, president of Linda Graff and Associates Inc. in Dundas, Ontario, "We are now recognizing that volunteering gives back important benefits to the person engaged in it, and to employers who encourage their employees to become involved." Her review of various studies indicates that volunteers can gain transferable job skills from doing charitable work, and that company-sponsored volunteerism can increase job satisfaction among employees.

A survey of Canadians by Investors Group found that "giving back to the community is very high up in the client's opinion of a corporation," but the firm is also aware of the team-building benefits of working together in a non-office environment, Ms. Brown says.

Markham, Ontario-based Timberland Canada Co. gives its employees 40 hours of paid leave a year for community service. This generous policy has helped to woo new employees like Evan Selby, who left his former employer to join Timberland two years ago when it opened a Canadian subsidiary. "It was one of the attractive things to me, because it shows the firm is dedicated to more than just making money," says the 33-year-old marketing manager, who has participated in company teams helping charities such as Habitat for Humanity.

Marlene Deboisbriand, president of Volunteer Canada, which promotes volunteerism, also points out that employees who work for companies that support volunteerism tend to be more loyal, which reduces the need to recruit and train replacements. Volunteer Canada (www.volunteercanada.ca) can provide advice on how to make a business case for volunteerism.

SOURCE: Shirley Won, "Doing Good Helps You Do Well at Work," The *Globe and Mail*, January 19, 2005, pp. C1, C9.

of Japan.[41] GE Fanuc Automation employs 1,500 people and maintains a strong commitment to quality. Its work design is based on the principle that employees who are closest to the work have the best ideas for improvement. To encourage these employees to contribute their ideas, the venture organized work into more than 40 work teams. The teams set their own goals and measure their success based on factors related to the venture's business goals. Each team spends at least one hour per week measuring performance relative to the goals and discussing ways to improve. Each function team within the business has a dedicated HR manager who helps the team develop its strategies, accompanies the team on sales calls, and supports the team as needed.

Recruitment and Selection

At a high-performance organization, recruitment and selection aim at obtaining the kinds of employees who can thrive in this type of setting. These employees are enthusiastic about and able to contribute to teamwork and knowledge sharing. Qualities such as creativity and ability to cooperate as part of a team may play a large role in selection decisions. High-performance organizations need selection methods that identify more than technical skills like ability to perform accounting and engineering tasks. Employers may use group interviews, open-ended questions, and psychological tests to find employees who innovate, share ideas, and take initiative.

Training and Development

When organizations base hiring decisions on qualities like decision-making and teamwork skills, training may be required to teach employees the specific skills they need to perform the duties of their job. Extensive training and development also are part of a learning organization, described earlier in this chapter. And when organizations delegate many decisions to work teams, the members of those teams likely will benefit from participating in team development activities that prepare them for their roles as team members. In the previous example of GE Fanuc Automation North America, training supports the effectiveness of the joint venture's work teams. All GE Fanuc employees receive more than 100 hours of training.[42]

Employee development is an important factor in IBM's top ranking in a study of the "Top 20 Companies for Leaders," jointly conducted by Hewitt Associates and *Chief Executive* magazine. According to Randall MacDonald, IBM's senior vice president of human resources, IBM had determined that leadership was one of four areas it had to focus on to achieve high performance. So the company charged all its ex-

FIGURE 12.8

Employee Performance as a Process

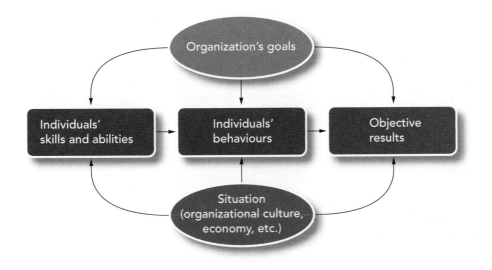

isting leaders with developing future leaders. Once a year, IBM calls together its top managers to select candidates for leadership development, and they work with the candidates to create a development plan that meets their personal goals. By making leadership development a part of the company's routine processes, IBM removes the fear that coaching one's replacement threatens one's own career. MacDonald points out that planning for leadership is at least as important as other types of planning: "The [chief financial officer], when he gives one of our line guys $3 billion to go build a new plant, he doesn't say, 'Go build the plant and do what you want with it.' No, that CFO and that line person are going to manage that asset. . . . Whatever happened to the concept of people being our most important asset? Well if they are, we ought to manage them."[43]

Performance Management

In a high-performance organization, employees know the organization's goals and what they must do to help achieve those goals. HR departments can contribute to this ideal through the design of the organization's performance management system. As we discussed in Chapter 7, performance management should be related to the organization's goals. For example, teamwork is central to the success of the joint venture at GE Fanuc Automation. Therefore, managers must support their teams, and support of teamwork is one performance measure in the managers' performance evaluations.[44] At Extreme Logic, high performance comes from clear communication about what kinds of behaviour are needed. On its intranet, the software company publishes attributes and behaviours associated with success in each job, as well as the performance standard for each attribute and behaviour. Employees can go online at any time to gauge whether they are meeting those standards.[45]

To set up a performance management system that supports the organization's goals, managers need to understand the process of employee performance. As shown in Figure 12.8, individual employees bring a set of skills and abilities to the job, and by applying a set of behaviours, they use those skills to achieve certain results. But success is more than the product of individual efforts. The organization's goals should influence each step of the process. The organization's culture and other factors influence the employees' abilities, behaviours, and results. Sometimes uncontrollable forces such as the current economic conditions enter the picture, it mustn't be forgotten—for example, a salesperson can probably sell more during an economic expansion than during an economic slowdown.

This model suggests some guidelines for performance management. First, each aspect of performance management should be related to the organization's goals. Business goals should influence the kinds of employees selected and their training, the requirements of each job, and the measures used for evaluating results. Generally, this means the organization identifies what each department must do to achieve the desired results, then defines how individual employees should contribute to their department's goals. More specifically, the following guidelines describe how to make the performance management system support organizational goals:[46]

To create high-performance work systems, organizations should establish performance goals that are linked to meeting customers' needs. Customers can be external or internal, such as the ones pictured here attending a training/orientation session conducted by someone in the company.

- *Define and measure performance in precise terms.* Focus on outcomes that can be defined in terms of how frequently certain behaviours occur. Include criteria that describe ways employees can add value to a product or service (such as through quantity, quality, or timeliness). Include behaviours that go beyond the minimum required to perform a job (such as helping coworkers).
- *Link performance measures to meeting customer needs.* "Customers" may be the organization's external customers, or they may be internal customers (employees receiving services from a coworker). Service goals for internal customers should be related to satisfying external customers.
- *Measure and correct for the effect of situational constraints.* Monitor economic conditions, the organization's culture, and other influences on performance. Measures of employees' performance should take these influences into account.

This approach gives employees the information they need to behave in ways that contribute to high performance. In addition, organizations should help employees identify and obtain the abilities they need to meet their performance goals.

Total Compensation and Rewards

Organizations can reinforce the impact of this kind of performance management by linking compensation in part to performance measures. Chapter 9 described a number of methods for doing this, including merit pay, gainsharing, and profit sharing. A small manufacturer called Headsets.com improved productivity by linking bonuses to sales volume; employees share a fixed percentage of the company's total sales.[47] Employees at Headsets.com can see that if the company grows by hiring more workers, rather than by using the same number of workers to produce and sell more, the bonus will be divided among more people. They can earn a bigger bonus if they get the same results by working more efficiently. Since starting this bonus plan, Headsets.com has been able to grow more profitably. Compensation systems also can help to create the conditions that contribute to high performance, including teamwork, involvement, and job satisfaction. For example, as discussed in Chapter 9, compensation can be linked to achievement of team objectives.

Organizations can increase employee satisfaction by including employees in decisions about compensation and by communicating the basis for decisions about pay. When the organization designs a pay structure, it can set up a task force that includes employees with direct experience in various types of jobs. Some organizations share financial information with their employees and invite them to recommend pay increases for themselves, based on their contributions. Employees also may participate in setting individual or group goals for which they can receive bonuses. Research has found that employee participation in decisions about pay policies is linked to greater satisfaction with the pay and the job.[48] And as we discussed in Chapter 9, when organizations explain their pay structures to employees, the communication can enhance employees' satisfaction and belief that the system is fair.

HRM Technology

LO5

Human resource departments can improve their own and their organization's performance by appropriately using new technology. New technology usually involves *automation*—that is, using equipment and information processing to perform activities that had been performed by people. Over the last few decades, automation has improved HRM efficiency by reducing the number of people needed to perform routine tasks. Information technology also provides ways to build and improve systems for knowledge generation and sharing, as part of a learning organization.

HRM Applications

New technologies continue to be introduced. In fact, so many HRM applications are developed for use on personal computers that publications serving the profession (such as *HR Magazine* and *Workforce Management*) devote annual issues to reviewing this software. Some of the technologies that have been widely adopted are transaction processing, decision support systems, and expert systems.[49]

transaction processing
Computations and calculations involved in reviewing and documenting HRM decisions and practices.

Transaction processing refers to computations and calculations involved in reviewing and documenting HRM decisions and practices. It includes documenting decisions and actions associated with employee relocation, training expenses, and enrolments in courses and benefit plans. Transaction processing also includes the activities required to meet government reporting requirements, such as filling out Employment Equity reports on which employers report information about Employment Equity group participation rates. Computers enable companies to perform these tasks more efficiently. Employers can fill out computerized forms and store HRM information in databases (data stored electronically in user-specified categories), so that it is easier to find, sort, and report.

decision support systems
Computer software systems designed to help managers solve problems by showing how results vary when the manager alters assumptions or data.

Decision support systems are computer software systems designed to help managers solve problems. They usually include a "what if?" feature that managers can use to enter different assumptions or data and see how the likely outcomes will change. This type of system can help managers make decisions for human resource planning. The manager can, for example, try out different assumptions about turnover rates to see how those assumptions affect the number of new employees needed. Or the manager can test a range of assumptions about the availability of a certain skill in the labour market, looking at the impact of the assumptions on the success of different recruiting plans. Possible applications for a decision support system include forecasting (discussed in Chapter 4) and succession planning (discussed in Chapter 8).

expert systems
Computer systems that support decision making by incorporating the decision rules used by people who are considered to have expertise in a certain area.

Expert systems are computer systems that incorporate the decision rules used by people who are considered to have expertise in a certain area. The systems help users make decisions by recommending actions based on the decision rules and the information provided by the users. An expert system is designed to recommend the same actions that a human expert would in a similar situation. For example, an expert system could guide an interviewer during the selection process. Some organizations use expert systems to help employees decide how to allocate their money for benefits (as in a flexible plan) and help managers schedule the labour needed to complete projects. Expert systems can deliver both high quality and lower costs. By using the decision processes of experts, an expert system helps many people to arrive at decisions that reflect the expert's knowledge. An expert system helps avoid the errors that can result from fatigue and decision-making biases, such as biases in appraising employee performance, described in Chapter 7. An expert system can increase efficiency by enabling fewer or less-skilled employees to do work that otherwise would require many highly skilled employees.

Proactive HR departments, transaction processing, decision support systems, and expert systems often are part of a human resource information system. Also, these technologies may be linked to employees through a network such as an intranet. The "E-HRM" box on page 398 describes how Labatt Breweries have created a dynamic HR portal that serves a variety of applications. Information systems and networks have been evolving rapidly; the following descriptions provide a basic introduction.

Human Resource Information Systems

A standard feature of a modern HRIS is the use of *relational databases*, which store data in separate files that can be linked by common elements. These common elements are fields identifying the type of data. Commonly used fields for an HR database include name, Social Insurance number, job status (full- or part-time), hiring date, position, title, rate of pay, job history, job location, mailing address, birth date, and emergency contacts. A relational database lets a user sort the data by any of the fields. For example, depending on how the database is set up, the user might be able to look up tables listing employees by location, rates of pay for various jobs, or employees who have completed certain training courses. This system is far more sophisticated than the old-fashioned method of filing employee data by name, with one file per employee.

The ability to locate and combine many categories of data has a multitude of uses in human resource management. Databases have been developed to track employee benefit costs, training courses, and compensation. The system can meet the needs of line managers as well as the HR department. On an oil rig, for example, management might look up data listing employee names along with safety equipment issued and appropriate skill certification. HR managers at headquarters might look up data on the same employees to gather information about wage rates or training programs needed. Another popular use of an HRIS is applicant tracking, or maintaining and retrieving records of job applicants. This is much faster and easier than trying to sort through stacks of résumés. With relational databases, HR staff can retrieve information about specific applicants or obtain lists of applicants with specific skills, career goals, work history, and employment background. Such information is useful for HR planning, recruitment, succession planning, and career development. Taking the process a step further, the system could store information related to hiring and terminations. By analyzing such data, the HR department could measure the long-term success of its recruiting and selection processes.

Human Resource Management Online: E-HRM

During the last decade or so, organizations have seen the advantages of sharing information in computer networks. At the same time, the widespread adoption of the Internet has linked people around the globe. As we discussed in Chapter 1, more and more organizations are engaging in e-HRM, providing HR-related information over the Internet. Because much human resource information is confidential, organizations may do this with an intranet, which uses Internet technology but allows access only to authorized users (such as the organization's employees). For HR professionals, Internet access also offers a way to research

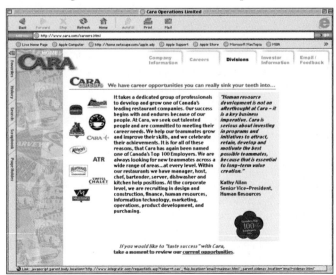

Cara Operations Ltd.'s career home page. Online recruiting offers potential benefits for companies. Employers can retrieve résumés at their own websites. They can also use online testing services to help make selection decisions. Potential employees benefit because they can read more about the company directly on the site and easily apply or submit their résumé.

From Filling in Forms to Brainstorming the Firm's Next Big Innovation

Vacation. Illness. Promotions. Many roads lead to the human resources department. But with the evolution of technology, more and more of these roads are leading employees to an HR portal. Every organization needs to manage employee information effectively to make the most of its diverse talents, services, and information. Originally designed to disseminate information quickly, the employee intranet has become a common feature of many workplaces.

Over time, this type of intranet has evolved from a static repository of company information to a collaborative meeting place where employees can ask HR-related questions and find the appropriate, up-to-date answers, fill in and file administrative forms and further develop their skills.

Through a dynamic HR portal, employees can find and communicate with key contacts and experts, by email and with instant messaging. Site content can be easily searched, and employees can receive alerts to tell them about changes or new information and documents on the portal. The online portal also allows for anonymity,

which can be helpful to employees searching for sensitive information. Through a portal, employees can quickly and easily share their ideas and contribute to projects, accessing the sites through the office intranet or outside work through a Web browser.

Labatt Breweries of Canada set up an intranet called "The Pub." Its goals were to improve overall communication with employees located in eight breweries from coast-to-coast, and eliminate silos of information between business units. Using the portal, Labatt was able to improve employee communications significantly and now 70 percent of its employees frequently visit The Pub. The Pub has also turned into a home for more than 30 team workspaces, where employees share information and collaborate on documents. With the new workspaces, various business units have a common point of access for project or departmental information, including documents, contacts, tasks, and discussions.

"Employee response to The Pub has been extremely positive," says Jonathan Starkey, data architecture centre of excellence manager

at Labatt. "Through our intranet, we've been able to deliver immense value to our employees by providing tools that enable them to make better informed decisions and increase their productivity. The business value of bringing employees closer together is apparent when you look at the individual contributions and recommendations for greater innovation that come in through The Pub."

Team building through virtual communities of interest created through the HR portal can also translate directly into improvements in the day-to-day functioning of a company. Work teams that may have members too busy to meet with the rest of the team, or perhaps even working from a different location, can meet online. This allows teams to be efficient and productive and ensures every individual on the team can meaningfully contribute to a project, increasing overall employee satisfaction.

SOURCE: Michael Bulmer, "From Filling in Forms to Brainstorming the Firm's Next Big Innovation," *Guide to HR Technology Canadian HR Reporter*, March 8, 2004, p. G2. © Copyright *Canadian HR Reporter*, March 8, 2004, by permission of Carswell, Toronto, Ontario, 1-800-387-5164, www.hrreporter.com.

new developments, post job openings, trade ideas with colleagues in other organizations, and obtain government documents. In this way, e-HRM combines company-specific information on a secure intranet with links to the resources on the broader Internet. Increasingly, organizations are enhancing their HR technology to provide for employee self-service. With self-service, employees are responsible for keeping their personal information up to date, thus freeing up the time of HR and increasing the accuracy of employee data.

A benefit of e-HRM including employee self-service is that employees and managers can help themselves to the information they need when they need it, instead of contacting an HR staff person. For example, employees can go online to enroll in or select benefits, submit insurance claims, or fill out employee satisfaction surveys. Using these HR self-service tools can be more convenient for the employees, as well as more economical for the HR department. This access to HR information can even be completely customized for the user. For example, the delivery of HR processes may be personalized for each employee's desktop according to his or her role—employee, manager, HR professional, executive. The result is a single place to go for easy access to all the resources needed related to human resource management.[50] Similarly, at Cisco Systems, many HR activities are automated online.[51] When employees join the company, they log on, visit the "New Hire" page, and sign up for benefits. They also see that the website is the place to file expense reports, look up project information, and more. The site lets employees know when it is time for their performance review and lets them start the process with their supervisor. The employee reviews an evaluation form, studies the expected behaviours, fills in needed information, and sends the form to the supervisor. If the form requires information from someone else in the company, the supervisor clicks on a link to request that information. The supervisor receives any requested information, completes the appraisal form, and meets with the employee to discuss the review. So much of the process is automated that supervisors have more time to focus on the actual meeting with the employee.

Most administrative and information-gathering activities in human resource management can be part of e-HRM. For example, online recruiting has become a significant part of the total recruiting effort, as candidates submit résumés online. Employers go online to retrieve suitable résumés from job search sites or retrieve information from forms they post at their own websites. For selection decisions, the organization may have candidates use one of the online testing services available; these services conduct the tests, process the results, and submit reports to employers. Online appraisal systems can help managers make pay decisions consistent with company policies and employee performance. Many types of training can be conducted online, as we discussed in Chapter 6. Online surveys of employee satisfaction can be quick and easy to fill out. Besides providing a way to administer the survey, an intranet is an effective vehicle for communicating the results of the survey and management's planned response.

Not only does e-HRM provide efficient ways to carry out human resource functions, it also poses new challenges to employees and new issues for HR managers to address. The Internet's ability to link people anytime, anywhere has accelerated such trends as globalization, the importance of knowledge sharing within organizations, and the need for flexibility.[52] These trends, in turn, change the work environment for employees. For example, employees are increasingly expected to be highly committed but flexible, able to move from job to job. Employees also may be connected to the organization 24/7. In the car, on vacation, in airports, and even in the bathroom, employees with handheld computers can deal with work demands. For example, Research in Motion recently added AIM and ICP instant messaging capabilities to the Blackberry.[53] Organizations depend on their human resource departments to help prepare employees for this changing work world through such activities as training, career development, performance management, and benefits packages that meet the need for flexibility and help employees manage stress.

LO6

Effectiveness of Human Resource Management

In recent years, human resource management at many organizations has been taking a customer-oriented approach. For an organization's human resource division, "customers" are the organization as a whole and its other divisions. They are customers of HRM because they depend on HRM to provide a variety of services that result in a supply of talented, motivated employees. Taking this customer-oriented approach, human resource management defines its customer groups, customer needs, and the activities required to meet those needs, as shown in Figure 12.9. These definitions give an organization a basis for defining goals and measures of success.

One company that uses this approach is Whirlpool Corporation. The company's HR managers identify their customer, define the need they can satisfy or the value they can provide, and identify the methods they must use to satisfy the customer. When Whirlpool planned to start a centralized service centre, its plan called for hiring of 100 to 150 employees to process service requests from customers owning Whirlpool appliances and to schedule service calls. Whirlpool gave an HR manager the responsibility for developing a selection system for call takers. The manager determined the customer in this instance was the operations manager in charge of phone service and the need was the delivery of qualified call takers. To meet this

FIGURE 12.9

Customer-Oriented Perspective of Human Resource Management

need, the HR manager decided to use a combination of structured interviews and paper-and-pencil tests. The company can evaluate the success of this program in terms of whether it efficiently produces enough qualified call takers.

Depending on the situation, a number of techniques are available for measuring HRM's effectiveness in meeting its customers' needs. These techniques include reviewing a set of key indicators, measuring the outcomes of specific HRM activity, and measuring the economic value or ROI (return on investment) of HRM programs.

Human Resource Management Audits

An **HRM audit** is a formal review of the outcomes of HRM functions. To conduct the audit, the HR department identifies key functions and the key measures of organizational performance and customer satisfaction that would indicate each function is succeeding. Table 12.3 lists examples of these measures for a variety of HRM functions: staffing, compensation, benefits, training, appraisal and development, and overall effectiveness. The audit may also look at any other measure associated with successful management of human resources—for instance, compliance with employment-related legislation, succession planning, maintaining a safe workplace, and positive labour relations. An HRM audit using customer satisfaction measures supports the customer-oriented approach to human resource management. When HR functions are outsourced, these audits need to look at both HR functions performed internally and those that are outsourced.

After identifying performance measures for the HRM audit, the staff carries out the audit by gathering information. The information for the key business indicators is usually available in the organization's documents. Sometimes the HR department has to create new documents for gathering specific types of data. The usual way to measure customer satisfaction is to conduct surveys. Employee attitude surveys provide information about the satisfaction of these internal customers. Many organizations conduct surveys of top line executives to get a better view of how HRM practices affect the organization's business success.

Analyzing the Effect of HRM Programs

Another way to measure HRM effectiveness is to analyze specific programs or activities. The analysis can measure a program's success in terms of whether it achieved its objectives and whether it delivered value in an economic sense. Increasingly HR is being called on to measure its impact. The Conference Board of Canada identifies "measurement" as one of the "hot HR issues" and indicates that HR measures must be meaningful due to the importance of HR's role in building organizational capabilities.[54]

Senior management and other organizational stakeholders are asking for metrics or measures that relate to the value of the firm's human capital and the return on investment in that human capital. A recent report from CFO Research Services and Mercer Human Resource Consulting revealed that chief financial officers' opinions of HR are improving—most of the 180 CFOs surveyed see human capital as a value driver rather than a cost. However, the survey also showed that just 16 percent of CFOs said they knew to a "considerable" or "great" extent the return on investments in human capital.[55]

"Traditional financial numbers are an indicator of past performance, but reliable measures of human capital are much better indicators of future performance, and

HRM audit
A formal review of the outcomes of HRM functions, based on identifying key HRM functions and measures of organizational performance.

TABLE 12.3

Key Measures of Success for an HRM Audit

BUSINESS INDICATORS	CUSTOMER SATISFACTION MEASURES
Staffing	
Average days taken to fill open requisitions	Anticipation of human resource needs
Ratio of acceptances to offers made	Timeliness of referring qualified workers to line supervisors
Ratio of Employment Equity target group applicant representation in local labour market	Treatment of applicants
Per capita requirement costs	Skill in handling terminations
Average years of experience/education of hires	Adaptability to changing labour market conditions
Compensation	
Per capita (average) merit increases	Fairness of existing job evaluation system
Ratio of recommendations for reclassification to number of employees	Competitiveness in local labour market
Percentage of overtime hours to regular time	Relationship between pay and performance
Ratio of average salary offers to average salary in community	Employee satisfaction with pay
Benefits	
Average workers' compensation payments	Promptness in handling claims
Benefit cost per payroll dollar	Fairness and consistency in the application of benefit policies
Percentage of sick leave to total pay	Communication of benefits to employees
	Assistance provided to line managers in reducing potential for unnecessary claims
Training	
Percentage of employees participating in training programs	Extent to which training programs meet the needs of employees and the company
Percentage of employees receiving tuition reimbursement	Communication to employees about available training opportunities
Training dollars per employee	Quality of introduction/orientation programs
Employee appraisal and development	
Distribution of performance appraisal ratings	Assistance in identifying management potential
Appropriate psychometric properties of appraisal forms	Organizational development activities provided by HRM department
Overall effectiveness	
Ratio of human resource staff to employee population	Accuracy and clarity of information provided to managers and employees
Turnover rate	Competence and expertise of staff
Absenteeism rate	Working relationship between organizations and HRM department
Ratio of per capita revenues to per capita cost	
Net income per employee	

SOURCE: Reprinted with permission excerpts from Chapter 1.5, "Evaluating Human Resource Effectiveness," pp. 187–227, by Anne S. Tsui and Luis R. Gomez-Mejia, from *Human Resource Management: Evolving Roles and Responsibilities*; edited by Lee Dyer. Copyright © 1988 by The Bureau of National Affairs, Inc., Washington DC 20037.

therefore growth, and therefore shareholder value," says Curt Coffman of the Gallup Organization.[56] The European Union is currently looking at human capital reporting measures. For example, Denmark requires publicly traded companies to report on the "human dimension" of their business to provide investors a background of the value of human capital and it is expected some type of reporting requirement will also be required in North America.[57]

However, caution about calculating the return on investment of specific, isolated HR initiatives is needed. When individual HR initiatives are evaluated in isolation on strictly quantitative terms, there may be a tendency to focus on cost containment only with a failure to consider qualitative considerations and indirect benefits. For example, if an investment in human capital such as a training program yields tangible results such as an increase in product quality and a decrease in product returns this only quantifies part of the return on investment. The ROI calculation may not fully capture the improved employee and/or customer satisfaction achieved as a result of the training program. Figure 12.10 provides the math for calculating the return on investment of an investment in human capital including both direct and indirect costs and benefits.

In general, HR departments should be able to improve their performance through some combination of greater efficiency and greater effectiveness. Greater efficiency means the HR department uses fewer and less-costly resources to perform its functions. According to Hewitt Associates, more than three-quarters of HR departments are experiencing pressure to reduce HR spending.[58] Greater effectiveness means that what the HR department does—for example, selecting employees or setting up a performance management system—has a more beneficial effect on employees' and the organization's performance.

HRM's potential to affect employees' well-being and the organization's performance makes human resource management an exciting field. As we have shown throughout the book, every HRM function calls for decisions that have the potential to help individuals and organizations achieve their goals. For HR managers to fulfill that potential, they must ensure that their decisions are well grounded. As an example, we discussed telework in Chapter 3, as an option for work design that many organizations have embraced to promote greater productivity and job satisfaction. At the same time, a review of the research literature shows that these assumptions about telework's benefits are largely untested.[59] Telework is but one example of an issue that can dramatically affect employees' lives and organizations' success yet remains open for future investigation. The field of human resource management provides tremendous opportunity to future researchers and managers who want to make a difference in many people's lives and contribute to the success of organizations.

$$\text{ROI \%} = \frac{\text{Realized direct/indirect benefits} - \text{Total direct/indirect costs}}{\text{Total direct/indirect costs}} \times 100$$

FIGURE 12.10

ROI Math: Formula for Calculating Return on Investment in Human Capital

SOURCE: Adapted from "ROI Math," *Canadian HR Reporter*, February 28, 2005, p. 15.

Summary

1. Define high-performance work systems and identify the elements of such a system.

   A high-performance work system is the right combination of people, technology, and organizational structure that makes full use of the organization's resources and opportunities in achieving its goals. The elements of a high-performance work system are organizational structure, task design, people, reward systems, and information systems. These elements must work together in a smoothly functioning whole.

2. Summarize the outcomes of a high-performance work system.

   A high-performance work system achieves the organization's goals, typically including growth, productivity, and high profits. On the way to achieving these overall goals, the high-performance work system meets such intermediate goals as high quality, innovation, customer satisfaction, job satisfaction, and reduced absenteeism and turnover.

3. Describe the conditions that create a high-performance work system.

   Many conditions contribute to high-performance work systems by giving employees skills, incentives, knowledge, autonomy, and employee satisfaction. Teamwork and empowerment can make work more satisfying and provide a means for employees to improve quality and productivity. Organizations can improve performance by creating a learning organization, in which people constantly learn and share knowledge so that they continually expand their capacity to achieve the results they desire. In a high-performance organization, employees experience satisfaction and engagement. Organizations also need to manage turnover and discipline effectively. For long-run high performance, organizations and employees must be ethical as well.

4. Explain how human resource management can contribute to high performance.

   Jobs should be designed to foster teamwork and employee involvement. Recruitment and selection should focus on obtaining employees who have the qualities necessary for teamwork and knowledge sharing. When the organization selects for teamwork and decision-making skills, it may have to provide training in specific job tasks. Training also is important because of its role in creating a learning organization. The performance management system should be related to the organization's goals, with a focus on meeting internal and external customers' needs. Total compensation and rewards should include links to performance, and employees should be included in decisions about compensation. Research suggests that it is more effective to improve HRM practices as a whole than to focus on one or two isolated practices.

5. Discuss the role of HRM technology in high-performance work systems.

   Technology can improve the efficiency of the human resource management functions and support knowledge sharing. HRM applications involve transaction processing, decision support systems, and expert systems, often as part of a human resource information system using relational databases, which can improve the efficiency of routine tasks and the quality of decisions. With Internet technology, organizations can use e-HRM to let all the organization's employees help themselves to the HR information they need whenever they need it.

6. Summarize ways to measure the effectiveness of human resource management.

   Taking a customer-oriented approach, HRM can improve quality by defining the internal customers who use its services and determining whether it is meeting those customers' needs. One way to do this is with an HRM audit, a formal review of the outcomes of HRM functions. The audit may look at any measure associated with successful management of human resources. Audit information may come from the organization's documents and surveys of customer satisfaction. Another way to measure HRM effectiveness is to analyze specific programs or activities. The analysis can measure success in terms of whether a program met its objectives and whether it delivered value in an economic sense, such as by leading to productivity improvements and generating a return on investment.

Review and Discussion Questions

1. What is a high-performance work system? What are its elements? Which of these elements involve human resource management?

2. As it has become clear that HRM can help create and maintain high-performance work systems, it appears that organizations will need two kinds of human re-

source professionals: One kind focuses on identifying how HRM can contribute to high performance. The other kind develops expertise in particular HRM functions, such as how to administer a benefits program that complies with legal requirements. Which aspect of HRM is more interesting to you? Why?

3. How can teamwork, involvement, knowledge sharing, satisfaction, and engagement contribute to high performance?

4. If an organization can win customers, employees, or investors through deception, why would ethical behaviour contribute to high performance?

5. How can an organization promote ethical behaviour among its employees?

6. Summarize how each of the following HR functions can contribute to high performance.
   a. Job design
   b. Recruitment and selection
   c. Training and development
   d. Performance management
   e. Total compensation and rewards

7. How can HRM technology make a human resource department more productive? How can technology improve the quality of HRM decisions?

8. Why should human resource departments measure their effectiveness? What are some ways they can go about measuring effectiveness?

What's Your HR IQ? www.mcgrawhill.ca/college/noe

The Online Learning Centre offers more ways to check what you've learned so far. Find experiential exercises as well as Test Your Knowledge Quizzes, Videos, and many other resources at www.mcgrawhill.ca/college/noe.

Case: Off-Duty Behaviour, At-Work Reprisals

When federal public servant Edith Gendron was fired by Heritage Canada for not stepping down as president of a separatist club, she was brought to the fore of one of the most intractable issues in employee relations. The issue: to what extent can employers sanction workers for their activities outside work? Whether it is political involvement, criminal acts of personal expressions online, or workers' activities off-hours, these activities have caused employers no small amount of grief and hand-wringing. Cases vary from employers who punish workers for such acts as cursing at a colleague at a local store to governments taking action against employees who campaign publicly against its policies.

When Edith Gendron was hired four years prior for a post in the Official Languages Division of Heritage Canada, she told the hiring manager, a director of operations, of her sovereigntist leanings. The director at the time didn't think Gendron's politics mattered in her day-to-day job, which was to handle funding requests—up to but not including making financial decisions for French language education for Acadian communities in the Atlantic provinces.

When the founding committee of a new sovereigntist group, Le Quebec, Un Pays! (which translates into "Quebec, A Country!"), set up shop in the western Quebec region and nominated her for its presidency, she consulted both her union and Heritage Canada's code of ethics. She then brought her concerns to management, requesting a confidential report be kept in her employee file that would state three conditions:

- The employer is aware of her outside activities.
- The employer confirms there is no conflict of interest.
- The employer would take measures to ensure the impartiality of her work at the department.

Gendron further placed two conditions on herself. First, she would never make any public criticism of her employer, Heritage Canada; if the occasion ever comes up, she would cede the spokesperson role to someone else in the group. Second, she is content never to have the power to make any funding decision; if she ever has to fill in for someone with authority over program funding, her decisions in the interim would be subject to review. In response to her request, management at the department issued the order that she step down as president of the new group. Gendron refused, and was fired after she defied employer orders to step down as president of a sovereigntist group. The department said it didn't object to her involvement as a member; but her position puts her in conflict with the department's mandate in fostering national unity. Gendron, however, maintained that as long as she fulfilled her duties, what she does outside work shouldn't be a concern of her employer. The federal public service union has filed grievances on Gendron's behalf, claiming unfair dismissal.

SOURCE: H. Uyen Vu, "Off-Duty Behaviour, At-Work Reprisals," *Canadian HR Reporter*, June 14, 2004, pp. 1, 2; "A Separatist in Their Midst," *Canadian HR Reporter*, June 14, 2004, p. 2. © Copyright *Canadian HR Reporter*, June 14, 2004, by permission of Carswell, Toronto, Ontario, 1-800-387-5164, www.hrreporter.com.

Questions

1. When do an employee's actions away from work become a legitimate employer concern?

2. Do you feel Heritage Canada made the right decision to terminate Edith Gendron's employment? Why or why not?

3. Could Heritage Canada's decision to terminate Gendron have any impact on the department's future performance?

Case: Air Canada's Collection Agency Threat

In a move not often seen in employee relations, Air Canada threatened to turn to a collection agency to recover meal allowances it had overpaid to some 5,100 employees. The company has since backed off from this threat, but the move generated considerable bad press for Air Canada.

The problem started with an "inputting error" in May 2004 that resulted in 5,100 flight attendants being paid for meals of which they weren't entitled. Some overpaid amounts were as little as $20, but the total was about $600,000. "The issue for the airline was the amount of overpayment was deemed to be significant enough that it would be really irresponsible of us not to try to recover the funds," said Air Canada spokesperson Laura Cooke. The airline approached the Canadian Union of Public Employees local representing flight attendants in July 2004 for co-operation in the matter but were "unsuccessful," said Cooke.

On November 26, 2004, the company issued a letter to flight attendants, asking the employees to either sign a form authorizing the company to recover the overpayment from their January 17, 2005 paycheques, or to remit personal cheques for the overpaid amounts. Failure to do either by January 1, 2005 "will result in your file being placed in the hands of a collection agency. You should be aware that this action may have an adverse effect on your personal credit status," states the letter.

Asked whether the airline regretted such a move, Cooke said only, "we were forced to take an unfortunate and unnecessary step." In a follow-up letter to employees dated December 6, 2004, however, vice-president of customer experience Susan Welscheid stated that in her view, the November 26 letter "should not have raised the possibility of using a collection agency to retrieve these monies."

Pamela Sachs, president of the Air Canada component of the Canadian Union of Public Employees, said what the union asked for all along was a breakdown of the overpayment. "It's not that we weren't being co-operative. We had no information," said Sachs. "It's an extremely time-consuming process if you have to go back and pull out all the files for 6,500 people. And they didn't say that was the reason but we know that's the reason. Air Canada had cut staff in all departments, and the few people who are left are doing all the work, and that's a humongous task."

Commenting on the case, Toronto-based HR consultant, Ian Turnbull said the threat of collection only prodded an open wound that still needed to heal after the difficult process of restructuring out of bankruptcy. But, he added, "I'm not sure Air Canada had a way to win this." If the company hadn't tried to recover the money, "it would have been setting up an unfortunate precedent. But from the perspective of employee relations, did they do as well as they could have? Employees don't react well to threats."

Turnbull doubts the company would have faced any privacy issues in turning to a collection agency, even though using such a service would have required the company to pass on the flight attendants' personal data to the agency. "The collection agency would have been acting as an agent for the company. But you never know. These are still the early days of the (federal privacy) legislation, and if someone issued a complaint, it's possible the commissioner would find for the complainant. But I don't think so. I think the decision would be that companies are allowed to use this kind of process."

SOURCE: Uyen Vu, "Air Canada Union Irate Following Collection Agency Threat," *Canadian HR Reporter*, January 17, 2005, pp. 1, 2. © Copyright *Canadian HR Reporter*, January 17, 2005, by permission of Carswell, Toronto, Ontario, 1-800-387-5164, www.hrreporter.com.

Questions

1. What impact might the collection agency threat have on Air Canada's ability to achieve the desired outcomes of a High-Performance Work System outlined in the text (Figure 12.2)?

2. How could proactive human resource management have avoided the union confrontation and affected the course of events described in this case?

CBC

VIDEO CASE

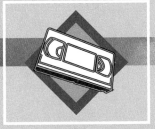

No Wal-Mart Wages

Unions such as the United Food and Commercial Workers Union (UFCW) are fighting for their future and for the standard of living of its members. According to the Canadian president of the UFCW, the union's power at the bargaining table for the grocery industry is eroding. Employers are demanding concessions from wages to health benefits to compete with non-unionized Wal-Mart. For example, the UFCW, in negotiations with Loblaw's Real Canadian Superstore, recently made a key concession that new hires will be paid less.

Employees in the grocery industry are concerned that their jobs may no longer offer the same hope for promotions or the ability to earn a wage that will keep their families above the poverty line.

For storeowners, pressure to keep labour costs down is fierce as Wal-Mart continues to expand and compete directly in their traditional grocery business. A parallel is drawn to the loss of North American manufacturing jobs to countries with cheaper labour costs.

While companies, unions, and people are trying to hold their ground, many are hoping that Wal-Mart's workforce of more than 1 million will become unionized. An epic struggle of union against non-union is occurring. The anti-union perspective raises the argument that a third-party intervention negatively affects a business's ability to operate successfully.

As mentioned in the video and discussed in Chapter 10, the UFCW has been working to certify Wal-Mart stores in Canada including a store in

Jonquiere, Quebec. Although this was the first Wal-Mart store to certify successfully in North America, Wal-Mart Canada recently announced the Jonquiere store would be closed for economic reasons.

SOURCE: Based on "No Wal-Mart Wages," CBC *Venture* 911, January 25, 2004.

Questions

1. Imagine that you are the senior human resource manager for Wal-Mart Canada. What might be your concerns about unionization?
2. If Wal-Mart became unionized do you think it would be possible for the UFCW and Wal-Mart to work together collaboratively? Explain your answer.
3. What is your reaction to Wal-Mart's announcement to close the Jonquiere store? Does this violate labour legislation?

Glossary

achievement tests Tests that measure a person's existing knowledge and skills.

action learning Training in which teams get an actual problem, work on solving it and commit to an action plan, and are accountable for carrying it out.

American Federation of Labor and Congress of Industrial Organizations (AFL-CIO) An association that seeks to advance the shared interests of its member unions at the international level.

apprenticeship A work-study training method that teaches job skills through a combination of on-the-job training and technical training.

aptitude tests Tests that assess how well a person can learn or acquire skills and abilities.

arbitration Conflict resolution procedure in which an arbitrator or arbitration board determines a binding settlement.

assessment centre A wide variety of specific selection programs that use multiple selection methods to rate applicants or job incumbents on their management potential; an assessment process in which multiple raters or evaluators (assessors) evaluate employees' performance on a number of exercises, usually as they work in a group at an off-site location.

assessment Collecting information and providing feedback to employees about their behaviour, communication style, or skills.

balanced scorecard An organizational approach to performance management that integrates strategic perspectives including financial, customer, internal processes, and learning and growth.

behavioural interview A structured interview in which the interviewer asks the candidate to describe how he or she handled a type of situation in the past.

behaviourally anchored rating scale (BARS) Method of performance measurement that rates behaviour in terms of a scale showing specific statements of behaviour that describe different levels of performance.

benchmarking A procedure in which an organization compares its own practices against those of successful competitors.

Benchmarks A measurement tool that gathers ratings of a manager's use of skills associated with success in managing.

Bill C-45 (Westray Bill) Amendment to the Criminal Code making organizations and anyone who directs the work of others criminally liable for safety offences.

bona fide occupational requirement (BFOR) A necessary (not merely preferred) requirement for performing a job.

broadbanding Reducing the number of levels in the organization's job structure.

Canada Industrial Relations Board (CIRB) Quasi-judicial tribunal responsible for the interpretation and enforcement of the Canada Labour Code (Part I—Industrial Relations).

Canada Pension Plan (CPP)/Quebec Pension Plan (QPP) A contributory, mandatory plan that provides retirement pensions, disability benefits, and survivor benefits.

Canadian Human Rights Act Federal legislation that protects individuals from discrimination on the basis of 11 protected grounds.

Canadian Human Rights Commission (CHRC) Provides individuals under federal jurisdiction a means to resolve complaints of discrimination.

Canadian Labour Congress (CLC) An association that seeks to advance the shared interests of its member unions at the national level.

career path The identified pattern or progression of jobs or roles within an organization.

cash balance plan Retirement plan in which the employer sets up an individual account for each employee and contributes a percentage of the employee's salary; the account earns interest at a predefined rate.

central tendency Incorrectly rating all employees at or near the middle of a rating scale.

checkoff provision Requirement that the employer, on behalf of the union, automatically deducts union dues from employees' paycheques.

closed shop Union security arrangement under which a person must be a union member before being hired.

coach A peer or manager who works with an employee to provide a source of motivation, help him or her develop skills, and provide reinforcement and feedback.

cognitive ability tests Tests designed to measure such mental abilities as verbal skills, quantitative skills, and reasoning ability.

collective bargaining Negotiation between union representatives and management representatives to arrive at an agreement defining conditions of employment for the term of the agreement and to administer that agreement.

commissions Incentive pay calculated as a percentage of sales.

compensatory model Process of arriving at a selection decision in which a very high score on one type of assessment can make up for a low score on another.

competency-based pay systems Pay structures that set pay according to the employees' levels of skill or knowledge and what they are capable of doing.

competency framework Competencies the entire organization requires to be successful.

competencies Knowledge, skills, abilities, and other characteristics associated with effective job performance.

conciliation Conflict resolution procedure in which a third party to collective bargaining reports the reasons for a dispute, the views and arguments of both sides, and possibly a recommended settlement, which the parties may decline.

concurrent validation Research that consists of administering a test to people who currently hold a job, then comparing their scores to existing measures of job performance.

constructive dismissal Occurs when the employer makes a significant change to a worker's condition of employment.

construct validity Capability of a test to measure a construct such as intelligence and the relationship of this construct to successful job performance.

content validity Consistency between the test items or problems and the kinds of situations or problems that occur on the job.

continuous learning Each employee's and each group's ongoing efforts to gather information and apply the information to their decisions in a learning organization.

contributory plan All costs of the plan are funded by employees, employers, and the plan's own investments; retirement plan funded by contributions from the employer and employee.

co-operative education A plan of higher education that incorporates paid work experience as an integral part of academic studies.

coordination training Team training that teaches the team how to share information and make decisions to obtain the best team performance.

core competency A set of knowledge and skills that provide the organization with a competitive advantage.

craft union Labour union whose members all have a particular skill or occupation.

criterion-related validity A measure of validity based on showing a substantial correlation between test scores and job performance scores.

critical-incident method Method of performance measurement based on managers' records of specific examples of the employee behaving in ways that are either effective or ineffective.

cross-cultural preparation Training to prepare employees and their family members for an assignment in a foreign country.

cross-training Team training in which team members understand and practise each other's skills so that they are prepared to step in and take another member's place.

culture shock Disillusionment and discomfort that occur during the process of adjusting to a new culture.

decision support systems Computer software systems designed to help managers solve problems by showing how results vary when the manager alters assumptions or data.

defined benefit plan Pension plan that guarantees a specified level of retirement income.

defined contribution plan Retirement plan in which the employer sets up an individual account for each employee and specifies the size of the investment into that account.

development The acquisition of knowledge, skills, and behaviors that improve an employee's ability to meet changes in job requirements and in customer demands.

differential treatment Differing treatment of individuals where the differences are based on a prohibited ground.

direct applicants People who apply for a vacancy without prompting from the organization.

direct compensation Financial rewards employees receive in exchange for their work.

direct discrimination Policies or practices that clearly make a distinction on the basis of a prohibited ground.

discrimination To treat someone differently or unfairly because of a personal characteristic.

diversity training Training designed to change employee attitudes about diversity and/or develop skills needed to work with a diverse workforce.

downsizing The planned elimination of large numbers of personnel with the goal of enhancing the organization's competitiveness.

downward move Assignment of an employee to a position with less responsibility and authority.

duty to accommodate An employer's duty to consider how an employee's characteristic such as disability, religion, or sex can be accommodated and to take action so the employee can perform the job.

e-learning Receiving training via the Internet or the organization's intranet.

electronic business (e-business) Any process that a business conducts electronically, especially business involving use of the Internet.

electronic human resource management (e-HRM) The processing and transmission of digitized HR information, especially using computer networking and the Internet.

employee assistance program (EAP) A referral service that employees can use to seek professional treatment for emotional problems or substance abuse.

employee benefits and services Compensation in forms other than cash.

employee development The combination of formal education, job experiences, relationships, and assessment of personality and competencies to help employees prepare for the future of their careers.

employee engagement The extent that employees are satisfied, committed to, and prepared to support what is important to the organization.

employee stock ownership plan (ESOP) An arrangement in which the organization distributes shares of stock to all its employees by placing it in a trust.

employee wellness program A set of communications, activities, and facilities designed to change health-related behaviours in ways that reduce health risks.

Employment Insurance (EI) A federally mandated program to provide temporary financial assistance to unemployed Canadians.

ergonomics The study of the interface between individuals' physiology and the characteristics of the physical work environment.

ethics The fundamental principles of right and wrong.

exit interview A meeting of a departing employee with the employee's supervisor and/or a human resource specialist to discuss the employee's reasons for leaving.

expatriates Employees who take assignments in other countries.

experiential programs A teamwork and leadership training program based on the use of challenging, structured outdoor activities.

expert systems Computer systems that support decision making by incorporating the decision rules used by people who are considered to have expertise in a certain area.

external labour market Individuals who are actively seeking employment.

externship Employee development through a full-time temporary position at another organization.

Fleishman Job Analysis System Job analysis technique that asks subject-matter experts to evaluate a job in terms of the abilities required to perform the job.

flexible benefits plan A benefits plan that offers employees a set of alternatives from which they can choose the types and amounts of benefits they want.

flexible staffing arrangements Methods of staffing other than the traditional hiring of full-time employees (for example, use of independent contractors, on-call workers, temporary workers, and contract company workers).

flextime A scheduling policy in which full-time employees may choose starting and ending times within guidelines specified by the organization.

forced-distribution method Method of performance measurement that assigns a certain percentage of employees to each category in a set of categories.

forecasting The attempts to determine the supply of and demand for various types of human resources to predict areas within the organization where there will be labour shortages or surpluses.

gainsharing Group incentive program that measures improvements in productivity and effectiveness and distributes a portion of each gain to employees.

generalizable Valid in other contexts beyond the context in which the selection method was developed.

glass ceiling Circumstances resembling an invisible barrier that keep most women and other members of the employment equity target groups from attaining the top jobs in organizations.

global organization An organization that chooses to locate a facility based on the ability to effectively, efficiently, and flexibly produce a product or service, using cultural differences as an advantage.

graphic rating scale Method of performance measurement that lists competencies and provides a rating scale for each competency; the employer uses the scale to indicate the extent to which an employee displays each competency.

green-circle rate Pay at a rate that falls below the pay range for the job.

grievance procedure The process for resolving union–management conflicts over interpretation or violation of a collective agreement.

group-building methods Training methods in which trainees share ideas and experiences, build group identity, understand interpersonal relationships, and learn the strengths and weaknesses of themselves and their coworkers.

halo error Rating error that occurs when the rater reacts to one positive performance aspect by rating the employee positively in all areas of performance.

hands-on methods Training methods which actively involve the trainee in trying out skills being taught.

harassment Any behaviour that demeans, humiliates, or embarrasses a person and that a reasonable person should have known would be unwelcome.

health spending account A specific amount of money set aside per employee by the employer to cover health-related costs.

high-performance work system An organization in which technology, organizational structure, people, and processes all work together to give an organization an advantage in the competitive environment.

home country The country in which an organization's headquarters is located.

horns error Rating error that occurs when the rater responds to one negative aspect by rating an employee low in other aspects.

host country A country (other than the home country) in which an organization operates a facility.

hot-stove rule Principle of discipline that says discipline should be like a hot stove, giving clear warning and following up with consistent, objective, immediate consequences.

hourly wage Rate of pay for each hour worked.

HRM audit A formal review of the outcomes of HRM functions, based on identifying key HRM functions and measures of organizational performance.

human capital An organization's employees, described in terms of their training, experience, judgment, intelligence, relationships, and insight.

human resource information system (HRIS) A computer system used to acquire, store, manipulate, analyze, retrieve, and distribute information related to an organization's human resources.

human resource management (HRM) The policies, practices, and systems that influence employees' behaviour, attitudes, and performance.

incentive pay Forms of pay linked to an employee's performance as an individual, group member, or organization member.

indirect compensation The benefits and services employees receive in exchange for their work.

indirect discrimination Policies or practices that appear to be neutral but have an adverse impact based on a prohibited ground.

industrial engineering The study of jobs to find the simplest way to structure work in order to maximize efficiency.

industrial union Labour union whose members are linked by their work in a particular industry.

instructional design A process of systematically developing training to meet specified needs.

interactional justice A judgment that the organization carried out its actions in a way that took the employee's feelings into account.

internal labour force An organization's workers (its employees and the people who work at the organization).

internal responsibility system Philosophy of occupational health and safety where employers and employees share responsibility for creating and maintaining safe and healthy work environments.

international organization An organization that sets up one or a few facilities in one or a few foreign countries.

internship On-the-job learning sponsored by an educational institution as a component of an academic program.

involuntary turnover Turnover initiated by an employer (often with employees who would prefer to stay).

job A set of related duties.

job analysis The process of getting detailed information about jobs.

job description A list of the tasks, duties, and responsibilities (TDRs) that a particular job entails.

job design The process of defining the way work will be performed and the tasks that a given job requires.

job enlargement Broadening the types of tasks performed in a job.

job enrichment Engaging workers by adding more decision-making authority to jobs.

job evaluation An administrative procedure for measuring the relative internal worth of the organization's jobs.

job experiences The combination of relationships, problems, demands, tasks, and other features of an employee's jobs.

job extension Enlarging jobs by combining several relatively simple jobs to form a job with a wider range of tasks.

job hazard analysis technique Safety promotion technique that involves breaking down a job into basic elements, then rating each element for its potential for harm or injury.

job involvement The degree to which people identify themselves with their jobs.

job posting The process of communicating information about a job vacancy on company bulletin boards, in employee publications, on corporate intranets, and anywhere else the organization communicates with employees.

job rotation Enlarging jobs by moving employees among several different jobs.

job sharing A work option in which two part-time employees carry out the tasks associated with a single job.

job specification A list of the competencies that an individual must have to perform a particular job.

job structure The relative pay for different jobs within the organization.

knowledge workers Employees whose main contribution to the organization is specialized knowledge, such as knowledge of customers, a process, or a profession.

labour relations Field that emphasizes skills managers and union leaders can use to minimize costly forms of conflict (such as strikes) and seek win–win solutions to disagreements.

Labour Relations Board (LRB) A specialized tribunal with authority to interpret and enforce the labour laws in their jurisdiction.

leaderless group discussion An assessment centre exercise in which a team of five to seven employees is assigned a problem and must work together to solve it within a certain time period.

leading indicators Objective measures that accurately predict future labour demand.

learning organization An organization in which people continually expand their capacity to achieve the results they desire.

leniency error Rating error of assigning inaccurately high ratings to all employees.

lockout A closure of a place of employment or refusal of the employer to provide work as a way to compel employees to agree to certain demands or conditions.

long-term disability insurance Insurance that pays a percentage of a disabled employee's salary after an initial period and potentially for the rest of the employee's life.

management by objectives (MBO) A system in which people at each level of the organization set goals in a process that flows from top to bottom, so employees at all levels are contributing to the organization's overall goals; these goals become the standards for evaluating each employee's performance.

material safety data sheets (MSDSs) Detailed hazard information concerning a controlled (hazardous) product.

mediation Conflict resolution procedure in which a mediator hears the views of both sides and facilitates the negotiation process but has no formal authority to dictate a resolution.

mentor An experienced, productive senior employee who helps develop a less experienced employee (a protégé/mentee).

merit pay A system of linking pay increases to ratings on performance appraisals.

mixed-standard scales Method of performance measurement that uses several statements describing each competency to produce a final score for that competency.

multinational company An organization that builds facilities in a number of different countries in an effort to minimize production and distribution costs.

multiple-hurdle model Process of arriving at a selection decision by eliminating some candidates at each stage of the selection process.

Myers-Briggs Type Indicator (MBTI) Psychological test that identifies individuals' preferences for source of energy, means of information gathering, way of decision making, and lifestyle, providing information for team building and leadership development.

National Occupational Classification (NOC) Tool created by the federal government to provide a standardized source of information about jobs in Canada's labour market.

needs assessment The process of evaluating the organization, individual employees, and employees' tasks to determine what kinds of training, if any, are necessary.

nepotism The practice of hiring relatives.

noncontributory plan Retirement plan funded entirely by contributions from the employer.

nondirective interview A selection interview in which the interviewer has great discretion in choosing questions to ask each candidate.

offshoring Setting up a business enterprise in another country (e.g., building a factory in China).

on-the-job training (OJT) Training methods in which a person with job experience and skill guides trainees in practising job skills at the workplace.

organization analysis A process for determining the appropriateness of training by evaluating the characteristics of the organization.

organizational behaviour modification (OBM) A plan for managing the behaviour of employees through a formal system of feedback and reinforcement.

orientation Training designed to prepare employees to perform their jobs effectively, learn about their organization, and establish work relationships.

outcome fairness A judgment that the consequences given to employees are just.

outplacement counselling A service in which professionals try to help dismissed employees manage the transition from one job to another.

outsourcing The practice of having another company (a vendor, third-party provider, or consultant) provide services.

paired-comparison method Method of performance measurement that compares each employee with each other employee to establish rankings.

panel interview Selection interview in which several members of the organization meet to interview each candidate.

pay equity Principle of non-discrimination in wages that require men and women doing work of equal value to be paid the same.

pay grades Sets of jobs having similar worth or content, grouped together to establish rates of pay.

pay level The average amount (including wages, salaries, and bonuses) the organization pays for a particular job.

pay policy line A graphed line showing the mathematical relationship between job evaluation points and pay rate.

pay ranges A set of possible pay rates defined by a minimum, maximum, and midpoint of pay for employees holding a particular job or a job within a particular pay grade or band.

pay structure The pay policy resulting from job structure and pay level decisions.

performance appraisal The measurement of specified areas of an employee's performance.

performance management The process of ensuring that employees' activities and outputs match the organization's goals.

Personal Information Protection and Electronic Documents Act (PIPEDA) Provides rules for how organizations can collect, use, or disclose information about you in the course of commercial activities.

person analysis A process for determining individuals' needs and readiness for training.

phased retirement A gradual transition into full retirement by reducing hours or job responsibility.

piecework rate Rate of pay for each unit produced.

Position Analysis Questionnaire (PAQ) A standardized job analysis questionnaire containing 194 questions about work behaviours, work conditions, and job characteristics that apply to a wide variety of jobs.

position The set of duties (job) performed by a particular person.

predictive validation Research that uses the test scores of all applicants and looks for a relationship between the scores and future performance of the applicants who were hired.

presentation methods Training methods in which trainees receive information provided by instructors or via computers or other media.

procedural justice A judgment that fair methods were used to determine the consequences an employee receives.

profit sharing Incentive pay in which payments are a percentage of the organization's profits and do not become part of the employees' base salary.

progressive discipline A formal discipline process in which the consequences become more serious if the employee repeats the offence.

promotion Assignment of an employee to a position with greater challenges, more responsibility, and more authority than in the previous job, usually accompanied by a pay increase.

protean career A career that frequently changes based on changes in the person's interests, abilities, and values and in the work environment.

psychological contract A description of what an employee expects to contribute in an employment relationship and what the employer will provide the employee in exchange for those contributions.

Rand Formula Union security provision that makes payment of labour union dues mandatory even if the worker is not a member of the union.

readiness for training A combination of employee characteristics and positive work environment that permit training.

realistic job preview Background information about a job's positive and negative qualities.

reality check Information employers give employees about their competencies and where these assets fit into the organization's plans.

recruiting Any activity carried on by the organization with the primary purpose of identifying and attracting potential employees.

recruitment The process through which the organization seeks applicants for potential employment.

red-circle rate Pay at a rate that falls above the pay range for the job.

referrals People who apply for a vacancy because someone in the organization prompted them to do so.

reliability The extent to which a measurement generates consistent results.

repatriation The process of preparing expatriates to return home from a foreign assignment.

sabbatical A leave of absence from an organization to renew or develop skills.

salary Rate of pay for each week, month, or year worked.

selection The process through which organizations make decisions about who will be chosen to fill job openings; the process by which the organization attempts to identify applicants with the necessary knowledge, skills, abilities, and other characteristics that will help the organization achieve its goals.

self-assessment The use of information by employees to determine their career interests, values, aptitudes, and behavioural tendencies.

self-service System in which employees have online access to information about HR issues and go online to enrol themselves in programs and provide feedback through surveys.

severance pay Compensation that recognizes the employee's years of service and compensates the employee for loss of job-related earnings.

sexual harassment Unwelcome behaviour that is of a sexual nature or is related to a person's sex.

short-term disability insurance Insurance that pays a percentage of a disabled employee's salary as benefits to the employee for six months or less.

similar-to-me error Rating error of giving a higher evaluation to people who seem similar to oneself.

simple ranking Method of performance measurement that requires managers to rank employees in their group from the highest performer to the lowest performer.

simulation A training method that represents a real-life situation, with trainees making decisions resulting in outcomes that mirror what would happen on the job.

situational interviews A structured interview in which the interviewer describes a situation likely to arise on the job, then asks the candidate what he or she would do in that situation.

social unionism Social unionism involves activities intended to influence social and economic policies of government.

standard hour plan An incentive plan that pays workers extra for work done in less than a preset "standard time."

stock options Rights to buy a certain number of shares of stock at a specified price.

strictness error Rating error of giving low ratings to all employees, holding them to unreasonably high standards.

strike A collective decision by union members not to work or to slow down until certain demands or conditions are met.

structured interview A selection interview that consists of a predetermined set of questions for the interviewer to ask.

succession planning The process of identifying and tracking high-potential employees who will be able to fill top management positions when they become vacant.

task analysis The process of identifying the tasks and competencies that training should emphasize.

task analysis inventory Job analysis method that involves listing the tasks performed in a particular job and rating each task according to a defined set of criteria.

teamwork The assignment of work to groups of employees with various skills who interact to assemble a product or provide a service.

technic of operations review (TOR) Method of promoting safety by determining which specific element of a job led to a past accident.

termination pay A lump sum payment equal to the regular wages for a regular work week that an employee would have earned during the notice period.

third country A country that is neither the home country nor the host country of an employer.

360-degree feedback Performance measurement that combines information from the employee's managers, peers, direct reports, self, and customers.

total compensation All types of financial rewards and tangible benefits and services employees receive as part of their employment.

total rewards Comprehensive approach to compensating and rewarding employees.

training An organization's planned efforts to help employees acquire job-related competencies with the goal of applying these on the job.

transaction processing Computations and calculations involved in reviewing and documenting HRM decisions and practices.

transfer of training On-the-job use of competencies enhanced in training.

transfer Assignment of an employee to a position in a different area of the company, usually in a lateral move.

transitional matrix A chart that lists job categories held in one period and shows the proportion of employees in each of those job categories in a future period.

transnational HRM system Type of HRM system that makes decisions from a global perspective, includes managers from many countries, and is based on ideas contributed by people representing a variety of cultures.

trend analysis Constructing and applying statistical models that predict labour demand for the next year, given relatively objective statistics from the previous year.

unfair labour practice A prohibited conduct of an employer, union, or individual under the relevant labour legislation.

union shop Union security arrangement that requires employees to join the union within a certain amount of time after beginning employment.

union steward An employee elected by union members to represent them in ensuring that the terms of the collective agreement are enforced.

unions Organizations formed for the purpose of representing their members' interests in dealing with employers.

utility The extent to which something provides economic value greater than its cost.

validity The extent to which performance on a measure (such as a test score) is related to what the measure is designed to assess (such as job performance).

virtual expatriates Employees who manage an operation abroad without permanently locating in the country.

virtual reality A computer-based technology that provides an interactive, three-dimensional learning experience.

voluntary turnover Turnover initiated by employees (often when the organization would prefer to keep them).

work flow design The process of analyzing the tasks necessary for the production of a product or service.

Workers' Compensation Acts Provincial programs that provide benefits to workers who suffer work-related injuries or illnesses.

workforce utilization review A comparison of the proportion of employees in protected groups with the proportion that each group represents in the relevant labour market.

workplace health and safety committee A committee jointly appointed by the employer and employees at large (the union) to address health and safety issues in a workplace.

workplace literacy Prose, document, and quantitative capabilities in the languages in which business is conducted.

yield ratio A ratio that expresses the percentage of applicants who successfully move from one stage of the recruitment and selection process to the next.

Notes

Chapter 1

1. *National Post*, January 26, 2004, p. A14.
2. www.ipsos-na.com/news/pressrelease.cfm. Retrieved: March 4, 2004.
3. www.rbc.com/aboutus/fastfacts.html. Retrieved: April 4, 2004.
4. Janice Cooney and Allison Cowan, "Training and Development Outlook 2003: Canadian Organizations Continue to Under-Invest," The Conference Board of Canada 2003, p. 1.
5. A. S. Tsui and L. R. Gomez-Mejia, "Evaluating Human Resource Effectiveness," in *Human Resource Management: Evolving Rules and Responsibilities*, ed. L. Dyer (Washington, DC: BNA Books, 1988), pp. 1187-227; M. A. Hitt, B. W. Keats, and S. M. DeMarie, "Navigating in the New Competitive Landscape: Building Strategic Flexibility and Competitive Advantage in the 21st Century," *Academy of Management Executive* 12, no. 4 (1998), pp. 22-42; J. T. Delaney and M. A. Huselid, "The Impact of Human Resource Management Practices on Perceptions of Organizational Performance," *Academy of Management Journal* 39 (1996), pp. 949-69.
6. W. F. Cascio, *Costing Human Resources: The Financial Impact of Behavior in Organizations*, 3rd ed. (Boston: PWS-Kent, 1991).
7. S. A. Snell and J. W. Dean, "Integrated Manufacturing and Human Resource Management: A Human Capital Perspective," *Academy of Management Journal* 35 (1992), pp. 467-504; M. A. Youndt, S. Snell, J. W. Dean Jr., and D. P. Lepak, "Human Resource Management, Manufacturing Strategy, and Firm Performance," *Academy of Management Journal* 39 (1996), pp. 836-66.
8. D. Ulrich, *Human Resource Champions* (Boston: Harvard Business School Press, 1998).
9. A. Halcrow, "Survey Shows HRM in Transition," Workforce, June 1998, pp. 73-80; J. Laabs, "Why HR Can Win Today," *Workforce*, May 1998, pp. 62-74; C. Cole, "Kodak Snapshots," *Workforce*, June 2000, pp. 65-72; Towers Perrin, *Priorities for Competitive Advantage: An IBM Study Conducted by Towers Perrin*, 1992.
10. David Brown, "HR Pulled in Two Directions at Once," *Canadian HR Reporter*, February 23, 2004, p. 1.
11. "Performance and Potential 2003-04: Defining the Canadian Advantage," A Special Report by the Conference Board of Canada, October 2003, pp. 5, 6.
12. J. Kahn, "The World's Most Admired Companies," *Fortune*, October 26, 1998, pp. 206-26; A. Fisher, "The World's Most Admired Companies," *Fortune*, October 27, 1997, p. 232.
13. M. Braxton, "HR's Role in a New Global Economy," HRTX iLinx, May/June 2001, pp. 1, 14.
14. C. Fleming and L. Lopez, "No Boundaries," *The Wall Street Journal*, September 9, 1998, p. R16.
15. J. L. Young, "Starbucks Expansion into China Is Slated," *The Wall Street Journal*, October 5, 1998, p. B13C.
16. Kamal Dib, "Diversity Works," *Canadian Business*, March 29–April 11, 2004, p. 54.
17. www.12.statcan/ca/english/census01/release/release5.cfm. Retrieved: April 2, 2004.
18. www.statcan.ca/english/Pgdb/demo46a.htm. Retrieved: April 3, 2004.
19. www.12.statcan/ca/english/Pgdb/demo46b.htm. Retrieved: April 3, 2004.
20. *Financial Post*, March 3, 2004, "The Generation Bomb," p. FP6.
21. National Association of Colleges and Employers, "Job Outlook 2002," www.jobweb.com.
22. Sean Silcoff, "Bombardier Examines Indian Option: 6000 Jobs Leaving? *Financial Post*, April 13, 2004, p. FP1.
23. "Canada's Edge Eroding," *Financial Post*, April 13, 2004, p. FP6.
24. "Canada's Edge Eroding."
25. "More HR Being Outsourced," *HR Daily News*, March 1, 2002, HRnext.com.
26. Uyen Vu, "Outsourcing Calls for New HR Skills," *Canadian HR Reporter*, March 22, 2004, pp. 1, 3.
27. www.cchra-ccarh.ca/phaseIreport/intro_ii.asp. Retrieved: March 23, 2004.
28. www.cchra-ccarh.ca/parc/en/section_4/ss41e.asp. Retrieved: April 8, 2004.
29. www.schra.ca/cert_process.htm. Retrieved: March 23, 2004.
30. Ibid.
31. R. Ricklees, "Ethics in America," *The Wall Street Journal*, October 31-November 3, 1983, p. 33.

32. www.statcan.ca/english/census01, Occupation 2001 National Occupational Classification for Statistics (720), Class of Worker (6) and Sex (3) for Labour Force 15 Years and Over. Retrieved: March 23, 30, 2004.

33. www.hrpao.org/About_Us/ar2003_significant achievements1.asp. Retrieved: March 31, 2004.

34. J. Wiscombe, "Your Wonderful, Terrible HR Life," *Workforce*, June 2001, pp. 32-38.

35. Andrew Wahl, "Leaders Wanted," *Canadian Business*, March 1-14, 2004, p. 31.

36. "Performance and Potential 2003-2004: Defining the Canadian Advantage," A Special Report by the Conference Board of Canada, October 2003, p. 9.

37. Andrew Wahl, "Leaders Wanted," p. 32.

38. Virginia Galt, "The Generational Divide," *The Globe and Mail*, March 31, 2004, pp. C1, C6.

39. B. Wooldridge and J. Wester, "The Turbulent Environment of Public Personnel Administration: Responding to the Challenge of the Changing Workplace of the Twenty-First Century," *Public Personnel Management* 20 (1991), pp. 207-24; J. Laabs, "The New Loyalty: Grasp It. Earn It. Keep It," *Workforce*, November 1998, pp. 34-39.

40. "Employee Dissatisfaction on Rise in Last 10 Years, New Report Says," *Employee Relations Weekly* (Washington, DC: Bureau of National Affairs, 1986).

41. D. T. Hall and J. Richter, "Career Gridlock: Baby Boomers Hit the Wall," *The Executive* 4 (1990), pp. 7-22.

42. S. Shellenbarger, "Companies Must Try Harder to Attract Older Employees," *The Wall Street Journal*, Interactive Edition, May 23, 2001.

43. Kamal Dib, "Diversity Works," *Canadian Business* March 29-April 11, 2004, p. 53.

44. Valerie Marchant, "The New Face of Work," *Canadian Business*, March 29-April 11, 2004, p. 42.

45. Andrew Wahl, "Opening Doors," *Canadian Business*, March 29-April 11, 2004, p.

46. www.statcan.ca/english/Pgdb/labor05.htm. Retrieved: April 2, 2004.

47. Valerie Marchant, "The New Face of Work," p. 40.

48. www.12.statcan.ca/english/census01/release/ release5.cfm. Retrieved: April 2, 2004.

49. www.chrc-ccdp.ca/discrimination/barrier_ freeen.asp. Retrieved: April 3, 2004.

50. "Industry Report 2000," *Training*, October 2000, p. 48.

51. J. A. Neal and C. L. Tromley, "From Incremental Change to Retrofit: Creating High-Performance Work Systems," *Academy of Management Executive* 9 (1995), pp. 42-54.

52. A. Carnevale and D. Desrochers, "Training in the Dilbert Economy," *Training & Development*, December 1999, pp. 32-36.

53. www.statcan.ca/english/Pgdb/educ45.htm. Retrieved: November 30, 2004.

54. Ray Turchansky, "Proof Education is Smart Investment," *Financial Post*, March 22, 2004, p. FP13.

55. M. J. Kavanaugh, H. G. Guetal, and S. I. Tannenbaum, *Human Resource Information Systems: Development and Application* (Boston: PWS-Kent, 1990).

56. S. Greengard, "When HRMS Goes Global: Managing the Data Highway," *Personnel Journal*, June 1995, pp. 91-106.

57. "Cashing in on Canadian Connectedness: The Move to Demonstrating Value," The Conference Board of Canada Briefing, April 2004, www.conferenceboard.ca/boardwise. Retrieved: April 1, 2004.

58. D. M. Rousseau, "Psychological and Implied Contracts in Organizations," *Employee Rights and Responsibilities Journal* 2 (1989), pp. 121-29.

59. D. Rousseau, "Changing the Deal While Keeping the People," Academy of Management Executive 11 (1996), pp. 50-61; M. A. Cavanaugh and R. Noe, "Antecedents and Consequences of the New Psychological Contract," *Journal of Organizational Behavior* 20 (1999), pp. 323-40.

60. Tejada, "For Many, Taking Work Home Is Often a Job without Reward."

61. www.cbc.ca/newwork/nomore9to5/234.html.

Chapter 2

1. Paul Samyn, "Tearing Down Barriers Big Job," *Winnipeg Free Press*, July 16, 2004, p. A3 and Paul Egan, "He's Breaking Barriers," *Winnipeg Free Press*, July 4, 2004, pp. A1, A2.

2. "Anti-Discriminatory Casebook," www.chrc-cdp.ca/Legis&Poli/AntiDiscriminationCasebook_ RecueilDeDecisions. Retrieved: February 18, 2004.

3. "Bona Fide Occupational Justifications-Canadian Human Rights Act," pp. 2, 3, www.chrc-ccdp.ca/ publications/BFOR. Retrieved: July 13, 2004.

4. www.pch.gc.ca/progs/pdp-hrp/Canada/gide/overview_e.cfm?nav. Retrieved: February 26, 2004.

5. www.chrc-ccdp.ca/employment_equity/ visibleminorities-en.asp. Retrieved: April 3, 2004.

6. www.chrc-ccdp.ca/employment_equity/aboriginal-en.asp. Retrieved: April 3, 2004.

7. www.chrc-ccdp.ca/employment_equity/disabilities-en.asp. Retrieved: April 3, 2004.

8. *Annual Report Employment Equity Act*, 2003, p. 31, www.hrsdc.gc.ca/en. Retrieved: July 13, 2004.

9. www.chrc-ccdp.ca/discrimination/grounds_en.asp. Retrieved: July 13, 2004.

10. David Brown, "Privacy Implications for Human Resources Still Unclear," *Canadian HR Reporter*, February 24, 2003, p. 11.

11. "A Guide for Canadians: What is the Personal Information Protection and Electronic Documents Act," www.privcom.gc.ca/information. Retrieved: March 31, 2004.

12. "Rights of Ontario Workers Backed by $300 Fines," *The Globe and Mail*, July 21, 2004.

13. www.chrc ccdp.ca/publications/employee_rights_en.asp. Retrieved: July 23, 2004.

14. Sarah Schmidt, "Report Says Male Profs Paid More Than Females," *Winnipeg Free Press*, July 17, 2004, p. A11.

15. Sarah Schmidt, "Report Says Male Profs Paid More Than Females."

16. David Brown, "New Rules Proposed for Pay Equity," *Canadian HR Reporter*, May 31, 2004, pp. 1, 3.

17. www.chrcccdp.ca/publications/employee_rights_en.asp. Retrieved: July 13, 2004.

18. "Privacy Commissioner of Canada-A Guide for Canadians," www.privcom.gc.ca/information. Retrieved: March 21, 2004.

19. Ron LeClair, "The Evolution of Accommodation," *Canadian HR Reporter*, February 24, 2003, p. 7.

20. "Bona Fide Occupational Requirements and Bona Fide Justifications under the Canadian Human Rights Act," pp. 4, 5, www.chrc-ccdp.ca/publications/BFOR. Retrieved: February 18, 2004.

21. "Anti-Harassment Policies for the Workplace: An Employer's Guide," p. 4, www.chrc-ccdp.ca/publications. Retrieved: February 26, 2004.

22. "Seneca Policies," p. 1, www.senecac.on/ca/about_seneca/policies/discrimination.cfm. Retrieved: July 13, 2004.

23. "Anti-Harassment Policies for the Workplace: An Employer's Guide."

24. Bernard Warner, "European Law Puts Employees on Hook for E-Mail Porn," *Financial Post*, April 28, 2004, p. FP14.

25. B. Carton, "At Jenny Craig, Men Are Ones Who Claim Sex Discrimination," *The Wall Street Journal*, November 29, 1995, p. A1; "Male-on-Male Harassment Suit Won," *Houston Chronicle*, August 12, 1995, p. 21A.

26. "2003 Employment Equity Annual Report," p. 24, www.hrsdc.gc.ca/en. Retrieved: July 13, 2004.

27. Wal-Mart Stores, "Diversity as a Way of Life," Wal-Mart website, February 13, 2002.

28. "Business Results Through Health and Safety," Ontario Workplace Safety and Insurance Board www.wsib.on.ca/wsib/website.nsf/. Retrieved: April 19, 2004

29. www.cchos.ca/oshanswers/legisl/ire_htm/. Retrieved: February 25, 2004.

30. "Information on Occupational Health and Safety," Government of Canada, http://info.load-otea.hrdc-drhc.gc.ca/publications/ohs/committees.pdf. Retrieved: February 25, 2004.

31. Mark Rogers, "Supporting Our Supervisors," p. 4, www.hrpao.org/Knowledge_Centre/kc_s04120403.asp. Retrieved: April 12, 2004.

32. "Initiative Puts Driver Safety First," *Canadian Occupational Health and Safety News*, August 2, 2004, www.ohscanada.com/article.asp?id=33374&issue=08032004. Retrieved: August 3, 2004.

33. "More Ontario Health and Safety Enforcers," *Canadian HR Reporter*, August 9, 2004, p. 2.

34. "Nova Scotia Gives Occupational Health and Safety Officers New Enforcement Tool," *Canadian HR Reporter*, February 2, 2004, www.hrreporter.com. Retrieved: February 5, 2004.

35. Ann Perry, "Workplace Safety Gets a Boost," *Toronto Star*, March 27, 2004, p. D10.

36. "Occupational Health and Safety: Labour Operations," http://info.load-otea.hrdc-drhc.gc.ca/~oshweb/homeen.shtml. Retrieved: February 26, 2004.

37. Uyen Vu, "Right to Refuse Dangerous Work Expands," *Canadian HR Reporter*, August 9, 2004, pp 1, 2.

38. "Ontario Responds to Alarming Increase in Construction Deaths, *Canadian HR Reporter*, www.hrreporter.com. Retrieved: February 10, 2004.

39. J. Roughton, "Managing a Safety Program through Job Hazard Analysis," *Professional Safety* 37 (1992), pp. 28-31.

40. M. A. Verespec, "OSHA Reform Fails Again," *Industry Week*, November 2, 1992, p. 36.

41. Roughton, "Managing a Safety Program."

42. R. G. Hallock and D. A. Weaver, "Controlling Losses and Enhancing Management Systems with TOR Analysis," *Professional Safety* 35 (1990), pp. 24-26.

43. H. Herbstman, "Controlling Losses the Burger King Way," *Risk Management* 37 (1990), pp. 22-30.

44. "Young Worker Awareness Program," www.young-worker.ca/English/index.htm. Retrieved: August 18, 2004.

45. T. Markus, "How to Set Up a Safety Awareness Program," *Supervision* 51 (1990), pp. 14-16.

46. J. Agnew and A. J. Saruda, "Age and Fatal Work-Related Falls," *Human Factors* 35 (1994), pp. 731-36.

47. Todd Humber, "WCBs Lawmakers Tackle Rising Death Toll," *Canadian HR Reporter*, April 19, 2004, p. 19.

48. R. King, "Active Safety Programs, Education Can Help Prevent Back Injuries," *Occupational Health and Safety* 60 (1991), pp. 49-52.

49. T. W. Turriff, "NSPB Suggests 10-Step Program to Prevent Eye Injury," *Occupational Health and Safety* 60 (1991), pp. 62-66.

50. "BC Firm Receives Safety Award," *Canadian Health and Safety News*, www.ohscanada.com/article.asp. Retrieved: August 13, 2004.

51. M. Janssens, J. M. Brett, and F. J. Smith, "Confirmatory Cross-Cultural Research: Testing the Viability of a Corporation-wide Safety Policy," *Academy of Management Journal* 38 (1995), pp. 364-82.

Chapter 3

1. "About SHRC," www.shrc.ca/about/about.html. Retrieved: December 12, 2004.

2. Ibid.

3. David Brown, "Trouble with Assessing IT Skills, Bad News as Demand Heats Up," *Canadian HR Reporter*, December 6, 2004, p. 1.

4. Ibid.

5. "SHRC Annual Report 2003-2004," www.shrc.ca/about/annual/AnnualRep_0304-e.pdf. Retrieved: December 12, 2004.

6. M. Fefer, "Bill Gates' Next Challenge," *Fortune*, December 14, 1992, pp. 30-41.

7. D. Shook, "Why Nike Is Dragging Its Feet," *BusinessWeek Online*, March 19, 2001; A. Bernstein, "Backlash: Behind the Anxiety over Globalization," *BusinessWeek*, April 20, 2000, pp. 38-43; A. Bernstein, "Low Skilled Jobs: Do They Have to Move?" *BusinessWeek*, February 26, 2001.

8. C. Joinson, "Refocusing Job Descriptions," *HR Magazine*, January 2001, downloaded from Findarticles.com.

9. www.managers-gestionnaires.gc.ca/career_development. Retrieved: December 14, 2004.

10. G. Koretz, "Perils of the Graveyard Shift: Poor Health and Low Productivity," *BusinessWeek*, March 10, 1997, p. 22; C. R. Maiwald, J. L. Pierce, and J. W. Newstrom, "Workin' 8 P.M. to 8 A.M. and Lovin' Every Minute of It," *Workforce*, July 1997, pp. 30-36.

11. A. O'Reilly, "Skill Requirements: Supervisor-Subordinate Conflict," *Personnel Psychology* 26 (1973), pp. 75-80; J. Hazel, J. Madden, and R. Christal, "Agreement between Worker-Supervisor Descriptions of the Worker's Job," *Journal of Industrial Psychology* 2 (1964), pp. 71-79.

12. www.hrdc-drhc.gc.ca/noc and "National Occupational Classification Training Tutorial," www.23.hrdc-drhc.gc.ca/2001/e/tutorial/NOC_TRAINING_TUTORIAL.pdf. Retrieved: April 27, 2004, p. 6.

13. *PAQ Newsletter*, August 1989.

14. E. Primhoff, *How to Prepare and Conduct Job Element Examinations* (Washington, DC: U.S. Government Printing Office, 1975).

15. E. Fleishman and M. Reilly, *Handbook of Human Abilities* (Palo Alto, CA: Consulting Psychologists Press, 1992); E. Fleishman and M. Mumford, "Ability Requirements Scales," in *The Job Analysis Handbook for Business, Industry, and Government*, pp. 917-35.

16. W. Cascio, *Applied Psychology in Personnel Management*, 4th ed. (Englewood Cliffs, NJ: Prentice Hall, 1991).

17. P. Wright and K. Wexley, "How to Choose the Kind of Job Analysis You Really Need," *Personnel*, May 1985, pp. 51-55.

18. www.rcmp-learning.org/howtouse.htm. Retrieved: March 11, 2004.

19. Canadian Human Rights Commission website, www.ccrc-ccdp.ca/discrimination/barrier_free-en.asp. Retrieved: April 3, 2004.

20. M. K. Lindell, C. S. Clause, C. J. Brandt, and R. S. Landis, "Relationship between Organizational Context and Job Analysis Ratings," *Journal of Applied Psychology* 83 (1998), pp. 769-76.

21. S. Caudron, "Jobs Disappear when Work Becomes More Important," *Workforce*, January 2000, pp. 30-32.

22. P. Gogoi, "Going to the Head of the Class," *Business Week*, December 10, 2001, pp. 53-54.

23. R. Hackman and G. Oldham, *Work Redesign* (Boston: Addison-Wesley, 1980).

24. M. A. Campion, G. J. Medsker, and A. C. Higgs, "Relations between Work Group Characteristics and Effectiveness: Implications for Designing Effective Work Groups," *Personnel Psychology* 46 (1993), pp. 823-50.

25. M. Werner, "Working at Home-the Right Way to Be a Star in Your Bunny Slippers," *Fortune*, March 3, 1997, pp. 165-66; P. Coy, "Home Sweet Office," *BusinessWeek*, April 6, 1998, p. 30; E. J. Hill, B. C. Miller, S. P. Weiner, and J. Colihan, "Influences of the Virtual Office on Aspects of Work and Work/Life Balance," *Personnel Psychology* 51 (1998), pp. 667-83.

26. Martin Patriquin, "Staff Get Along Without Meeting in Person," *Special to The Globe and Mail-Telework*, March 4, 2004, www.globeandmail.com. Retrieved: April 22, 2004.

27. Ibid.

28. Kevin Marron, "Remote Access System Lets Health Care Professionals Make More Accurate Off-Site Diagnoses," Special to *The Globe and Mail—Telework*, March 4, 2004, www.globeandmail.com. Retrieved: April 22, 2004.

29. D. May and C. Schwoerer, "Employee Health by Design: Using Employee Involvement Teams in Ergonomic Job Redesign," *Personnel Psychology* 47 (1994), pp. 861-86.

30. S. F. Brown, "International's Better Way to Build Trucks," *Fortune*, February 19, 2001, pp. 210k-210v.

31. C. Haddad, "OSHA's New Regs Will Ease the Pain for Everybody," *BusinessWeek*, December 4, 2000, pp. 90-94.
32. Canadian Centre for Occupational Health and Safety website, www.ccohs.ca/oshanswers/ergonomics. Retrieved: April 28, 2004.
33. "SPAM Volume Doubles," March 14, 2004, www.ipsos-na.com/news/pressrelease.cfm?id=2084. Retrieved: April 21, 2004.
34. Kevin Restivo, "35% of PC Users Open Junk E-Mail: New Survey," *Financial Post*, March 16, 2004.
35. E. Weinstein, "Rising Flood of Office E-Mail Messages Threatens to Drown the Unorganized," *The Wall Street Journal*, Interactive Edition, January 10, 2002; Associated Press, "With Mountain of Junk Mail Set to Grow, Companies Promote Tools to Reduce 'Spam,'" *The Wall Street Journal*, Interactive Edition, December 17, 2001

Chapter 4

1. Wallace Immen, "Immigrants Welcome, Roadblocks Ahead," *The Globe and Mail*, February 18, 2004, p. C1. Reprinted with permission from *The Globe and Mail*.
2. "Ontario Pumps $4 Million into Program to Help Immigrants with Foreign Credentials," *Canadian HR Reporter*, January 20, 2004, www.hrreporter.com. Retrieved: May 11, 2004.
3. B. Schlender, "Matsushita Shows How to Go Global," *Fortune*, July 11, 1994, pp. 159-66.
4. P. Smith, "Salariless Man," *The Economist*, September 16, 1995, p. 79.
5. M. Conlin, "Savaged by the Slowdown," *BusinessWeek*, September 17, 2001, pp. 74-77.
6. "Nortel in Talks to Sell Off Factories," *Information Week*, January 22, 2004, www.informationweek.com. Retrieved: May 10, 2004.
7. W. F. Cascio, "Whither Industrial and Organizational Psychology in a Changing World of Work?" *American Psychologist* 50 (1995), pp. 928-39.
8. Allan Swift and Kevin Restivo, "Montreal Loses More Tech Jobs Overseas," *Financial Post*, April 7, 2004, p. FP6.
9. K. P. DeMeuse, P. A. Vanderheiden, and T. J. Bergmann, "Announced Layoffs: Their Effect on Corporate Financial Performance," *Human Resource Management* 33 (1994), pp. 509-30.
10. P. P. Shaw, "Network Destruction: The Structural Implications of Downsizing," *Academy of Management Journal* 43 (2000), pp. 101-12.
11. R. T. King, "Is Job Cutting by Drug Makers Bad Medicine?" *The Wall Street Journal*, August 23, 1995, pp. B1-B3.
12. W. F. Cascio, "Downsizing: What Do We Know? What Have We Learned?" *Academy of Management Executive* 7 (1993), pp. 95-104.
13. J. Schu, "Internet Helps Keep Goodwill of Downsized Employees," *Workforce*, July 2001, p. 15.
14. D. Skatlicki, J. H. Ellard, and B. R. C. Kellin, "Third Party Perceptions of a Layoff: Procedural, Derogation, and Retributive Aspects of Justice," *Journal of Applied Psychology* 83 (1998), pp. 119-27.
15. R. Folger and D. P. Skarlicki, "When Tough Times Make Tough Bosses: Managerial Distancing as a Function of Layoff Blame," *Academy of Management Journal* 41 (1998), pp. 79-87.
16. R. Stodghill, "The Coming Job Bottleneck," *BusinessWeek*, March 24, 1997, pp. 184-85.
17. S. Kim and D. Feldman, "Healthy, Wealthy, or Wise: Predicting Actual Acceptances of Early Retirement Incentives at Three Points in Time," *Personnel Psychology* 51 (1998), pp. 623-42.
18. D. Fandray, "Gray Matters," *Workforce*, July 2000, pp. 27-32.
19. www.adecco.com/Channels/adecco/press+office/corporate. Retrieved: May 14, 2004.
20. www.adecco.com/Channels/adecco/investor+relations. Retrieved: March 4, 2004.
21. G. Flynn, "Contingent Staffing Requires Serious Strategy," *Personnel Journal*, April 1995, pp. 50-58.
22. G. Koretz, "Overtime versus New Factories," *BusinessWeek*, May 4, 1998, p. 34.
23. Nurjehan Mawani, "The Federal Public Service: Opportunities for All Canadians," June 1, 2003, http://globeandmail.workopolis.com. Retrieved: February 17, 2004.
24. A. E. Barber, *Recruiting Employees* (Thousand Oaks, CA: Sage, 1998).
25. J. D. Olian and S. L. Rynes, "Organizational Staffing: Integrating Practice with Strategy," *Industrial Relations* 23 (1984), pp. 170-83.
26. "Employers Take Recruiting Seriously," http://globeandmail.workopolis.com. Retrieved: March 16, 2004.
27. Rifka Rosenwein, "Help (Still) Wanted," Inc., April 2001, pp. 51-52, 54-55.
28. G. T. Milkovich and J. M. Newman, Compensation (Homewood, IL.: Richard D. Irwin, 1990).
29. S. J. Marks, "After School," *Human Resources Executive*, June 15, 2001, pp. 49-51.
30. J. Kaufman, "A McDonald's Owner Becomes a Role Model for Black Teenagers," *The Wall Street Journal*, August 23, 1995, p. A1.
31. K. Clark, "Reasons to Worry about Rising Wages," *Fortune*, July 7, 1997, pp. 31-32.
32. Dale Buss, "Help Wanted: Top Talent Apply Within," www.brandchannel.com. Retrieved: January 4, 2005.

33. S. L. Rynes and A. E. Barber, "Applicant Attraction Strategies: An Organizational Perspective," *Academy of Management Review* 15 (1990), pp. 286-310; J. A. Breaugh, *Recruitment: Science and Practice* (Boston: PWS-Kent, 1992), p. 34.

34. www.recruitingforces.gc.ca. Retrieved: May 15, 2004.

35. D. M. Cable, L. Aiman-Smith, P. Mulvey, and J. R. Edwards, "The Sources and Accuracy of Job Applicants' Beliefs about Organizational Culture," *Academy of Management Journal* 43 (2000), pp. 1076-85.

36. M. A. Conrad and S. D. Ashworth, "Recruiting Source Effectiveness: A Meta-Analysis and Re-examination of Two Rival Hypotheses," paper presented at the annual meeting of the Society of Industrial/Organizational Psychology, Chicago, 1986.

37. Breaugh, Recruitment.

38. Susan Singh, "Looking Inside for Leaders at CCL, Alliance Atlantis," *Canadian HR Reporter*, January 12, 2004, www.hrreporter.com. Retrieved: February 17, 2004.

39. Breaugh, Recruitment, pp. 113-114.

40. R. S. Schuler and S. E. Jackson, "Linking Competitive Strategies with Human Resource Management Practices," *Academy of Management Executive* 1 (1987), pp. 207-19.

41. "Quebec Targets Health Care Workers in France, Switzerland" *Canadian HR Reporter*, November 20, 2003, www.hrreporter.com. Retrieved: January 23, 2004.

42. C. R. Wanberg, R. Kanfer, and J. T. Banas, "Predictors and Outcomes of Networking Intensity among Job Seekers," *Journal of Applied Psychology* 85 (2000), pp. 491-503.

43. A. Halcrow, "Employers Are Your Best Recruiters," *Personnel Journal* 67 (1988), pp. 42-49.

44. G. Flynn, "Do You Have the Right Approach to Diversity?" *Personnel Journal*, October 1995, pp. 68-75.

45. Breaugh, *Recruitment*, p. 87.

46. Steve Jones, "You've Come a Long Way Baby: What the Industry Offers Today," *Canadian HR Reporter*, November 5, 2001, www.hrreporter.com. Retrieved: May 16, 2004.

47. J. Mitchell, "BMW Names 2 Honda Executives to Oversee New U.S. Assembly Plant," *The Wall Street Journal*, November 29, 1992, p. B4.

48. http://globeandmail.workopolis.com. Retrieved: February 17, 2004.

49. J. Reingold, "Casting for a Different Set of Characters," *BusinessWeek*, December 8, 1997, pp. 38-39.

50. J. Greenwald, "Invasion of the Body Snatchers," *Time*, April 23, 1984, p. 41.

51. www.recruiting.forces.gc.ca. Retrieved: May 15, 2004.

52. Uyen Vu, "The Drug Sector's Staffing Remedies," *Canadian HR Reporter*, February 10, 2003, p. 1.

53. P. Smith, "Sources Used by Employers When Hiring College Grads," *Personnel Journal*, February 1995, p. 25.

54. J. W. Boudreau and S. L. Rynes, "Role of Recruitment in Staffing Utility Analysis," *Journal of Applied Psychology* 70 (1985), pp. 354-66.

55. D. Anfuso, "3M's Staffing Strategy Promotes Productivity and Pride," *Personnel Journal*, February 1995, pp. 28-34.

56. www.rim.net. Retrieved: May 15, 2004.

57. http://client.njoyn.com/cl/xweb/XWeb.asp. Retrieved: December 12, 2004.

58. "Half of Resumes Coming by E-Mail," *Canadian HR Reporter*, February 23, 2004, p. 2.

59. J. Smith, "Is Online Recruiting Getting Easier?" *Workforce*, September 2, 2001, p. 1.

60. "Workopolis, CareerBuilder.com Team Up," *Canadian HR Reporter*, February 20, 2004, www.hrreporter.com. Retrieved: February 24, 2004.

61. S. Bills, "A Wider Net for Hiring," *CNN/Money Online*, July 26, 2000, p. 1.

62. A. Salkever, "A Better Way to Float Your Résumé," *BusinessWeek Online*, October 9, 2000, pp. 1-2.

63. Todd Humber, "New Standards for Recruitment Technology to Debut Soon," *Canadian HR Reporter*, March 8, 2004, p. G3.

64. http://c0dsp.westjet.com/internet/sky/jobs/index. Retrieved: March 28, 2004.

65. R. Hawk, *The Recruitment Function* (New York: American Management Association, 1967).

66. C. K. Stevens, "Effects of Preinterview Beliefs on Applicants' Reactions to Campus Interviews," *Academy of Management Journal* 40 (1997), pp. 947-66.

67. M. S. Taylor and T. J. Bergman, "Organizational Recruitment Activities and Applicants' Reactions at Different Stages of the Recruitment Process," *Personnel Psychology* 40 (1984), pp. 261-85; C. D. Fisher, D. R. Ilgen, and W. D. Hoyer, "Source Credibility, Information Favorability, and Job Offer Acceptance," *Academy of Management Journal* 22 (1979), pp. 94-103.

68. L. M. Graves and G. N. Powell, "The Effect of Sex Similarity on Recruiters' Evaluation of Actual Applicants: A Test of the Similarity-Attraction Paradigm," *Personnel Psychology* 48 (1995), pp. 85-98.

69. R. D. Tretz and T. A. Judge, "Realistic Job Previews: A Test of the Adverse Self-Selection Hypothesis," *Journal of Applied Psychology* 83 (1998), pp. 330-37.

70. P. Hom, R. W. Griffeth, L. E. Palich, and J. S. Bracker, "An Exploratory Investigation into Theoretical Mechanisms Underlying Realistic Job Previews," *Personnel Psychology* 51 (1998), pp. 421-51.

71. G. M. McEvoy and W. F. Cascio, "Strategies for Reducing Employee Turnover: A Meta-Analysis," *Journal of Applied Psychology* 70 (1985), pp. 342-53; S. L. Premack and J. P. Wanous, "A Meta-Analysis of Realistic Job Preview Experiments," *Journal of Applied Psychology* 70 (1985) , pp. 706-19.

72. P. G. Irving and J. P. Meyer, "Reexamination of the Met-Expectations Hypothesis: A Longitudinal Analysis," *Journal of Applied Psychology* 79 (1995), pp. 937-49.

73. R. W. Walters, "It's Time We Become Pros," *Journal of College Placement* 12 (1985), pp. 30-33.

74. S. L. Rynes, R. D. Bretz, and B. Gerhart, "The Importanceof Recruitment in Job Choice: A Different Way of Looking," *Personal Psychology* 44 (1991), pp. 487-522.

Chapter 5

1. "Entrepreneur," Special Feature to *National Post-Financial Post*, June 11, 2004, p. FP20.

2. "Intelligence Officers" and "Stages in the IO Recruitment Process," www.csis-scrs.gc.ca. Retrieved: June 23, 2004.

3. J. C. Nunnally, *Psychometric Theory* (New York: McGraw-Hill, 1978).

4. N. Schmitt, R. Z. Gooding, R. A. Noe, and M. Kirsch, "Meta-Analysis of Validity Studies Published between 1964 and 1982 and the Investigation of Study Characteristics," *Personnel Psychology* 37 (1984), pp. 407-22.

5. C. H. Lawshe, "Inferences from Personnel Tests and Their Validity," *Journal of Applied Psychology* 70 (1985), pp. 237-38.

6. D. D. Robinson, "Content-Oriented Personnel Selection in a Small Business Setting," *Personnel Psychology* 34 (1981), pp. 77-87.

7. F. L. Schmidt and J. E. Hunter, "The Future of Criterion-Related Validity," *Personnel Psychology* 33 (1980), pp. 41-60; F. L. Schmidt, J. E. Hunter, and K. Pearlman, "Task Differences as Moderators of Aptitude Test Validity: A Red Herring," *Journal of Applied Psychology* 66 (1982), pp. 166-85; R. L. Gutenberg, R. D. Arvey, H. G. Osburn, and R. P. Jeanneret, "Moderating Effects of Decision-Making/ Information Processing Dimensions on Test Validities," *Journal of Applied Psychology* 68 (1983), pp. 600-8.

8. "A Guide to Screening and Selection in Employment," *Canadian Human Rights Commission*, www.chrc-ccdp.ca/publications/employment_equity-en.asp. Retrieved: April 3, 2004.

9. T. W. Dougherty, D. B. Turban, and J. C. Callender, "Confirming First Impressions in the Employment Interview: A Field Study of Interviewer Behavior," *Journal of Applied Psychology* 79 (1994), pp. 659-65.

10. J. B. Copeland, "Revenge of the Fired," *Newsweek*, February 16, 1987, pp. 46-47.

11. S. Greengard, "Are You Well Armed to Screen Applicants?" *Personnel Journal*, December 1995, pp. 84-95.

12. A. Ryan and M. Lasek, "Negligent Hiring and Defamation: Areas of Liability Related to Pre-employment Inquiries," *Personnel Psychology* 44 (1991), pp. 293-319.

13. A. Long, "Addressing the Cloud over Employee References: A Survey of Recently Enacted State Legislation," *William and Mary Law Review* 39 (October 1997), pp. 177-228.

14. "Companies Step Up Checks as Applicants Turn to Fraud," *The Globe and Mail*, March 24, 2004, p. C5.

15. "Cheating on Resumes Goes High-Tech," *Financial Post*, March 15, 2004, p. FP11.

16. "PRSI Screening News,"November 2002, p. 1, www.prsinet.com/newsletter. Retrieved: February 13, 2004.

17. Nancy Dunne, "Screeners Wanted," *Financial Post*, May 3, 2004, p. FP5.

18. L. C. Buffardi, E. A. Fleishman, R. A. Morath, and P. M. McCarthy, "Relationships between Ability Requirements and Human Errors in Job Tasks," *Journal of Applied Psychology* 85 (2000), pp. 551-64; J. Hogan, "Structure of Physical Performance in Occupational Tasks," *Journal of Applied Psychology* 76 (1991), pp. 495-507.

19. www.psc-cfp.gc.ca/ppc/assessment. Retrieved: February 13, 2004.

20. M. J. Ree, J. A. Earles, and M. S. Teachout, "Predicting Job Performance: Not Much More than *g*," *Journal of Applied Psychology* 79 (1994), pp. 518-24; L. S. Gottfredson, "The g Factor in Employment," *Journal of Vocational Behavior* 29 (1986), pp. 293-96; J. E. Hunter and R. H. Hunter, "Validity and Utility of Alternative Predictors of Job Performance," *Psychological Bulletin* 96 (1984), pp. 72-98; Gutenberg et al., "Moderating Effects of Decision-Making/Information Processing Dimensions on Test Validities"; F. L. Schmidt, J. G. Berner, and J. E. Hunter, "Racial Differences in Validity of Employment Tests: Reality or Illusion," *Journal of Applied Psychology* 58 (1974), pp. 5-6; J. A. LePine, J. A. Colquitt, and A. Erez, "Adaptability to Changing Task Contexts: Effects of General Cognitive Ability, Conscientiousness, and Openness to Experience," *Personnel Psychology* 53 (2000), pp. 563-93.

21. F. L. Schmidt and J. E. Hunter, "The Validity and Utility of Selection Methods in Personnel Psychology: Practical and Theoretical Implications of 85 Years of Research Findings," *Psychological Bulletin* 124 (1998), pp. 262-74.

22. W. S. Dunn, M. K. Mount, M. R. Barrick, and D. S. Ones, "Relative Importance of Personality and General Mental Ability on Managers' Judgments of Applicant Qualifications," *Journal of Applied Psychology* 79 (1995), pp. 500-9; P. M. Wright, K. M. Kacmar, G. C. McMahan, and K. Deleeuw, "$P = f(M \times A)$: Cognitive Ability as a Moderator of the Relationship between Personality and Job Performance," *Journal of Management* 21 (1995), pp. 1129-39.

23. M. Mount, M. R. Barrick, and J. P. Strauss, "Validity of Observer Ratings of the Big Five Personality Factors," *Journal of Applied Psychology* 79 (1994), pp. 272-80.

24. Todd Humber, "Psychometric Testing Often Misused in Recruitment," *Canadian HR Reporter*, May 17, 2004, p. G5.

25. R. Gatewood and H. Feild, *Human Resource Selection* (Fort Worth, TX: Dryden, 1998); A. Rafaeli and R. Klimoski, "Predicting Sales Success through Handwriting Analysis: An Evaluation of the Effects of Training and Handwriting Sample Content," *Journal of Applied Psychology* 68 (1983), pp. 212-17.

26. D. S. One, C. Viswesvaran, and F. L. Schmidt, "Comprehensive Meta-Analysis of Integrity Test Validities: Findings and Implications for Personnel Selection and Theories of Job Performance," *Journal of Applied Psychology* 78 (1993), pp. 679-703; H. J. Bernardin and D. K. Cooke, "Validity of an Honesty Test in Predicting Theft among Convenience Store Employees," *Academy of Management Journal* 36 (1993), pp. 1079-1106.

27. www.chrc-ccdp.ca/legislation. Retrieved: May 31, 2004.

28. Canadian Human Rights Commission, www.chrc-ccdp.ca/legislation. Retrieved: May 31, 2004.

29. M. A. McDaniel, F. P. Morgeson, E. G. Finnegan, M. A. Campion, and E. P. Braverman, "Use of Situational Judgment Tests to Predict Job Performance: A Clarification of the Literature," *Journal of Applied Psychology* 86 (2001), pp. 730-40; J. Clavenger, G. M. Perreira, D. Weichmann, N. Schmitt, and V. S. Harvey, "Incremental Validity of Situational Judgment Tests," *Journal of Applied Psychology* 86 (2001), pp. 410-17.

30. M. A. Campion, J. E. Campion, and J. P. Hudson, "Structured Interviewing: A Note of Incremental Validity and Alternative Question Types," *Journal of Applied Psychology* 79 (1994), pp. 998-1002; E. D. Pulakos and N. Schmitt, "Experience-Based and Situational Interview Questions: Studies of Validity," *Personnel Psychology* 48 (1995), pp. 289-308.

31. J. Cleaver, "What Kind of Question Is That?" *Chicago Tribune*, April 24, 2002, sec. 6, pp. 1, 4.

32. Todd Humber, "How BMO Financial Selects Employees," *Canadian HR Reporter*, December 6, 2004, p. G2.

33. Hunter and Hunter, "Validity and Utility of Alternative Predictors of Job Performance."

34. R. Pingitore, B. L. Dugoni, R. S. Tindale, and B. Spring, "Bias against Overweight Job Applicants in a Simulated Interview," *Journal of Applied Psychology* 79 (1994), pp. 184-90.

35. M. A. McDaniel, D. L. Whetzel, F. L. Schmidt, and S. D. Maurer, "The Validity of Employment Interviews: A Comprehensive Review and Meta-Analysis," *Journal of Applied Psychology* 79 (1994), pp. 599-616; A. I. Huffcutt and W. A. Arthur, "Hunter and Hunter (1984) Revisited: Interview Validity for Entry-Level Jobs," *Journal of Applied Psychology* 79 (1994), pp. 184-90.

36. Y. Ganzach, A. N. Kluger, and N. Klayman, "Making Decisions from an Interview: Expert Measurement and Mechanical Combination," *Personnel Psychology* 53 (2000), pp. 1-21; G. Stasser and W. Titus, "Effects of Information Load and Percentage of Shared Information on the Dissemination of Unshared Information during Group Discussion," *Journal of Personality and Social Psychology* 53 (1987), pp. 81-93.

37. A. Cuneo, "Diverse by Design," *BusinessWeek*, June 6, 1992, p. 72.

Chapter 6

1. www.pcl.com. Retrieved: February 7, 2005.

2. www.engineering.ualberta.ca. Retrieved: February 7, 2005.

3. www.pcl.com/html/homesection/careers/college_of_construct. Retrieved: February 7, 2005.

4. "Developing Skills in the Canadian Workplace," *Canadian Workplace Gazette*, Volume 2, No. 1, p. 98, http://labour-travail.hrdc-drhc.gc.ca. Retrieved: Februaury 28, 2004.

5. Janice Cooney and Allison Cowan, "The Conference Board of Canada: Training and Development Outlook 2003: Canadian Organizations Continue to Under-Invest," May 2003, ISBN 0-88763-584-9.

6. Uyen Vu, "Marking Staff on a Bell Curve," *Canadian HR Reporter*, July 14, 2003.

7. Janice Cooney, Allison Cowan, "The Conference Board of Canada: Training and Development Outlook 2003: Canadian Organizations Continue to Under-Invest," May 2003, p. 3, ISBN 0-88763-584-9.

8. Asha Tomlinson, "T&D Spending up in U.S. as Canada Lags Behind," *Canadian HR Reporter*, March 25, 2002.

9. Uyen Vu, "Marking Staff on a Bell Curve."

10. "Performance and Potential 2003-04: Defining the Canadian Advantage A Special Report by The Conference Board of Canada," October 2003, p. 31, http://www.conferenceboard.ca. Retrieved: March 2, 2004.

11. I. L. Goldstein, E. P. Braverman, and H. Goldstein, "Needs Assessment," in *Developing Human Resources*, ed. K. N. Wexley (Washington, DC: Bureau of National Affairs, 1991), pp. 5-35-5-75.

12. D. Stamps, "Deep Blue Sea," *Training*, July 1999, pp. 39-43.

13. J. Z. Rouillier and I. L. Goldstein, "Determinants of the Climate for Transfer of Training" (presented at Society of Industrial/Organizational Psychology meetings, St. Louis, MO, 1991); J. S. Russell, J. R. Terborg, and M. L. Powers, "Organizational Performance and Organizational Level Training and Support," *Personnel Psychology* 38 (1985), pp. 849-63; H. Baumgartel, G. J. Sullivan, and L. E. Dunn, "How Organizational Climate and Personality Affect the Payoff from Advanced Management Training Sessions," *Kansas Business Review* 5 (1978), pp. 1-10.

14. R. A. Noe, "Trainees' Attributes and Attitudes: Neglected Influences on Training Effectiveness," *Academy of Management Review* 11 (1986), pp. 736-49; T. T. Baldwin, R. T. Magjuka, and B. T. Loher, "The Perils of Participation: Effects of Choice on Trainee Motivation and Learning," *Personnel Psychology* 44 (1991), pp. 51-66; S. I. Tannenbaum, J. E. Mathieu, E. Salas, and J. A. Cannon-Bowers, "Meeting Trainees' Expectations: The Influence of Training Fulfillment on the Development of Commitment, Self-Efficacy, and Motivation," *Journal of Applied Psychology* 76 (1991), pp. 759-69.

15. L. H. Peters, E. J. O'Connor, and J. R. Eulberg, "Situational Constraints: Sources, Consequences, and Future Considerations," in *Research in Personnel and Human Resource Management*, ed. K. M. Rowland and G. R. Ferris (Greenwich, CT: JAI Press, 1985), vol. 3, pp. 79-114; E. J. O'Connor, L. H. Peters, A. Pooyan, J. Weekley, B. Frank, and B. Erenkranz, "Situational Constraints' Effects on Performance, Affective Reactions, and Turnover: A Field Replication and Extension," *Journal of Applied Psychology* 69 (1984), pp. 663-72; D. J. Cohen, "What Motivates Trainees?" *Training and Development Journal*, November 1990, pp. 91-93; Russell, Terborg, and Powers, "Organizational Performance."

16. J. B. Tracey, S. I. Trannenbaum, and M. J. Kavanaugh, "Applying Trade Skills on the Job: The Importance of the Work Environment," *Journal of Applied Psychology* 80 (1995), pp. 239-52; P. E. Tesluk, J. L. Farr, J. E. Mathieu, and R. J. Vance, "Generalization of Employee Involvement Training to the Job Setting: Individuals and Situational Effects," *Personnel Psychology* 48 (1995), pp. 607-32; J. K. Ford, M. A. Quinones, D. J. Sego, and J. S. Sorra, "Factors Affecting the Opportunity to Perform Trained Tasks on the Job," *Personnel Psychology* 45 (1992), pp. 511-27.

17. B. Mager, *Preparing Instructional Objectives*, 2nd ed. (Belmont, CA: Lake Publishing, 1984); B. J. Smith and B. L. Delahaye, *How to Be an Effective Trainer*, 2nd ed. (New York: Wiley, 1987).

18. "Community Report 2003: NAIT/Bring on the Future," www.nait.ab.ca. Retrieved: March 1, 2004.

19. R. Zemke and J. Armstrong, "How Long Does It Take? (The Sequel)," *Training*, May 1997, pp. 69-79.

20. C. Lee, "Who Gets Trained in What?" *Training*, October 1991, pp. 47-59; W. Hannum, *The Application of Emerging Training Technology* (San Diego, CA: University Associates, 1990); B. Filipczak, "Make Room for Training," *Training*, October 1991, pp. 76-82; A. P. Carnevale, L. J. Gainer, and A. S. Meltzer, *Workplace Basics Training Manual* (San Francisco: Jossey-Bass, 1990).

21. Janice Cooney and Allison Cowan, "The Conference Board of Canada: Training and Development Outlook 2003: Canadian Organizations Continue to Under-Invest," May 2003, p. 14, ISBN 0-88763-584-9.

22. J. M. Rosow and R. Zager, *Training: The Competitive Edge* (San Francisco: Jossey-Bass, 1988).

23. T. Skylar, "When Training Collides with a 35-Ton Truck," *Training*, March 1996, pp. 32-38.

24. G. Yohe, "The Best of Both?" *Human Resource Executive*, March 6, 2002, pp. 35, 38-39.

25. D. Filipowski, "How Federal Express Makes Your Package Its Most Important," *Personnel Journal*, February 1992, pp. 40-46.

26. "More about DiscoverU," *Corporate Reports*, Sunday, February 6, 2005, www.vancity.com/Community/AboutUs/CorporateReports. Retrieved: February 6, 2005.

27. "WG11: Computing Managed Instruction," http://ltsc.ieee.org/wg11. Retrieved: March 2, 2004.

28. "New Research Reveals that Over 85% of Lecturers Believe e-Learning Improves Teaching Creativity and Student Learning Success," www.webct.com. Retrieved: March 2, 2004.

29. R. W. Glover, *Apprenticeship Lessons from Abroad* (Columbus, OH: National Center for Research in Vocational Education, 1986).

30. Human Resources Development Canada-Red Seal Program, www.red-seal.ca/English/redseal_e.shtml. Retrieved: March 21, 2004.

31. Ibid.

32. www.sauder.ubc.ca/ccc/employers/mba_internships.cfm. Retrieved: March 9, 2004.

33. www.uregina.ca/coop/students/current/handbook.shtml. Retrieved: March 11, 2004.

34. W. J. Rothwell and H. C. Kanzanas, "Planned OJT Is Productive OJT," *Training and Development Journal*, October 1990, pp. 53-56.

35. B. Filipczak, "Who Owns Your OJT?" *Training*, December 1996, pp. 44-49.

36. A. F. Cheng, "Hands-on Learning at Motorola," *Training and Development Journal*, October 1990, pp. 34-35.

37. N. Adams, "Lessons from the Virtual World," *Training*, June 1995, pp. 45-48.

38. Ibid.

39. A. Richter, "Board Games for Managers," *Training and Development Journal*, July 1990, pp. 95-97.

40. G. P. Latham and L. M. Saari, "Application of Social Learning Theory to Training Supervisors through Behavior Modeling," *Journal of Applied Psychology* 64 (1979), pp. 239-46.

41. www.peaktraining.com/corp/home.html. Retrieved: March 9, 2004.

42. P. F. Buller, J. R. Cragun, and G. M. McEvoy, "Getting the Most out of Outdoor Training," *Training and Development Journal*, March 1991, pp. 58-61.

43. C. Clements, R. J. Wagner, C. C. Roland, "The Ins and Outs of Experiential Training," *Training and Development*, February 1995, pp. 52-56.

44. P. Froiland, "Action Learning," *Training*, January 1994, pp. 27-34.

45. C. E. Schneier, "Training and Development Programs: What Learning Theory and Research Have to Offer," *Personnel Journal*, April 1974, pp. 288-93; M. Knowles, "Adult Learning," in *Training and Development Handbook*, 3rd ed., ed. R. L. Craig (New York: McGraw-Hill, 1987), pp. 168-79; R. Zemke and S. Zemke, "30 Things We Know for Sure about Adult Learning," *Training*, June 1981, pp. 45-52; B. J. Smith and B. L. Delahaye, *How to Be an Effective Trainer*, 2nd ed. (New York: Wiley, 1987).

46. K. A. Smith-Jentsch, F. G. Jentsch, S. C. Payne, and E. Salas, "Can Pretraining Experiences Explain Individual Differences in Learning?" *Journal of Applied Psychology* 81 (1996), pp. 110-16.

47. W. McGehee and P. W. Thayer, *Training in Business and Industry* (New York: Wiley, 1961).

48. R. M. Gagne and K. L. Medsker, *The Condition of Learning* (Fort Worth, TX: Harcourt-Brace, 1996).

49. J. C. Naylor and G. D. Briggs, "The Effects of Task Complexity and Task Organization on the Relative Efficiency of Part and Whole Training Methods," *Journal of Experimental Psychology* 65 (1963), pp. 217-24.

50. "1998 Workplace Literacy Best Practices Reader," www.conferenceboard.ca/education/best-practices/pdf/litread.pdf. Retrieved: March 9, 2004.

51. Asha Tomlinson, "Math, Reading Skills Holding Employees Back," *Canadian HR Reporter*, October 21, 2002, www.hrreporter.com. Retrieved: February 11, 2005.

52. "Awards for Excellence in Workplace Literacy Large Business Winner, 2002 Palliser Furniture: Case Study December 2002," The Conference Board of Canada, www.conferenceboard.ca. Retrieved: February 28, 2004.

53. Levels of training evaluation by Janice Cooney and Allison Cowan, "The Conference Board of Canada: Training and Development Outlook 2003: Canadian Organizations Continue to Under-Invest," May 2003, pp. 15, 16, ISBN 0-88763-584-9.

54. Janice Cooney and Allison Cowan, "The Conference Board of Canada: Training and Development Outlook 2003: Canadian Organizations Continue to Under-Invest," May 2003, p. 15, ISBN 0-88763-584-9.

55. K. Mantyla, *Blended E-Learning* (Alexandria, VA: ASTD, 2001).

56. Adapted from "Measurement Standards: Training Evaluation and Effectiveness Reporting," (c) Copyright 2003 TD Bank Financial Group Learning and Development Measurement 2003, www.cstd.ca/networks/Eva/sampleTD.doc. Retrieved: March 10, 2004.

57. M. R. Louis, "Surprise and Sense Making: What Newcomers Experience in Entering Unfamiliar Organizational Settings," *Administrative Science Quarterly* 25 (1980), pp. 226-51.

58. Pillsbury engineering orientation program.

59. www.fusionproductions.com/case/elearning/arthritisfoundation. Retrieved: March 10, 2004.

60. S. M. Paskoff, "Ending the Workplace Diversity Wars," *Training*, August 1996, pp. 43-47; H. B. Karp and N. Sutton, "Where Diversity Training Goes Wrong," *Training*, July 1993, pp. 30-34.

61. Paskoff, "Ending the Workplace Diversity Wars."

62. S. Rynes and B. Rosen, "A Field Study of Factors Affecting the Adoption and Perceived Success of Diversity Training," *Personnel Psychology* 48 (1995), pp. 247-70.

63. S. Rynes and B. Rosen, "What Makes Diversity Programs Work?" *HR Magazine*, October 1994, pp. 67-73; Rynes and Rosen, "A Field Survey of Factors Affecting the Adoption and Perceived Success of Diversity Training"; J. Gordon, "Different from What? Diversity as a Performance Issue," *Training*, May 1995, pp. 25-33.

64. "Recognizing Commitment to Diversity," *Canadian HR Reporter*, November 3, 2003, http://www.hrreporter.com. Retrieved: March 3, 2004.

Chapter 7

1. "RCMP Supervisor's Handbook-Helping Your Employees Develop a Learning Strategy," p. 2, www.rcmp-learning.org/doc/s_book.htm. Retrieved: July 13, 2004.

2. C. Lee, "Performance Appraisal: Can We Manage Away the Curse?" *Training*, May 1996, pp. 44-49.

3. "Measuring People Power," Fortune, October 2, 2000.

4. G. Bylinsky, "How Companies Spy on Employees," *Fortune*, November 4, 1991, pp. 131-40; T. L. Griffith, "Teaching Big Brother to Be a Team Player: Computer Monitoring and Quality," *Academy of Management Executive* (1993), pp. 73-80.

5. Karen Williams and Caroline Beach, "Laborious Task of Tracking Skills and Performance Streamlined by Technology," *Canadian HR Reporter*, May 3, 2004, p. 12.

6. www. performancereview.com/pfasp/main.asp. Retrieved: May 24, 2004.

7. Mike Moralis, "Trainers Morph Into New Role," *Canadian HR Reporter*, November 22, 2004, www.hrreporter.com. Retrieved: February 15, 2005.

8. Claudine Kapel and Catherine Shepherd, "Four Keys to Goals and Performance," *Canadian HR Reporter*, February 23, 2004, www.hrreporter.com. Retrieved: February 15, 2005.

9. David Brown, "Performance Management Elusive for Public-Sector HR," *Canadian HR Reporter*, February 23, 2004, www.hrreporter. Retrieved: February 15, 2005.

10. Uyen Vu, "Marking Staff on a Bell Curve," *Canadian HR Reporter*, July 14, 2003, www.hrreporter.com. Retrieved: March 5, 2004.

11. Ibid.

12. P. Smith and L. Kendall, "Retranslation of Expectations: An Approach to the Construction of Unambiguous Anchors for Rating Scales," *Journal of Applied Psychology* 47 (1963), pp. 149-55.

13. K. Murphy and J. Constans, "Behavioral Anchors as a Source of Bias in Rating," *Journal of Applied Psychology* 72 (1987), pp. 573-77; M. Piotrowski, J. Barnes-Farrel, and F. Estig, "Behaviorally Anchored Bias: A Replication and Extension of Murphy and Constans," *Journal of Applied Psychology* 74 (1989), pp. 823-26.

14. D. C. Anderson, C. Crowell, J. Sucec, K. Gilligan, and M. Wikoff, "Behavior Management of Client Contacts in a Real Estate Brokerage: Getting Agents to Sell More," *Journal of Organizational Behavior Management* 4 (2001), pp. 580-90; F. Luthans and R. Kreitner, *Organizational Behavior Modification and Beyond* (Glenview, IL: Scott-Foresman, 1975).

15. K. L. Langeland, C. M. Jones, and T. C. Mawhinney, "Improving Staff Performance in a Community Mental Health Setting: Job Analysis, Training, Goal Setting, Feedback, and Years of Data," *Journal of Organizational Behavior Management* 18 (1998), pp. 21-43.

16. J. Komaki, R. Collins, and P. Penn, "The Role of Performance Antecedents and Consequences in Work Motivation," *Journal of Applied Psychology* 67 (1982), pp. 334-40.

17. S. Snell, "Control Theory in Strategic Human Resource Management: The Mediating Effect of Administrative Information," *Academy of Management Journal* 35 (1992), pp. 292-327.

18. R. Pritchard, S. Jones, P. Roth, K. Stuebing, and S. Ekeberg, "The Evaluation of an Integrated Approach to Measuring Organizational Productivity," *Personnel Psychology* 42 (1989), pp. 69-115.

19. G. Odiorne, MOBII: *A System of Managerial Leadership for the 80's* (Belmont, CA: Pitman Publishers, 1986).

20. R. Rodgers and J. Hunter, "Impact of Management by Objectives on Organizational Productivity," *Journal of Applied Psychology* 76 (1991), pp. 322-26.

21. P. Wright, J. George, S. Farnsworth, and G. McMahan, "Productivity and Extra-role Behavior: The Effects of Goals and Incentives on Spontaneous Helping," *Journal of Applied Psychology* 78, no. 3 (1993), pp. 374-81.

22. G. Latham and K. Wexley, *Increasing Productivity through Performance Appraisal* (Boston: Addison-Wesley, 1981).

23. "What is a Balanced Scorecard?" www.2gc.co/UK/pdf/2GC-FAQ1.pdf. Retrieved: July 14, 2004.

24. Mehrdad Derayeh and Stephane Brutus, "Learning from Others' 360-Degree Experiences," *Canadian HR Reporter*, February 10, 2003, www.hrreporter.com. Retrieved: February 15, 2005.

25. R. Heneman, K. Wexley, and M. Moore, "Performance Rating Accuracy: A Critical Review," *Journal of Business Research* 15 (1987), pp. 431-48.

26. T. Becker and R. Klimoski, "A Field Study of the Relationship between the Organizational Feedback Environment and Performance," *Personnel Psychology* 42 (1989), pp. 343-58; H. M. Findley, W. F. Giles, K. W. Mossholder, "Performance Appraisal and Systems Facets: Relationships with Contextual Performance," *Journal of Applied Psychology* 85 (2000), pp. 634-40.

27. K. Wexley and R. Klimoski, "Performance Appraisal: An Update," in *Research in Personnel and Human Resource Management*, vol. 2, ed. K. Rowland and G. Ferris (Greenwich, CT: JAI Press, 1984).

28. F. Landy and J. Farr, *The Measurement of Work Performance: Methods, Theory, and Applications* (New York: Academic Press, 1983).

29. G. McEvoy and P. Buller, "User Acceptance of Peer Appraisals in an Industrial Setting," *Personnel Psychology* 40 (1987), pp. 785-97.

30. D. Antonioni, "The Effects of Feedback Accountability on Upward Appraisal Ratings," *Personnel Psychology* 47 (1994), pp. 349-56.

31. John Kiska, "Do an Employee Self-Assessment," *HR Professional Magazine*, February/March 2004, www.hrpao.org/knowledge_Centre/HR_Professional/2003_issues. Retrieved: May 28, 2004.

32. R. Steel and N. Ovalle, "Self-Appraisal Based on Supervisor Feedback," *Personnel Psychology* 37 (1984), pp. 667-85; L. E. Atwater, "The Advantages and Pitfalls of Self-Assessment in Organizations," in *Performance Appraisal: State of the Art in Practice*, ed. J. W. Smither (San Francisco: Jossey-Bass, 1998), pp. 331-65.

33. Geoff Kirbyson, "Market Research Firm Lands Major Contract, *Winnipeg Free Press*, July 19, 2004, p. D7.

34. J. Bernardin, C. Hagan, J. Kane, and P. Villanova, "Effective Performance Management: A Focus on Precision, Customers, and Situational Constraints," in *Performance Appraisal: State of the Art in Practice*, pp. 3-48.

35. K. Wexley and W. Nemeroff, "Effects of Racial Prejudice, Race of Applicant, and Biographical Similarity on Interviewer Evaluations of Job Applicants," *Journal of Social and Behavioral Sciences* 20 (1974), pp. 66-78.

36. D. Smith, "Training Programs for Performance Appraisal: A Review," *Academy of Management Review* 11 (1986), pp. 22-40.

37. G. Latham, K. Wexley, and E. Pursell, "Training Managers to Minimize Rating Errors in the Observation of Behavior," *Journal of Applied Psychology* 60 (1975), pp. 550-55.

38. E. Pulakos, "A Comparison of Rater Training Programs: Error Training and Accuracy Training," *Journal of Applied Psychology* 69 (1984), pp. 581-88.

39. S. W. Gilliland and J. C. Langdon, "Creating Performance Management Systems That Promote Perceptions of Fairness," in *Performance Appraisal: State of the Art in Practice*, pp. 209-43.

40. S. W. J. Kozlowski, G. T. Chao, and R. F. Morrison, "Games Raters Play: Politics, Strategies, and Impression Management in Performance Appraisal," in *Performance Appraisal: State of the Art in Practice*, pp. 163-205.

41. K. Wexley, V. Singh, and G. Yukl, "Subordinate Participation in Three Types of Appraisal Interviews," *Journal of Applied Psychology* 58 (1973), pp. 54-57; K. Wexley, "Appraisal Interview," in *Performance Assessment*, ed. R. A. Berk (Baltimore: Johns Hopkins University Press, 1986), pp. 167-85.

42. D. Cederblom, "The Performance Appraisal Interview: A Review, Implications, and Suggestions," *Academy of Management Review* 7 (1982), pp. 219-27; B. D. Cawley, L. M. Keeping, and P. E. Levy, "Participation in the Performance Appraisal Process and Employee Reactions: A Meta-analytic Review of Field Investigations," *Journal of Applied Psychology* 83, no. 3 (1998), pp. 615-63; W. Giles and K. Mossholder, "Employee Reactions to Contextual and Session Components of Performance Appraisal," *Journal of Applied Psychology* 75 (1990), pp. 371-77.

43. Bill Curry, "Health Canada Fires Three Whistleblowers," *Winnipeg Free Press*, July 15, 2004, p. A1.

44. S. E. Forrer and Z. B. Leibowitz, *Using Computers in Human Resources* (San Francisco: Jossey-Bass, 1991).

45. Uyen Vu, Employees, "Resistant to Any Form of Computer Video Monitoring, Study Says," *Canadian HR Reporter*, March 8, 2004, p. 2.

Chapter 8

1. "Irving Oil Receives Human Resource Innovation Award,"www.irvingoilco.com/media_releases/MVP. htm. Retrieved: February 17, 2005.

2. Kevin Cox, "Irving Oil Fuels Its Leaders," *The Globe and Mail*, April 21, 2004, pp. C1, C3.

3. M. London, *Managing the Training Enterprise* (San Francisco: Jossey-Bass, 1989).

4. R. W. Pace, P. C. Smith, and G. E. Mills, *Human Resource Development* (Englewood Cliffs, NJ: Prentice Hall, 1991); W. Fitzgerald, "Training versus Development," *Training and Development Journal*, May 1992, pp. 81-84; R. A. Noe, S. L. Wilk, E. J. Mullen, and J. E. Wanek, "Employee Development: Issues in Construct Definition and Investigation of Antecedents," in *Improving Training Effectiveness in Work Organizations*, ed. J. K. Ford (Mahwah, NJ: Lawrence Erlbaum, 1997), pp. 153-89.

5. J. H. Greenhaus and G. A. Callanan, *Career Management*, 2nd ed. (Fort Worth, TX: Dryden Press, 1994).

6. M. B. Arthur, P. H. Claman, and R. J. DeFillippi, "Intelligent Enterprise, Intelligent Careers," *Academy of Management Executive* 9 (1995), pp. 7-20.

7. "CEOs Talk—Leadership Development," *Canadian HR Reporter*, December 1, 2003, pp. 1, 2, www.hrreporter.com. Retrieved: February 17, 2004.

8. Ibid.

9. R. J. Campbell, "HR Development Strategies," in *Developing Human Resources*, ed. K. N. Wexley (Washington, DC: BNA Books, 1991), pp. 5-1–5-34; M. A. Sheppeck and C. A. Rhodes, "Management Development: Revised Thinking in Light of New Events of Strategic Importance," *Human Resource Planning* 11 (1988), pp. 159-72; B. Keys and J. Wolf, "Management Education: Current Issues and Emerging Trends," *Journal of Management* 14 (1988), pp. 205-29; L. M. Saari, T. R. Johnson, S. D. McLaughlin, and D. Zimmerle, "A Survey of Management Training and Education Practices in U.S. Companies," *Personnel Psychology* 41 (1988), pp. 731-44.

10. T. A. Stewart, "GE Keeps Those Ideas Coming," *Fortune*, August 12, 1991, pp. 41-49; N. M. Tichy, "GE's Crotonville: A Staging Ground for a Corporate Revolution," *The Executive* 3 (1989), pp. 99-106; General Electric website, www.ge.com.

11. http://business.queensu.ca/emba/nation/index.htm. Retrieved: February 25, 2005.

12. "CEOs Talk—Leadership Development."

13. David Brown, "Banking on Leadership Development," *Canadian HR Reporter*, January 27, 2005, p. 7.

14. J. Reingold, "Corporate America Goes to School," *BusinessWeek*, October 20, 1997, pp. 66-72.

15. A. Howard and D. W. Bray, *Managerial Lives in Transition: Advancing Age and Changing Times* (New York: Guilford, 1988); J. Bolt, *Executive Development* (New York: Harper Business, 1989); J. R. Hinrichs and G. P. Hollenbeck, "Leadership Development," in *Developing Human Resources*, pp. 5-221–5-237.

16. Joyce Rowlands, "Soft Skills Give Hard Edge," *The Globe and Mail*, June 9, 2004, p. C8.

17. Ibid.

18. A. Thorne and H. Gough, *Portraits of Type* (Palo Alto, CA: Consulting Psychologists Press, 1993).

19. D. Druckman and R. A. Bjork, eds., *In the Mind's Eye: Enhancing Human Performance* (Washington, DC: National Academy Press, 1991); M. H. McCaulley, "The Myers-Briggs Type Indicator and Leadership," in *Measures of Leadership*, ed. K. E. Clark and M. B. Clark (West Orange, NJ: Leadership Library of America, 1990), pp. 381-418.

20. G. C. Thornton III and W. C. Byham, *Assessment Centers and Managerial Performance* (New York: Academic Press, 1982); L. F. Schoenfeldt and J. A. Steger, "Identification and Development of Management Talent," in *Research in Personnel and Human Resource Management*, vol. 7, ed. K. N. Rowland and G. Ferris (Greenwich, CT: JAI Press, 1989), pp. 151-81.

21. Thornton and Byham, *Assessment Centers and Managerial Performance*.

22. P. G. W. Jansen and B. A. M. Stoop, "The Dynamics of Assessment Center Validity: Results of a Seven-Year Study," *Journal of Applied Psychology* 86 (2001), pp. 741-53; D. Chan, "Criterion and Construct Validation of an Assessment Centre," *Journal of Occupational and Organizational Psychology* 69 (1996), pp. 167-81.

23. R. G. Jones and M. D. Whitmore, "Evaluating Developmental Assessment Centers as Interventions," *Personnel Psychology* 48 (1995), pp. 377-88.

24. C. D. McCauley and M. M. Lombardo, "Benchmarks: An Instrument for Diagnosing Managerial Strengths and Weaknesses," in *Measures of Leadership*, pp. 535-45.

25. C. D. McCauley, M. M. Lombardo, and C. J. Usher, "Diagnosing Management Development Needs: An Instrument Based on How Managers Develop," *Journal of Management* 15 (1989), pp. 389-403.

26. S. B. Silverman, "Individual Development through Performance Appraisal," in *Developing Human Resources*, pp. 5-120–5-151.

27. B. Pfau and I. Kay, "Does 360-Degree Feedback Negatively Affect Company Performance?" *HR Magazine* 47 (2002), pp. 54-59; J. F. Brett and L. E. Atwater, "360-Degree Feedback: Accuracy, Reactions, and Perceptions of Usefulness," *Journal of Applied Psychology* 86 (2001), pp. 930-42.

28. "Telus Awarded for Development System," *Canadian HR Reporter*, March 8, 2004, p. 16.

29. M. W. McCall Jr., *High Flyers* (Boston: Harvard Business School Press, 1998).

30. R. S. Snell, "Congenial Ways of Learning: So Near yet So Far," *Journal of Management Development* 9 (1990), pp. 17-23.

31. M. McCall, M. Lombardo, and A. Morrison, *Lessons of Experience* (Lexington, MA: Lexington Books, 1988); M. W. McCall, "Developing Executives through Work Experiences," *Human Resource Planning* 11 (1988), pp. 1-11; M. N. Ruderman, P. J. Ohlott, and C. D. McCauley, "Assessing Opportunities for Leadership Development," in *Measures of Leadership*, pp. 547-62; C. D. McCauley, L. J. Estman, and P. J. Ohlott, "Linking Management Selection and Development through Stretch Assignments," *Human Resource Management* 34 (1995), pp. 93-115.

32. C. D. McCauley, M. N. Ruderman, P. J. Ohlott, and J. E. Morrow, "Assessing the Developmental Components of Managerial Jobs," *Journal of Applied Psychology* 79 (1994), pp. 544-60.

33. Sue Nador, "Don't Let Strengths Go to Waste," *Canadian HR Reporter*, June 14, 2004, p. 13.

34. Andrew Wahl, "Leaders Wanted," *Canadian Business*, March 1-14, 2004, pp. 33, 34.

35. M. Frase-Blunt, "Ready, Set, Rotate," *HR Magazine*, October 2001, pp. 46-53; G. B. Northcraft, T. L. Griffith, and C. E. Shalley, "Building Top Management Muscle in a Slow Growth Environment: How Different Is Better at Greyhound Financial Corporation," *The Executive* 6 (1992), pp. 32-41.

36. M. London, Developing Managers (San Francisco: Jossey-Bass, 1985); M. A. Camion, L. Cheraskin, and M. J. Stevens, "Career-Related Antecedents and Outcomes of Job Rotation," *Academy of Management Journal* 37 (1994), pp. 1518-42; London, *Managing the Training Enterprise*.

37. Andrew Wahl, "Leaders Wanted."

38. Ibid.

39. L. Cheraskin and M. Campion, "Study Clarifies Job Rotation Benefits," *Personnel Journal*, November 1996, pp. 31-38.

40. R. A. Noe, B. D. Steffy, and A. E. Barber, "An Investigation of the Factors Influencing Employees' Willingness to Accept Mobility Opportunities," *Personnel Psychology* 41 (1988), pp. 559-80; S. Gould and L. E. Penley, "A Study of the Correlates of Willingness to Relocate," *Academy of Management Journal* 28 (1984), pp. 472-78; J. Landau and T. H. Hammer, "Clerical Employees' Perceptions of Intraorganizational Career Opportunities," *Academy of Management Journal* 29 (1986), pp. 385-405; J. M. Brett and A. H. Reilly, "On the Road Again: Predicting the Job Transfer Decision," *Journal of Applied Psychology* 73 (1988), pp. 614-20.

41. J. M. Brett, "Job Transfer and Well-Being," *Journal of Applied Psychology* 67 (1992), pp. 450-63; F. J. Minor, L. A. Slade, and R. A. Myers, "Career Transitions in Changing Times," in *Contemporary Career Development Issues*, ed. R. F. Morrison and J. Adams (Hillsdale, NJ: Lawrence Erlbaum, 1991), pp. 109-20; C. C. Pinder and K. G. Schroeder, "Time to Proficiency Following Job Transfers," *Academy of Management Journal* 30 (1987), pp. 336-53; G. Flynn, "Heck No-We Won't Go!" *Personnel Journal*, March 1996, pp. 37-43.

42. R. E. Silverman, "Mercer Tries to Keep Employees through Its 'Externship' Program," *The Wall Street Journal*, November 7, 2000, p. B18.

43. B. Bounds, "Give Me a Break," *The Wall Street Journal*, May 5, 2000, pp. W1, W4.

44. D. B. Turban and T. W. Dougherty, "Role of Protégé Personality in Receipt of Mentoring and Career Success," *Academy of Management Journal* 37 (1994), pp. 688-702; E. A. Fagenson, "Mentoring: Who Needs It? A Comparison of Protégés' and Nonprotégés' Needs for Power, Achievement, Affiliation, and Autonomy," *Journal of Vocational Behavior* 41 (1992), pp. 48-60.

45. A. H. Geiger, "Measures for Mentors," *Training and Development Journal*, February 1992, pp. 65-67.

46. K. E. Kram, *Mentoring at Work: Developmental Relationships in Organizational Life* (Glenview, IL: Scott-Foresman, 1985); L. L. Phillips-Jones, "Establishing a Formalized Mentoring Program," *Training and Development Journal* 2 (1983), pp. 38-42; K. Kram, "Phases of the Mentoring Relationship," *Academy of Management Journal* 26 (1983), pp. 608-25; G. T. Chao, P. M. Walz, and P. D. Gardner, "Formal and Informal Mentorships: A Comparison of Mentoring Functions and Contrasts with Nonmentored Counterparts," *Personnel Psychology* 45 (1992), pp. 619-36.

47. Keynote presented by Nancy Nazer, Consultant Bell Canada-Mentoring Connections National Conference, www.mentorcanada/ca/en/en_keynote/nnazer.ppt. Retrieved: March 29, 2004.

48. R. A. Noe, D. Greenberger, and S. Wang, "Mentoring: What We Know and Where We Might Go," in G. R. Ferris and J. J. Martocchio, eds., *Research in Personnel and Human Resources Management*, vol. 21 (Oxford: Elsevier Science, forthcoming).

49. M. Murray, "GE Mentoring Program Turns Underlings into Teachers of the Web," *The Wall Street Journal*, February 15, 2000, pp. B1, B16.

50. D. B. Peterson and M. D. Hicks, *Leader as Coach* (Minneapolis: Personnel Decisions, 1996).

51. David Brown, "Mentoring Boosts Retention, T&D . . . But It's a Long-Term Game," *Canadian HR Reporter*, July 12, 2004, p. 7.

52. J. S. Lublin, "Building a Better CEO," *The Wall Street Journal*, April 14, 2000, pp. B1, B4.

53. B. Baumann, J. Duncan, S. E. Former, and Z. Leibowitz, "Amoco Primes the Talent Pump," *Personnel Journal*, February 1996, pp. 79-84.

54. Janice Cooney and Allison Cowan, "Training and Development Outlook 2003," *The Conference Board of Canada*, p. 16, ISBN 0-88763-584-9.

55. Ford Motor , "Personal Development Roadmap," Ford Brochure, Detroit, 1998.

56. Claudine Kapel and Catherine Shepherd, "Career Ladders Create Common Language for Defining Jobs," *Canadian HR Reporter*, June 14, 2004, p. 15.

57. "Women Have Little Clout in Large Organizations," *The Worklife Report*, Ottawa 2000, Vol. 12, Issue 3, p. 9, ISSN: 0834292X, http://proquest.umi.com. Retrieved: February 26, 2004.

58. P. J. Ohlott, M. N. Ruderman, and C. D. McCauley, "Gender Differences in Managers' Developmental Job Experiences," *Academy of Management Journal* 37 (1994), pp. 46-67.

59. L. A. Mainiero, "Getting Anointed for Advancement: The Case of Executive Women," *Academy of Management Executive* 8 (1994), pp. 53-67; J. S. Lublin, "Women at Top Still Are Distant from CEO Jobs," *The Wall Street Journal*, February 28, 1995, pp. B1, B5; P. Tharenov, S. Latimer, and D. Conroy, "How Do You Make It to the Top? An Examination of Influences on Women's and Men's Managerial Advancements," *Academy of Management Journal* 37 (1994), pp. 899-931.

60. U.S. Department of Labor, *A Report on the Glass Ceiling Initiative* (Washington, DC: Labor Department, 1991); R. A. Noe, "Women and Mentoring: A Review and Research Agenda," *Academy of Management Review* 13 (1988), pp. 65-78; B. R. Ragins and J. L. Cotton, "Easier Said than Done: Gender Differences in Perceived Barriers to Gaining a Mentor," *Academy of Management Journal* 34 (1991), pp. 939-51.

61. D. McCracken, "Winning the Talent War for Women," *Harvard Business Review*, November-December 2000, pp. 159-67.

62. Andrew Wahl, "Leaders Wanted," p. 33.

63. W. J. Rothwell, *Effective Succession Planning*, 2nd ed. (New York: AMACOM, 2001).

64. B. E. Dowell, "Succession Planning," in *Implementing Organizational Interventions*, ed. J. Hedge and E. D. Pulakos (San Francisco: Jossey-Bass, 2002), pp. 78-109.

65. C. B. Derr, C. Jones, and E. L. Toomey, "Managing High-Potential Employees: Current Practices in Thirty-Three U.S. Corporations," *Human Resource Management* 27 (1988), pp. 273-90; K. M. Nowack, "The Secrets of Succession," *Training and Development* 48 (1994), pp. 49-54; J. S. Lublin, "An Overseas Stint Can Be a Ticket to the Top," *The Wall Street Journal*, January 29, 1996, pp. B1, B2.

66. B. Gerber, "Who Will Replace Those Vanishing Execs?" *Training*, July 2000, pp. 49-53.

67. M. W. McCall Jr. and M. M. Lombardo, "Off the Track: Why and How Successful Executives Get Derailed," *Technical Report*, no. 21 (Greensboro, NC: Center for Creative Leadership, 1983); E. V. Veslo and J. B. Leslie, "Why Executives Derail: Perspectives across Time and Cultures," *Academy of Management Executive* 9 (1995), pp. 62-72.

68. L. W. Hellervik, J. F. Hazucha, and R. J. Schneider, "Behavior Change: Models, Methods, and a Review of Evidence," in *Handbook of Industrial and Organizational Psychology*, vol. 3, 2nd ed., ed. M. D. Dunnette and L. M. Hough (Palo Alto, CA: Consulting Psychologists Press, 1992), pp. 823-99.

69. D. B. Peterson, "Measuring and Evaluating Change in Executive and Managerial Development," paper presented at the annual conference of the Society for Industrial and Organizational Psychology, Miami, 1990.

Chapter 9

1. David Brown, "Soft Side of Rewards has Hard Impact," *Canadian HR Reporter*, April 5, 2004, pp. 5, 7. © Copyright *Canadian HR Reporter*, April 5, 2004, by Carswell, Toronto, Ontario, 1-800-387-5164, www.hrreporter.com.

2. Todd Humber, "Banking on a Benefits Redesign," *Canadian HR Reporter*, February 23, 2004, www.hrreporter.com. Retrieved: March 3, 2004.

3. Strategic Rewards in Canada: Building the Optimal Reward Plan-Watson Wyatt's 2004 Survey of Canadian Strategic Rewards and Pay Practices in "Why Firms Develop a Total Rewards Strategy," *Canadian HR Reporter*, February 14, 2005, p. R5.

4. "Cost Containment in the Works for Compensation," *InsideEdge*, Newsletter of The Conference Board of Canada, Winter 2004, p. 8, www.conferenceboard.ca. Retrieved: March 10, 2004.

5. B. Gerhart and G. T. Milkovich, "Organizational Differences in Managerial Compensation and Financial Performance," *Academy of Management Journal* 33 (1990), pp. 663-91; E. L. Groshen, "Why Do Wages Vary among Employers?" *Economic Review* 24 (1988), pp. 19-38.

6. G. A. Akerlof, "Gift Exchange and Efficiency-Wage Theory: Four Views," *American Economic Review* 74 (1984), pp. 79-83; J. L. Yellen, "Efficiency Wage Models of Unemployment," *American Economic Review* 74 (1984), pp. 200-5.

7. J. S. Adams, "Inequity in Social Exchange," in *Advances in Experimental Social Psychology*, ed. L. Berkowitz (New York: Academic Press, 1965); P. S. Goodman, "An Examination of Referents Used in the Evaluation of Pay," *Organizational Behavior and Human Performance* 12 (1974), pp. 170-95; J. B. Miner," *Theories of Organizational Behavior* (Hinsdale, IL: Dryden Press, 1980).

8. J. P. Pfeffer and A. Davis-Blake, "Understanding Organizational Wage Structures: A Resource Dependence Approach," *Academy of Management Journal* 30 (1987), pp. 437-55.

9. This section draws freely on B. Gerhart and R. D. Bretz, "Employee Compensation," in *Organization and Management of Advanced Manufacturing*, ed. W. Karwowski and G. Salvendy (New York: Wiley, 1994), pp. 81-101.

10. E. E. Lawler III, *Strategic Pay* (San Francisco: Jossey-Bass, 1990); G. Ledford, "3 Cases on Skill-Based Pay: An Overview," *Compensation and Benefits Review*, March-April 1991, pp. 11-23; G. E. Ledford, "Paying for the Skills, Knowledge, Competencies of Knowledge Workers," *Compensation and Benefits Review*, July-August 1995, p. 55.

11. B. C. Murray and B. Gerhart, "An Empirical Analysis of a Skill-Based Pay Program and Plant Performance Outcomes," *Academy of Management Journal* 41, no. 1 (1998), pp. 68-78.

12. Ibid.; N. Gupta, D. Jenkins, and W. Curington, "Paying for Knowledge: Myths and Realities," *National Productivity Review*, Spring 1986, pp. 107-23.

13. B. Gerhart and G. T. Milkovich, "Organizational Differences in Managerial Compensation and Financial Performance," *Academy of Management Journal* 33 (1990), pp. 663-91.

14. "Salary Surveys 101," *Canadian HR Reporter*, September 29, 2004, www.hrreporter.com.

15. G. T. Milkovich and A. K. Wigdor, *Pay for Performance* (Washington, DC: National Academy Press, 1991); Gerhart and Milkovich, "Employee Compensation"; C. Trevor, B. Gerhart, and J. W. Boudreau, "Voluntary Turnover and Job Performance: Curvilinearity and the Moderating Influences of Salary Growth and Promotions," *Journal of Applied Psychology* 82 (1997), pp. 44-61.

16. Kathy Chu, "What's Good Work Worth These Days," *Financial Post*, June 16, 2004, p. FP14.

17. "Who's Answering the Phone? Your Company's Fortunes Hang on It," *Gallup Management Journal*, Fall 2001.

18. R. D. Bretz, R. A. Ash, and G. F. Dreher, "Do People Make the Place? An Examination of the Attraction-Selection-Attrition Hypothesis," *Personnel Psychology* 42 (1989), pp. 561-81; T. A. Judge and R. D. Bretz, "Effect of Values on Job Choice Decisions," *Journal of Applied Psychology* 77 (1992), pp. 261-71; D. M. Cable and T. A. Judge, "Pay Performance and Job Search Decisions: A Person-Organization Fit Perspective," *Personnel Psychology* 47 (1994), pp. 317-48.

19. E. A. Locke, D. B. Feren, V. M. McCaleb, K. N. Shaw, and A. T. Denny, "The Relative Effectiveness of Four Methods of Motivating Employee Performance," in *Changes in Working Life*, ed. K. D. Duncan, M. M. Gruenberg, and D. Wallis (New York: Wiley, 1980), pp. 363-88.

20. Gerhart and Milkovich, "Employee Compensation."

21. R. D. Bretz, G. T. Milkovich, and W. Read, "The Current State of Performance Appraisal Research and Practice," *Journal of Management* 18 (1992), pp. 321-52; R. L. Heneman, "Merit Pay Research," *Research in Personnel and Human Resource Management* 8 (1990), pp. 203-63; Milkovich and Wigdor, *Pay for Performance*.

22. Bretz et al., "Current State of Performance Appraisal Research."

23. W. E. Deming, *Out of the Crisis* (Cambridge, MA: Center for Advanced Engineering Study, Massachusetts Institute of Technology, 1986), p. 110.

24. J. Bennett, "A Career on Commission Can Be a Hard Sell," *Chicago Tribune*, March 24, 2002, sec. 5, p. 5.

25. T. L. Ross and R. A. Ross, "Gainsharing: Sharing Improved Performance," in *The Compensation Handbook*, 3rd ed., ed. M. L. Rock and L. A. Berger (New York: McGraw-Hill, 1991).

26. Leah Janzen, "Huge Payday for Brick Staff," *Winnipeg Free Press*, July 17, 2004, p. A3.

27. T. M. Welbourne and L. R. Gomez-Mejia, "Team Incentives in the Workplace," in *The Compensation Handbook*, 3rd ed.

28. L. R. Gomez-Mejia and D. B. Balkin, *Compensation, Organizational Strategy, and Firm Performance* (Cincinnati: South-Western, 1992).

29. This idea has been referred to as the "share economy." See M. L. Weitzman, "The Simple Macroeconomics of Profit Sharing," *American Economic Review* 75 (1985), pp. 937-53. For supportive research, see the following studies: J. Chelius and R. S. Smith, "Profit Sharing and Employment Stability," *Industrial and Labor Relations Review* 43 (1990), pp. 256S-73S; B. Gerhart and L. O. Trevor, "Employment Stability under Different Managerial Compensation Systems," working paper (Cornell University Center for Advanced Human Resource Studies, 1995); D. L. Kruse, "Profit Sharing and Employment Variability: Microeconomic Evidence on the Weitzman Theory," *Industrial and Labor Relations Review* 44 (1991), pp. 437-53.

30. American Management Association, *CompFlash*, April 1991, p. 3.

31. Gerhart and Milkovich, "Organizational Differences in Managerial Compensation."

32. Steve Maich, "Nortel's Final Victim," August 2, 2004, www.mcleans.ca/topstories/business. Retrieved: September 20, 2004.

33. http://c3dsp.westjet.com/internet/sky/jobs/whywestjetTemplate.jsp. Retrieved: February 28, 2005.

34. M. A. Conte and J. Svejnar, "The Performance Effects of Employee Ownership Plans," in *Paying for Productivity*, pp. 245-94.

35. Ibid.; T. H. Hammer, "New Developments in Profit Sharing, Gainsharing, and Employee Ownership," in *Productivity in Organizations*, ed. J. P. Campbell, R. J. Campbell, et al. (San Francisco: Jossey-Bass, 1988); K. J. Klein, "Employee Stock Ownership and Employee Attitudes: A Test of Three Models," *Journal of Applied Psychology* 72 (1987), pp. 319-32.

36. E. Raimy, "A Plan for All Seasons," *Human Resource Executive*, April 2001, pp. 34-38.

37. R. T. Kaufman, "The Effects of Improshare on Productivity," *Industrial and Labor Relations Review* 45 (1992), pp. 311-22; M. H. Schuster, "The Scanlon Plan: A Longitudinal Analysis," *Journal of Applied Behavioral Science* 20 (1984), pp. 23-28; J. A. Wagner III, P. Rubin, and T. J. Callahan, "Incentive Payment and Nonmanagerial Productivity: An Interrupted Time Series Analysis of Magnitude and Trend," *Organizational Behavior and Human Decision Processes* 42 (1988), pp. 47-74.

38. C. R. Gowen III and S. A. Jennings, "The Effects of Changes in Participation and Group Size on Gainsharing Success: A Case Study," *Journal of Organizational Behavior Management* 11 (1991), pp. 147-69.

39. D. I. Levine and L. D. Tyson, "Participation, Productivity, and the Firm's Environment," in *Paying for Productivity*.

40. T. Welbourne, D. Balkin, and L. Gomez-Mejia, "Gainsharing and Mutual Monitoring: A Combined Agency-Organizational Justice Interpretation," *Academy of Management Journal* 38 (1995), pp. 881-99.

41. "Benefits—United States," Hewitt Associates website, http://was.hewitt.com, downloaded August 27, 2002.

42. B. Gerhart and G. T. Milkovich, "Employee Compensation: Research and Practice," in *Handbook of Industrial and Organizational Psychology*, vol. 3, 2nd ed., ed. M. D. Dunnette and L. M. Hough (Palo Alto, CA: Consulting Psychologists Press, 1992).

43. "Canadian Employers Rate Health Plans Over Cash," *The Globe and Mail*, May 12, 2004, p. C2.

44. Judith MacBride-King and Nicole Wassink, "Beyond Band-Aid Solutions: Managing Organizations' Health Benefit Costs," The Conference Board of Canada, April 2004, www.conferenceboard.ca. Retrieved: June 15, 2004.

45. Jacqueline Taggart, "No Easy Answer for Cost Conundrum," *Canadian HR Reporter*, April 19, 2004, p. 11.

46. J. V. Nackley, *Primer on Workers' Compensation* (Washington, DC: Bureau of National Affairs, 1989); T. Thomason, T. P. Schmidle, and J. F. Burton, *Workers' Compensation* (Kalamazoo, MI: Upjohn Institute, 2001).

47. John Greenwood, "Software Giant Cuts into Worker Perks," *Financial Post*, June 14, 2004, p. FP5.

48. Ibid.

49. Virginia Galt, "Discontent Over Rising Benefit Costs," *The Globe and Mail*, May 26, 2004, p. C2.

50. "Starbucks to Raise N.A. Prices about US 11Cents a Cup," *Financial Post*, September 28, 2004, p. FP2.

51. Mary Teresa Bitti, "Alternative Health Plan Benefits Small Firms," *National Post*, March 8, 2004, pp. FE1, FE4.

52. Nikki Pavlov, "A Healthy Workplace Means Recognizing Stress is the Enemy," *Canadian HR Reporter*, April 9, 2001, www.hrreporter.com. Retrieved: September 29, 2004.

53. Ibid.

54. J. C. Erfurt, A. Foote, and M. A. Heirich, "The Cost-Effectiveness of Worksite Wellness Programs for Hypertension Control, Weight Loss, Smoking Cessation and Exercise," *Personnel Psychology* 45 (1992), pp. 5-27.

55. D. Wessel, "Enron and a Bigger Ill: Americans Don't Save," *The Wall Street Journal Online*, March 7, 2002, http://online.wsj.com.

56. Gary Norris, "Study Warns Pensions May Come Up Short," *Financial Post*, June 16, 2004, p. FP9.

57. "Phased Retirement: Aligning Employer Programs with Worker Preferences—2004 Survey Report," www.watsonwyatt.com/research/resrender.asp. Retrieved: April 21, 2004.

58. Richard W. Yerema, *Canada's Top 100 Employers 2004*, MediaCorp Canada Inc., ISBN 1-894450-17-5, p. 353.

59. Ibid, p. 131.

60. "Study: The Sandwich Generation," Statistics Canada—*The Daily*, September 28, 2004, www.statcan.ca/Daily/English/040928/d040928b.htm. Retrieved: October 1, 2004.

61. "Part-Time Work and Family-Friendly Practices in Canadian Workplaces—June 2003," Government of Canada, p. 1, www.11.sdc.gc.ca/en/cs/sp/arb/publications/research/2003-000183/page03.shtml. Retrieved: September 30, 2004.

62. E. E. Kossek, "Diversity in Child Care Assistance Needs: Employee Problems, Preferences, and Work-Related Outcomes," *Personnel Psychology* 43 (1990), pp. 769-91.

63. E. E. Kossek, *The Acceptance of Human Resource Innovation: Lessons from Management* (Westport, CT: Quorum, 1989).

64. Richard W. Yerema, *Canada's Top 100 Employers 2004*, p. 131.

65. R. Broderick and B. Gerhart, "Nonwage Compensation," in *The Human Resource Management Handbook*, ed. D. Lewin, D. J. B. Mitchell, and M. A. Zadi (San Francisco: JAI Press, 1996).

66. Todd Humber, "Perquisites No Longer a Prerequisite," *Canadian HR Reporter*, February 10, 2003, pp. G7, G9.

67. Ibid.

68. www.intuit.com/canada/carrers_benefits.shtml. Retrieved: October 1, 2004.

69. B. T. Beam Jr. and J. J. McFadden, *Employee Benefits*, 6th ed. (Chicago: Real Estate Education Co., 2001).

70. Cathy O'Bright, "Flex Benefits Drive Culture Change, Contain Costs at Superior Propane," *Canadian HR Reporter*, September 8, 2003, www.hrreporter.com. Retrieved: March 21, 2004.

71. David Johnston, "Poorly Communicated Plans Worse Than None at All," *Canadian HR Reporter*, February 14, 2005, p. R7.

72. "Salary Surveys 101," *Canadian HR Reporter*, September 9, 2004, www.hrreporter.com. Retrieved: September 29, 2004.

73. M. Wilson, G. B. Northcraft, and M. A. Neale, "The Perceived Value of Fringe Benefits," *Personnel Psychology* 38 (1985), pp. 309-20; H. W. Hennessey, P. L. Perrewe, and W. A. Hochwarter, "Impact of Benefit Awareness on Employee and Organizational Outcomes: A Longitudinal Field Experiment," *Benefits Quarterly* 8, no. 2 (1992), pp. 90-96.

74. Todd Humber, "The Power to Change," *Supplement to Canadian HR Reporter*, May 31, 2004, pp. G1, G10.

75. Sinclair Steward, "Godsoe's Nest Egg Worth $122 Million," *The Globe and Mail*, January 31, 2004, pp. B1, B6.

76. Perri Capell, "Compensation Packages Get Harder to Compare," *Financial Post*, September 12, 2004, p. FP11.

77. "Executive Pay Announced," *The Globe & Mail*, March 24, 2004, p. B8.

78. "Canadian Companies Reward High-Performing CEOs Better than Low-Performing CEOs," October 27, 2003, www.watsonwyatt.com/canada-english/news/press. Retrieved: February 19, 2004.

79. Ibid.

80. Barbara Shecter, "Royal Bank's Nixon Gets $7.75M Package," *Financial Post*, January 27, 2005, p. FP4.

81. Drew Hasselback, "Inco Chief Takes Home $6.1 Million," *Financial Post*, March 23, 2004.

82. Gerhart and Milkovich, "Organizational Differences in Managerial Compensation."

83. "Canadian Companies Rewarded High-Performing CEOs Better Than Low-Performing CEOs," October 27, 2003, www.watsonwyatt.com/Canada-english/news/press. Retrieved: February 19, 2004.

84. Eastman Kodak 1996 proxy statement.

85. "Canadian Companies Rewarded High-Performing CEOs Better Than Low-Performing CEOs."

86. Wojtek Dabrowski and Mark Evans, "Nortel Execs Keep Millions," *Financial Post*, January 13, 2005, p. FP1.

87. "Happy Shareholders, Happy Employees," *Canadian HR Reporter*, February 10, 2003, p. C9.

Chapter 10

1. Hollie Shaw, "Wal-Mart Closes First Union Store in Quebec," *Financial Post*, February 10, 2005, pp. A1, A9. Material reprinted with permission of: "The National Post Company," a CanWest Partnership.

2. J. T. Dunlop, *Industrial Relations Systems* (New York: Holt, 1958); C. Kerr, "Industrial Conflict and Its Mediation," *American Journal of Sociology* 60 (1954), pp. 230-45.

3. See A. M. Glassman and T. G. Cummings, *Industrial Relations: A Multidimensional View* (Glenview, IL: Scott, Foresman, 1985); W. H. Holley Jr. and K. M. Jennings, *The Labor Relations Process* (Chicago: Dryden Press, 1984).

4. T. A. Kochan, Collective *Bargaining and Industrial Relations* (Homewood, IL: Richard D. Irwin, 1980), p. 25; H. C. Katz and T. A. Kochan, *An Introduction to Collective Bargaining and Industrial Relations* (New York: McGraw-Hill, 1992), p. 10.

5. Whether the time the union steward spends on union business is paid for by the employer, the union, or a combination is a matter of negotiation between the employer and the union.

6. "History of Unions in Canada," www.maple-leafweb.com/education/spotlight/issue_51/history. Retrieved: March 5, 2005.

7. Suzanne Payette, "Yesterday and Today: Union Membership," excerpt from the *Workplace Gazette*, Vol. 5, No. 3, Fall 2002, www.rhdcc.gc.ca. Retrieved: November 5, 2004.

8. "Study: The Union Movement in Transition," *The Daily*, August 31, 2004, www.statcan.ca/Daily/English/040831/d040831b.htm. Retrieved: November 6, 2004.

9. Suzanne Payette "Yesterday and Today: Union Membership."

10. Katz and Kochan, *An Introduction to Collective Bargaining*, building on J. Fiorito and C. L. Maranto, "The Contemporary Decline of Union Strength," *Contemporary Policy Issues* 3 (1987), pp. 12-27; G. N. Chaison and J. Rose, "The Macrodeterminants of Union Growth and Decline," in *The State of the Unions*, ed. G. Strauss et al. (Madison, WI: Industrial Relations Research Association, 1991).

11. T. A. Kochan, R. B. McKersie, and J. Chalykoff, "The Effects of Corporate Strategy and Workplace Innovations in Union Representation," *Industrial and Labor Relations Review* 39 (1986), pp. 487-501; Chaison and Rose, "The Macrodeterminatnts of Union Growth and Decline"; J. Barbash, *Practice of Unionism* (New York: Harper, 1956), p. 210; W. N. Cooke and D. G. Meyer, "Structural and Market Predictors of Corporate Labor Relations Strategies," *Industrial and Labor Relations Review* 43 (1990), pp. 280-93; T. A. Kochan and P. Capelli, "The Transformation of the Industrial Relations and Personnel Function," in *Internal Labor Markets*, ed. P. Osterman (Cambridge, MA: MIT Press, 1984).

12. "Study: The Union Movement in Transition," *The Daily*, August 31, 2004, www.statcan.ca/Daily/English/040831/d040831b.htm. Retrieved: November 6, 2004.

13. Charlotte Yates, "Unions Going After Private Service Sector," *Canadian HR Reporter*, October 6, 2003, www.canadianhrreporter.com. Retrieved: January 23, 2004.

14. "Union Recruiters Hit the Road," *Leader-Post*, November 20, 2004, p. F8.

15. Ibid.

16. C. Brewster, "Levels of Analysis in Strategic HRM: Questions Raised by Comparative Research," Conference on Research and Theory in HRM, Cornell University, October 1997.

17. J. T. Addison and B. T. Hirsch, "Union Effects on Productivity, Profits, and Growth: Has the Long Run Arrived?" *Journal of Labor Economics* 7 (1989), pp. 72-105; R. B. Freeman and J. L. Medoff, "The Two Faces of Unionism," *Public Interest* 57 (Fall 1979), pp. 69-93.

18. L. Mishel and P. Voos, *Unions and Economic Competitiveness* (Armonk, NY: M. E. Sharpe, 1991); Freeman and Medoff, "Two Faces"; S. Slichter, J. Healy, and E. R. Livernash, *The Impact of Collective Bargaining on Management* (Washington, DC: Brookings Institution, 1960).

19. A. O. Hirschman, *Exit, Voice, and Loyalty* (Cambridge, MA: Harvard University Press, 1970); R. Batt, A. J. S. Colvin, and J. Keefe, "Employee Voice, Human Resource Practices, and Quit Rates: Evidence from the Telecommunications Industry," *Industrial and Labor Relations Review* 55 (1970), pp. 573-94.

20. R. B. Freeman and J. L. Medoff, *What Do Unions Do?* (New York: Basic Books, 1984); E. E. Herman, J. L. Schwatz, and A. Kuhn, *Collective Bargaining and Labor Relations* (Englewood Cliffs, NJ:Prentice Hall, 1992); Addison and Hirsch, "Union Effects on Productivity"; Katz and Kochan, *An Introduction to Collective Bargaining*; P. D. Lineman, M. L. Wachter, and W. H. Carter, "Evaluating the Evidence on Union Employment and Wages," *Industrial and Labor Relations Review* 44 (1990), pp. 34-53.

21. B. E. Becker and C. A. Olson, "Unions and Firm Profits," *Industrial Relations* 31, no. 3 (1992), pp. 395-415; B. T. Hirsch and B. A. Morgan, "Shareholder Risks and Returns in Union and Nonunion Firms," *Industrial and Labor Relations Review* 47, no. 2 (1994), pp. 302-18.

22. "Eighth Biennial National Labor-Management Conference," *Monthly Labor Review*, January 1999, pp. 29-45; "Companies Breaking Records in Hard Times," *Milwaukee Journal Sentinel* (October 13, 2001).

23. "Perspectives on Labour and Income," August 31, 2004, www.statcan.ca/Daily/English/04031/b040831a. htm. Retrieved: November 6, 2004.

24. Buzz Hargrove, "Stand Up and Fight for Anti-Semitism," *Financial Post*, November 1, 2004, p. FP17.

25. "History and Development of Unions in Canada-The Rand Formula," www.law-faqs.org/nat/u50.htm. Retrieved: March 5, 2005.

26. S. Webb and B. Webb, *Industrial Democracy* (London: Longmans, Green, 1987); J. R. Commons, *Institutional Economics* (New York: Macmillan, 1934).

27. "Sweeping Labour Law Changes in Ontario," *Canadian HR Reporter*, November 4, 2004, www. hrreporter.com. Retrieved: November 5, 2004.

28. "Frequently Asked Questions," Canada Industrial Relations Board website, www.cirb-ccri.gc.ca/fqu/index_e.asp. Retrieved: November 5, 2004.

29. "Trade Union Application for Certification," www.sdc.gc.ca. Retrieved: November 1, 2004.

30. R. B. Freeman and M. M. Kleiner, "Employer Behavior in the Face of Union Organizing Drives," *Industrial and Labor Relations Review* 43, no. 4 (April 1990), pp. 351-65.

31. Freeman and Medoff, *What Do Unions Do?*; National Labor Relations Board annual reports for 1980s and 1990s.

32. J. A. Fossum, *Labor Relations*, 5th ed. (Homewood, IL: Richard D. Irwin, 1992), p. 149.

33. Department of Justice Canada website, http://laws.justice.gc.ca/en/L-2/16931.html. Retrieved: November 6, 2004.

34. Labour Relations Board British Columbia website, www.lrb.bc.ca/mediation/new_cert.htm. Retrieved: November 8, 2004.

35. Fossum, *Labor Relations*, p. 262.

36. R. E. Walton and R. B. McKersie, *A Behavioral Theory of Negotiations* (New York: McGraw-Hill, 1965).

37. C. M. Steven, *Strategy and Collective Bargaining Negotiations* (New York: McGraw-Hill, 1963): Katz and Kochan, *An Introduction to Collective Bargaining.*

38. Chris Sorensen, "Air Canada Unions Cause Flap," *Financial Post*, March 3, 2005, p. FP6.

39. Kochan, *Collective Bargaining and Industrial Relations*, p. 272.

40. Katz and Kochan, *An Introduction to Collective Bargaining.*

41. T. A. Kochan, H. C. Katz, and R. B. McKersie, *The Transformation of American Industrial Relations* (New York: Basic Books, 1986), chap. 6; E. Appelbaum, T. Bailey, and P. Berg, *Manufacturing Advantage: Why High-Performance Work Systems Pay Off* (Ithaca, NY: Cornell University Press, 2000).

42. L. W. Hunter, J. P. MacDuffie, and L. Doucet, "What Makes Teams Take? Employee Reactions to Work Reforms," *Industrial and Labor Relations Review* 55 (2002), pp. 448-472.

43. J. B. Arthur, "The Link between Business Strategy and Industrial Relations Systems in American Steel Minimills," *Industrial and Labor Relations Review* 45 (1992), pp. 488-506; M. Schuster, "Union Management Cooperation," in *Employee and Labor Relations*, ed. J. A. Fossum (Washington, D.C.: Bureau of National Affairs, 1990); E. Cohen-Rosenthal and C. Burton, *Mutual Gains: A Guide to Union-Management Cooperation*, 2nd ed. (Ithaca, NY: ILR Press, 1993); T. A. Kochan and P. Osterman, *The Mutual Gains Enterprise* (Boston: Harvard Business School Press, 1994); E. Applebaum and R. Batt, *The New American Workplace* (Ithaca, NY: ILR Press, 1994).

44. Eric Beauchesne, "Public Unions in Volatile Mood," *Financial Post*, December 17, 2004, p. FP2.

45. Allan Swift, "Bombardier, Union Reach Deal," *The Globe and Mail*, March 3, 2005, p. B6.

46. Frederic Tomesco and Theo Argitis, "Bombardier Workers Agree to New Contract," *The Globe and Mail*, March 7, 2005, p. B5.

47. A. E. Eaton, "Factors Contributing to the Survival of Employee Participation Programs in Unionized Settings," *Industrial and Labor Relations Review* 47, no. 3 (1994), pp. 371-89.

48. "Preventive Mediation—Nova Scotia Industrial Relations Conciliation Services," www.gov.ns.ca/enla/conciliation/prevbro.htm. Retrieved: March 5, 2005.

49. Judith Lendvay-Zwicki, "The Canadian Industrial Relations System: Current Challenges and Future Options," Document Highlights: Conference Board Document, April 2004, www.conferenceboard.ca. Retrieved: April 19, 2004.

Chapter 11

1. www.rim.net/company/index.shtml and www.rim.com. Retrieved: September 23, 2004.

2. Towers Perrin, *Priorities for Competitive Advantage: A Worldwide Human Resource Study* (Valhalla, NY: Towers Perrin, 1991).

3. Vladimir Pucik, "Human Resources in the Future: An Obstacle or a Champion of Globalization," *Tomorrow's HR Management*, eds. Dave Ulrich, Michael R. Losey, and Gerry Lake (John Wiley & Sons, Inc. New York, 1997), pp. 326-327.

4. "Hewitt Associates Study Highlights Global Sourcing Trends and Outcomes," March 2, 2004, http://was4.hewitt.com/resource/newsroom/presrel. Retrieved: March 3, 2004.

5. R. Kopp, "International Human Resource Policies and Practices in Japanese, European, and United States Multinationals," *Human Resource Management* 33 (1994), pp. 581-99.

6. Murray McNeill, "Loewen Opens Door to Area Job Seekers," *Winnipeg Free Press*, July 9, 2004, p. B4.

7. "Canadian Tire to Open Office in Shanghai," *The Globe and Mail*, June 26, 2004, p. B4.

8. "CN Rail Opens Offices in China," *Leader-Post*, October 23, 2004, p. D6.

9. "Bank of Nova Scotia Buys Fourth Largest Bank in Central America," *Leader-Post*, October 23, 2004, p. D9.

10. www.bp.com. Retrieved: March 19, 2005.

11. "Molson Coors: 11 Executives Leave in Merger's Wake," *Leader-Post*, March 19, 2005, p. D9.

12. N. Adler and S. Bartholomew, "Managing Globally Competent People," *The Executive* 6 (1992), pp. 52-65.

13. V. Sathe, *Culture and Related Corporate Realities* (Homewood, IL: Richard D. Irwin, 1985); M. Rokeach, *Beliefs, Attitudes, and Values* (San Francisco: Jossey-Bass, 1968).

14. N. Adler, *International Dimensions of Organizational Behavior*, 2nd ed. (Boston: PWS-Kent, 1991).

15. G. Hofstede, "Dimensions of National Cultures in Fifty Countries and Three Regions," in *Expectations in Cross-Cultural Psychology*, eds. J. Deregowski, S. Dziurawiec, and R. C. Annis (Lisse, Netherlands: Swets and Zeitlinger, 1983); G. Hofstede, "Cultural Constraints in Management Theories," *Academy of Management Executive* 7 (1993), pp. 81-90.

16. Hofstede, "Cultural Constraints in Management Theories."

17. W. A. Randolph and M. Sashkin, "Can Organizational Empowerment Work in Multinational Settings?" *Academy of Management Executive* 16, no. 1 (2002), pp. 102-115.

18. Ibid.

19. National Center for Education Statistics (NCES), "International Comparisons of Education," *Digest of Education Statistics*, 2000, chapter 6, NCES website, http://nces.ed.gov, downloaded September 23, 2002.

20. Adler and Bartholomew, "Managing Globally Competent People."

21. B. O'Reilly, "Your New Global Workforce," *Fortune*, December 14, 1992, pp. 52-66.

22. P. Conrad and R. Peiper, "Human Resource Management in the Federal Republic of Germany," in *Human Resource Management: An International Comparison*, ed. R. Peiper (Berlin: Walter de Gruyter, 1990).

23. Uyen Vu, "Calling 18,000 Venezuelan Workers to Oilsands," *Canadian HR Reporter*, February 28, 2005, www.hrreporter.com. Retrieved: March 5, 2005.

24. I. M. Kunii, "Under the Knife," *BusinessWeek*, September 10, 2001, p. 62; C. Dawson, "Saying Sayonara," *BusinessWeek*, September 24, 2001, pp. 108-9; I. M. Kunii, "Japan's Jobless Need More than a Handout," *BusinessWeek*, September 24, 2001, p. 110.

25. B. Ettore, "Let's Hear It for Local Talent," *Management Review*, October 1994, p. 9; S. Franklin, "A New World Order for Business Strategy," *Chicago Tribune*, May 15, 1994, sec. 19, pp. 7-8.

26. West and Bogumil, "Foreign Knowledge Workers as a Strategic Staffing Option."

27. W. A. Arthur Jr. and W. Bennett Jr., "The International Assignee: The Relative Importance of Factors Perceived to Contribute to Success," *Personnel Psychology* 48 (1995), pp. 99-114; G. M. Spreitzer, M. W. McCall Jr., and J. D. Mahoney, "Early Identification of International Executive Potential," *Journal of Applied Psychology* 82 (1997), pp. 6-29.

28. J. S. Black and J. K. Stephens, "The Influence of the Spouse on American Expatriate Adjustment and Intent to Stay in Pacific Rim Overseas Assignments," *Journal of Management* 15 (1989), pp. 529-44.

29. P. Caligiuri, "The Big Five Personality Characteristics as Predictors of Expatriates' Desire to Terminate the Assignment and Supervisor-Rated Performance," *Personnel Psychology* 53 (2000), pp. 67-88.

30. C. Lachnit, "Low-Cost Tips for Successful Inpatriation," *Workforce*, August 2001, pp. 42-44, 46-47.

31. J. Flynn, "E-mail, Cell Phones, and Frequent-Flier Miles Let 'Virtual' Expats Work Abroad but Live at Home," *The Wall Street Journal*, October 25, 1999, p. A26.

32. D. M. Gayeski, C. Sanchirico, and J. Anderson, "Designing Training for Global Environments: Knowing What Questions to Ask," *Performance Improvement Quarterly* 15, no. 2 (2002), pp. 15-31.

33. B. Filipczak, "Think Locally, Train Globally," *Training* (January 1997), pp. 41-48.

34. J. S. Black and M. Mendenhall, "A Practical but Theory-Based Framework for Selecting Cross-Cultural Training Methods," in *Readings and Cases in International Human Resource Management*, eds. M. Mendenhall and G. Oddou (Boston: PWS-Kent, 1991), pp. 177-204.

35. D. D. Davis, "International Performance Measurement and Management," in *Performance Appraisal: State of the Art in Practice*, ed. J. W. Smither (San Francisco: Jossey-Bass, 1998), pp. 95-131.

36. N. Shirouzu and J. Bigness, "7-Eleven Operators Resist System to Monitor Managers," *The Wall Street Journal*, June 16, 1997, pp. B1, B5.

37. M. Gowan, S. Ibarreche, and C. Lackey, "Doing the Right Things in Mexico," *Academy of Management Executive* 10 (1996), pp. 74-81.

38. L. S. Chee, "Singapore Airlines: Strategic Human Resource Initiatives," in *International Human Resource Management: Think Globally, Act Locally*, ed. D. Torrington (Upper Saddle River, NJ: Prentice Hall, 1994), pp. 143-59.

39. C. M. Solomon, "Global Compensation: Learn the ABCs," *Personnel Journal*, July 1995, p. 70; R. A. Swaak, "Expatriate Management: The Search for Best Practices," *Compensation and Benefits Review*, March-April 1995, p. 21.

40. Sparks, Bikoi, and Moglia, "A Perspective on U.S. and Foreign Compensation Costs in Manufacturing."

41. See, for example, A. E. Cobet and G. A. Wilson, "Comparing 50 Years of Labor Productivity in U.S. and Foreign Manufacturing," *Monthly Labor Review*, June 2002, pp. 51-63.

42. P. Wonacott, "China's Secret Weapon: Smart, Cheap Labor for High-Tech Goods," *The Wall Street Journal*, March 14, 2002, pp. A1, A6.

43. "Mexican Labour Relationship," www.solutions-abroad.com/d_mexicanlaborlaws.asp.

44. "Taxation of European Stock Options," *The European Commission*, June 26, 2001, http://europa.eu.int; D. Woodruff, "Europe: A Latecomer, Embraces Options Even as Market Swoons," *The Wall Street Journal*, May 15, 2001, www.wsj.com; "Eager Europeans Press Their Noses to the Glass," *BusinessWeek Online*, April 19, 1999, www.businessweek.com.

45. "Employers Compensating Employees in High-Risk Areas," August 5, 2003, www.hrreporter.com. Retrieved: January 23, 2004.

46. Paul Glader and Kris Maher, "Unions Look for Cross-Border Allies," *The Globe and Mail*, March 15, 2005, p. B17.

47. P. J. Dowling, D. E. Welch, and R. S. Schuler, *International Human Resource Management*, 3rd ed. (Cincinnati: South-Western, 1999), pp. 235-36.

48. Ibid.; J. La Palombara and S. Blank, *Multinational Corporations and National Elites: A Study of Tensions* (New York: Conference Board, 1976); A. B. Sim, "Decentralized Management of Subsidiaries and Their Performance: A Comparative Study of American, British and Japanese Subsidiaries in Malaysia," *Management International Review* 17, no. 2 (1977), pp. 45-51; Y. K. Shetty, "Managing the Multinational Corporation: European and American Styles," *Management International Review* 19, no. 3 (1979), pp. 39-48; J. Hamill, "Labor Relations Decision-Making within Multinational Corporations," *Industrial Relations Journal* 15, no. 2 (1984), pp. 30-34.

49. Dowling, Welch, and Schuler, *International Human Resource Management*, p. 231.

50. P. Wonacott, "PetroChina Unit, after Job Cuts, Is Besieged by Protesters," *The Wall Street Journal*, March 14, 2002, pp. A9, A12.

51. J. K. Sebenius, "The Hidden Challenge of Cross-Border Negotiations," *Harvard Business Review*, March 2002, pp. 76-85.

52. Ibid.

53. R. Tung, "Selection and Training Procedures of U.S., European, and Japanese Multinational Corporations," *California Management Review* 25, no. 1 (1982), pp. 57-71.

54. L. Copeland and L. Griggs, *Going International* (New York: Random House, 1985).

55. M. Mendenhall, E. Dunbar, and G. R. Oddou, "Expatriate Selection, Training, and Career-Pathing: A Review and Critique," *Human Resource Management Review* 25, no. 1 (1982), pp. 57-71; A. Halcrow, "Expats: The Squandered Resource," *Workforce*, April 1999, pp. 42-44, 46, 48.

56. M. Harvey and M. M. Novicevic, "Selecting Expatriates for Increasingly Complex Global Assignments," *Career Development International* 6, no. 2 (2001), pp. 69-86.

57. M. Mendenhall and G. Oddou, "The Dimensions of Expatriate Acculturation," *Academy of Management Review* 10 (1985), pp. 39-47.

58. Arthur and Bennett, "The International Assignee."

59. J. I. Sanchez, P. E. Spector, and C. L. Cooper, "Adapting to a Boundaryless World: A Developmental Expatriate Model," *Academy of Management Executive* 14, no. 2 (2000), pp. 96-106.

60. "Work Week," *The Wall Street Journal*, September 5, 1995, p. A1.

61. "Ten Years of Global Relocation Trends: 1993-2004," GMAC Global Relocation Services, October 2004, http://24.227.160.195/gmac//WhitePapers. Retrieved: March 20, 2005.

62. "Employers Compensating Employees in High-Risk Areas," *Canadian HR Reporter*, August 5, 2003 www.hrreporter.com. Retrieved: September 23, 2004.

63. Ibid.

64. P. Dowling and R. Schuler, *International Dimensions of Human Resource Management* (Boston: PWS-Kent, 1990).

65. Sanchez, Spector, and Cooper, "Adapting to a Boundaryless World."

66. Ibid.; Lachnit, "Low-Cost Tips for Successful Inpatriation."

67. P. Evans, V. Pucik, and J.-L. Barsoux, *The Global Challenge: Frameworks for International Human Resource Management* (New York: McGraw-Hill/Irwin, 2002), p. 131; F. Higgins, "Survey on Expatriate Compensation and Benefits, 1996," cited in B. Fitzgerald-Turner, "Myths of Expatriate Life," *HRMagazine* 42, no. 6 (June 1997), pp. 65-74.

68. J. Flynn, "Multinationals Help Career Couples Deal with Strains Affecting Expatriates," *The Wall Street Journal*, August 8, 2000, p. A19; C. Solomon, "The World Stops Shrinking," *Workforce*, January 2000, pp. 48-51; C. Solomon, "Unhappy Trails," *Workforce*, August 2000, pp. 36-41.

69. "Ten Years of Global Relocation Trends: 1993–2004."

70. "Minimizing Expatriate Turnover," *Workforce Management Online*, August 2004, www.workforce.com/section/09/article/23/81/28.html. Retrieved: March 22, 2005.

71. Adler, *International Dimensions of Organizational Behavior*.

72. L. G. Klaff, "The Right Way to Bring Expats Home," *Workforce*, July 2002, pp. 40-44.

73. C. Solomon, "Repatriation: Up, Down, or Out?" *Personnel Journal*, 1995, pp. 28-37.

Chapter 12

1. "Do Something Extraordinary for Canada and the World," *Financial Post*, April 14, 2004, p. FP13. Reprinted with permission of the Vancouver Organizing Committee for the 2010 Olympic and Paralympic Winter Games.

2. S. Snell and J. Dean, "Integrated Manufacturing and Human Resource Management: A Human Capital Perspective," *Academy of Management Journal* 35 (1992), pp. 467-504.

3. M. A. Huselid, "The Impact of Human Resource Management Practices on Turnover, Productivity, and Corporate Financial Performance," *Academy of Management Journal* 38 (1995), pp. 635-72; U.S. Department of Labor, *High-Performance Work Practices and Firm Performance* (Washington, DC: U.S. Government Printing Office, 1993).

4. R. N. Ashkenas, "Beyond the Fads: How Leaders Drive Change with Results," *Human Resource Planning* 17 (1994), pp. 25-44.

5. "Client Testimonials," www.sgcicom.com. Retrieved: March 26, 2005.

6. SGCI correspondence with author received in an email from Judy Ells on April 4, 2005.

7. J. Arthur, "The Link between Business Strategy and Industrial Relations Systems in American Steel Mini-Mills," *Industrial and Labor Relations Review* 45 (1992), pp. 488-506.

8. Wallace Immen, "Managers Hold Key to Keep Staff Happy," *The Globe and Mail*, June 16, 2004, p. C3.

9. D. McCann and C. Margerison, "Managing High-Performance Teams," *Training and Development Journal*, November 1989, pp. 52-60; S. Sheman, "Secrets of HP's 'Muddled' Team," *Fortune*, March 18, 1996, pp. 116-20.

10. T. Stewart, "Brace for Japan's Hot New Strategy," *Fortune*, September 21, 1992, pp. 62-76.

11. T. T. Baldwin, C. Danielson, and W. Wiggenhorn, "The Evolution of Learning Strategies in Organizations: From Employee Development to Business Redefinition," *Academy of Management Executive* 11 (1997), pp. 47-58; J. J. Martocchio and T. T. Baldwin, "The Evolution of Strategic Organizational Training," in *Research in Personnel and Human Resource Management* 15, ed. G. R. Ferris (Greenwich, CT: JAI Press, 1997), pp. 1-46.

12. T. A. Judge, C. J. Thoresen, J. E. Bono, and G. K. Patton, "The Job Satisfaction—Job Performance Relationship: A Qualitative and Quantitative Review," *Psychological Bulletin* 127 (2001), pp. 376-407; R. A. Katzell, D. E. Thompson, and R. A. Guzzo, "How Job Satisfaction and Job Performance Are and Are Not Linked," *Job Satisfaction*, ed. C. J. Cranny, P. C. Smith, and E. F. Stone (New York: Lexington Books, 1992), pp. 195-217.

13. C. Ostroff, "The Relationship between Satisfaction, Attitudes, and Performance," *Journal of Applied Psychology* 77, no. 6 (1992), pp. 963-74.

14. Watson Wyatt Worldwide, *WorkUSA 2002: Weathering the Storm* (Watson Wyatt, October 2002, www.humancapitalonline.com).

15. Frances Horibe, "What If HR Has No Effect?" *Canadian HR Reporter*, October 11, 2004, p. 19.

16. "The Link Between Employee Engagement and Business Results," Hewitt Associates, http://was4.hewitt.com/hewitt/resource/rptspubs/hewitt_magazine/vol6. Retrieved: November 29, 2004.

17. Ibid.

18. R. P. Quinn and G. L. Staines, *The 1977 Quality of Employment Survey* (Ann Arbor, MI: Survey Research Center, Institute for Social Research, University of Michigan, 1979).

19. T. Judge and T. Welbourne, "A Confirmatory Investigation of the Dimensionality of the Pay Satisfaction Questionnaire," *Journal of Applied Psychology* 79 (1994), pp. 461-66.

20. Suzanne Wintrob, "Reward A Job Well Done," *Financial Post*, May 10, 2004, p. FP7.

21. John Thackray, "Feedback for Real," March 15, 2001, http://gmj.gallup.com/content/default.asp?ci=811. Retrieved: November 28, 2004.

22. Ibid.

23. J. Applegaste, "Plan an Exit Interview," *CNNMoney.com*, November 13, 2000, pp. 1-2.

24. H. E. Allerton, "Can Teach Old Dogs New Tricks," *Training & Development*, November 2000, downloaded from FindArticles.com.

25. "Wrongful Dismissal Law in Canada," Duhaime's Employment and Labour Law Centre, www.duhaime.org/Employment/ca-wd.aspx. Retrieved: March 28, 2005.

26. "Termination of Employment and Severance Pay," Ontario Ministry of Labour, www.gov.on.ca/LAB/english/es/factsheets/fs_termination.html. Retrieved: March 24, 2005.

27. A. Q. Nomani, "Women Likelier to Face Violence in the Workplace," *The Wall Street Journal*, October 31, 1995, p. A16.

28. Uyen Vu, "Off-Duty Behaviour Cases," *Canadian HR Reporter*, June 14, 2004, www.hrreporter.com. Retrieved: March 25, 2005.

29. N. Orkin and M. Heise, "Weingarten through the Looking Glass," *Labor Law Journal* 48, no. 3 (March 1997), pp. 157-63.

30. C. Hymowitz, "CEOs Must Work Hard to Maintain Faith in the Corner Office," *The Wall Street Journal*, July 9, 2002, p. B1.

31. K. Maher, "Wanted: Ethical Employer," *The Wall Street Journal*, July 9, 2002, pp. B1, B8.

32. Ibid.

33. www.cibc.com/ca/inside-cibc/governance/governance-practices/code-of-conduct.html. Retrieved: October 22, 2004.

34. www.cibc.com/ca/pdf/about/code-ethic-dir.pdf. Retrieved: October 22, 2004.

35. "Corporate Ethics: CIBC-Style Programs Work; Focus Above All on Account and Senior Executive Fraud," BDO Dunwoody/Chamber Weekly CEO/Business Leader Poll by COMPAS in the *Financial Post* for Publication March 1, 2004, www.compas/ca/poll/040301-BLCorpEthics-PB.htm. Retrieved: May 4, 2004.

36. Barrie McKenna and Richard Bloom, "Fearful Boeing Axes Amorous Leader," *The Globe and Mail*, March 8, 2005, p. A1.

37. W. F. Cascio, *Costing Human Resources: The Financial Impact of Behavior in Organizations*, 3rd ed. (Boston: PWS-Kent, 1991); Watson Wyatt Worldwide, *Watson Wyatt's Human Capital Index: Human Capital as a Lead Indicator of Shareholder Value*, 2001/2002 Survey Report (Watson Wyatt, October 2002, www.humancapitalonline.com).

38. Watson Wyatt, *Watson Wyatt's Human Capital Index*.

39. B. Becker and M. A. Huselid, "High-Performance Work Systems and Firm Performance: A Synthesis of Research and Managerial Implications," in *Research in Personnel and Human Resource Management* 16, ed. G. R. Ferris (Stamford, CT: JAI Press, 1998), pp. 53-101.

40. B. Becker and B. Gerhart, "The Impact of Human Resource Management on Organizational Performance: Progress and Prospects," *Academy of Management Journal* 39 (1996), pp. 779-801.

41. G. Flynn, "HR Leaders Stay Close to the Line," *Workforce*, February 1997, p. 53; General Electric Company, "World Class Excellence," GE Fanuc Corporate Profile, GE website, www.ge.com/gemis/gefanuc.

42. Flynn, "HR Leaders Stay Close to the Line"; GE, "World Class Excellence."

43. "Leadership: Ripe for Change," *Human Resource Executive*, 2002, pp. 60, 62+ (interview with Randall MacDonald).

44. Flynn, "HR Leaders Stay Close to the Line"; GE, "World Class Excellence."

45. C. M. Solomon, "HR's Push for Productivity," *Workforce*, August 2002, pp. 28-33.

46. H. J. Bernardin, C. M. Hagan, J. S. Kane, and P. Villanova, "Effective Performance Management: A Focus on Precision, Customers, and Situational Constraints," in *Performance Appraisal: State of the Art in Practice*, ed. J. W. Smither (San Francisco: Jossey-Bass, 1998), p. 56.

47. J. Bailey, "Entrepreneurs Share Their Tips to Boost a Firm's Productivity," *The Wall Street Journal*, July 9, 2002, p. B4.

48. L. R. Gomez-Mejia and D. B. Balkin, *Compensation, Organizational Strategy, and Firm Performance* (Cincinnati: South-Western, 1992); G. D. Jenkins and E. E. Lawler III, "Impact of Employee Participation in Pay Plan Development," *Organizational Behavior and Human Performance* 28 (1981), pp. 111-28.

49. R. Broderick and J. W. Boudreau, "Human Resource Management, Information Technology, and the Competitive Edge," *Academy of Management Executive* 6 (1992), pp. 7-17.

50. "What's on the Horizon in HR Technology," *Canadian HR Reporter*, September 22, 2003, www.hrreporter.com. Retrieved: January 23, 2004.

51. Solomon, "HR's Push for Productivity," p. 31.

52. Gephart, "Introduction to the Brave New Workplace."

53. "America Online Inc. and Research in Motion to Deliver AOL Instant Messaging Via Blackberry," Press Release, www.rim.com/news/press/2005/pr-14_03_2005-02.shtml. Retrieved: March 28, 2005.

54. "Hot HR Issues for the Next Two Years," The Conference Board of Canada, September 2004.

55. "CFOs Showing More Interest in HR," *Canadian HR Reporter*, October 25, 2004, p. 4.

56. David Brown, "Measuring Human Capital Crucial, ROI Isn't, Says New Think-Tank Paper," *Canadian HR Reporter*, October 25, 2004, p. 4.

57. Ibid.

58. "As Pressure to Reduce Costs Continues, HR Works to Save, But Struggles to Measure, According to Hewitt," Press Release Hewitt Associates, February 17, 2004, http://was4.hewitt.com/hewitt/resource/newsroom/ presrel/2004. Retrieved: February 24, 2004.

59. D. E. Bailey and N. B. Kurland, "A Review of Telework Research: Findings, New Directions, and Lessons for the Study of Modern Work," *Journal of Organizational Behavior* 23 (2002), pp. 383-400

Photo Credits

Name/Company Index

(Included in this index are names of government agencies, institutions, organizations, and publications)

See also SUBJECT INDEX

Note: Titles of specific books or publications and names of specific acts of legislation or legal cases can be found in the SUBJECT INDEX.

Subject Index